Cover:
Batalha Monastery, detail of the cloister.

PORTUGAL   Museum With No Frontiers Exhibition Trails
THE GREAT PATRONS OF ARTS

THE MANUELINE
Portuguese Art during the Great Discoveries

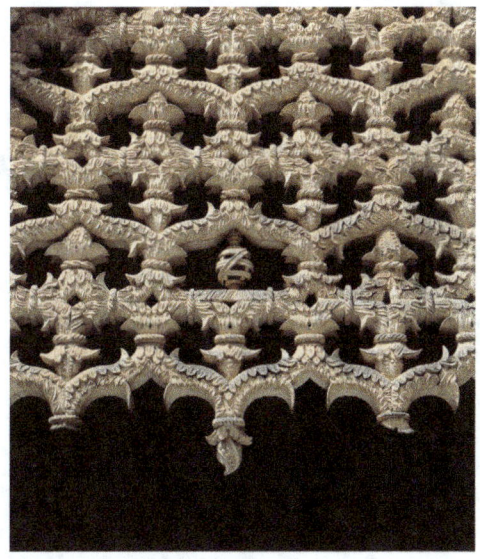

Museum With No Frontiers (MWNF)

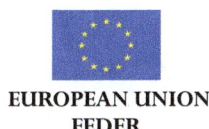
The MWNF Exhibition Trail "THE MANUELINE: Portuguese Art during the Great Discoveries" has been cofinanced by the European Union

and has received the support of the following Portuguese institutions:

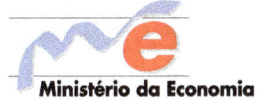
Portuguese State Secretariat for Tourism.

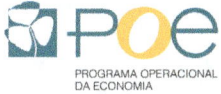
Economic Operational Programme.

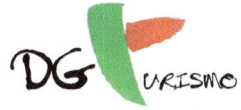
Produced by the Programme for the Development of Cultural Tourism (PICT) with the assistance of the Directorate General for Tourism of Portugal.

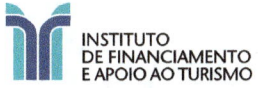
The project has equally benefited from the financial support of the Institute for the Financing and Support of Tourism in Portugal.

First edition
© 2002 Museum With No Frontiers & Programme for the Development of Cultural Tourism, Lisbon, Portugal
(texts and illustrations)
© 2002 Museum With No Frontiers & Electa (Grijalbo Mondadori S.A.), Madrid, Spain

Second edition
© 2017 Museum Ohne Grenzen | Museum With No Frontiers (MWNF), Vienna, Austria

All rights reserved.
ISBN: 978-3-902782-98-4 (paper back)
ISBN: 978-3-902782-96-0 (eBook)

Information: www.museumwnf.org
               www.mwnfbooks.net

While every effort has been made to ensure that the information contained within this book is accurate, MWNF makes no warranty, representation or undertaking whether expressed or implied, nor does it assume any legal liability, whether direct or indirect, or responsibility for the accuracy, completeness, or usefulness of any information.

Idea and overall concept of the Museum With No Frontiers Programme
Eva Schubert

Head of the Project
Flávio Lopes
Programme for the Development of Cultural Tourism (PICT)

Curatorial Co-ordination
Pedro Dias

Curatorial Committee
Dalila Rodrigues, Fernando Grilo, Nuno Vassallo e Silva

Catalogue

Introduction
Pedro Dias

Presentation of the Itineraries
Pedro Dias, Coimbra
Dalila Rodrigues, Viseu
Nuno Vassallo e Silva, Lisbon
Fernando Grilo, Lisbon

Technical texts
Maria José Machado Santos, Lisbon

Historical Personalities
Maria João Bonina

Translation
Margaret Kelting, Lisbon

Technical revision
John Elliott, Lisbon

Copy editor
Mandi Gomez, London

Photography
António Cunha, Beja (A.C.)
Jorge Barros, Lisbon (J.B.)
Maurício Abreu, Setúbal (M.A.)
Rui Cunha, Lisbon (R.C.)
Laura Castro Caldas e Paulo Cintra, Lisbon (L.C.C.+P.C.)

IPM, Lisbon
Abreu Nunes (A.N.)
Carlos Monteiro (C.M.)
Delfim Ferreira (D.F.)
Francisco Matias (F.M.)
José Pessoa (J.P.)
José Rubio (J.R.)
Luís Pavão (L.P.)
Manuel Palma (M.P.)

Sketches
José Russo, Lisbon

Layout and design
Agustina Fernández, Madrid

Editorial Co-ordination
Sakina Missoum, Madrid

Technical Co-ordination

Production Manager, Cultural Heritage
Teresa Gamboa, Lisbon

Production Manager, legal area
Isabel Menezes, Lisbon

Cultural dynamisation and co-ordination of events
Rita Morgado, Lisbon

Technical control
Miguel García López, Madrid

Acknowledgements

The PICT would like to thank the following organisations, without which the realisation of this project would not have been possible:

The Town Councils of Alcochete, Almeida, Alvito, Angra do Heroísmo, Arraiolos, Barcelos, Batalha, Beja, Braga, Bragance, Calheta, Caminha, Castro Marim, Celorico da Beira, Coimbra, Condeixa-a-Nova, Évora, Faro, Freixo de Espada à Cinta, Funchal, Golegã, Guarda, Guimarães, Lamego, Lisbonne, Machico, Mafra, Meda, Miranda do Douro, Mogadouro, Montemor-o-Novo, Montemor-o-Velho, Moura, Palmela, Pinhel, Pombal, Ponta Delgada, Portimão, Porto, Praia da Vitória, Ribeira Brava, Santa Cruz, Santarém, Santiago do Cacém, Serpa, Setúbal, Silves, Sines, Sintra, Tarouca, Tavira, Tomar, Torre de Moncorvo, Torres Novas, Torres Vedras, Viana do Alentejo, Viana do Castelo, Vidigueira, Vila do Bispo, Vila do Conde, Vila Franca do Campo, Vila Nova da Barquinha, Vila Nova da Cerveira, Vila Nova de Foz Côa et Viseu;

The Institute for the Finance and Support of Tourism, the Confederation of Tourism, the General Directorate of Buildings and National Monuments, ICEP – Investments, Commerce and Tourism of Portugal, the Portuguese Institute for the Performing Arts, the Portuguese Institute of Museums, the Portuguese Institute of Architectural Heritage and of Regional Tourism.

Practical Advice

The exhibition trail "THE MANUELINE: Portuguese Art during the Great Discoveries" covers the entire Portuguese territory, including the Azores and Madeira.

This travel book is organised into fourteen independent itineraries, each dedicated to a specific region. The sequence follows a geographic order and can be modified according to your specific interests.

Each itinerary can be completed in one or two days, depending on the distances to be covered and the number and kind of monuments to be visited.

The monuments, sites and museums included in each itinerary provide a detailed overview of the existing Manueline heritage in each area. However, since the MWNF travel books aim for thematic coherence rather than providing an exhaustive inventory, some Manueline remains are not featured in this publication. Visitors who wish to deepen their knowledge about Manueline heritage beyond the information provided in this book are advised to contact the local Tourism Offices.

Thematic text boxes are used to further describe the context of the various places or to call the traveller's attention to landscapes that are of particular interest for a better understanding of the region.

The book provides practical information, including how to get to the various places within each city or village, opening hours and telephone numbers. We recommend that you supplement this information with road maps and city plans. We also advise you to check in advance opening hours and terms of visit as these may change without warning.

Please note that national museums and important Portuguese monuments are closed on Mondays.

On Sundays and religious holidays services are held in many of the churches presented in this book and you are advised to visit these places outside the hours of worship.

Terms in italic in the text without an accompanying translation or explanation can be found in the glossary.

For kings and queens, the usual Portuguese designation of D. (Dom/Dona) has been used and the name of the monarch has been kept in Portuguese (e.g. D. Afonso).

We wish you a most enjoyable voyage to Manueline Portugal.

The MWNF Travel Team

INDEX

15 **D. Manuel I and the Overseas Discoveries**
Pedro Dias

22 **Manueline Art**
Pedro Dias

39 **Itinerary I** (two days)
The Beach of Adventure
Pedro Dias, Dalila Rodrigues, Nuno Vassallo e Silva, Fernando Grilo
D. Manuel I
Pedro Dias

69 **Itinerary II** (two days)
Lands of the Order of Christ
Pedro Dias, Dalila Rodrigues, Nuno Vassallo e Silva, Fernando Grilo
The Order of Christ and the Discoveries
Pedro Dias

93 **Itinerary III** (two days)
In the Footsteps of Boytac
Pedro Dias, Dalila Rodrigues, Nuno Vassallo e Silva, Fernando Grilo
The Legend of Inês de Castro
Pedro Dias

121 **Itinerary IV**
Discovering Grão Vasco
Pedro Dias, Dalila Rodrigues, Nuno Vassallo e Silva, Fernando Grilo
Grão Vasco, the Painter-Hero
Pedro Dias

137 **Itinerary V** (two days)
Biscayans in Northern Portugal
Pedro Dias, Dalila Rodrigues, Nuno Vassallo e Silva, Fernando Grilo
Legend of the Barcelos Cock
Pedro Dias

163 **Itinerary VI**
Looking Towards Galicia
Pedro Dias, Dalila Rodrigues, Nuno Vassallo e Silva, Fernando Grilo
Manorial Towers of Alto Minho
Pedro Dias

177 **Itinerary VII**
Lands of the Sabor and the Douro
Pedro Dias, Dalila Rodrigues, Nuno Vassallo e Silva, Fernando Grilo
The *Livro das Fortalezas* by Duarte D'Armas
Pedro Dias

195 **Itinerary VIII** (two days)
Frontier Churches and Castles
Pedro Dias, Dalila Rodrigues, Nuno Vassallo e Silva, Fernando Grilo
Mudejar Ceilings
Pedro Dias

215 **Itinerary IX** (two days)
Évora: City of the Court
Pedro Dias, Dalila Rodrigues, Nuno Vassallo e Silva, Fernando Grilo
Painted Houses: Mural Painting in the House of Vasco da Gama
Pedro Dias

237 **Itinerary X** (two days)
White Towns
Pedro Dias, Dalila Rodrigues, Nuno Vassallo e Silva, Fernando Grilo
Queen D. Leonor
Pedro Dias

265 **Itinerary XI** (two days)
Algarve
Pedro Dias, Dalila Rodrigues, Nuno Vassallo e Silva, Fernando Grilo
Prince Henry the Navigator
Pedro Dias

283 **Itinerary XII**
The Military Order of Santiago
Pedro Dias, Dalila Rodrigues, Nuno Vassallo e Silva, Fernando Grilo
Vasco da Gama
Pedro Dias

301 **Itinerary XIII** (two days)
The Island of Madeira: between Portugal and Flanders
Pedro Dias, Dalila Rodrigues, Nuno Vassallo e Silva, Fernando Grilo
Porto Santo

325 **Itinerary XIV** (two days)
The Azores on the Routes West and the East
Pedro Dias, Dalila Rodrigues, Nuno Vassallo e Silva, Fernando Grilo
The 16th-Century Furniture Factory on the Island of Terceira
Pedro Dias

343 **Glossary**
347 **Kings and Queens of Portugal**
348 **Chronology**
353 **Historical Personalities**
361 **Bibliography**
364 **Authors**

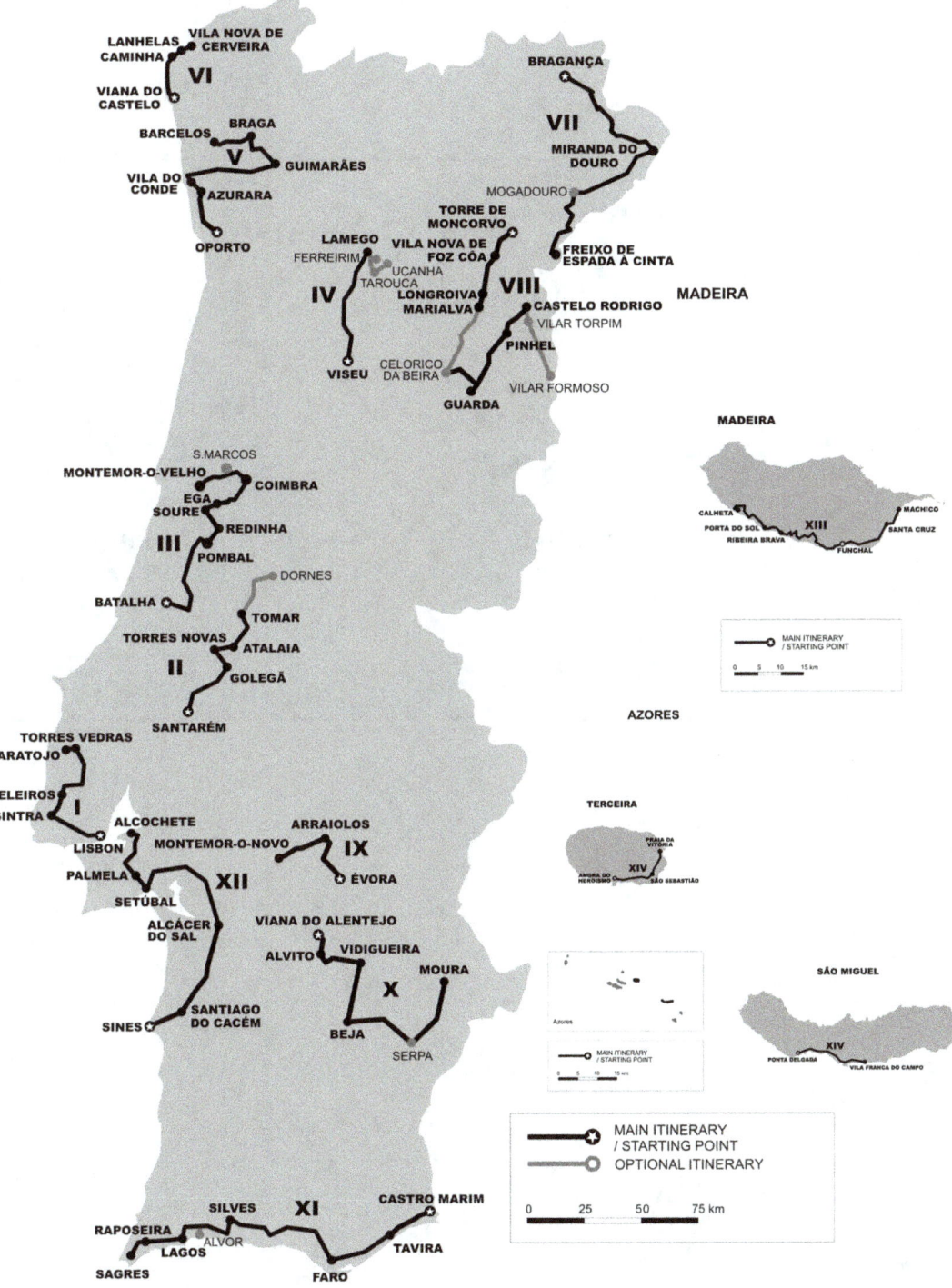

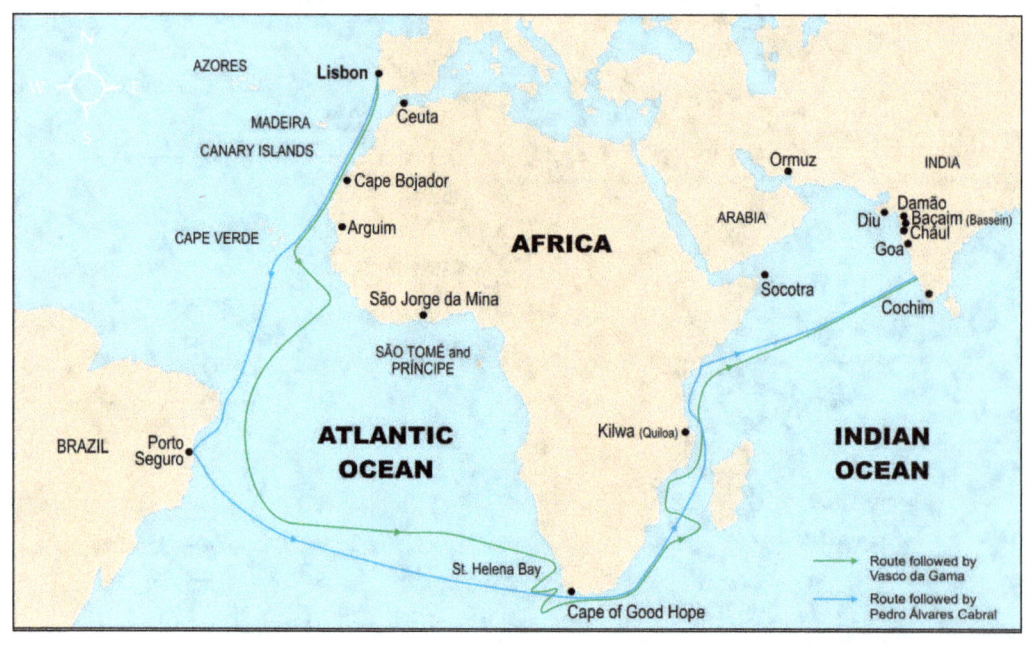

Voyages of the Portuguese discoverers.

D. MANUEL I AND THE OVERSEAS DISCOVERIES

Pedro Dias

D. Manuel I, known as "the Fortunate", was King of Portugal at a time when the Middle Ages was giving way to a dynamic new age of exploration and discovery that would change the face of the world.

It was thanks to his government that the maritime links between Europe and the Far East was established, thus fulfilling the long-held dream of his great uncle Prince Henry the Navigator. This fact was to radically alter the lives of the people of Europe and all those who inhabited North and South America, Africa and Asia.

The Portuguese maritime discoveries were to become one of the most remarkable sagas in the history of humankind and would establish closer contacts between people of all continents who had previously not known each other, or who had only the vaguest knowledge of each other's existence and whose impressions were frequently clouded with somewhat fantastic notions. They represented the embryo of the modern era, the age of globalisation, which now seems to be about to change once more. Arnold Toynbee wrote that the history of the world is divided into two great eras: before and after Vasco da Gama, i.e. the one that preceded the great ocean-going voyages and the one coming after the admiral's remarkable journey in 1498.

Much of Portugal's success in attaining world importance was due to its geographical position at the extreme south west of Europe, facing towards Africa and the Americas, as well as to its condition as a stopping-off point for ships sailing between Northern Europe and the Mediterranean. Its long coastline with sheltered estuaries had attracted traders from the time of the Phoenicians, who sailed the high seas and rounded the Straits of Gibraltar. First came fishing and then trade, transforming the Por-

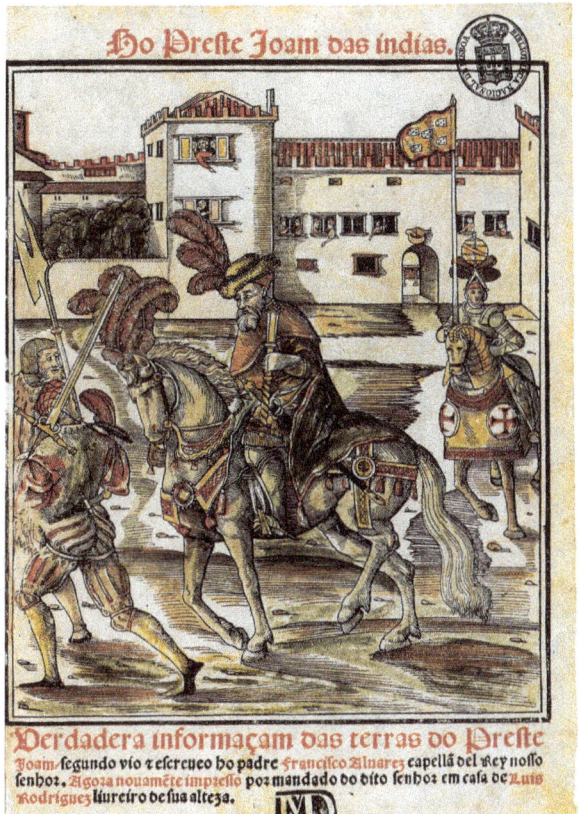

"Verdadeira Informação das Terras do Preste João"(True Information about the Land of Prester John), Padre Francisco Álvares, Luís Rodrigues, Lisbon, 1540.

tuguese into a practical race in matters relating to the sea and ocean voyages, which greatly facilitated its overseas expansion when the time was right. Portuguese boats were already sailing to the ports of Northern Europe as early as the 12th century, transporting the produce of both land and sea, especially salt; a precious commodity considered to be essential in the cementing of a continued guarantee of the economic independence of the newly formed kingdom.

The Maghreb was only a short distance away, the land of Portugal's traditional enemies, who laid waste to villages, towns and cities along the coast, killing and pillaging indiscriminately. For this reason, a strong and permanent fleet was needed to patrol the coast and protect it against these bloody attacks. The country's presence on the sea was therefore important from the time of the first King, D. Afonso Henriques, when the fleet was led by the mythical Admiral D. Fuas Roupinho.

The policy of naval development was a constant concern of the Portuguese Crown. In 1317, D. Dinis called on Admiral Pessanha from Genoa, who brought with him two dozen seafarers to improve the structure and organisation of the navy. Throughout the 15th century, this foreign presence in Portugal grew ever larger and included Iberian, Italian and Northern European specialists, both Christians and Jews, who worked together in creating a genuine nautical science. But, whilst men from other nations came to Lisbon and Lagos, the reverse was also true, with Portuguese technicians and pilots establishing themselves in other kingdoms and playing a decisive role in the development of these kingdom's respective navies.

International trading and fishing agreements were signed, forests were planted to provide wood for shipbuilding, and even a form of marine insurance was introduced between 1370 and 1380. All this took place in a reasonably stable and cohesive Portugal, whilst, further north, other European countries were becoming embroiled in interminable wars.

Only because of this situation was it possible for the Portuguese to reach the Canary Islands in 1341, at the initiative of D. Afonso IV. Later, when the dynastic crisis of 1383-1385 was resolved and D. João I ascended the throne, the Portuguese Crown turned its attention towards overseas expansion, with the occupation, or Christian Reconquest in 1415, of the city of Ceuta in the Staights of Gibraltar representing its first great action in this enterprise.

The proselytising spirit of the Portuguese adventure is sometimes looked upon as a continuation of the Mediaeval Crusades, undertaken in the Holy Land at the instigation of the Pope. It is true that the Turkish forces represented a real danger and that they had already partly devastated Eastern Europe, but this was not a a major reason for Portuguese expansion. The religious zeal of Henry the Navigator, D. Afonso V, D. João II and the princes that followed them is well documented, as was their wish to form an alliance with the legendary Christian ruler, Prester John, against Islam. Their final aim was to establish the Christian Empire, which would include the Indian Christians of São Tomé and those of the Island of Sete Cidades, who lived on the frontier between East and West. There were, of course, other more important reasons, one of which was the change of mentality, indeed the change in Philosophy illustrated by the battle between "realists" and "nominalists". The triumph of the latter and the actions of the Franciscan monks led to the European awareness of the vital need to know more about the world and to base this knowledge on direct observation and experience, thus sowing the seed that would make curiosity the mainspring of all Portuguese action.

With the occupation of Ceuta on the Straits of Gibraltar in 1415, Portugal's horizons expanded to include the whole of the North African Atlantic coast. The conquest of the port was, however, only completed in 1514, in the time of D. Manuel I. The nearest islands in the Atlantic represented the next stage of expansion, with the men from the House of Prince Henry the Navigator reaching the islands of Porto Santo, in 1418, Madeira in 1425, and the Azores in 1427. Year by year, the list grew, as systematic voyages probed the coast of Sub-Saharan Africa, leading to the rounding of Cape Bojador by Gil Eanes in 1434, after 15 earlier failures.

To make all this possible, the Crown commissioned Portuguese and foreign mathematicians, mapmakers and naval technicians, and information was constantly updated by the first-hand accounts of returning mariners. Mathematics, Cartography, Astronomy and, naturally, shipbuilding made unprecedented progress, facilitating navigation of the open sea in increasingly sophisticated, safer, faster and larger vessels. In the space of 100 years, small vessels with oars were replaced by caravels with triangular or

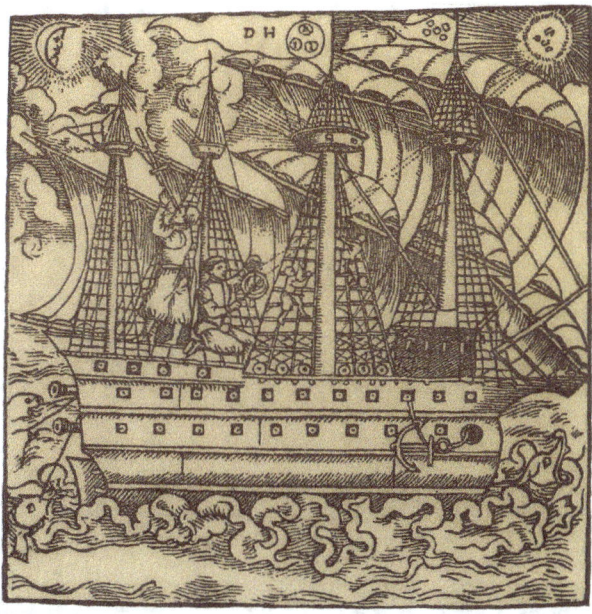

Representation of the use of the astrolabe and the cross-staff, engraving in "Wahrhaftige Historia und Beschreibung eyner Landschafft der wilden nacketen grimmigen Menschfresser Leuthen", Hans Staden, Marburg, 1557.

"Livro de Traças de Carpintaria (Book of Carpentry Sketches with all the models and measurements needed for making all navigation, both in large ships and in rowing boats), Manuel Fernandes. 1616.

"Guia Náutico de Évora" (Nautical Guide of Évora), Germão Galharde, Lisbon, c.1516.

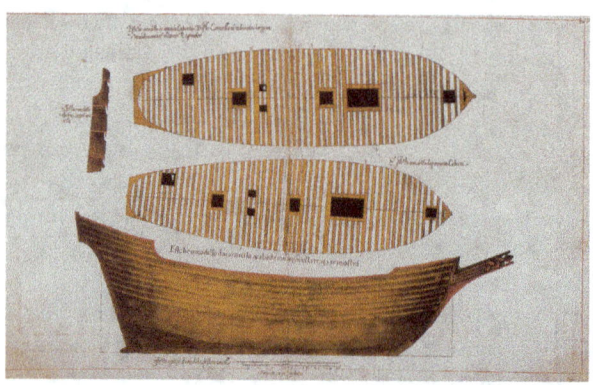

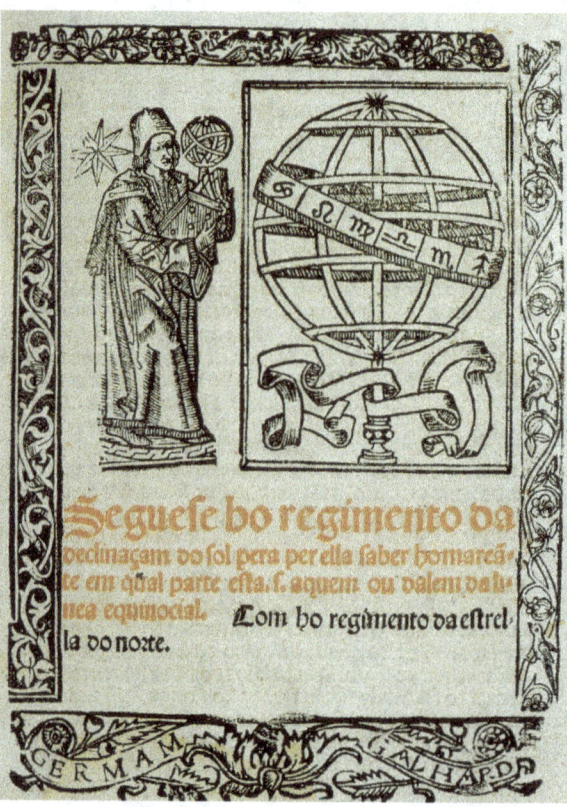

lateen sails that enabled them to sail against the wind. They were superseded, in turn, by the great carracks and galleons of the later voyages to India.

Nautical instruments were developed to pinpoint the position of vessels, by measuring the altitude of the noonday sun or known polar stars, to obtain latitude, just as magnetic declination was later used to determine longitude. Wind systems, currents and tides were studied, whilst charts of rivers, bars and coastlines were drawn up, and some maps were made even of the surface of the sea itself, in order to choose the most convenient and safest routes and to determine the best times for sailing. All this knowledge was condensed into nautical almanacs, sailing directions and treatises that were printed and used by seafarers of many nations.

The support given to shipping and navigation led to the formation of various industries, especially in coastal cities and towns, designed to supply and outfit ships, whilst, at the same time, trade intensified with the inland areas of the Iberian Peninsula, Flanders and the Germanic States. Utensils, weapons and manufactured products were exchanged for indigenous products brought back from overseas. Portugal, on her own, was unable to outfit and supply or finance her ships, which led to the involvement of many other Europeans in the country's high seas adventures. In Lisbon and other ports, traders, merchants, artists and craftsmen, soldiers of fortune and bankers from Italy and Germany all flourished, and, from the mid-15th century onwards, were often partners in rigging the ships that set sail for Africa, the Far East and Brazil.

The Portuguese Discoveries showed something of the actual dimension of the world and the great diversity of its inhabitants, plants and animals. They also made it possible to explode some of the myths that still existed in the minds of European men at the dawning of the Modern Age. It was still thought, for example, that the equatorial region was uninhabited, that there were no antipodes, and even that monsters dwelt in certain lands and under the sea. All novelties that were discovered were religiously noted down and this knowledge was later transmitted to the Court in Lisbon. Returning mariners brought back animals and new plant species, men of unknown races, and even samples of water for analysis.

The experimental nature and consequent exceptional growth in technical and scientific knowledge was perhaps the most important contribution made by the great Portuguese adventure of the 15th and 16th centuries.

The holds of caravels, carracks, hookers and galleons arriving in Lisbon were laden with astonishing treasures: embroidered silks, velvets and satins, jewels, ivory carvings, gold and rock crystal, furniture made with rare or unknown woods inlaid with ivory, or covered with tortoise-shell or mother-of-pearl. All these extremely valuable works of art aroused admiration and fuelled the curiosity of the more cultured classes, so that the rich and powerful filled their palaces with them all over Renaissance and Mannerist Europe.

Prince Henry the Navigator masterminded the political, administrative and scientific machine of the Discov-

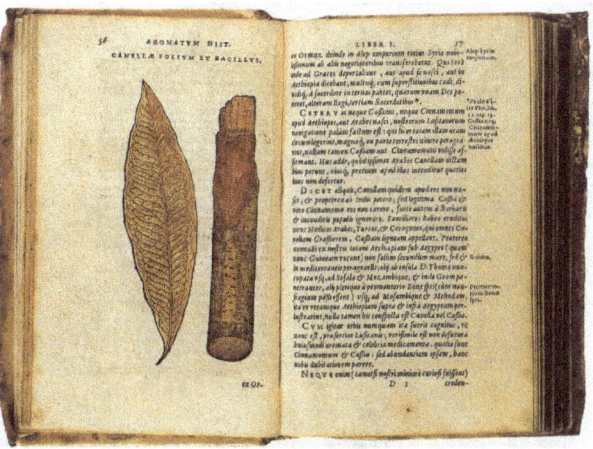

Treatise on Drugs and Medicines from the East Indies, Cristóvão da Costa, Burgos, Martín de Victoria, 1578.

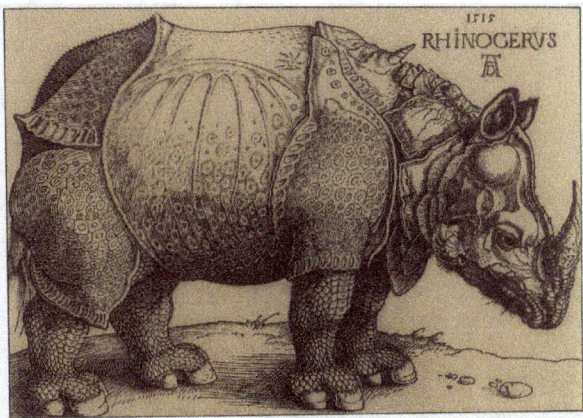

"Rhinoceros", engraving by Albrecht Dürer, based on a Portuguese drawing.

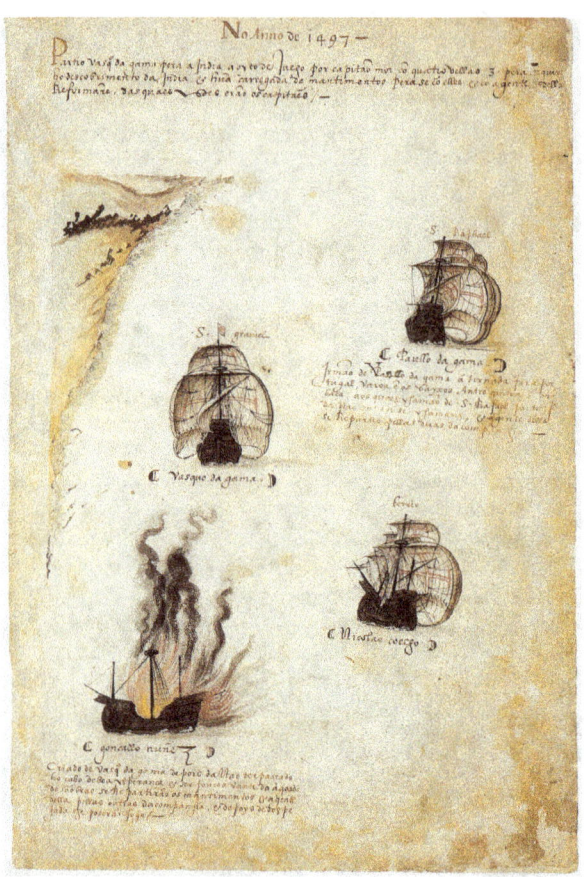

Fleet of Vasco da Gama's first voyage to India, "Memórias das Armadas" (Memories of the Fleets), c.1568, Lisbon Academy of Sciences.

The first important trading post, or factory, was set up on the African coast at Arguim, to be replaced by São Jorge da Mina, the centre for the gold trade, in 1482.

Christopher Columbus, in the service of Castile, learnt the art of navigation in Portugal, where he married the daughter of one of the most illustrious navigators, Bartolomeu Perestrelo, the lord proprietor of Porto Santo. Although his attempt to reach India by navigating west was a complete failure, he nonetheless had the virtue of introducing Europe to North America, though documented sources, such as the writings of the scientist and navigator Duarte Pacheco Pereira and other contemporary witnesses, show that the Portuguese Crown already knew of its existence.

This event led to a dispute between Portugal and Castile, resolved by the Treaty of Tordesillas (1494), which divided the world of discovered and undiscovered lands between the two countries. The treaty received the indispensable Papal blessing, needed for it to be considered valid as an international law amongst the Christian community. From then on, Portuguese feats of navigation were directed towards the Far East and a voyage to India by the Cape route was prepared. The Cape of Good Hope was finally rounded by Bartolomeu Dias in 1489, whilst, in April 1500, a fleet under the command of Pedro Álvares Cabral set out for Malabar, but, either by accident or design, it

eries until 1460. His major objective was the Orient, particularly India, which, he was convinced, could be reached by following a route around the south of Africa. In his day, the first settlers (including Flemish and German citizens) were installed on many of the deserted islands of the archipelagos of Madeira, the Azores, Cape Verde, as well as on other islands, such as São Tomé, Príncipe, Fernando Pó (Bioko) and Ano Bom (Annobón).

sailed too far to the south west and officially discovered Brazil, before returning to its original course.

Historical research has frequently concentrated on both the transport and trade in overseas products, particularly from the Orient, with the result that another important aspect of the Portuguese Discoveries has tended to be somewhat overlooked. Indeed, the spices, textiles, wood and other precious goods brought from Asia began to arrive in Europe in large numbers and at exceptional prices, so that the curiosity about their origin was one of the major causes of expansion. Yet, the Portuguese played a significant part, too, in disseminating plants and encouraging their cultivation. Eating habits changed, not only in Europe, but also in Africa, Asia and North and South America, with the planting of economically viable crops, such as corn, manioc, potatoes, beans and tobacco.

All this brought great splendour and more or less lasting wealth to the nations of Central and Northern Europe, including those which either did not take part in the attempts being made to brave uncharted seas and inhospitable lands or else were only just beginning to do so, on a smaller scale and in clearly demarcated geographical areas. The Portuguese Crown, however, can claim great credit for its investment in men and equipment, and for the extraordinary adventure of the Discoveries, which reached their apogee during the reign of D. Manuel I, between 1495 and 1521.

The Discoveries also brought about the realisation that creativity was not the prerogative of Christians, Europeans and even less that of the white man.

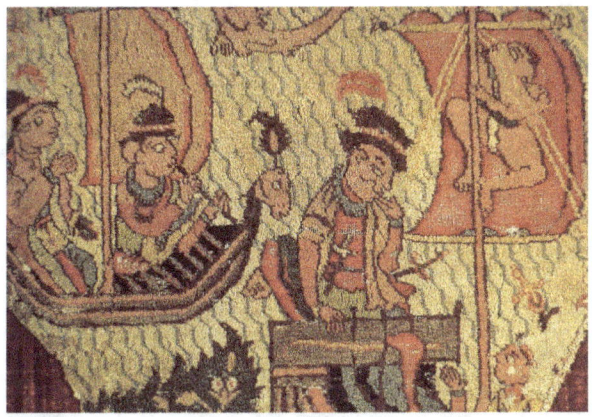

Persian tapestry, 16th-century, Portuguese figures.

MANUELINE ART

Pedro Dias

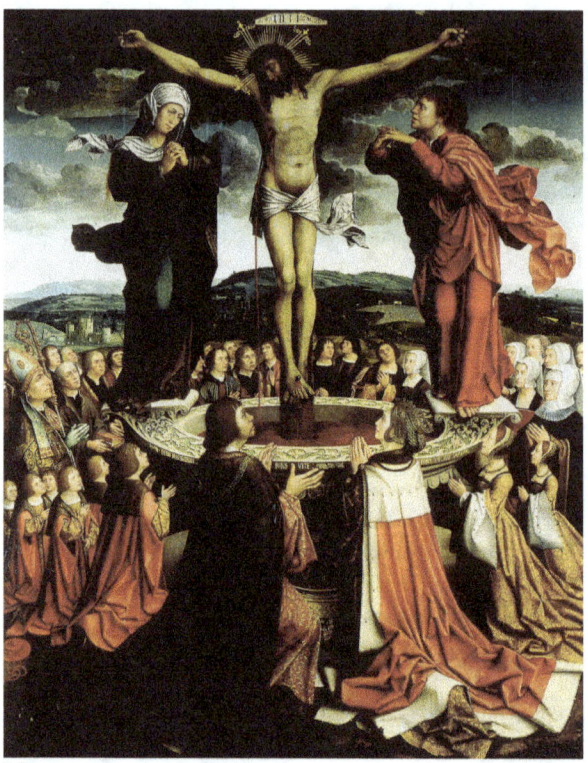

D. Manuel I and his family worshipping the "Fons Vitae", Flemish workshop, early 16th century, Misericórdia do Porto.

Manueline art flourished during the reign of D. Manuel I (hence its name) and the early years of the reign of D. João III, until about 1535, the peak of Portuguese imperial power. The king, nobility and clergy set great store by architectural undertakings and it is easy to understand how they became the emblems of this epoch and the new empire.

Closely imitating Caesar's vision from Classical Antiquity and transferring it to the Modern Era, D. Manuel I created an imperial policy that decreed that not only should territory be extended, but also the True Faith. Just as it had been for Augustus, the idea of Empire, or the mastery of the vast territories of the known world, was constantly propagated by the king's panegyrists, being reinforced by his titles and those of his predecessors, *"King of Portugal and the Algarves here and beyond the Seas"*, and later, *"Lord of Guinea and of the Trade, Conquests and Navigations of Arabia, Persia and India"*.

In the embassy he sent to Pope Leo X in 1514, D. Manuel I was presented as the leading figure in the expansion of the Faith, though he was careful to back this image up by more prosaic things such as the firepower of his ships' cannons. The king saw himself as the active and visible arm of the expansion of Christian Rome, the successor of Constantine, seeking to embody the imperial figure that would later be recreated by Charles V, albeit with some variants.

The *imperium* of D. Manuel I presupposed that power is not autonomous, that it only exists in so far as it is exercised, in might not deeds, and that it needs to be recognised by permanent symbols or acts, even though these are always only of limited duration. Art and, in particular architecture, were an excellent device whereby both the existence and the characteristics of the powerful were conveyed.

The Image of the King

D. Manuel I, and other rulers of his time, Maximilian of Austria, Charles V of Spain, and the Catholic Monarchs, Ferdinand and Isabella, before him, shared the same views about the use of painting, sculpture and tapestry, religious vestments and objects in silver and gold; religious, civil and military edifices; books and documents; festivals and ceremonies, for everything visible bore their stamp. The symbols of royalty, or the mission, with which God had apparently entrusted the king, were moulded on façades and in the chancels of churches and the frontispieces of manuscripts and printed books. Before designating D. Manuel his successor, D. João II, had granted him the coat of arms of Portugal as a blazon and the armillary sphere as a device to indicate the universality of his mission. His name was also *Manuel* or *Emmanuel*, in imitation of the name of Christ, which means *"God in me"*, heralding another redemption, that of Christianity, which was in fact faced with a serious crisis at that time, as well as announcing the emergence of a new and brilliant Golden Age, the Empire of the Holy Spirit.

The king's image appeared everywhere. One still visible image, a statue sculpted by the Frenchman, Nicolas Chanterène, is to be found on the west door of the Mosteiro dos Jerónimos in Lisbon. Another image appears painted in a family *polyptych*, the work of an unknown painter for the Palace at Almeirim, but now largely lost; sometimes D. Manuel is even depicted as one of the Wise Men. The king surfaces on retables painted by Jorge Afonso and some of his most direct followers: in the *Fons Vitae* at the Misericórdia charity organisation in Oporto, kneeling next to the young Queen D. Leonor; and in the painting at the Misericórdia in Lisbon, where he is depicted with the same queen, his third wife. D. Manuel was also portrayed in the stained glass windows of the Mosteiro da Batalha; in the frontispieces of chronicles, on the pages of *Leitura Nova*; and in the engravings of the *Ordenações Manuelinas*. He also figured in some of the

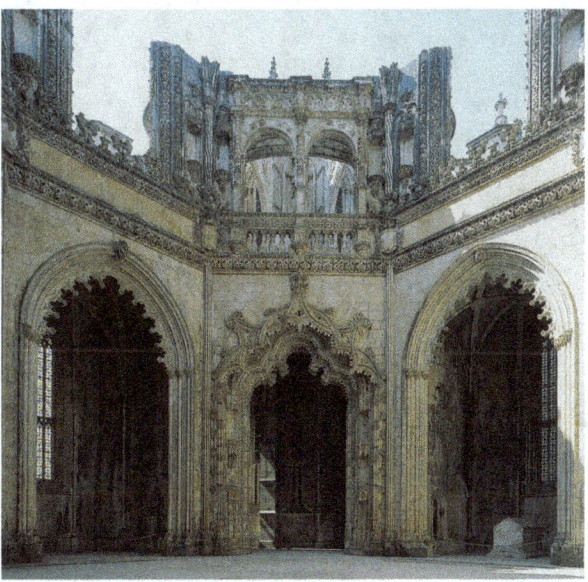

Unfinished Chapels, Batalha Monastery.

R. C.

Manueline Art

Former Cathedral, Elvas.

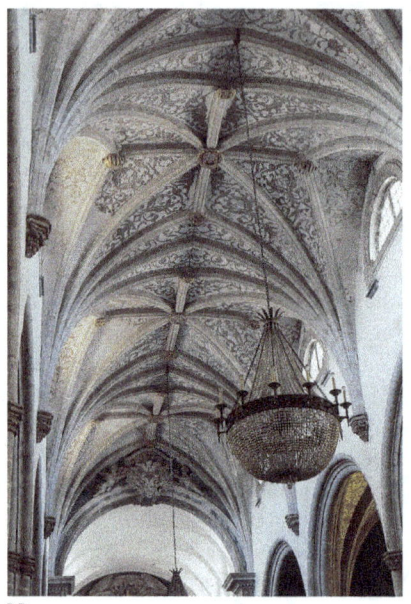

P.D.

26 scenes of the tapestries that he commissioned from Flanders, which depicted Vasco da Gama's voyage to India and were said to be *"in the Portuguese and Indian Style"*, being intended for the walls of the Royal Cloister of the Mosteiro dos Jerónimos.

Architecture

D. Manuel I was also greatly interested in architecture for, along with festivals, it attracted considerable public attention and again conveyed the message of power.

The *Manueline* — and here we are restricting the scope of this term to the field of architecture — was not an actual style, nor was it exclusive to Portugal. And, furthermore, in its magical decoration, there are no explicit references to Portuguese Expansion and the Overseas Discoveries. The ropes that so delighted art historians appeared not only on boats, but also on ox carts. The anchors repeated by Revivalist architects in the last century are nowhere to be found in any truly Manueline structure; and suggested sails are a figment of overactive imaginations.

The Portuguese building style at the beginning of the 16th century was no different from that of other European countries such as Castile, France, Bohemia or Flanders. Late Gothic structures endured both in Portugal and abroad, although vaulting tended towards the horizontal and the internal pillars of churches and great halls were pared down, almost unifying the space. Illumination was increased by the use of ever-larger windows and by the unity of the vaulting, with its new curved ribs.

The 14th-century Flamboyant Gothic decoration became heavier, more abundant and exceptionally exuberant. Throughout Europe, there appeared examples of decorative excesses, with the use of elements drawn from nature, towards which humankind was beginning to turn its attention. The splendour of the Late Gothic differed from place to place, depending on the prevailing conditions in each region. In France and England, there was little change, while in Castile and Burgundy the number of edifices gradually increased through aristocratic patronage and the flourishing craftsmen's guilds. These latter organisations were particularly important in Flanders and the Netherlands.

Islamic decorative forms were revived, especially in Andalusia. Moorish craftsmen were still working in Portugal even after the definitive Conquest of the Algarve, in 1349, but the outbreak of *Mudejar* revivalism corresponds to a fashion that was imported from Castile, particularly in Court circles. In Portugal, the *Mudejar* influence is mostly to be found in Sintra and Évora, where it became popular after D. Manuel I had visited Spain, in 1498. There was a return to surmounted arches, decorative tiles from Seville, ornamented ceilings and Moroccan carpets to re-create Muslim-style interiors.

The reigns of D. Afonso V and D. João II were not so fertile in terms of civil and religious architecture, at least on European territory, since these kings were less interested in this activity than D. Manuel I, who, even before becoming king, had already shown clear evidence of his enthusiasm for artistic endeavours. On ascending the throne, D. Manuel ordered work to begin on a series of suitably majestic buildings, some being specially designed, whilst others were either reconstructions or additions. As Portugal was short of skilled craftsmen, hundreds of foreign builders came from Castile, France, Germany or Flanders to form part of the workforce directed by Portuguese or Spaniards. Among these men were the brothers, Francisco and Diogo Arruda, the sons of the Master craftsman at Batalha, João de Arruda. They built the Chapter House of the Convento de Cristo in Tomar and also the Torre de Belém in Lisbon. Mateus Fernandes, father and son, worked on the monastery at Batalha, the training ground for many leading artists. There were also foreigners such as the Frenchman, Boytac, who was the Master

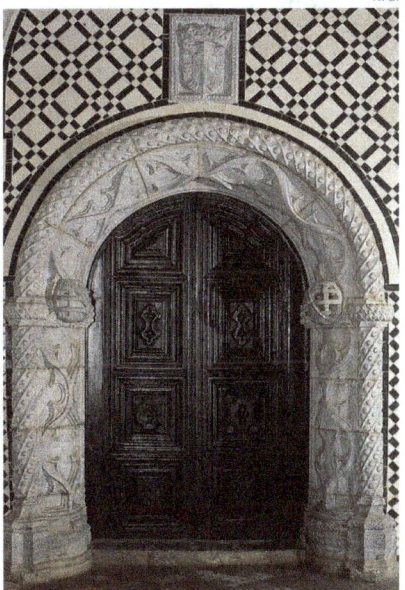

A.C.

Convent of Nossa Senhora da Conceição, refectory door, Beja.

Manueline Art

Window of the Convent of Christ, detail, Tomar.

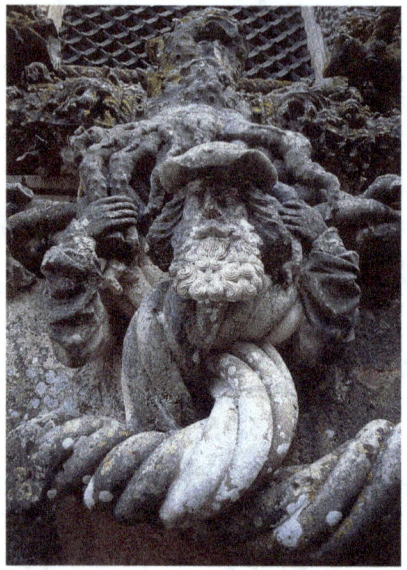

J. B.

craftsman at Batalha, Coimbra and Jerónimos. João de Castilho (Juan del Castillo) from Biscay concluded the formidable buildings of Tomar and Belém and introduced the figure of the modern architect, on adopting the Renaissance style and imposing the principles demanded by D. João III.

D. Manuel I's enthusiasm for the arts was aped by the nobility, who built new palaces, improved old ones, rebuilt and enlarged the churches and chapels of which they were patrons. This sudden surge of building would have been impossible without adequate funds, but, during D. Manuel's reign, Portugal was brimming with commodities and goods that generated the money to finance these artistic undertakings.

Overseas expansion not only enriched the king and those closest to him, but also the population in general; merchant communities and workers in the riverside areas also rebuilt and enriched their churches and houses, which they considered as emblems of their prosperity. This is to be seen all along the Atlantic coast, in places such as Caminha, Viana, Vila do Conde and Azurara in the Minho, Setúbal and Sines to the south of the River Tagus, and Portimão, Alvor, Tavira, Cacela and Loulé in the Algarve, as well as scores of other cities, towns and simple villages.

Inland, in the north and centre of the country, and apart from the cathedrals, the lesser nobility who had made money out of overseas adventure tended to transform only the chancels or side chapels of parish churches. In the Ribatejo, Lower Estremadura and the Alentejo provinces, however, many new churches were built from scratch or completely rebuilt in keeping with the new artistic taste. Patrons had the task of maintaining and ornamenting the chancel, sacristy, stores and priest's dwellings, while the faithful congregation were responsible for maintaining the main vessel of the church. As a consequence, many churches in villages and old towns in the north and centre of Portugal have Manueline apses and Renaissance or Baroque naves, for the population living in these areas only felt economic improvement in their everyday lives when new crops, such as corn, were produced.

Manueline architecture went far beyond Europe, however. It appeared almost immediately in the recently created towns on the islands of Madeira and the Azores, in fortresses, churches, chapels, town halls, hospitals, charity organisations and palaces. A number of these buildings have been completely or partially conserved up to this day, with the 15th-century cathedral in Funchal being a prime example. But there are also the Parish Churches of Machico, Santa Cruz, Ponta do Sol and Loreto.

Manueline architecture is to be found in the Azores in the Parish Churches of Ponta Delgada, Praia da Vitória and São Sebastião da Terceira, to name just a few. Yet, the masters of Manueline also went to the Canary Islands, and the archipelagos of Cape Verde and São Tomé and Principe. In 1503, a fortress and trading post were built at Cochim, in India.

In Morocco, great architects of the day, such as the Arruda brothers, Boytac, Francisco Danzilho and Bastião Luís, erected a series of fortresses in Ceuta, Asilah, Tangier, Azamor and Safi, and so on. Built in the typical Portuguese style, these were exactly like those found elsewhere in the kingdom.

It was in the Portuguese cities in India that the Manueline style most successfully outlived the time frame of its European period. In the sands of Ormuz, the entire structure of the cistern of an old fortress is still to be seen; in Goa, there is the monumental portal of the Church of the Convento de São Francisco, *c.*1521. The ribbed vaulting in the Churches in Chaul and Baçaim (Bassein), and even in the Capela do Baluarte on the island of Mozambique, were built at least 30 or 40 years later. Master builders such as Tomé Fernandes left Portugal to settle on the shores of the Indian Ocean, and, at a time when architectural treatises were still rare, they prolonged the fashion by continuing to practice what they had learned before leaving Lisbon.

It seems reasonable, therefore, to talk of a Manueline architecture, or the Manueline. Not because it was a specific style, or because it had unity

Bastion of Asilah walls, Morocco.

P.D.

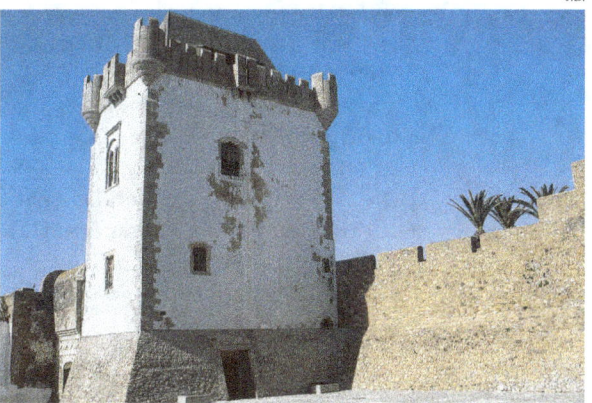

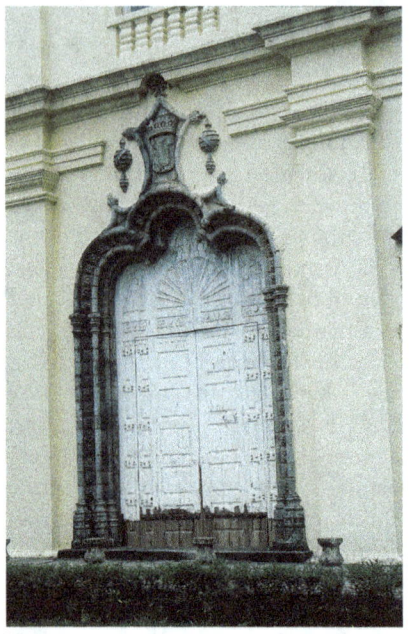

Convent of São Francisco, monumental portal, Goa.

P.D

and peculiarities that might be regarded as exclusive to Portugal and the reign of D. Manuel I, but because it represents a phenomenon defined in time and space, namely at the beginning of the 16th century and in Portuguese European territory and her islands, cities and fortresses overseas.

There is, however, something that distinguishes the Manueline from other contemporary versions of the Late Gothic: vernacular characteristics in the ornamentation and even some of the structural elements. The need to complete so many constructions, in as short a time as possible, meant that inadequately trained builders and workmen were employed. Never having completed their apprenticeship, they found themselves almost overwhelmed by problems to which they had to find, for better or worse, empirical solutions. They over-embellished decorative elements, over-used exuberant forms, joined columns and colonettes to piers for no functional purpose, interpreted common schemes badly, all of which resulted in anti-erudite and even ingenuous art.

Contrary to legend, the ropes and sails of the vessels that set out on the Discoveries are not depicted in Manueline edifices, though if it were not for such ropes and vessels there would not be so many, nor such fascinating, Manueline buildings to be seen today.

Sculpture

Manueline sculpture is also Gothic in essence, although Renaissance works were being executed during the lifetime of D. Manuel I, mainly by Nicolas Chanterène, who worked on the Mosteiro dos Jerónimos, as well as in Coimbra, Sintra and Évora. The leading workshops were in Coimbra, where the influence of the Gothic style hindered the development of new styles from Italy and Flanders. Diogo Pires the Elder and Diogo Pires the Younger headed the small multitude of men who, from stonemasons to tilers,

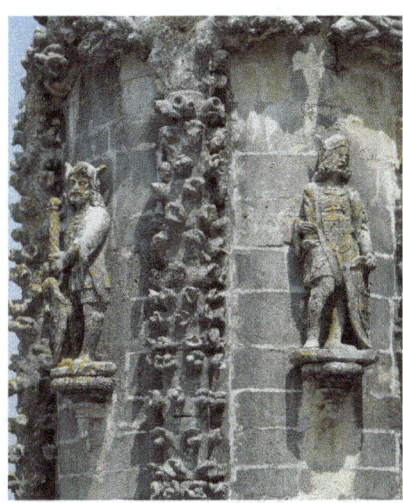

Convent of Cristo, sculptures, Tomar.

supplied almost 70 per cent of the national production. Chanterène lived in the city, from 1518 to 1526, and after that nothing was ever the same again especially as Jean de Rouen (João de Ruão), who was to dominate the sculptural scene until almost 1580, also settled there in 1526.

Imports from Italy were few and confined to Court circles, for they were almost always from the Florentine workshops of the Della Robbia. Work from Flanders was very common and statuary in polychrome wood and small retables from Northern Europe were to be found all over Portugal and the overseas territories. The polychrome, gold and dramatic effect of these images suited the inherent piety of the people, quite different from the rationality that was to hold sway in the following decades when decorum, proportion and the norm were more highly valued. Many masters, aware there was a good potential market, made their way to Portugal, where they settled for a number of years or stayed all their lives. An outstanding figure among them was Oliver of Ghent, the creator of the formidable retable in the chancel of Coimbra Cathedral and the imagery of the Charola, the original 16-sided rotunda Church of the Templars, in the Convento de Cristo in Tomar. There was also a certain Orte Maginário, who worked in Jerónimos; German John (João Alemão), active in Coimbra and Alcobaça, as well as Arnau de Carvalho, who partnered the legendary painter Vasco Fernandes (Grão Vasco) in making fine

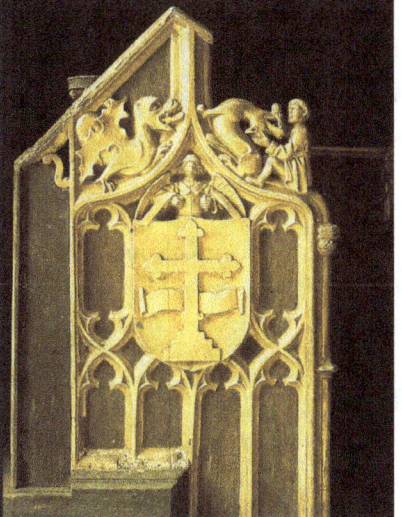

Church of Santa Cruz, detail of the choir stalls, Coimbra.

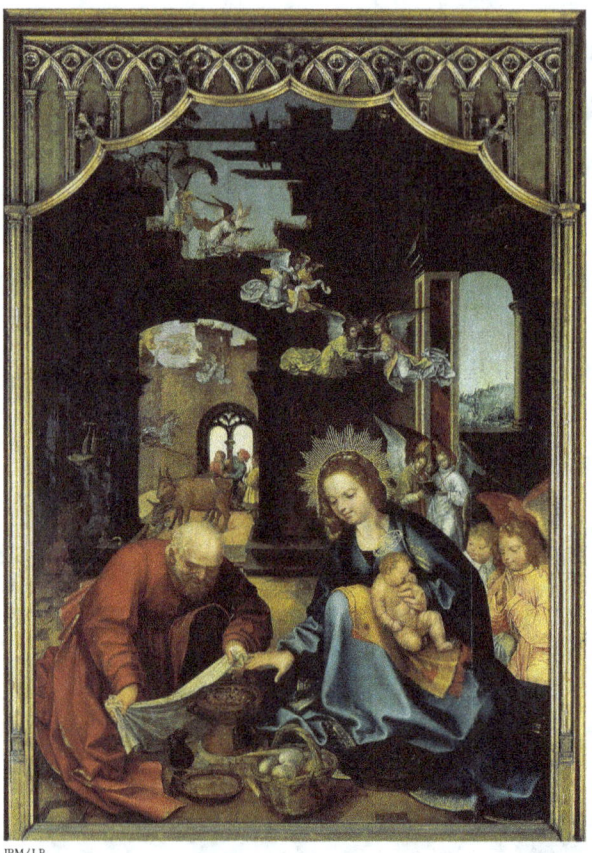

IPM/J.P.

Gregório Lopes and Workshop, "Nativity", from the retable originating from the Convent of Paraíso, oil on oak, 16th century, Museu Nacional de Arte Antiga, Lisbon.

retables in the Beira and Douro provinces.

Painting, Illumination and Engraving

The Flemish influence was more strongly felt in painting, in its various forms, than in any other branch of the arts. In the early years of the 15th century, when the painter Jan Van Eyck visited Portugal, Bruges, Ghent, Ypres, Malines, Brussels and Antwerp were well-known centres for buying works of art and this increased significantly after the marriage of Princess D. Isabel of Portugal to the Duke of Burgundy, Philip the Good. Flemish studios in Hainaut and Brabant also had agents in the North and South of Europe, from where they acquired most of their production. Over a period of 150 years, Portugal, like Spain, acquired thousands of paintings and retables that were sent, as were sculptures, to her churches in Africa, the Far East and Brazil.

Flemish painters descended on Lisbon and Évora, became Portuguese and adopted Portuguese names such as Francisco Henriques and Frei Carlos. They set up workshops where young Portuguese were trained, which meant this art was largely influenced by the Gothic style, first from Ghent and Bruges and then later from Antwerp. By the end of the first third of the 16th century, Renaissance influences were dominant in the leading workshops, but even the Italian style was second-hand, as most of those bringing it to Portugal were Flemish, mainly second-generation artists from Antwerp.

Lisbon, Évora, Viseu and Coimbra were the most active centres, with emphasis on the Court where, during the Manueline period, Jorge Afonso was the great influence, after the overwhelming example of Nuno Gonçalves, who stood head and

shoulders above everyone else during the second half of the 15th century.
In Évora, Francisco Henriques, a craftsman working in the Flemish style, competed with the authors of the fantastic imported panels that filled many of the chapels in the cathedral and other churches in the city. In Coimbra, he set up a vernacular school, with Vicente Gil and Manuel Vicente and, in the province of Beira, Vasco Fernandes covered the whole range of styles from the last of the Flamboyant Gothic to burgeoning Mannerism.

Painting on wood reached an exceptional level rarely attained in Portugal, with Garcia Fernandes, Gregório Lopes, Cristóvão de Figueiredo and the enigmatic Masters of Lourinhã and Palmela. Fresco painting, which spread all over Portugal, was even more impressive. Though the great majority of this work has disappeared, there are still examples dating from the beginning of the 15th century and this has allowed for atmospheric, albeit hypothetical, reconstructions of churches and noble residences.

Another highly successful sub-discipline was illumination. Many of the illuminated books, mainly Books of Hours, were imported from France, Flanders and Italy, though some fine examples were also produced in various *scriptoria* in Lisbon, Coimbra and Alcobaça. When D. Manuel I ascended the throne and undertook his great reform of the State, illumination flourished at a time when in other countries it was beginning to lose ground to printing. The king ordered legislation, new charters, old chronicles of past kings and heraldic tomes to be copied in luxurious volumes, with exuberantly decorated frontispieces, which led to the setting up of a huge and highly active studio. The *Leitura Nova*, the lettering then used, and the legislative codices, show not only the

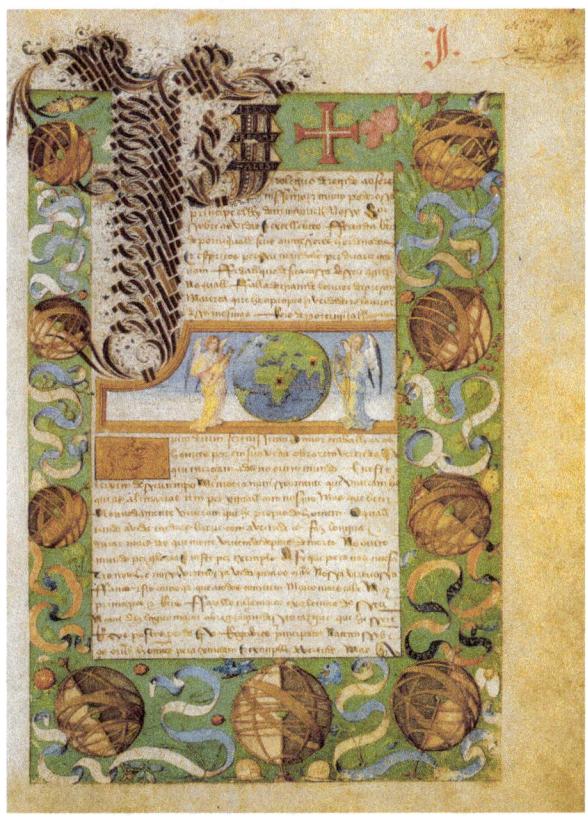

Illumination, frontispiece of the "Crónica" (Chronicle) by Duarte Galvão, early 16th century, National Archives/ Torre do Tombo, Lisbon.

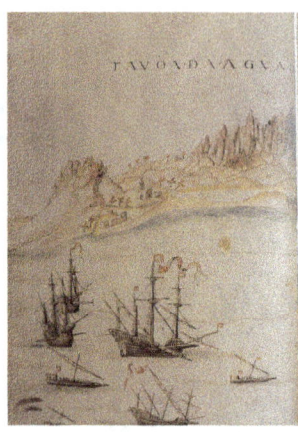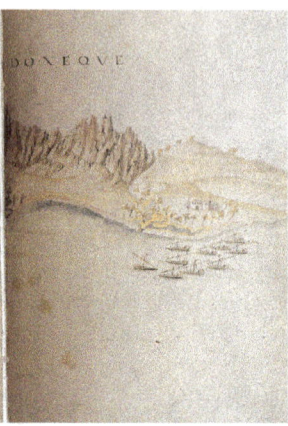

"Roteiro"(Sailing Directions) by D. João de Castro.

evolution from Gothic to Mannerism, but also the Flemish and Italian influences and the brilliance of the Portuguese illuminators.

Cartographic decoration had very similar characteristics to illumination, but was not always executed by the same technique. The charts used on ships at the time of the Discoveries whether on long voyages or on trading vessels were not objects of great aesthetic concern, except for those kept at Court or drawn up as gifts to other princes or for use as political propaganda. Unfortunately, very few examples of the abundant Portuguese map production remain from the beginning of the 16th century. Even so, those from the mid-16th century and the second half of the century are sufficiently elucidative to evaluate Manueline production.

Topographical drawings or city views, often of a distinct aesthetic value, were important records, sometimes appearing in codices, such as the *Livro das Fortalezas* (*Book of Fortresses*) by Duarte D'Armas. The high point of this art was, however, attained overseas, with works like the *Roteiros* (*Sailing Directions*) of D. João de Castro and the *Códice Casamatense* dating from the time of D. João III.

While it is not entirely within the framework of painting, but nonetheless also based on drawing, engraving began to evolve, brought and developed by German printers who soon opened wood-engraving presses, to produce volumes or enliven the pages of text with illustrations. Gradually, engraving became autonomous and took its place as a form of book illustration, later being used for devotional or promotional prints.

Goldware, Silverware and Jewellery

These decorative arts always take a great step forward whenever the economy is sound, as was the case in the 15th and 16th centuries, when pieces could be commissioned in precious metals with expensive stones, whether for the ornamentation of Man or in praise of God. Civil jewellery, goldware and silverware and religious objects were particularly important, because this was a period of marked social stratification, when the display of wealth was regarded as an imperative and not just an act of vanity.

It should not be forgotten, however, that the treasures of the Church were plundered at various times, whenever silver was "requisitioned", as occurred in the reigns of D. João I, D. João II and, later, D. João III. This, like the constant modernisation it provoked, caused many older objects to disappear, although there were many that, for one reason or another, were saved from being melted down.

Gold and silver religious pieces were similar in style to those of Castile, which is partially explained by the fact that many artists who came to work in Lisbon hailed from there and were often commissioned by the royal family. These pieces were also highly mobile, as the clergymen carried them around with them when they travelled, as did people of importance who had private chapels.

In the early years of the 16th century, the court of D. Manuel I suddenly developed a taste for oriental jewellery, when an Indian craftsman came to Lisbon and attracted the king's attention with his superb, exotic art.

D. Manuel I, as patron of hundreds of churches that stretched from Lisbon to Malacca, commissioned hundreds, even thousands, of religious works in gold and silver, the most emblematic of which is the Monstrance of Belém, made from

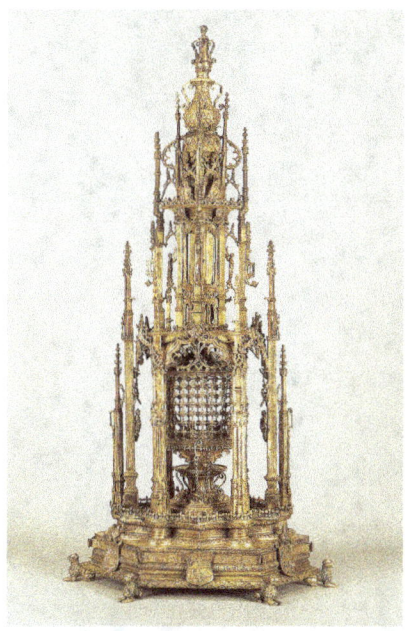

Monstrance, silver-gilt, Portuguese production, 1527, Museu Nacional Machado de Castro, Coimbra.

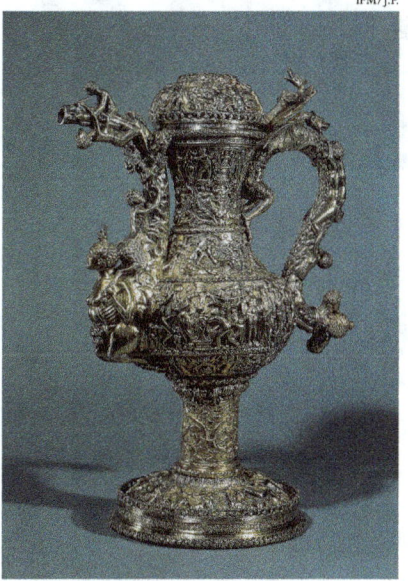

Ewer, silver-gilt, Portuguese work, 16th century, Palácio Nacional da Ajuda, Lisbon.

Manueline Art

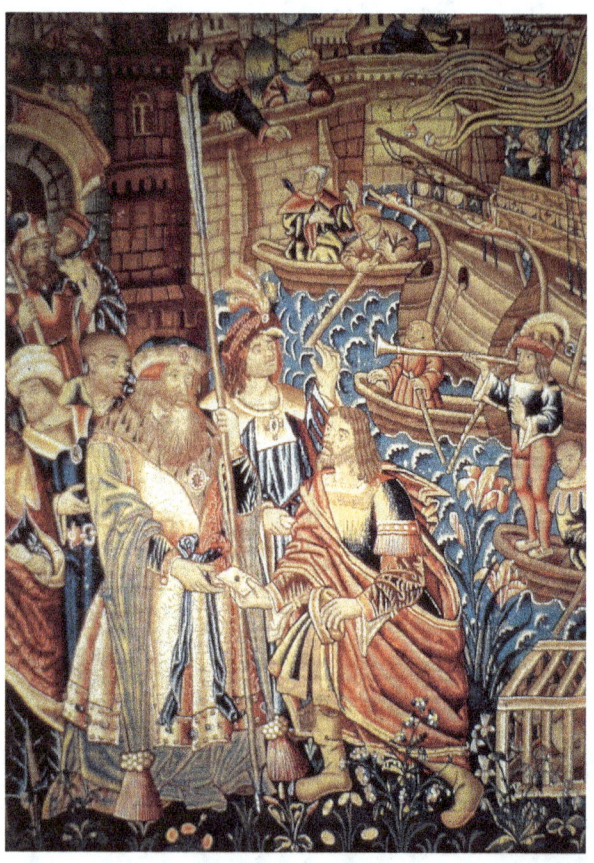

"The Disembarkation", tapestry in the Indian and Portuguese Style, Museu do Caramulo.

the first gold tributes from Kilwa (Quiloa). It was designed and made by Gil Vicente, who was also the founder of the Portuguese Theatre.

Tapestries and Fabrics

The Portuguese imported most of the fabrics they needed for the domestic market and also in order to re-export, for they were used for bartering in Africa and the Far East in exchange for spices, gold, copper, ivory, and so on. Altar cloths and frontals in white or printed linen, and richer materials, such as velvet, gold or silver brocade used for the clothes of the nobility or liturgical vestments, came from Flanders. Italy and Flanders were highly competitive suppliers to Portuguese merchants.

During the 15th and 16th centuries, hundreds, if not thousands, of tapestries were exported to Portugal from workshops in Tournai, Brussels, Audenard and, before 1477, also from Arras. In 1580, the ambassadors from the *Signoria* of Venice, the knights Trom and Lippomani, were in Portugal and were impressed that 40,000 *cruzados* a year were spent on tapestries.

Tapestries were used in the interiors of monastery churches, convents and cathedrals, to make them more comfortable, and also for aesthetic reasons in the streets, covering façades and flanking streets during processions. They were also used at bullfights, jousts and other sporting occasions to mark enclosed spaces.

There is extensive documentation about direct commissions, but tapestries also arrived in Portugal through organised trade, mainly with a common iconography of sacred or ancient history or simply landscapes.

When Vasco da Gama received the King of Malindi on his carrack in the Indian Ocean, he had the poop deck covered with tapestries. A few years later, in 1505, D. Francisco de Almeida, the first Viceroy of Portuguese India, also received the King of Vijayanagara in a throne room hung with Flemish tapestries. It was as gifts to Asiatic and African potentates that Flemish tapestries reached the far corners of the world.

D. Manuel I ordered a series of 26 scenes recounting the inaugural voyage of Vasco da Gama to India, which was so successful that the workshops of Brussels made many others with the same scenes that were sold all over Europe and were described as being *"in the Portuguese and Indian style"*.

When commissioning tapestries, the Portuguese always sought the best contemporary artists to draw the cartoons, and though they invariably went to Flanders for them, this did not prevent D. Manuel I from requesting a cartoon from Leonardo da Vinci.

The Meeting of Aesthetics

Art, in the reign of D. Manuel I, or, more generally speaking, at the time of the Discoveries, was based on the meeting of several aesthetics, from Europe, on the one hand, and from Africa and the Far East, on the other. In this small kingdom, such a meeting produced specimens that were often free of the Western canons on which Portuguese art had always been based. Imports from Castile, the East of the Iberian Peninsula and Andalusia were constant, as were purchases from Northern European cities, above all those from Flanders, Brabant and the southern region of present-day Germany. The arrival of artists from these areas was not, as we have seen above, an occasional occurrence.

With the passage of time, and most of all with the opening of the maritime route to India, the arrival of

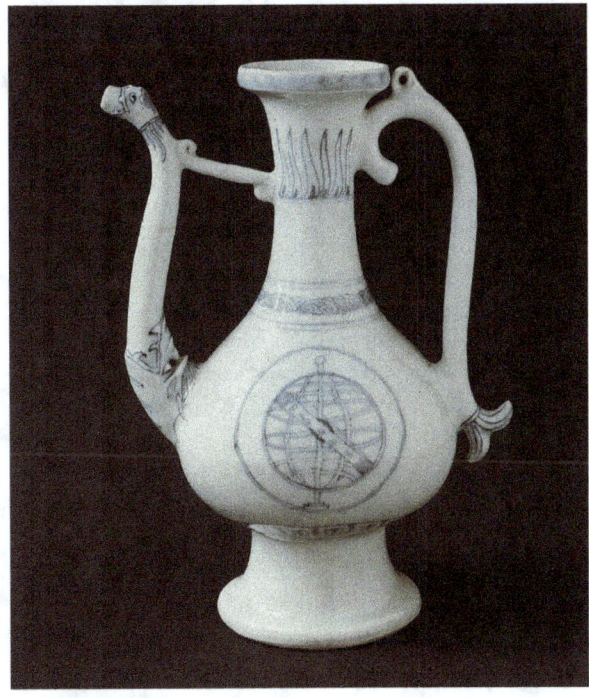

Ewer, blue-and-white porcelain, with the armillary sphere, China, Ming Dynasty, c.1519, Fundação Medeiros e Almeida, Lisbon.

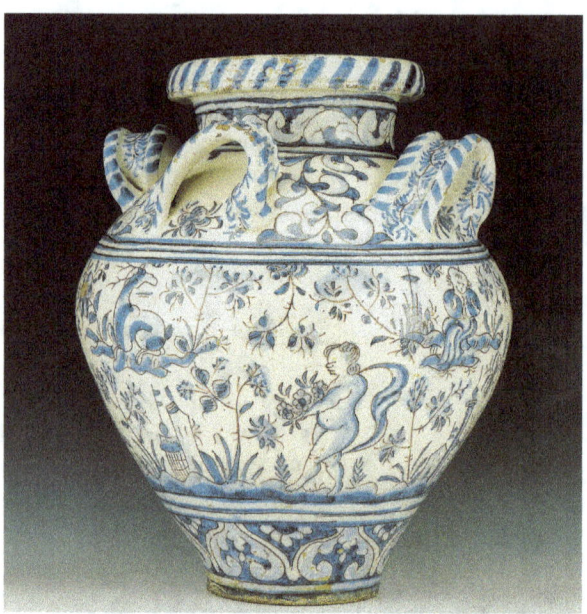

Earthenware jar decorated with Chinese motifs, manufactured in Lisbon, 17th century, private collection.

Attributed to Kano Domi, "Namban" screen, detail, leaves with tempera painting on rice paper covered with gold leaf, c.1600, Museu Nacional de Arte Antiga, Lisbon.

artefacts and articles from the Far East stimulated the imagination of Portuguese artists and had a distinct effect on the development of local arts and crafts. This did not happen immediately during the reign of D. Manuel I, but during the reigns of succeeding monarchs. Lisbon potters imitated Ming designs on glazed pottery; the carpet makers of Arraiolos made carpets with Persian patterns and the embroidered coverlets from Castelo Branco acquired Hindustani patterns.

At the same time, men and women covered themselves in jewellery from India and Ceylon, wore silks and brocades from China and the Middle East, reclined on *cochins*,

amid fountains and ornamental pools reminiscent of those in Andalusia and the Maghreb.

The Portuguese presence in other places also motivated local artists and craftsmen to produce new products with other uses, but with their own traditional stamp. This led to the production of Indo-Portuguese furniture, followed by the Japanese *Namban* style. In the same way, Middle-Kingdom painters of porcelain began to decorate valuable blue and white vases with the coats of arms and device of the Kings of Portugal, and with phrases in praise of the Virgin Mary. In Africa, talented artists from Benin and Sierra Leone invented salt-cellars, spoons, and wafer-boxes for the sacred Host. There were also innumerable objects in which Europeans were represented, which were sold in

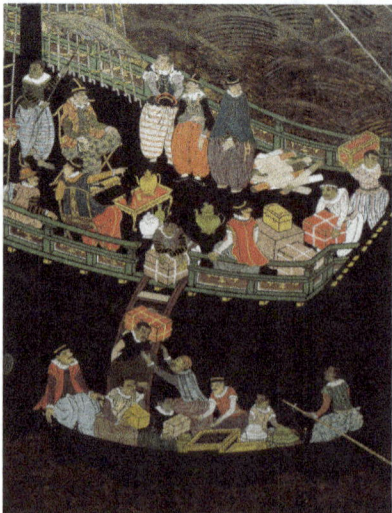

Manueline Art

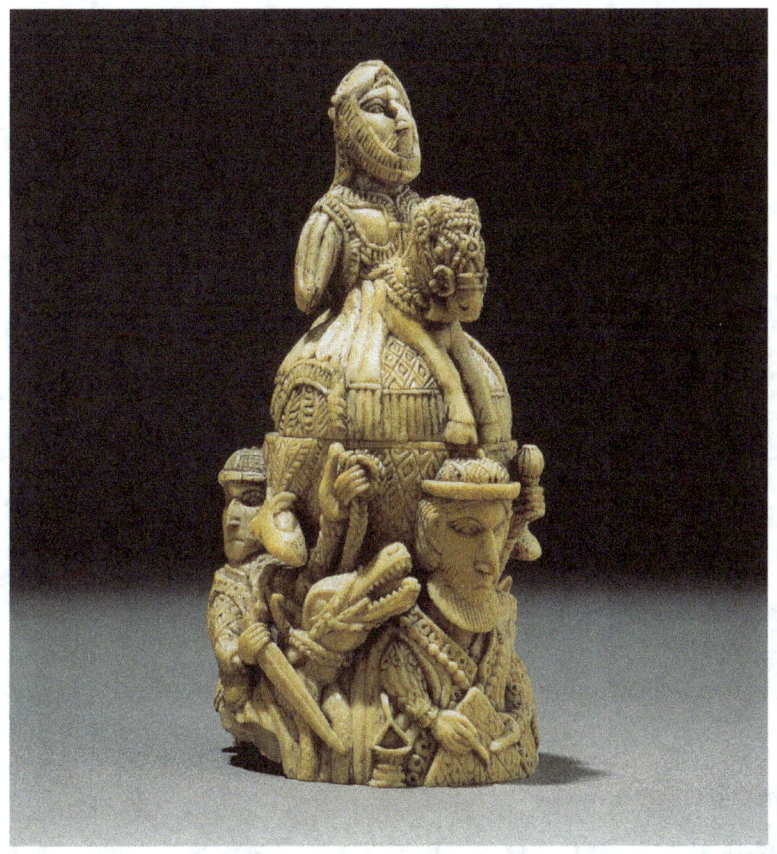

Incomplete double salt-cellar, Afro-Portuguese, ivory, 16th century, Museu Nacional de Arte Antiga, Lisbon.

a way that anticipated the modern concept of the souvenir.
The treasures of the Lords of Persia, Indian rajas, Japanese daimyos, and even the Great Mogul, included European precious rarities. Equally, in European Courts, chambers were filled with previously unknown, splendid valuables that travelled in chests in the cabins of the captains commanding the carracks that sailed on the India route.

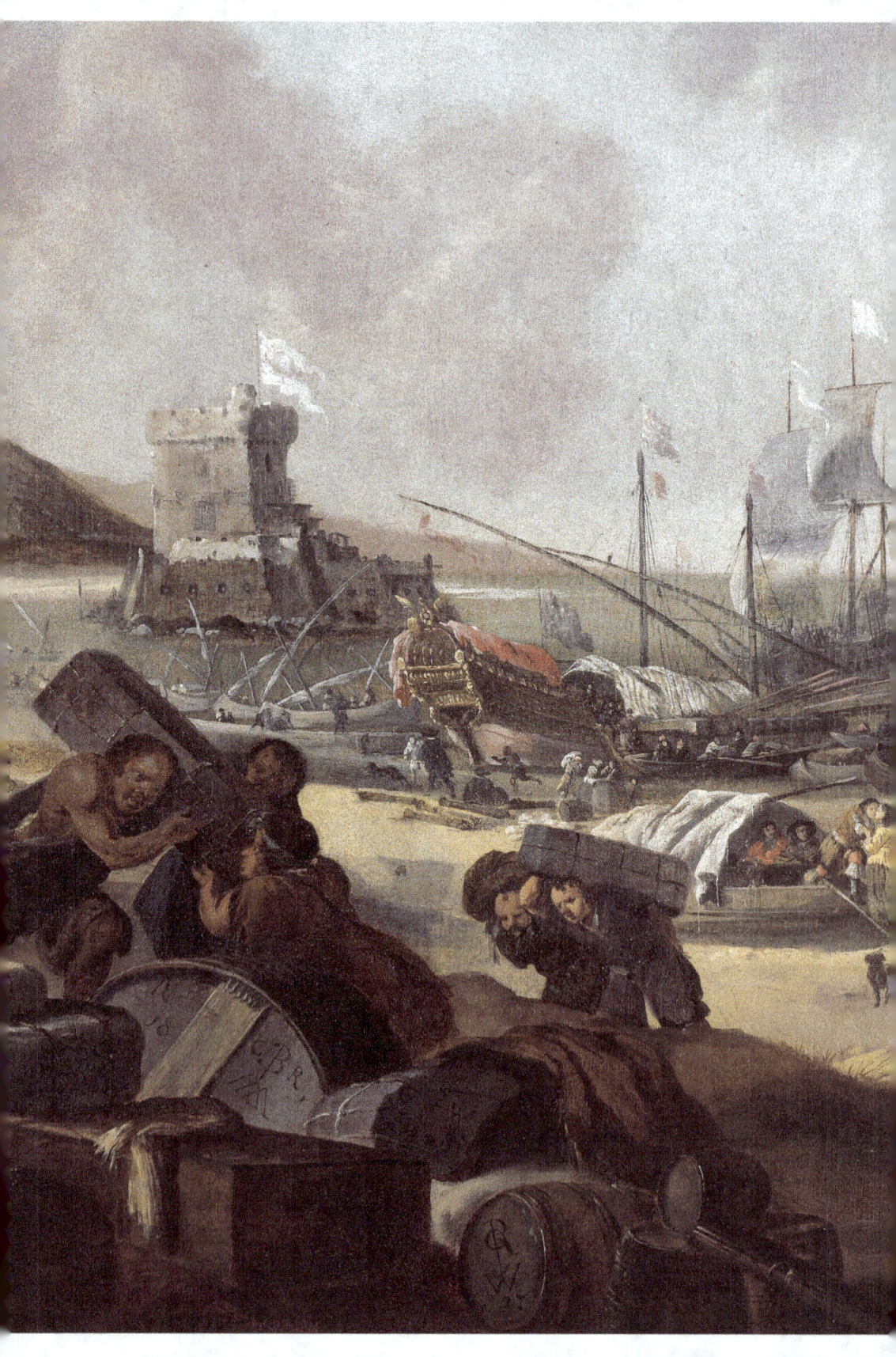

ITINERARY I

The Beach of Adventure

Pedro Dias, Dalila Rodrigues,
Nuno Vassallo e Silva, Fernando Grilo

First day

I.1 LISBON

      I.1.a Monastery of Jerónimos
      I.1.b Museu da Marinha (Naval Museum)
      I.1.c Tower of Belém
      I.1.d Museu Nacional de Arte Antiga
      I.1.e Portal of the Church of Conceição Velha
      I.1.f Casa dos Bicos
      I.1.g Castelo de São Jorge (St George's Castle)

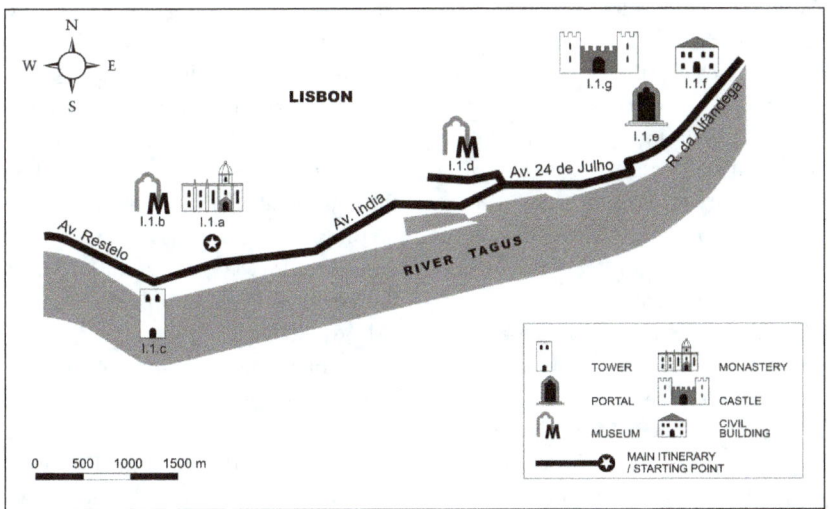

Detail of a painting by Weenix, showing the Torre de Belém and the anchorage of Restelo, private collection, Lisbon.

ITINERARY I   *The Beach of Adventure*

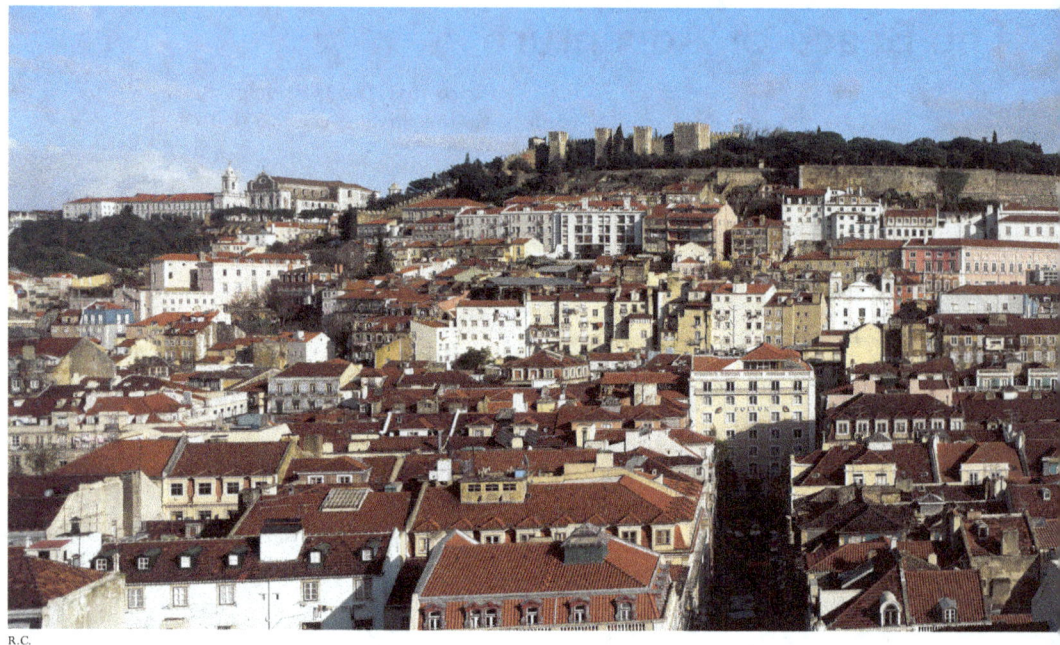

R.C.

General view of Lisbon.

Praia do Restelo, on the River Tagus, was the poet's *"Beach of Adventure"*. The Infante Dom Henrique, who was to become known as Prince Henry the Navigator, founded a chapel there for the spiritual and moral support of returning or departing navigators. Even today, the sea commands respect and awe, so how much more terrifying it must have been at a time when images of Mediaeval monsters were only just being erased from the communal imagination.

The small chapel grew to be the parish church and was then transformed by D. Manuel I, into a large monastic complex, a hymn to glorious majesty. A votive offering to the Virgin of Estrela or Belém, for Vasco da Gama's successful voyage to India and the future profits this would produce in gold and souls.

This was the setting in which the immortal Portuguese poet Camões placed his long-bearded old man, grumbling about all those who ventured forth on the high seas. The *Velho do Restelo* (the Old Man of Restelo), later depicted by the equally talented Columbano, gained mythical status and has entered Portuguese history as the personification of those who prefer to stay put rather than risk adventure.

Manueline memorials such as the Mosteiro dos Jerónimos and the Torre de Belém or, more generically, those connected with the era of the Discoveries, such as the Museu da Marinha (Na-

ITINERARY 1   *The Beach of Adventure*
Lisbon

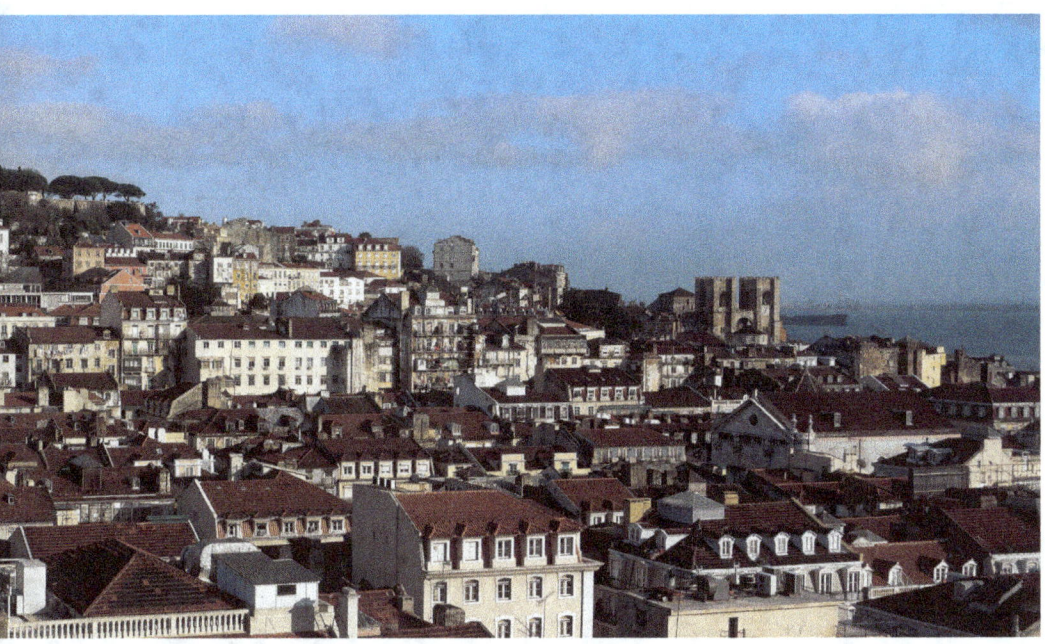

1.1 LISBON

Today, Lisbon, the Portuguese capital, has a population of about one million. Though the city dates back thousands of years, the Roman and, later, the Islamic eras gave it the structures that made it, at the time of D. Manuel I, one of the most important cities in Europe and the link between the old continent and recently discovered lands.

After the Arab Conquest of 711 to 713, the city developed from the castle hill and Alfama down to the banks of the River Tagus, eventually covering an area of 30 hectares with a population of some 25,000.

val Museum), are not confined to Restelo. Belém was and is an extension of Lisbon, the capital of the kingdom and the centre of the great 16th-century Maritime Empire. With the castle crowning its highest hill, the Christian and Jewish areas built over traces of the Roman, Visigothic and Moorish occupations, spread down to the river and then stretched up to Alfama, Bairro Alto and other areas.

Time and natural catastrophes have destroyed many of the magnificent buildings erected during this period, water and fire engulfing the treasures they contained, but there are still traces that recall this time and its many and varied peoples.

41

ITINERARY I   *The Beach of Adventure*
Lisbon

Monastery of Jerónimos, main façade, Lisbon.

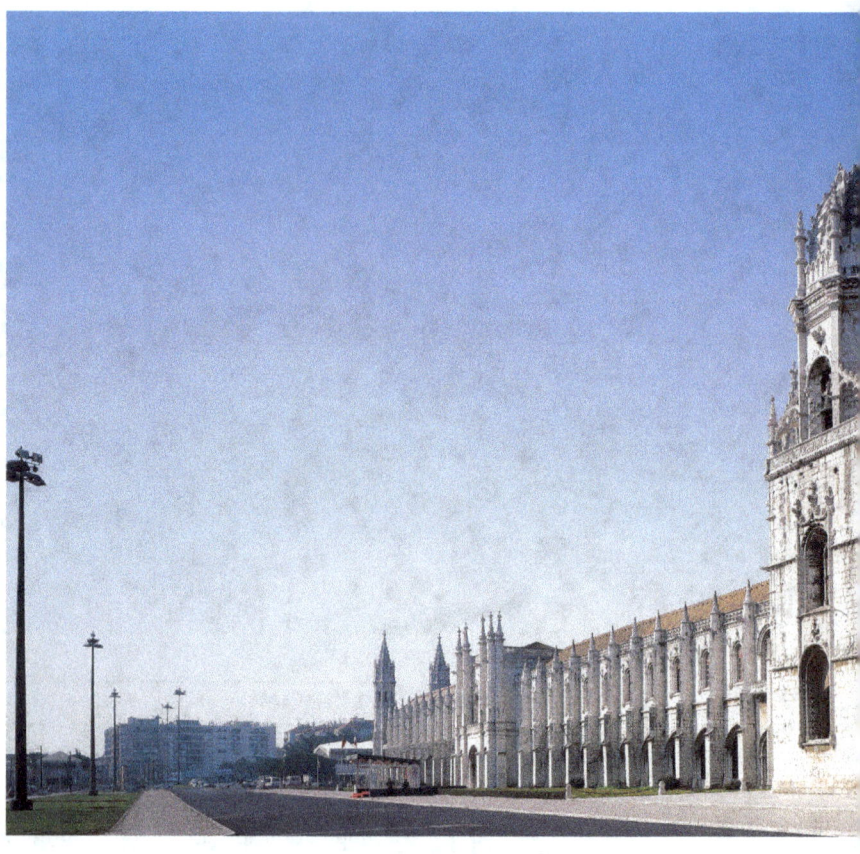

One of the high points of the Christian Reconquest towards the South was the taking of Coimbra, in 1064. This forced the Moors to set up defensive lines, but the Christians under the command of D. Afonso Henriques, who was to become the first King of Portugal, took Lisbon in 1147, to establish a new frontier along the Tagus.

The young king, realising the importance of Lisbon and its port, moved to the city, strengthening its surrounding walls, rebuilding the palace and churches and even building a new cathedral, though Coimbra remained the official capital for another century and a half.

Lisbon grew in its number of merchants, the establishment of religious orders and a fast burgeoning port activity. D. Afonso III established his Court in the Castle of the Alcáçova, the old Moorish fortress, and the city became the capital of the king-

ITINERARY I *The Beach of Adventure*
Lisbon

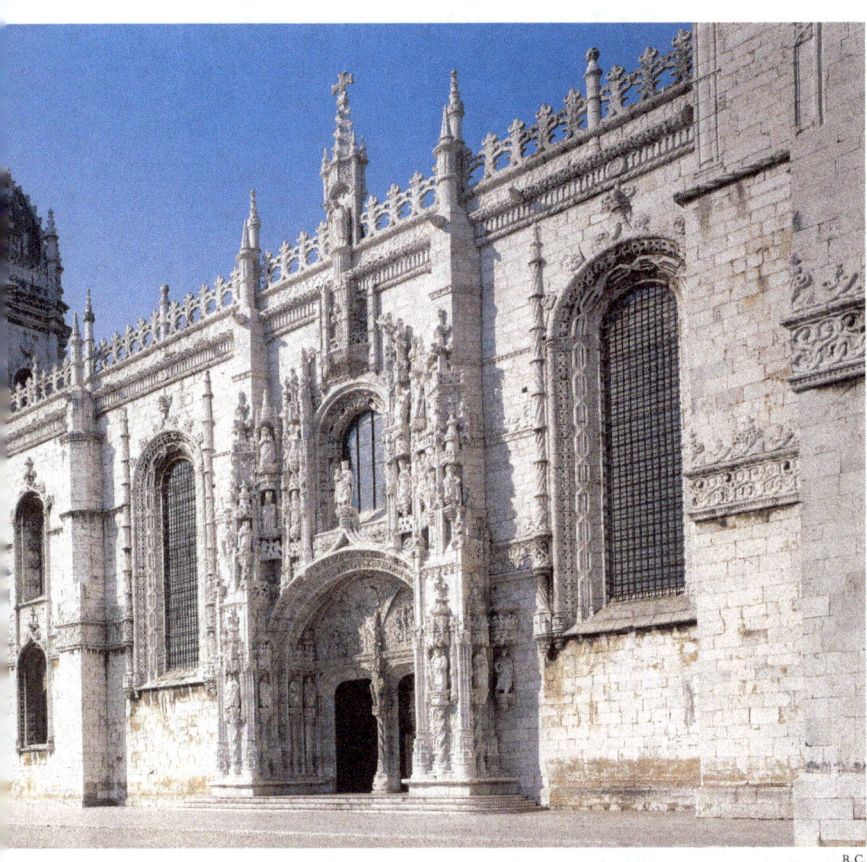
R.C.

dom. By the end of the Middle Ages, the life of its population centred on the royal residence, Paço da Ribeira, down by the river, to which D. Manuel I moved in 1498. The warehouses of the Casa da Índia (India House), the Arsenal, and Ribeira das Naus were built nearby. Roads stretched as far as Alfama, Mouraria, the castle and Vila Nova de Andrade, more popularly known as Bairro Alto, and the city began to spread along the river. There, the nobility built second residences and developed *quintas* (estates), monks and nuns built convents and monasteries that were gradually linked by houses to form a single urban agglomerate. Today, the Greater Lisbon area includes municipalities stretching practically from Vila Franca de Xira to Cascais, Loures to Odivelas, and from Almada to Barreiro on the opposite bank of the river.

ITINERARY I   *The Beach of Adventure*
Lisbon

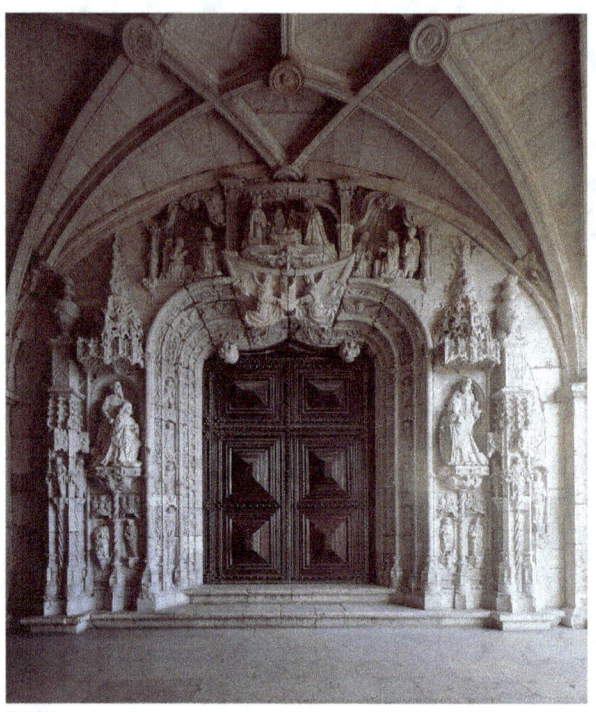

IPM/C.M.

Monastery of Jerónimos, southern portal, Lisbon.

I.1.a **Monastery of Jerónimos**

Praça do Império, Belém. (Tel: 21 3620034). Designated a National Monument and a UNESCO World Heritage Site since 1983. Photography permitted.
Admission charge to cloister, refectory and upper choir. Opening hours: 10.00-18.30, May-September and 10.00-17.00, October-May. Visitors admitted up to 30 minutes before closing time. Closed on Mondays and January 1st, Easter, May 1st and December 25th. The church is open for worship.

The Monastery of Jerónimos, with its almost 200-metre-long façade facing the River Tagus, dominates the Praça do Império. The author of the original plan, altered in 1510 and again in 1516, is unknown. The Church, Royal Cloister and the dormitory facing the river, were the work of the Master Builder Boytac, but the roof casing and work undertaken after 1517 were by the Spaniard, João de Castilho. In later years, when other styles from the Renaissance to Romantic Revivalism were in fashion, further work was carried out to enhance and modernise the building.

The west side contains the enormous two-storey monks' dormitory, which today houses the National Museum of Archaeology and the Naval Museum. The structure is essentially as it was originally planned and as Boytac began to build it before 1514, but the two neo-Manueline towers and the cupola which complete this end of the building were added in the mid-19th century.

The church has two main doorways in cretaceous limestone, and, though both were begun in 1517 and executed simultaneously, they reveal different inspirations and understanding of architectural sculpture. While, clearly, both demonstrate the principal characteristics of Manueline art, and the work of various artists can be distinguished, there is a remarkably uniform inspiration and execution that reveals the quality of the artists, of different nationalities, assembled by João de Castilho.

The south door with its profusion of images and decorative motifs is regularly and accurately described as a jewel of Portuguese 16th-century architectural sculpture. For, even taking into consideration the influence of earlier portals, such as that of the Convent of Christ in Tomar, the south door is on a scale without parallel in Portuguese art of the period. It is like a retable celebrating Our Lady of Bethlehem attended by the Apostles, Sybils and Evangelists and also includes the emblematic figure of Prince Henry the Navigator on the central pillar.

The west door, canonically the most important, was the first work carried out in Portugal by the French Master Nicolas Chanterène. This highly cultured multi-faceted artist, arrived in Portugal at the king's invitation, and at once introduced some of the most important features of Renaissance sculpture, such as the portrait statues of D. Manuel I and his second wife, Queen D. Maria, presented by their patron saints on corbels flanking the central bay. Reliefs of the Apostles and scenes from the *Childhood of Christ*, in the second register, are also of remarkable quality.

This is the most perfect Portuguese *hall-church*, and one of the most remarkable in Europe, with very slender octagonal pillars covered with Renaissance decoration in low relief supporting the depressed ribbed vaulting erected by João de Castilho, in 1522. Below the late Gothic upper choir lie the tombs of the epic poet Camões and the navigator Vasco da Gama, both of which are by Costa Mota, and both neo-Manueline and dating from the end of the 19th century.

There are two exceptional, late Gothic pulpits in the transept, made by João de Castilho's assistants. A door here leads into the sacristy, which has a very fine vaulted ceiling, supported by a portly pier covered with early Renaissance *grotesque* carvings.

The chancel and the two arms of the transept, containing the tombs of D. Manuel I, D. João III, their wives and a number of royal children, were re-modelled in the

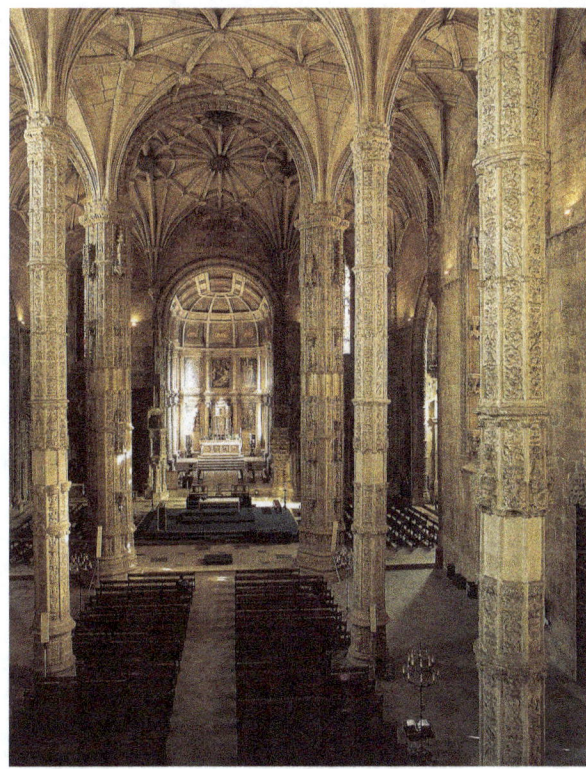

Church of the Monastery of Jerónimos, interior, Lisbon.

M.A.

ITINERARY I   The Beach of Adventure
Lisbon

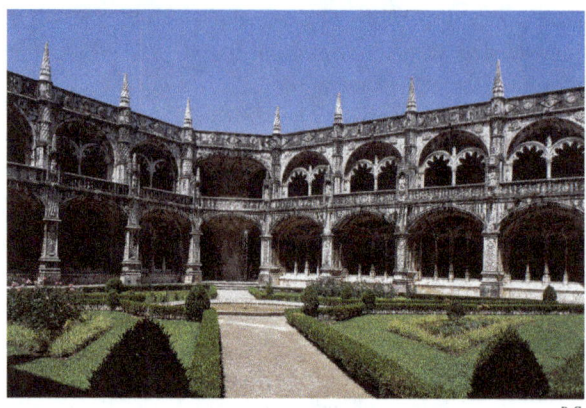

Monastery of Jerónimos, Royal Cloister, Lisbon.

Museu de Marinha (Naval Museum), interior, Lisbon.

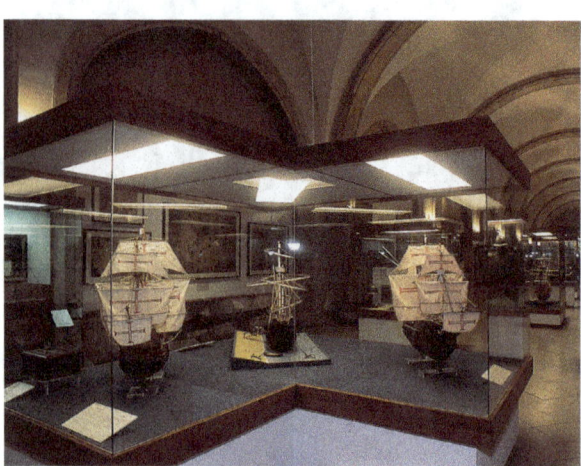

Mannerist style by the architect Jerome of Rouen and inaugurated in 1572. The great retable contains a remarkable series of Mannerist paintings by Lourenço Salzedo. The tombs of the Kings D. Sebastião and D. Henrique and various princes are in the transept chapels.

The two-storey, late Gothic, Royal Cloister has foliate Manueline decoration alternating with Renaissance themes. Boytac, João de Castilho and Diogo de Torralva successively carried out work here, the last-mentioned being responsible for the Renaissance *plaitband* on the upper floor. The maple stalls in the upper choir, made in 1550 by Diego de Zarza to a design by Torralva, are perhaps the finest example of Portuguese Mannerist woodwork. The choir loft also contains an exceptional Crucifixion by the Flemish sculptor Philippe de Vries and was offered to the monastery by Prince D. Luís.

Leonardo Vaz was responsible for the late Gothic refectory, on the ground floor, off the Royal Cloister. The Chapter House, also off the cloister, has a very lovely portal sculpted by Rodrigo de Pontezilla, and contains the neo-Gothic tomb of the 19th-century historian, Alexandre Herculano.

I.1.b **Museu da Marinha (Naval Museum)**

Praça do Império, next to the Mosteiro dos Jerónimos. (Tel: 21 3620019). Photography permitted.
Admission charge. Opening hours: 10.00-18.00 in the summer months, and 10.00-17.00, October-May. Closed on Mondays and national holidays.

The Naval Museum is housed in the west wing of the old dormitory of the Mosteiro dos Jerónimos and also in more modern buildings. It contains a series of

ITINERARY I   *The Beach of Adventure*
Lisbon

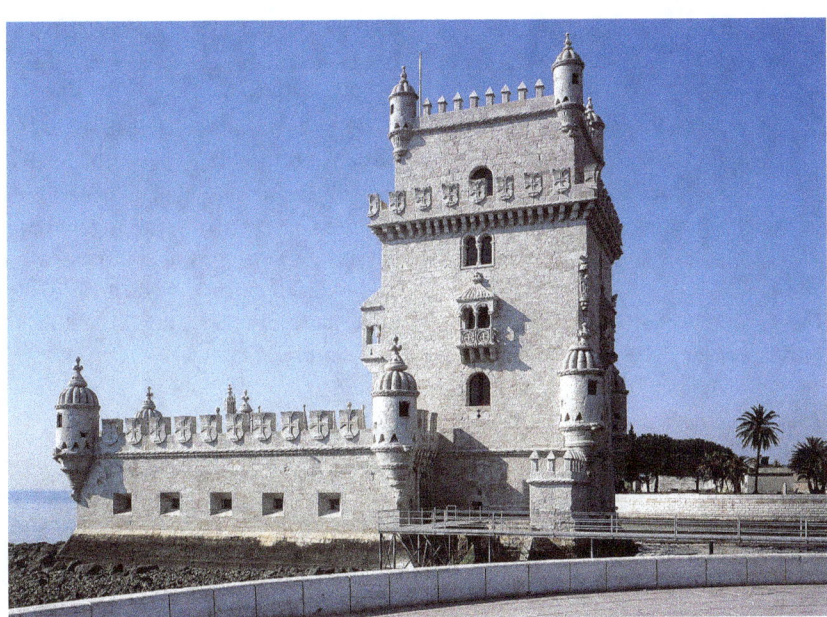

Tower of Belém, general view, Lisbon.

model ships dating from the Middle Ages to the present day, with special emphasis on vessels from the time of the Discoveries. Also on display are nautical instruments, weapons and cannon, items related to the sea, as well as memorials, marker stones and other original pieces brought from overseas' forts and cities. The collection also contains a number of maps and nautical charts, as well as an image of St Raphael that was on one of the vessels that made the first voyage to India under the command of Vasco da Gama. Royal brigs, barges and other craft are on display in the new part of the museum along with the aircraft *Lusitânia*, in which Gago Coutinho and Sacadura Cabral made their first crossing of the South Atlantic.

I.1.c **Tower of Belém**

Belém, near the River Tagus. (Tel: 21 3620034). Designated a National Monument. Designated

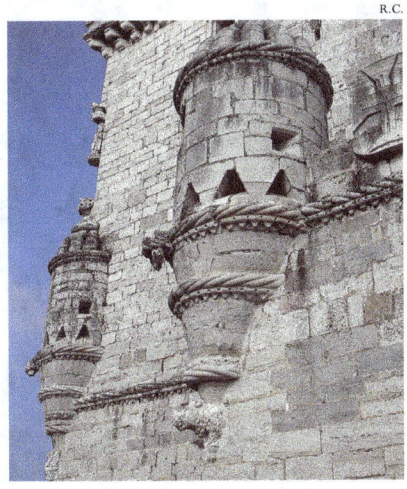

Tower of Belém, detail with head of rhinoceros, Lisbon.

47

ITINERARY I   *The Beach of Adventure*
Lisbon

a UNESCO World Heritage Site since 1983. Photography permitted.
Admission charge. Opening hours: 10.00-18.30, May-September, and 10.00-17.00, October-April. Closed on Mondays and January 1st, Easter, May 1st and December 25th. Visitors admitted up to 30 minutes before closing.

The Torre de Belém, built to defend the entrance to the Tagus with crossfire from the old fortress of Outão, is one of the most emblematic examples of Manueline architecture. A short distance from the Monastery of Jerónimos, and even closer to the royal palace built on the orders of D. Manuel I, it was designed and built by Francisco de Arruda between 1515 and 1519 and consists of a modern, polygonal bulwark with casemates and a keep-like square watchtower. The Court no doubt used the original building when attending ceremonies to mark the arrival and departure of the fleets.

In 1848, considerable changes were made to the building giving it a festive air with *merlons* shaped like shields bearing the Cross of Christ, a loggia with elegant tracery and Arabic-inspired sentry boxes, all exclusively the fruit of the rather fanciful imagination of 19th-century restorers.

I.1.d **Museu Nacional de Arte Antiga**

Rua das Janelas Verdes. (Tel: 21 3964151). The Museum, the former residence of the Counts of Alvor, is classified as a Building of Public Interest. Cafeteria and restaurant. Admission charge. Open Wednesday-Sunday

Nuno Gonçalves, polyptych of São Vicente de Fora, mixed media on oak, 1470-1480, Museu Nacional de Arte Antiga, Lisbon.
a) Monks' Panel.
b) Fishermen's Panel.
c) Prince's Panel.
d) Archbishop's Panel.
e) Knights' Panel.
f) Relic Panel.

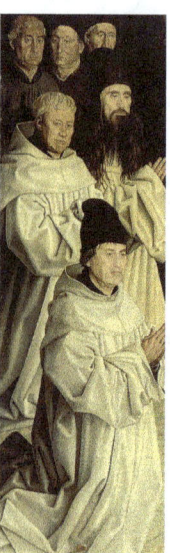
a)

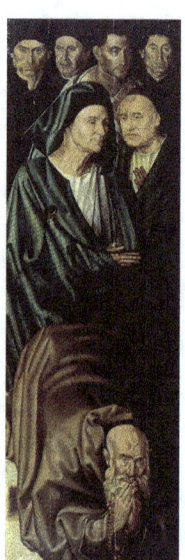
b)

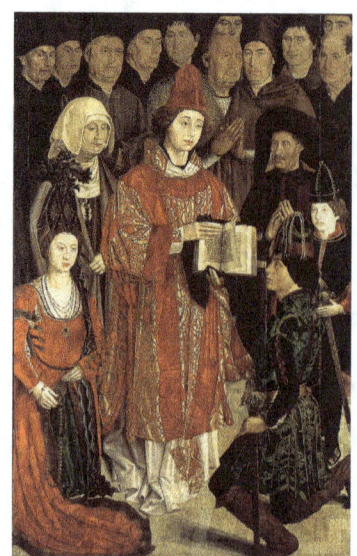
c)

10.00-18.00 and Tuesday 14.00-18.00. Closed on Monday and Tuesday mornings and national holidays: January 1st, Easter, May 1st and December 25th.

The National Museum of Ancient Art contains one of the most important collections of Portuguese Manueline art from the time of the Discoveries, as well as pieces that are the result of the meeting of European culture with that of the peoples of Africa, the Americas and Asia.

St Vincent Panels

These panels were rediscovered at the end of the 19th century and originally belonged to the altar of St Vincent in the *Sé* (cathedral) de Lisboa. They are one of the most extraordinary examples of western painting. The panels have become an emblem of the Portuguese Discoveries, although there has been considerable conjecture as to their authorship, original location, chronology and the identity of the various personages depicted.

Available information seems to indicate that Nuno Gonçalves, painter to D. Afonso V, active between 1450 and 1492, was responsible for this superb royal commission, possibly designed as a votive offering in gratitude for the protection of the saint, and for Portuguese victories in Morocco. The saint appears on the two central panels as the protective figure, around which the others are placed, highlighting the two personages occupying the foreground and depicted with one knee

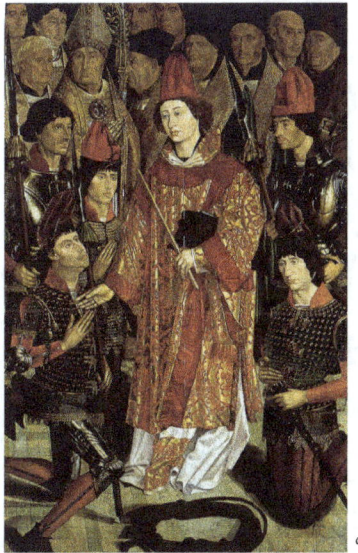
d)

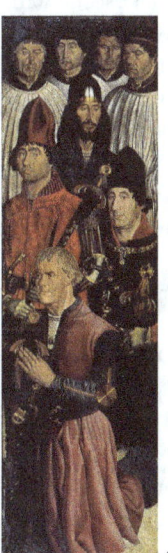
e)

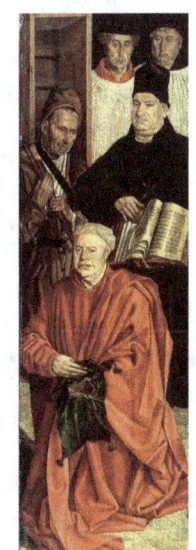
f)

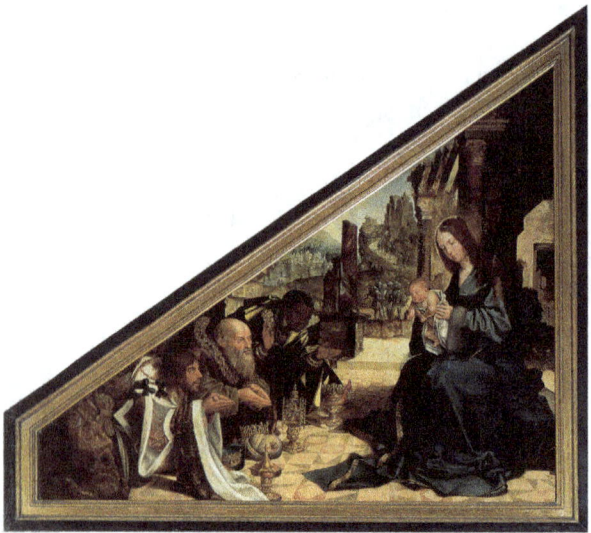

Jorge Afonso, "Adoration of the Magi", retable from Madre de Deus, oil on oak, c.1515, Museu Nacional de Arte Antiga, Lisbon.

on the ground. The insertion of the figures, in a squared perspective on a dark background, is not at all arbitrary.

The Prince's Panel, a Court scene with Prince Henry, can be interpreted as being the swearing of an oath to, or be seen as a veneration of, the Royal Family, as St Vincent is showing one of the leading figures, possibly D. Afonso V, the Gospel. The saint, against a wall of very expressive faces that is prolonged into the other panels, is flanked by figures that correspond to portraits of Prince Henry, his sister D. Isabel, Duchess of Burgundy, Prince João, the future D. João II, as well as Queen D. Isabel, facing the king.

The Archbishop's Panel has been interpreted as a war-like exaltation. St Vincent holds a commander's baton, the Book is closed, while the main figures wear military uniform and are armed with lances and a sword. This may be a specific allusion to military power and war with the sanction of the Church, the hierarchy of which is amply represented in this and other panels.

The four smaller lateral panels are a continuation of the two at the centre in both formal values and significance. The Knights' Panel, on the right, and that of the Fishermen, on the left, emphasise the involvement of Portuguese society in what possibly corresponds to the military campaigns in Africa; at Álcacer Seguer in 1458, and Asilah and Tangier in 1471.

The two end panels, a coherent part of the ensemble, give new meaning to the work. The Relic Panel and that of the Monks contain significant elements that, while not consensual, can be directly related to the cult of St Vincent, namely the Cross that appears in the first, and the relic and coffin that appear in the second. The powerful and innovative expressive resources of Nuno Gonçalves stand out in this masterly pictorial discourse, dating back to *c.*1470-1480.

Manueline Painting

Painting underwent a significant creative thrust from the mid-15th century onwards, although visible results, in an already diverse framework, were only to be seen in the period corresponding to the reign of D. Manuel I.

Imported paintings, mainly Flemish, were commissioned or acquired on the open market, and many fine examples are on display in this museum. They include *St. Jerome* by Albrecht Durer, *The Virgin and Child* by Hans Memling, the *Retable of the Passion* by Quentin Metsys, and the *polyptych* by Jan Provost from the Misericórdia in Funchal, Madeira should also be added to the list. The arrival of Flemish artists in Portugal and the subsequent training of Portuguese painters, provoked decisive changes in artistic circles.

Many examples of work undertaken under the patronage of D. Manuel I, the Dowager Queen D. Leonor, and high-ranking members of the regular and secular clergy are in this collection. They are displayed in isolation or in groups according to what is thought to have been their retabular organisation, and are mainly from the Lisbon workshops of Portuguese or Flemish artists active in Portugal. The great retable from the Convento da Madre de Deus, of which seven panels remain, is a good example of the best that was produced in the workshops in Lisbon during the Manueline period and also of the effect that Flemish painting had in Portugal. The retable was the work of the Court Painter Jorge Afonso, active between 1504 and 1540. *Christ Appearing to the Virgin,* one of the finest examples in this series, is dated 1515.

The panels from the altarpiece of Santa Auta are from the same convent, and were commissioned by the same patron, Queen D. Leonor, for the chapel that contained her relics. The *Arrival of the Relics of Santa Auta* depicts the scene with the ceremonial reception at which the queen is present, seated in a tribune on the left, while, paradoxically, it is the seductive figure of the martyr Santa Auta that occupies the foreground.

Many of the Portuguese painters of the Manueline period represented in this collection trained in the studio of the influential Jorge Afonso. These include Cristovão de Figueiredo, whose masterpiece *Deposition of Christ* was painted for the Church of Santa Cruz de Coimbra; Gregório Lopes, Court Painter to both D. Manuel I and D. João III, with his retables of São Bento and Santos-o-Novo, as well as Garcia Fernandes, who produced the *Presentation in the*

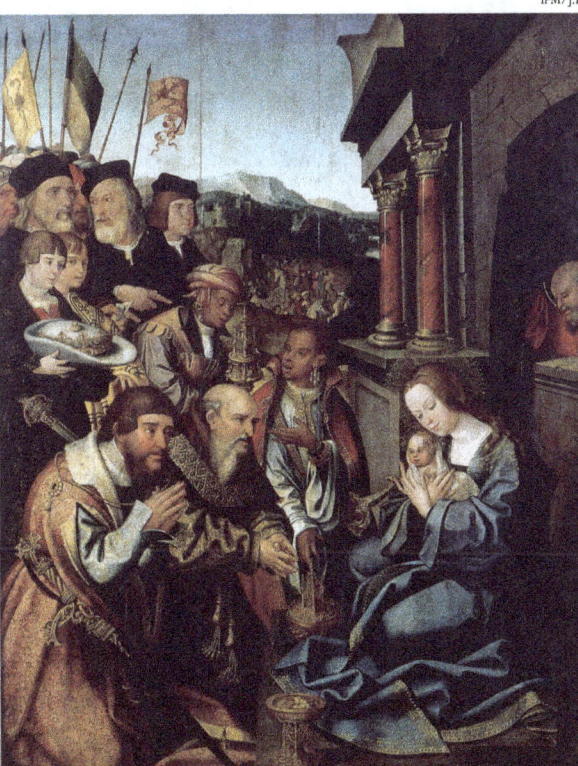

Jorge Leal and Gregório Lopes, "Adoration of the Magi", from the retable of São Bento, oil on oak, c.1524-25, Museu Nacional de Arte Antiga.

IPM/J.P.

ITINERARY I   The Beach of Adventure
Lisbon

Unknown painter, "Hell", oil on oak, 16th century, Museu Nacional de Arte Antiga, Lisbon.

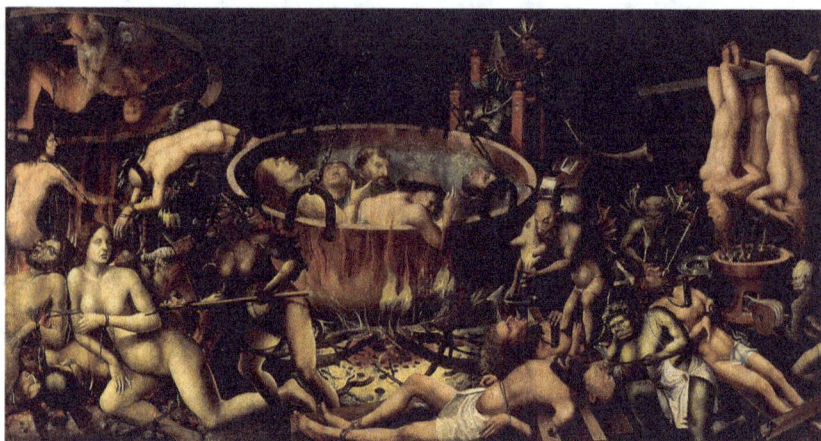

IPM/L.P.

Temple. The Flemish painter, Francisco Henriques, painted panels for the retable of the Church of São Francisco in Évora. These painters were related to Jorge Afonso, and they more or less constantly worked together. The similarity of style in a significant number of works may be accounted for by this teamwork.

Among other works on display are several by the Flemish monk, Frei Carlos, whose workshop was at the Convento do Espinheiro in Évora, namely the *Annunciation*, *Resurrection* and the *Good Shepherd*, as well as works by another Nordic painter, the Master of Lourinhã. These include the very lovely *St John in Patmos* from the Convento das Berlengas and the *Retable of the life of St James* from the Church of Palmela Castle.

Gold and Silver

The Monstrance of Belém, named after the monastery within which it was conserved when D. Manuel died, is undoubtedly one of most famous works of all Manueline craftsmanship in precious metals, and of Portuguese art in general.

The Royal Testament, dated 1517, informs us of the name of the author, Gil Vicente. D. Manuel I organised the delivery to Vicente's workshop of the first gold tribute brought back from the Kingdom of Quiloa by Vasco da Gama in 1503. For three years, the master craftsman and his assistants worked on the monstrance, which, according to the inscription on the base, was finished in 1506: O MUITO ALTO. PRICIPE E. PODEROSO. SENHOR. REI. D. MANUEL I. A. MDOU. FAZER. DO. OURO. DAS. PARIAS. DE. QUILOA. AQUABOU. CCCCCVI *("The very high prince and powerful lord, King D. Manuel I ordered it to be made from the gold of the tributes of Quiloa. Completed in 1506.")*.

Iberian late Gothic in style, as can be seen by the vertical cylinder, the base is ellipsoidal with six lobules covered with mezzo-reliefs in gold, enamelled with fruit, flowers, snails and peacocks and six armillary spheres, the king's personal device. On the base of the highly architectural upper part, the 12 Apostles kneel round the crystal cylinder containing the Host. Minuscule figures depicting the Annunciation, the Angel Gabriel and the Virgin appear on the two *pilasters* that flank this group. On the upper level, in a triple *baldachin*, a dove represents the Holy Ghost, and above is the figure of the Eternal Father.

The monstrance, described in the chronicles of King D. Manuel, associates the symbols of his power, such as the armillary spheres and the legend round the base with the religious sphere that marks the upper part, to become one of the monarch's most powerful politico-religious messages.

Other outstanding items from the Manueline era include a silver hour-glass with the Royal coat of arms and armillary sphere; a *porta-pax* dated 1515 from the Convento do Espinheiro in Évora; and the Renaissance style reliquary of Santo Lenho, in the form of a template in gold, enamel and precious stones that belonged to Queen D. Leonor and was very probably made by Mestre João.

Sculpture

The Manueline sculptures from the workshops of Coimbra are particularly fine, primarily those of Diogo Pires the Elder,

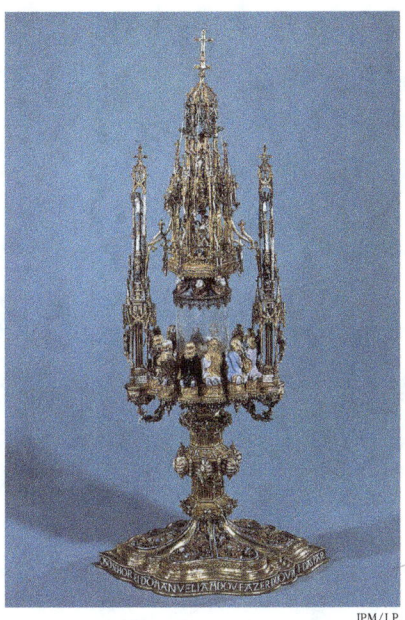

Workshop of Gil Vicente, Belém Monstrance, gold and enamel in "ronde bosse", 1503–06), Museu Nacional de Arte Antiga, Lisbon.

IPM/J.P.
J.B.

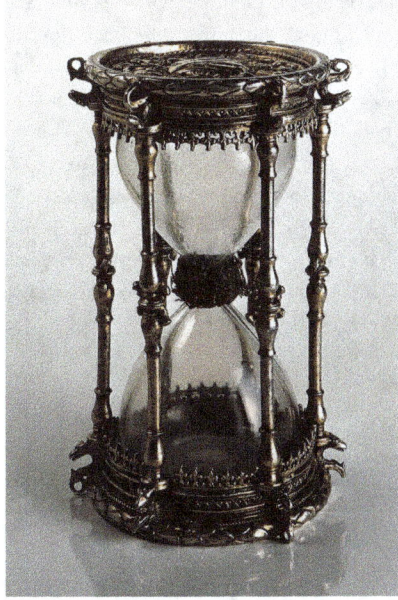

Manueline hourglass, Museu Nacional de Arte Antiga, Lisbon.

ITINERARY I   *The Beach of Adventure*
Lisbon

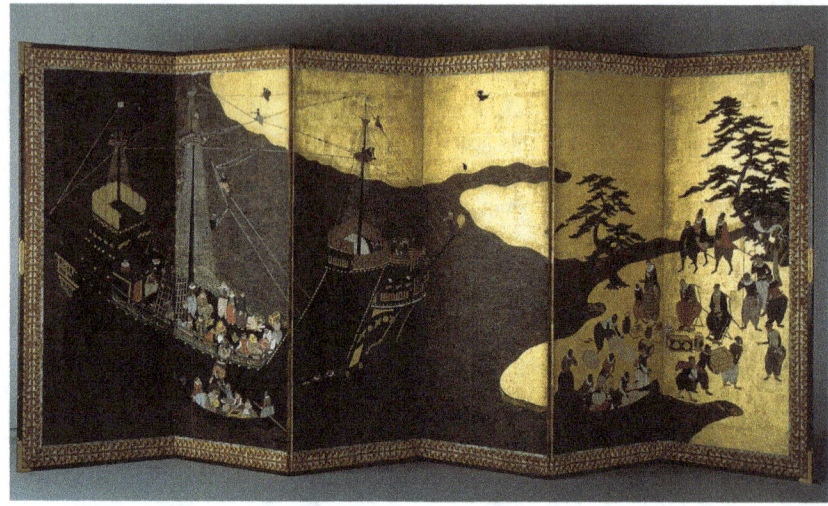

Attributed to Kano Domi, "Namban" Screen, leaves with tempera painting on rice paper covered with gold leaf, 1593-1600, Museu Nacional de Arte Antiga, Lisbon.

for example, his *São Tiago* (St James), in polychrome Ançã limestone, and a superb *São Miguel* (St Michael) by Diogo Pires-the-Younger. Flemish works include *São Mateus* (St Matthew) by Cornelius de Holanda. There are Della Robbia medallions, a series of *tondi,* the tabernacle frontal from the Convento da Madre de Deus and the collection of Queen D. Leonor. Not to mention the statues of *São Leonardo* (St Leonard) and *Nossa Senhora da Estrela*, presented by Pope Leo X to D. Manuel I, which were formerly in the Mosteiro dos Jerónimos.

Luso-African and Luso-Oriental Art

The contents of convents and monasteries suppressed in 1834, provided the National Museum of Ancient Art with an important collection of works imported from Africa, India, China and Japan after the Portuguese Discoveries. Acquisitions and donations have added to this section, now one of the most important in the museum and indispensable to all those who wish to know more about the art of Africa and the Far East.

Portuguese contacts with Sierra Leone are represented by three works in ivory: two horns of ivory, one ornamented with the Cross of the Order of Christ, and the base of a salt-cellar, ornamented with figures of Portuguese, one on horseback serving as the lid.

Indian pieces are the richest and most numerous and include religious objects in silver and gold, coffers in filigree and tortoiseshell, all kinds of furniture, ivory pieces, and painted and embroidered vestments that illustrate the evolution of art over four centuries. The Treasury of the Convent of Vidigueira produced an oratory-reliquary, a missal stand and a *porta-pax*, all made of silver and donated to the convent by Padre André Coutinho, who brought them back from India at the end of the 16th century. Pieces from India also include furniture in exotic woods inlaid with ivory, cabinets, desks, tables and ivory statues, many of them of the Child Jesus – the Good Shepherd.

From distant China there is a fine selection of blue and white porcelain dating back to the Ming Dynasty, and important 18th-century polychrome Export Ware, along with lacquerware and enamel items made in Canton, especially for European customers.

Japanese contacts with Portugal produced fine works of art, including a fascinating pair of late 16th-century *Namban* screens that depict Portuguese carracks leaving Goa and arriving in Japan. The Museum also has a good collection of *Namban* lacquer referring to the *Nambam-jin*, or the "Barbarians from the South" as the Portuguese were known, along with coffers, desks, trays and other pieces.

I.1.e Portal of the Church of Conceição Velha

Rua da Alfândega in the Pombaline Centre of Lisbon. (Tel: 21 8870202). Designated a National Monument. Photography permitted. Opening hours: 8.00-18.00 on weekdays, 8.00-13.00 on Saturdays and 10.00-13.00 on Sundays. Mass is at 12.00 from Tuesday to Friday inclusive. Normally closed during August.

The Church of Conceição Velha was granted to the Knights of the Order of Christ, who enlarged and enriched it to such an extent in the 16th century, that it became one of the most remarkable in Lisbon. The earthquake of 1755 left little standing other than the fine portal built shortly after 1518, so it is probable that some of the artists who had worked on the Mosteiro dos Jerónimos had a hand in it, under the direction of João de Castilho.

The portal is composed of a central arch with two finely sculpted *archivolts* defining a *tympanum* and central pillar divided by a sculpted pillar. Two typically Manueline pillars with niches and *baldachins* depicting the Annunciation, flank the doorway. The fine sculpture of Nossa Senhora da Misericórdia shelters under her mantle, on one side representatives of the clergy, including a

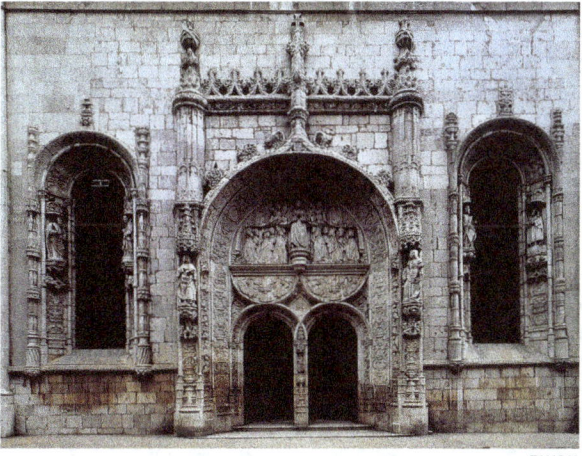

Church of Conceição Velha, portal, Lisbon.

pope, cardinal and bishops, while on the other side are a king, queen and members of the nobility. This is clearly the work of a sculptor of the very highest quality, who remains unknown, but who certainly proved capable of representing the most essential elements of his theme by placing under the protection of the Virgin's robe different social classes: on the one hand, ecclesiastic representatives, for instance a pope, a cardinal and various bishops; on the other hand, the emperor, kings and other members of the aristocracy.

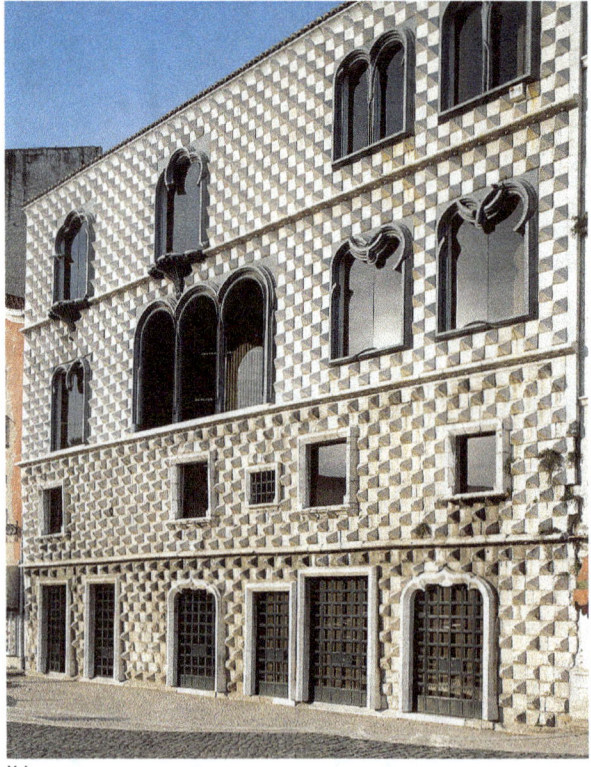

General view of the Casa dos Bicos, Lisbon.

I.1.f Casa dos Bicos

Rua dos Bacalhoeiros. (Tel: 21 8810900 / 21 8884827). Designated a National Monument. Used for temporary exhibitions.
Opening hours: 9.30-17.30 on weekdays.

This unusual building, a little further to the east along the former Terreiro do Trigo, is covered in diamond-shaped bosses (*bicos*) and is a remarkable example of architecture dating from the beginning of the 16th century. Similar buildings are to be found in other parts of Europe, namely Ferrara and Segovia. Built for Brás Afonso de Albuquerque, the son of Afonso de Albuquerque, Governor of India, it stood against the old Late-Mediaeval wall on the site of some former salt-pans. The upper floors of the building collapsed during the earthquake of 1755, but were reconstructed in 1983 according to old pictures, though the window frames have been made in metal.

I.1.g Castelo de São Jorge (St. George's Castle)

Enter the castle by the São Jorge gateway in Rua do Chão da Feira. Designated a National Monument. Currently under restoration.
Opening hours: daily 10.00-18.00 in winter and 10.00-21.00 in summer.
A multimedia show about the history of the city of Lisbon is held daily in Olissipónia, on the site of the old Royal Palace at 10.00 and 18.00, except on January 1st, May 1st and December 25th.
The city of Lisbon can be seen through a periscope with a 360°-viewing angle from the Torre de Ulisses in the upper part of castle.

ITINERARY I   *The Beach of Adventure*
Lisbon

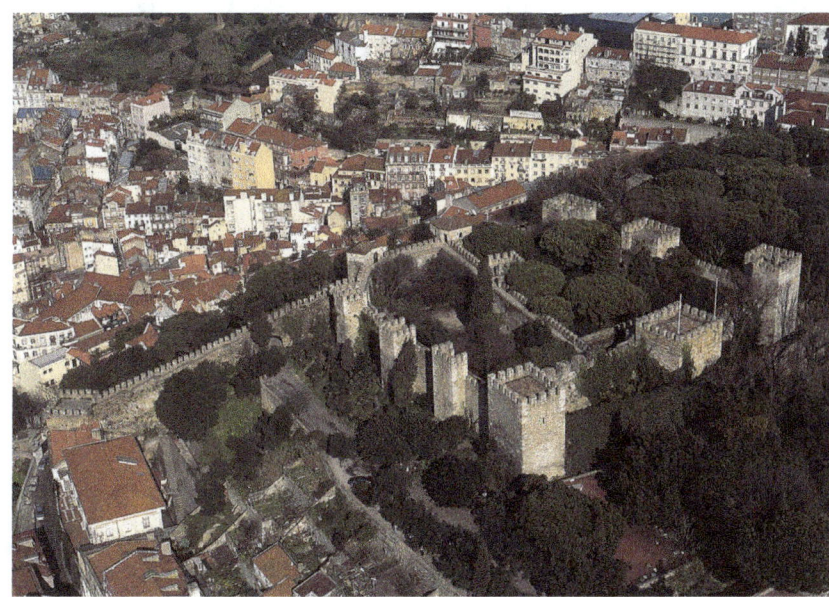

Aerial view of São Jorge Castle, Lisbon.

A.C.

Opening hours: daily 10.00-16.30, except on January 1st, May 1st and December 25th. (Tel: 21 8877244 / 21 8882831).

The Castle of São Jorge dates back to the Islamic period and was the site of the *alcáçova*, a fortress, which occupied about four hectares. The defensive Moorish walls of the city, some of which still remain to the east by the Church of Menino Deus, stretched out from this point. After the Reconquest of Lisbon in 1147, the Portuguese kings took up residence in the castle and made extensive alterations. The last were carried out in the time of D. Manuel I, though in the early years of the 16th century he went to live by the river in the Paço da Ribeira. Some kings such as D. Sebastião, preferred to live in the old castle for longer or shorter periods.

To get to Sintra by car, take the IC19 (25 km.). Trains also run regularly from Rossio station in central Lisbon (45 mins.).

57

ITINERARY I

The Beach of Adventure

Pedro Dias, Dalila Rodrigues,
Nuno Vassallo e Silva, Fernando Grilo

Second day

I.2 SINTRA
    I.2.a Palácio da Vila
    I.2.b Palácio da Pena

I.3 CHELEIROS
    I.3.a Church of Cheleiros

I.4 TORRES VEDRAS
    I.4.a Castle
    I.4.b Church of São Pedro
    I.4.c Varatojo Convent

D. Manuel I

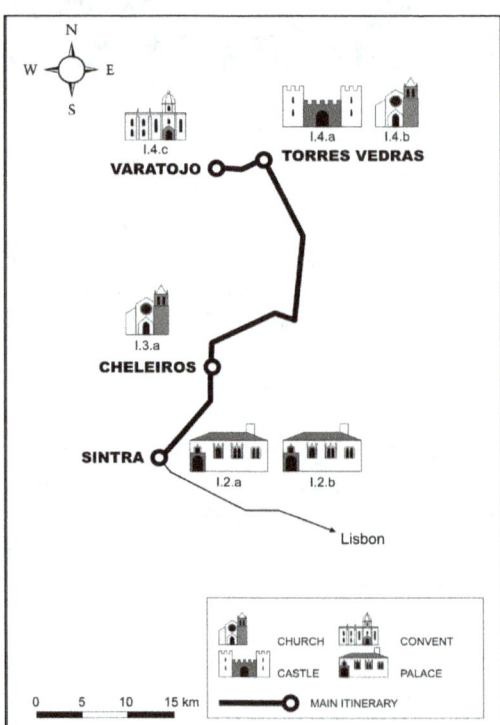

ITINERARY I *The Beach of Adventure*
Sintra

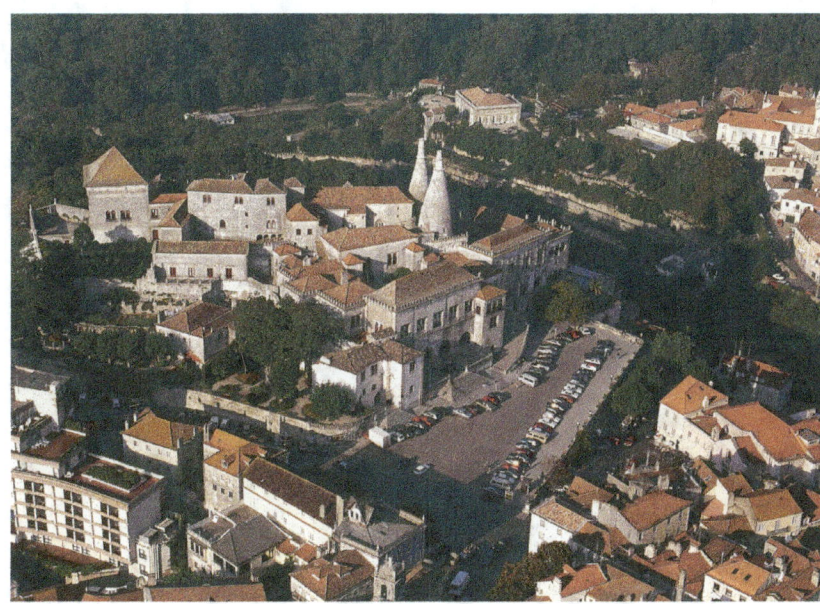

General view of Sintra.

R.C.

I.2 SINTRA

Sintra was an important Arab settlement, which fell to the forces of D. Afonso Henriques in 1147. The king garrisoned the 11th-century Moorish castle on the hillside, as well as the Palácio da Vila, which was a fortified construction dating from the same period.

The pleasant countryside, mild climate and abundance of game made the town a favourite with the Portuguese kings in the early Middle Ages. Over the centuries, the palace was added to and enlarged, making Sintra into a prosperous town by the 15th century.

In the Manueline era, the palace at Sintra was complementary to the Paço da Ribeira in Lisbon. The Court resided there for long periods, and churches and convents were either built or reconstructed in the vicinity, most notably Pena and Penha Longa, as well as the Town Hall and a leper hospital and many residences belonging to the upper aristocracy.

In the 19th century, D. Fernando II, the Romantic king, introduced the Neo-Gothic and other Revivalist styles to the town that enchanted travellers such as the poet, Lord Byron, and cultured personalities, such as Queen Amélia. The last three kings of Portugal brought new life to the Palácio da Vila, turning it into a favoured royal residence.

ITINERARY I *The Beach of Adventure*
Sintra

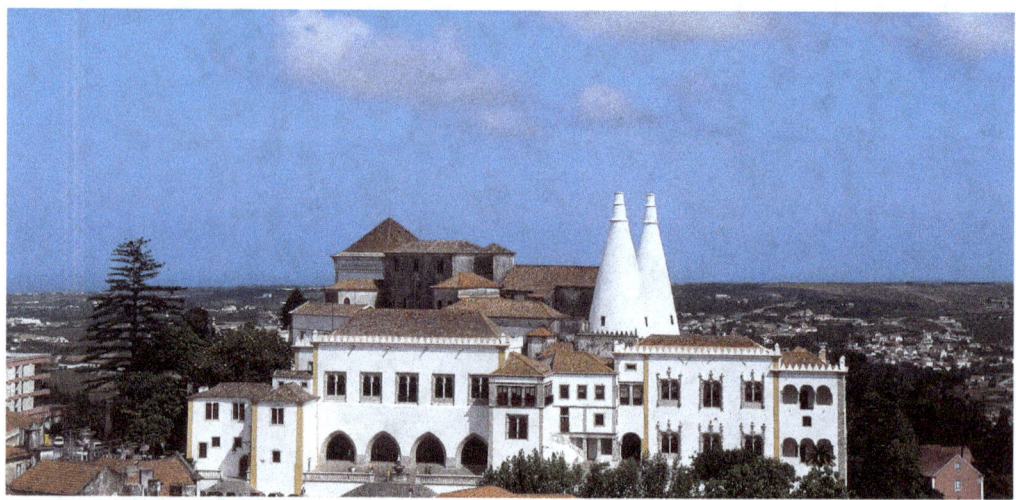

A.C.

Palácio da Vila, Sintra.

I.2.a **Palácio da Vila**

Largo Rainha D. Amélia, in the centre of Sintra. (Tel: 21 9106840/2). Designated a National Monument.
Admission charge. Opening hours: daily 10.00-17.30. Last admission 30 minutes before closing. Closed on Wednesdays and January 1st, Easter, May 1st, June 29th and December 25th.

The Palácio da Vila was a Muslim building used by the Portuguese Crown immediately after the Reconquest of 1147. In the early years of the 15th century, D. João I added to the building and D. Manuel I made changes at least twice, once immediately on ascending the throne, which gave the building the look it retains to this day. D. João III made further improvements and others were introduced following the earthquake of 1755.

On the main façade facing the square, note the brattishing of the *Mudejar* battlements in the Córdoba style and the paired balcony windows with exuberant naturalistic Manueline frames. Steps lead to the main floor below a Gothic arcade.
Note also the two large kitchen chimneys and the complexity and lack of cohesion in the various juxtaposed buildings. Courtyards with ornamental pools and fountains, gardens and cool corners, link each area. The Pátio dos Cisnes, the Pátio da Carranca and the Jardim da Preta were constructed by D. Manuel I, who hankered after a Moorish palace like those he had seen in Castile, especially at Aragon, and Andalusia. The chapel has a *Mudejar* tracery ceiling, and all over the palace are walls covered in Hispano-Arabic tiles made in Seville such as those in the Sala da Sereia and the Sala dos Árabes, which also has an

ITINERARY I   *The Beach of Adventure*
Sintra

elegant fountain. The Jardim da Preta has a twisted stone pillar with foliate decoration, surrounded by exotic vegetation.
The delightful decoration of the Sala das Pegas with magpies painted on the ceiling, panelling shaped by ridged tiles, and an Italian Renaissance marble fireplace, is noteworthy, as is the ceiling of the Sala dos Brasões, depicting the armorial bearings of the Manueline nobility. Other 16th-century constructions are the atrium and the Sala das Galés, its ceiling decorated with Portuguese sailing vessels.

I.2.b **Palácio da Pena**

Estrada da Pena, on top of the ridge, 2 km. south of Sintra. From the gate, it is possible to walk to the top or take a minibus. The no. 434 bus leaves the train station every 40 minutes, from 10.20 daily, going through the town centre, passing the Moorish Castle and the Palácio da Pena and returning to the station. (Tel: 21 9105340). Designated a National Monument.
Admission charge. Opening hours: 10.00-17.00 in winter and 10.00-18.30 in summer. Closed on Monday and public holidays: January 1st, Good Friday, Easter

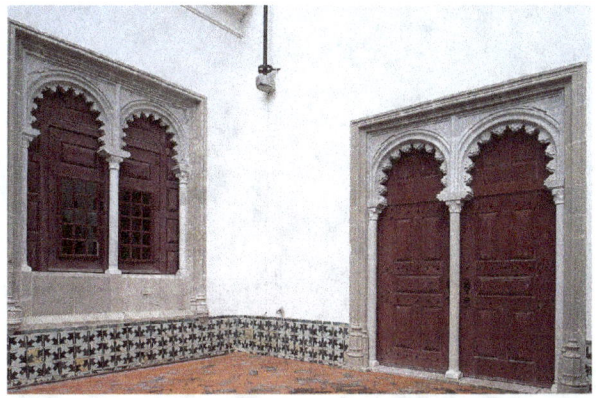

Palácio da Vila, courtyard, Sintra.

Palácio da Pena, general view of the Revivalist constructions, Sintra.

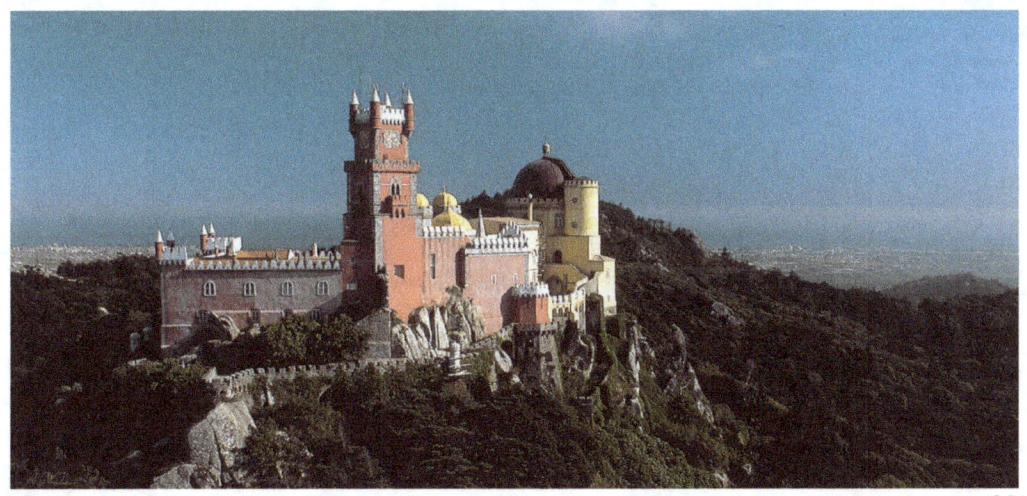

ITINERARY I   The Beach of Adventure
Sintra

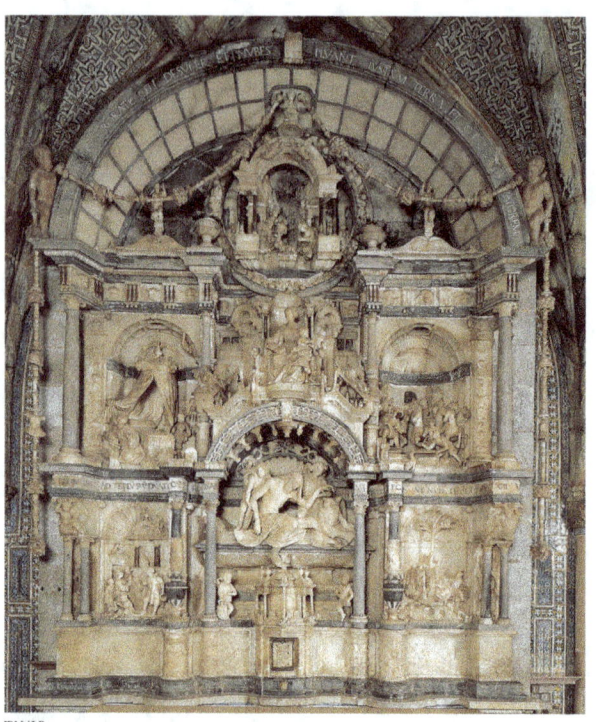

Nicolas Chanterène, Renaissance retable from the Chapel at Palácio da Pena, alabaster, 1529-32, Sintra.

Sunday, May 1st, June 29th and December 25th.

The Palácio da Pena, with its complex structure, bright colour and extravagant forms, was the invention of D. Fernando II and his faithful right-hand man, Baron Eschwege, who drew up the plans and directed the work in the Romantic spirit of the time. Manueline structures in the old convent were, however, conserved. These works, attributed to Boytac and largely completed by 1511, include the church, choir, sacristy and cloister.

Nicolas Chanterène executed the alabaster altarpiece in the chapel, a masterpiece of Renaissance sculpture, in a formal, rather Italianate style. He began work on it at the end of 1528 after acquiring the alabaster, the best in the Iberian Peninsula, in Aragon.

Four registers in height, the Court sculptor carved the *Last Supper* and the *Descent into Limbo* in very low relief, and highlighted the importance of the tabernacle, a perfect example of Classical architecture even to the columns, pediments and a small cupola. The reliefs on the second and third register are also quite remarkable for the profusion of figures and the sensation of movement they create, especially in the *Annunciation* and the *Adoration of the Three Kings*. In the centre, *Christ Supported by two Angels*, shows the sculptor at the height of his powers, perfectly representing the human body. The image of the Virgin *in sedia* holding a restless Child is also of great artistic quality.

To reach Cheleiros follow the EN9.

Mafra and Torres Vedras Area

The fertile countryside to the north of the Serra de Sintra, next to the Atlantic coast, supplied Lisbon with meat and agricultural produce from the end of the Middle Ages onwards, hence the development of towns such as Mafra, Torres Vedras and

Ericeira. Various religious orders were established in the region, the Franciscans in particular making a decisive contribution, leasing their property but watching over it with the zeal of good administrators. This land of plenty, abundant with bread, wine, meat and fish, stretched to Alenquer, Caldas da Rainha and Óbidos.

I.3 CHELEIROS

I.3.a Church of Cheleiros

Next to the Estrada Nacional. Designated as a Building of Public Interest. To visit the Church, contact Senhora D. Guiomar Baleia, at Rua do Arco da Ponte, 16. (Tel: 219 670052 Monday to Friday 9.00-12.30 or at the weekend). Alternatively, contact Senhora D. Hermenegilda Maria, at Rua do Chafariz. (Tel: 219 270281 at the same times).
Opening hours: mass celebrated on Wednesdays at 19.30 and on Sundays at 13.00.

The Church of Cheleiros is very typical of those found in medium-sized settlements in Manueline times. The portal is well designed with good stonework, the long vessel of the church is covered with wood and the chancel has new Renaissance touches, though the ribbed vaulting is still Gothic in style.

To continue to Torres Vedras take the EN9 in the direction of Alcainça / Malveira. Continue on the EN8 in the direction of Gradil / Turcifal to Torres Vedras.

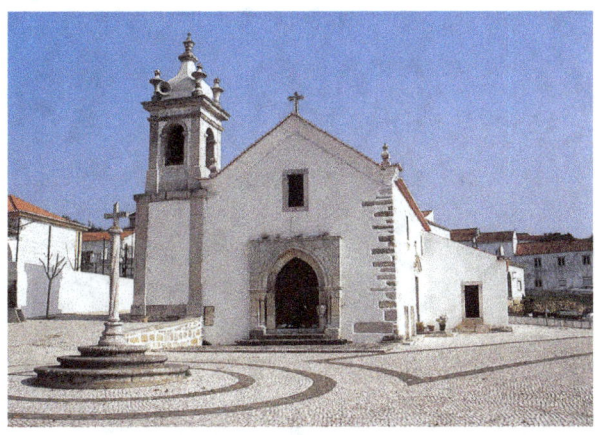

Church of Cheleiros, main façade.

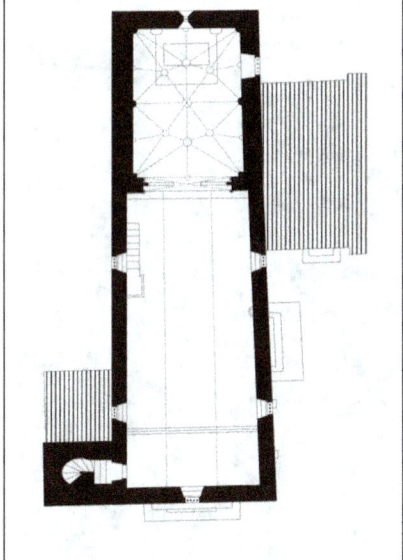

Church of Cheleiros, plan at choir level, Boletim da Direcção-Geral dos Edifícios e Monumentos Nacionais, No. 48, Lisbon, 1947.

ITINERARY I *The Beach of Adventure*
Torres Vedras

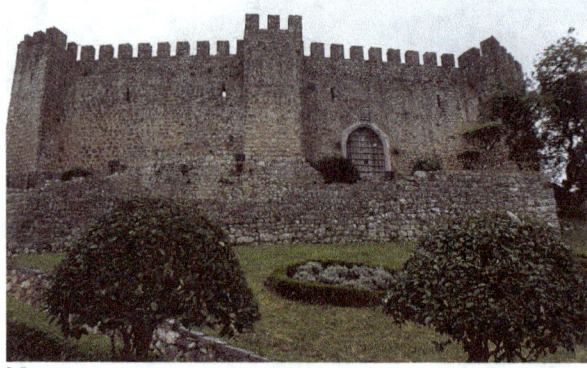

Castle of Torres Vedras.

Church of São Pedro, main portal, Torres Vedras.

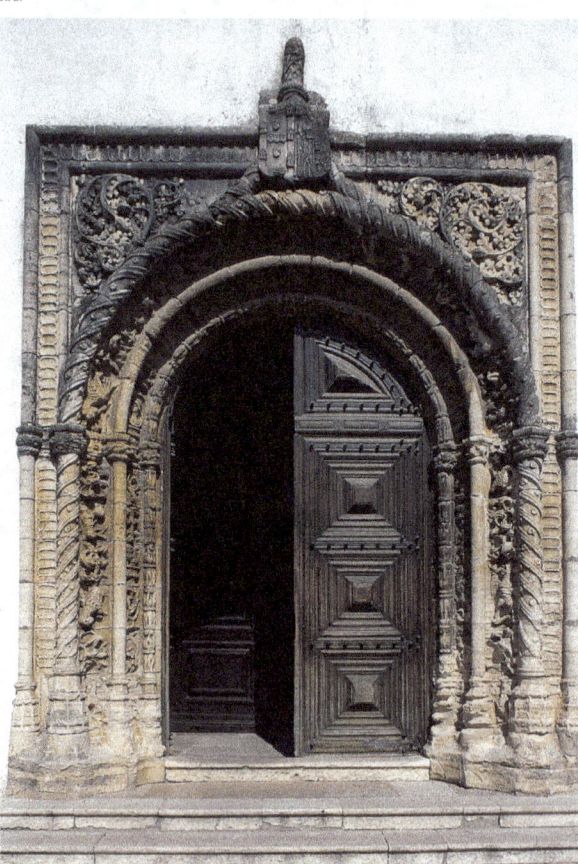

I.4 TORRES VEDRAS

I.4.a Castle

The Castle at Torres Vedras has largely retained its Manueline structure. Built before Portugal became a nation, it was conquered by D. Afonso Henriques in 1147 and rebuilt at the same king's orders, being later altered and improved by Kings D. Dinis and D. Fernando.
Note the two rounded bastions or bulwarks that gird the gateway, bearing the blazon and device of D. Manuel I. These were erected as part of the Manueline building programme that took place some time around 1516. The castle, looking over the town it defended, was also the governor's residence.
Much of the castle was laid to ruin by the devastating earthquake of 1755. Its walls have since been restored and now surround a wooded garden.

I.4.b Church of São Pedro

Largo de S. Pedro. (Tel: 261 322386). Designated a National Monument.
Opening hours: daily 8.30-12.00 and 15.00-17.00.

In the plains at the bottom of the hill were the houses of the ordinary folk and the churches, such as that of São Pedro, which still retains important Manueline traces, for example in the exuberant naturalistic doorway. The interior has a late Gothic oratory containing the tomb of João Lopes Perestrelo. The 16th-century main vessel of the church has Renaissance arches and other decorative motifs from later periods, namely Baroque painted tiles and gilded Rococo woodwork.

1.4.c Varatojo Convent

Situated at Lugar do Varatojo. (Tel: 261 314120). Designated a National Monument.
Opening hours: daily 9.00-12.00 and 15.00-18.30.

The Varatojo Convent, formerly on the outskirts of Torres Vedras, has now been almost absorbed into the town centre. Founded by D. Afonso V, the first stone was laid in 1470 and the main construction work was completed in four years. Little now remains of this period, or that of the Manueline, other than the atrium, wich is covered with a *Mudejar* tracery ceiling and a late Gothic portal, in the finest Late Gothic style that was used at Batalha.

The late Gothic cloister that dates from the beginning of the 16th century, was, undoubtedly, sponsored by the D. Manuel I.

One of the most curious elements is a corner window with a Gothic frame, called the "D. Afonso V window", though, in truth, it is already very characteristic of the Manueline period.

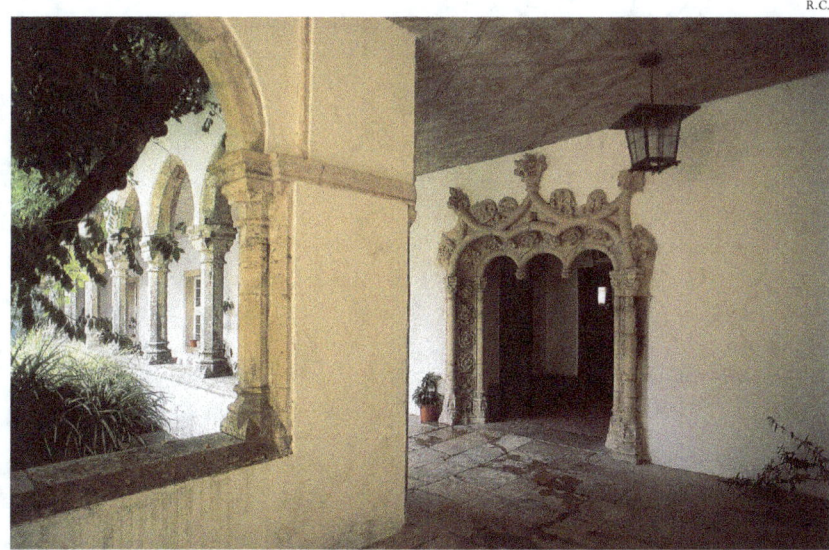

Convent of Varatojo, cloister and portal, Torres Vedras.

D. MANUEL I

Pedro Dias

D. Manuel I ascended the throne of Portugal as the result of a series of implausible historical accidents. He was the ninth and youngest child of D. Fernando, Duke of Beja, brother of D. Afonso V, and D. Beatriz, the daughter of Prince D. João and, therefore, also a great-granddaughter of D. João I. Prince D. Afonso, heir to D. João II, D. Manuel's cousin, was killed in a riding accident shortly after his marriage. The king's natural son, Prince D. Jorge was kept out of the running by palace intrigues, primarily, the machinations of Queen D. Leonor, D. Manuel's sister. D. Manuel's father died prematurely, and his two elder brothers were killed after plotting against the king, their cousin. When D. João II died at the age of only 45, D. Manuel, by then Duke of Beja, ascended the throne to lead the country through a period of glory that it had never seen before, and would never see again.

Born in Alcochete, on May 31 1469, D. Manuel was proclaimed King in Alcácer do Sal on October 27 1495, and died in Lisbon on December 13 1521. When his brother Diogo was executed, D. Manuel was made Duke of Beja, Lord of Viseu, Covilhã and Vila Viçosa, Constable of the Realm and Adminstrator General of the Order of Christ.

In 1497, he married the widow of Prince D. Afonso, D. Isabel, daughter of Ferdinand and Isabella and heir presumptive to the thrones of León, Castile and Aragon. D. Isabel died in childbirth in Saragossa and their son, Miguel da Paz, died shortly afterwards. D. Manuel I then married his sister-in-law, D. Maria in 1500 and produced 10 children, including the future D. João III. Widowed for a third time, in 1517, he married D. Leonor, sister of Charles V.

D. Manuel I was one of the most remarkable Portuguese politicians of all time. He surrounded himself with cultured, able men who advised and helped him to modernise the State by reforming its administrative, judicial and economic structures. He handled his overseas victories wisely and used them to underpin his position in Europe and form effective partnerships with other crowned heads. He continued the work of his great-uncle, Prince Henry and of his cousin, D. João II, by fostering and supporting nautical and mercantile activities. During his reign and under his personal direction, Portuguese mariners reached China and America, to make Portugal the greatest maritime power of the day and the establishment of a thalassocracy, never before known and never repeated in history.

D. Manuel was a great patron and protector of artists and men of letters, inviting many from other countries to his Court and leaving a remarkably rich heritage to the nation.

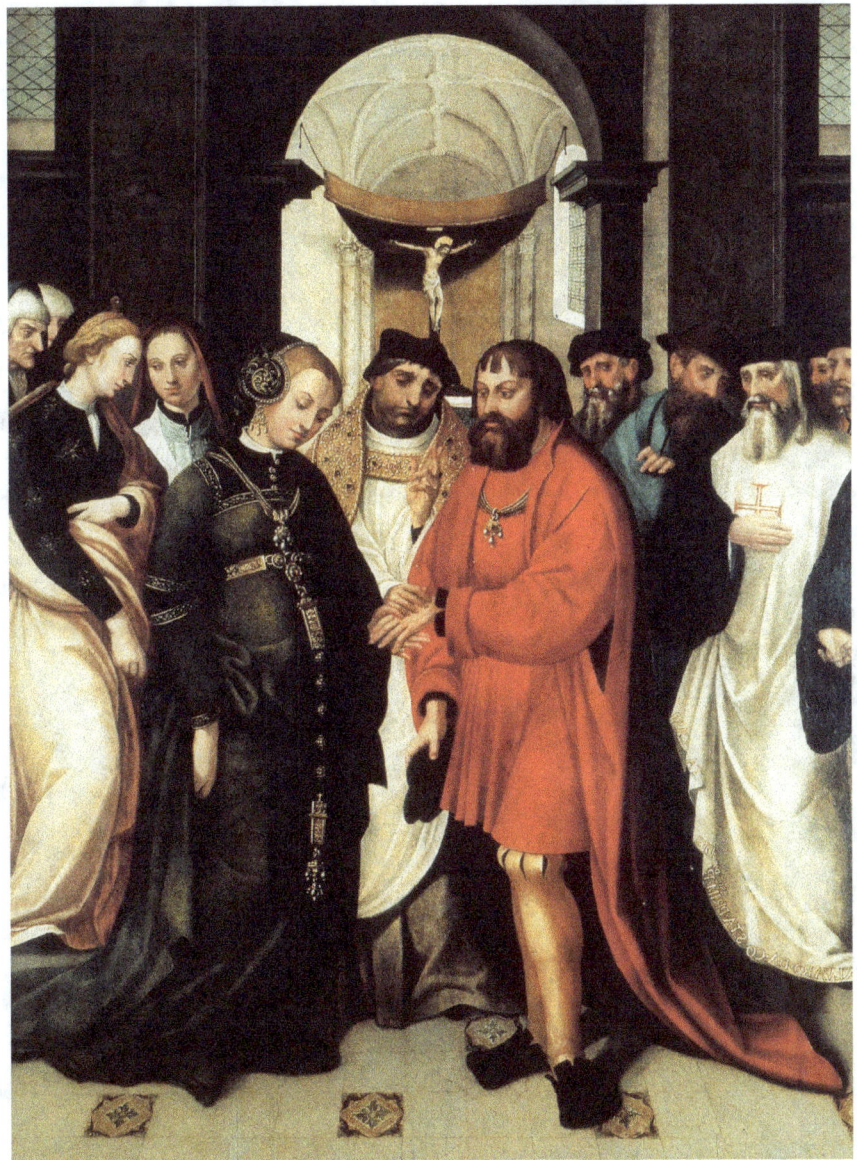
Garcia Fernandes, "Wedding of D. Manuel I", oil on wood, 16th century, Museu de São Roque, Lisbon.

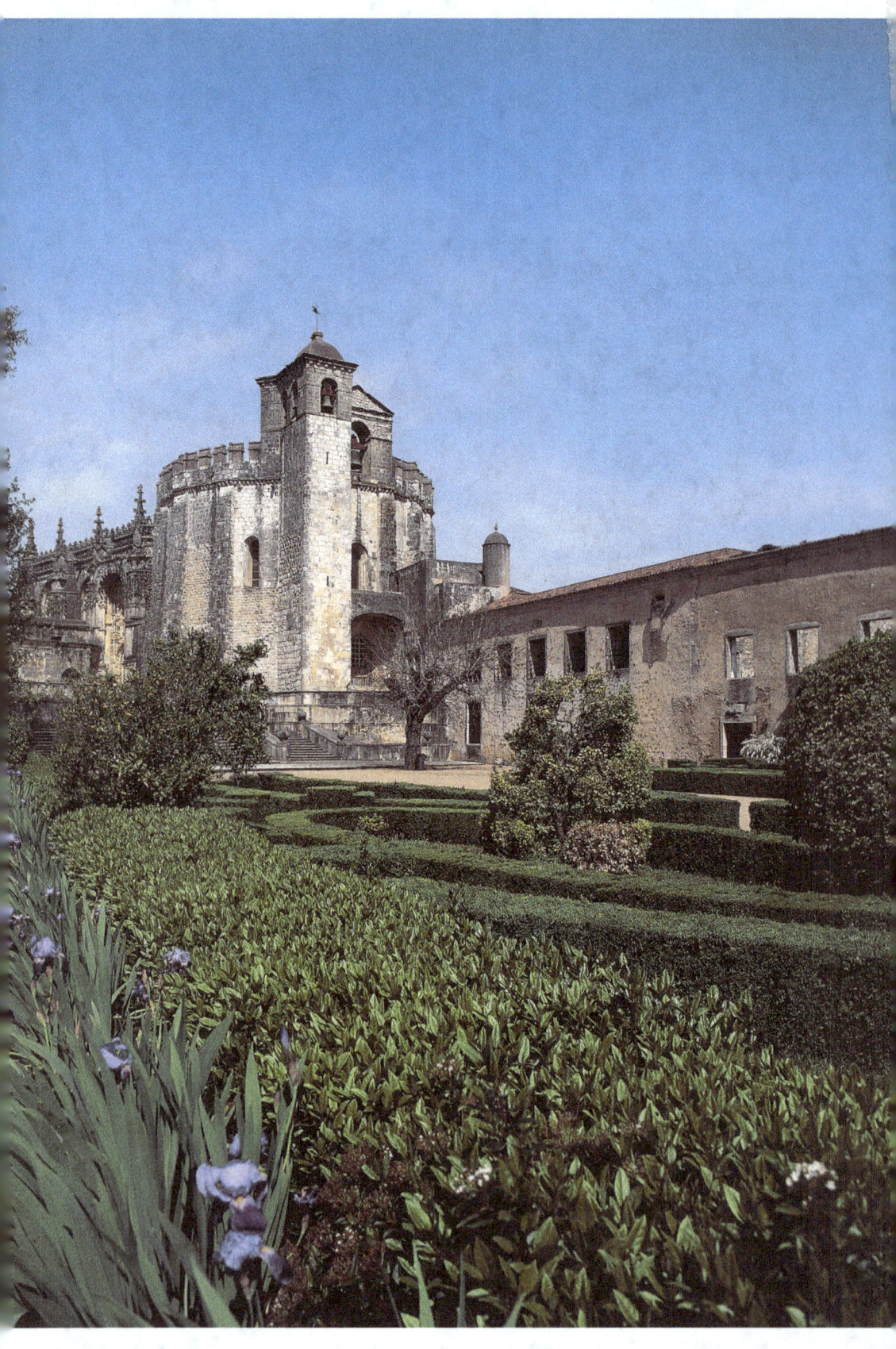

ITINERARY II

Lands of the Order of Christ

Pedro Dias, Dalila Rodrigues,
Nuno Vassallo e Silva, Fernando Grilo

First day

II.1 SANTARÉM
        II.1.a Church of Santa Maria de Marvila
        II.1.b Municipal Museum of São João de Alporão
        II.1.c Torre das Cabaças (Calabash Tower)
        II.1.d Church of Nossa Senhora da Graça

II.2 GOLEGÃ
        II.2.a Nossa Senhora da Conceição (Golegã Parish Church)

II.3 TORRES NOVAS
        II.3.a Castle

II.4 ATALAIA
        II.4.a Nossa Senhora da Assunção (Atalaia Parish Church)

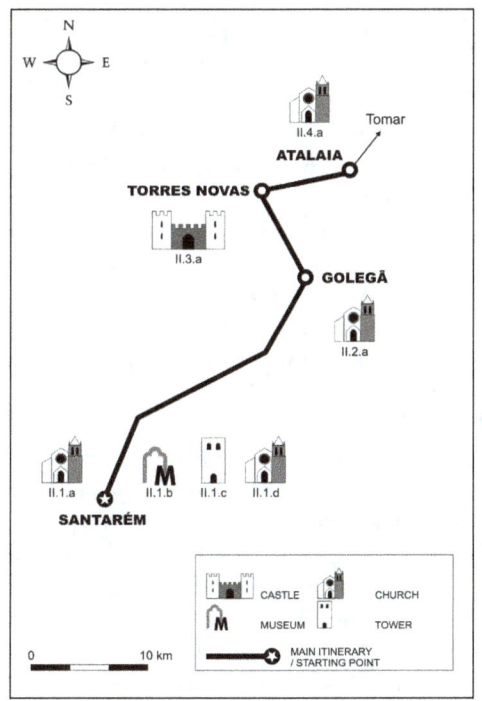

Convent of Cristo, general view of the mediaeval buildings, Tomar.

ITINERARY II   Lands of the Order of Christ

Santarém

King D. Dinis founded the Military Order of Christ after the Pope disbanded the Order of the Knights Templar, which had performed sterling service in Portugal in the fight to regain land occupied by the Moors. While the Knights Templar definitively disappeared in the rest of Europe the poet-king created a new Order, based on the same principles, and granting it the property and revenue of the old.

The Order of Christ set up its headquarters in Tomar and the former Templar Monastery was greatly enriched, primarily after Prince Henry the Navigator was made Administrator General. The Order was responsible for spreading Christianity to overseas territories and strengthened its role when D. Manuel I, the Duke of Beja, and another Administrator, ascended to the throne on the death of D. João II.

Even today, Tomar remains something of a mythical spot, where fantastic tales of underground passages and the fabulous treasures of the Templars still echo. The real treasures are not hidden, however, as they are still to be seen. They are visible in the stone tracery around the portals and windows, the soaring vaulting, the delicacy of the carving of corbels and bosses, in the paintings in the rotunda, and in the magical garments and realistic flesh colours of the Flemish sculptures also in the Knights' Rotunda.

The years after the reign of D. Manuel I also added splendour to the Convent of Christ, which also boasts some superb examples of Renaissance and Mannerist architecture.

The Military Order of Christ owned extensive lands and churches and, even though some of the edifices in this area did not come within its patronage, the artists and craftsmen who worked on the edifices on the fortified hilltop influenced local builders, leaving memories of their skills amidst the vines and estates that once were owned by the knights. Convent lands stretched as far as the banks of the River Tagus and the countryside around Santarém famed for its Gothic churches. We shall begin with this historical city.

II.1 SANTARÉM

Nowadays, Santarém is busily engaged in cattle breeding, agricultural activities and the food industry, but in former times its interests were rather different. It was the key to an extensive frontier area between the interior and the coast, forming a natural barrier against invasion from the sea and transit between the Christian North and the Islamic South.

Even in Roman and Muslim times, its position and the navigability of the Tagus made it the second town in the country after Lisbon, a position it maintained throughout the Middle Ages. The Roman *Scallabis*, founded by Junius Brutus in 138 BC, a strong fortified town or *oppidum*, was the headquarters of a con-

ITINERARY II Lands of the Order of Christ
Santarém

ventus, and a rich and populous Muslim *Xantarim* that managed to resist until March 15th 1147, before being taken by D. Afonso Henriques, although it had been in Christian hands previously from 1093 to 1110.

Santarém developed in the 16th century with the textile industry and benefited from its proximity to the Royal residences at Almeirim and Salvaterra. By 1537, it was the fourth largest town in the country with some 13,000 inhabitants. It thrived during the Mannerist period, at the end of the 16th and the first half of the 17th centuries, due to commissions from the Society of Jesus and the patronage of the nobility and Court, which was only slightly reduced in the mid-18th century.

Unfortunately, this rich heritage was to be severely diminished as a result of the suppression of the religious orders in Portugal in 1835, but what remains from the 14th, 15th and 16th centuries bears witness to a proud Arab past and the persistence of the *Mozarab* population.

All buildings of interest are situated in the historic centre of Santarém and are within walking distance of each other.

II.1.a Church of Santa Maria de Marvila

Largo de Marvila. Designated a National Monument. Information: Department of Culture at the Câmara Municipal de Santarém (Town Hall Tel: 243 304400/4).
Opening hours: Tuesday, Wednesday, Saturday and Sunday 9.30-12.30 and 14.00-17.30; Thursday and Friday 10.00-12.30 and 14.00-17.30. Closed on Mondays.

The Church of Santa Maria de Marvila was one of the first to be built in Santarém after the Conquest of 1147, but it was completely rebuilt in Manueline times. Only the east end and a fine portal remain from this period, as further work was carried out on the main vessel of the church, no doubt due to the earthquake of 1531.

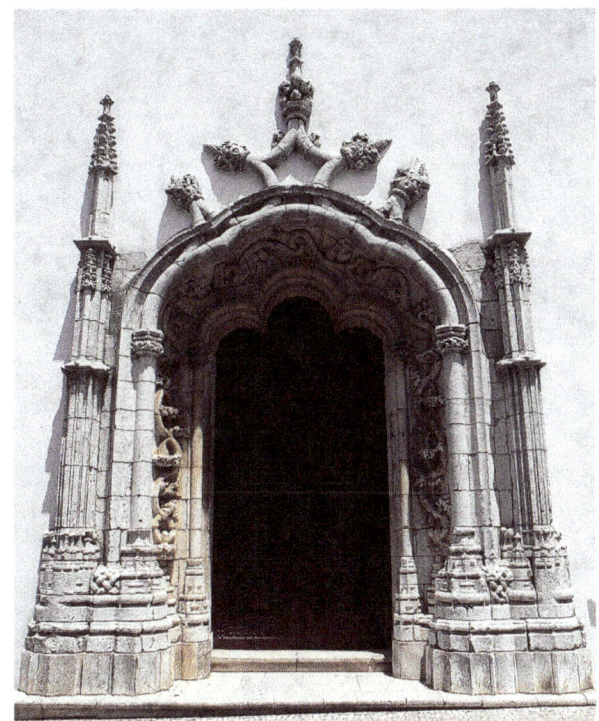

Church of Santa Maria de Marvila, portal, Santarém.

M.A.

ITINERARY II   Lands of the Order of Christ
Santarém

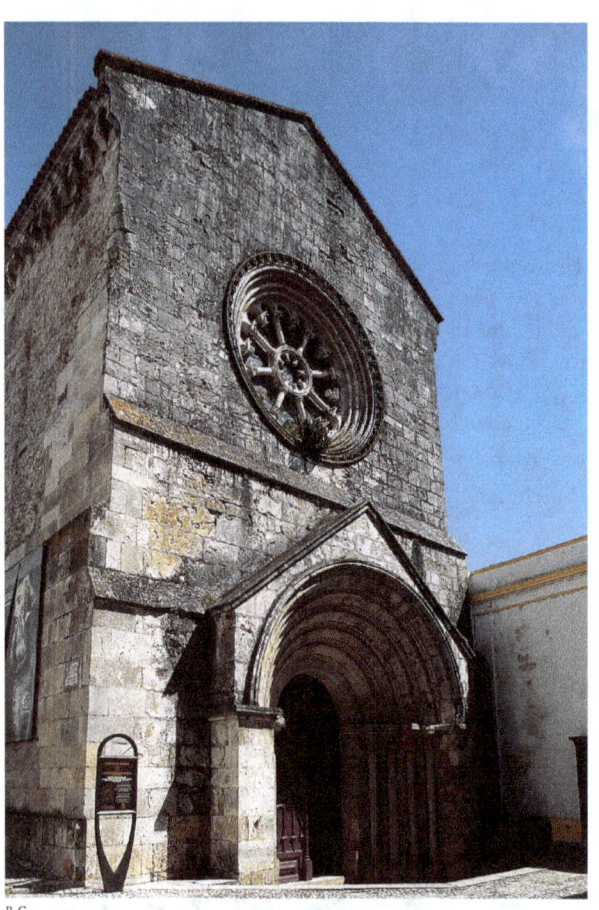

Church of São João de Alporão, Santarém.

the 17th-century tiles, among the best of Lisbon production of the time.

II.1.b Municipal Museum de São João de Alporão

Housed in the Igreja de São João de Alporão, Largo Zeferino Sarmento. Designated a National Monument. Information Tel: 243 304400. Admission charge. Opening hours: Tuesday, Wednesday, Saturday and Sunday 9.30-12.30 and 14.00-17.30; Thursday and Friday 10.00-12.30 and 14.00-17.30. Closed on Mondays.

Work was begun on the church during the Romanesque period, and the lateral walls and lower part of the façade with one of the first *hood mould* Gothic portals in Portugal, undoubtedly date from this period. The upper part of the church was completed in the 14th and 15th centuries, when the chancel rotunda was built. Nothing remains of the changes made during the Manueline period.

The exuberant naturalistic portal includes architectural elements reminiscent of the Monastery of Batalha. The interior boasts a *triumphal arch* in the chancel and late Gothic vaulting in the main and collateral chapels.

The fine early Renaissance longitudinal nave arcades are worthy of note, as are

The contents of the museum are largely made up of archaeological finds and lapidary stones, many items coming from ruined or disaffected monasteries. There are Arab, Gothic and fine Manueline naturalistic capitals and others imported from Genoa at the beginning of the 16th century, as well as the tomb of Duarte de Meneses, Captain of Alcácer-Ceguer and two other 15th-century tombs of João and Martim Docem respectively.

ITINERARY II Lands of the Order of Christ
Santarém

II.1.c Torre das Cabaças (Calabash Tower)

Avenida 5 de Outubro.
Admission charge. Opening hours: daily 9.30-12.30 and 14.00-17.30, except on Mondays and national holidays.

The 22-metre-high tower, next to the Mediaeval Church of São João de Alporão, was erected, complete with sun-dial, by the municipality in the 14th century. A tower probably already existed on the site as part of the old wall, and there is documentary evidence dating it back to 1462. Some writers date it back to the 16th century when changes were undoubtedly made to the structure during the Manueline period.
Built on a square plan, it is crowned by an iron framework designed to hold eight earthenware vessels that increased the sound of the bell.

Follow the signposts to the Portas do Sol, cross the garden and, from the walls, there is a good view over the River Tagus and the flat lands of the Ribatejo.

II.1.d Church of Nossa Senhora da Graça

Largo Pedro Álvares Cabral, also known as Largo da Graça. (Tel: 243 304400/4). Designated a National Monument.
Opening hours: Tuesday, Wednesday, Saturday and Sunday 9.30-12.30 and 14.00-17.30; Thursday and Friday 10.00-12.30 and 14.00-17.30. Closed on Mondays.

The Church is interesting not only because of its 14th- and 15th-century architecture,

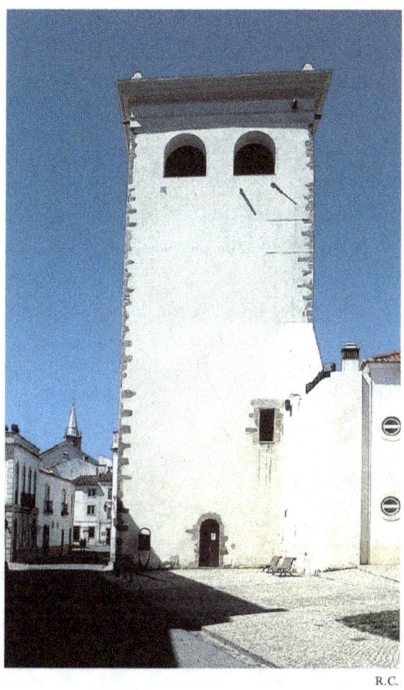

Torre das Cabaças (Calabash Tower), Santarém.

R.C.

particularly the Flamboyant Gothic façade, but also for the tombs it contains. One is that of the first Captain and Governor of Ceuta, D. Pedro de Meneses, and another is that of Pedro Álvares Cabral, the

Church of Nossa Senhora da Graça, axionometric drawing, Santarém, Catalogue of the 18th Exhibition of Art, Science and Culture, "The Portuguese Discoveries and Renaissance Europe", Lisbon, 1983.

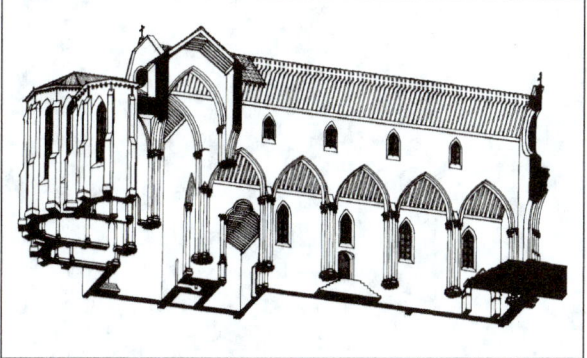

ITINERARY II Lands of the Order of Christ
Golegã

Commander of the Fleet that set sail for India but landed on and claimed Terra de Santa Cruz, modern-day Brazil, for the Portuguese Crown in 1500.
The interior of the church bears a remarkable similarity to the architecture of Batalha under its first Master Builder, Afonso Domingues.

To reach Golegã, follow the EN365 towards Alcanhões / Vale de Figueira / Pombalinho / Azinhaga to Golegã (32 km.).

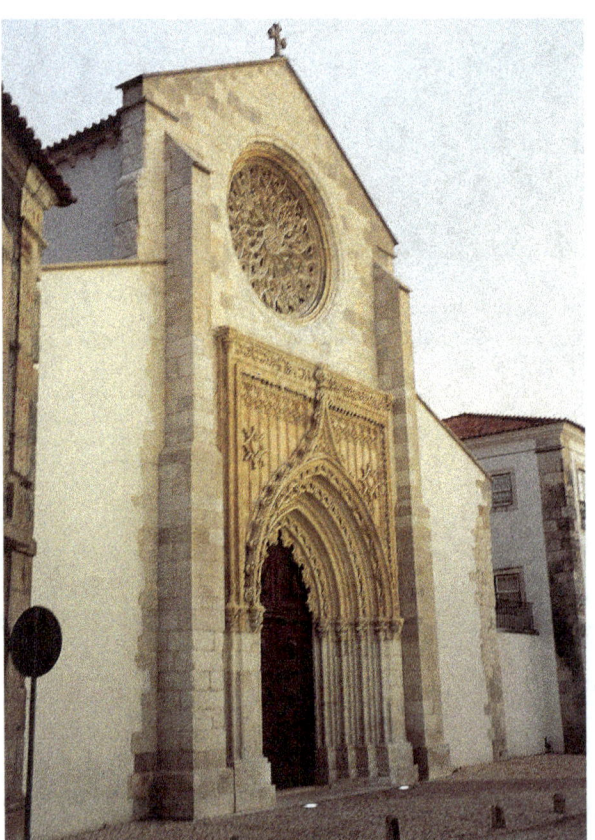

Church of Nossa Senhora da Graça, façade, Santarém.

II.2 GOLEGÃ

II.2.a Nossa Senhora da Conceição (Golegã Parish Church)

Largo da Imaculada Conceição. Designated a National Monument. Information: Golegã Parish Church (Tel: 249 976193).
Opening hours: daily from 8.30-17.00. Mass is held on Tuesdays and Thursdays at 19.00, on Saturdays at 19.30 and on Sundays at 12.00.

Golegã initially developed due to its position on the Ribatejo road network, and had already attained some importance by the reign of D. Manuel I. Nowadays, the area is particularly well known for bull- and horse-breeding activities. The most important monument in the town is the Parish Church of Nossa Senhora da Conceição, a very good example of a medium-sized Manueline church. Nothing is known as to the builder or date of construction, but the architectural lines suggest it belongs to the Batalha period of Mateus Fernandes or Boytac; the beginning of the 16th century.
The façade, the three-aisled main vessel, and apse, have remained unaltered, which is rare, particularly as much of the decoration, namely superb tiles, date from the Baroque period.
The portal with its twisted pillars, lettered parchments and inevitable allu-

ITINERARY II *Lands of the Order of Christ*
Torres Novas

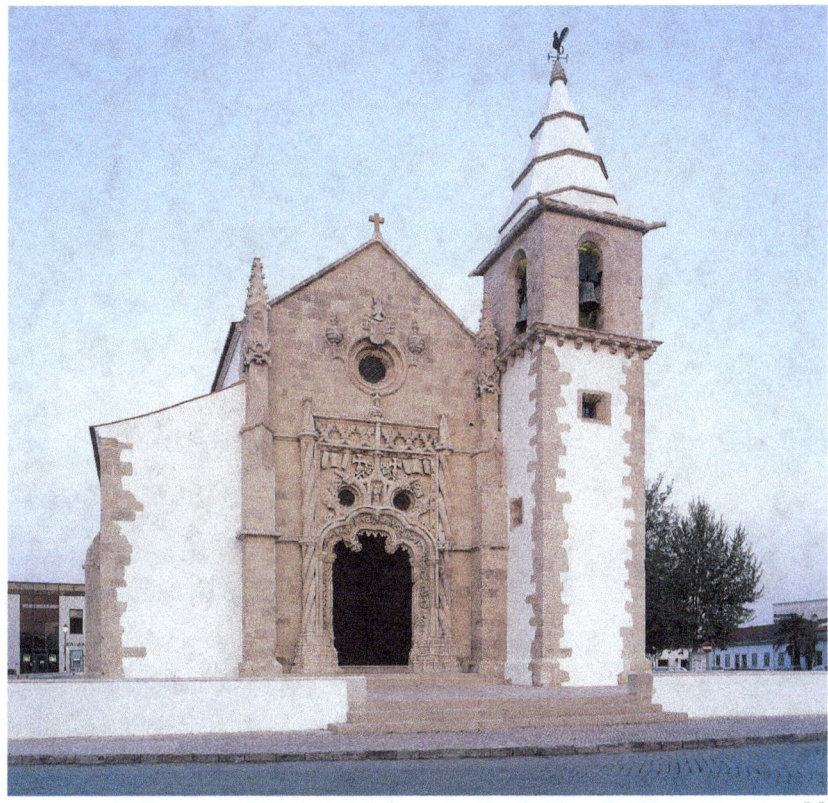

Church of Nossa Senhora da Conceição, main façade, Golegã.

sions to D. Manuel I, specifically the Cross of Christ and armillary spheres, is of a robust, rich naturalism. Note the plain arches in the aisles with their bare pillars and the ribbed vaulting in the chancel. A sculpture evocative of the Virgin and Child from the Manueline workshops in Coimbra, stands on a corbel.

For Torres Novas, take the EN365, then the E243 in the direction of Riachos, then finally the E3 to Torres Novas (10 km.).

II.3 TORRES NOVAS

II.3.a **Castle**

The castle can be reached by Rua do Conde de Torres Novas. Designated a National Monument. Information: Municipal Council (Tel: 249 839430).
Opening hours: daily 9.00-17.00.

In relation to our itinerary, the main feature of interest in Torres Novas is

ITINERARY II   *Lands of the Order of Christ*
Atalaia

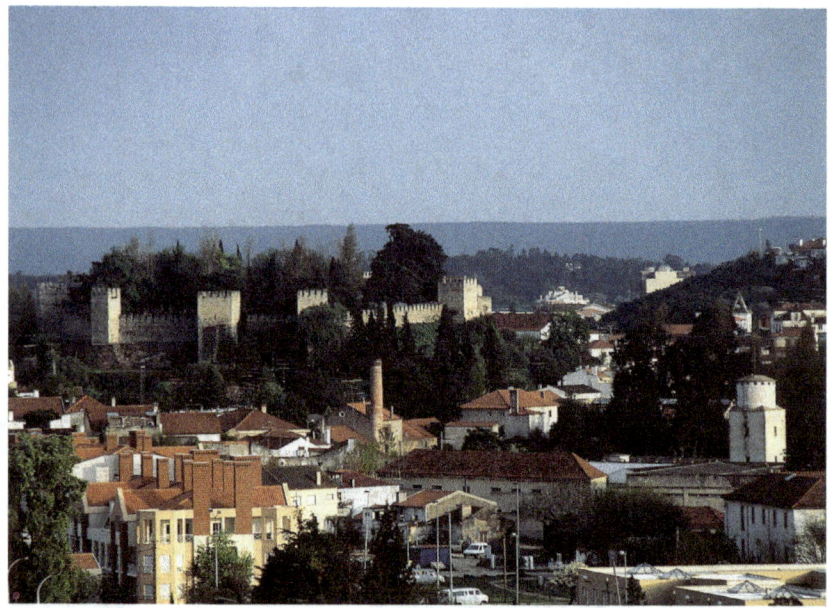

Torres Novas Castle.

its original Muslim Castle. Conquered from the Moors by D. Afonso Henriques, it was enlarged and modernised, in the course of succeeding centuries, mainly by extending the enclosure and raising the walls and towers. Today it remains pretty much as it was in Manueline times when the last changes took place. Then, all the Late Mediaeval structures were replaced, except for part of the Old Chapel of São Jorge, founded in the 12th century, today part of the Church of São Salvador, and some pillars in the Church of São Pedro.

The Castle dominates the town, which grew around the fortress and spread to the lower ground.

Take the EN3 to Entroncamento and then follow the IC3 to Atalaia.

II.4 ATALAIA

II.4.a Nossa Senhora da Assunção (Atalaia Parish Church)

Rua Patriarca D. José. Designated a National Monument.

Opening hours: the Parish Church is open for religious services daily at 15.00 and on Sundays at 9.15. To make an appointment to visit the church, call D. Silviana Vital (Tel: 249 710201).

ITINERARY II Lands of the Order of Christ
Atalaia

As far as can be seen, according to the coat of arms on one of the bosses of the vaulted ceiling, the church was built at the orders of D. Pedro de Meneses, Lord of Cantanhede and Tancos, in about 1528, the date carved on one of the *pilasters* that flank the chancel.

The church consists of only one nave; the apse is vaulted in the Manueline style, and is in fact, very similar to the one to be found at the Convent of Christ in Tomar. It may well have been the work of João de Castilho or one of his disciples in the 1520s.

The portal was the first work executed by the Frenchman, Jean de Rouen (João de Ruão), in Portugal. Built in the 16th century, it displays the superb visual and compositional qualities that were to mark all of his future work. The broad, coffered arch has high relief busts of St Peter and St Paul in soffits on the *pilasters*.

Also noteworthy is the stylistic and technical mastery of the overall decoration, which displays strong Italian influences, as well as the remarkable quality of the busts, contained within a circular frame, which clearly testify to the sculptor's highly developed artistic skill. This same skill is to be noted in later works such as the retable of the Church of Nossa Senhora da Varziela, commissioned by the same patron.

To reach Tomar, take the IC3 to Asseiceira, then continue on the EN110.

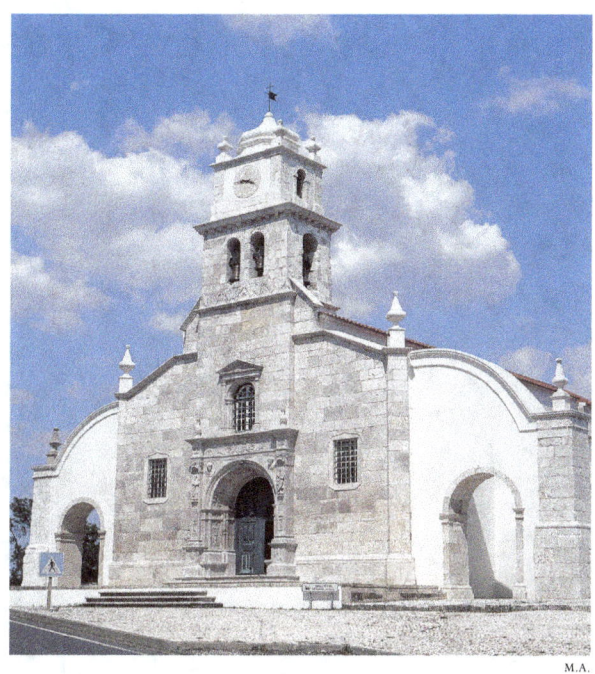

Church of Nossa Senhora da Assunção, Renaissance façade, Atalaia.

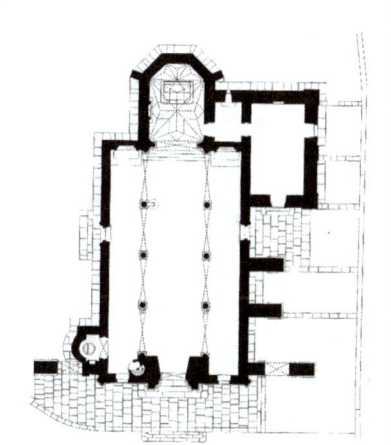

Church of Nossa Senhora da Assunção, plan, Atalaia, Boletim da Direcção-Geral dos Edifícios e Monumentos Nacionais, No. 24, Lisbon, 1941.

ITINERARY II

Lands of the Order of Christ

Pedro Dias, Dalila Rodrigues,
Nuno Vassallo e Silva, Fernando Grilo

Second day

II.5 TOMAR
    II.5.a Old Urban Centre
    II.5.b São João Baptista (Tomar Parish Church)
    II.5.c Ermida de São Gregório (Chapel of St Gregório)
    II.5.d Synagogue
    II.5.e Estaus Arches
    II.5.f Convento de Cristo (Convent of Christ)

II.6 DORNES (option)
    II.6.a Tower of Dornes

The Order of Christ and the Discoveries

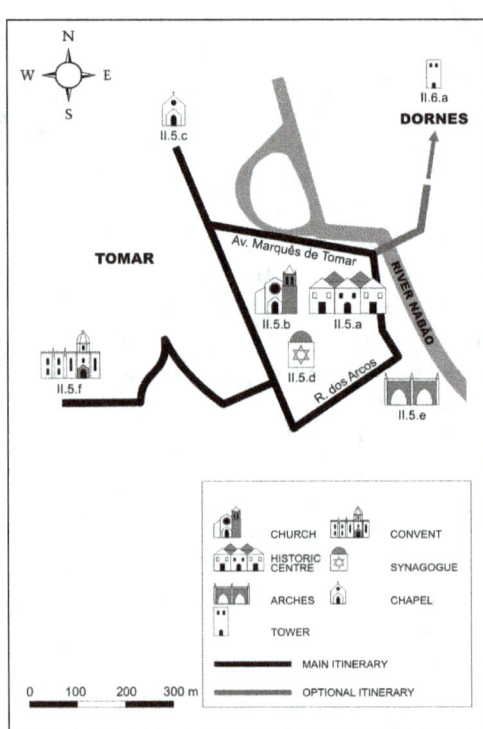

ITINERARY II *Lands of the Order of Christ*
Tomar

II.5 TOMAR

Information: Tourist Office (Tel: 249322427).

The origin of Tomar as an important Roman settlement is verified not only by the information from the 3rd-century *Antonin's Itinerary*, but also by many archaeological finds. It was known then as *Sellium,* on the military road that led from *Olisipo,* Lisbon, to *Bracara Augusta,* Braga, and was integrated into the *Conventus Scallabitanus.* It was also called *Nabância* during the period of occupation by the Suevi about 570, and was then taken by the Visigoths. Conquered by the Muslims, probably in 716, it only attained any real importance after the Reconquest in 1147 and developed rapidly when it became the headquarters of the Mmilitary Order of the Knights Templar.

The Master, Gualdim Pais, installed the Order on the hillock on which the Convent of Christ now stands. After the disbanding of the Templars throughout Europe, the successor Military Order of Christ, created by the King of Portugal in 1317, was granted all its property and revenue. The siting of their headquarters here breathed life into the town, which spread down towards the River Nabão and, by the mid-16th century, formed a compact and organised centre between the river banks and the foothills of the castle. The knights-friars lived in the town at this period, though with the reform of the Order in 1529, they took up residence in the monastery and the town was left to labourers, servants, administrators and an important Jewish community. Nonetheless, it is fair to say

M.A.

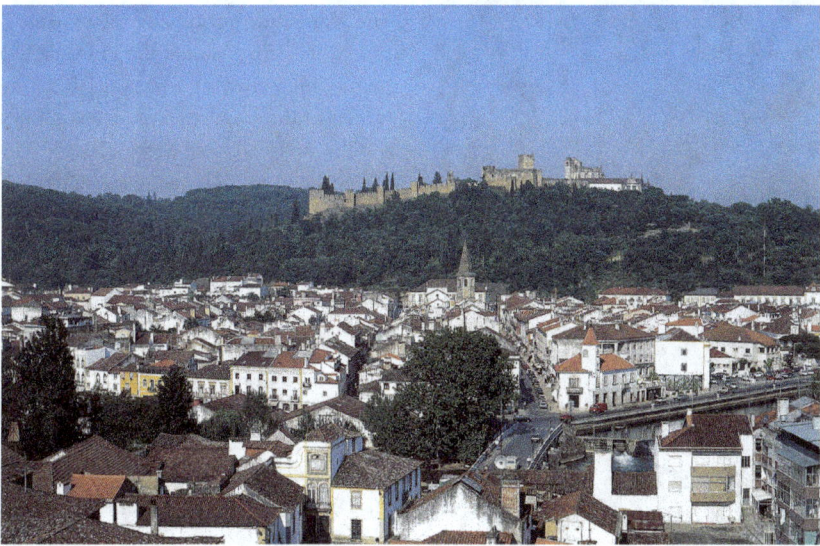

General view of the old urban centre of Tomar.

79

ITINERARY II   *Lands of the Order of Christ*
Tomar

that the Convent of Christ was to determine the town's appearance forever more.

It is advisable to park your car and walk round the Old Town (except for the Convent of Christ). The nearest car park is behind the Town Hall, with access to Praceta D. Afonso Henrique or Largo do Pelourinho via Rua do Dr. Sousa. The route is signposted.

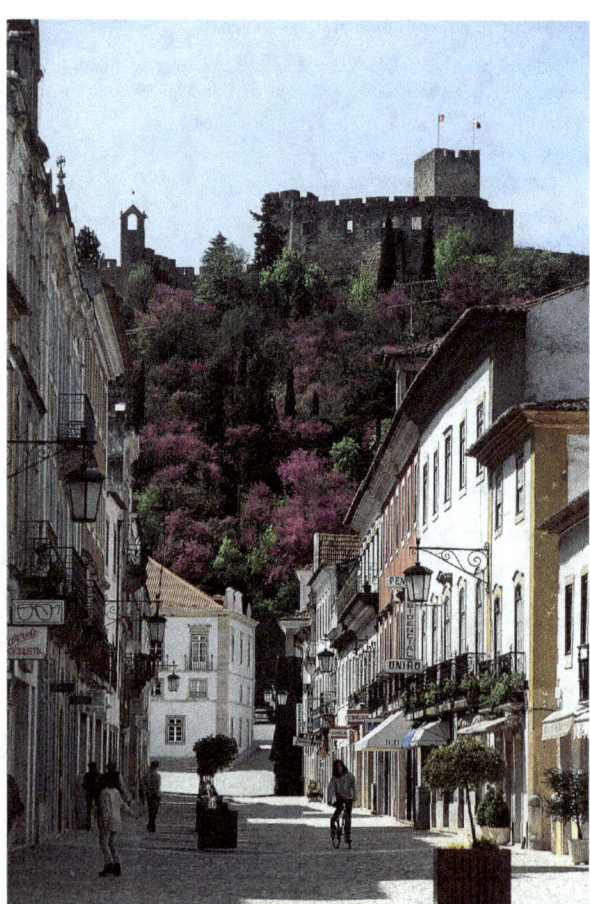

Tomar historic centre.

II.5.a **Old Urban Centre**

Between the hill on which the Templar Castle stands and the banks of the river, many of the old streets and buildings date back to the Middle Ages. The installations set up by Prince Henry the Navigator, from 1420 onwards are of particular interest. They include Paços da Ribeira, the Estaus (inns, in which the kings or important visitors were accommodated when travelling), the bridge over the river, soapworks, granaries and a hospital. The houses belonging to the servants of the Order, industrial workers and tradesmen gradually filled this tightly knit space dotted with chapels and the Church of St John the Baptist, as well as an important synagogue that exists to this day. It was only in the 16th century that Tomar extended into the agricultural land and across the river.

The Manueline period saw the construction of the Town Hall in the Praça de São João, which encompassed the old pharmacies of the market place, a new pillory and the well-endowed Misericórdia Charity Hospital. In 1504, wine and oil presses were built, along with windmills and shortly afterwards ironworks, to manufacture armaments.

II.5.b **São João Baptista
(Tomar Parish Church)**

Praça da República, in the Old Quarter. (Tel: 249 312611). Designated a National Monument.

ITINERARY II *Lands of the Order of Christ*
Tomar

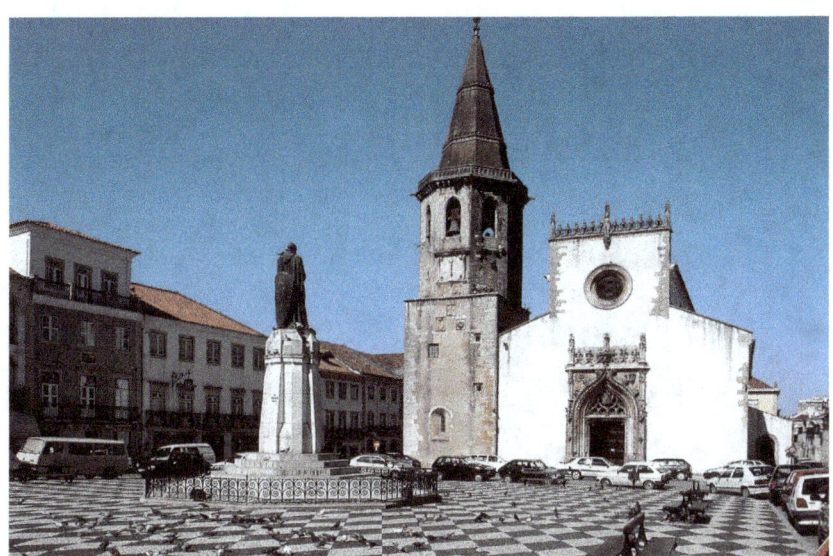

São João Baptista, Tomar Parish Church, main façade.

São João Baptista, Tomar Parish Church, axionometric drawing, Catalogue of the 18th Exhibition of Art, Science and Culture "The Portuguese Discoveries and Renaissance Europe", Lisbon, 1983.

Opening hours: 9.00-12.00 and 15.00-18.30 except on Thursdays, Fridays and Saturdays, when it closes at 19.30.

The Parish Church is one of the oldest in Tomar, although it was completely rebuilt at the beginning of the 16th century, the axial door, on the left, being completed in 1510. It is Manueline in style, based on the Flamboyant Gothic, reminiscent of the art of the Church of Batalha dating from the second half of the 15th century. The axial portal is superbly Flamboyant Gothic in style, the same as the left axial doorway. Inside, well-designed arcades separate the aisles, the carved stone pulpit is also Flamboyant Gothic, one of the few examples that still exist in Portugal, and the chancel has Gothic vaulting.
Six paintings have been conserved from the old retable painted by Gregório

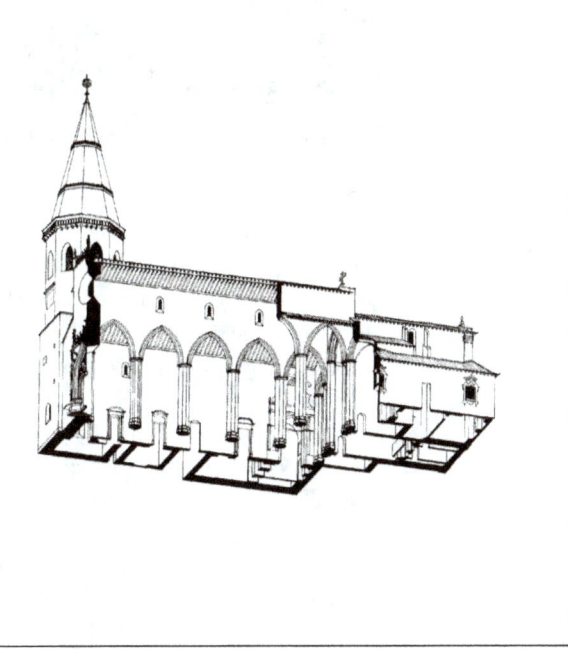

ITINERARY II   Lands of the Order of Christ
Tomar

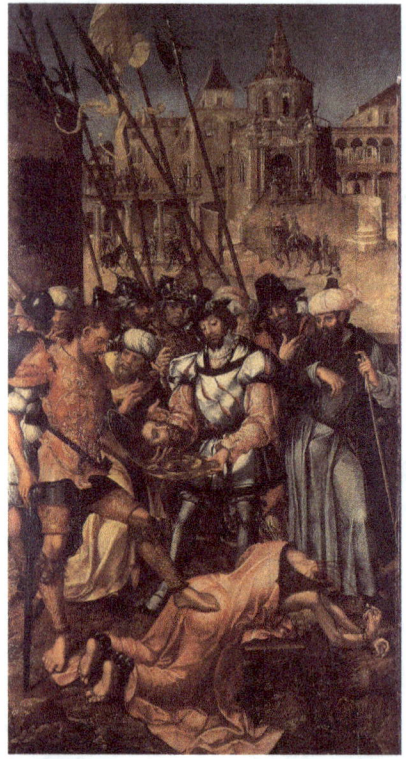

Gregório Lopes, "Beheading of St John the Baptist", 16th century, church of São João Baptista, Tomar.

IPM/M.P.

well represented in the *Presentation of the Head of St John the Baptist*. The gestures and poses of the figures are gracefully conceived, even down to the amusing pages in the foreground. The Renaissance architecture is another characteristic of this series of works by Gregório Lopes, Court painter and Knight of the Order of Santiago.

II.5.c Ermida de São Gregório (Chapel of St Gregório)

Estrada do Prado, next to the hotel. If the chapel is closed, please contact the Tourist Office Tel: 249 322427. Designated a Building of Public Interest.

This is one of the most interesting of the small chapels in the city and the only one

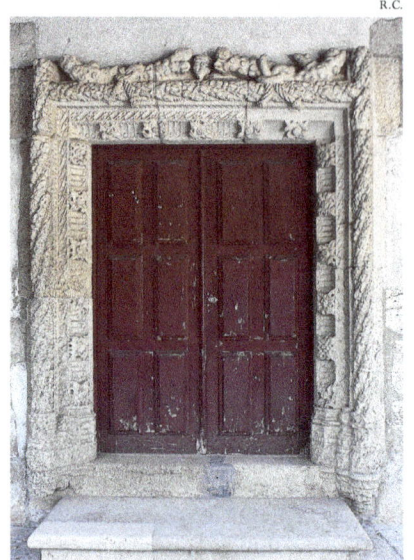

R.C.

Lopes, very probably after he had completed the rotunda in the Convent of Christ *c.*1538. Three themes from the Eucharist on the side walls include, on the left, the *Mass of St Gregory*, *The Last Supper* and *Abraham and Melchizedek*, and, on the right, *Gathering Manna*, the *Martyrdom of St John the Baptist* and the *Presentation of the Head of St John the Baptist to Herodias*.

Lopes' finest work here, in a vibrant palette with a remarkable play of light and colour, is undoubtedly that of *The Last Supper*. The palatial, Courtly atmosphere of the period is

Ermida de São Gregório, portal, Tomar.

ITINERARY II — Lands of the Order of Christ
Tomar

that has essentially retained its Manueline structure, with its octagonal vaulted main vessel and the very lovely foliate portal. The classical porch, in a pared down Mannerist style, was either added or renewed at a later date. The Chapel is dedicated to St Gregory.

II.5.d Synagogue

Rua Dr. Joaquim Jacinto, in the Old Town. Designated a National Monument. Information: Tourist Office (Tel: 249 322427). Opening hours: 10.00-13.00 and 14.00-18.00.

The Jewish community was once concentrated in the Rua Nova area where the Synagogue is situated. The structure of the building has remained intact and the annexes have recently been excavated. After prohibition enforced during the Manueline period, the building was confiscated and used for secular and religious purposes, being in turn a jail, chapel and one of the town granaries.

It is built on an almost square plan, measuring 9 x 8 m., with brick vaulting supported by elegant pillars and decorated capitals, the same shape as the lateral corbels, recalling the workmanship at Batalha, and similar to the crypt of the Ourém Collegiate Church. It probably dates from c.1460. Today, the floor is lower than the street elevation and, inside there is still an acoustic system with small cavities in the corners, where earthenware pots increased the sound and added resonance.

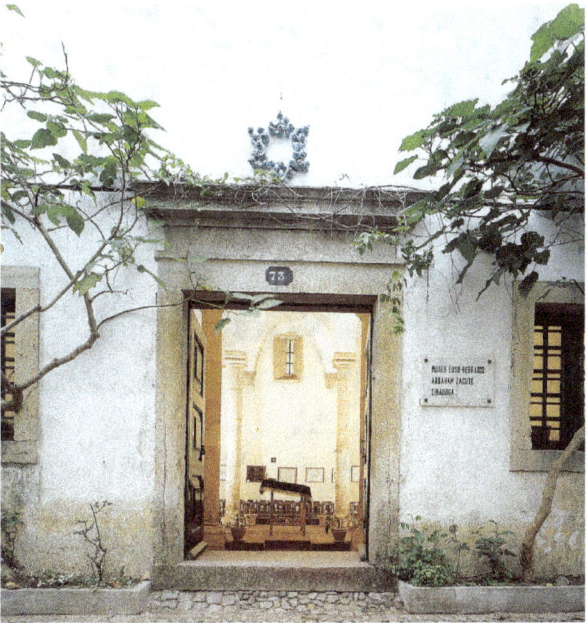

Synagogue, entrance, Tomar.

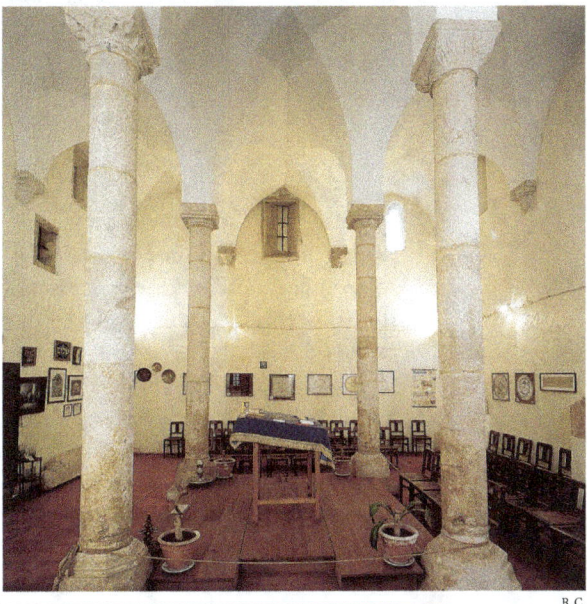

Synagogue, interior, Tomar.

ITINERARY II   Lands of the Order of Christ
Tomar

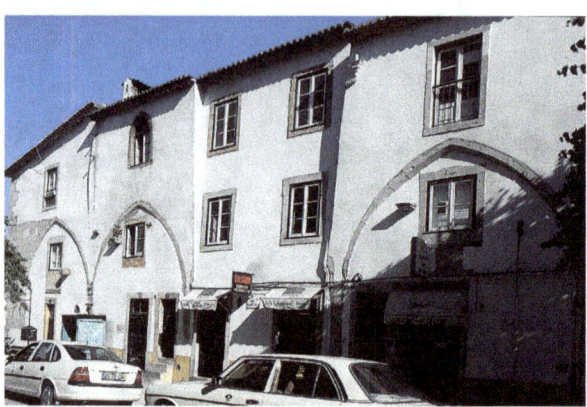

R.C.
Estaus Arches, Tomar.

of the free fair set up by the prince in 1420. What remains of this sober structure is nonetheless a highly impressive construction, making it possible for us to imagine the whole complex, which must have been quite vast for that particular period.

II.5.f **Convento de Cristo (Convent of Christ)**

Set on the hill overlooking the town. The route is signposted. (Tel: 249 315089). Designated a National Monument since 1907 and a UNESCO World Heritage Site since 1983. Flash photography is prohibited, although other photographs may be taken.
Admission charge. Opening hours: 9.00-17.30 in winter and 9.00-18.30 from June to September. Last visitors admitted 30 minutes before closing time. Closed on January 1st, Good Friday, Easter, May 1st and December 25th.

The synagogue is lit by elegant window slits in the north- and south-facing walls with keel-shaped arches.

II.5.e **Estaus Arches**

Five large arches are visible in Rua dos Arcos and a further three are incorporated into buildings in Rua Torres Pinheiro. There is a Gothic window on top of a second arch in Rua dos Arcos. Designated as a Building of Public Interest.

The Rua dos Estaus was on the main road in Tomar at the end of the Middle Ages. Today, close to the river, it is possible to see the powerful Gothic arches of this extremely large construction built by Prince Henry the Navigator to house visiting dignitaries, especially those accompanied by servants and a military guard, and to avoid their having to stay with local residents. The number of people visiting the town increased considerably during the period

The Convent of Christ dates back to the end of the 12th century, when the Knights Templar was installed in the castle after abandoning the neighbouring hill at Ceras. The Master of the Order, Gualdim Pais, and his troops defended this hill in 1190, against the Muslim invasions of Al-Mansur. The church was built in this period, on a centred plan in the shape of a central octagon, surrounded by an *ambulatory* or circular nave, marked on the outside by a polygon with 16 sides. During this first phase, it also served as a defensive tower to which other convent build-

ITINERARY II   Lands of the Order of Christ
Tomar

ings were linked, particularly after the Order of Christ succeeded the Order of the Knights Templar in 1315. The Ablutions and Cemetery Cloisters were built in the mid-15th century when Prince Henry was Administrator General of the Order. The former cloister has two storeys and was built in a very simple style; the latter is smaller and has one storey only, but the decoration is more interesting. Both cloisters were the work of master builders trained at the Monastery of Batalha. The name of one, Fernão Gonçalves, is inscribed on the base of one of the columns in the second cloister, which also contains the luxuriantly naturalist Manueline tomb of D. Diogo da Gama, chaplain to the king. The rotunda was extensively altered during the Manueline period, not only by a decorative programme that included paintings and sculptures, but also by linking it to the terrace and opening an arch giving onto the large choir. In 1510, Diogo de Arruda began work on the

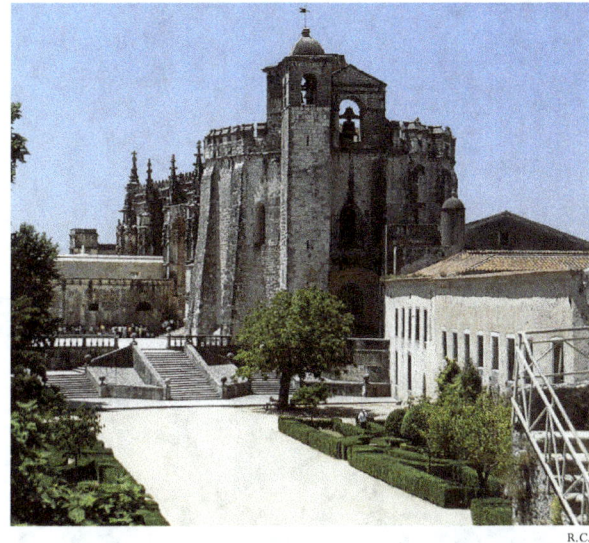

Convent of Christ, general view of the mediaeval buildings, showing the exterior of the Rotunda, Tomar.

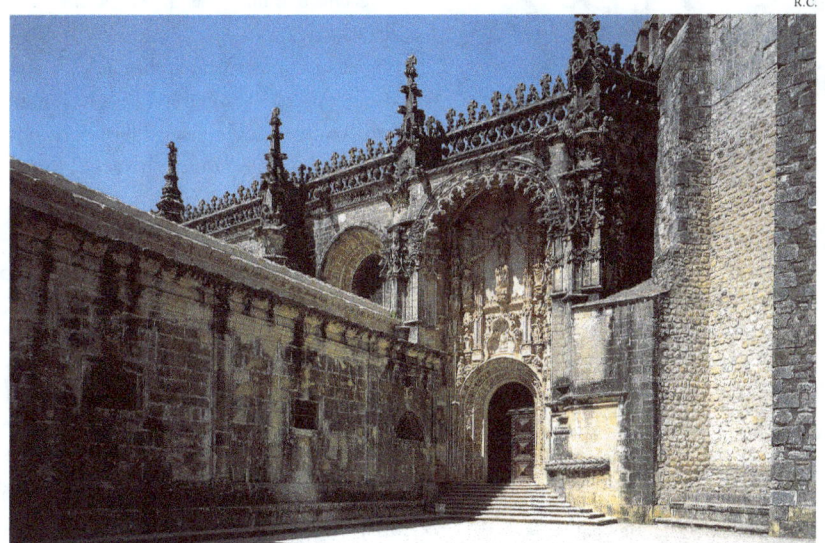

Church of the Convent of Christ, entrance, Tomar.

85

ITINERARY II   Lands of the Order of Christ
Tomar

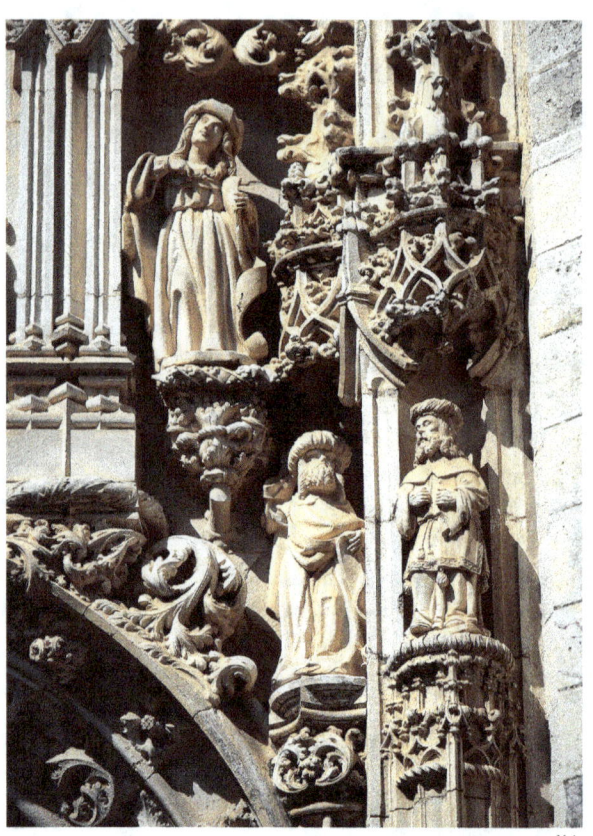

Convent of Christ, detail of the portal, Tomar.

wide, deep main vessel, which is remarkable for the unusual, if not unique, Baroque naturalism of the façade, an explosion of foliate forms turned into architectural elements, the frame of the frontal window being particularly exuberant. High up, four kings in armour recall the attributes of D. Manuel I, though they are often erroneously identified as the Kings D. Afonso Henriques, D. Dinis and D. Manuel I, himself, as well as Prince Henry the Navigator.

The lateral window by the Royal Cloister is fantastic in outline and the frame very naturalistic, although less intensely so. Diogo de Arruda was responsible for the vaulting that divides this part of the building into two levels, although he never finished the work. In 1515, João de Castilho, who made the curved rib vaulting with naturalistic corbels and also introduced an important heraldic and emblematic component, replaced Arruda. He also produced the exterior door very much in the Castilian style of the time and embellished it with fine sculptures of the Virgin, prophets and saints.

Castilho was also responsible for the incomplete Chapter House and the cloisters next to these constructions, as the Royal Cloister, a masterpiece of Portuguese Classical architecture that substituted his original, was the work of Diogo de Torralva.

The *charola*, or rotunda, has an extraordinary pictorial heritage that has been rediscovered and conserved over recent years. The filling up of surfaces almost seems to be the result of a dislike of emptiness but, over the years, the significant works also highlight the essential function of painting: the symbolic qualification of architecture. The geometric patterns, the successive repainting of Oriental-style decoration, in the "Byzantine manner", certainly took place during the Manueline period, and was combined with various figurative themes that were adapted to the difficult structure of the walls and covering of the Knights' Rotunda.

Changes introduced at the beginning of the 16th century began with the impressive decoration of the vaulting that surrounds the central octagonal. Executed in *grisaille* on a large figurative scale, and re-covering the 16 trusses of the vaulting, the painting simulates architectural elements combined with recurrent themes in the painting of the time, some of which were clearly designed to promote the sovereign image of the king. Heraldry, basically the royal shield, the cross of Christ, and the armillary sphere, and some expressive human and animal figures, appear on the most varied, fantastic architectural forms that are interwoven by ropes, branches and ribbons. A programme centred on Christ, formed by the instruments of the Passion and displayed by 16 angels, is visible on the upper walls of the central tambour.

Another programme, dating from 1510 to 1515, relative to the Life of Christ but executed in oil on wood, was conceived for the large paintings in the blind arches of the facing walls.

Paintings by Gregório Lopes dating from about 1536 to 1538 occupied the same wall but at a lower register. His panels of *St Anthony Praying to the Fish* and *St Bernard* are still in the convent, though *The Virgin of the Angels* and *The Martyrdom of St Sebastian* are now to be seen in the National Museum of Ancient Art in Lisbon.

The rotunda of the Convent of Christ also has a series of superb 16th-century polychrome wood sculptures around the walls, quite unique in European terms. The 16 images, each about 2 m. in height, and representing in the central figures Our Lady and St John, as well as the Apostles, the Doctors of the Church and the Prophets, were executed between 1511 and 1514 by Oliver of Ghent (Olivier de Gand) and Fernan Muñoz.

Also part of this ensemble, were choir stalls that were destroyed in the early years of the 19th century during the Peninsula War; now only two angels remain, one of which bears the coat of

M.A.

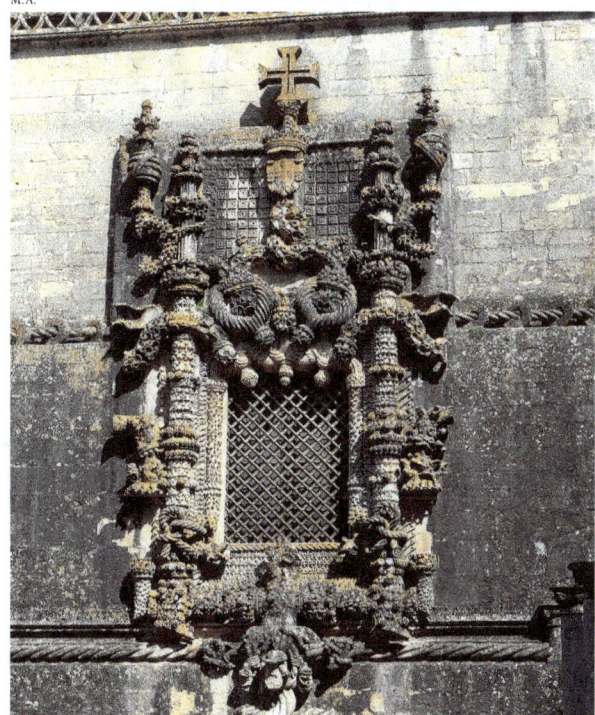

Convent of Christ, Manueline window, Tomar.

ITINERARY II   *Lands of the Order of Christ*
Dornes

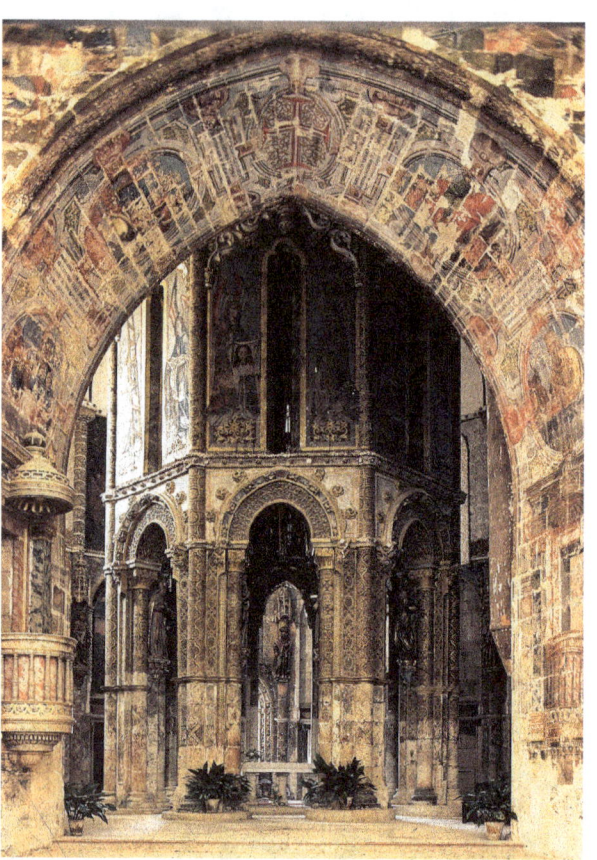

Convent of Christ, interior of the Rotunda (before restoration work), Tomar.

arms of Portugal and the other the arms of the Order of Christ. These sculptures demonstrate the three main facets that distinguished Northern European artists in Portugal during the Manueline period: painting, seen in the polychrome of the statues, sculpture and woodwork, and which are highly visible in the central structure of the building. All these aspects harmonise in a magnificent, iconographically significant discourse.

The statues along the walls of the rotunda, around a central group representing Our Lady and St John, have an extraordinary dignity emphasised by the plastic quality of each one and the careful polychromy they still show.

The rotunda and the sculptures form a fundamental document for the understanding of Manueline artistic production not only for their exceptional quality and excellent state of conservation, but essentially for the artistic and cultural postulate that is revealed, placing them squarely in the Northern sphere of influence.

To visit Dornes take the EN110 in the direction of Pereiro. Turn right onto the EN238 towards Águas Belas. After the Águas Belas crossroads and before Casal da Madalena, on the left, is the junction of two roads. The Dornes road is the second of these.

II.6 **DORNES** (option)

II.6.a **Tower of Dornes**

Next to Dornes Church. Designated as a Building of Public Interest. The Tower can only be seen from outside. Information: Tourist Office (Tel: 249 366677).

The origin of the tower is unknown but according to tradition it was originally a Roman observation post, though it seems

ITINERARY II   Lands of the Order of Christ
Dornes

more probable that it was a Mediaeval watchtower belonging to the Templars or the Order of Christ, on whose land it stands.
It overlooks a considerable area, particularly the artificial lake of the dam at Castelo de Bode, and was used in Manueline times as a bell tower, and then the church was built alongside. It is built of local schist on a square plan, with marked angles, and, on the upper floor, there are large windows and brick vaulting.

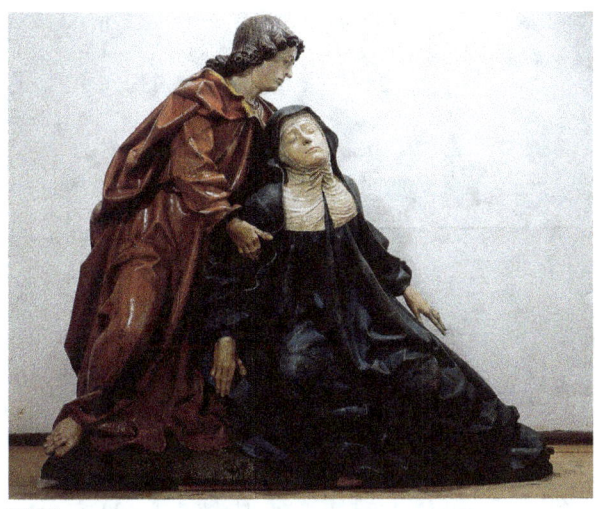

IPM/C.M.

Oliver of Ghent, "St. John and the Virgin Mary", 16th century, Convent of Christ, Tomar.

"Santarém is a book in stone, in which the most interesting and most poetic of our chronicles are written. Rich in manuscript illuminations, indentations, fleurons, images, arabesques and perfect tracery, the book is the most beautiful and most valuable in Portugal. Bound in green enamel and silver by the Tagus and by its streams, held fast by the bronze clasp of its strong Gothic walls, the magnificent book should last forever provided the hand of the Creator does not stretch out to erase the creature's memories.
But this Nineveh was not destroyed, this Pompeii was not submerged by a great catastrophe. The people whose history is the book, still exist, but these people behaved childishly. They were given the book to play with, they tore it, despoiled it, pulled it apart page by page, and made parrots and dolls and hats. There is no other way to describe what these people called government, called administration, have been doing and allowing to be done in Santarém for more than a hundred years.

The ruins of time are sad and beautiful; the solemn stamp of history marks those that are caused by revolutions. But the brutal degradation and the even more brutal ignorant repairs, the paltry patching of parasitic art, these debase, they take away all prestige.
This is the general impression I have of this place. Let's lunch, I can hear them calling, and afterwards let us go and see whether I am wrong. At lunch the conversation naturally turned to the most obvious subject, Santarém. D. Afonso Henriques and his brave men, Friar Gil and the Divine Miracle, Alfageme and the High Constable, King D. Fernando and Queen D. Leonor. Camões was born here, Pedr'Álvares Cabral, the Docens, almost all the great figures of our history passed in review. In the end, I also saw Santa Iria, the patron saint of this land, whose name here makes one forget that of the Romans and the Celts."

Almeida Garrett (1799-1854),
Travels in My Homeland, Lisbon, 1846.

89

THE ORDER OF CHRIST AND THE DISCOVERIES

Pedro Dias

The origin of the Order of Christ lies in the Order of the Knights Templar, founded to fight against the Infidel in the Holy Land. In the 13th century, on the return of the Templars to their native lands, many entered into conflict with various monarchs, who succeeded in destroying the Order, particularly Philippe the Good of France. In Portugal, King D. Dinis did not share the general view and to avoid any problems that might be caused by the lack of an armed militia, as had been seen during the Reconquest, he decided to create a new Portuguese Order. He called it the Order of Christ and granted it all Templar property and revenues. So, in 1319, the Order of Christ was set up and, a century later, it was to play a most important role in introducing Christianity into overseas territories. The headquarters of the order moved definitively to Tomar in 1357.

When Prince Henry the Navigator accepted the post of Administrator General of the Order of Christ, its importance increased. He saw to it that the Order was granted the patronage of the churches on the Atlantic Islands and, later, of many others in conquered or discovered lands or in overseas continental territory. Equally, the Portuguese Court was interested in channelling its revenue in the kingdom to the defence of the forts in the Maghreb, and also to the struggle against Islam overseas. When D. Manuel I took over the administration of the Order, just as his great-uncle had, the Policy of Vicariates continued, granting these overseas churches many religious objects and works of art bought in Northern European markets, with particular emphasis on Flanders.

Many of those who took part in the overseas discoveries were linked to the Order of Christ, or to the Order of Santiago. Others were thanked with the gift of a commandery or made a knight after performing great deeds, a distinction that was extended, from the 15th century onwards, to many princes and royal personages and even to non-Europeans, namely Africans and Indians.

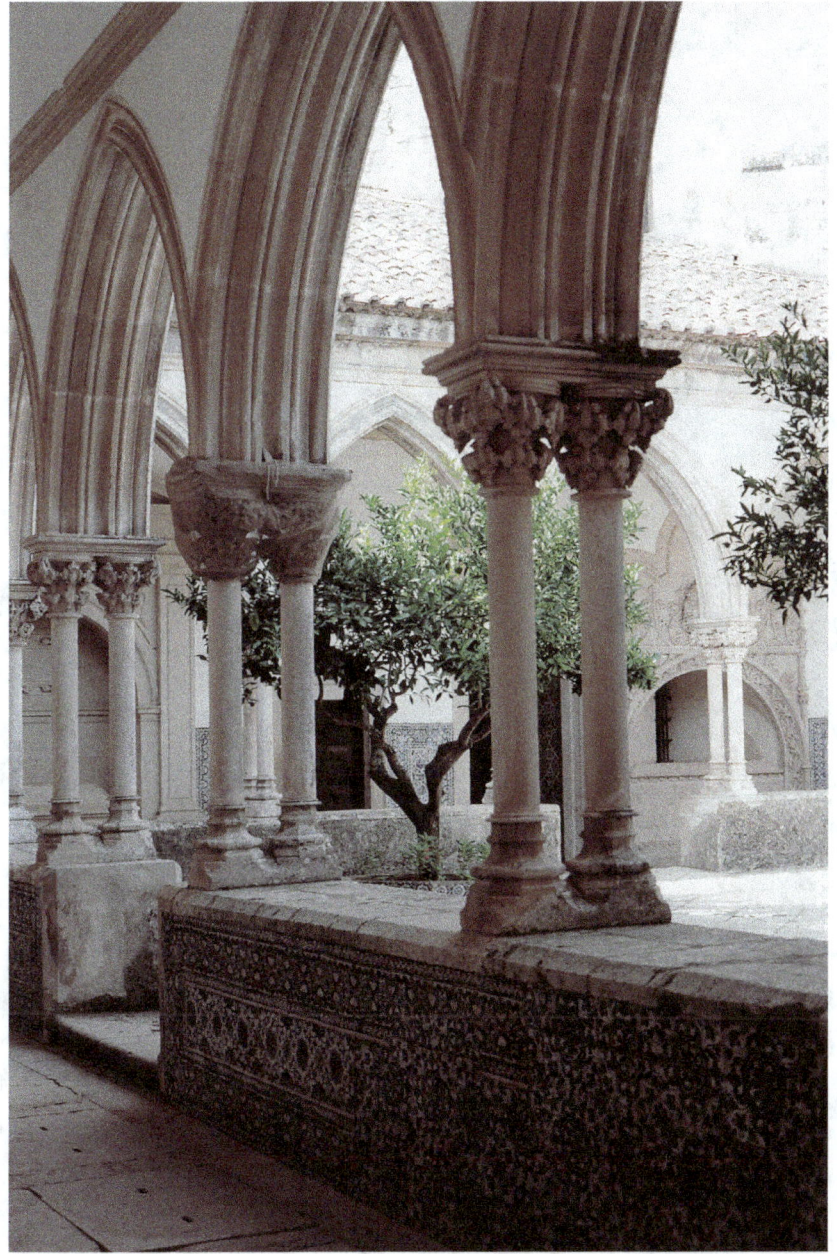

Convent of Christ, cemetery cloister, Tomar.

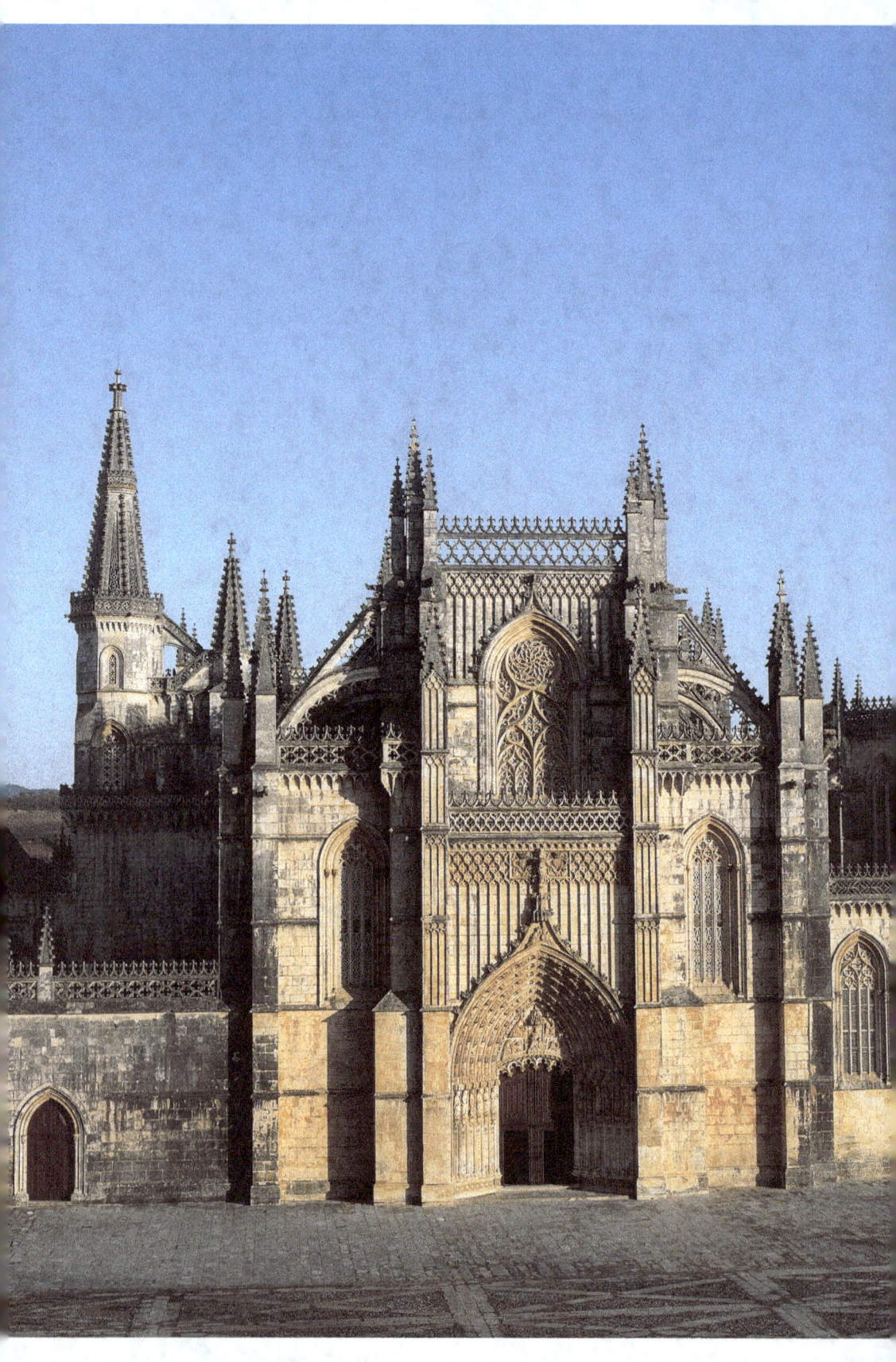

ITINERARY III

In the Footsteps of Boytac

Pedro Dias, Dalila Rodrigues,
Nuno Vassallo e Silva, Fernando Grilo

First day

III.1 BATALHA
    III.1.a Batalha Monastery
    III.1.b Exaltação da Santa Cruz (Batalha Parish Church)

III.2 POMBAL
    III.2.a Castle

III.3 REDINHA
    III.3.a Nossa Senhora da Conceição (Redinha Parish Church)

III.4 SOURE
    III.4.a Castle
    III.4.b São Tiago (Soure Parish Church)

III.5 EGA
    III.5.a Paço dos Comendadores (Residence of the Commanders)
    III.5.b Nossa Senhora da Graça (Ega Parish Church)

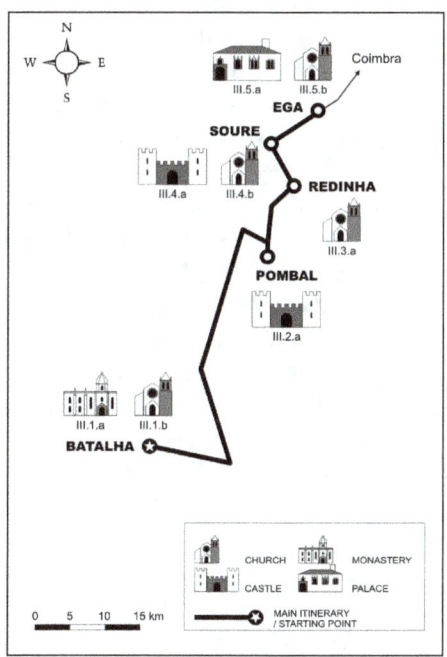

Monastery of Batalha, main façade.

ITINERARY III   *In the Footsteps of Boytac*

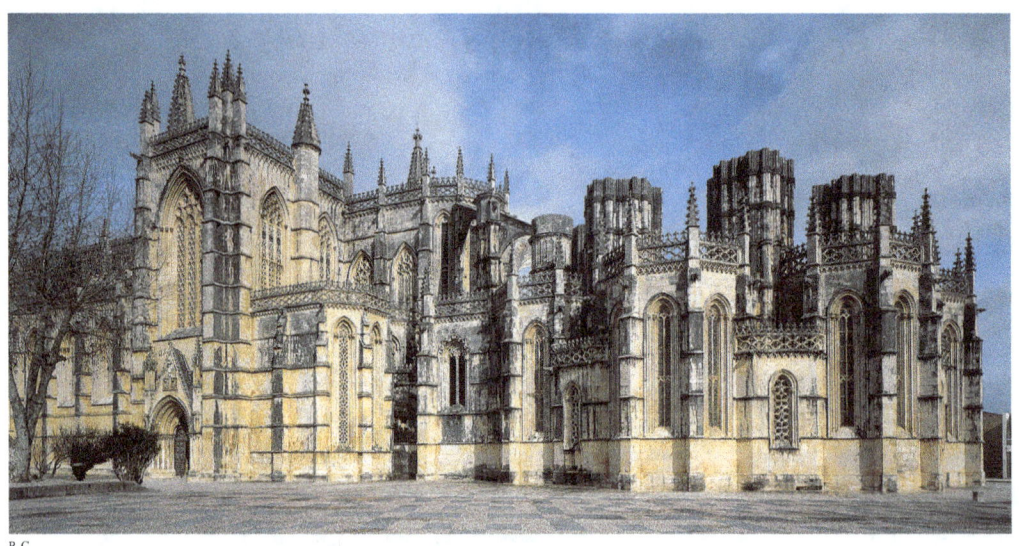

General view of the Unfinished Chapels, Batalha Monastery.

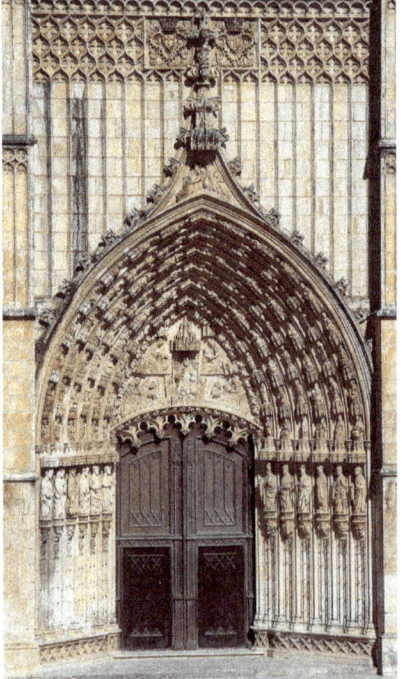

Batalha Monastery, main portal.

Manueline architecture reached its peak in the second decade of the 16th century, with the power of the king D. Manuel I now stabilised, and overseas expansion providing economic benefits. Tomar, Lisbon and Tavira were among a number of artistic centres that affected building methods, though the most important was Batalha, where the greatest monastery ensemble in Portugal, the Mosteiro de Santa Maria da Vitória was begun in 1389. The site became a school where the major 15th-century and Manueline master builders were trained and it was there that D. Manuel I recruited architects, whom he later sent to Morocco, Africa and parts of India. One of these was Boytac.

Boytac, or Diogo de Boytac, was not of Portuguese origin, but he arrived in the country while still young and served his

ITINERARY III *In the Footsteps of Boytac*
Batalha

apprenticeship with João de Arruda and Mateus Fernandes. He served D. João II and, after his death, continued in the service of D. Manuel I, making his name building forts in Morocco, though he also built palaces and churches in Portugal.

Some of Boytac's most important works, and those of his leading disciples, are to be found in the provinces of Estremadura and Beira Litoral, particularly Coimbra, though he is also said to have been one of the first master builders to work on the Mosteiro dos Jerónimos in Lisbon.

III.I BATALHA

III.1.a Batalha Monastery

Classified as a National Monument since 1907, the building has been listed as a World Heritage Site by UNESCO since 1983. (Tel: 244 765497). Photography permitted. Admission charge. Opening hours: summer 09.00-18.00, October-March 09.00-17.00. Closed on January 1st, Good Friday, Easter, May 1st, December 24th and 25th.

D. João I founded the Mosteiro de Santa Maria da Vitória, better known as the Mosteiro da Batalha, to thank the Virgin Mary for his victory over the Castilians at Aljubarrota, in 1385, which resolved the Portuguese dynastic crisis. The monastery was granted to the monks of the Dominican Order, many of whom were among

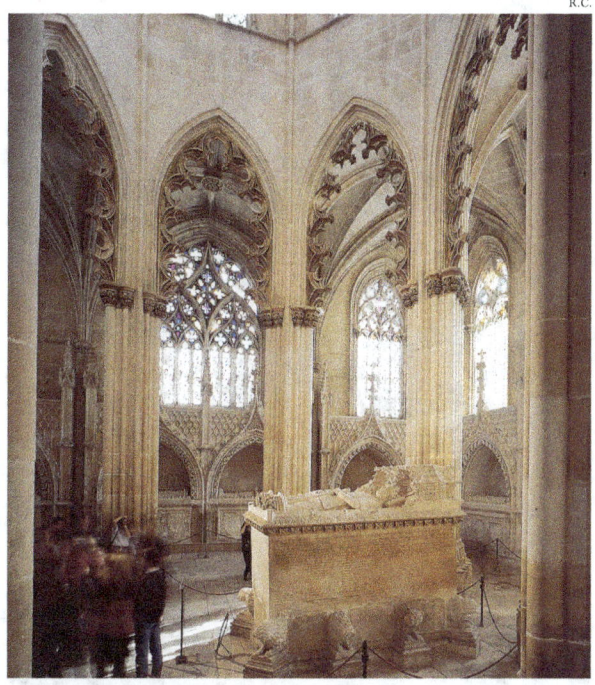

Founder's Chapel, Batalha Monastery.

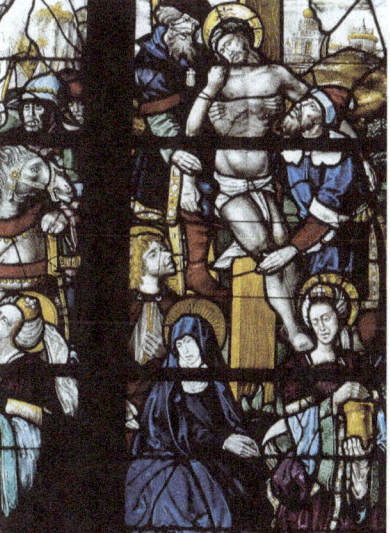

"Descent from the Cross", stained-glass window in the Chapter House, 1514, Batalha Monastery.

ITINERARY III   In the Footsteps of Boytac
Batalha

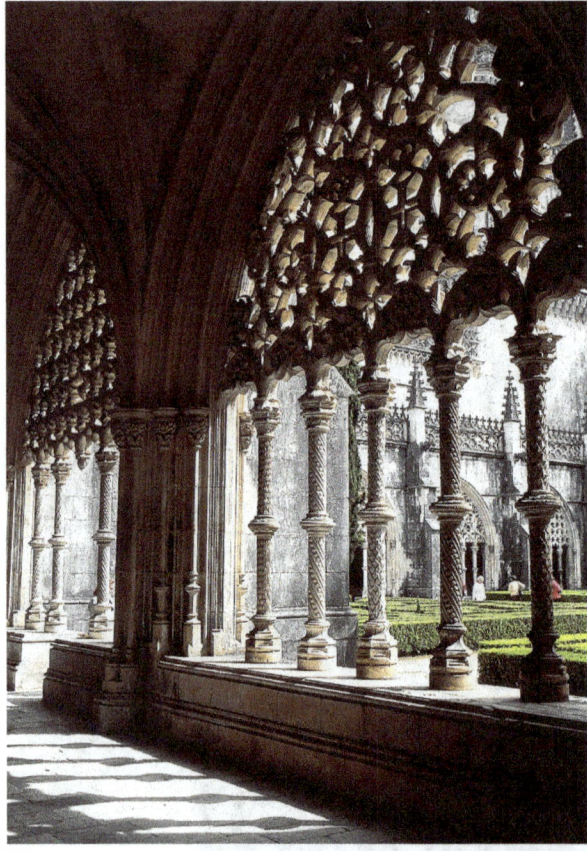

Cloister of the Batalha Monastery.

M.A.

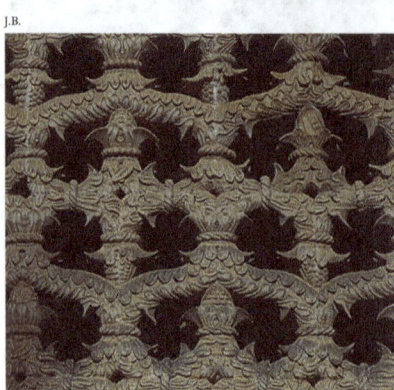

J.B.

Cloister of the Batalha Monastery, detail.

the king's closest followers. In 1389, the foundations were laid by the Master Builder Afonso Domingues, who was succeeded by other masters, the second being Huguet, who introduced the Flamboyant Gothic.

Mateus Fernandes and Boytac also worked at Batalha during the Manueline period. Both of them settled in the town that had grown around the monastery and it was here that their children grew up, who later also became builders themselves.

The Batalha Monastery is the most important Portuguese Gothic building, started in the Rayonnant period and moving on to the Perpendicular, Flamboyant Gothic, and finishing with the Manueline.

The ensemble, which survived the ravages of two opposing armies during the Peninsular War, is made up of the Abbey Church and the Founder's Chapel, the Royal and the D. Afonso V Cloisters, the Chapter House, refectory, dormitory and other buildings. The centrally planned Gothic Founder's chapel contains the tombs, with recumbent figures, of D. João I and his English Queen, Philippa of Lancaster. On the south wall lie the restored tombs of their children, the Princes of Avis, namely Prince Henry the Navigator, and also D. João II and his ill-fated heir, Prince D. Afonso.

The main portal of the church is a fine example of the architectural sculpture that is such a feature of Batalha.

The work of Mateus Fernandes is remarkable because it was he who introduced lush foliate decoration into the late Gothic style as can be seen in the tracery filling the

ITINERARY III   *In the Footsteps of Boytac*
Batalha

arches of the Royal Cloister and the great portal leading to the Unfinished Chapels, planned as a royal pantheon. If this last work is based on a Flamboyant Gothic structure that is clearly influenced by central European styles, the shafting of the unfinished vaulting is clearly Vernacular, and one of the high points of this truly naturalist exuberance, that so marks the period, and Manueline art. Unfortunately the death of D. Manuel I, in 1521, led to the cancellation of this fantastic undertaking.

III.1.b Exaltação da Santa Cruz (Batalha Parish Church)

Near the Monastery. (Tel: 244 765140). Designated a National Monument.
Opening hours: daily 10.00-16.00. Mass is at 08.30 from Monday to Friday, at 19.30 on Saturdays and 08.00 and 11.00 on Sundays.

The Church of Santa Cruz was built for the workers and their families who lived in the town that grew up around the site of the Mosteiro da Batalha. It was considerably altered and enhanced during the Manueline period and work continued up until 1532. Note the elegant portal, with heavy foliate decoration, and also two shields one with an armillary sphere and the other with the cross of the Order of Christ, as well as the chancel which is in the best tradition of the Portuguese late Gothic. It is possible that Boytac may have been the master builder in charge of construction.

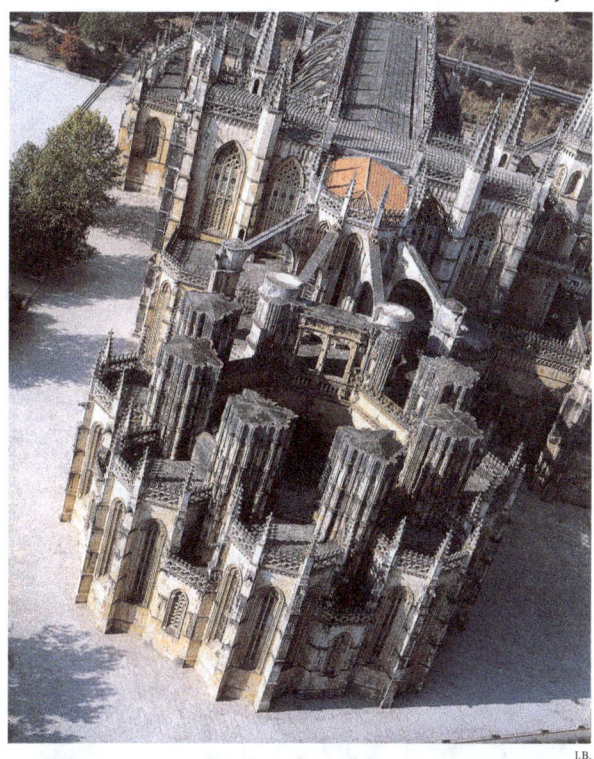

Aerial view of the Unfinished Chapel, Batalha Monastery.

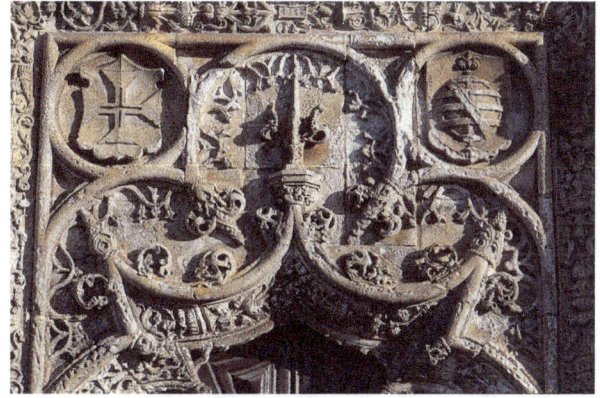

Exaltação da Santa Cruz, detail of the main portal, Batalha.

97

ITINERARY III   *In the Footsteps of Boytac*
Pombal/Redinha

Church of Exaltação da Santa Cruz, plan, Batalha, Boletim da Direcção-Geral dos Edifícios e Monumentos Nacionais, No. 13, Lisbon, 1938.

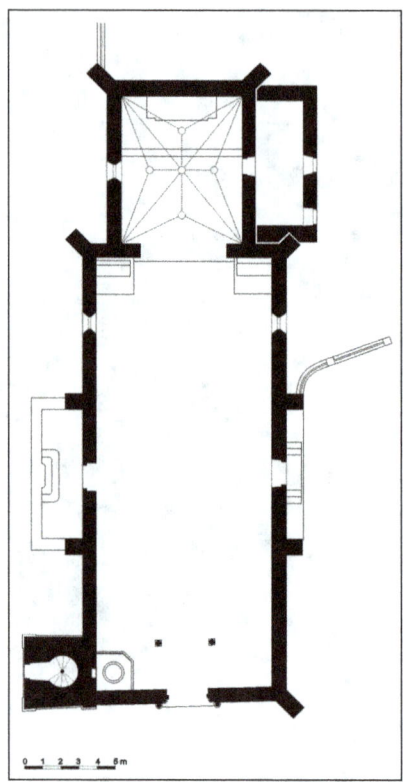

To reach Pombal follow the EN1 in the direction of Porto (42 km.).

III.2 POMBAL

III.2.a Castle

Situated on Monte do Castelo. Designated a National Monument. Information: Pombal Tourist Office (Tel: 236 213230).
Opening hours: the Castle can be visited at any time.

The importance of Pombal during the early years of the kingdom of Portugal derived from its position between the River Mondego and the Muslim lands on the route of the Tagus. The castle was built or rebuilt in 1161, by Gualdim Pais and held by the Knights Templar. In 1319, it was handed over to the Order of Christ, which maintained it as head quarters of one of its commanderies. D. Manuel I, Administrator General of the Order, restored the castle at the beginning of the 16th century, and granted the town a charter in 1512.

For Redinha follow the EN1. After the exit for Pelarga / Verigo, there is a crossroads. Take the Estrada Municipal to Redinha (11 km.).

III.3 REDINHA

III.1.a Nossa Senhora da Conceição (Redinha Parish Church)

Largo da Igreja. Designated as a Building of Public Interest.
Open for mass on Sundays at 10.00. To visit the church, ask for the key at the residence of the Parish Priest, or make an appointment (Tel: 236 911121).

This settlement grew up around a fort built by the Knights Templar, that was

ITINERARY III *In the Footsteps of Boytac*
Redinha

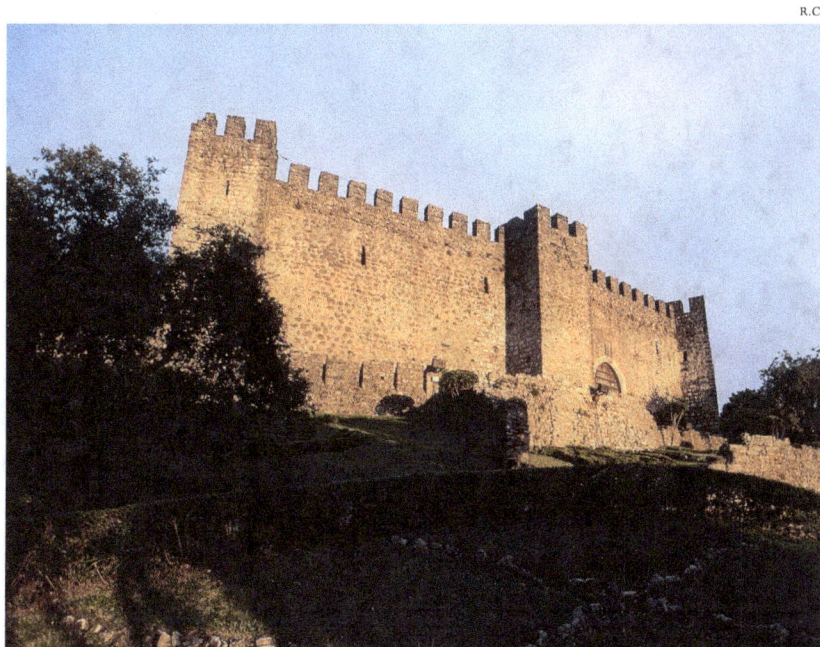

Pombal Castle, general view.

handed over to the Order of Christ in the 14th century. The first charter was granted to Gualdim Pais, Master of the Order, in 1159, who re-built the small castle and the Romanesque bridge that still exists here.

The Romanesque Parish Church was considerably altered during the Manueline period. The general structure dates from the 16th century, as do the simple outer doorways with foliate decoration that is typical of this period.

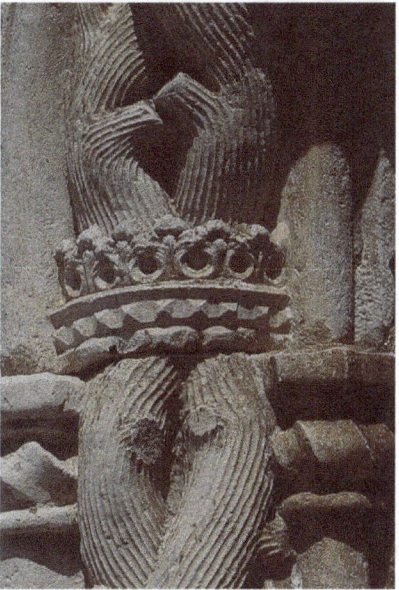

For Soure, follow the EN1 in the direction of Venda Nova. Turn left in the direction of Paleão along the EN348 to Soure (12 km.).

Nossa Senhora da Conceição, detail of the portal, Redinha.

ITINERARY III   In the Footsteps of Boytac
Soure

Soure Castle.

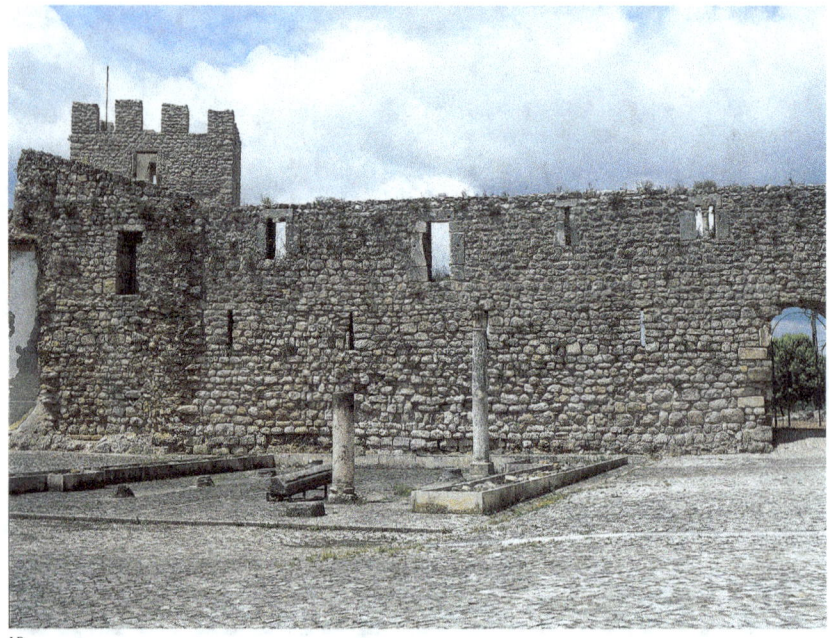

J.B.

III.4 SOURE

III.4.a Castle

The Castle is reached via the churchyard. Designated a National Monument.
Opening hours: it may be visited at any time. For a guided tour, make an appointment at the Museu Municipal Tel: 239 509190, between the hours of 9.00-12.30 and 14.00-17.30.

The town of Soure was built on the site of a Roman settlement and the area was also inhabited during the Visigothic period. Its importance increased in the 12th century when it stood on the frontier between the Christian North and the Islamic South.

Queen D. Teresa granted the town a charter in 1111, and in 1128, it was donated to the Knights Templar along with its castle. Prince Henry the Navigator ordered the castle, which contains a number of *Mozarab* elements, to be rebuilt in the 15th century. It was rebuilt again some 50 years later by D. Manuel I as it was the headquarters of a commandery of the Military Order of Christ. Except for parts that have gradually fallen into ruin, the character of the building is much as it was in Manueline times.

III.4.b São Tiago (Soure Parish Church)

Praça Miguel Bombarda (Tel: 239 502226).
Opening hours: daily 09.00-17.00. For a

ITINERARY III   *In the Footsteps of Boytac*
Ega

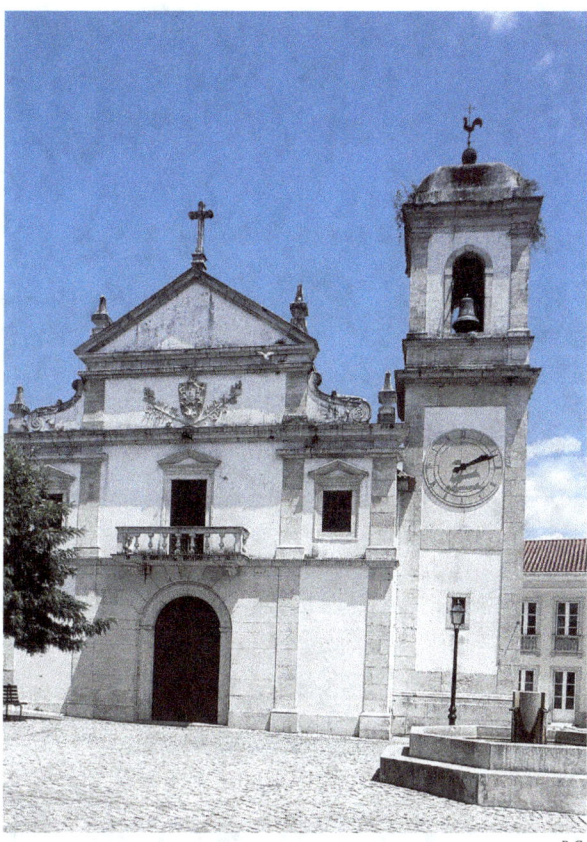

São Tiago, Soure Parish Church, main façade.

guided tour, make an appointment through the Museu Municipal (Tel: 239 509190), between the hours of 09.00-12.30 and 14.00-17.00.

D. Manuel I had the Parish Church of São Tiago built in 1490, when he was Administrator General of the Order of Christ, and it seemed unlikely that he would ascend the throne. All that remains of the early church are the arcades that divide the three aisles of the main vessel, as well as two lapidary stones referring to the construction of the building. These are emblazoned with D. Manuel's armorial bearings and device as Duke of Beja.

For Ega follow the EN342, towards Condeixa (8 km.).

III.5 **EGA**

III.5.a **Paço dos Comendadores (Residence of the Commanders)**

At Ega, on the road from Condeixa to Soure, behind the Parish Church.

When D. Afonso Henriques granted this settlement to the Knights Templar, it was one of the first lines of defence south of the River Mondego. It later came into the possession of the Order of Christ and became a commandery, the manor or estate of an Order of Knights, and was granted a new charter by D. Manuel I in 1514, due to its strategic importance. The Paço dos Comendadores stands on a hill overlooking the old village. It is now

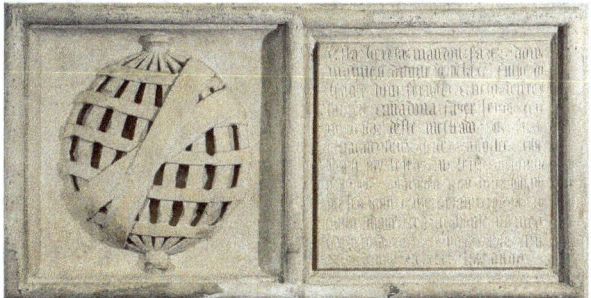

Emblazoned stone referring to the building of São Tiago, Soure Parish Church.

101

ITINERARY III In the Footsteps of Boytac
Ega

Residence of the Commanders, general view, Ega.

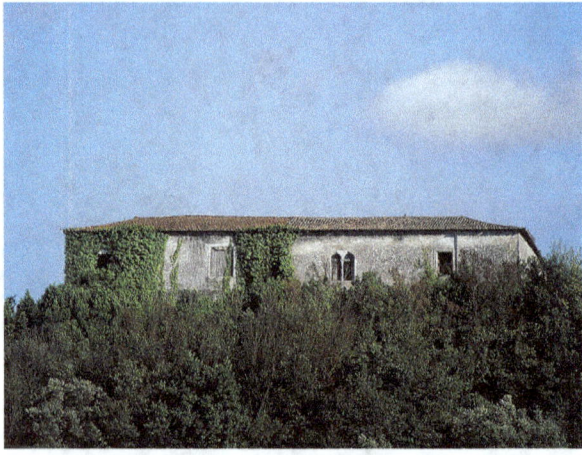
J.B.

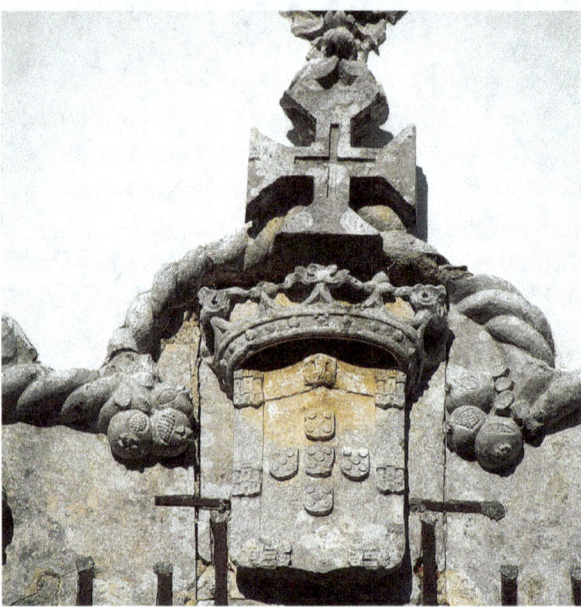
J.B.

Nossa Senhora da Graça, detail of the portal, Ega.

sadly in ruins but a number of Manueline doors and windows can still be seen.
Lower down the hill, the stone column of the old pillory is topped by a naturalist pinecone.

III.5.b Nossa Senhora da Graça (Ega Parish Church)

Classified as a Building of Public Interest. Further information can be obtained by telephoning the Priest (Tel: 239 944441).
Opening hours: daily for mass at 19.00, and on Sunday at 12.00. To arrange a visit the church, enquire at the house next door, or at the residence of the Parish Priest nearby.

The Parish Church, which is not far from the Paço dos Commendadores, was entirely altered at the beginning of the 16th century; the work being completed by Diogo de Castilho, on the death of Marcus Pires, in 1521. Pires was a disciple and collaborator of Boytac and completed his work at the Mosteiro de Santa Cruz and the Royal Palace in Coimbra. The Manueline portal is particularly fine with its plaited columns, the chancel has a naturalist *triumphal arch* also adorned by plaited columns and *archivolts*, and elegant *quadripartite vaulting*. The altar triptych which dates to *c.*1543, painted by a Court artist, and includes a portrait of the Commander, D. Afonso de Lencastre.

To reach Coimbra take the EN342 in the direction of Condeixa and from there follow the N1.

ITINERARY III

In the Footsteps of Boytac

Pedro Dias, Dalila Rodrigues,
Nuno Vassallo e Silva, Fernando Grilo

Second day

III.6 COIMBRA
- III.6.a Paço Real (Royal Palace)
- III.6.b Museu Nacional Machado de Castro
- III.6.c Sé Velha (Old Cathedral)
- III.6.d House of Sub-Ripas
- III.6.e Santa Cruz Monastery

III.7 SÃO MARCOS (option)
- III.7.a São Marcos Monastery

III.8 MONTEMOR-O-VELHO
- III.8.a Castle
- III.8.b Convent of Santa Maria dos Anjos
- III.8.c Former Hospital da Misericórdia

The Legend of Inês De Castro

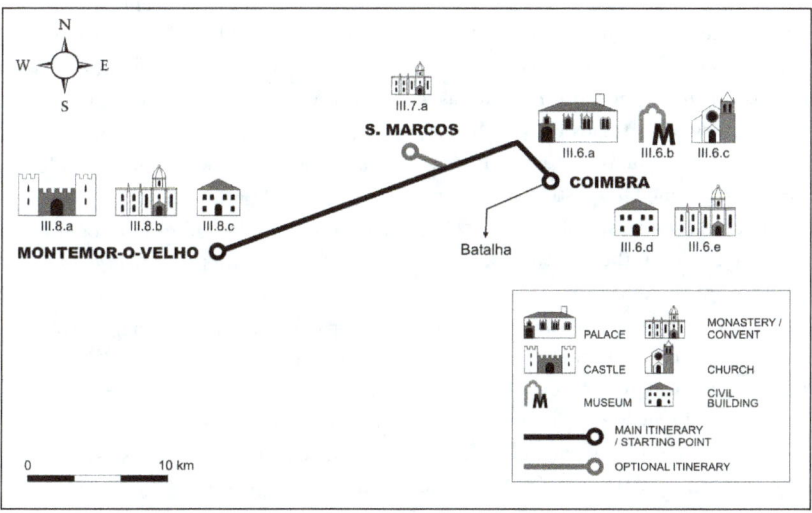

ITINERARY III   In the Footsteps of Boytac
Coimbra

Oliver of Ghent, high-altar retable, detail, 1499-1500, Sé Velha, Coimbra.

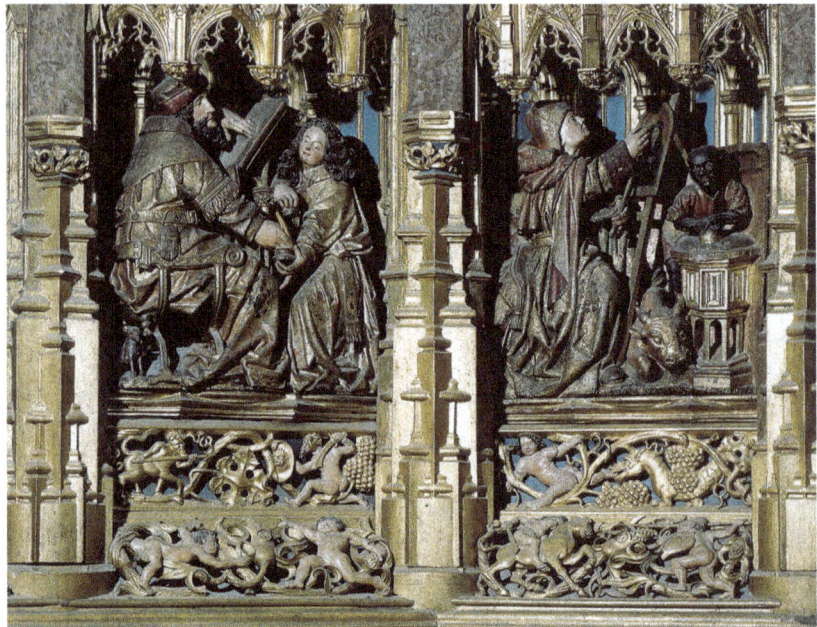

III.6 COIMBRA

During the Manueline period, Coimbra was not as important in the national context as it is today, nor as important as it had been two centuries earlier. It had, nevertheless, flourished since Roman times and retained interesting artistic and architectural remains, maintaining its key position between the North and South, until the mid-12th century.

In 713, Coimbra was occupied by the Arabs, who remained there until 1064, when it was taken by Fernando the Great, Emperor of León, and his troops, among which was the great warrior El Cid.

The first King of Portugal, D. Afonso Henriques chose Coimbra as the seat of the Court and it was capital of the kingdom until the mid-13th century. The university was established in the time of D. Dinis, largely due to the prestigious reputation of monastic seats of learning, such as the Mosteiro de Santa Cruz.

As from 1505, Coimbra developed apace. D. Manuel I had religious and administrative buildings built or rebuilt, as well as constructing a bridge over the River Mondego and a hospital. All this activity and royal patronage attracted many artists, architects and sculptors of national and international stature, who not only influenced the Mondego area, but also the Beira provinces and the Upper Estremadura region.

ITINERARY III In the Footsteps of Boytac
Coimbra

To best enjoy a visit to Coimbra, we suggest that you park in one of the car parks after the viaduct, next to the Casa do Sal. Take the "Eco Via", a small bus that goes up to the highest part of the city and then, from there, follow the suggested route on foot.

III.6.a Paço Real (Royal Palace)

Largo da Porta Férrea, University of Coimbra. Designated a National Monument. Information Tel: 239 859800. Cafeteria.
There is an admission charge; teachers and students are exempt. Opening hours: daily 09.30-12.00 and 14.00-17.00, except on December 25th.

The Royal Palace in Coimbra dates back to the time of the first King of Portugal, D. Afonso Henriques, who lived and possibly died here. There was, however, a fort on this site many centuries earlier and some of its remains were incorporated into the Manueline buildings. The round towers on the exterior wall facing the old cathedral, the Sé Velha, date from this period, as do the large windows, visible in the Via Latina and belonging to what used to be the Throne Room, now the Ceremonial Hall, as well as a number of interesting doorways and arches on the ground floor in the area now occupied by the Instituto Jurídico.
The most interesting building is the Chapel of São Miguel with its Manueline portal and *triumphal arch* with rope carving. This was the work of Marcos Pires,

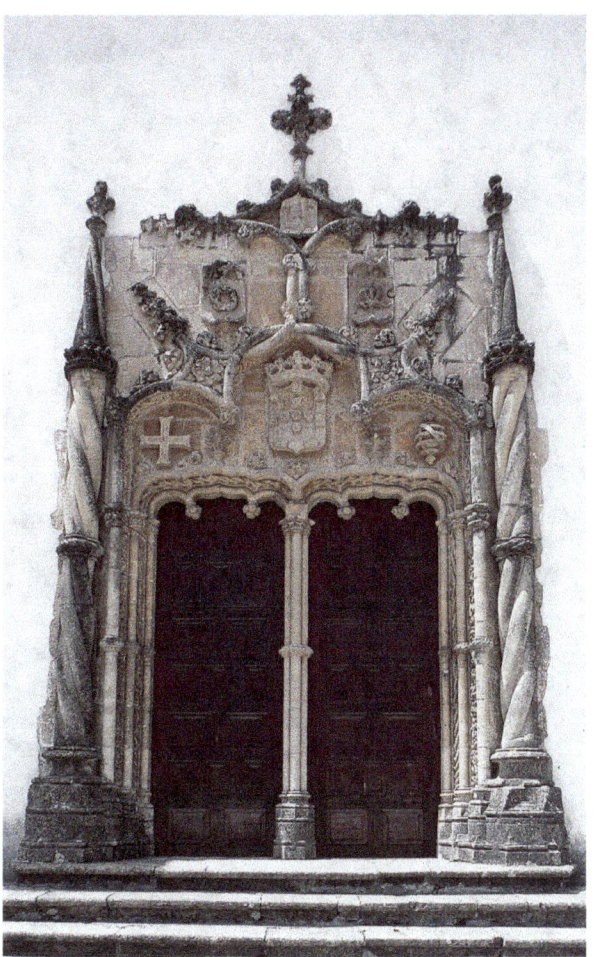

Boytac's leading disciple, who worked there from 1517 to 1521.

Paço Real, portal, Coimbra.

R.C.

III.6.b Museu Nacional Machado de Castro

Admission charge. Largo Dr. José Rodrigues. (Tel: 239 823727). Once the Episcopal

ITINERARY III — *In the Footsteps of Boytac*
Coimbra

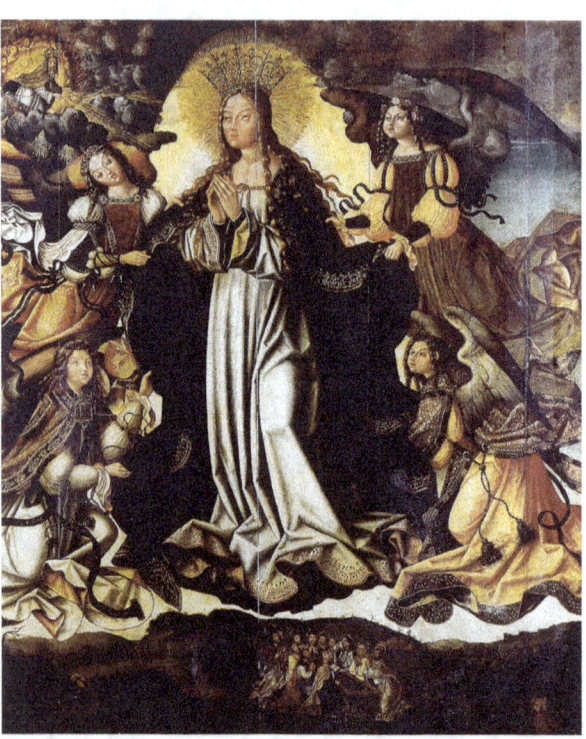

Vicente Gil, "Assumption of the Virgin", oil on wood, c.1520, Museu Nacional Machado de Castro, Coimbra.

co and courtyard with its large terrace overlooking the river, still exist from this time. The Museum contains a comprehensive collection dating from the High Middle Ages up to the present day.

One of the most important sections is that consisting of the Treasury of the Cathedral, which dates back to the 12th century and has been progressively enriched by valuable items. A very fine example of the Late Gothic, typical of the Manueline period, is to be seen in the superb, silver-gilt monstrance donated to the Cathedral by D. Jorge de Almeida in 1527. Its structure is reminiscent of a Manueline edifice with three registers, set on a broad base supported by lions. A legend around the base refers to its donation and it also bears the coat of arms of the bishop-count. The wafer box is in the shape of a small temple, and the Host can be seen through a very fine grid.

Among a number of silver-gilt chalices are fine examples from the Monastery of Santa Clara, and the Treasury of D. Catarina de Eça, Abbess of Lorvão.

The collection contains important 16th-century Portuguese and imported paintings, a number from the most traditionalist workshop in the Manueline period, probably situated in Coimbra. From the *Assumption of the Virgin*, *St Bartholomew* and the six panels from the Monastery of Celas *polyptych*, it is possible to pick out characteristics that define all the workshop's production.

Palace, the building has been classified as a National Monument since 1910.
Opening hours: 09.30-12.30 and 14.00-17.30. Closed on Mondays and on January 1st, Easter, May 1st, December 25th.

The Museum is installed in the old Episcopal Palace, which in turn rests on a large, imposing Roman *cryptoporticus*. This artificial platform was used in the 12th century for the building of the Church of São João de Almedina, with its respective cloisters and annexes. The last work was carried out at the end of the 16th century, and the porti-

ITINERARY III In the Footsteps of Boytac
Coimbra

Despite the superior quality of some of the paintings, as in the case of the *Assumption of the Virgin*, the arrangement of figures tends to be rigid. There is difficulty with composition; faces are simplified and repetitive with little character, while the anatomical structure of the figures is deficient, with recourse to traditional angular folds of drapery. The superb treatment of brocade, ornamented with precious stones and pieces of jewellery, must be highlighted, however, in a finely detailed work of great density. It seems to be the result of a traditionalist concept of painting, conceived as a materially valuable object.

What is today called the "Masters of Coimbra" corresponds to the former designation the "School of the Master of Sardoal", a name derived from the fact that the Parish Church there contained a valuable group of paintings, the origin of all the surviving school's production, some 40 in all. It seems likely that Vicente Gil, painter to D. João II, active in Coimbra between 1498 and 1525, and his son Manuel Vicente, who worked in the city from 1521 to 1530, headed a workshop operating in this region.

The museum also contains an admirable collection of sculpture including works by the master, Oliver of Ghent (Olivier de Gand) and those within his circle. Sculptures such as *St Barbara, St Jerome* and *St Gregory*, although miniature and belonging to the imposing altarpiece in the old Cathedral, the Sé Velha, are highly representative of his aesthetic. A monumental *Prophet* although

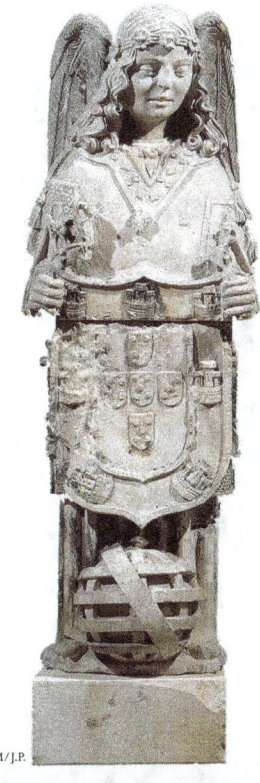

Diogo Pires the Younger, "Heraldic Angel", limestone, 1518-20, Museu Nacional Machado de Castro, Coimbra.

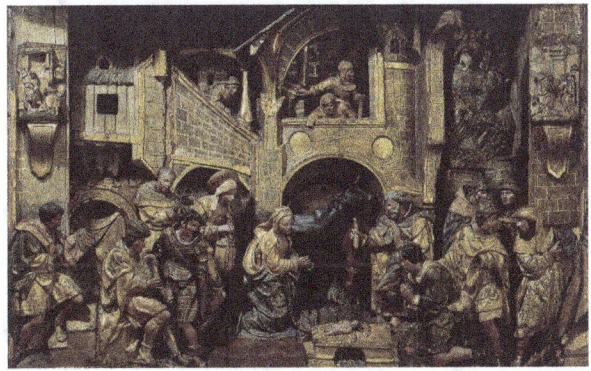

Antwerp Workshop, "Retable of the Nativity", 16th century, Museu Nacional Machado de Castro, Coimbra.

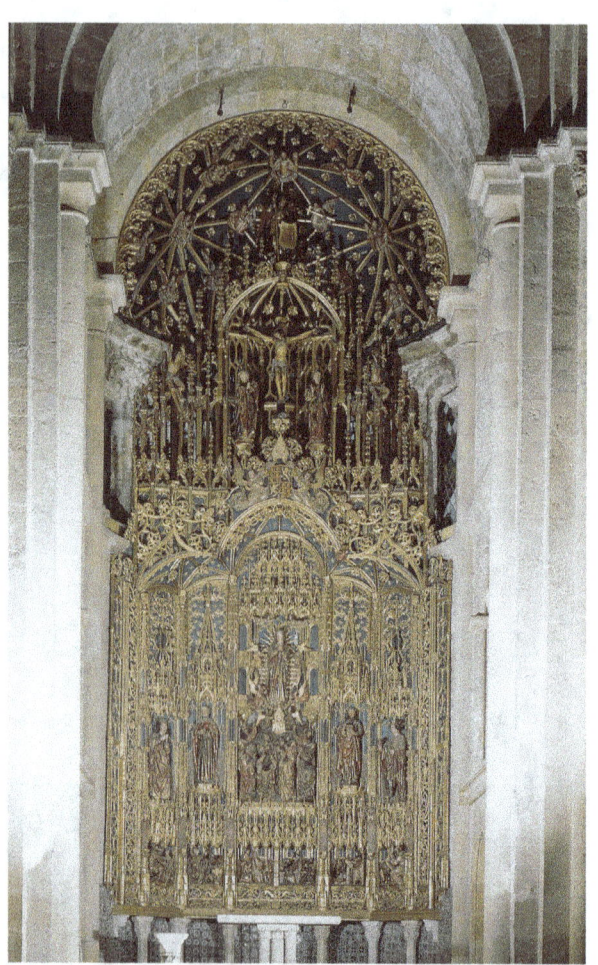

Oliver of Ghent and Jean of Ypres, high-altar retable, 1499-1500, Sé Velha, Coimbra.

incomplete, *Our Lady* and *St John*, as well as a remarkable *St Matthew* from the Parish Church in Botão, are other examples of this Flemish master's influence on the Coimbra area. The magnificent *Nativity* altarpiece is representative of the large number of sculptural works imported from Northern Europe in Manueline times. The quality of the retable, in carved polychrome wood, indicates that it came from one of the most important workshops in Antwerp at the beginning of the 16th century.

III.6.c Sé Velha (Old Cathedral)

Largo da Sé Velha. (Tel: 239 825273). Designated a National Monument.
Admission charge to cloister; students are exempt. Opening hours: daily 10.00-13.00 and 14.00-18.00. Closed on Sunday.

The Old Cathedral in Coimbra dates back to the 6th-century Visigothic period, and was replaced by the edifice constructed in 1164 by the Bishop, D. Miguel Salomão. It was always a sacred place even before the Visigothic period, almost certainly being a Roman temple and, later, an Arab mosque.

Essentially completed by 1184, it was further enriched by a cloister at the beginning of the 13th century, and underwent considerable changes between 1483 and 1543 due to the efforts of the Bishop, D. Jorge de Almeida.

During his time in the Diocese of Coimbra, besides architectural works by Pero and Filipe Henriques, sons of one of the master craftsman at Batalha, Mateus Fernandes, in 1498, the bishop ordered the high altar retable to be renovated by Jean of Ypres and Oliver of Ghent. The work was completed in

1502. In the following year, he acquired some 10,000 tiles from Seville to cover the interior of the cathedral, though they were later stripped and only a few remain in place. The polychrome *Mudéjar, cuenca* tiles were made by Fernán Quijarro and Pedro de Herrera, ceramists from the Triana area of Seville.

In about 1500, Oliver of Ghent, the sculptor and woodworker, and Jean d'Ypres, painter and gilder, were commissioned to execute a new retable for the high altar, which, immediately, brought different stylistic influences to bear.

This grandiose work executed in polychrome wood and gilt, is one of the high points of Portuguese late Gothic art. The monumentality of the retable is based on a number of factors that include the quality of the sculpture, the perfect symbiosis between the structure of the woodwork in architectural form and the sculptures, the painstaking polychrome and the gilding in keeping with the overall magnificence. In the middle, in a flight of angels, *Our Lady of the Assumption* is carried to heaven leaving the inconsolable Apostles demonstrating their grief, to form one of the many emotional reactions that this type of altarpiece sparks in the believer. The monumental effect is created not only by the scale, but also the symbiosis between the sculpture, polychrome and the remarkable gilded woodwork.

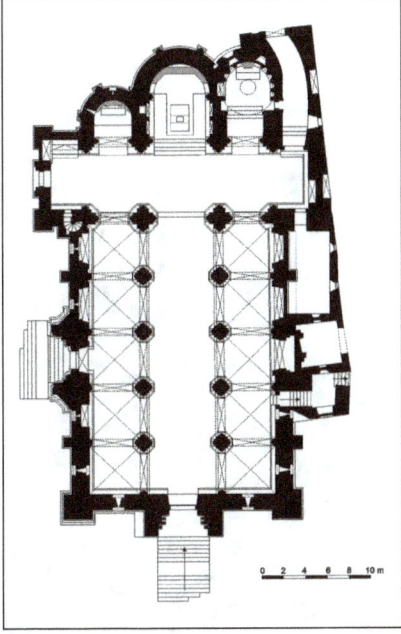

Sé Velha at Coimbra, plan at entrance level, Boletim da Direcção-Geral dos Edifícios e Monumentos Nacionais, No. 109, Lisbon, 1962.

III.6.d House of Sub-Ripas

Rua de Sub-Ripas. Designated a National Monument. Information: Tourist Office (Tel: 239 832591). This building can only be seen from the outside.

Few Manueline houses have been conserved in Coimbra, but this very fine example is one of the best in the country. Like many of the houses of the bourgeoisie or the lower nobility, it was also built on the battlement of the wall and included one of the towers. Work on the building took place soon after 1515, and the builder stamped it with the exuberant foliage, so typical of the work at Batalha. The windows and balconies are all different and strongly

ITINERARY III — *In the Footsteps of Boytac*
Coimbra

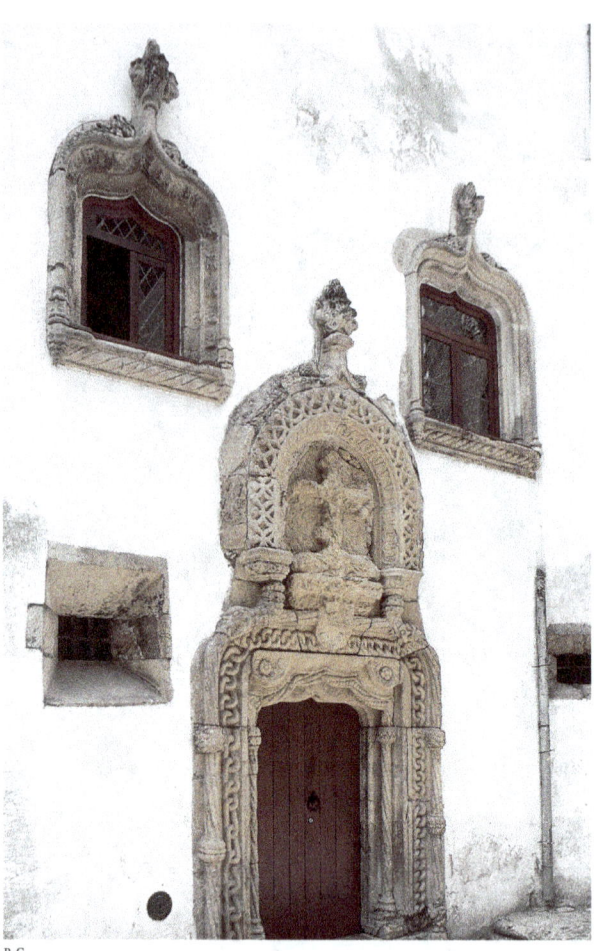

R.C.

House of Sub-Ripas, Coimbra.

naturalistic in style, and the interior has largely retained the original divisions.

Later, in Renaissance times, the Casa de Cima or Casa do Arco was built, and includes on the outer walls of both, dozens of medallions and low relief work from the workshop of Jean of Rouen, an artist whose workshop was nearby.

III.6.e Santa Cruz Monastery

Praça 8 de Maio. (Tel: 239 822941). Designated a National Monument.
Admission charge to cloister. Opening hours: 9.00-12.00 and 14.00-17.30 Mondays-Saturdays and 16.00-18.00 on Sundays.

Work began on the Monastery on July 28th 1131, on the site of what was almost certainly the Muslim or Roman Royal Baths. D. Afonso Henriques, the first King of Portugal, was responsible for the initiative, and it was here that the young prince brought together the leading intellectuals and politicians in the kingdom. Among them were D. João Peculiar, D. Miguel Salomão, the Archdeacon D. Telo, and São Teotónio (St Theotonius), first Prior of the Monastery, which was granted to the Augustine Canons.

Following a visit by D. Manuel I in 1502, profound alterations were made to the physical structure of the monastery, rebuilding the church, cloisters and dwellings from the very foundations. The promoter was the Prior and Bishop of Guarda, D. Pedro Gavião, whilst D. Manuel I was the patron and principal financier, and Boytac was the Master Builder.

The Mediaeval façade was erected between 1507 and 1513; the portal was added in 1522. Designed and constructed by Diogo de Castilho, it was completed with statues by Nicolas Chanterène. The interior of the Church is spacious, although there is only one aisle. The

ITINERARY III In the Footsteps of Boytac
Coimbra

vaulting, completed in 1513, was the work of Boytac. The ribbed vault is typically Late Gothic, but the bosses and spiral corbels are not at all like Boytac's work. Diogo de Castilho constructed the upper choir over the entrance, in 1530.

The chancel is also covered by a similar type of vault to that of the nave, and the key stones bear the royal coat of arms, armillary spheres and the cross of the Order of Christ, all alluding to the royal patronage. The tombs of D. Afonso Henriques and his son D. Sancho I, are on the lateral walls, although initially, they were in the nave, but were transferred to this more important location in 1535. D. Manuel I wished to highlight his ancestors and commissioned these two formidable reminders of the ascendancy of the Royal House, from João de Castilho, at that time in charge of works at the Mosteiro dos Jerónimos. Work was carried out between 1518 and 1522 and was overseen by Diogo de Castilho, younger brother of the Court architect. The superb recumbent statues were the work of the French sculptor, Nicolas Chanterène, and the remainder of the statuary was undertaken by other Portuguese and Spanish artists who had come from Jerónimos: Diogo Francisco, Pêro Anes, Diogo Fernandes, João Fernandes and Juan de la Faya. There is a contrast here between the aesthetics of the Late Gothic, obvious in the structures and some of the decoration, and that of the Renaissance, as can be seen in the recumbent statues and other sculptures, namely those of *Our Lady* and the *Virtues*. Another Manueline work of considerable importance is the Cloister of Silence by Marcos Pires, though it is possible that the design was by Boytac, his master, who, in 1513, had left Coimbra to work on the

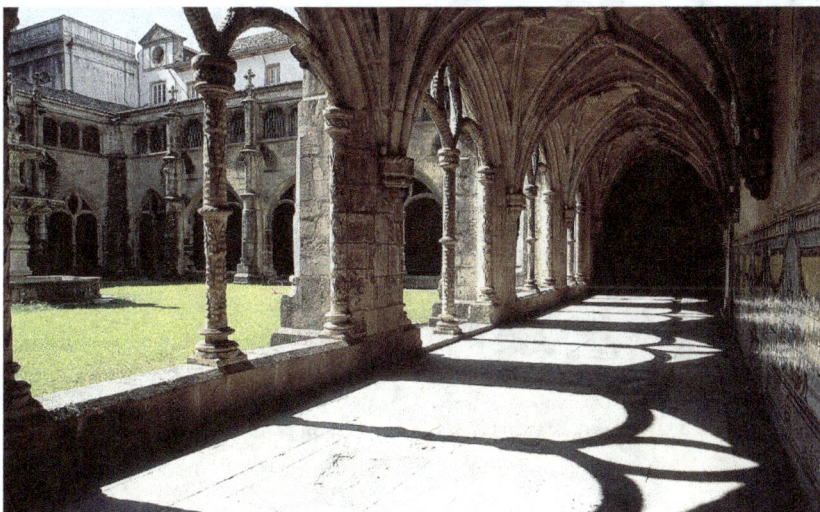

M.A.

Santa Cruz Monastery, Cloister of Silence, Coimbra.

ITINERARY III   In the Footsteps of Boytac
São Marcos

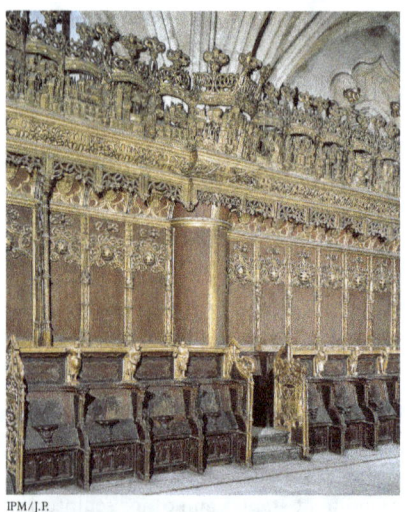

João Alemão Machim and Francisco Lorete, choir stall of Santa Cruz Monastery, 1513-1518, Coimbra.

IPM/J.P.

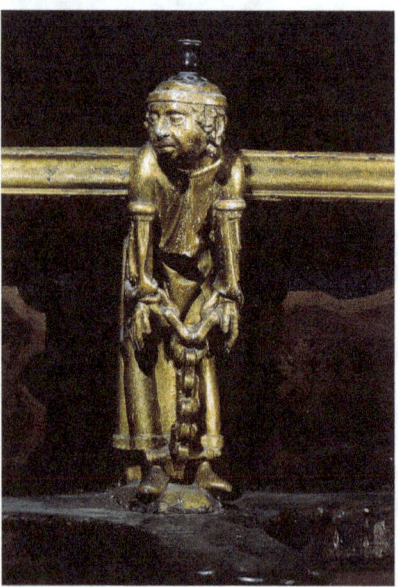

João Alemão Machim and Francisco Lorete, choir stall of Santa Cruz Monastery, detail, 1513-1518, Coimbra.

IPM/J.P.

The cloister opens onto the upper choir, where the stalls made for the chancel 20 years earlier, by the Flemish woodworker Machim, were moved in 1531. This brilliant work with very rich cresting evokes the maritime voyages of the Portuguese and the cities to which they sailed, some clearly defined as Oriental or Muslim. On the chair arms, sculpted figures of Moorish, Asiatic and African kings are depicted in chains to display Portuguese sovereignty over their lands.

III.7 SÃO MARCOS (option)

III.7.a São Marcos Monastery

At Quinta de S. Marcos, on the Coimbra / Figueira da Foz road, about 15 km. from Coimbra. (Tel: 239 963293).
Opening hours: 08.00-12.00 and 13.00-17.00 Mondays-Fridays. Closed on national holidays and at weekends, unless by prior request.

The São Marcos (St Mark) Monastery dates back to 1441 when mass was said in a small chapel on the site. In 1452, D. Beatriz da Silva donated the chapel to the Hieronymite Friars, and extensive work was carried out under the Master, Gil de Sousa. The early structure was, however, profoundly altered in the Manueline era, with the church doorway *c.*1510, in the Late Gothic style, with a strong natural-

forts in North Africa. The cloister is totally Gothic, both in structure and decoration, vigorous in form and with exuberant foliate decoration.

istic component, being the oldest remaining part.

Despite further alterations in the mid-16th century, the Gothic chancel and sacristy have both been conserved. This has left intact the ribbed vaulting and highly decorated key stones, both completed in 1521, the year D. Manuel I died.

The tombs of João da Silves and Aires Gomes da Silva, dating from the same period, were the work of Diogo Pires the Younger, the leading sculptor in Coimbra in the Manueline period. Despite the Late Gothic fondness for foliate naturalism, there are already signs of Renaissance elements here. This was due to Pires' contact with Nicolas Chanterène, who, at the same time, was carving the lovely high altar retable commissioned by Aires Gomes da Silva, one of the finest classical works in Portugal.

Other tombs in the church are of considerable interest and artistic value, ranging from the Flamboyant Gothic of that of Fernão Teles de Meneses, to those in the Capela dos Reis Magos, dated 1572 and Mannerist in style, the last great works of the sculptor Jean of Rouen.

To continue to Montemor-o-Velho, follow the EN111.

Lower Mondego

The lower course of the River Mondego from Portela, almost at the entrance to Coimbra, is characterised by an ever wider alluvial plain. After passing through the narrow lands of the Penacova valley, on reaching Ceira, the waters that rise in the Serra da Estrela are set free from the girdle of hills, and, in the winter, used to overflow the banks and flood the fertile fields of Montemor and Vila Verde.

In recent years, with the construction of the Aguieira Dam, the flow appears to be under control and the old towns of Ereira and Maiorca are no longer regularly turned into isolated islands. The landscape remains the same, with its largely flat rice-growing lands, although other valuable crops are also grown here.

This agricultural land was occupied in prehistoric times, as can be seen by the remains of the hill-fort of Santa Eulália. The main towns of Montemor-o-Velho, Tentúgal and Buarcos were at one time occupied by Muslims, but were definitively taken by the Christians in 1064. This was due to the *Mozarab* D. Sesnando, who built castles, cleared land, and fixed settlements in the Lower Mondego.

The fertility of the land attracted both institutions and individuals, such as the Monastery of Santa Cruz, the University and the Dukes of Aveiro, who owned considerable property in the area. There are still many important reminders of these periods of prosperity.

ITINERARY III   *In the Footsteps of Boytac*
Montemor-o-Velho

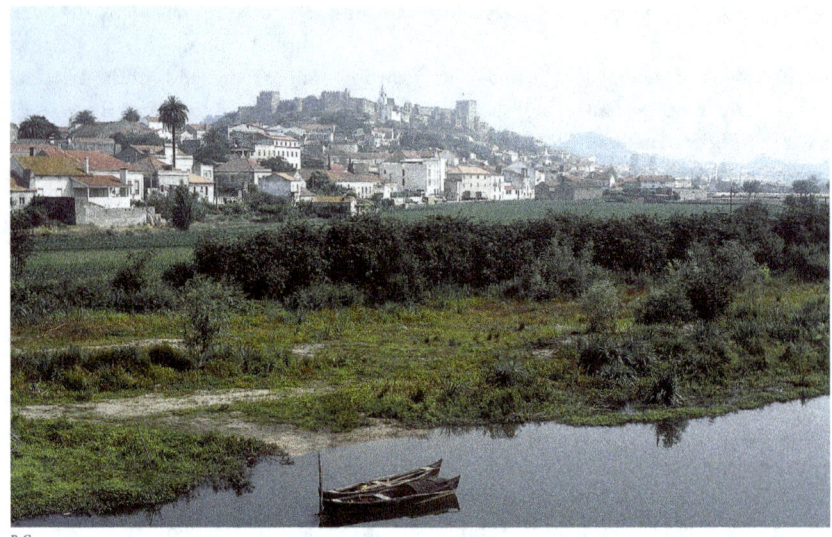

General view of Montemor-o-Velho.

R.C.

III.8 MONTEMOR-O-VELHO

The history of the town has been documented since Roman times, but the fortress became important only at the time of the Muslim Occupation when, along with Coimbra, it was an important point on the route of the River Mondego. Taken by the Christians in 878, but lost again, it was eventually conquered by Fernando the Great, Emperor of León, in 1064.

Over the years, the Castle was enlarged and developed at the top of the hill that dominates the countryside, making it the centre of this rich agricultural land and a highly important focal point for the *Mozarab* community. Integrated into the county of Portucalense, it was granted its first charter in 1095 by D. Raimundo, the son-in-law of the Emperor of León and the Governor of Coimbra at that time. Eventually it passed into the hands of the daughters of D. Sancho I of Portugal, D. Teresa and D. Sancha.

The royal residence built in the castle was a favourite with the kings of the first dynasty. It was here that D. Afonso IV gave the order for the murder of Inês de Castro, in one of the most tragic and beautiful love stories that poets such as Camões and António Ferreira have never tired of telling. Another resident was the Duke of Coimbra, D. Pedro, one of the sons of D. João I and regent during the minority of D. Afonso V, an enthusiast for overseas discoveries and expansion.

An outstanding figure in Manueline times was Diogo de Azambuja, a *fidalgo* (nobleman) who served three kings and established Portuguese sovereignty in São Jorge de Mina, Safi, Mogador and Aguz.

ITINERARY III *In the Footsteps of Boytac*
Montemor-o-Velho

The town was granted a new charter by D. Manuel I in 1517.

III.8.a Castle

Follow Rua de Coimbra to walk up to the Castle, or take Rua do Castelo if continuing by car. (Tel: 239 680380). Designated a National Monument.
Opening hours: daily, except Mondays 10.00-20.00 in summer and 10.00-12.30 and 14.00-17.00 in winter. Appointments to visit the Castle can be made through the Cultural Department of the Municipal Council (Tel: 239 687316).

The remaining Mediaeval structure is divided into the uppermost part of the castle, the main enclosure, the surrounding *barbican*, the northern enclosure and the lower redoubt. These, and the basic design that has been conserved, must have been due to work carried out in the 14th century, but there are older parts such as the keep, where Roman masonry was re-used. The *barbican* gate dates from the Manueline period.

The Church of Santa Maria da Alcáçova within the *enceinte*, was founded by D. Sesnando in the 11th century and was restored at the beginning of the 16th century by Francisco Pires, a former assistant of Boytac at Santa Cruz de Coimbra, on the orders of D. Jorge de Almeida, the Bishop of Coimbra.

Note the three aisles separated by twisted pillars, similar to the corbels in the style of Boytac, the same type of ornamentation on the east-end chapels, and the elegant lateral portal, where the builder left his initials on the lintel. There are a number of inscribed Mediaeval stones on the inner

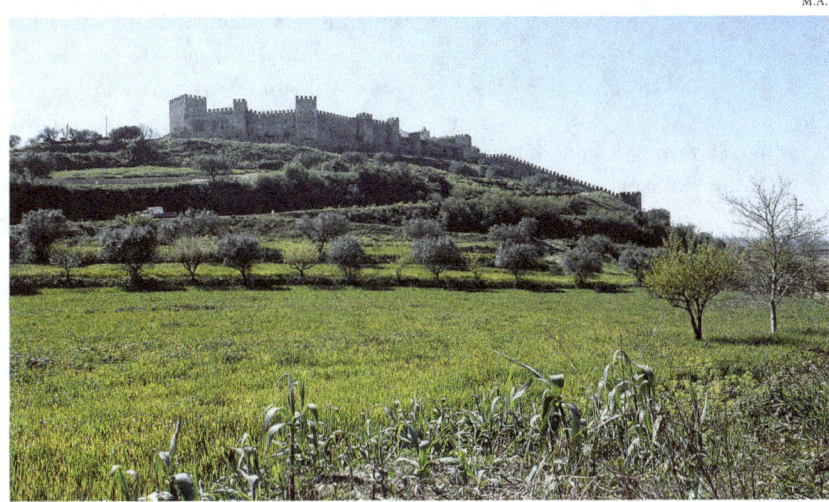

M.A.

Castle, general view, Montemor-o-Velho.

115

ITINERARY III   *In the Footsteps of Boytac*
Montemor-o-Velho

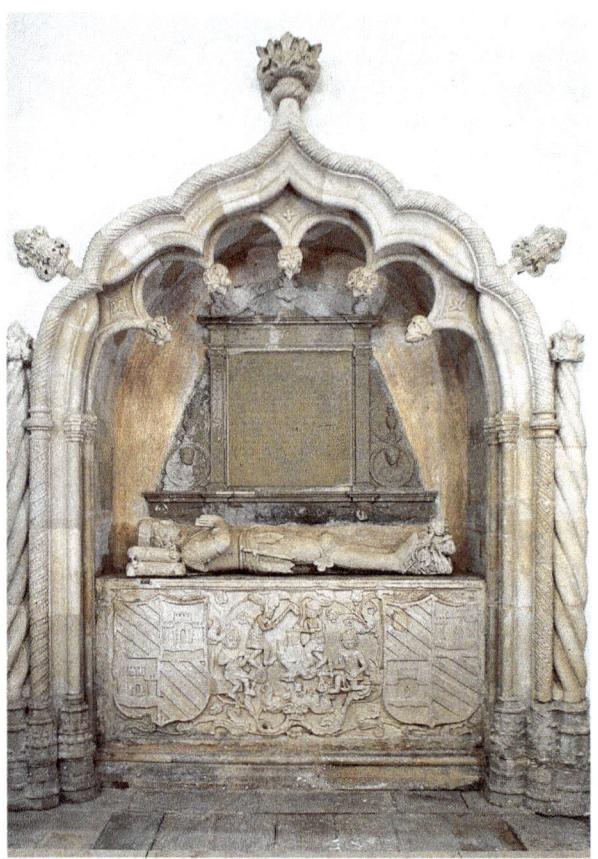

Convent of Santa Maria dos Anjos, Tomb of Diogo de Azambuja, Montemor-o-Velho.

walls and, 50 years ago, some *Mudejar* tiles from Seville were applied, from amongst those that were removed from the Old Cathedral in Coimbra.

III.8.b Convent of Santa Maria dos Anjos

Largo dos Anjos.
Opening hours: the Convent is open for special ceremonies and for Mass at 20.00 on

Saturday. Visits to the Monastery are by appointment only through the Cultural Department of the Municipal Council (Tel: 239 687316).

The Hermit Brothers of St Augustine canonically founded this Convent in 1494. The nobleman Diogo de Azambuja ordered the chancel to be built as his pantheon in 1511, according to the inscription on the keystone of the typically Late Gothic ribbed vaulting. The crossing arch, however, rises from naturalist bases that include vases with flowers evocative of Our Lady. The remainder of the church was completely altered. Flanking chapels were built, containing remarkable decorative Renaissance and Coimbra-style Mannerism sculptures, primarily the work of Jean de Rouen (João de Ruão) and Tomé Velho. The main item of interest is the tomb of Diogo de Azambuja; the work of Diogo Pires the Younger. This tomb dates back to about 1518, the year in which this distinguished nobleman died. Somewhat later, in the 1530s, an early Renaissance inscribed stone, attributed to Jean de Rouen, was added with the story of the founder of São Jorge da Mina in 1482.
The tomb is made up of an arched wall niche defined by a rope adornment and a large sarcophagus with a recumbent figure. The design already shows awareness of the Renaissance style, which had only just arrived in Portugal, although the frontal, clearly dating from a later period, is equally of interest to the visitor. D. Diogo requested that represented on his tomb should be natives, shown working

with gold from extraction to selling on the Costa da Mina. In this way, the memory of one of his major contributions to Portuguese overseas expansion was preserved for the appreciation of future generations.

III.8.c **Former Hospital da Misericórdia**

Av. Bombeiros Voluntários, currently used as an old people's home. Designated a Building of Public Interest.
Opening hours: 10.00-18.00. Appointments can be made though the Cultural Department of the Municipal Council (Tel: 239 687316).

The Hospital of the Santa Casa da Misericórdia in Montemor was founded in the Town Square in the early years of D. Manuel I's reign and under his patronage. However, little now remains of this original edifice, since it was almost entirely rebuilt in the 18th century from the foundations up.
Despite the uniformity created through the use of a base formula, the retable by the Masters of Coimbra is diverse in character, as regards the overall effect. This is a good example of teamwork both in the larger panels and the smaller ones of the predellas where there are busts of various saints, both male and female, accompanied in one way of another by their distinguishing attributes. The work of less talented painters can be identified by the way in which the figures and faces are depicted.

In the narrative scenes, there is also considerable difficulty with the structure and spatial organisation of the composition, particularly noticeable in the scaling and simplification of the figures on the panel depicting the *Adoration of the Magi*. On the side panels, representing *St Peter* and *St John the Baptist* respectively, the representational values are remarkable in the monumentality of volume, the

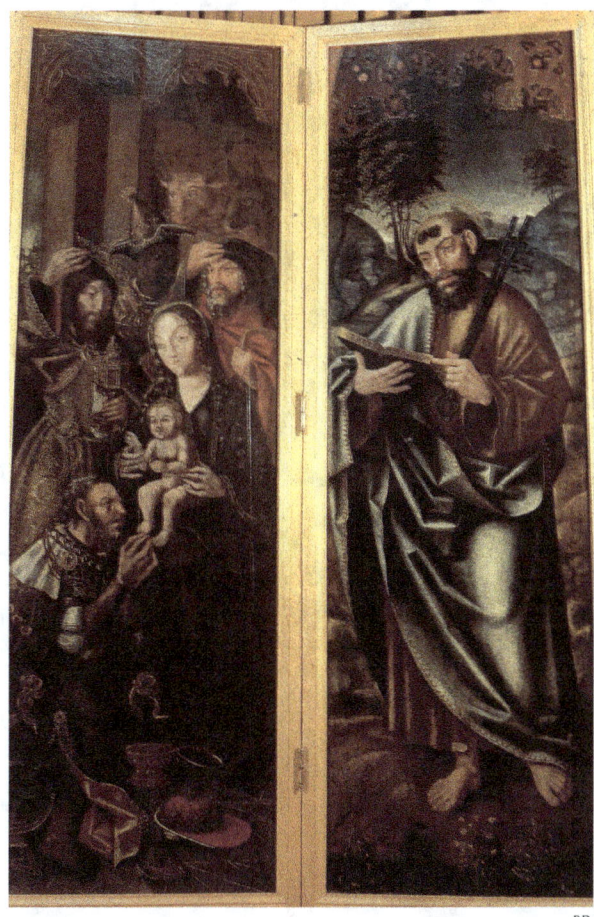

Vicente Gil and Manuel Vicente, retable of the Former Hospital da Misericórdia, Montemor-o-Velho.

delicate modelling of the drapery, and the artist's attempts to give character to the faces and the foalite elements of the landscape.
In the retable, the most visible feature is the martyred body of Christ, sustained and displayed by the figures participating in the scene, their theatrical gestures and emotional force, giving rise to a definite feeling of empathy with the spectator.

Forest of Buçaco
The very lovely Forest of Buçaco, 400 hectares surrounded by a wall 5,750 m. long, was founded in the 17th century. In 1628, the Bishop of Coimbra gave permission to the Barefoot Carmelites to make a deserted domain in the hills near Vacariça. They not only built a small monastery, but also planted the forest with various exotic, rare and native species of trees, and to protect them, they obtained a Papal Bull threatening anyone damaging the trees with excommunication. The text of the Bull, dated 1643, was posted on all the gates so that this botanical heritage would come to no harm. Some trees came from Spain, others from the Americas and others from the Azores. The **Cupressus lusitanicus**, *the Mexican cedar, is one of the most abundant and largest, with various other types originating from Crete, the Lebanon, the Himalayas and Afghanistan. In 1879, new species were planted, including a 46-m.-high American sequoia, next to the Santa Teresa Fountain.*

Women were prohibited from entering the enclosure, a ban that remained in force until the dissolution of religious orders in Portugal in 1835.
The Barefoot Carmelites wanted to make the land into an earthly paradise centred on the monastery, which gradually grew in size as the number of monks increased. The initial work on the building seems to have been carried out by the brothers Alberto da Virgem and António das Chagas. Chapels were constructed in the more isolated areas for periods of prayer.
A new building was erected on the site of the old monastery as a hunting lodge for the Royal Family, and was converted later into an hotel. Work began in 1898, to a plan by the Italian Luigi Manini, a set designer, who envisaged it in the Revivalist Manueline style to honour the Discoveries, emphasising its symbology and hypernaturalistic decoration. It is a fantastic structure, in a singular setting, to which the skill and technique of the stonemasons and sculptors of Coimbra have again contributed.

THE LEGEND OF INÊS DE CASTRO

Pedro Dias

Political motives along with reasons of State led Prince D. Pedro, the son and heir of D. Afonso IV, to marry D. Constança, the Princess of Castile. In the princess's retinue, in 1340, there also came D. Inês de Castro, with whom D. Pedro fell in love. Thereafter, D. Pedro and D. Inês de Castro were to live a beautiful and tragic love story. D. Constança died in 1345 and D. Pedro went to live with D. Inês de Castro in Coimbra. They had four children together. However, palace intrigues, together with the king's refusal to sanction the marriage, led to the latter ordering the assassination of D. Inês in 1355. This event gave rise to the Civil War of 1355-1356, in which the prince took up arms against his father, D. Afonso IV, culminating in D. Pedro's accession to the throne. As soon as he became king, D. Pedro sought revenge on those of his father's advisers who had been involved in the assassination and ordered their hearts to be cut out and removed from their bodies. D. Inês was made queen posthumously. Her body was exhumed and crowned, and the whole Court was forced to kneel before her corpse.

History and legend become confused at this point and it is said that, in the place where the two lovers met, a spring was formed, the Fonte dos Amores (the Fountain of Love), in the garden of the Quinta das Lágrimas (the Estate of Tears), a site that can currently be visited in the surroundings of Coimbra.

At the express wishes of D. Pedro, his tomb and that of D. Inês de Castro were placed in the Mosteiro de Alcobaça facing one another, waiting for the chance to meet again on the day of final judgement.

R.C.

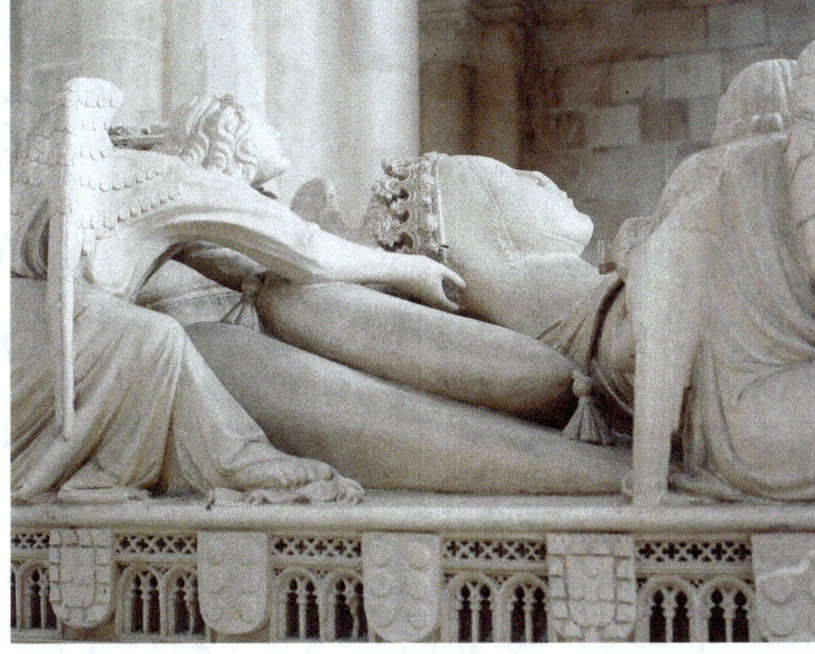

Tomb of D. Inês de Castro, detail, Monastery of Alcobaça.

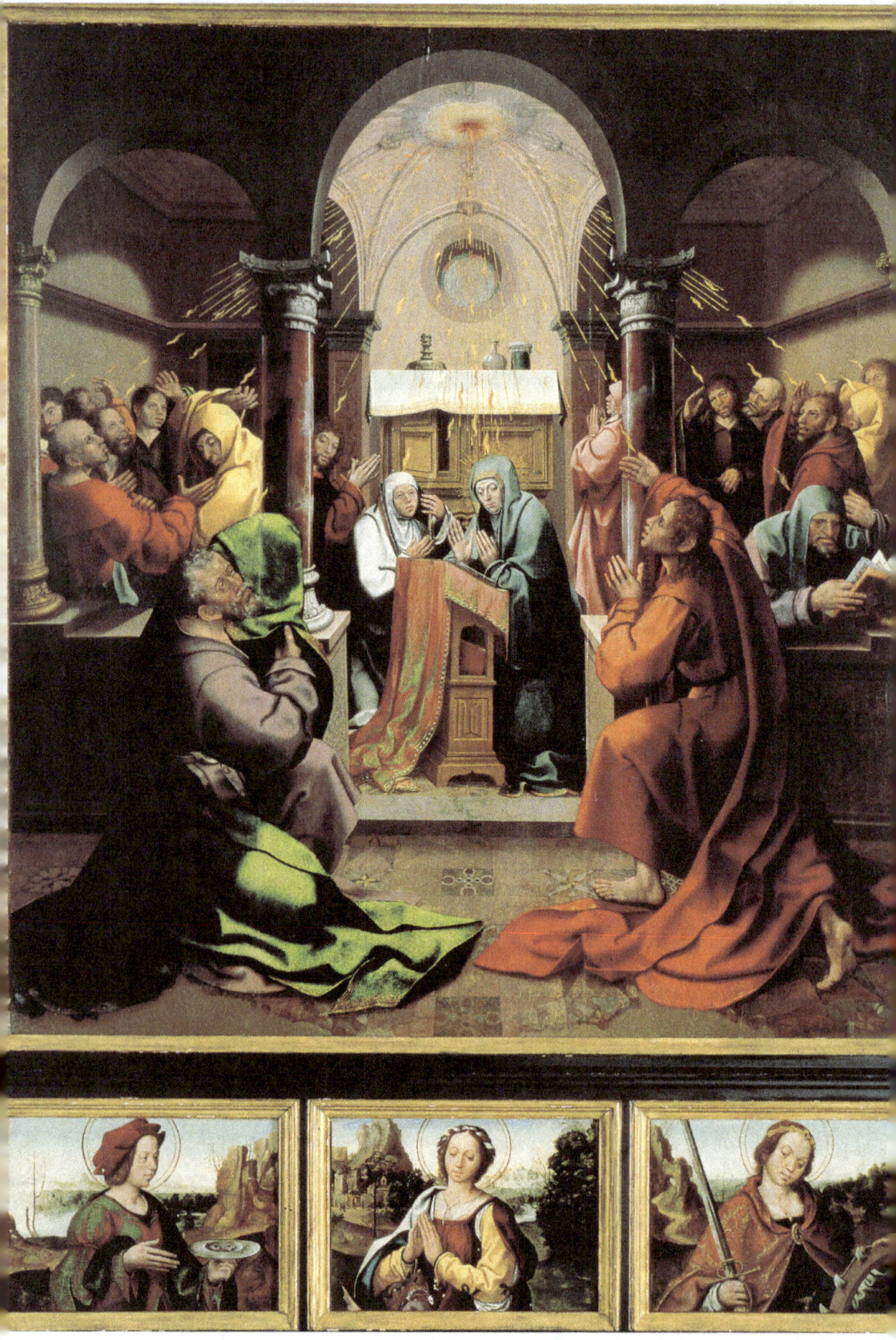

ITINERARY IV

Discovering Grão Vasco

Pedro Dias, Dalila Rodrigues,
Nuno Vassallo e Silva, Fernando Grilo

IV.1 VISEU
- IV.1.a Historic Centre
- IV.1.b Viseu Cathedral
- IV.1.c Grão Vasco Museum

IV.2 LAMEGO
- IV.2.a Cathedral
- IV.2.b Houses in Rua do Poço
- IV.2.c Lamego Museum

IV.3 FERREIRIM (option)
- IV.3.a Santo António (Ferreirim Parish Church)

IV.4 TAROUCA (option)
- IV.4.a São João de Tarouca Convent

IV.5 UCANHA (option)
- IV.5.a Ucanha Bridge

Grão Vasco, the Painter-Hero

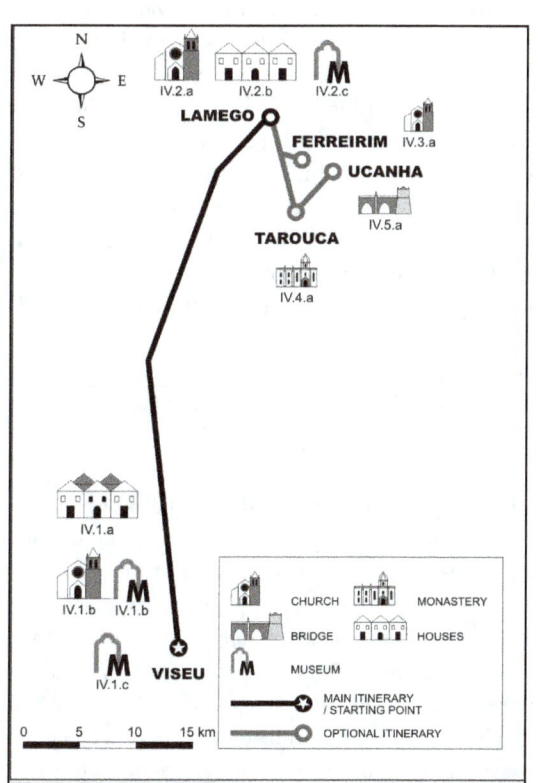

Vasco Fernandes, "Pentecost", in the predellas are the saints St Luzia, St Margarida and St Catarina, oil on chestnut, 1535-40, Museu Grão Vasco, Viseu.

Vasco Fernandes, or Grão (Great) Vasco, acquired a mythical status amongst Portuguese painters. For many years, until the beginning of the last century, any ancient painting of quality was immediately attributed to Grão Vasco. Although, nowadays, this is known to be false, legend and history have together left us the legacy of his great work, which combined tradition and picturesque regional landscapes, whilst also incorporating the new prevailing influences from Flanders and Italy.

The painter was born and spent most of his life in Viseu, though he is known to have worked for a time at the studio of the Court Painter, Jorge Afonso, in Lisbon. In Viseu and also in Lamego, slightly further north, he found wealthy and powerful patrons, among them the poet, antiquarian and man of letters, D. Miguel da Silva, who later went to Rome where he became a cardinal and was one of those largely responsible for introducing the Renaissance into Portuguese arts.

In the Manueline period, Viseu was a developing, prosperous regional centre. Although far from the sea, it was at the centre of a road network and a rich agricultural region. Prince Henry the Navigator was one of the Dukes of Viseu, as was a brother of D. Manuel I, and D. Duarte was actually born in the town.

There are still many traces of the Manueline style in the city including the knotted vaulting in the cathedral church, the work of João de Castilho, commissioned by the Bishop, D. Diego Ortiz de Villegas, Court Cosmographer. The painted panels belonging to the high altar retable are on display in the Museu de Grão Vasco and were the work of Grão Vasco and his Lisbon and Flemish disciples, as were the great Renaissance fascias in the side chapels, commissioned and paid for by D. Miguel da Silva. The Manueline monstrance from the cathedral is in the Museu de Arte Sacra (Museum of Sacred Art), whilst the Museu de Grão Vasco contains an ivory *pyx* made by craftsmen in Benin at the beginning of the 16th century.

Vasco Fernandes worked all over the provinces of Beira Alta and Alto Douro, from the Lamego Cathedral to the Monasteries of Santa Maria de Salzedas and Orgens, and the Parish Church at Freixo de Espada à Cinta, where the retable for the chancel is almost complete. This is one of the richest regions in the country as regards painting, architecture, sculpture, tapestry and gold and silver work from the Manueline period.

IV.I VISEU

Grão Vasco is the most famous of Portuguese painters, whom legend has surrounded with a mythical and timeless aura. According to the available historical information, he appears to have lived and had a flourishing workshop in Viseu for some 40 years, at least from 1501 to 1543. Commissions from rich and powerful patrons who carried out reforms in

ITINERARY IV *Discovering Grão Vasco*
Viseu

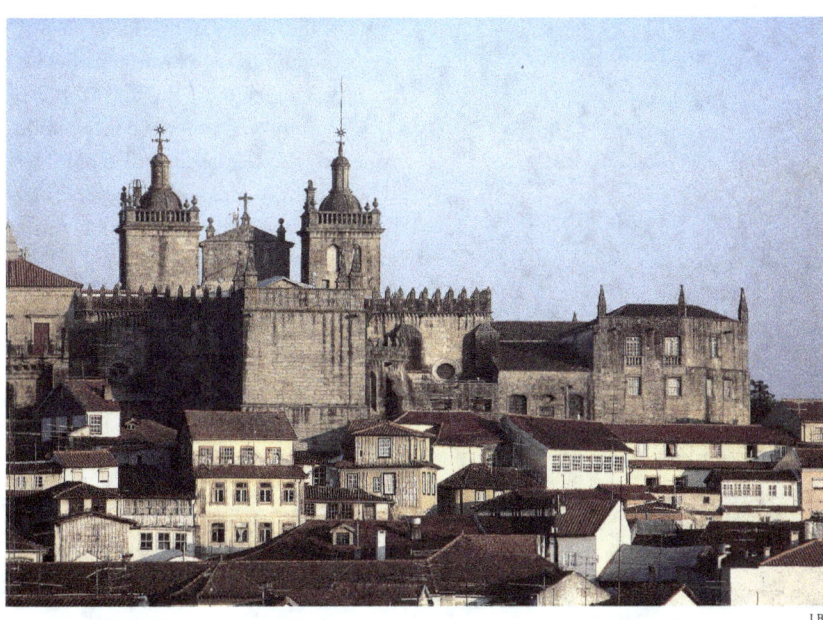

General view of Viseu historic centre.

cathedrals, churches and monasteries in the Beira and Alto Douro regions, enabled him to produce exceptional retable paintings.

In the first 30 years of the century, the vigorous figurative realism of the Flemish style marked his production, just as it did the work of the cosmopolitan painters in Lisbon, with whom Grão Vasco maintained close relations. About 1530, however, the work of Vasco Fernandes began to display Italian Renaissance values. This was due largely to the influence of his patron, the illustrious humanist D. Miguel da Silva, who had been Portuguese Ambassador to the Papal Court, before he became Bishop of Viseu in 1526, and was one of the leading figures behind the introduction of the Renaissance into Portuguese art. The Bishop commissioned great retables for the cathedral, namely the famous *St Peter*, and also for the Chapel of the Bishop's Quinta de Fontelo, before he left to live in Rome permanently in 1540.

Vasco Fernandes reveals his sensitivity and vision of the world in the expressive character of form, in his poetic or dramatic strength, in the mystery of light, the intensity of colours and the simple outlines of figures or distant landscapes. In recognition of his technical ability and his remarkable expressive resources he was commissioned, in 1535, to paint the four retables for the Mosteiro de Santa Cruz in Coimbra. The only remaining panel of this series is that of the exceptional *Pentecost*, which currently hangs in the Sacristy

ITINERARY IV Discovering Grão Vasco
Viseu

Manueline window, Viseu historic centre.

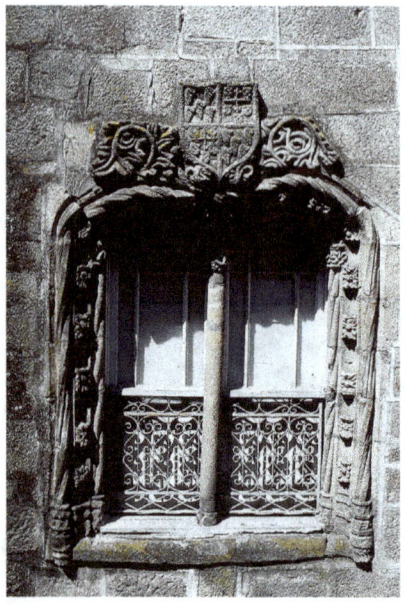

J.B.

there and is signed in the Latin style, *"Velascus"*.

Viseu can be visited on foot, as the monuments are close together near the Cathedral. Information: Tourist Office (Tel: 232 420950).

IV.1.a **Historic Centre**

Viseu is the see of one of the oldest and most important Dioceses in the country and the various restoration programmes carried out during the Manueline period were basically due to the patronage of its bishops.
Centred on the cathedral and various areas directly associated with the spiritual and temporal needs of the clergy, especially of the bishop and resident chapter, these alterations had a profound effect on the city. Though the 17th- and 18th-century restorations and new constructions are more visible, there is still a considerable amount of Manueline art particularly in the historic centre, which still retains some of its 15th-century walls.

D. Fernando Gonçalves de Miranda and, more so, D. Diego Ortiz de Villegas, carried out an ambitious programme of reforms on the old cathedral that included the construction of a new façade, the old one having been destroyed in a storm in 1635. The vaulting, an emblem of Manueline art in the city, was built, and a large retable was acquired for the chancel, of which 14 panels can be seen in the Museu Grão Vasco. Secular architecture in the city, inspired by these programmes and forms, adopted the same decorative solutions.

In the urban grid around the cathedral and on about ten 16th-century houses, there are a number of windows, portals and arches displaying the exuberant decoration of the period. The most ornamented window is to be found on a house in the former Rua da Cadeia, which was erroneously associated by tradition with the birthplace of D. Duarte, as can be seen by the presence of the coat of arms of its owner, Canon Pero Gomes de Abreu. There is now no trace left in the city of the former palace of the first Duke of Viseu, Prince Henry the Navigator.

A new phase began in the city with the introduction of the Renaissance by

Bishop D. Miguel da Silva. He employed the Italian architect Francesco da Cremona on his building projects for the cathedral, which included a very fine Renaissance cloister, the upper choir and the choir stalls.

IV.1.b Viseu Cathedral

Largo da Sé. (Tel: 232 422984). Designated a National Monument.
Opening hours: daily 09.00-12.00 and 14.00-17.00.

The architect who planned the "knotted vaulting" that was built on already existing pillars to unite the three aisles of the cathedral into a *hall-church* is unknown. Despite its bold style, which some identify with the work of João de Castilho, the most remarkable characteristic is the way in which the ribs are carved into ropes with huge knots, in the middle of each bay. One of the keystones is inscribed with the date when the work was completed, 1513, and the name of the founder Bishop, D. Diego Ortiz de Villegas.

The depressed vaulting of the upper choir at the entrance to the church is in the Manueline style, although it was built at the time of D. João III, under the patronage of D. Miguel da Silva. One of the most noteworthy works is the Renaissance cloister, completed in 1532. Its classicist vocabulary and perfect mastery of the visual language of the Renaissance are due to the taste of the same illustrious patron and the skill of its architect, Francesco da Cremona, who had accompanied the bishop on his return to Portugal from Rome.

The Manueline portal, described by a local chronicler in 1630 has disappeared, and the great 16th-century retables in the apse chapels by Grão Vasco have been dismounted. The cathedral has retained its *azulejos*, carved gilded woodwork and 17th- and 18th-century imagery. The Gothic image of the *Virgin with Child* still remains on the high altar, although it was transferred from the central niche of the Manueline retable to the Baroque retable. The Museu de Arte Sacra in the cathedral contains two valuable evangelistary covers in chased silver. There is also a beautiful silver-gilt monstrance dated 1533, donated by D. Miguel da Silva. Just like D. Jorge de Almeida in Coimbra, D. Miguel da Silva was responsible for intro-

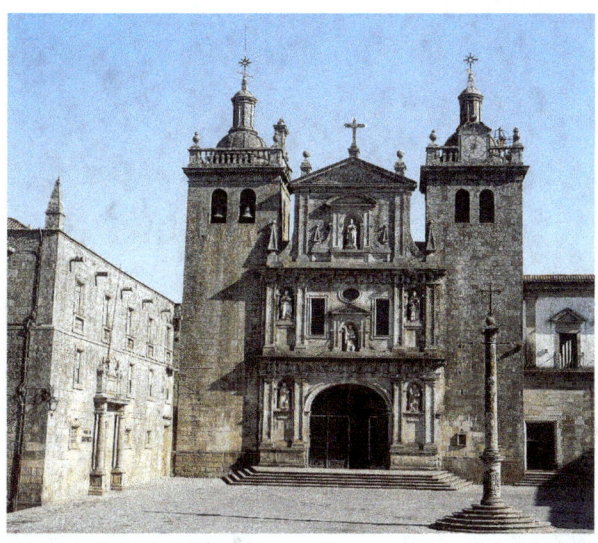

J.B.

Viseu Cathedral and the former Episcopal Palace.

ITINERARY IV *Discovering Grão Vasco*
Viseu

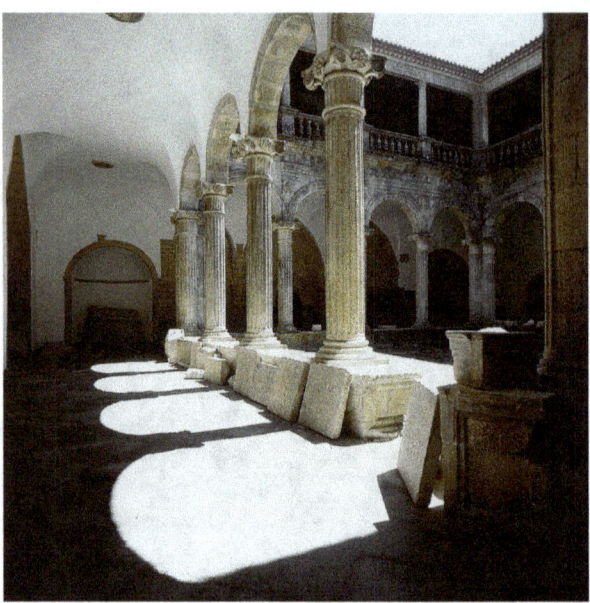

Viseu Cathedral, Renaissance cloister.

ducing Renaissance art into his Diocese, although his legacy of liturgical objects is highly conservative in style, unlike other artistic renovations, of which the cloister that he founded in the cathedral, designed by Francesco da Cremona, is the finest example.

IV.1.c **Grão Vasco Museum**

Largo da Sé. (Tel: 232 422049). Designated a National Monument. This Museum is closed for restoration until 2004. The entire collection is, however, in the meantime on display in the north wing of the Igreja da Misericórdia next to the Museum.
Admission charge. Opening hours: 09.10-12.30 and 14.00-17.30. Closed on Mondays and public holidays: January 1st, Easter Sunday, May 1st and December 25th.

The Museum, installed in a late 16th-century building that was originally intended as a seminary, completes the visit to the cathedral, from which a substantial part of the museum's extraordinary collection originates, namely the best known of all the paintings by Vasco Fernandes.
The 14 panels of equal size that make up the first part of the collection were part of the retable commissioned for the chancel in 1506 by the Bishop D. Fernando Gonçalves de Miranda, and concluded by his successor D. Diego Ortiz de Villegas. Overall the panels appear to have a direct relationship and to display appropriation of processes in vogue in Flemish workshops in Ghent and Bruges at the time. These range from the general structure of each panel, the most diverse elements and figurative strategies, the sometimes bizarre perspectives, anatomical structure (conceived in baggy drapery), the physiognomy of figures, types of apparel and ornaments and the superb technique with which the details are transcribed. This must be related not only to the prevailing trend and its influence on Portuguese artists, but also to the direct participation of Flemish artists. The Master craftsman, possibly Vasco Fernandes, who was resident in the city at that time, also called on a woodcarver and sculptor, Arnau de Carvalho and João de Utreque, respectively, to create the carved, gilded-wood structure that held and framed the panels of this collective work of art.

ITINERARY IV *Discovering Grão Vasco*
Viseu

The didactic and liturgical elements within the pictorial scheme include one of the most important narrative scenes alluding to the Life of the Virgin and the Childhood and Passion of Christ. The most relevant detail, which greatly contributed to the popularity of this work, is that of the Brazilian Amerindian substituting the traditional black figure of Balthazar in the *Adoration of the Magi*. This is, in fact, the first Western representation of a native of Brazil, two or three years after the region's discovery by the Portuguese.

Another example of the expressive resources of Grão Vasco in his first phase, is the well identified work representing the *Assumption of the Virgin*, c. 1515.

The two panels from the Chapel of the Episcopal Palace at Fontelo, *Christ in the House of Martha* and *The Last Supper*, produced in his workshop in the 1530s, reveal a significant increase in formal repertoires and a gradual moving away from the Flemish processes dominant in his early work. The iconographic complexity of *The Last Supper* seems to indicate that D. Miguel da Silva, both masterminded and commissioned it. Indeed the portrait of this patron in *Christ in the House of Martha*, where he is seated at the table, to the right of Christ, a presence emphasised by his coat-of-arms on the plinths of the columns, seems to suggest a direct relationship with the painter.

The very large paintings that Fernandes produced, under the patronage of D. Miguel, for the apse chapels and the cloister of Viseu Cathedral, of which five large retables remain in this collection, are centred on the expressive potentialities of form, and experiment with new methods of organising space and composition.

In the famous *St Peter*, one of the high points of his creative achievement, the expressive strength of the work is concentrated in the monumental, austere

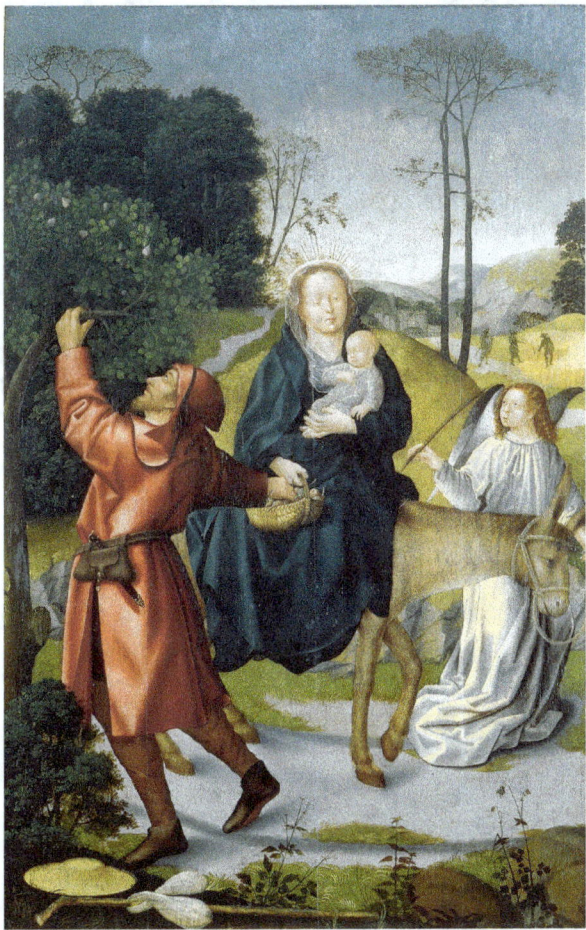

Workshop of Vasco Fernandes (Grão Vasco), "Flight into Egypt", from the retable of Viseu Cathedral, oil on oak, 1506-10, Grão Vasco Museum, Viseu.

IPM/C.M.

127

ITINERARY IV   *Discovering Grão Vasco*
Viseu

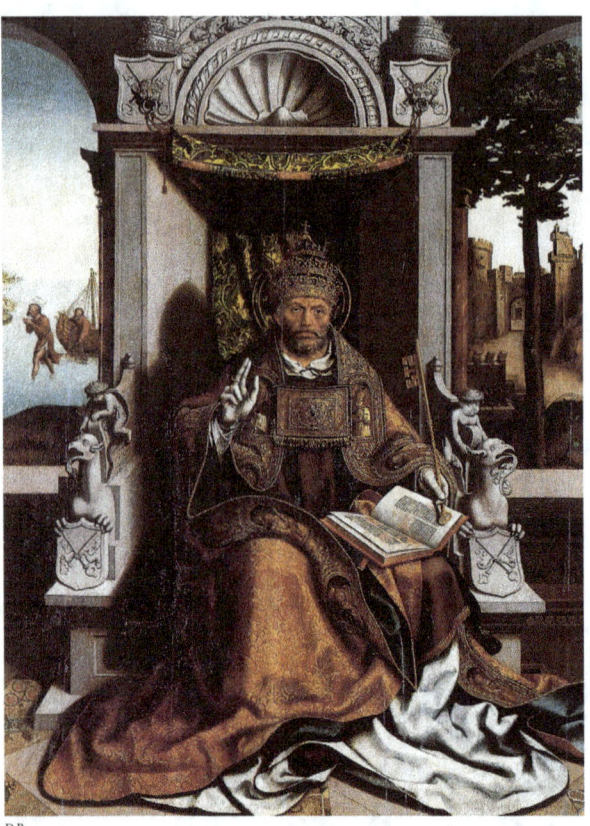

D.R.

Vasco Fernandes, "St Peter", oil on chestnut, 1535-40, Grão Vasco Museum, Viseu.

composition in relation to the spectator, opting for theatrical concentration and a greater monumentality of the figures, spacing them with patches of colour, burnished by the light.

St Sebastian, a poetic nude representation, is the perfect expression of his approach to the expressive methods of Italian painting.

The *Pentecost* panel, similar, with few variations, to that in the Sacristy of the Church of Santa Cruz in Coimbra and signed "Velascus", is also worthy of note. With the representation of the Manueline vaulting of the cathedral, he seeks to accentuate the relationship between the spectator and the painting, between real, and virtual space.

In the miniature paintings of the *predella* of these huge retables in the form of a pall, the form of which highlights the transition from the Nordic to the Italian, a synthesis can be identified between a language that does not hide either the teachings of the Flemish school or the assimilation of the Italian style.

gravity of the Holy Patriarch, seated on an Italian-style throne, severe and firm, almost intimidating. The light coming from the right plays a determinant role in the sculptural modelling of the figure and its autonomy in relation to the throne, which is basically underpinned by the projected shadow and the vigorous triangular structure.

In *Calvary*, representing a spectacle of dramatic pain and grief, among other strategies, the artist significantly elevates the

Among the remaining Manueline works of art in the Museum, there are some sculptures in Ança limestone from workshops in Coimbra, today minus their original polychrome. There is also a 15th-century relief plaque in alabaster imported from Nottingham, and a very rare 16th-century Afro-Portuguese ivory *pyx* made in Sierra Leone where local craftsmen copied a Portuguese model, almost certainly in silver. The iconography,

ITINERARY IV *Discovering Grão Vasco*
Lamego

however, is taken from engravings from a Book of Hours printed in France in 1498. Note also the Portuguese Royal coat of arms, the cross of the Order of Christ and the inscription *"Ave (Maria) Gratia Plena"*.

On leaving Viseu, follow the N2 in the direction of Castro Daire. About 13 km. outside the town, join the IP3 to Lamego.

IV.2 LAMEGO

The city was important in distant times, at least from the Visigothic period in the 7th century onwards, for coins were minted here in the reign of Sisebuto. When the Muslims began to take over the Peninsula in 713, Lamego was occupied soon afterwards and was only definitively reconquered by the army of Fernando the Great, Emperor of León, in 1057. In 1071, it became the see of the Diocese.
The development of Lamego in Mediaeval times was, in a first phase, due to Egas Moniz, who lived nearby in Britiande and was tutor to the first Portuguese King, D. Afonso Henriques. In 1191, D. Sancho I granted the town its first charter in an attempt to attract a fixed population to this, a depressed area.
Until the 19th century, the town was never very large and any social life was related to the cathedral.
The 12th-century castle stands on a frontier hill. It was frequently restored in the Middle Ages and further work, mainly consolidation, was carried out in Manueline times, giving it the look that it has retained to this day.

IV.2.a Cathedral

Largo de Sé. (Tel: 254 612766). Designated a National Monument.
Opening hours: daily 08.00-13.00 and 15.00-19.00.

Lamego Cathedral dates back to the 11th century, but everything to be seen nowa-

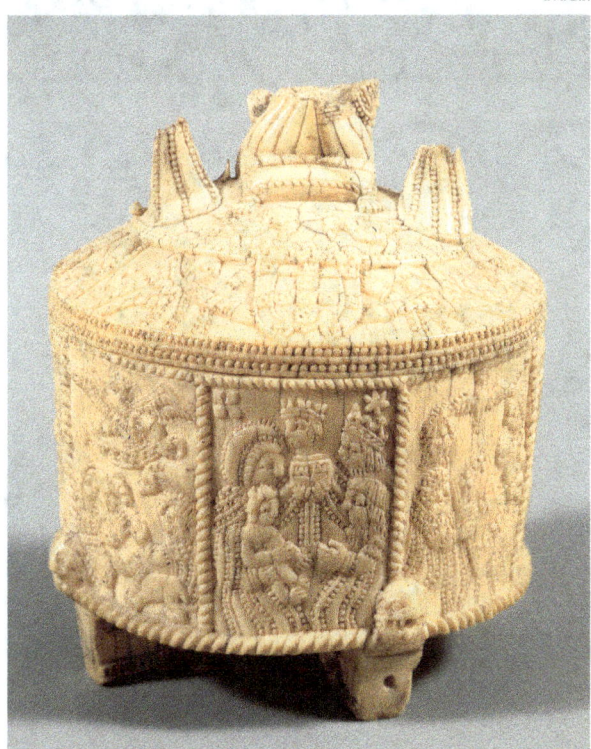

Pyx, Sierra Leone, ivory, c.1500, Grão Vasco Museum, Viseu.
IPM/D.F.

129

ITINERARY IV Discovering Grão Vasco
Lamego

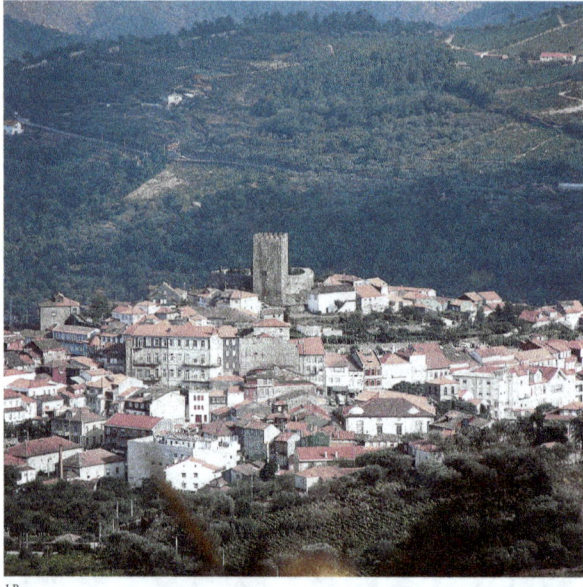

General view of the historic centre of Lamego.

J.B.

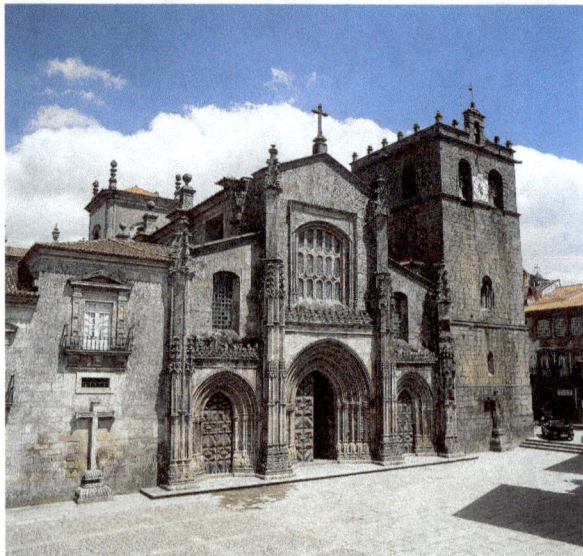

R.C.

Lamego Cathedral, main façade.

days is from a later date, the oldest part being the base of the tower. The new façade with its three beautiful Late Gothic portals dates from the Manueline period, in 1508, and the following years. João Lopes was the Master Craftsman and Juan de Vargas and Juan de Pamenes, Spaniards from Cantabria, assisted him. Part of the cloister is also Manueline, begun at the end of 1524 by Duarte Coelho.

IV.2.b Houses in Rua do Poço

Next to the Cathedral in the heart of the city, in Rua do Poço there are a number of houses with some of the most important Manueline windows in the region. They are rather unusual in line, with naturalist decorative elements, along with others that were to be found in traditional constructions in this region several centuries earlier.

IV.2.c Lamego Museum

Largo de Camões. (Tel: 254 600230). Opening hours: 10.00-12.30 and 14.00-17.00. Closed on Mondays and public holidays: January 1st, Easter Sunday, May 1st and December 25th.

The Museum holds a number of important collections, though only those related to the Manueline era of the Maritime Discoveries are discussed here.

ITINERARY IV   *Discovering Grão Vasco*
Lamego

Some of the most interesting items are the early 16th-century wool and silk tapestries, made in workshops in Brussels that used to hang in the Episcopal Palace. Excellently drawn, they are based on mythological themes: *The Temple of Leto*, *Laius consulting the Oracle*, *Oedipus in Corinth*, *Oedipus in Thebes*, and *Oedipus and Queen Jocasta,* and there is another, perhaps the most spectacular of all, an *Allegory to Music*. The syncretism between classical culture, Paganism and the new humanistic vision of the Catholic Church is evident.

J.B.

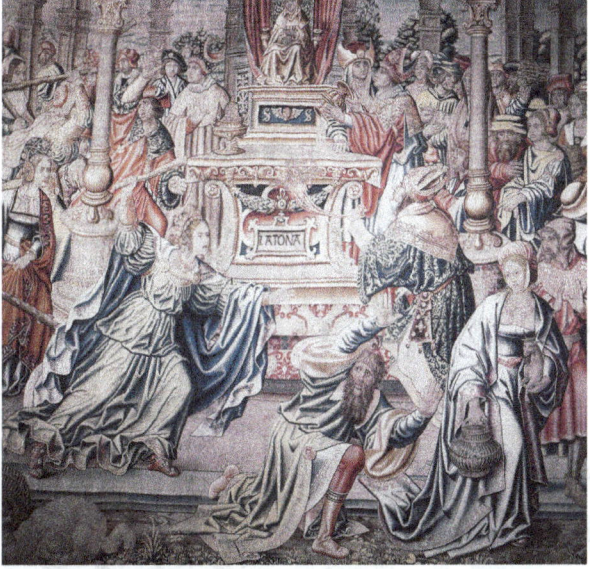

Brussels workshop, "The temple of Leto", Flemish tapestry, 16th century, Lamego Museum.

J.B.

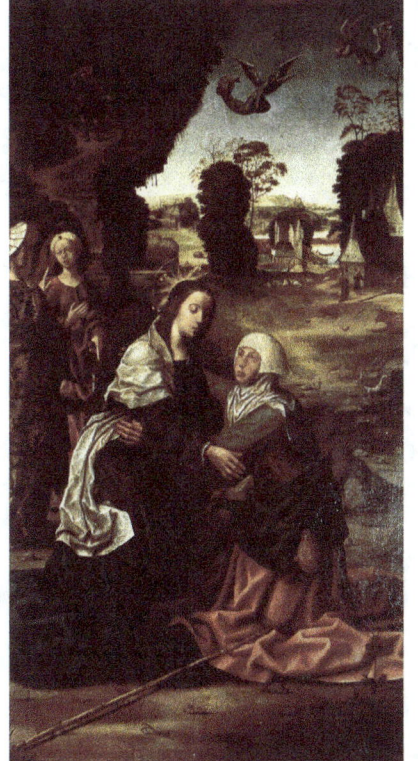

Five panels by Vasco Fernandes, or Grão Vasco, represent outstanding works in the painting collection in this Museum. The five panels that once belonged to the retable in the chancel of Lamego Cathedral were commissioned by Bishop D. João Carmelo de Madureira in 1506, and were completed in 1511. They reveal some fundamental elements towards an understanding of Vasco's art and his creative process, in the initial phase of his long career.

From these five remaining panels, it is not difficult to imagine the sumptuousness of the original retable, which was made up of 20 panels, two of which, along with a sculpture that has since disappeared, occupied the central axis and which were, therefore, larger in size.

Vasco Fernandes, "Visitation", from the retable of Lamego Cathedral, oil on wood, 1506-11, Lamego Museum.

ITINERARY IV   *Discovering Grão Vasco*

Lamego

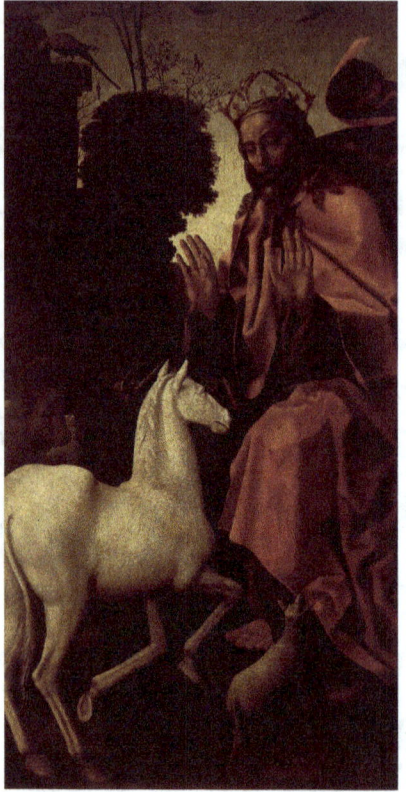

Vasco Fernandes, "The Creation of Animals", from the retable of Lamego Cathedral, oil on wood, 1506-11, Lamego Museum.

Flemish Realism can also be identified by the form, in the way in which the texture of the fabrics is represented, by the transparency of glass and in the reflections on the surface of metal objects. Recourse to various inspirational sources can be identified by elements such as the Nordic detail of the background landscape with architecture in *The Visitation*, while he opts for the mythical unicorn in *The Creation of Animals*.

To confirm the importance that painting had at this time as a means of personal and social promotion, the figure holding the child Jesus in the *Circumcision* corresponds to the portrait of the Bishop who commissioned this work. His coat of arms is also included, at his express wish, in the carved structure of the retable.

Leave Lamego and head towards Ferreirim on the EN226.

Fernandes's essential concern with formal harmony and representative rigour are to be noted in the spatial organisation of the compositions, where his use of light to focus on intermediate planes is masterly. An example of this is to be seen in the flooring in the *Annunciation* and the strategic positioning of the stove as a source of light. Also impressive is the balanced distribution of colour and the way in which the figures are wrapped in full drapery and modelled with remarkable plasticity.

Douro Region

A little further north of Lamego, the River Douro flows through its deep, narrow, schistose valley cut by an infinity of terraces where grapes grow to provide the regional wines, the most famous of which is a port wine, named after Porto or Oporto. On the south bank live hard-working people with a very rich artistic heritage. The Cistercian Order was the first to take an interest in the area. They built abbeys, some of which still remain and recall their period of grandeur. Some were enriched, erasing the Mediaeval and Manueline traces, while conserving them in others.

IV. 3 **FERREIRIM** (option)

IV.3.a **Santo António (Ferreirim Parish Church)**

Lugar do Convento. Classified as a Building of Public Interest.
Opening hours: Thursday-Sunday 10.00-13.00 and 14.00-18.00. If you wish to make a guided visit, you should first make an appointment with Sr. Fernando Cardoso (Tel: 254 699130).

There is little left of the work carried out in the Parish Church in the Manueline period, for considerable remodelling was done later. The nearby tower dates back to the 15th century, as do the general structure of the church and the Late Gothic tomb of D. Francisco Coutinho. Dated a little later than this, in 1533, the paintings commissioned by the Cardinal-Infante D. Henrique from the Court painters Cristóvão de Figueiredo, Gregório Lopes and Garcia Fernandes belonged to the convent of which he was Prior-Commendatary. Of particular note are *The Annunciation*, *The Birth of Jesus* and the *Passing of Our Lady*.

IV.4 **TAROUCA** (option)

IV.4.a **São João de Tarouca Convent**

São João de Tarouca. Designated a National Monument. Information: Sr. Caetano (Tel: 254 678766).
Opening hours: 10.00-12.30 and 14.00-18.00. Closed on Mondays and on Tuesdays until 14.00.

All that remains of the Abbey of São João de Tarouca, the first foundation of the Cistercian Order in Portugal, is the Romanesque church with its magnificent interior and the ruins of other parts of the Convent. Founded in 1154, it must have been either completed, or at least close to completion, in 1169 according to an inscription inside, by the main door. The church follows the austere architectural lines of Clairvaux, with three apse chapels, a wide transept and three aisles covered by ogival-arch vaulting. This was an innovation with regard to the Portuguese Romanesque because of the structural and spatial solutions and the decorative austerity, which must have been planned by a monk-architect, probably of French origin.
The interior of the church is very rich, containing as it does the imposing tomb of D. Pedro, the Count of Barcelos, one of the most impressive examples of 14th-century Portuguese funerary sculpture. There are also panels of painted tiles,

carved gilded woodwork and imagery, as well as some 16th-century paintings, 1530-1535, by Gaspar Vaz, a pupil of Vasco Fernandes.

Trained in the workshop of the Court painter Jorge Afonso, this Master worked in the Viseu region at least between the dates of 1522 and 1568, so it is not surprising that these paintings show the direct influence of Fernandes's models. In the *St Peter* the similarities are more obvious when compared to that of *St Peter* in the collection in the Museu de Grão Vasco; they are less obvious in the graceful panels set in Baroque carved gilded woodwork of the altar of *Nossa Senhora da Glória* or even in that of *St Michael*. Despite the similarity of the figure of the saint – which lay at the root of the controversial attribution of this painting in Tarouca to Vasco Fernandes – the differences in the formal values of the two panels are quite evident.

Besides the use of a more traditionalist, archaic style in the Gothic decoration of the throne and the presence of foliate elements, unlike the flooring in perspective in the work in Viseu, there are visible differences in the concept of volume and in the handling of light. The timid figure of the saint, the lack of anatomical vigour, the simplistic juxtaposition of the planes, minimising the integrating value of the light, show a painter with expressive resources quite different from those of Vasco Fernandes. It is reasonable to consider that these are two versions from the same model, done by two painters with different resources and technical skills and, a point no less important, from different locations.

The search for balance and grace, a slight affectedness and theatricality of gesture, more accentuated in the *St Michael*, by Gaspar Vaz, mark the lack of vigour and expressive dynamism, two features that characterise the production of Vasco Fernandes.

To reach Ucanha, take the EN226. Ucanha is about 2 km. past the turning for Tarouca.

IV.5 **UCANHA** (option)

IV.5.a **Ucanha Bridge**

Designated a National Monument.

The Ponte de Ucanha, the loveliest of Portugal's Mediaeval bridges, crosses the River Varoza in the enclosure of the Mosteiro de Salzedas. It was built by order of the Abbot D. Fernando in the mid-15th century, and besides the tower for defence and collecting tolls, almost 9 m. wide at the side, it has three arches with cutwaters and a trestle roadway.

GRÃO VASCO, THE PAINTER-HERO

Pedro Dias

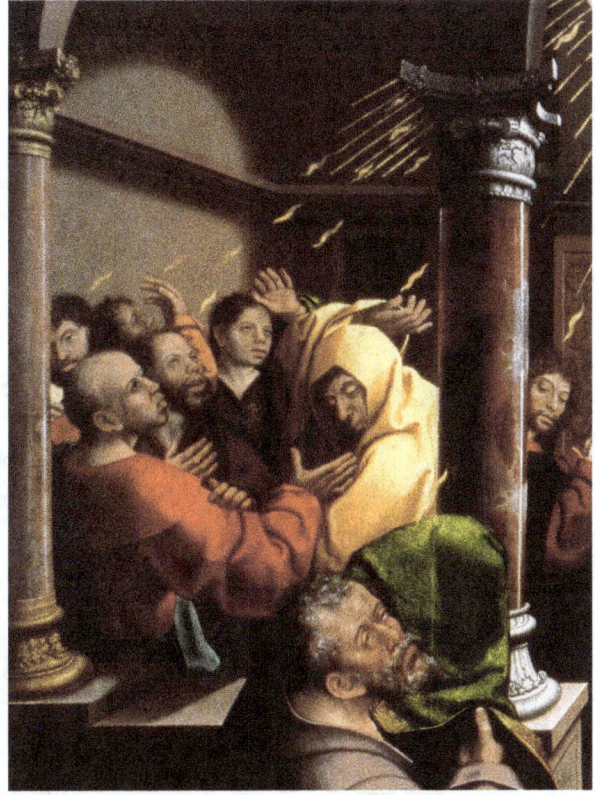

Vasco Fernandes, "Pentecost", oil on chestnut, 1535-40, detail, Grão Vasco Museum, Viseu.

Until the end of the 19th century, the real identity of the painter from Viseu called Grão Vasco, or simply Vasco, as his surname had been lost, was unknown. A series of tales dating back to the beginning of the 17th century transformed the author of the paintings in the cathedral into a mythical painter-hero to whom, in the absence of information about other painters, all the painting of antiquity in Portugal was attributed. Oral tradition developed some ideas based on local chroniclers, who had adapted the biographies of the great Renaissance masters to praise the qualities of the cathedral paintings and the genius of their authors. By the end of the 19th century, a romantic image survived that had changed the famous painter Vasco into the poor, but brilliant son of a miller who lived near the city.

According to one story, Vasco painted a donkey laden with sacks on the door of the house so well, that when his father returned home as night was falling he tried in vain to coax the "donkey" into the cottage.

Another tale tells of his adventures in Italy where he was said to have studied. He went into a painter's house and asked for a job. The ragged clothes he was wearing, along with his miserable demeanour, did not please the owner of the house, but he gave him some paints to mix. At dinner-time everyone went out and Vasco painted a fly, so well on a painting that when all the people of the house returned they tried to get rid of the fly before realising their mistake. They all agreed that it could only be the work of the great "Vasco".

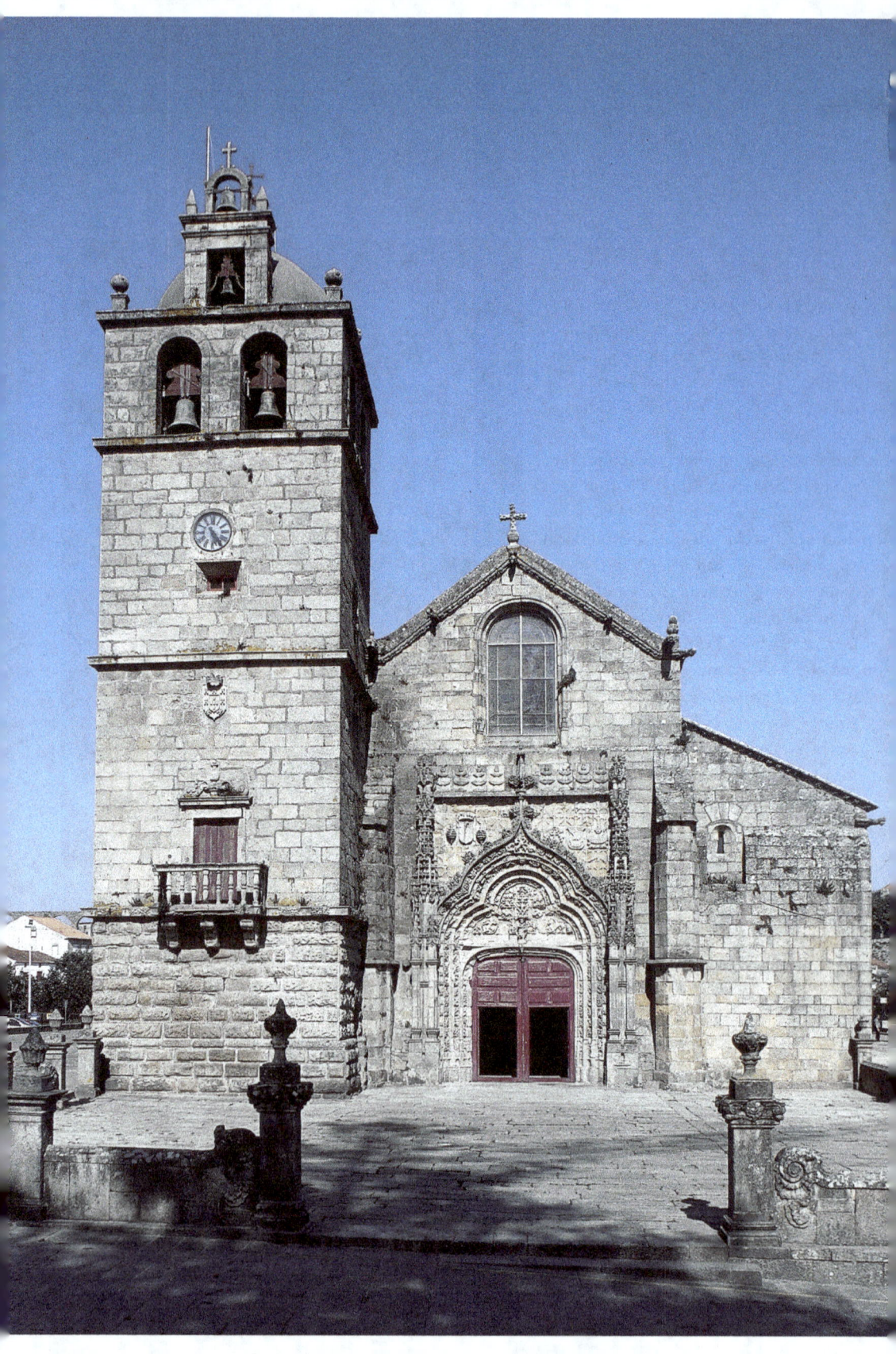

ITINERARY V

Biscayans in Northern Portugal

Pedro Dias, Dalila Rodrigues,
Nuno Vassallo e Silva, Fernando Grilo

First day

V.1 OPORTO
  V.1.a Chapel of João Carneiro, Church of the Convent of São Francisco
  V.1.b Tesouro da Misericórdia

V.2 AZURARA
  V.2.a Santa Maria (Azurara Parish Church)

V.3 VILA DO CONDE
  V.3.a Historic Centre
  V.3.b São João Baptista (Vila do Conde Parish Church)
  V.3.c Convent of Santa Clara

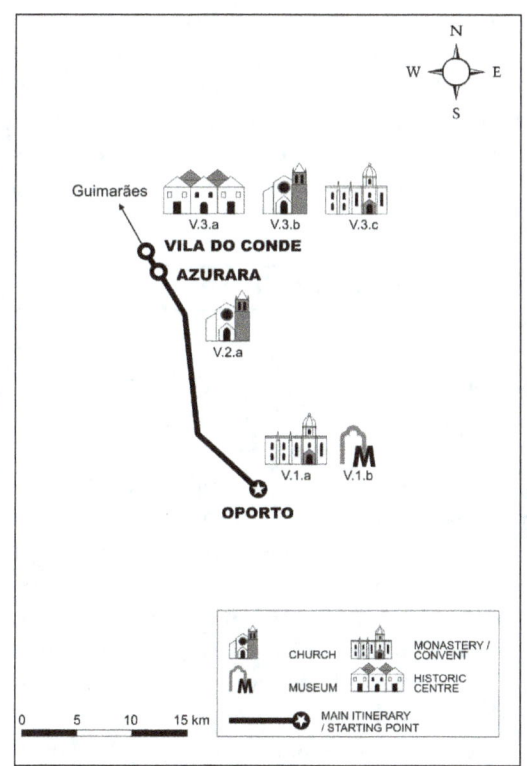

São João Baptista, Vila do Conde Parish Church.

ITINERARY V   Biscayans in Northern Portugal
Oporto

Northern Portugal played a highly important role in Portuguese expansion. Prince Henry the Navigator recruited many of the men who took part in the first overseas expedition, in 1415, in Oporto. The city also supplied many of the provisions for the fleet, and Prince Henry himself was born in the riverside area known as Ribeira, in Oporto. The fact that the inhabitants had handed over all their meat and been left with only the *tripas* or innards of the animals is said to account for one of the best known of Portuguese traditional dishes: tripe or *tripas à moda do Porto*.

These maritime peoples, trading since the 12th century, exporting agricultural products to Flanders and to Britain, and importing cargoes from there or from the Bay of Biscay, suddenly found their businesses taking off. Northern ports and towns such as Gaia, Vila do Conde, Caminha, Viana do Lima and Valença were suddenly more prosperous and this was reflected in pious works and simple pageantry.

Men who sailed the seas and those who tilled the land took an equal part in the overseas adventure. For every man who embarked, two or three had to stay and prepare for their journeys both outbound and homewards. They made rope, sails and casks, helped widows and cared for orphans, whose salt tears were evoked by the 20th-century poet Fernando Pessoa.

This prosperity was reflected in the architecture, but, due to the close relationship with Galicia and Biscay, the master builders who erected churches, chapels, houses, bridges and Town Halls mostly came from these areas. Even works commissioned by D. Manuel I, in 1505, when he travelled through the region on the way to Santiago de Compostela, spoke the aesthetic languages of the north, Galico-Portuguese or Basque. It was an architecture that ignored political frontiers and extended without a break to the other side of the River Minho, and the same can be said of painting, sculpture, gold and silver and the other arts.

João de Castilho worked on the Parish Church of Vila do Conde, and, a little further inland, in Guimarães, Braga and Barcelos, the presence of these master builders is still evident in the churches and cathedrals today.

V.I OPORTO

The historic centre of the city of Oporto has been classified as a World Heritage site, and since the 12th century has been the principal pole of development in the Northern Portugal. The port was enormously important until the beginning of the 20th century, for it was both the entry and exit for people and merchandise, creating within its walls, an active, hard-working population, who earned the area the title of the "capital of work" for the city.

ITINERARY V   *Biscayans in Northern Portugal*
Oporto

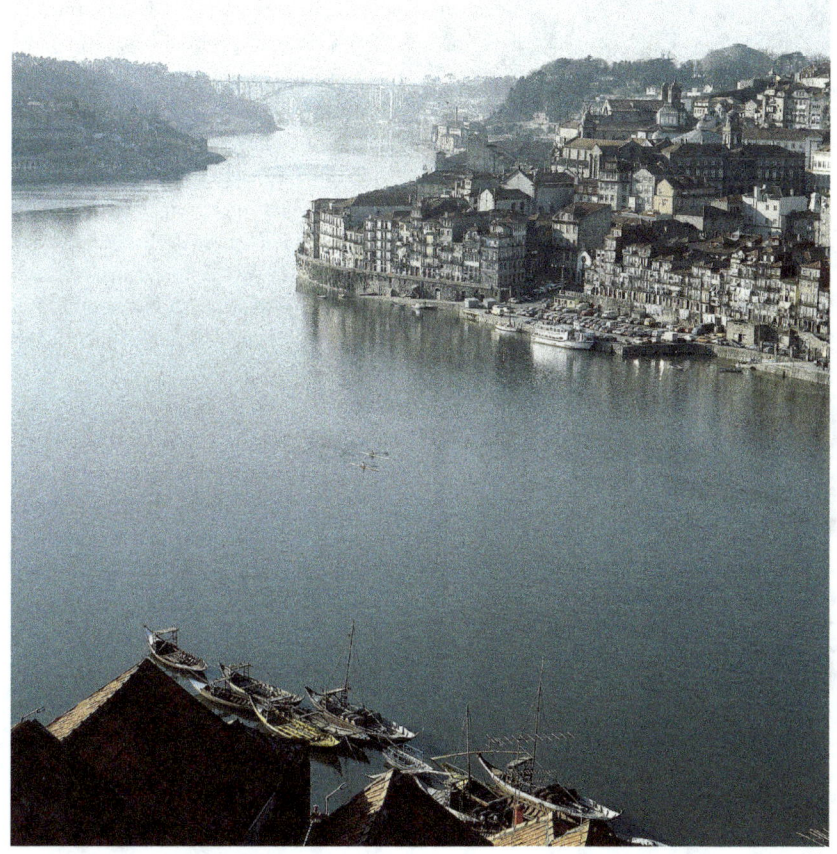

Panoramic view of the bank of the River Douro, Oporto.

It was from here that generation after generation of Portuguese left to settle in overseas territories, particularly Brazil. The city is linked to expansion for a number of other reasons too, not only because it was the birthplace of Prince Henry the Navigator, but also because of trade. Agricultural products, such as wine, were loaded here, together with manufactured goods, whilst ocean-going ships were built and outfitted, consolidating various industries closely linked to the Voyages. These ranged from modest cooperage to the more complex production of gold and silver objects and statues that were sent to churches in Portuguese territories in the four corners of the world.

Development after the 16th century provoked great changes in the city; other buildings, larger and richer, substituted the Manueline. Not only the clergy, but also some bourgeois families were ele-

Oporto

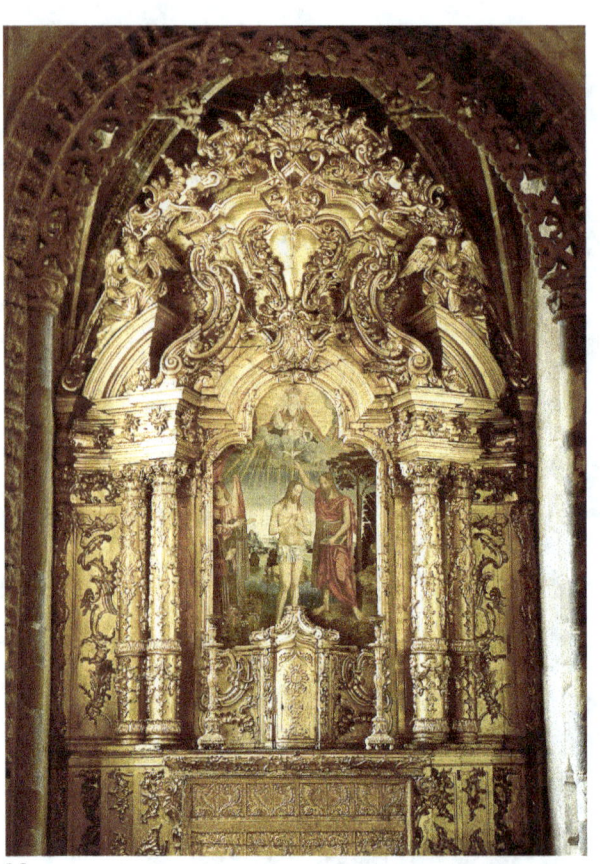

R.C.
Chapel of João Carneiro, Church of the Convent of São Francisco, Oporto.

V.1.a Chapel of João Carneiro, Church of the Convent of São Francisco

Rua do Infante D. Henrique. (Tel: 22 2062100). Designated a National Monument. The admission charge includes a visit to the catacombs and the Museu de Arte Sacra, as well as to the church. Opening hours: November-February 09.30-17.00, March-October 09.00-18.00. Closed on Sundays and December 25th and January 1st.

The Church of the Convent of São Francisco is one of the oldest of Portuguese Early Gothic buildings, but its original structure is covered by magnificent carved gilded woodwork dating from the Baroque to the Rococo. In the midst is a small but highly important Manueline work, an architectural jewel: the chapel of the schoolmaster of Braga Cathedral, João Carneiro, also known as the Chapel of Redress.

According to an inscribed stone, it was founded canonically in 1500, with one of João's brother's acting as the executor of his will. This highly influential family gave Portuguese politics a number of important figures at the time of the Discoveries, such as António Carneiro, who was the confidential scribe to D. João II and donatory of the Island of Príncipe. He was also Secretary of State to D. Manuel I, as was Pêro de Alcáçova Carneiro, who was also later Secretary of State to D. João III. Together with their brother Francisco Carneiro, they were vated to the nobility and appointed to high positions in public governance. They were responsible for many important buildings, such as chapels in convents and monasteries and even brotherhoods and the Misericórdia charitable organisation itself.

While not a lot is left of the Manueline art, historical places remain, with the waters of the River Douro testifying to the success or the sorrow of such an adventure.

ITINERARY V *Biscayans in Northern Portugal*
Oporto

responsible for overseeing trade with India.

Stylistically speaking, the architecture of the church can be attributed to the circle of Diogo de Castilho, who, in about 1526, settled in the city of Oporto after marrying the daughter of a rich Basque iron merchant. He lived in Rua das Flores and only returned definitively to Coimbra in about 1535. The Biscayan master produced a solid and elegant structure, even though not in line with the latest trends.

The painting on the high altar in oil on wood, representing the Baptism of Christ, now swathed in Baroque carved gilded woodwork, dates from the same period, c.1530. The master and his helpers, active in Entre Douro e Minho and Galicia, produced a series of works that were greatly influenced by Late Gothic work from the Flemish workshops in Ghent and Bruges. The donor of the painting, João Carneiro, is represented on the left, set back from the main scene as the river water is sprinkled onto the head of the Messiah.

V.1.b **Tesouro da Misericórdia**

The Misericórdia is at No. 5 Rua das Flores. (Tel: 22 2074710). The Misericórdia Church is classified as a Building of Public Interest. There is an admission charge, though study visits booked beforehand are free. Opening hours: Monday-Saturday 09.00-12.00 and 14.00-18.00. Closed on Sundays and public holidays.

The Misericórdia charitable organisation in the city of Oporto was founded at the beginning of the 16th century and the brotherhood used to meet regularly from 1502, in the chapel of St James in the cathedral cloisters. Some of its exceptional Manueline pieces are to be seen in the Sala do Despacho of its 18th-century headquarters now in the Rua de Santa Catarina das Flores.

The most emblematic work in this institution is an enormous painting in oil on wood, measuring 2.65 m. x 2.10 m., a *Fons Vitae* from Brussels, very similar to the work of Bernard van Orley. The paint-

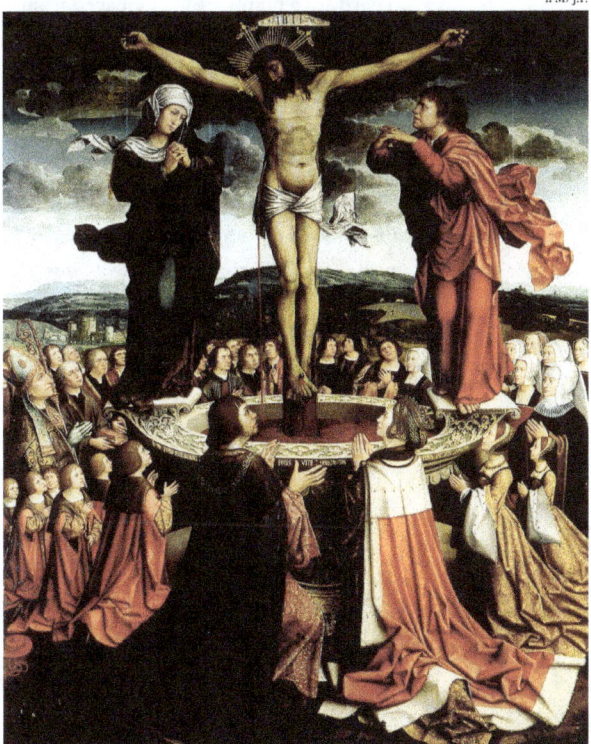

Brussels workshop, "Fons Vitae", 16th century, Santa Casa da Misericórdia, Oporto.

IPM/J.P.

ing is remarkable for the quality of the brushwork, its size and monumental structure, the impressive gallery of faces and even the landscapes in the background. Much of its interest centres on the fact that it portrays the Portuguese Royal Family and the Bishop of Oporto, D. Pedro da Costa, a great patron of the arts, who commissioned the work.

The central theme is the Fountain of Life, here depicted as a vessel with the blood of Christ, from which the Cross, on which He lies dead, can be seen emerging. Flanking Him are a serene Mary and Joseph, very much in the Flemish Renaissance manner. There are a number of personages around the vessel: facing the spectator are men and women with Flemish faces and dress, whilst seen from the back or in three-quarter profile are the Portuguese Royal Family. D. Manuel I and Queen D. Leonor, his third wife, are visible, together with the Crown Prince, D. João, and other princes and princesses, as well as the Bishop of Oporto, who donated the painting. The work must be dated some time after 1518 and before 1521.

The painting actually arrived unfinished and the faces of the Portuguese monarch and his family were only put in later, which also occurred with other examples of Flemish painting.

Other items of interest include two silver gilt chalices and the respective patens that belonged to the Mosteiro de Arouca, and were commissioned by the Abbess D. Melícia de Melo, as can be seen by the legends and coat of arms. The richest chalice has a round base with 12 semicircular sections, the six largest with a representation of Christ and five Apostles. The six smaller ones are decorated with floral motifs and daisies in silver. A six-sided structure with a smaller section joins the architectural-style knot. The images of the other Apostles in silver are set in niches.

The other chalice is simpler, but it is still one of the richest Late Gothic pieces in Portugal. On the base, there are quite exceptional figures of the *Resurrection*, *St John the Baptist* and *St Benedict*. Both chalices date back to the 1520s.

There is also a silver gilt salver dated c.1500, possibly from Oporto, decorated with finely chased arbutus berries and placed on a later structure made up of a lower dish, frame and foot.

Also belonging to the Manueline period are two Flemish-inspired sculptures, one of *St Stephen* and the other of a *Saint-Bishop* in polychrome wood, 1.6 m. high, which may have belonged to the original Chapel of the Misericórdia Brotherhood.

For Azurara, head in the direction of Maia and follow the EN13 towards Vila do Conde. Azurara is near a junction with the EN104.

V.2 AZURARA

V.2.a **Santa Maria (Azurara Parish Church)**

Rua Mouzinho de Albuquerque, next to the EN13. Designated a National Monument.

Information: Centro Paroquial, Vila do Conde (Tel: 252 640810).

The Parish Church of Azurara lies on the south bank of the River Ave and is larger than that of Vila do Conde, which apparently served as a model. The main vessel of the church has three aisles and five bays with simple longitudinal arcades on eight-sided pillars, covered in wood and of different heights. The east end of the church has Late Gothic ribbed vaulting, and the Royal Arms, armillary sphere, and the Cross of Christ in the chancel, confirm the patronage of D. Manuel I.

According to an inscription, Gonçalo Lopes built the church in 1522, and was the founder of a veritable dynasty of stonemasons and master builders.

The main door is quite simple with foliate elements in the inter-columnation and plaited pillars. The bell tower, begun at the same time, was only completed towards the end of the century.

For Vila do Conde, follow the EN13 in the direction of Vila do Conde / Póvoa do Varzim.

V.3 VILA DO CONDE

The city was originally a hill fort overlooking the River Ave and the lower area later became the site of a Roman villa, a large agricultural complex. In the first document that refers to Vila do Conde, dated 953, the most heavily populated area corresponds to the upper area. By the mid-13th century, the town had more than 50 pinnaces for fishing and transporting goods, the basis of the local economy, along with salt and salted fish.

At the beginning of the 14th century, the town became the domain of D. Afonso Sanches, the natural son of D. Dinis and

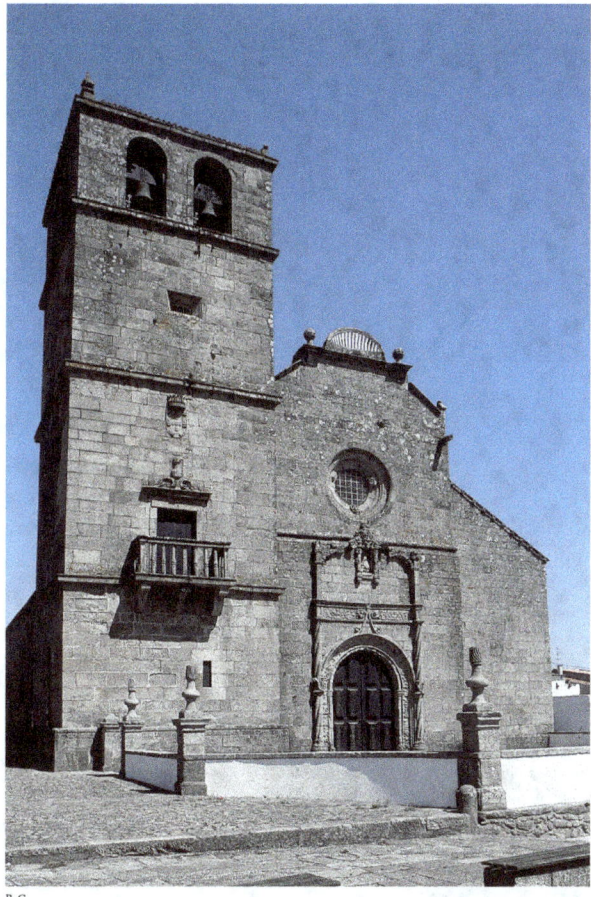

Church of Santa Maria, Azurara Parish Church, main façade.

ITINERARY V   Biscayans in Northern Portugal
Vila do Conde

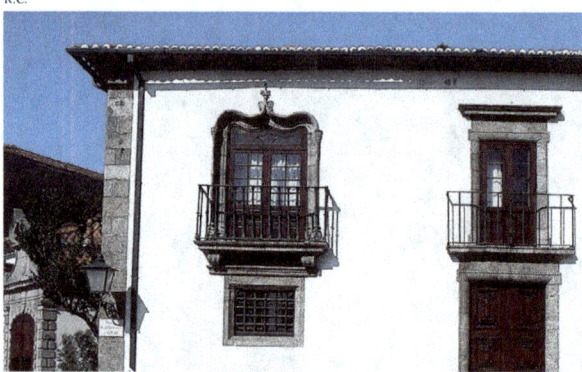

Manueline window, Azurara historic centre.

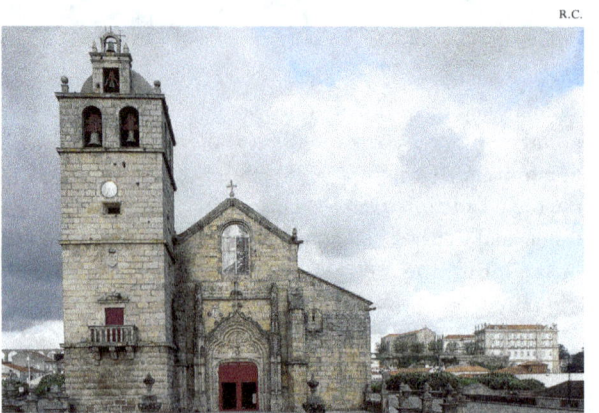

São João Baptista, main façade, Vila do Conde.

his wife, D. Teresa Martins, daughter of the Count of Barcelos.

With expansion into the Atlantic, followed by the Indian Ocean, the maritime activities of the port were of prime importance, and in this context there was considerable restoration and construction work carried out during the Manueline period, when many houses were built near the mouth of the river. D. Manuel I granted the town a charter on 10th September 1516, giving it autonomy from the seigniorial rights of the nuns of Santa Clara.

V.3.a Historic Centre

Information: Tourist Office (Tel: 252 248473).

There are a number of 16th-century houses down by the river with Manueline doors and windows, although some date from after the mid-16th century. The taste for embellishing bourgeois houses began during this period, as can be seen from these examples, although there is not the decorative exuberance here as seen in other ports.

These houses are spread throughout the town's older streets, such as Rua da Igreja, Rua da Misericórdia, Rua da Costa, Rua do Socorro, and Largo de São Roque.

V.3.b São João Baptista (Vila do Conde Parish Church)

Rua da Igreja. (Tel: 252 631327). Designated a National Monument.
Opening hours: daily 09.00-12.00 and 14.00-20.00.

The Parish Church is one of the most interesting of those built by the masters from Biscay and it has the advantage of being very much as it was, whilst information is also available as to who worked there and when. The church to be seen today was designed by João Rianho who began to construct the building, although the work was handed over to his compatriot, Sancho Garcia, in 1500. He was succeeded by the Basques: Rui Garcia de Penagós, who worked there until 1511,

Biscayans in Northern Portugal
Vila do Conde

when it was handed over definitively to João de Castilho, the man who was to complete the Mosteiro dos Jerónimos and the Convento de Cristo in Tomar. Paid by the municipality, Castilho and 20 masons, almost all of them from Biscay, completed the aisles in either February or March 1514, together with their respective arches and the axial door. Among the masons were João Garcia, André de la Cota and João de Quintanilha

The door in this church is the same as that of the Church of Azuaga, in Spain, which means that one was copied from the other. So, it seems most likely that João de Castilho also made, or at least designed, the Spanish portal.

The three aisles of the church are separated by a simple series of arches and a wooden ceiling with evolved Manueline ribbed vaulting similar to that of Braga Cathedral in the triple apse, chancel and side chapels. The crossing chapels, which form a false transept, date from the same period and are in the same style, with curved ribs and finely decorated foliate and heraldic keystones.

V.3.c Convent of Santa Clara

Situated on the slope overlooking the city in Largo D. Afonso Sanches. (Tel: 252 631016). Designated a National Monument.
Opening hours: daily 09.00-12.30 and 14.00-16.30.

This important building, founded by the natural son of D. Dinis, D. Afonso Sanches, and his wife D. Teresa Martins, has largely retained its Gothic structure, along with some extensive and impressive work carried out in the 18th century. Sanches, who the king wanted to succeed him in detriment to D. Afonso, had already chosen the monastery overlooking the River Ave as his pantheon.

Of particular interest to visitors is the chapel, where his mortal remains are

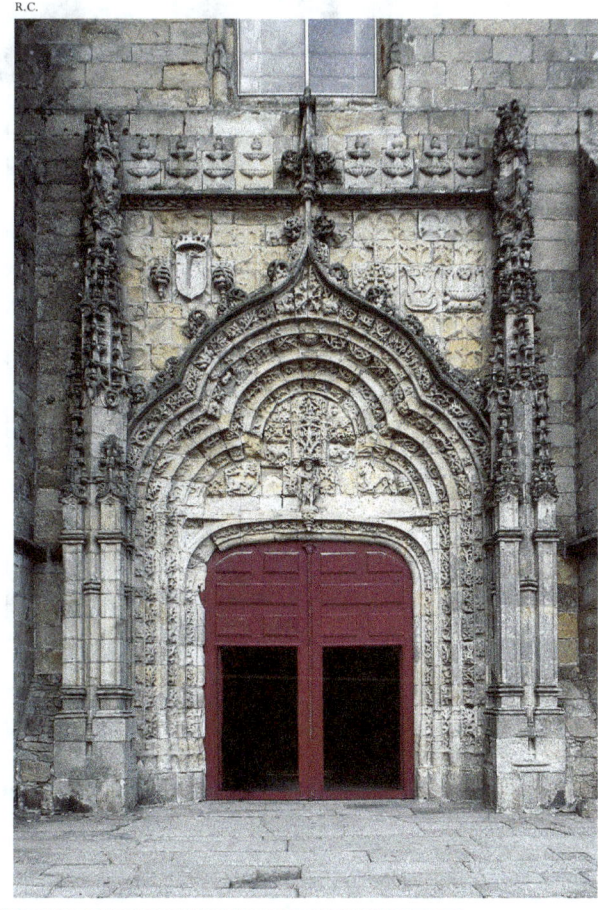

São João Baptista, main portal, Vila do Conde.

R.C.

ITINERARY V   Biscayans in Northern Portugal
Vila do Conde

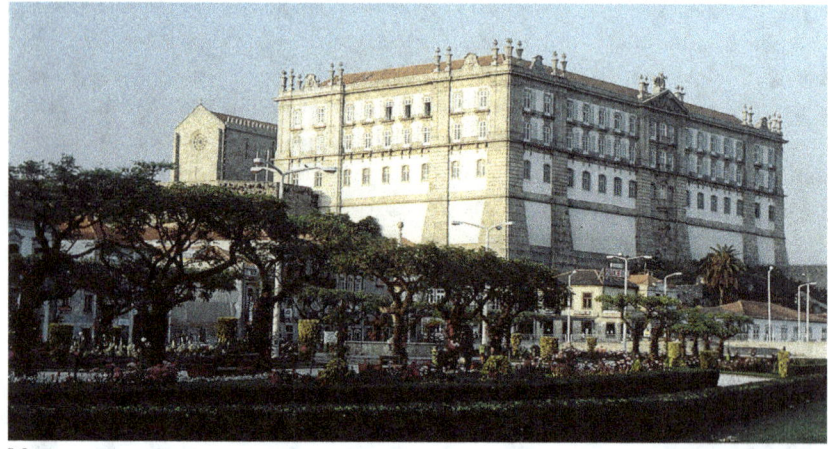

Convent of Santa Clara, general view, Vila do Conde.

R.C.

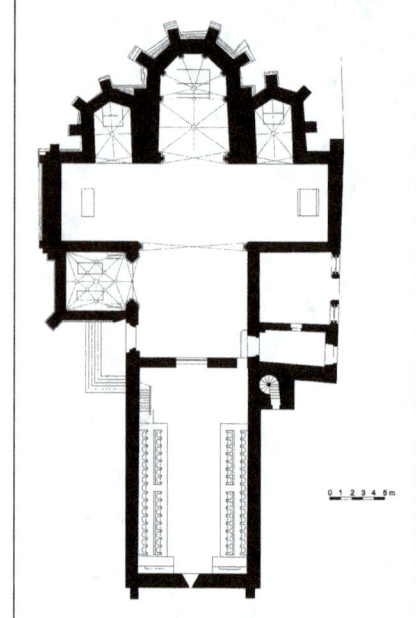

Church of Santa Clara, plan at lower choir level, Vila do Conde, Boletim da Direcção-Geral dos Edifícios e Monumentos Nacionais, No. 14, Lisbon, 1938.

Life of Christ. These works, in the transition from the Gothic to the Renaissance, may have been from the Coimbra workshop of Diogo Pires the Younger, as they are made in the local. Ançã limestone.

The chapel, dating to c.1526, which houses these masterful statues, was built at the side of the Monastery Church by the Abbesses D. Isabel de Castro and D. Catarina de Lima. It is completely Late Gothic in the Manueline tradition, with the entrance arch edged with tracery in the style of Batalha and quadrifoliate ribbed vaulting, with curved and straight segments, with the armorial bearings of D. Afonso Sanches on the central keystone.

to be found together with those of his descendants. The recumbent statues of the prince and his wife lie on their tombs decorated with scenes from the

For Guimarães, follow the EN309 to Vila Nova de Familicão; then the EN206 to Guimarães.

ITINERARY V

Biscayans in Northern Portugal

**Pedro Dias, Dalila Rodrigues,
Nuno Vassallo e Silva, Fernando Grilo**

Second day

V.4 GUIMARÃES
  V.4.a Paço dos Duques de Bragança
  V.4.b Alberto Sampaio Museum

V.5 BRAGA
  V.5.a Cathedral
  V.5.b Cathedral Museum of Sacred Art
  V.5.c Chapel of the Coimbras

V.6 BARCELOS
  V.6.a Paço dos Duques de Bragança
  V.6.b Santa Maria Maior (Barcelos Parish Church)
  V.6.c Solar dos Pinheiros

Legend of the Barcelos Cock

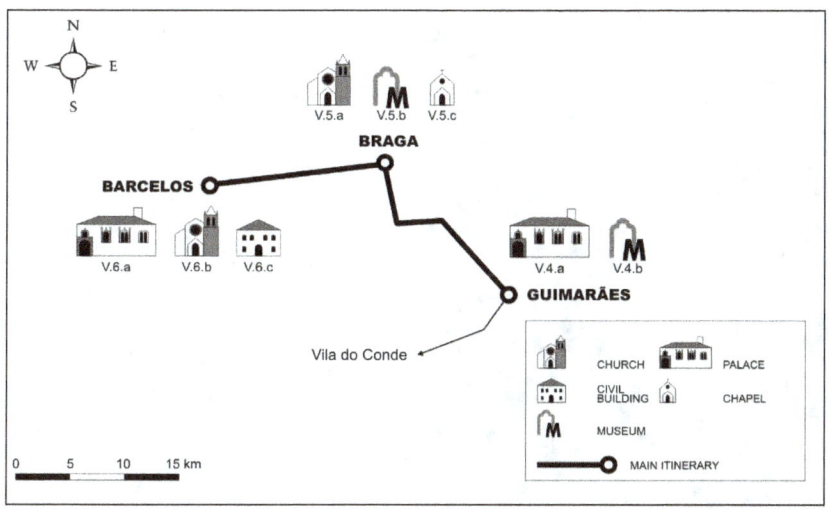

V.4 GUIMARÃES

Guimarães is one of Portugal's most mythical cities, as it was the birthplace of the first King of Portugal, D. Afonso Henriques, son of Count Henry of Burgundy and Teresa, daughter of the Emperor of León. He gained independence from his mother, and the Galician warlords who fought by her side, at the Battle of São Mamede in 1128, thus beginning his effective domination over the territory that was to give birth to the Portuguese nation.

The city was important throughout the Middle Ages, being in the centre of fertile agricultural land and close to other large centres of population, particularly the Archdiocese of Braga. Of the various institutions in the city, the Collegiate Church of Nossa Senhora da Oliveira is of interest, being a favourite of Countess Mumadona, who held sway in this region. One of its priors was João das Regras and one of its patrons was D. João I.

The development of Guimarães is also closely associated with a number of religious orders that were installed here, such as the Dominicans and Franciscans. In the Manueline period, it was remarkable for its urban grid of streets and houses and also for the Ducal Palace belonging to the House of Bragança.

Head for the Paço dos Duques, nearby, which has free parking and then walk the remainder of the distance. Walk to Largo da Condessa de Mumadona, and then follow Avenida Alberto Sampaio to the Museum.

V.4.a Paço dos Duques de Bragança

Rua Conde D. Henrique. (Tel: 253 412273). Designated a National Monument. Admission charge. Opening hours: daily 09.30-12.00 and 14.00-17.00. Closed on the following public holidays: January 1st, Easter Sunday, May 1st and December 25th.

The building was constructed by order of D. Afonso, Count of Barcelos, in 1401. He was later to become the Duke of Bragança and to create the Royal House that represents the throne of Portugal even today. The natural son of D. João I, he wanted to build a Gothic Palace equal to any in Europe, and altered the original plans a number of

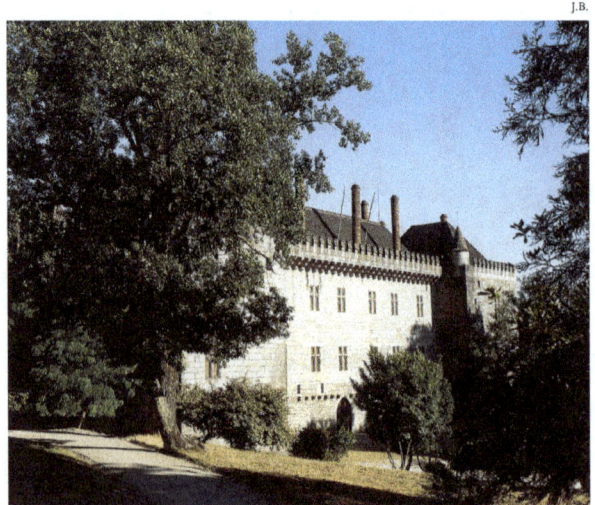

Paço dos Duques de Bragança. Guimarães.

J.B.

times before sending for a French builder, referred to in contemporary documents as Master Anton.
The scale of the undertaking was such that the palace remained incomplete, so that what is to be seen today was mostly carried out in the 1940s. Built round a large arcaded courtyard with a private chapel, the building has high walls with battlemented cresting and strong towers at the corners. Inside, there is a collection of artwork from various periods bought expressly for the palace or brought from other Portuguese palaces and museums. It includes Persian carpets, Chinese porcelain, European and Oriental furniture, and Flemish tapestries, even copies of the famous Pastrana tapestries, made in 1471 to commemorate the Portuguese Conquests of Asilah and Tangiers.

V.4.b Alberto Sampaio Museum

Rua Alfredo Guimarães. (Tel: 253 423910). Admission charge. Opening hours: 10.00-12.30 and 14.00-17.30, except on Mondays and the following public holidays: January 1st, Easter, May 1st and December 25th.

This important collection of 16th-century painting not only demonstrates the activity of regional painters, but also indicates the importance attributed to images both in public and private spaces. Worthy of note are the *São Brás Triptych* and the small panel of the *Virgin with Child* from the Collegiate Church of Nossa Senhora da Oliveira. Two altar panels represent *The Virgin between St Benedict and St Jerome* and *St Michael and St Margaret* from the Church of São Miguel do Castelo; and there is also a panel of *St Martin, St Vincent and St Sebastian* from the Monastery of Santa Marinha da Costa.

The collection also contains some mural paintings that demonstrate the various technical solutions used in the Manueline period. Conservation criteria of half a century ago, led to the separation of these paintings from walls of the Convento do São Francisco in Guimarães, and the

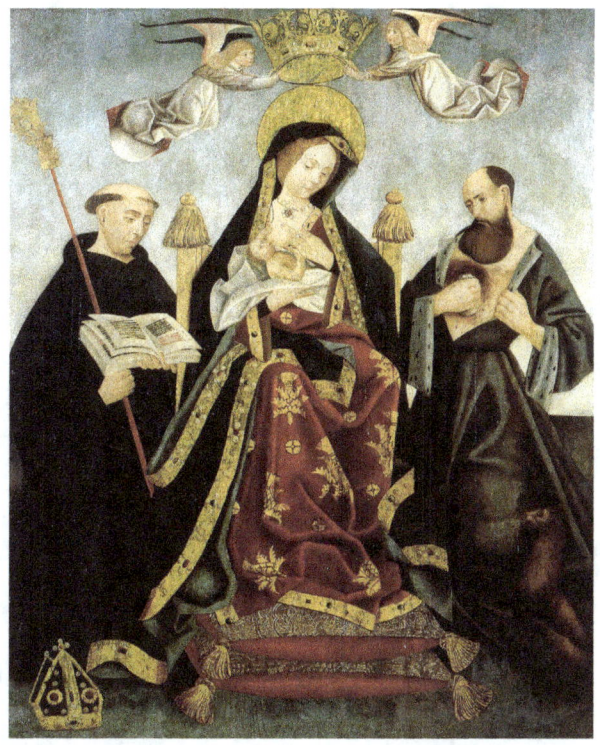

IPM/J.P.

"The Virgin between St Benedict and St Jerome", from the Church of São Miguel do Castelo, oil on chestnut, c.1500, Alberto Sampaio Museum, Guimarães.

ITINERARY V   Biscayans in Northern Portugal
Guimarães

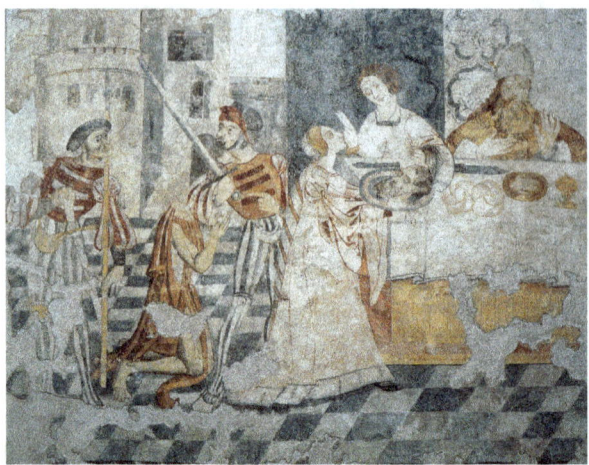

"Beheading of St John the Baptist", from the Church of São Miguel do Castelo, fresco, 1510-1530, Alberto Sampaio Museum, Guimarães.

Churches of Fonte Arcada and São Salvador in Bravães.
All the paintings were originally on display in places of public worship, except for a small panel in the *Virgin with Child* that belonged to the Private Chapel of the priors of the collegiate Church. The *Lamentation of Christ* originally in the triptych in the Chapel of São Brás in the Collegiate Church has an extraordinary dramatic sense. Its anonymous author expresses the pain associated with the death of Christ that, although in a more pictorial hand, is centred on stylised form and ornamental value rather than figurative realism, and is, therefore, out of touch with trends in other parts of the country. His body is offered here, clearly inviting the spectator's emotional response and provoking a sense of pious compassion. The presence of the monumental figures of São Brás and St

Jerome in the same triptych, is probably related to the Church's need to provide the public with edifying examples of moral conduct, through the former's miraculous ability to cure, and the latter's conspicuous bodily penance. When closed, the triptych represents the *Annunciation*.
Since, with rare exceptions, this activity was a largely anonymous exercise, little is known about the authors of this group of Portuguese regional paintings. The concept of form and the usual distorted expressions of the *São Brás Triptych* would seem to indicate that their anonymous author is also responsible for the two paintings from the Church of São Miguel do Castelo and the fresco of the *Beheading of St John the Baptist*.
It also seems probable that there was a small workshop actually in Guimarães at

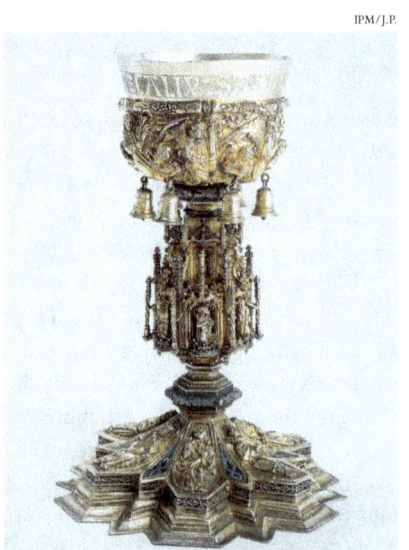

Silver-gilt chalice, c. 1520, Alberto Sampaio Museum, Guimarães.

the beginning of the 16th century, that painted both altarpieces in oil on wood and produced frescoes. The idea that there was a frontier of specialisation between painters, depending on their use of the two separate techniques, tends to be contradicted by examples such as this one.

It is also likely that the author of the *Virgin with Child* was a disciple of Vasco Fernandes according to the name [ANTO.VAZ] visible in a small *phylactery* held in the beak of one of the small birds. The author of the panel with the three saints (*St Martin, St Vincent and St Sebastian*) uses similar figurative strategies, but only to make it easier to identify them. The affinities with the production of the Flemish monk Frei Carlos, leave no doubt that this painting came from the workshop in the Hieronymite Monastery of Espinheiro, in Évora.

The Museu de Alberto Sampaio contains some very fine works in silver dating from the Manueline period, almost all from the Treasury of the Collegiate Church of Nossa Senhora da Oliveira. It is known that D. Manuel I gave the church many religious objects, including ornate candlesticks, an aspersorium, a *thurible* and an *incense boat*, though none have survived as they were almost certainly damaged and melted down in the 17th century to make new ones.

Dating from the early 16th century, is the chalice donated to the Collegiate Church by the Precentor, Fernão Álvares that appeared in inventories

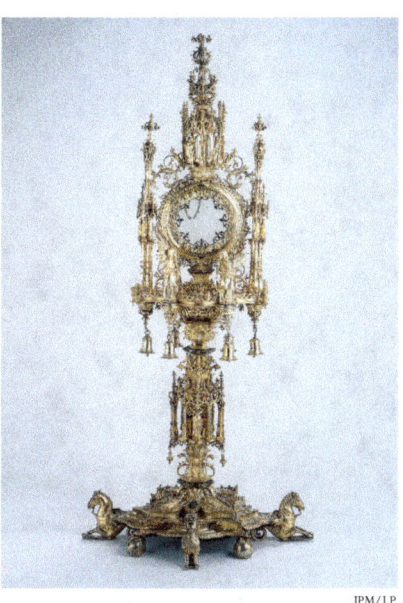

Silver-gilt and enamel monstrance, c.1530, Alberto Sampaio Museum, Guimarães.

IPM/J.P.

from 1527. The silver-gilt monstrance, finished in 1534 and commissioned by Canon Gonçalo Anes for the Chapel of the Holy Sacrament, is an excellent example of the taste of the time. It is quite remarkable from the technical point of view, with a profusion of silver dematerialised into typically Manueline adornment, and a rich ornamental and iconographic repertoire that transforms it into a unique object.

One of the final objects of the Manueline period is the processional cross made in Oporto, in 1547, in accordance with the will of Canon Gonçalo Anes. Rather out of the normal time frame, the general concept remains faithful to the Late Gothic, with a profusion of architectural elements, the surface decorated with Renaissance

ITINERARY V   Biscayans in Northern Portugal
Braga

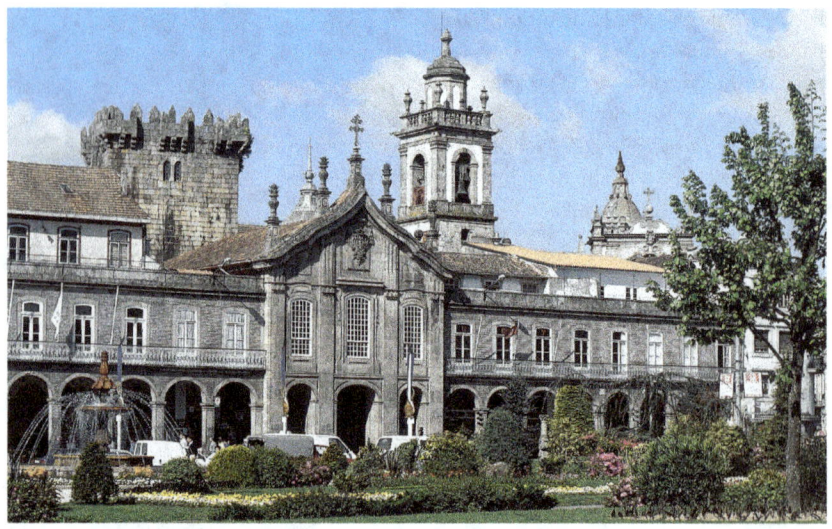

Braga historic centre.

R.C.

motifs and low reliefs of the *Passion of Christ* after engravings by Albrecht Dürer.

For Braga, take the EN101 in Guimarães in the direction of Caldas das Taipas / Esporões to Braga (20 km.).

V.5 BRAGA

Braga, the ancient *Bracara*, was a very important city in the Hispano-Roman period. Named *Augusta* at the time of Caesar, it became the headquarters of the new province of *Gallaecia*, Galicia, in 216, during the reign of the Emperor Caracalla.
It was also one of the main centres of Christianity and had a resident bishop, D. Paterno, in 400. In 448, under Rechiarius, King of the Suevi, the *Bracara conventus*, a smaller unit of a province, became the first Orthodox Christian Kingdom in Europe.
Taken by the Arabs, it was under constant attack from Asturia, even before 765, but the area was resettled and developed under Bishop D. Pedro, who governed the diocese from 1070 to 1091, when the first cathedral was constructed to replace the one built before the Suevo-Visigothic period.
In the Middle Ages, the city was poised between royal ownership and that of the archbishops, the latter with the title of Primates of Spain, which they contested, with the archbishops of Toledo.
The 15th century was an era of rapid development, stimulated by the archbishop, D. Fernando da Guerra (1416-

ITINERARY V   *Biscayans in Northern Portugal*
Braga

1467), with new constructions going up both inside and outside the city walls and constant improvements and additions being made to the cathedral and Episcopal Palace, fountains and gates. The Manueline period was even more spectacular under Archbishop D. Diogo de Sousa (1505-1532), back from Rome and imbued with the Renaissance spirit for splendour and luxury.

The archbishop planned and built new streets and squares, donated fountains, built hospitals, such as the Hospital de São Marcos, shelters for muleteers, a leper hospital, a large Town Hall, churches and monasteries of which he was patron, such as São Jerónimo de Montélios and Vilar de Frades. Not to mention setting up schools and a printing press.

The wealth of the cathedral and the Misericórdia under his administration also made these institutions the richest artistically in the entire Peninsula.

We suggest that you use the car park next to Arco de Porta Nova and walk round the monuments in Braga. Take Rua D. Diogo de Sousa as far as the Cathedral. For the Capela dos Coimbras, go round the Cathedral and along Rua de S. João.

V.5.a **Cathedral**

Rua D. Paio Mendes. (Tel: 253 263317). Designated a National Monument.

Opening hours: daily 08.30-19.00.

The origins of the Cathedral in Braga date back to the fall of the Roman Empire and the time of the Suevi Occupation. In the following centuries, not only the church was enlarged, but also the surrounding area, from the cloisters to the Episcopal palace. When D. Diogo de Sousa became archbishop in 1505, he found a rather dilapidated Late Romanesque church, with a collection of other buildings that

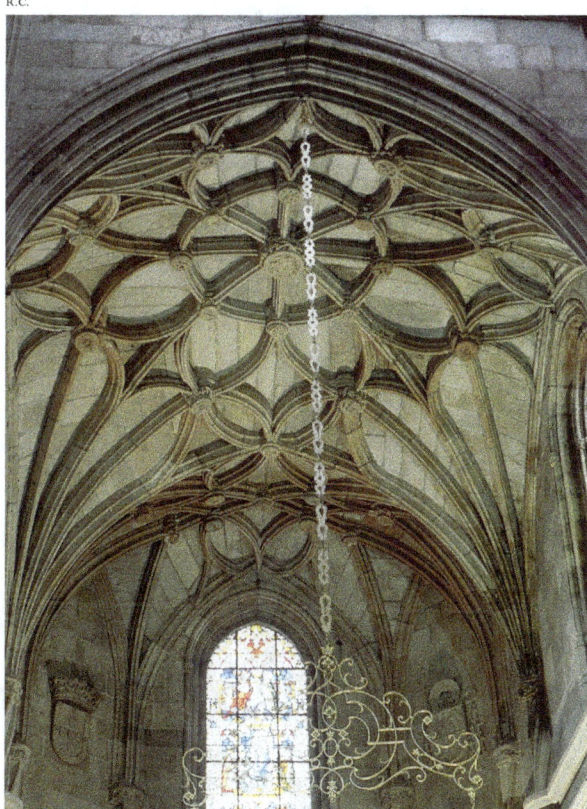

Braga Cathedral, vaulted ceiling of the chancel.

R.C.

153

Braga

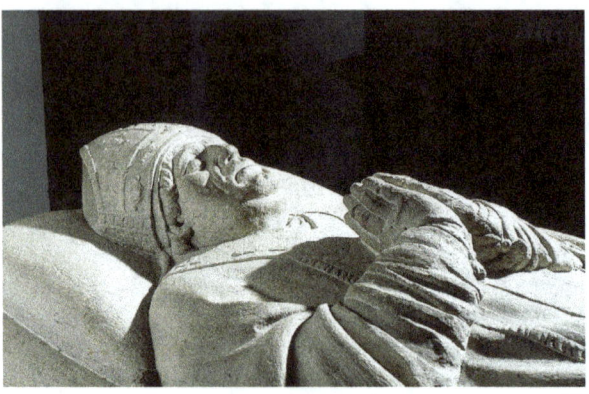

Recumbent statue of D. Diogo de Sousa, Funerary Chapel, Braga Cathedral.

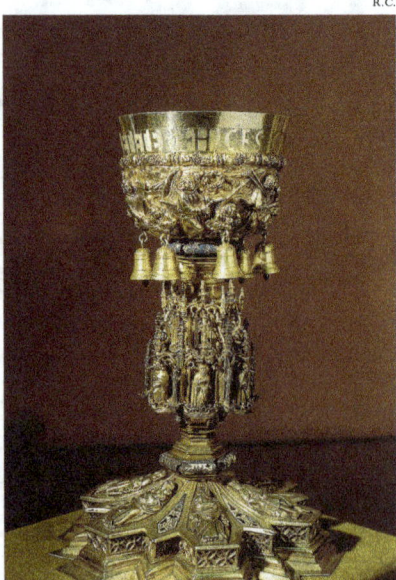

Manueline chalice, silver-gilt, c.1520, Museu de Arte Sacra, Braga.

ranged from the good to the modest. In 1509, the Spanish Master Builder, João de Castilho, was in Braga just setting out on his brilliant career.

Castilho had been working on the cathedral in Seville and later worked in Vila do Conde in 1511, Tomar, in 1515, and the following year he was in charge of works on the Mosteiro dos Jerónimos in Lisbon. D. Diogo de Sousa commissioned him to modernise the church in Braga, as there was not enough money at that time for a new cathedral. Castilho planned and built the *galilee*, with its three frontal arches and the *crossed rib vaulting*. He also constructed a chancel, high and strong, with the outer brattishing made up of a flamboyant garland. On the extrados of the wall, at the bottom, there is a Coimbra sculpture of Our Lady, with the coat of arms of the archbishop and the date, 1509. The interior of the chancel has a curved ribbed vault that forms petals, the first of its kind in Portugal.

D. Diogo de Sousa also commissioned an altarpiece in white limestone, the so-called Ançã stone, from the Flemish sculptor Machim, of which some images of great plasticity and anatomical rigour remain, as well as the decoration of the niches in the Flamboyant Gothic style.

V.5.b Cathedral Museum of Sacred Art

In the cathedral, on Rua D. Paio Mendes. (Tel: 253 263317).
Admission charge. Opening hours: 08.30-17.30 in winter and 08.30-18.30 in summer.

The Treasury of Braga Cathedral, one of the oldest in Portugal, was enriched by successive donations, Archbishop D. Diogo de Sousa no doubt contributing most. One of his offerings in 1509 was a monumental, silver-gilt chalice for High Mass, engraved with his coat of arms.

No less remarkable is the altar stone in alabaster and silver engraved with an exceptional *Calvary*, where the arms of the donor appear under the crucifix, which was given to the Treasury in 1527.

V.5.c Chapel of the Coimbras

Largo de S. João de Souto. Designated a National Monument.
The Chapel is private property, and can only be seen from the outside. It is, however, open to the public during Holy Week, and outside this period permission to visit it may be obtained by telephoning Sr. Manuel da Silva Macedo (Tel: 253 263704).

Dr. João Coimbra, who was Provisor to the Archbishop of Braga, founded the Chapel of Nossa Senhora da Conceição between 1525 and 1528. The structure of the tower and its porch are Mediaeval in line and for stylistic reasons, namely the vaulting, it can be attributed to Diogo de Castilho, as one of his final works in the north of the country. The house, which stretches along the road, has very fine windows framed in Late Gothic elements of great complexity and naturalistic exuberance.

Works by two of the most important French sculptors who lived in 16th-century Portugal can be seen here, though they are in the Renaissance style. On the *cornice* and the tower, there are a series of sculptures by Houdart and, inside, the high altar retable is by Jean of Rouen.

Take the EN103 straight to Barcelos (15 km.)

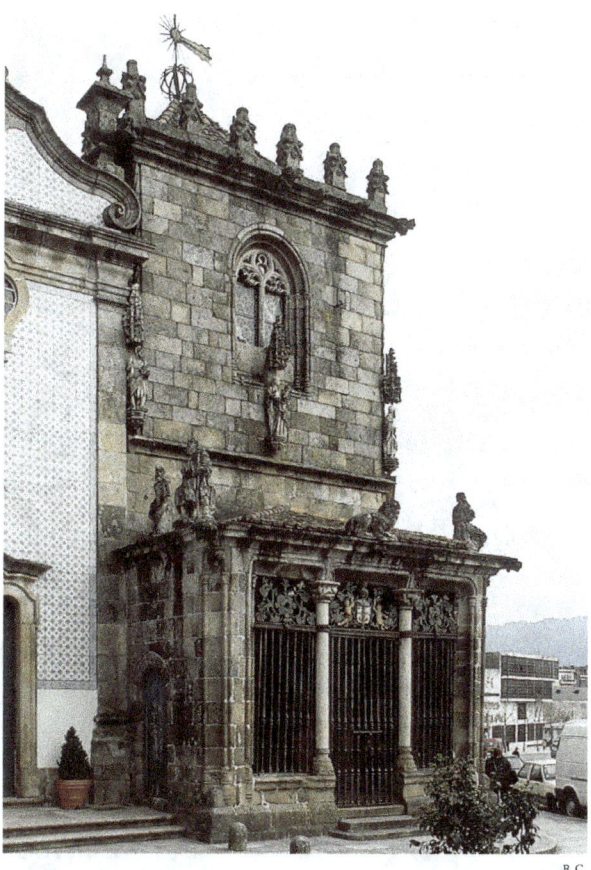

Chapel of the Coimbras, Braga.

Barcelos

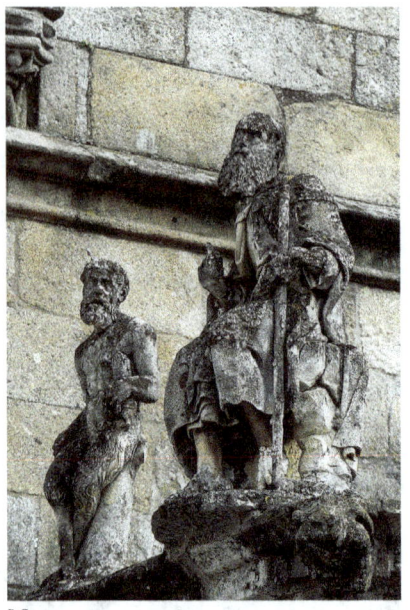

Chapel of the Coimbras, exterior detail of the sculptures by Houdart, Braga.

By the end of the Middle Ages, Barcelos had developed considerably through the activities of the Dukes of Bragança and their representatives, and Jewish and Christian families who built or rebuilt houses within the walls, while in the surrounding countryside agriculture prospered. It was a time when the bourgeoisie and lower classes settled in the new peripheral areas of *Porta do Vale*, Cruz and Salvador.

Enter Barcelos via Barcelinhos. Cross the Ponte Velha over the Cávado, which provides a good view of the old part of the town. After the bridge, turn left to the Largo do Município. Parking is available next to the Parish Church or the Ducal Palace. All the monuments can be visited on foot as they are in quite close proximity to one another.

V.6 BARCELOS

In the 13th century, Barcelos was a walled town, a strategic point on the road that linked the Douro coastal area with Galicia, dominating the plains of the River Cávado. D. Dinis granted these Crown lands to the High Steward of the Kingdom, João Afonso, whom he named a Count in 1298. The land and title re-entered the orbit of the Royal Family in 1314, when they were passed to D. Pedro, the natural son of D. Dinis, poet and author of *Nobiliário*. The title of Count of Barcelos also passed into, and remains, in the House of Bragança, through Prince D. Afonso, the son of D. João I.

V.6.a Paço dos Duques de Bragança

Rua Dr. Miguel Fonseca. (Tel: 253 824741). Designated a National Monument. It is now the Museu Lapidar de Barcelos or the Museu Arqueológico (Archaeological Museum).
Opening hours: daily 09.00-17.30, except on January 1st, Good Friday, Easter Sunday, May 1st and December 25th.

The Old Palace is set on the right bank of the River Cávado and, as can be seen by its 16th-century iconography, it defended the old bridge. In 1510, it was set into the walls and was the last redoubt. Most of the work on the residence was carried out by order of D.

ITINERARY V *Biscayans in Northern Portugal*
Barcelos

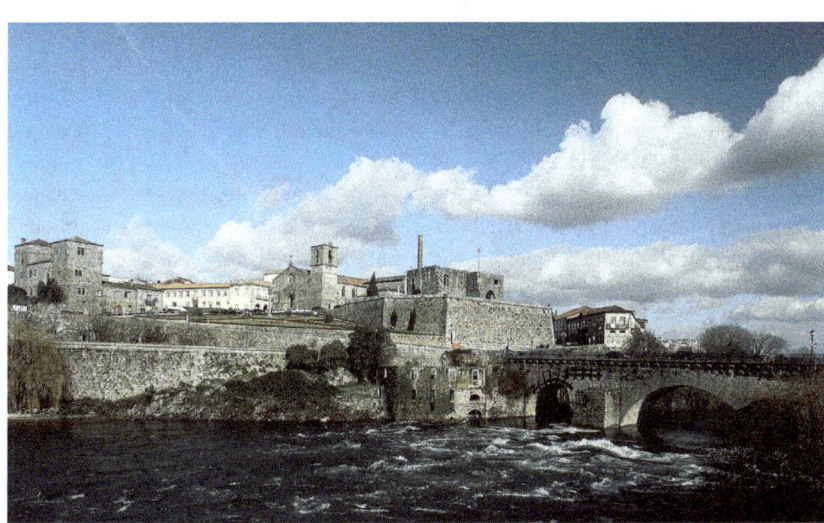

Panoramic view, Barcelos historic centre.

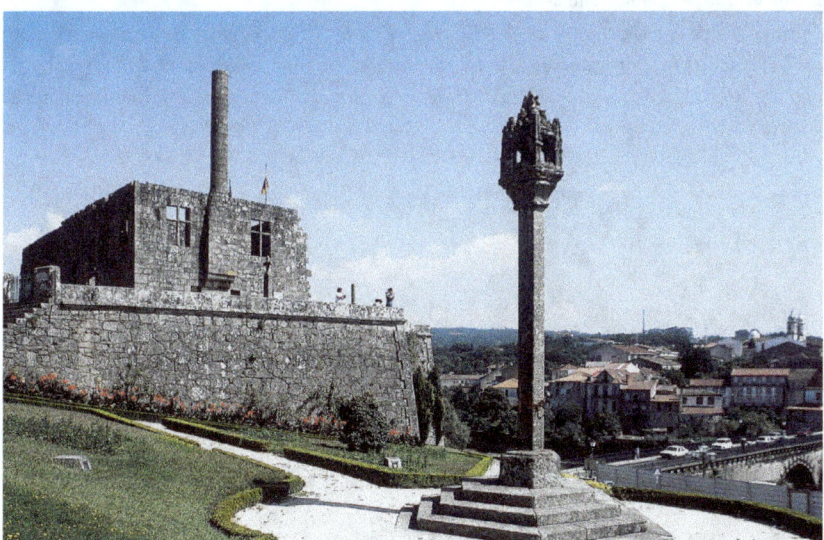

Paço dos Duques de Bragança and Pillory, Barcelos.

Fernando, the 9th Count of Barcelos and Marquis of Vila Viçosa, as well as his son, also called Fernando, who later plotted against D. João II and was killed as a result of this in 1483. Works were continually being carried out, as can be seen by the letter from the Duke of Bragança; D. Jaime, to the Archbishop of Braga in 1530 indicating that the count wanted to enlarge his residence.

ITINERARY V Biscayans in Northern Portugal

Barcelos

All that remains today is the artificial platform and the central part of the building with cross-beam windows, serving as clear proof that work was still being carried out some time between 1530 and 1540.

Various archaeological pieces have been placed around the building and nearby there is the Manueline pillory with its head in the form of a cage.

V.6.b Santa Maria Maior (Barcelos Parish Church)

Largo do Município. (Tel: 253 811451). Designated a National Monument.
Opening hours: Monday-Friday 10.00-12.00 and 15.00-20.00, Saturday 09.30-12.30 and 14.30-18.00, Sunday 09.00-12.30 and 15.00-18.00.

The Parish Church, once a Collegiate Church, dates back to the 14th century, but it is now an architectural mixture from various periods. The oldest part is the front, and the structure corresponding to three Gothic bays, but the chancel and the next bay are Manueline, although built on 14th-century structures.

The date 1504 and the name Gil da Costa are carved on the central keystone in the chancel. As far as can be seen, he must have been one of the men who paid for the renovation of the church.

V.6.c Solar dos Pinheiros

Rua Dr. Miguel Fonseca, on the corner, with Rua Duques de Bragança. Designated a National Monument. Information: Tourist Office (Tel: 253 812135).

R.C.

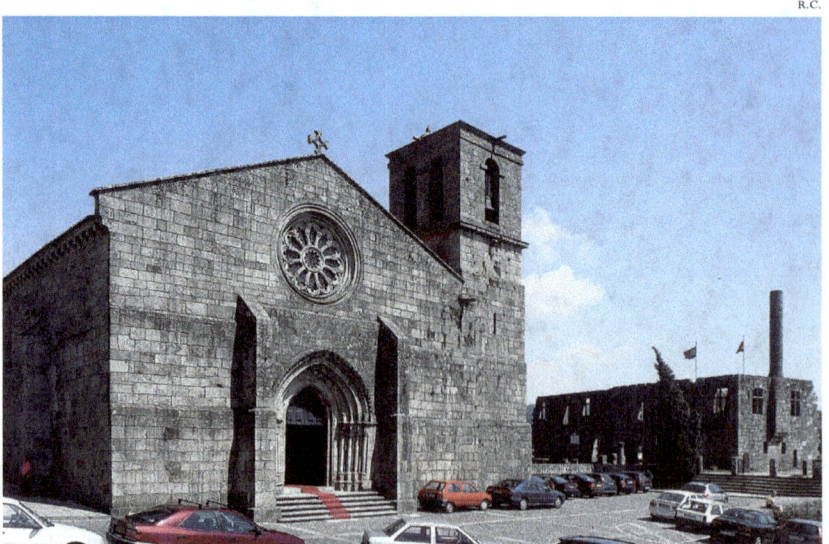

Church of Santa Maria Maior, Barcelos Parish Church, main façade.

ITINERARY V *Biscayans in Northern Portugal*
Barcelos

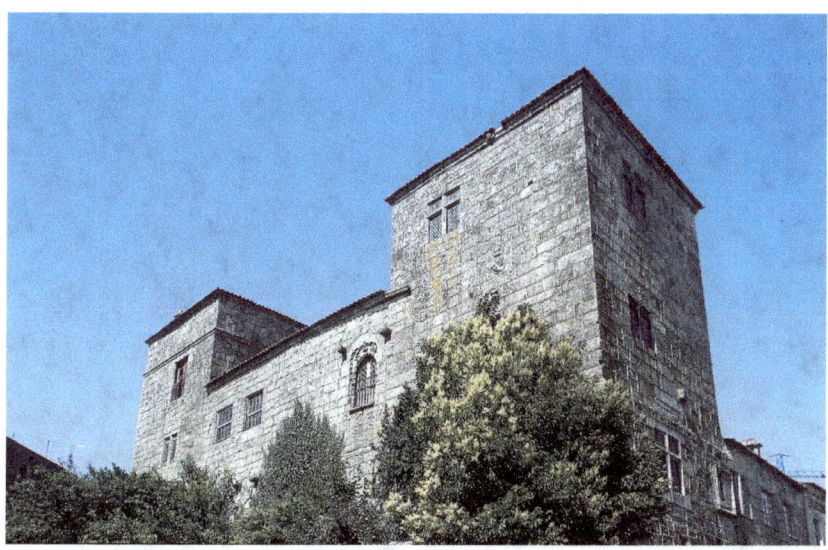

Solar dos Pinheiros, Barcelos.

The magistrates of the Duke of Bragança and the *alcaides* of the town built this grand house next to the Paço dos Duques and the Parish Church. It is very much in line with the houses built by Pedro Esteves, in 1448, and it was later enlarged by Álvaro Pinheiro, the owner's son, when it took on its present-day appearance.

The two-storey main front, faces west and is flanked by two imposing, square towers that are four storeys high. Despite the alterations that it has naturally undergone, the structure is still Manueline, with good dressed stonework in excellent local granite, whilst the door and window surrounds are of a regular design though not always symmetrical. Two lower wings stretch out behind the towers to form a courtyard.

Next to the coat of arms of Álvares Pinheiro on the south tower, is a sculpture of a praying figure and two male busts are included on the *cornice*, one with a long beard. This is one of the best examples of Portuguese domestic architecture of the Manueline period.

LEGEND OF THE BARCELOS COCK

Pedro Dias

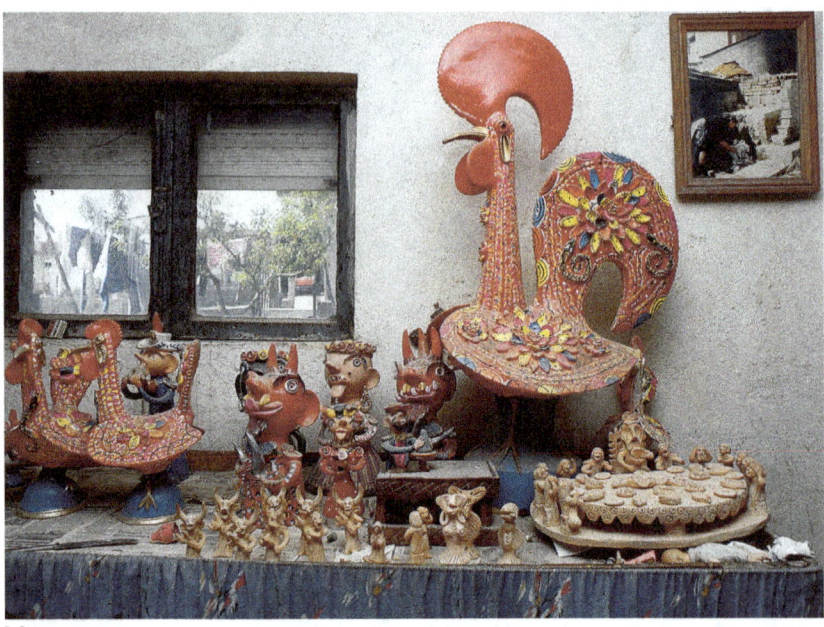

Barcelos Cock.

The Barcelos cock is one of Portugal's best-known icons. With its ingenuous air and bright colours, it is also an emblem of the modern Portuguese Diaspora. The legend, however, is old and comes from the oral tradition.

"In that area, by the edge of the old road, perhaps in the same place as Senhor do Galo, there was an inn much praised by travellers for the loveliness of its owner, a graceful wench, whose beauty was known for many leagues around and no one had anything to say against her. One day, the Devil (who else but he) made a pilgrim enter the inn, from all appearances a Galician, accompanied by a comely youth, his son, filled with faith on his way to keep a vow to St James. The owner of the inn in an instant was bewitched by the youth, though the son of the Galician was not devoured by the same passion that led her to the point that the reader will shortly see.

She tried to persuade the pilgrim to stay a few more days, but to no avail. When she realised they would stay no longer than the time required to rest, she used all her womanly wiles to try and persuade the son to stay there until his father returned. When the obstinacy of the father was followed by the indifference of the son, the landlady formed a diabolical plan that she immediately put into effect.

The pilgrims paid their bill and said goodbye to the innkeeper, who bade them farewell with a smile, and they continued on their pious way. They had not gone far when, at a bend in the

road, there appeared a band of men from the court of justice and going up to the young man they cried,
"We arrest you in the name of the King."
Astonished, father and son asked what was the meaning of all this, and were even more surprised to hear the young man denounced as a thief and to see silver knives and forks taken from their bags just as the innkeeper had told the men.
The pilgrim, unperturbed, continued his journey to Santiago after embracing his son who was led off to jail, to be condemned to hang according to the justice of the day.
On the day when the sentence was to be carried out, the pilgrim returned from Santiago and was filled with despair at the news at what was to happen. He went in search of a judge to convince him of his son's innocence, but the judge was eating. Not wanting to be disturbed, the judge declared that he would believe the boy innocent if the roast chicken on the table would get up and crow. When he said that, the cock got to its feet, shook off the parsley and in an instant began to crow.
The judge leapt up, looked at the clock and saw that it was the exact time fixed for the execution. He started to run to the execution site, followed by the father, but, as they drew nearer, they realised they had arrived too late and the condemned man was hanging there…
Not that it mattered, however. St James was holding the youth, supporting his feet with his head and hands."

Domingos J. Pereira, *Nova História da Vila de Barcelos*, 1817.

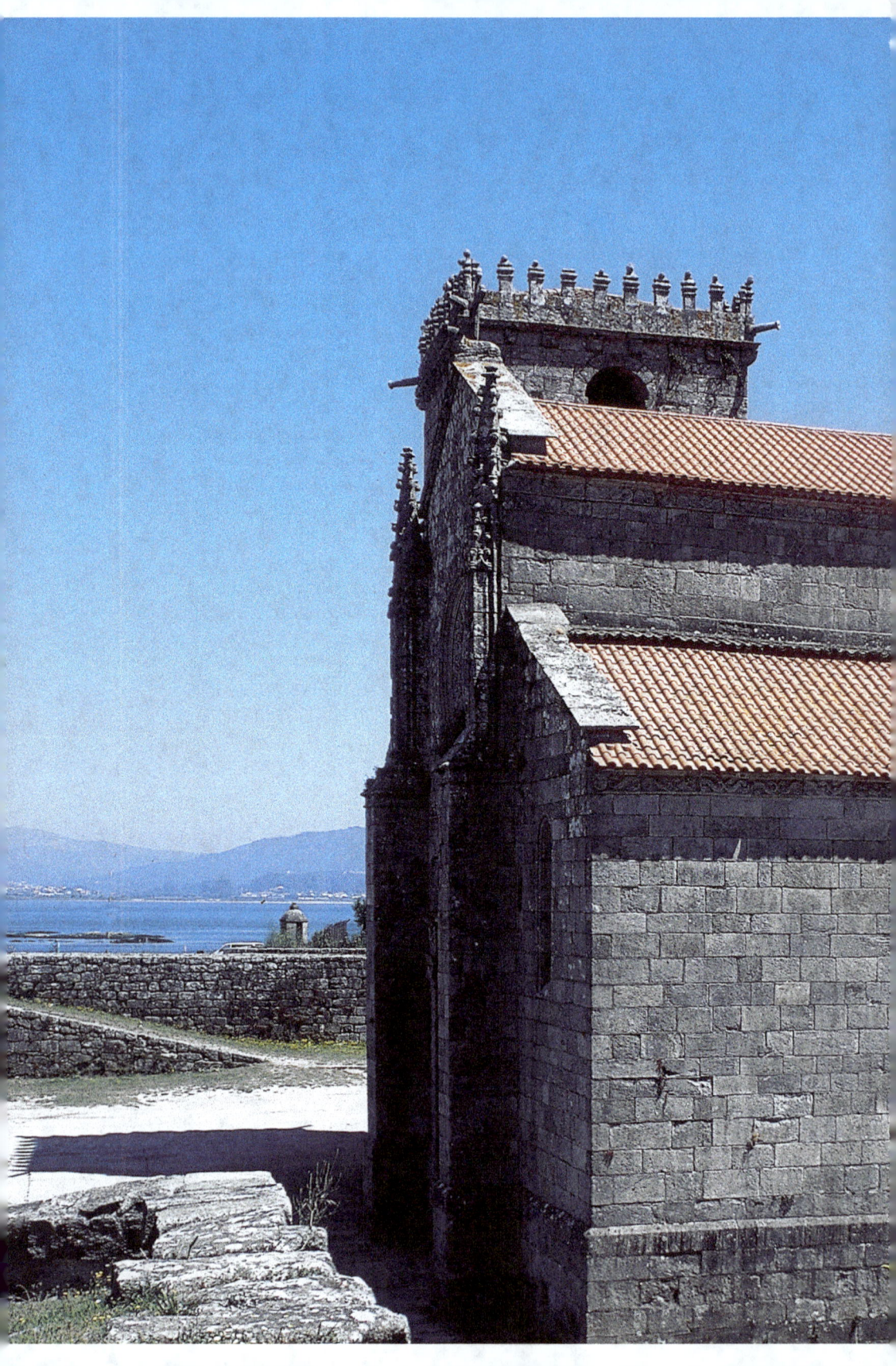

ITINERARY VI

Looking Towards Galicia

Pedro Dias, Dalila Rodrigues,
Nuno Vassallo e Silva, Fernando Grilo

VI.1 VIANA DO CASTELO
    VI.1.a Historic Centre
    VI.1.b Cathedral
    VI.1.c Roqueta Castle

VI.2 CAMINHA
    VI.2.a Historic Centre
    VI.2.b Nossa Senhora da Assunção
    (Caminha Parish Church)

VI.3 LANHELAS
    VI.3.a Casa da Torre

VI.4 VILA NOVA DE CERVEIRA
    VI.4.a Castle

Manorial Towers of Alto Minho

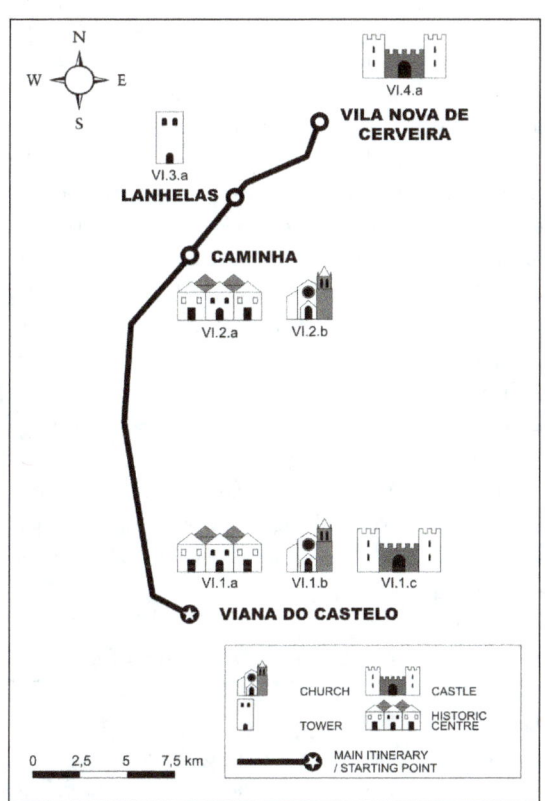

Caminha Parish Church with Galicia in the background.

ITINERARY VI   *Looking Towards Galicia*
Viana do Castelo

The River Minho, rather than separating the people of the Minho and Galicia, has united them for centuries. Even in wintertime, when the river's current was strong, people from each bank with much in common including the language, would come and go frequently, so that even nowadays they seem to speak to each other like twin brothers.

It was impossible to ford the river but there was always a small boat ready to carry people either to trade, legally or illegally, to visit their families or friends or to take part in religious services, on one bank or the other.

When the kingdom of Portugal was founded at the beginning of the 12th century, there were still parishes on the south bank that came under the jurisdiction of the Diocese of Tuy in Spain. The stonemasons, who erected its cathedral in about 1200, had already built Romanesque churches at Sanfins, Ganfei, Longos Vales and other places in the Minho.

The Sanctuary at Santiago de Compostela was the most important in the far western part of Europe, and Portuguese pilgrims ignored the frontier and eventual state of war between Castile and Portugal to pray and fulfil their vows there. It was also there that the announcements were made for the public and private building contracts in the Minho and Entre Douro-e-Minho provinces.

So, it is not surprising to find similar works of art in these neighbouring lands, produced at the end of the 15th and the beginning of the 16th centuries, i.e. during the Late Gothic and proto-Renaissance artistic periods, emblems of the transition between the Middle Ages and the Modern Era.

The main doorway of the Parish Church in Viana do Castelo is clearly derived from the Galician tradition of proto-Gothic portals. Tomé de Tolosa, Francisco Fial, Fernão Muñoz and Pêro Galego all worked on the church in Caminha, the last-named being the master builder of the Church of the Convent of Santana in Viana. Similarities also extend to cover sculpture imported from Coimbra; painting, the leading artist being André de Padilha; and, of course, gold and silver work and luxurious textiles.

This is an area with many estates and highborn families dating back to the founding of Portugal. During this period, the houses were added to and modernised to make them more comfortable, but in line with new needs and tastes. The proud towers of Lapela, Lanheses and Giela are still to be seen today between vineyards and on rocky crags.

Look towards Galicia, see it, enjoy it, go there to buy something or to have something made, make the same, or sell it, make it there, such was the intricate equation of a particular region, time and river.

VI.I **VIANA DO CASTELO**

Viana do Castelo, or Viana do Lima, as many of its inhabitants like to call it,

ITINERARY VI *Looking Towards Galicia*
Viana do Castelo

started out as a small fishing village called Átrio, which existed in the 12th century. D. Afonso III named it Viana when he granted it a charter in 1258, and from then on it developed rapidly, especially during the Manueline Period. The town was, therefore, a Crown estate and, for the first phase of its settlement with new inhabitants, the actions of João Gonçalves proved to be crucial. The king's representative in the region, he justly came to be known as "the Settler" of Viana.

Its excellent anchorage at the mouth of the River Lima first attracted inter-European trading vessels, and then, later, ships carrying goods and people to and from Africa, Brazil and the Far East, at the same time as European trade increased apace. It was an essential trading port for cloth and metal goods from Flanders, England and Germany. This wealth, however, attracted pirates, mainly from France and the Biscay area, so when D. Manuel I passed through the town on a pilgrimage to Santiago do Compostela, he ordered a fort to be constructed on the bar of the estuary.

This golden period created a mercantile and manufacturing class and craftsmen's guilds, which left their mark on the historic centre of the city. The wealth, piety and devotion of the citizens of the town, along with their personal and professional affirmation, are reflected in churches and many other buildings in the area.

Take a walk through the historic centre of Viana do Castelo and visit the Church of Santa Maria. The Castelo da Roqueta is about 1 km. away, towards the mouth of the River Lima.

R.C.

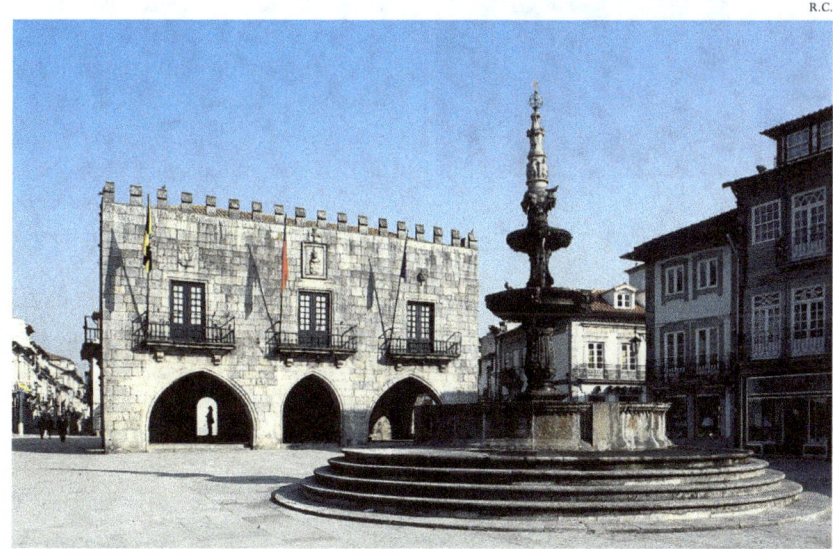

Former Town Hall, Viana do Castelo.

ITINERARY VI *Looking Towards Galicia*
Viana do Castelo

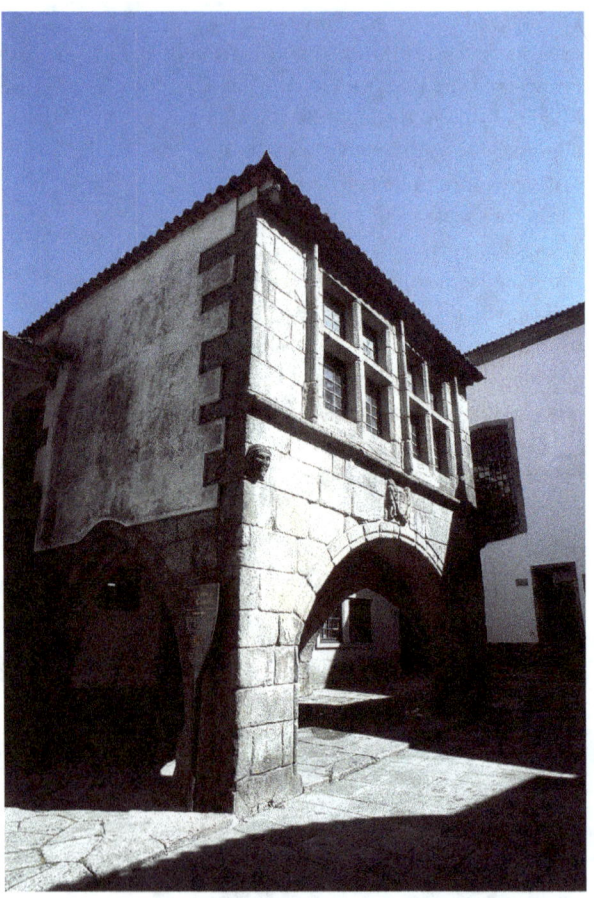

R.C.

Casa de João Velho, Viana do Castelo historic centre.

VI.1.a Historic Centre

You may begin your tour of the city on foot, starting in Rua de São Pedro (close to the Cathedral), where you will find the Casa dos Costa Barros. From here continue along Rua Grande to Viela da Parenta, where you will find the Casa de Pêro Galego. Next follow Rua do Hospital Velho as far as Rua do Tourinho in order to visit the Casa de Pedro Tourinho.

From here, you should continue along Rua Sacadura Cabral, where you will see the Casa dos Medalhões or the Casa dos Lunas, and then immediately after the Cathedral is the Casa de João Velho. Continue on to Praça da República, where you will find the former Casa da Câmara (Town Hall) and then from here walk along Rua Cândido dos Reis, where you can see the Casa da Carreira (the building that currently houses the Municipal Council). Contact the Tourist Office (Tel: 258 822620).

The structure of Manueline Viana is easily seen today by studying the roads in the historic centre. They form an oblong, corresponding to the outline of the 14th-century walls that surrounded rectangular blocks of dwellings defined by a perpendicular grid, widening parallel to the river. The Porta de São Crispim opened at this side and the road crossed the town in a straight line in front of the New Parish Church to the Praça Velha and the Porta do Forno or the Porta de São Tiago, which led into Campo do Forno. Rua de São Pedro and Rua Grande ran in perpendicular lines to the other gates, Porta da Ribeira or Porta de São João, and Porta das Atafonas.

The defending wall, built, essentially, between 1263 and 1374, has since disappeared, although its outline can still be traced. The names of some of the masters of works who worked there towards the end of this period are known, such as António Fernandes and João Domingues.

Looking Towards Galicia
Viana do Castelo

Some of the Late Gothic houses in this area are of particular interest. The Casa dos Costa Barros, in Rua de São Pedro has splendid Manueline windows, that have something profoundly Baroque about them, on the main floor. In front of the Parish Church is the Casa dos Medalhões or the Casa dos Lunas, already Renaissance in style. The Casa de João Velho, at the side of the church, has a segmental arch on the ground floor and cross-headed windows that were quite common in the Late Gothic period. D. Manuel I stayed in this house in 1506 when he visited Viana.

Some of the houses in this area have added historic interest; for example, the Casa de Pêro Galego in Viela da Parenta has a caravel carved in relief on the door lintel. In the Rua do Tourinho there is the Gothic Casa de Pedro Tourinho, the home of one of the first *donatários* or lord proprietors in Brazil, specifically of Porto Seguro.

Just outside the walled perimeter there are other buildings, which either date back to or were heavily restored during the early 16th century. This is the case with the elegantly fronted Gothic Casa da Câmara, the Town Hall in the former Campo do Forno, now the Praça da República. Meetings used to be held under the triple arcade on the main floor. In view of the limited space available within the town's walls, the market also began to be held here when the population increased dramatically in Manueline times.

One of the best Manueline houses, although heavily restored later on, is the Casa da Carreira (in Rua Cândido dos Reis) built in 1527, by Fernão Brandão, who served in the forts at Safi and Azamor in North Africa. The façade retains some Late Manueline door and window frames.

R.C.

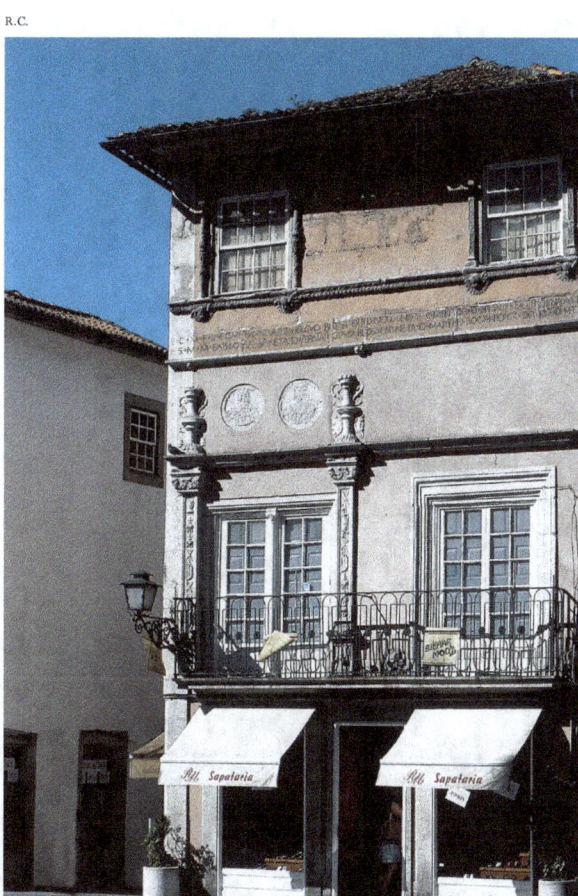

Casa dos Luna, Viana do Castelo historic centre.

Viana do Castelo

VI.1.b Cathedral

Largo Instituto Histórico do Minho. (Tel: 258 822436). Classified as a Building of Public Interest.
Opening hours: Monday-Friday 09.00-11.30 and 15.00-18.00, Mass is celebrated at 12.00-13.00. On Saturday and Sunday, the Cathedral is open 09.30-12.00 and 16.30-17.00, mass is celebrated at 18.30.

The Old Church of Santa Maria Maior, the Parish Church of Viana do Lima, was a Collegiate Church until the 19th century. Work began on it in the 1430s and it was completed in the reign of D. João II (1482-1495). The arms and devices of this monarch can be seen on the front, together with the shield of D. Justo Baldino, the Bishop of Ceuta, who, in 1478, was nominated Administrator of the Valença district (to which Viana belonged at that time). Also to be seen are the Manueline Chapels of the Mareantes (Mariners), Santo Cristo, the Fagundes and Camaridos.

Two strong towers, rather like castle keeps, flank the austere façade and there is a fine late 15th-century portal with the Apostles, similar to the Galician sculptures to be found in Santiago, Tuy, and the suburbs of these two sees of the respective dioceses. It is most probable that Galicians helped to build this cathedral, although their identities are unknown.

The interior of the church is in the form of a Latin cross, with three aisles divided by lightly structured arcades and the ceiling is in wood. The Mariners' Chapel, donated to the Brotherhood by the Velho family in the 15th century, is in the north arm of the transept. The altar boasts a quite remarkable series of Flemish sculptures, forming a scene of the *Lamentation on the Dead Body of Christ*, that were probably produced in an Antwerp workshop,

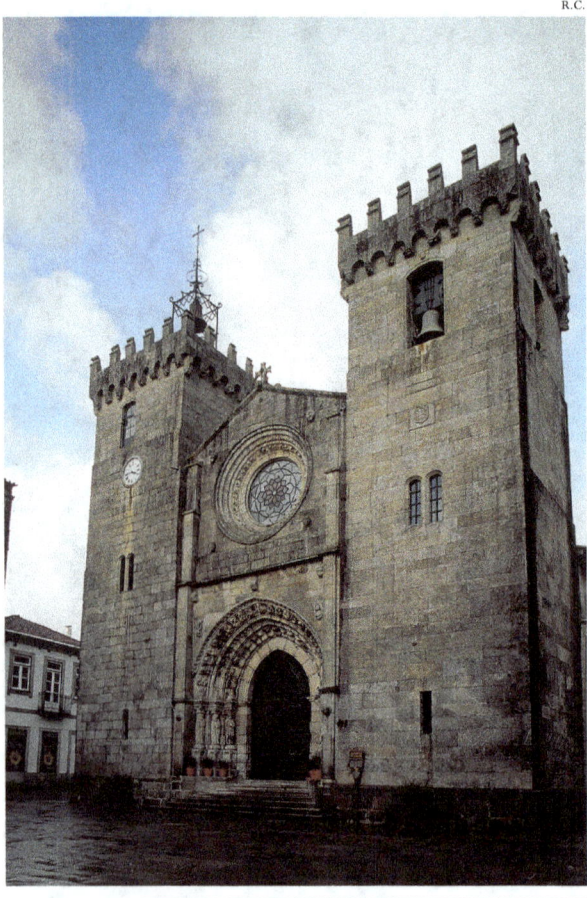

Viana do Castelo Cathedral.

in c.1520. The chapel was remodelled at various times later, but still contains the tomb of João Velho.

The Capela do Santo Cristo is a traditional Gothic structure and was founded in the second decade of the 16th century by João Álvares Fagundes, a navigator who sailed the North Atlantic and explored the coast of Canada and Newfoundland.

Martim Fernandes Correia, the heir to the Carreira family's estate, founded the Capela dos Camaridos, remarkable for the double arch with slender, plaited columns at the entrance, and for the Late Gothic ribbed vaulting. The founders donated the very lovely Brussels altarpiece attributed to the circle of Jan Provost, dating back to about 1530. The retable is large with a fine landscape background, the figures of *St John the Baptist* and *Our Lady of the Rosary* dominating the foreground, an unusual combination but no doubt commissioned as such.

VI.1.c Roqueta Castle

The Castle is accessible from Campo or Largo do Castelo and is part of the fortress of Santiago da Barra. Classified as a Building of Public Interest. Currently occupied by one of the public services.
Opening hours: Monday-Friday 09.00-12.30 and 14.00-17.30.

The remains of the Castle built on the rocks by D. Manuel I to defend the bar of the River Lima from marauding pirates is part of the modern-day bastioned Fortress of Santiago da Barra. A curious structure, similar to the Torre de Belém in Lisbon, with a Mediaeval tower and bulwark to the south, it demonstrates the evolution of fortifications in Portugal at this period of transition from more rudimentary weapons to the use of pyro-ballistics, of which there are few examples still remaining.

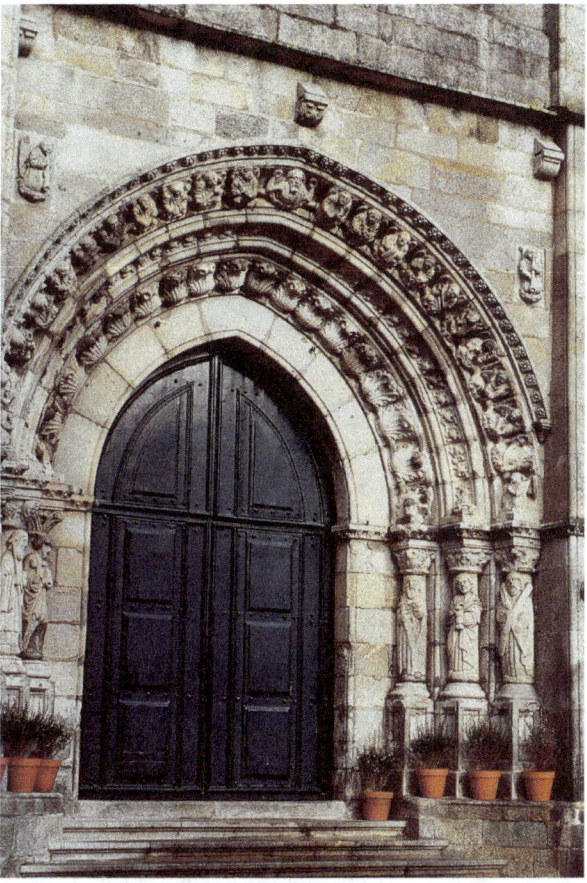
R.C.

Viana do Castelo Cathedral, portal.

Caminha and the estuary of the River Minho.

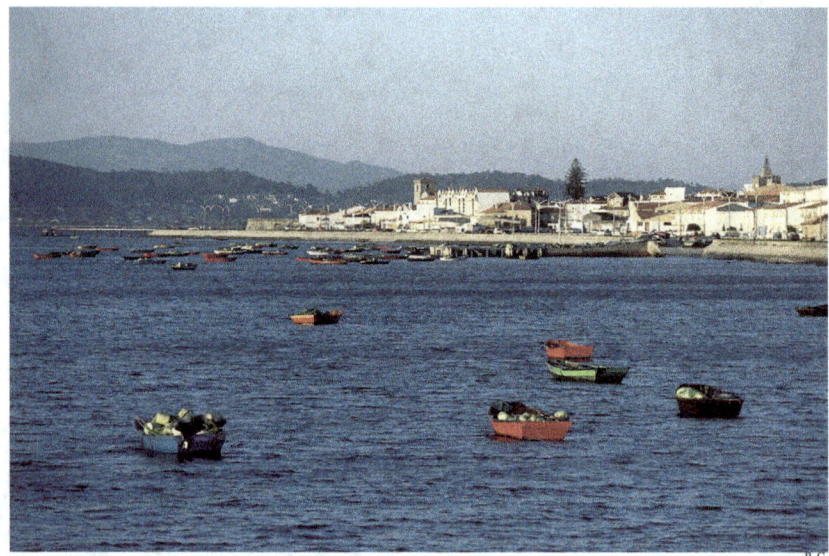

Although it is difficult to date the castle, there is little doubt that it was built at around the same time as the Torre de Belém around 1510-1520, although, originally, it was thought that it was built somewhat later.

Follow the EN13 in the direction of Santa Luzia / Carreço / Vila Praia de Âncora / Vilarinho / Cristelo to Caminha (22 km.).

VI.2 CAMINHA

The old town of Caminha stands at the mouth of the River Minho, facing Galicia and the imposing Monte de Santa Tecla, in Spain. It was an important Mediaeval town that, along with many others, prospered greatly during the era of the Discoveries. The small fishing port that already existed in the 10th century had undergone its first real development thanks to the efforts of D. Afonso III in fortifying and settling the frontiers by creating a defensive frontier cordon that also included Melgaço and Valença beyond the river line. The first wall round Caminha dates from this period. D. Dinis granted the town a charter in 1284. By this time, a clear division had been formed between the original village, located at Vilarelhe, and the new town, which was to develop into modern-day Caminha.

In 1507, Duarte D'Armas depicted Caminha as an oval town with a wall and twelve towers as the first line of defence.

ITINERARY VI *Looking Towards Galicia*
Caminha

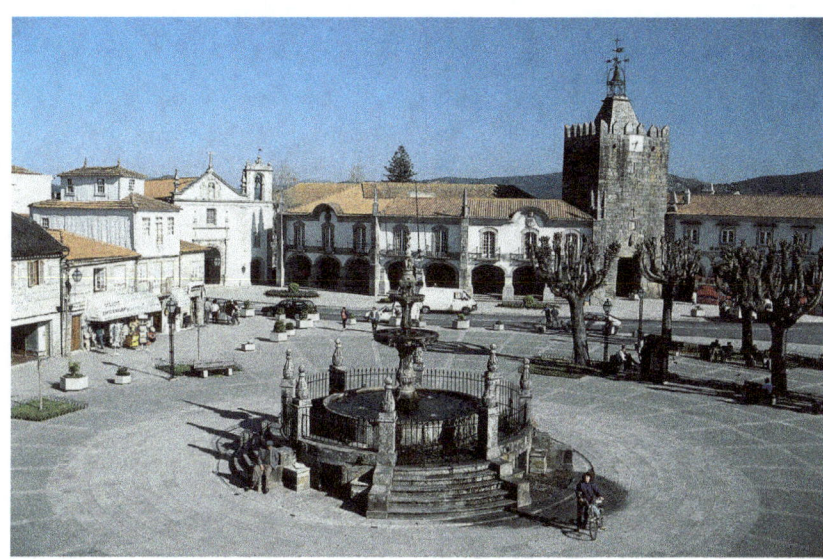

Caminha historic centre.

The keep, rising from a low *barbican* and begun in the time of D. João I, was very much stronger and was concluded in half of the entire *enceinte*. This part of the wall was studded with dozens of embrasures. Outside the walls, a few dwellings belonging to fishermen are shown, as well as some shipbuilding activities, for, in this particular case, the author drew a caravel undergoing extensive alterations.

VI.2.a Historic Centre

Information: Tourist Office (Tel: 258 724100).

The old part of the town is similar to that of Vila do Conde or Viana, having been based on a rectangular grid of dwellings with narrow but straight streets. The fortress changed the area around the Parish Church, the façade of which faces the fort's parade ground instead of the usual square.

The built-up area was, and still is, the main street known as Rua Direita, which begins by the old keep, today the clock tower, Torre do Relógio, at the southern edge of the Mediaeval enclosure. On the other side was the Porta do Sol; the other two parallel streets are Rua do Poço and Rua dos Cavaleiros.

Another important spot in times gone by was the Campo da Feira, where the market was held, originally founded by D. Dinis in 1291. This place marks the site of the town's first great expansion.

ITINERARY VI *Looking Towards Galicia*
Caminha

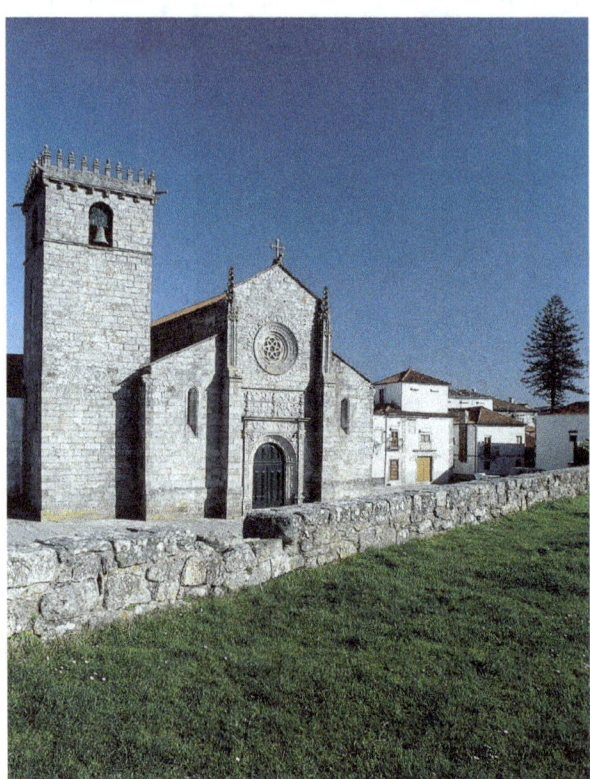

Nossa Senhora da Assunção, Caminha Parish Church.

Nossa Senhora da Assunção, Caminha Parish Church, plan, Boletim da Direcção-Geral dos Edifícios e Monumentos Nacionais, No. 6, Lisbon, 1936.

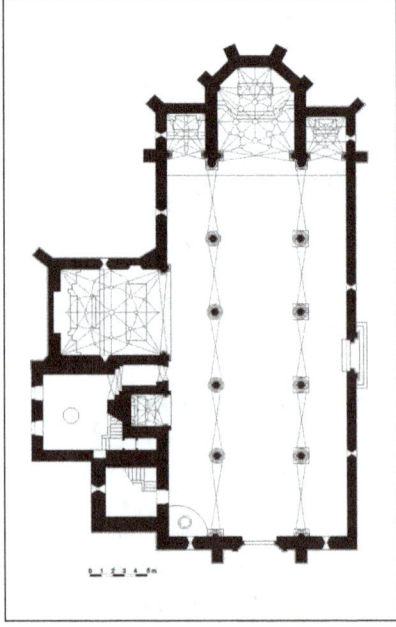

day at 12.00 and at 18.00 in winter and 19.00 in summer.

Work began on the Parish Church in 1488; led by Tomé de Tolosa from Biscay and continued by Pêro Galego, who worked on a number of buildings in Alto Minho. Francisco Fial was yet another Spaniard who worked on the church.
The portals were not concluded until the 1540s, the entrance arch to the Mariners' Chapel is from a similar time period, probably 1551, though it is dated 1151, no doubt a slip on the part of the stonemason. The bell tower probably also served as a watchtower, for its position in relation to the sea certainly suggests this possibility.

In Rua Direita, a number of houses with typically chamfered lintels in the doors and windows have been conserved from the Manueline period.

VI.2.b Nossa Senhora da Assunção (Caminha Parish Church)

Rua Ricardo Joaquim de Sousa. Designated a National Monument. Information: Tourist Office (Tel: 258 921952).
Opening hours: for mass Monday-Saturday at 18.00 in winter and 19.00 in summer, Sun-

The interior with three aisles has a fine, maple Mudéjar ceiling, carved, dated and signed by Fernão Muñoz from Tuy, in 1565. The profile of the longitudinal arcades is of good quality, as are the ribbed vaults of the apse chapels.
On the left, the Chapel of the Brotherhood of Navigators has a depressed rib vault, probably dating from 1530-1540, one of the most elegant examples of the Late Gothic ceiling in Alto Minho, and similar to others in Galicia.
Outside, take note of the very elegant brattishing at the east end, clearly inspired by Braga Cathedral.

Take the EN13 again in the direction of Seixas for Lanhelas (6.5 km.).

VI.3 LANHELAS

VI.3.a Casa da Torre

Next to the EN13, in Lanhelas. Classified as a Building of Public Interest.

One of the oldest houses in the region is the Casa da Torre, a fortified manor house dating from the end of the Middle Ages, but restored at the beginning of the 16th century. The date 1531 is inscribed on one of the towers. Built to a simple rectangular plan, it probably had thinner interior walls forming a courtyard of common rooms and servant's dwellings. The towers are in the Mediaeval tradition, like others still to seen on both sides of the River Minho.

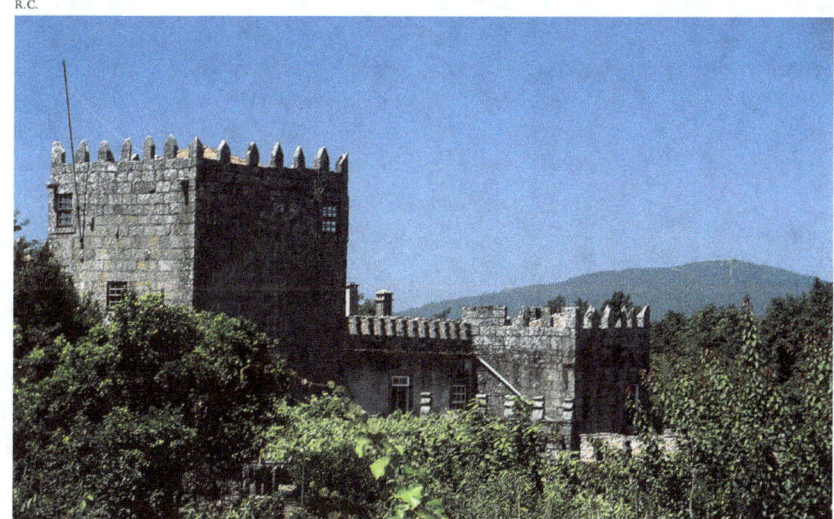

Casa da Torre, Lanhelas.

ITINERARY VI *Looking Towards Galicia*
Vila Nova de Cerveira

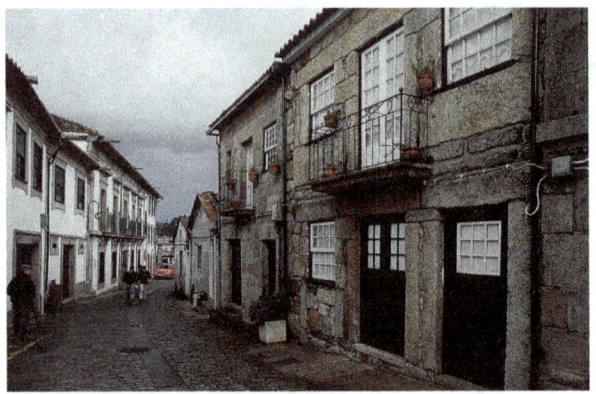

Vila Nova de Cerveira historic centre.

For Vila Nova de Cerveira take the IC1 in the direction of Gondarém / Loivo to Vila Nova de Cerveira (6 km.).

VI.4 VILA NOVA DE CERVEIRA

D. Dinis decided to create a fishing village of about 100 people here in 1320 and, in the following year, the king granted the settlement a charter,

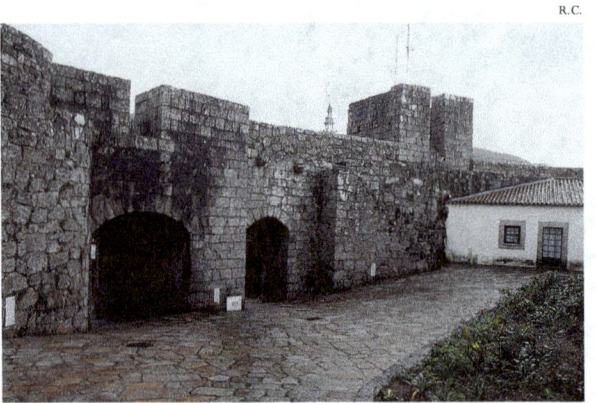

Vila Nova de Cerveira Castle.

renewed by D. Manuel I in 1512. One of the founder's main concerns was to build a walled redoubt or castle, and this project was carried out immediately afterwards. It still retained its 15th-century structure when Duarte D'Armas drew it, depicting a number of houses and churches already spreading beyond the town walls.

Cerveira was not only an important village because of its links with fishing and trading, but also for military activities on a coast that was frequently attacked by pirates.

VI.4.a Castle

Largo do Terreiro. The Castle is now the Pousada D. Dinis. (Tel: 251 708120). Designated a National Monument.

There may have been a Castle in Cerveira before the time of D. Dinis, but only the constructions begun at that period have survived. Some fragments of the elliptical walls that surrounded the old town still remain, as well as the main gateway or the Porta de Nossa Senhora da Ajuda.

The crenellated towers, the type of stone used, and their rectangular shape above the parapet, indicate the castle's 14th-century origin. On the north side, fewer buildings impede the view of the walls, which makes it easier to study their original design and layout. Some fragments of the surrounding *barbican* still remain.

MANORIAL TOWERS OF ALTO MINHO

Pedro Dias

Even today on the banks of the River Minho and throughout the region of Entre Minho-e-Lima, there are a whole host of palaces dating back to the Middle Ages, to the time when Portugal was beginning to take shape as a nation.

These palaces were the residences of the lords of the region and were initially little more than sober-looking square towers with two or three storeys, where the nobles protected themselves against the attacks of their neighbours, who fought with them over possession of farmland, watercourses, forests and serfs, not to mention the favours of the king.

The *inquirições* (surveys of aristocratic patrimony) and the *confirmações* (ratifications), ordered by the Crown in the mid-13th century, provide us with accounts concerning the deeds of these nobles and the oppression that they exercised over the common people, whilst at the same time evading the payment of the taxes due, and, more generally, the king's authority as a whole. Placed at strategic points, overlooking the surrounding countryside, these towers were used as watchtowers and simultaneously served as symbols of their inhabitants' power. Even so, those who lived in them dwelt in extremely precarious conditions, in a situation that was unthinkable, even for the simple bourgeoisie of the 15th and 16th centuries. Despite their modest living conditions, the manorial towers stood as emblems of the ancestral line of the families whose roots were firmly planted in these estates or *quintas*. Indeed, it was frequent for the serfs' huts and cottages to accumulate around them, together with some chapels or churches.

Thus, when they reached a new era, a time when concern for the body and physical comfort became more important than

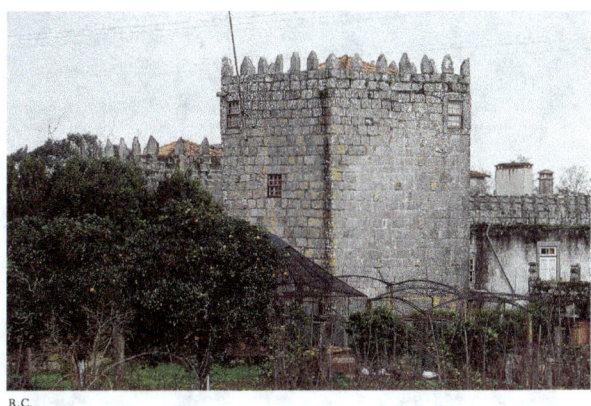

Torre de Lanheses.

concern for spiritual well-being, the nobility of the Minho, just as their Galician counterparts had done before them, enlarged their palaces, conferring upon them a certain grandeur and much greater comfort, but preserving their fortified nature, because times were still uncertain. The walls of the new halls and chambers were crowned with battlements in an evocation of their inhabitants' warlike past.

The next few centuries continued to be a period of grandeur and renewal, but not even the luxurious nature of Baroque decoration was sufficient to bring down these towers, which were now incorporated into genuine palace complexes and remained as both reminders and guarantees of their owners' nobility.

The Casa do Paço de Geraz do Lima; the Paço do Courutelo de Freixo; the Paço de Bertiandos; the Casa de Quintela, in Nogueira; the Casa da Torre de Aguiã; the Paço de Giela, in Arcos; the Casa da Torre in Lanhelas; and the Torre de Lapela are just some of the examples to be found in a long list of Late Gothic buildings that have left their distinctive mark on the landscape of Alto Minho.

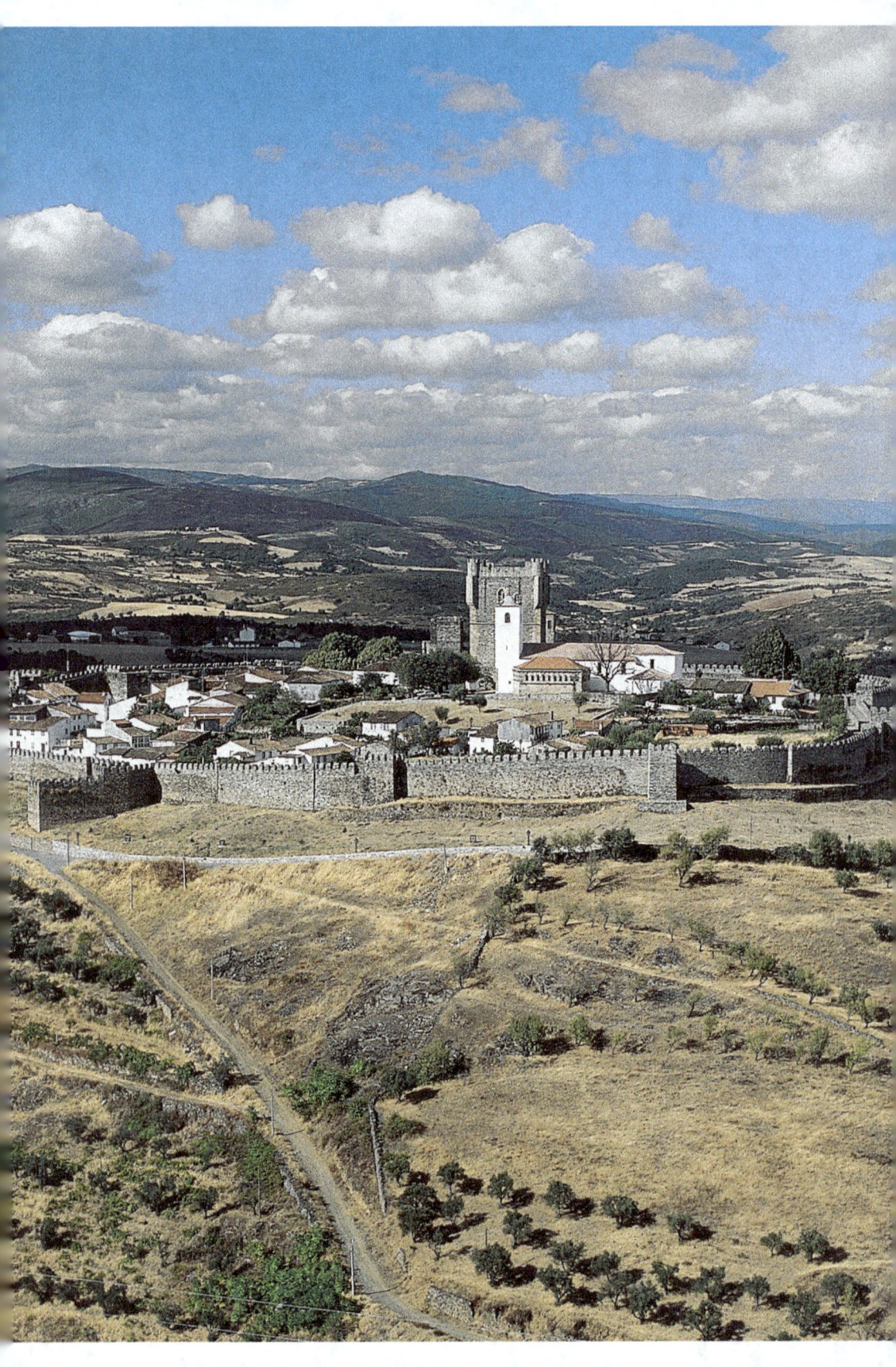

ITINERARY VII

Lands of the Sabor and the Douro

Pedro Dias, Dalila Rodrigues,
Nuno Vassallo e Silva, Fernando Grilo

VII.1 BRAGANÇA
    VII.1.a Castle
    VII.1.b Church of Santa Maria

VII.2 MIRANDA DO DOURO
    VII.2.a Historic Centre
    VII.2.b Castle

VII.3 MOGADOURO (option)
    VII.3.a Castle
    VII.3.b São Mamede (Mogadouro Parish Church)

VII.4 FREIXO DE ESPADA À CINTA
    VII.4.a Historic Centre
    VII.4.b Castle
    VII.4.c São Miguel (Freixo de Espada à Cinta Parish Church)
    VII.4.d Church of Misericórdia

The Livro das Fortalezas *by Duarte D'Armas*

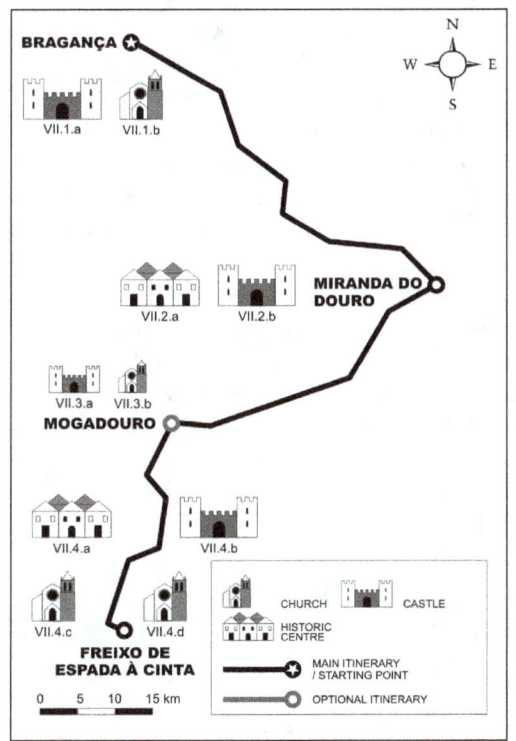

Panoramic view of Bragança Castle.

ITINERARY VII   *Lands of the Sabor and the Douro*
Bragança

The lands bordered by the River Sabor to the west, and the River Douro to the east, make up a unit with quite unique characteristics. Hot in the summer and capable of plummeting to Alpine temperatures in the chill of winter, girdled by stern and almost insurmountable valleys, they have a cultural and social character that has a surprising vitality. It is somehow quite right that here, around Miranda, the other language of Portugal is spoken, *Mirandês*, recently recognised as an official language.

Politically dependent on León until the 12th century, even after the Treaty of Zamora was signed in 1143, the region continued to live turned towards the east, in permanent dialogue with the people of Zamora, León and other inhabitants of important cities and towns like Toro and Sahagún.

D. Sancho I wished to develop the region, granting charters to various towns, but the definitive turnabout, an attraction towards the coast, had to wait until the Manueline era. The dry ports, meanwhile, continued to be the most important in the kingdom, and D. Manuel I, known as the "Fortunate", ordered the reform of a ring of castles, to defend the ports and simultaneously remind his parents-in-law, Ferdinand and Isabella of Spain, that they were in his domain.

Few of the fortresses from that time have survived, but they are known about through the drawings made in 1507 by Duarte D'Armas. At the foot of these castles, villages spread, churches were built, and urban systems were put into place.

The Benedictine monks settled in Bragança, where they developed more prosperous agriculture, guaranteeing their self-sufficiency. On the banks of the River Douro, the Order of Christ had the task of settlement and administration, and many artistic references to the time of the commendaries and commendators have survived to be admired today.

Three places are of particular note: Bragança, today the capital of north-east, Miranda, which was the see of the first diocese in Trás-os-Montes, and Freixo de Espada à Cinta (literally, the "ash-tree of the girt sword"), were all equally important at the beginning of the 16th century, but destined to change in the following centuries. Manueline fortresses still mark the landscape and, within them, are Late Gothic churches and chapels different from those on the coast or in the south. Working on them were great artists from León and Castile, like Gregório Fernandez, or from Biscay, like João de Castilho, as well as some Portuguese artists, such as the legendary Grão Vasco, whose magnificent retable, by one of his disciples, is today an emblem of Freixo.

VII.I BRAGANÇA

Like most settlements in the Trás-os-Montes region, Bragança seems to

Lands of the Sabor and the Douro
Bragança

have already been settled in the Prehistoric period, certainly since Neolithic, if not Palaeolithic times. This does not mean that there was an important community, but that there were some family groups or small populations. In the Bragança area, the Hill-Fort of Castro de Avelãs, perhaps lying in the original position of the Mediaeval town, seems to have been the most important.

Due to its strategic, and primarily military importance, but also in order to control traffic between the young Kingdom of Portugal and the neighbouring Kingdom of León and Castile, D. Dinis granted the town its first charter in 1187, a charter that was successively renewed, firstly by D. Afonso III, in 1253, and later by D. Manuel I, in 1514.

During the first dynasty, development was partially due to the annual fair, initiated by D. Afonso III, in 1272, and the free fair started by D. Fernando in 1383, which lasted a month. The fact of the matter was that it was extremely difficult to attract people to this area, far from the coast, with a harsh climate and a rather delicate geographical position. It was also very close to the frontier and was one of the first areas of confrontation whenever Peninsular governments had a disagreement. Nevertheless, agricultural activity and cattle breeding were significant, as was trade with Castile.

In 1442, on the creation of the House of the Dukes of Bragança, the town, later

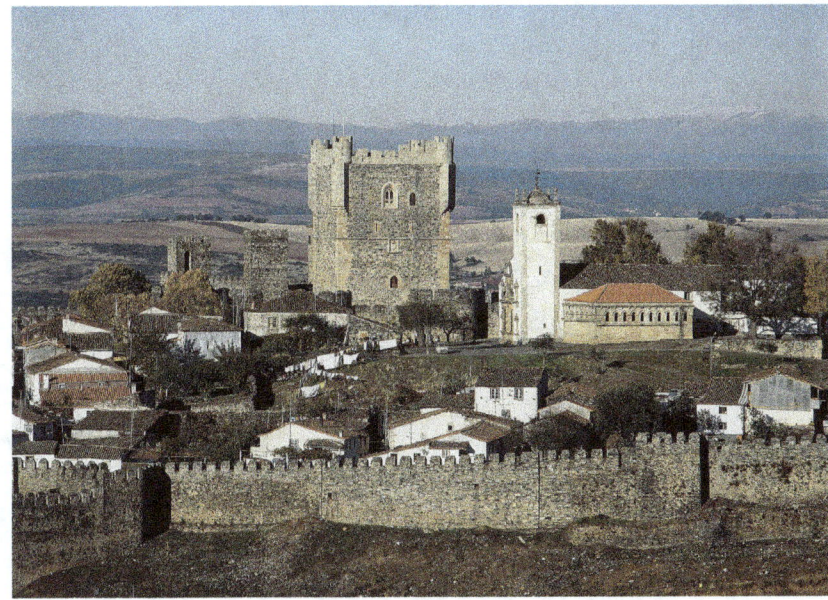

Bragança.

ITINERARY VII *Lands of the Sabor and the Douro*

Bragança

Panoramic view of Bragança Castle.

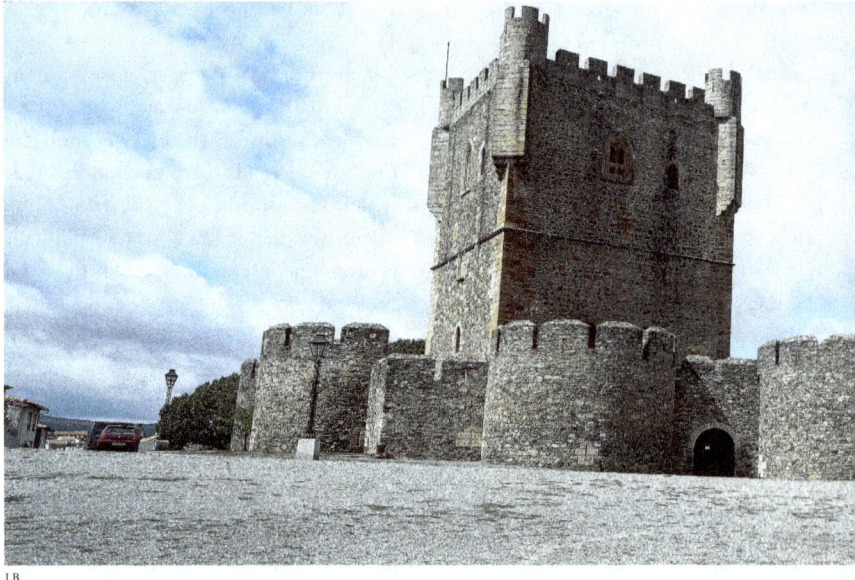

J.B.

made a city, came into the possession of D. Afonso, the first duke, until it returned to the Crown, when the eighth duke ascended the throne as D. João IV, in 1640.

As in all the frontier towns and villages, the Manueline peace provided a considerable increase in economic activities and a subsequent growth in population, largely of Jewish origin, so that, by 1530, it numbered 2,000 inhabitants.

VII.1.a **Castle**

The Military Museum is in the keep. (Tel: 273 322378). Designated a National Monument. Admission charge. Opening hours: 09.00-12.00 and 14.00-17.00, except on Thursdays and public holidays.

The Mediaeval castle is at the heart of Bragança, as it has been for over 700 years. It has undergone successive phases of construction, the most important being that which took place in the mid-15th century, even though it was a continuation of those ordered by D. João I. The *Livro das Fortalezas* by Duarte D'Armas, shows what the castle and settlement were like in the time of D. Manuel I.

The upper part of the castle was the strongest and was adapted as living quarters for the *alcaide* and the dukes when they made their rare visits to their dukedom. The first work must date

ITINERARY VII   *Lands of the Sabor and the Douro*
Bragança

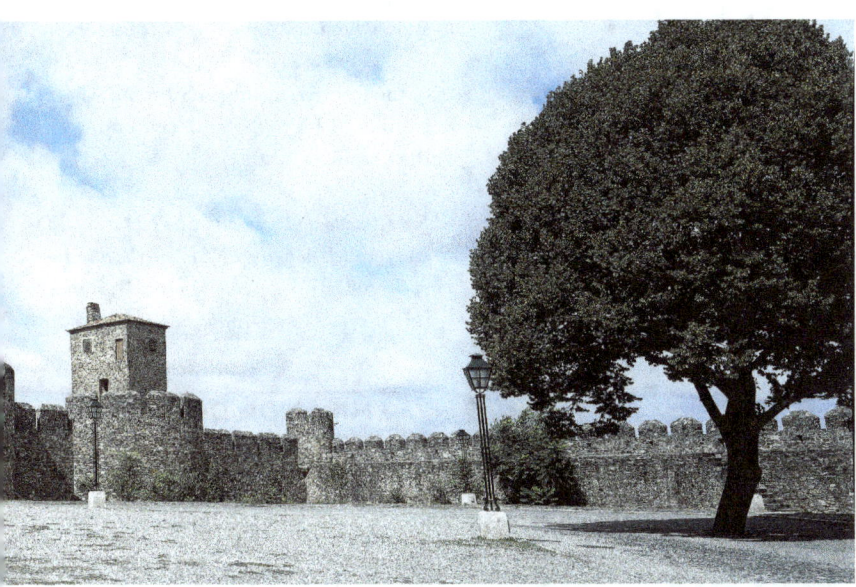

back to the reign of D. Sancho I, and further work was done during the reign of D. Afonso III. To the side was the centre of the city, the oldest part with narrow streets that formed a radiating network marked by a street joining the two gateways. The Church of Santa Maria stands inside the fortress proper, immediately abutting the cistern with, on the upper floor, the council chamber or *domus municipalis* with pierced rounded arches.

The large tower of the keep, 30 m. high and 16 m. at the base seems to have been built between 1409 and 1449, and remains much the same today: dominating and gigantic. There are large rooms on the upper floors and a terrace with projecting towers at the corners. The keep is linked to the first enclosure by passages around the five-sided castle, with straight *curtain walls* with forward cubes or low, semi-circular towers with embrasures to allow sweeping fire with primitive firearms.

The remodelled, high Princess Tower that existed in 1507, is also important, standing well above the parapet and prepared for living quarters when not required for military purposes.

The walls of the town occupied the remainder of the hillock, significantly increasing available defended space in the Mediaeval tradition. The wall is high, wide and surmounted by battlements with irregularly placed towers that protected the 2-m.-wide parapet.

ITINERARY VII Lands of the Sabor and the Douro
Miranda do Douro

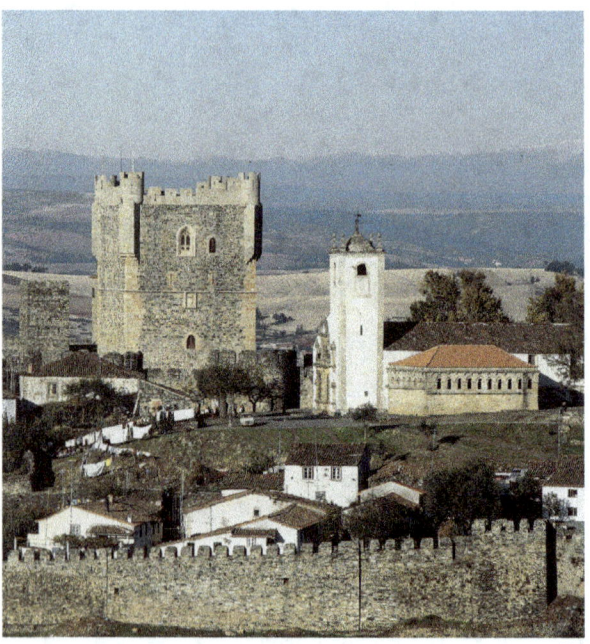

Church of Santa Maria, Bragança.

VII.1.b Church of Santa Maria

Situated inside the castle walls. Information: Junta de Freguesia (Parish Council Tel: 271 322181).
Opening hours: 09.00-12.00 and 14.00-18.00, except Thursdays.

This is the only church in Bragança that has retained its Manueline structure, as it benefited from numerous improvements in later eras. The first documentation dates back to 1258. At the beginning of the 16th century, the duke contracted a master builder to construct the arcade that marks the vessel of the church and divides the three aisles. This work was done in brick, in the *Mudejar* tradition, a style which continued for a considerable time in this area and also on the other side of the frontier, mainly in Sahagún, where, from the 12th to the 16th century, it was the dominant aesthetic.

For Miranda do Douro take the E217 to Izeda and turn left onto the EN317, in the direction of Santulhão / Carção to Vimioso. From there, take the EN218 to Miranda do Douro.

VII.2 MIRANDA DO DOURO

The history of Miranda do Douro goes back to the time of the first King D. Afonso Henriques, who set up an enclosure of shelters to encourage settlers, in a harsh, remote area where there was only a small hamlet. There was little success at first and it was only in the time of D. Dinis, in 1286, that the settlement was raised to town status. Its position on the frontier with the neighbouring kingdom encouraged trade and local craftsmanship and eventually the town was made the see of the diocese in 1545.

The Manueline era, a time of peaceful association with Castile, was one of great prosperity and a large number of both Portuguese and Spanish Jews, converted or not, settled here. New houses and churches were built, as well as public buildings, such as the Customs House, and naturally the defences were completely overhauled and renovated. This led to a polarisation between Miranda and Bragança and a healthy dispute between primacies, privi-

ITINERARY VII   *Lands of the Sabor and the Douro*
Miranda do Douro

leges and development. A large part of the city's Manueline heritage disappeared with the explosion of the gun powder store at the Castle on 8th May 1762.

VII.2.a Historic Centre

Information: Tourist Office (Tel: 273 431132).

More than any single Manueline building, the historic centre is worth visiting for the whole ensemble of the Old Town that includes edifices from the time of D. Manuel I, or later, though still in the Late Gothic style. The Castle is on the high ground with the remains of the old wall. In Rua da Costanilha, which leads to Praça D. João III, and in the side streets, there are a number of well-conserved 16th-century houses with pointed or rounded doors and window frames, or straight lintels that, chronologically speaking, must have been built later than 1521.

VII.2.b Castle

The Castle can be reached from Largo do Castelo. Classified as a Building of Public Interest. Information: Tourist Office (Tel: 273 431132). Opening hours: the Castle may be visited at any time.

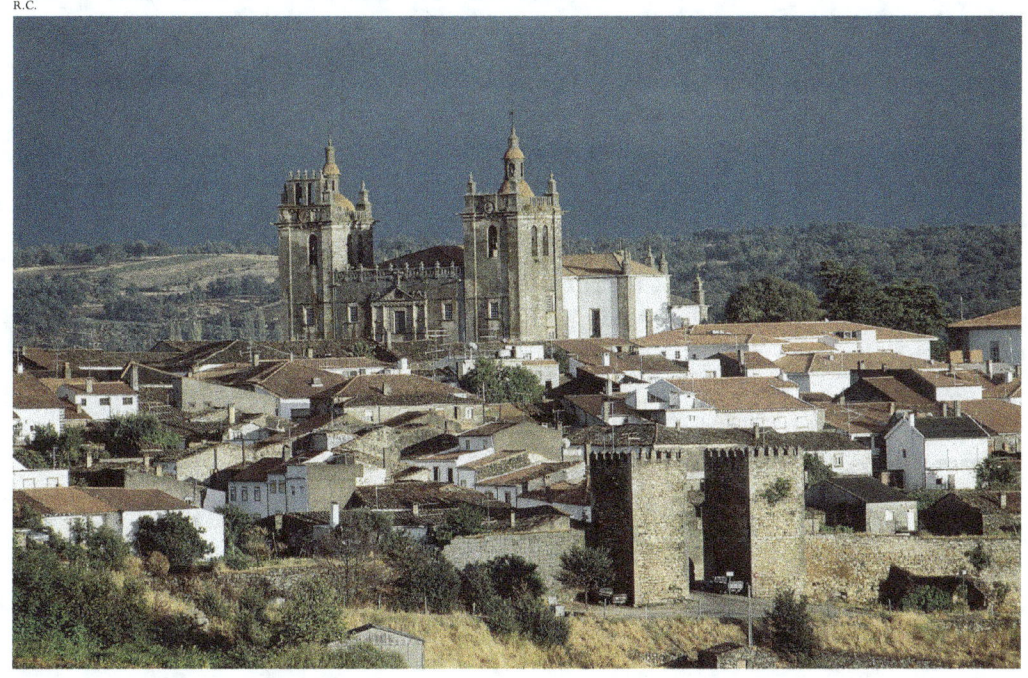

Partial view, Miranda do Douro.

ITINERARY VII   *Lands of the Sabor and the Douro*
Mogadouro

Miranda do Douro Castle and historic centre.

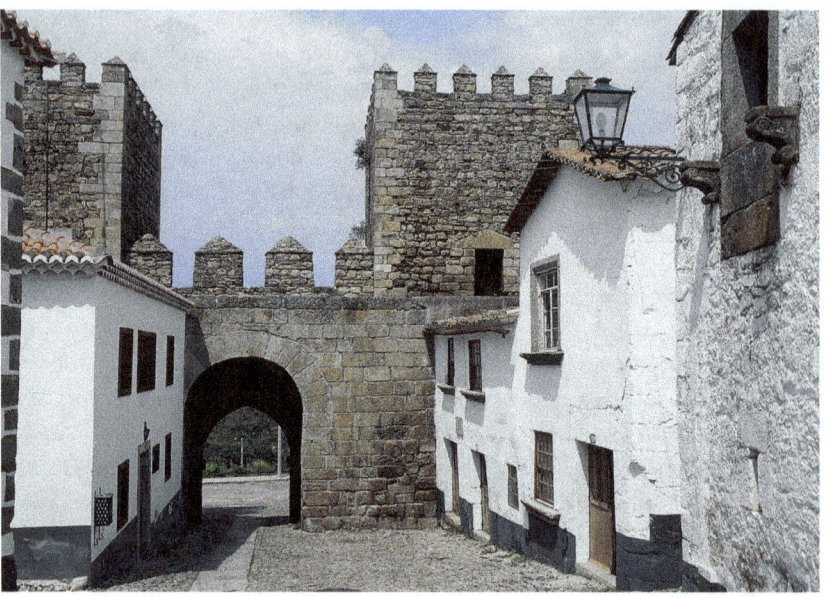

The Castle probably dates back to the period when the settlement was raised to town status, but it was enlarged and improved throughout the first and second dynasties, mainly in the reign of D. João I, when the structure was reinforced.

New and extensive work took place later as part of the Manueline policy of strengthening the frontier with Castile, and the *curtain walls* that do still exist, and the keep in the old fortress, date from this time. According to the plan drawn by Duarte D'Armas, the fort at that time was quadrangular in shape, with towers at the corners, probably built in the time of D. Dinis. There were also *barbicans*, passageways and even a polygonal bulwark with embrasures. This latter feature was probably the first of its kind in Portugal, although it, too, has unfortunately disappeared.

All that remains of the Manueline work on the Castle and the walls facing the Douro is the Porta do Amparo, strong and well defended by flanking towers that rise above the parapet.

For either Mogadouro or Freixo de Espada à Cinta, take the EN221, passing through part of the Douro Natural Park.

VII.3 **MOGADOURO** (option)

Mogadouro became important on the regional scene after it received a charter from D. Afonso III in the 13th century. Despite the fact that the parish depended on the Diocese of Zamora, a commendatory of the Knights Templar was set up here, and, with the extinction of the Order by the Pope, it was transferred to the Order of Christ at the initiative of D. Dinis. It was during this period that the town developed, and improvements were carried out on the castle and the town walls.

In the 15th century, the town was dominated by the Távoras, one of the most powerful families in the country, who built a residence within the walls. Franciscan friars also built a monastery here, which was unfortunately destroyed by fire in the 19th century.

As occurred with all the commendaries of the Order of Christ, Mogadouro was greatly improved following a visit paid to the town by D. Manuel I, the Administrator of the Order, in 1510.

VII.3.a Castle

Largo do Castelo. Designated a National Monument. Information: Câmara Municipal (Town Hall Tel: 279 340100).

Opening hours: the castle can be visited at any time.

Very little is left of the Mediaeval and Manueline castle other than the remains of the *curtain walls* and the rectangular and sturdy keep. It was the centre of the old castle, which also accommodated the commendator, a courtyard, and barracks for the garrison. A short distance away, there is a short *barbican*, in a line with the higher walls.

VII.3.b São Mamede (Mogadouro Parish Church)

Opening hours: the Church is open on the 1st and 3rd Sunday in each month, 11.00-12.00, for the celebration of mass. To see the Church at any other time, please contact the Câmara Municipal (Town Hall Tel: 279 340100).

The old Manueline Parish Church was altered during the Baroque period, but the main structure still remains. Note the very simple main door and the chancel with an excellent rib vault with the royal coat of arms of D. Manuel I on the central boss.

Leave Mogadouro by the EN221 heading southwards and passing through Figueira / Meirinhos / Fornos and Mazouco. Freixo de Espada à Cinta is 6 km. further on.

VII.4 FREIXO DE ESPADA À CINTA

The town dates back to the time of D. Afonso Henriques, who encouraged settlement in 1152 at a time when there was said to be a castle there. This castle must obviously have been a small defensive structure, which did not withstand the ravages of time. The town became a cen-

ITINERARY VII   Lands of the Sabor and the Douro
Freixo de Espada à Cinta

General view of Freixo de Espada à Cinta including the historic centre.

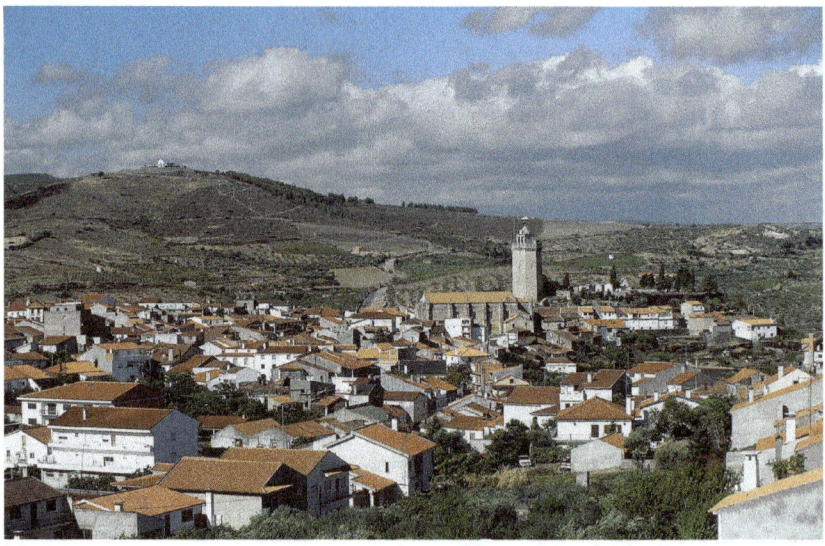

tre for trade with León and Old Castile, and was granted a new charter by D. Afonso III in 1272.

The negotiations between D. Dinis and Alfonso X, that culminated in the lands of Riba-Côa entering the Portuguese orbit, made Freixo more important and called for a new series of fortifications. The castle, however, was still not completed in 1342.

The area around the town dealt in the production of cereal and cattle rearing, whilst within the walls there was a budding silk- and wool-weaving industry, which encouraged trade with other regions and the frontier area of Castile. In 1527, Freixo was the most important town in the area with 447 dwellings. Many people set out from there on Manueline maritime adventures, the most important of them all being Jorge Álves who served brilliantly in the East.

VII.4.a Historic Centre

Information: Câmara Municipal (Town Hall Tel: 279 658070).

In the historic centre of the town of Freixo is a remarkable ensemble of 16th-century houses, with narrow streets, such as Rua Flores and Rua Direita that converge at the Parish Church and the Old Castle. The town is built on a radiating grid, the civic centre being between the Parish Church and the Santa Casa da Misericórdia. The houses usually have two storeys; the ground floor used for commercial activities, handicrafts or to shelter animals. Manueline Late Gothic lintels and doorposts are frequently bordered by naturalistic elements, some dating to 1552; the date carved on the Casa dos Carrascos, and even later dates. This style continued in religious architecture, as can be seen by the private Church of the Misericórdia. No doubt this was due not only to influences from across the border, but also to the master builders who worked in Portugal.

VII.4.b Castle

Praça Jorge Álves. Designated a National Monument. Information: Sr. Gouveia, Biblioteca de Freixo de Espada à Cinta (Library Tel: 279 653445).
Opening hours: daily 8.30-16.00.

Only some half-destroyed *curtain walls* and a beautiful seven-sided tower remain from the old walls and enclosure that existed in Manueline times, with a parapet projecting over the terrace. The Manueline *barbican* was integrated in the *enceinte* at the point of greatest vigilance in the town, close to the Parish Church, so that all the surrounding countryside could be seen. The castle, built on an almost circular plan, was probably built in the 13th century, but was extensively remodelled and enlarged during the reign of D. Manuel I.

VII.4.c São Miguel (Freixo de Espada à Cinta Parish Church)

Praça Jorge Álvares. Designated a National Monument. Information: Sr. Gouveia, Biblioteca de Freixo de Espada à Cinta (Library Tel: 279 653445).
Opening hours: 09.30-12.30 and 14.00-17.30. The Church is closed on Mondays and

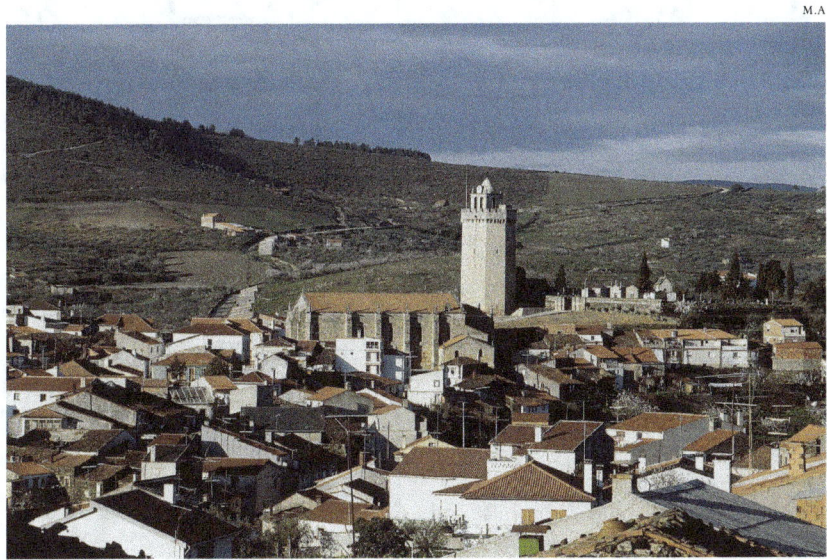

Freixo de Espada à Cinta historic centre.

ITINERARY VII *Lands of the Sabor and the Douro*
Freixo de Espada à Cinta

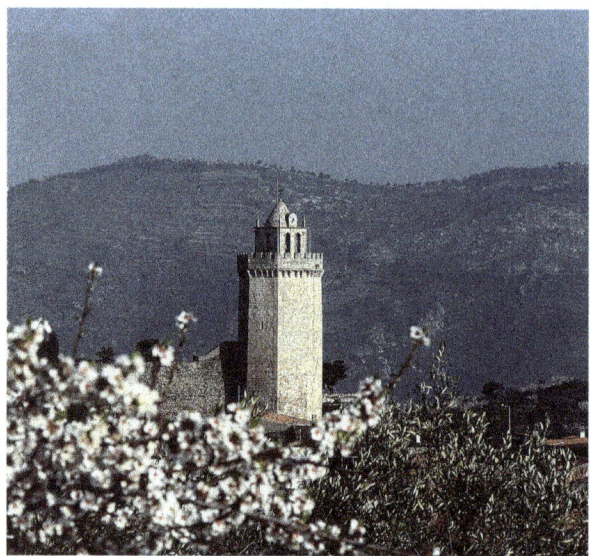

Tower of the castle, Freixo de Espada à Cinta.

on Tuesday mornings, and on January 1st, Easter, May 1st and December 25th.

This Late Gothic Parish Church was begun in the reign of D. Manuel I, and, therefore, some time before 1521. It took a while to complete, the vault dating from the time of D. João III.

Its plan is, however, homogeneous and may have possibly been by a Biscayan architect or master builder, perhaps even João Castilho, who married a young woman from the neighbouring Spanish town of Quintanilla.

It is a *hall-church*, with depressed vaulting supported by elongated piers, which demonstrate the great technical skill of those responsible. The portal and decorative elements are more vernacular and rude, built by less erudite men.

Freixo de Espada à Cinta Parish Church, plan, Boletim da Direcção-Geral dos Edifícios e Monumentos Nacionais, No. 70.

The interior of the church is divided into three aisles and five bays, the vaulting being linked to the outside buttresses. The apse has three parallel chapels with simple angled vaulting, whilst the vault in the chancel is more developed with the royal coat of arms on the central boss, and the armillary sphere on the intermediate ribs.

In the chancel, 16 panels have been preserved amongst the Baroque carved-gilded woodwork. These belonged to the 16th-century retable, which was located in this chapel until the early 18th century. They are currently distributed in a random fashion, bearing no relationship to the organisation that they would have had in the original retable. Because of their narrative sequence and their unequal sizes, the scenes from the *Life of the Virgin*

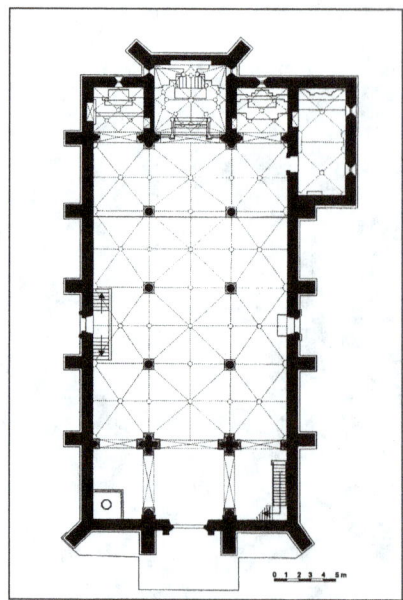

188

ITINERARY VII Lands of the Sabor and the Douro
Freixo de Espada à Cinta

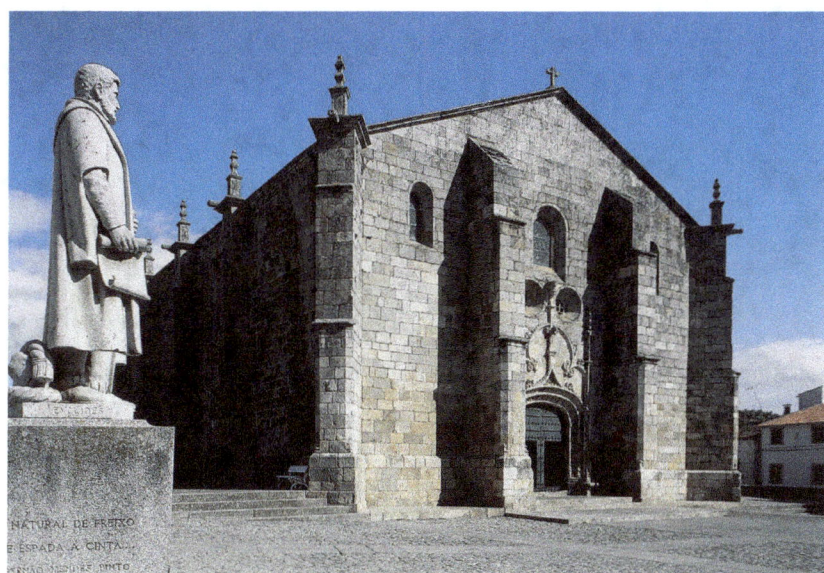

São Miguel, Freixo de Espada à Cinta Parish Church, main façade.

and the *Childhood and Passion of Christ* were placed in rows and had an essentially pedagogical and decorative function.

There is no historical information available as to the date and author of this work. However, its visual language and the figurative models used, allow us to place it amidst the production of Vasco Fernandes's workshop in Viseu, and to propose a date somewhere around 1535. Despite the poor state of conservation of these panels and some already irrecoverable losses, as is the case with the *Assumption of the Virgin,* they reveal a remarkable sensitivity to the effects of light, which is used with great mastery to create space between the figures. This effect can be seen, for example, in the *Presentation at the Temple* and *Calvary.*

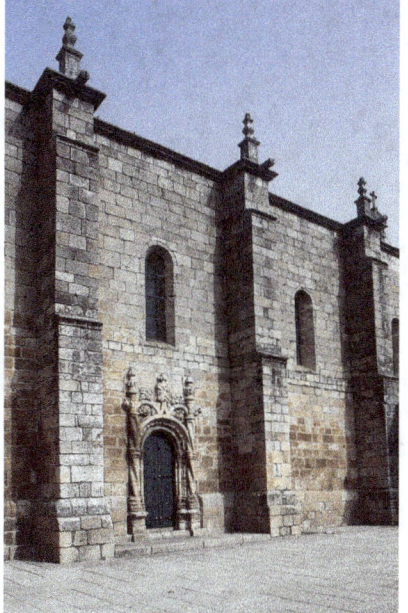

São Miguel, Freixo de Espada à Cinta Parish Church, side portal.

Freixo de Espada à Cinta

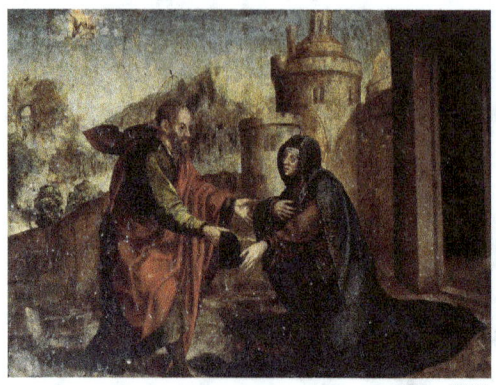

"St Anne and St Joachim", from the retable of Freixo de Espada à Cinta Parish Church.

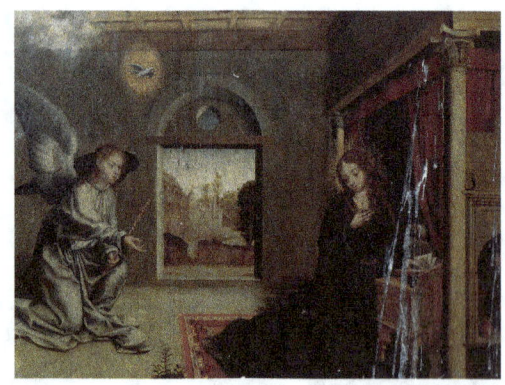

"The Annunciation", from the retable of Freixo de Espada à Cinta Parish Church.

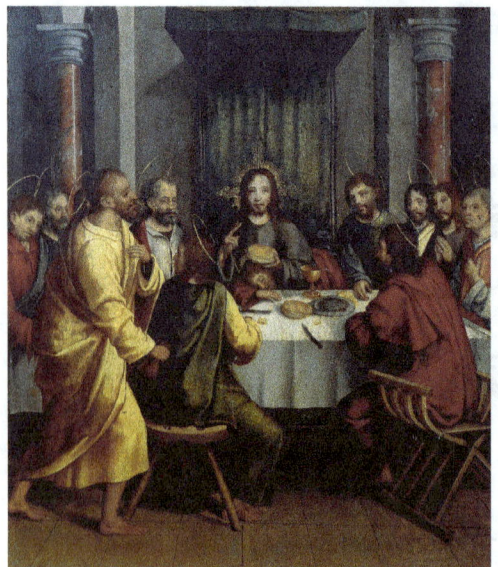

"The Last Supper", from the retable of Freixo de Espada à Cinta Parish Church.

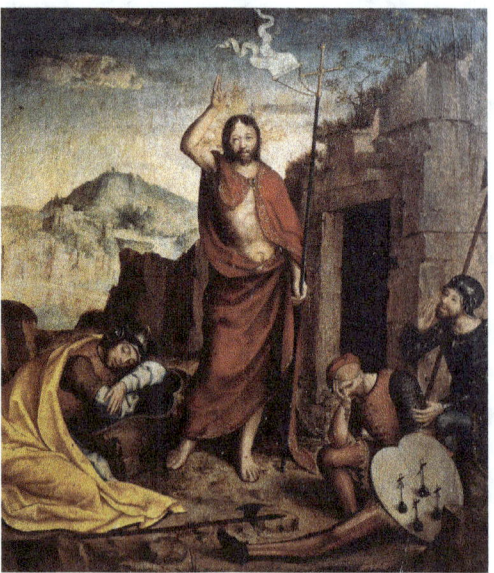

"Resurrection", from the retable of Freixo de Espada à Cinta Parish Church.

The fragment of carved gilded woodwork, depicting the four writers of the Gospels, which currently stands on the altar of the right-hand chapel, might have been part of the structure of the original retable. It was probably the work of the Flemish sculptor and wood carver, Arnau de Carvalho, who worked with the painters from Viseu and made a series of retables for various churches in the region.

VII.4.d Church of Misericórdia

The Misericórdia Church is in the same square as the Parish Church. Those wishing to visit the church should contact the Santa Casa da Misericórdia (Tel: 279 653016). Designated a Building of Public Interest.

The Misericórdia Church is one of the finest examples of how the Late Gothic style continued to be used throughout the second half of the 16th century, following a type that had become crystallised at the height of the Manueline period. The church has a simple main vessel,

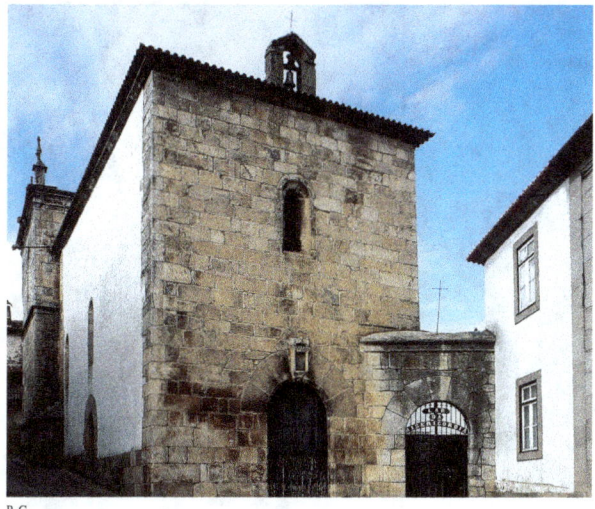

R.C.

with its façade facing onto the square, a large plain portal with wide *voussoirs* in the Castile style, and a vaulted chancel. However, the documentary evidence is quite clear, showing that this beautiful example of thick, curved rib vaulting was only completed in 1555. Its bosses, either merely decorative or heraldic in design, are already from the Renaissance period.

Church of Misericórdia, Freixo de Espada à Cinta.

THE *LIVRO DAS FORTALEZAS*, BY DUARTE D'ARMAS

Pedro Dias

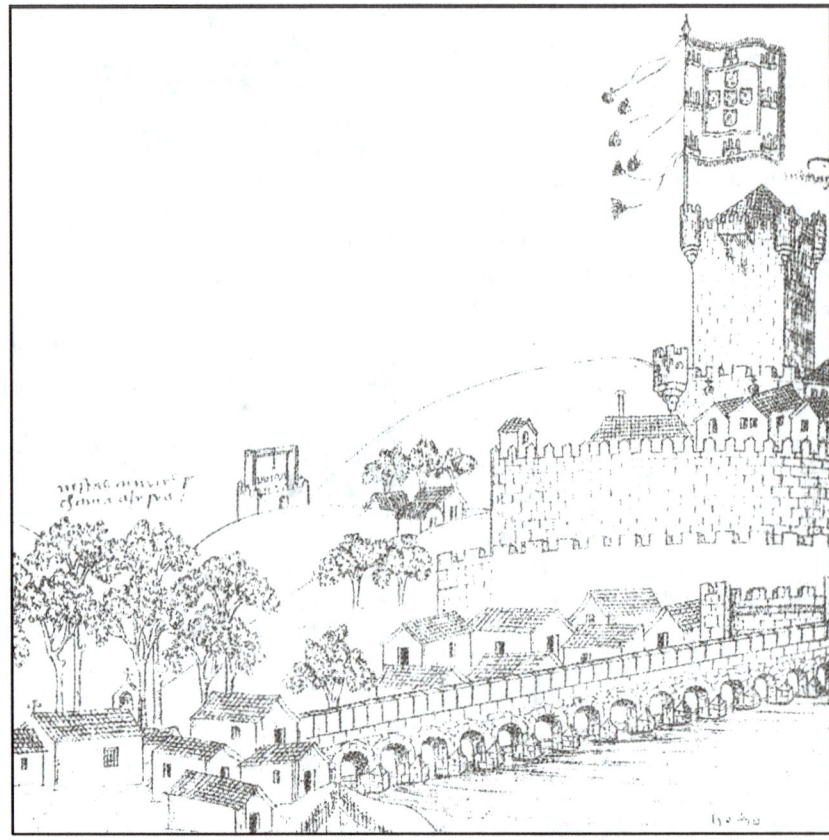

Duarte D'Armas, "Livro das Fortalezas", 16th-century drawing of Chaves, detail.

Duarte D'Armas, a squire to the House of D. Manuel I, had an enormous talent for drawing and was, therefore, used in systematic campaigns for the drawing of the general views of cities and even for topographical and hydrographic surveys of lands overseas, at least in Morocco and the Azores. His fame was such that the chronicler João de Barros mentioned him in his *Crónica de D. Manuel*.

One of his main tasks was to study the fortresses built along the frontier and condense all this information into one single book, which he called quite simply the *Livro das Fortalezas* (Book of Fortresses). Two copies of this book have been preserved until the present day, one at the Instituto dos Arquivos Nacionais/Torre do Tombo (National Archives) in Lisbon, and the other at the National Library in Madrid. Both are known by the same name and have 110 panoramic views of cities and 51 plans of castles, situated between Castro Marim and Caminha, in the so-called 'A' manuscript, which also includes two non-frontier towns, Sintra and Barcelos. In this copy of the book, the drawing is more detailed and there is much more information than in the 'B' manuscript, where there are only 57 views of 29 fortresses. It should also be noted that the author depicted himself on various occasions, during this journey that he made in 1509, which resulted in the most perfect and complete portrait of Manueline rural Portugal.

The Stonemason
"The stonemason from the Douro region takes delight in his work, taking great pains to be perfect in his finishing touches, piling stone upon stone as if he were composing a mosaic — using the schist that, as soon as it is washed after the first rain, shines with metallic reflections, ranging from the warm colour of copper to the moonlit tones of silver. These surfaces stretch for mile after mile, following one another like the waves of a petrified sea, always composed with the same taste, but no less dazzling because of this. There is a continuous uniformity in the interweaving of these surfaces, akin to the beauty of a curtain that constantly repeats the same colour and pattern, unalterable yet perfect.

The artist adds more to the merely functional requirements of his work, taking delight in composing such vast sections of wall, perfect in the use of his skilful, sensitive hands, enamoured with and fully cognisant of the stone's secrets. The way in which he manipulates this stone, not imprisoned by any form of mortar, piling block upon block, with the certain support of the small cracked stones wedged in between them, all clearly points to how much he appreciates the value and uses of the raw material with which he is working. But, in choosing the stone, in making the most elegant composition and careful gradation of the colour, he achieves truly magnificent mottled effects, with gentle hues, displaying his artistic taste. His pleasure and, at the same time, his awareness of the work he is doing are more than evident, visible in the touching respect that he shows for the material with which he is working and, above all, in his exemplary devotion to his craft. These walls are quite admirable, providing us with a lesson in the humble and simple process of their making, but they also display the enchantment produced by someone who takes pride in his art, however primitive and rustic it may be. Man projects himself in all his work, in the passion or contempt that may be contained within his feelings. (...)

The loving hand that works the stone, even knowing it to be limited in its possibilities, feels that in some way he may be able to highlight its beauty. He then composes the masonry, just as blankets are woven from rags on the rustic loom, whether he is building the walls of a house or laying in place the lintel of the door or window, or raising the walls of the terraced vineyards. The effect is like vast tapestries of natural colour, producing an intense dark brown here, sometimes fading into yellow hues, other times with flecks of grey, or even a rare, strange, surprising blue."

Manuel Mendes, Roteiro Sentimental: Douro, *Lisbon, 1964.*

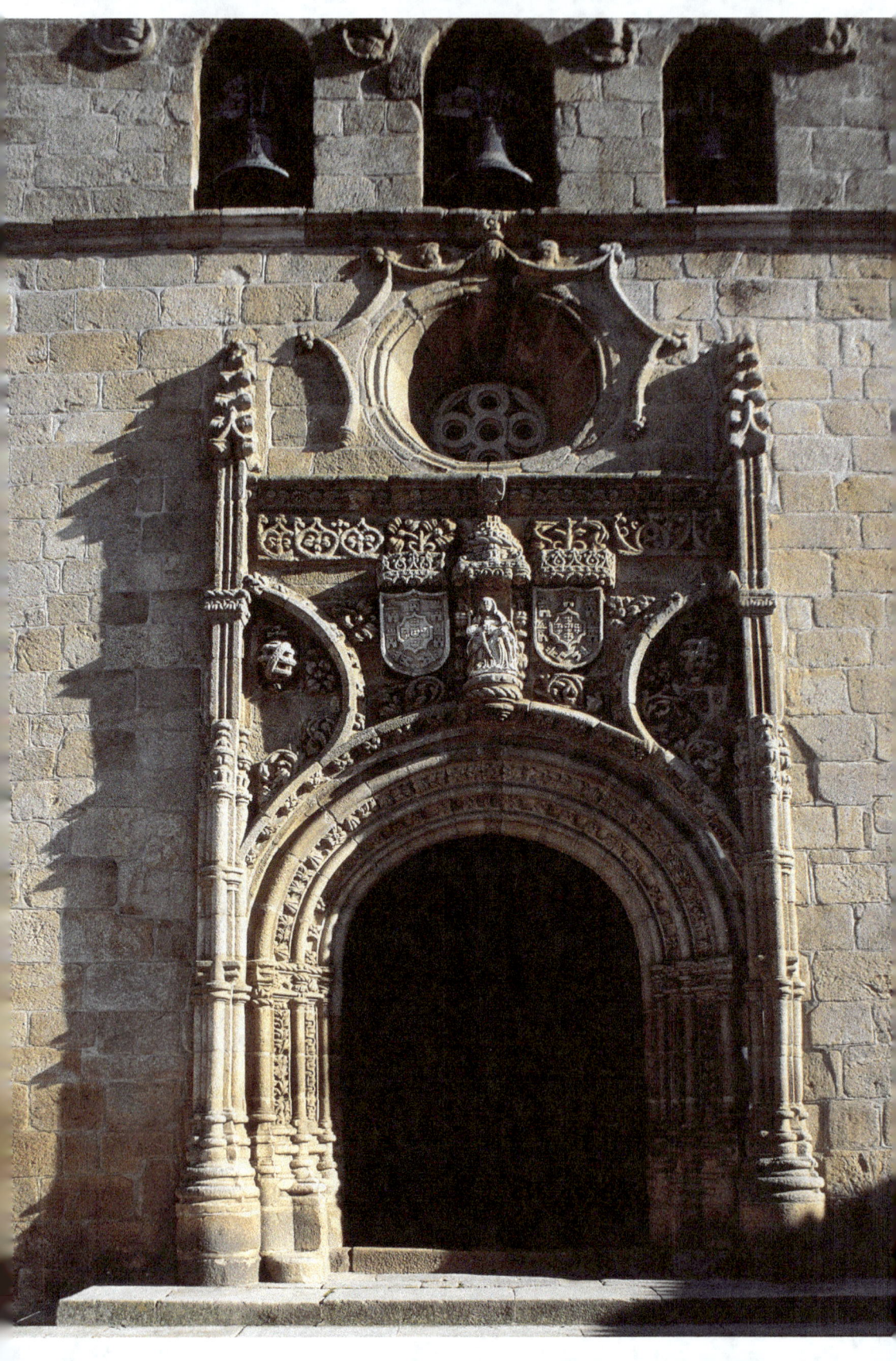

ITINERARY VIII

Frontier Churches and Castles

Pedro Dias, Dalila Rodrigues,
Nuno Vassallo e Silva, Fernando Grilo

First day

VIII.1 TORRE DE MONCORVO
    VIII.1.a Flemish triptych, Nossa Senhora da Assunção (Torre de Moncorvo Parish Church)

VIII.2 VILA NOVA DE FOZ CÔA
    VIII.2.a Nossa Senhora do Pranto (Vila Nova de Foz Côa Parish Church)
    VIII.2.b Pillory

VIII.3 LONGROIVA
    VIII.3.a Castle
    VIII.3.b Pillory

VIII.4 MARIALVA
    VIII.4.a Castle
    VIII.4.b Pillory

VIII.5 CELORICO DA BEIRA (option)
    VIII.5.a Castle

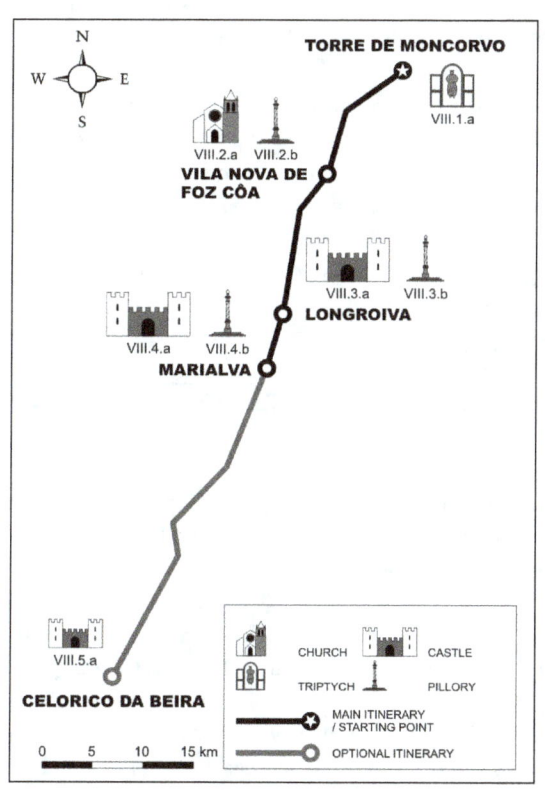

Vila Nova de Foz Côa Parish Church, main portal.

ITINERARY VIII   *Frontier Churches and Castles*
Torre de Moncorvo

The area along the frontier of the Douro and Beira regions, commonly known as *Raia* (the borderland), faced León and Old Castile, reaching out to the north of Spanish Extremadura, on the southerly limit.

Far from the coast and the main cities, there were periods of great depression in this area, and after the Christian Reconquest the land was almost deserted. Life was hard, the climate harsh, and there was little to attract people on the other side of the frontier, unlike the villages on the north bank of the River Minho, and even beyond the valleys of Miranda do Douro. Only because of the insistence of the Crown, particularly at the time of D. Sancho I, did a few settlers go there, almost all of them fugitives, who preferred a hard life of freedom to one of imprisonment.

But times changed. Trade with Castile began to prosper, settlements grew and, by the end of the Middle Ages, there were some towns, today cities, with a reasonable amount of movement, people and economic activity based on agriculture, the grazing of cattle and handicrafts. The Crown established important castles, primarily after three wars and the dynastic crisis of 1383-1385. This was also an area chosen by many Jewish families, who built up communities here away from the intolerance of the coastal towns and even some cities such as Lisbon and Coimbra.

There are many artistic traces of the maritime discoveries in this northern area bounded by Torre de Moncorvo and Guarda, where the sons of the Master of Royal Works at Batalha erected a cathedral. At Castelo Rodrigo and Pinhel, the Mediaeval castles were extensively remodelled at the time of D. Manuel I. This land of brilliant hard granite, guards and exhibits treasures that range from regional or Lisbon-based painting, fine sculptures from Flanders or Coimbra, tombs with recumbent statues, to pillories and bridges of Roman origin.

Works with local, even vernacular, characteristics are mixed with more sophisticated offerings, undoubtedly the work of some of the best artists in the country at the end of the 15th and the beginning of the 16th centuries.

One of the greatest sanctuaries of prehistoric art in the country is to be found at Vale do Côa in this area, as well as Late Romanesque churches such as that at Mileu, near Guarda, or Gothic churches such as the imposing Cistercian Monastery of Santa Maria de Aguiar.

VIII.1 TORRE DE MONCORVO

The present town of Torre de Moncorvo dates back at least to the 12th century and the beginnings of the Portuguese nationality, but nearby there are villages, such as Santa Cruz, that lay at the origins of the modern town. Its first charter was granted in 1062, confirmed by D. Afonso Henriques between 1128 and 1140. D. Dinis renewed this charter in 1285 and D.

ITINERARY VIII   *Frontier Churches and Castles*
Torre de Moncorvo

Manuel I granted the town a new charter in 1512.

The development of the town was largely due to the cultivation of flax and cereals, as well as to the mining of iron ore. Yet, due to its geographical position, it also soon became an important trading centre. It is, therefore, not surprising to discover that D. João I granted the town the right to hold a free fair, in 1385.

During the Manueline period, rope that supplied many of the vessels involved in the Discoveries and maritime expansion was manufactured here, with the result that the town, with 300 houses in 1507, soon spread beyond its Mediaeval walls.

VIII.1.a Flemish triptych, Nossa Senhora da Assunção (Torre de Moncorvo Parish Church)

Largo General Claudino and Dr. Balbino Rêgo. Designated a National Monument. Information: Tourist Office (Tel: 800 252289). Opening hours: daily 9.00-12.00 and 14.00-17.30, except on Monday and Tuesday mornings.

Amongst other features of interest, the Parish Church, one of the most imposing buildings in the Portuguese Mannerist style, contains a remarkable Flemish retable imported from Antwerp, in *c*.1520, as is confirmed by the mark of origin, two hands and a tower, on the reverse side. This remarkable triptych of the *Family of*

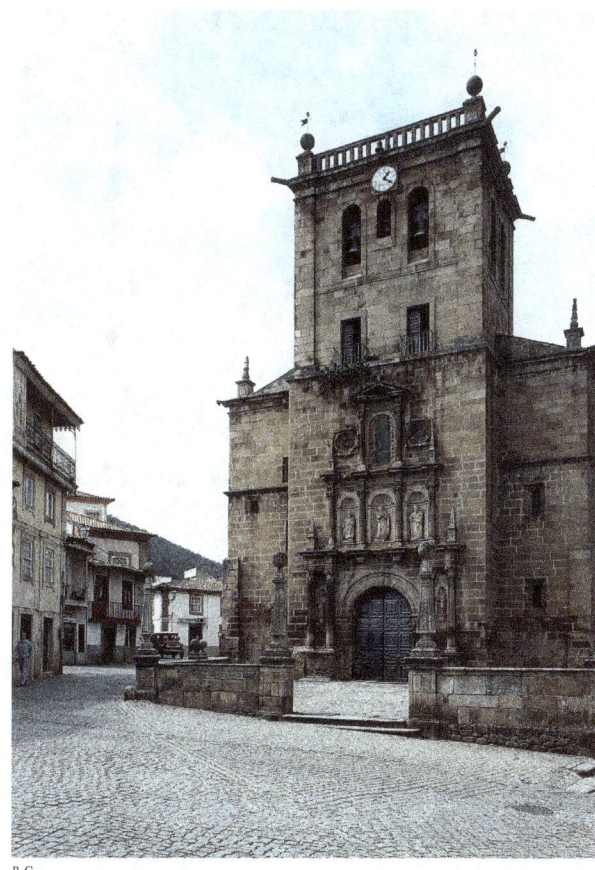

R.C.

Torre de Moncorvo Parish Church.

St Anne must have belonged to the private oratory of a member of the local nobility. The images are of excellent quality, being small but well defined and typical of this type of work, with the rich, precise polychrome that was, no doubt, wondrous in the 16th century and still delights people today.

To reach Vila Nova de Foz Côa, take the EN220 towards the dam of Barragem do

ITINERARY VIII   *Frontier Churches and Castles*
Vila Nova de Foz Côa

Nossa Senhora do Pranto, Vila Nova de Foz Côa Parish Church.

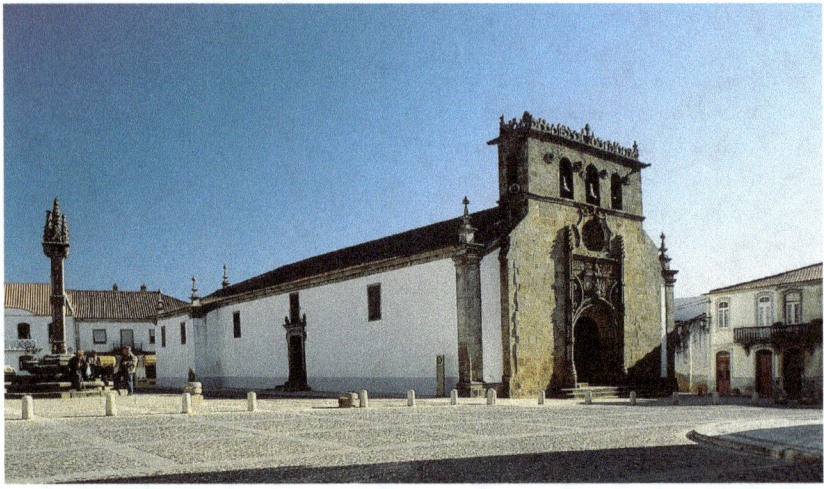

Pocinho. *Turn left on reaching the EN102 and then follow the road. After crossing the River Douro, Vila Nova de Foz Côa is about 7 km. further on.*

VIII.2 VILA NOVA DE FOZ CÔA

Vila Nova de Foz Côa was granted a town charter in 1299, in the time of D. Dinis. The definitive acquisition of this area from Castile encouraged settlement and development, castles were built, and administrative and ecclesiastical reorganisation carried out. The catalyst for much of this development was provided by a large, active Jewish community, which settled near the castle.

Although it was some distance from the sea, one of the most important economic activities of the town was the production of rope. In the first quarter of the 16th century, Foz Côa had 44 families living within the walls and 108 families living outside the walls. The walls that defined the urban grid were destroyed in the 19th century and along with them, some of the most remarkable material remains of the Middle Ages and the Manueline era.

VIII.2.a **Nossa Senhora do Pranto (Vila Nova de Foz Côa Parish Church)**

Largo do Município. (Tel: 279 762226). Designated a National Monument.
Opening hours: 08.00-17.00 in winter, and until 21.00 in summer.

Built at the beginning of the 16th century, the Church has altered over time and today it only retains the original façade. The building is highly influenced by the style prevalent in neighbouring Castile, as can be seen by the brattishing with three openings for the bells and a Renaissance garland. The portal is Naturalist Manueline, with small columns framing the *archivolts* and the *pinnacle* with the royal arms and Manueline armillary sphere.

VIII.2.b **Pillory**

Next to the Parish Church, in Largo do Município. Designated a National Monument.

The pillory is one of the most handsome monuments in the area with a square column set on a four-step podium, crowned at the top by a lantern turret surmounted by a cross. Architecturally impressive and heavily decorated, the work matches that on the church doorway.

For Longroiva, retake the EN102, in the direction of Celorico da Beira. Approx. 12 km.

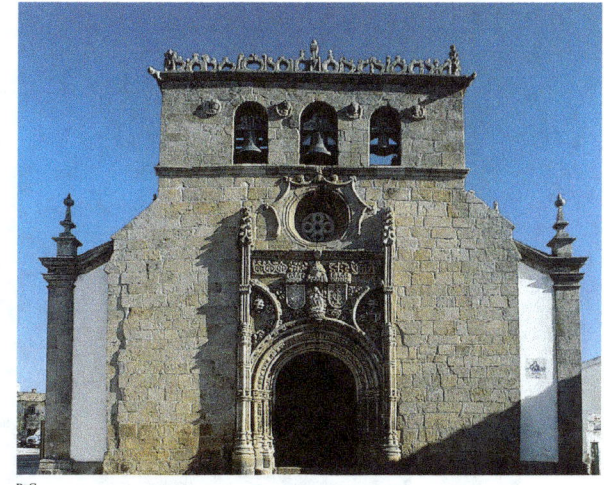

Nossa Senhora do Pranto, Vila Nova de Foz Côa Parish Church, main façade.

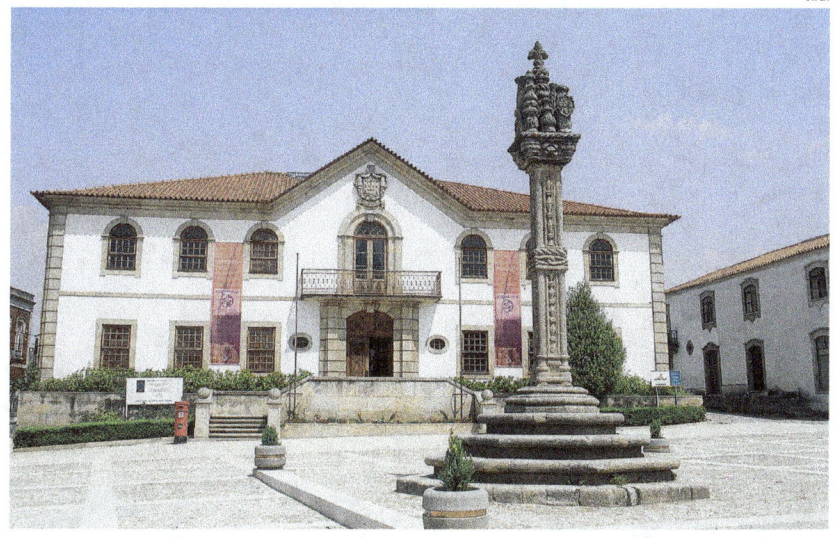

Foz Côa Pillory.

ITINERARY VIII *Frontier Churches and Castles*
Longroiva

Longroiva Castle.

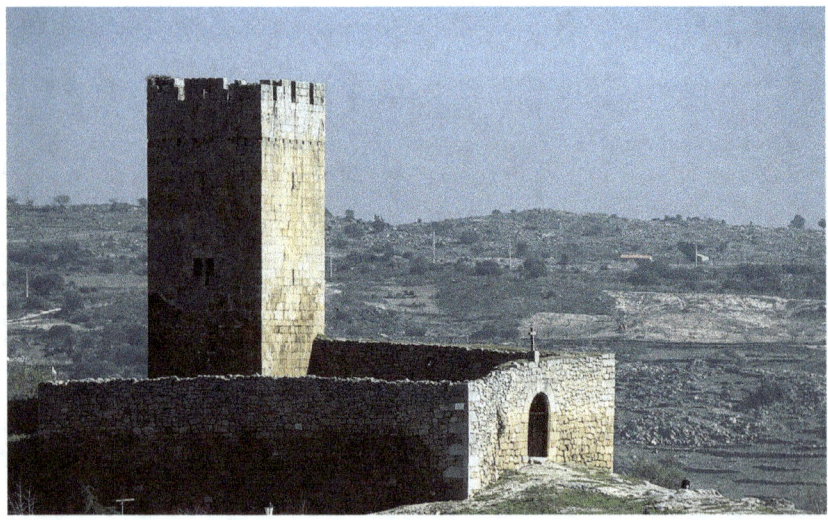

R.C.

ahead on the right, the exit leads to the EN331 to Longroiva.

VIII.3 **LONGROIVA**

VIII.3.a **Castle**

The Castle may be visited at any time. Information: Câmara Municipal (Town Hall Tel: 279 883525). Designated a National Monument.

This small, fortified Castle, re-constructed at the beginning of the 16th century, stands on a hill dominating the surrounding area. D. Manuel I ordered it to be repaired, as it was the headquarters of a commendary of the Order of Christ. The nature of the reconstruction is easi-ly understood from records in the Manueline cartulary. It was surrounded by a small enclosure and a square keep was built that also served as the residence of the commendator. The Knights Templar erected the original tower in about 1170. The village grew next to this, beyond the walls.

VIII.3.b **Pillory**

In the centre of Longroiva, facing the Capela de São Pedro. Classified as a Building of Public Interest.

Belonging to the Manueline era, Longroiva has a simple pillory consisting of a column with the royal coat of arms of Manuel I on top, and the chamfered Gothic entrance arch of the Parish Church.

ITINERARY VIII   Frontier Churches and Castles
Marialva

For Marialva, retake the EN102, towards Celorico da Beira. After 7.5 km., turn right onto the EN324. Marialva is 3 km. further on.

VIII.4 MARIALVA

VIII.4.a Castle

Designated a National Monument. Information: Tourist Office (Tel: 279 858020). The castle may be visited at any time.

The Castle, built on the site of a Romanised hill fort, dates back to the 12th century, certainly to the reign of D. Afonso Henriques, who granted the first charter to the town, in 1179. D. Manuel I later, in 1512, renewed the charter, as happened with most other towns. As the castle was located in the Portuguese frontier zone before the signing of the Alcanices Peace Treaty on 12th September 1297, it played an important role as a first line of defence.

The *enceinte* on the line of the hillock occupied considerable space; the *curtain walls* were elevated irregularly to create a wide parapet and battlements. There are two gateways, Porta do Anjo da Guarda and Porta do Monte, linked by a causeway, and, with two wicket gates, which provided rapid access to the surrounding countryside. The fortress and the four towers are in ruins; the last restoration probably having taking place

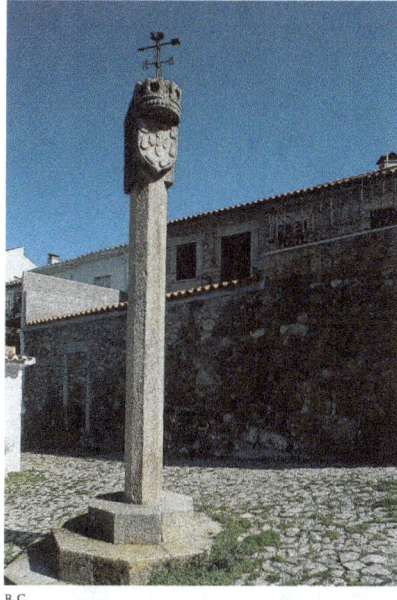

Longroiva Pillory.

R.C.
R.C.

Marialva Castle and Pillory.

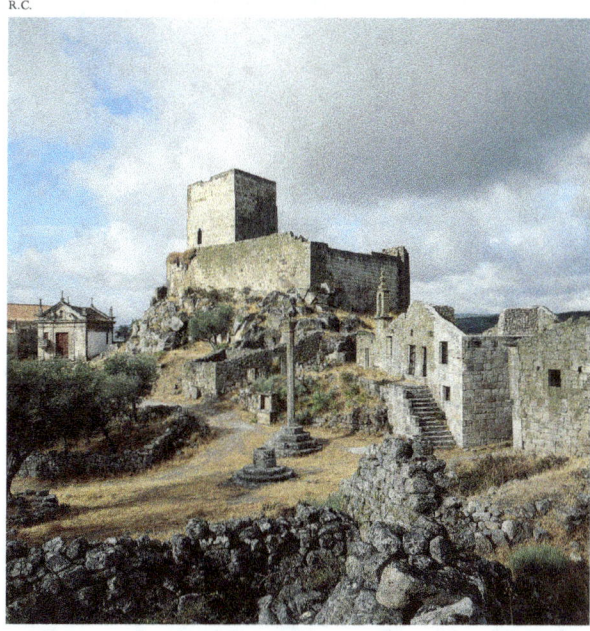

201

at the end of the 15th century and continuing into the Manueline period.
The remains of the old quarters are still visible inside the enclosure, as well as the cistern, pillory and two 18th-century churches.

VIII.4.b Pillory

The Pillory is inside the castle enclosure. Classified as a Building of Public Interest.

This Manueline Pillory has an octagonal column on a pedestal with four steps; the top is in the form of a lantern turret, but with less evolved architectural elements than those usually found in other pillories in neighbouring towns.

For Celorico, retake the EN102 heading south. If going on to Guarda, go through Celorico and after 4 km. join the IP5.

VIII.5 CELORICO DA BEIRA
(option)

VIII.5.a Castle

Information: Câmara Municipal (Town Hall Tel: 271 742105). Designated a National Monument.

This Castle, which already existed in the 12th century, was successively restored, namely by D. Dinis at the end of the 13th century. It finally began to take definite shape in the Manueline era.
The large quadrangular tower, which is not the original keep, has been preserved, along with other lesser towers built to reinforce the corners, and the complete set of walls built on the highest point of the 550-m.-high plateau. Two gateways communicated with the town, one facing west and the other south.

ITINERARY VIII

Frontier Churches and Castles

Pedro Dias, Dalila Rodrigues,
Nuno Vassallo e Silva, Fernando Grilo

Second day

VIII.6 GUARDA
VIII.6.a Historic Centre
VIII.6.b Castle
VIII.6.c Cathedral

VIII.7 PINHEL
VIII.7.a Castle
VIII.7.b Church of Misericórdia and Pillory

VIII.8 CASTELO RODRIGO
VIII.8.a Castle
VIII.8.b Nossa Senhora do Reclamador (Castelo Rodrigo Parish Church) and Pillory

VIII.9 VILAR TORPIM (option)
VIII.9.a Nossa Senhora dos Prazeres (Vilar Torpim Parish Church)

VIII.10 VILAR FORMOSO (option)
VIII.10.a São João Baptista (Vilar Formoso Parish Church)

Mudejar *Ceilings*

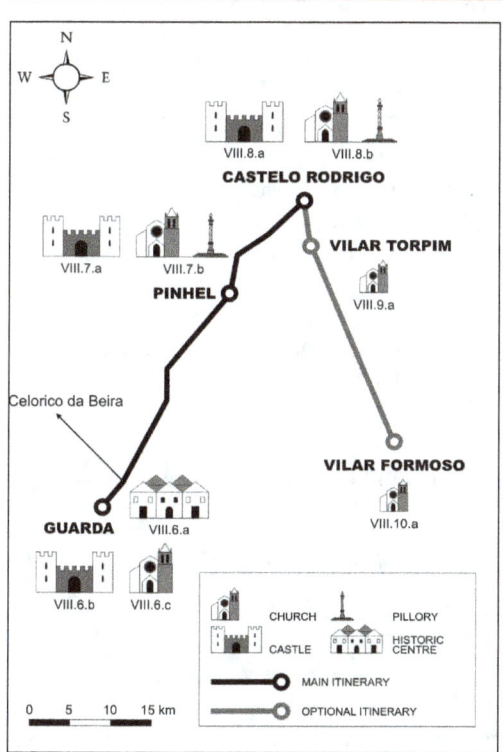

ITINERARY VIII   Frontier Churches and Castles
Guarda

General view of the historic centre, including the cathedral, Guarda.

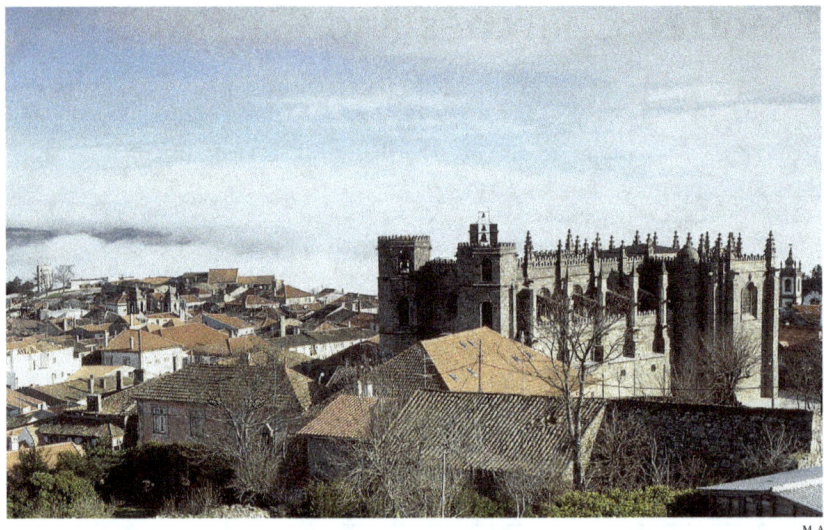

M.A

VIII.6 **GUARDA**

The origins of the modern city date back to the policy of D. Sancho I, which was to fortify the eastern frontier of the kingdom with people and castles, conforming to a clear line of separation with León and with Castile. In order to re-organise the territory that was sparsely populated, he created new towns, one of which was established on the top of the platform where the old town is situated. He also moved the see of the Diocese of Egitania from Idanha-a-Velha to Guarda in about 1203.

Guarda became the most important Portuguese frontier settlement between the River Douro and the River Tagus, with a significant military garrison, and it also carried out the task of economic development, chiefly in the form of trade. Its geographical situation, in the communications corridor between Portugal and Castile, meant that it fell prey to various attacks and struggles in times of crisis, the greatest of which eventually elevated D. João I to the throne, in 1384.

As the Episcopal city, the activity of its clergy was always highly relevant, and the appointment of D. Pedro Gavião as bishop, in 1496, brought considerable benefits.

VIII.6.a **Historic Centre**

Information: Tourist Office (Tel: 271 205530).

The oldest part of the settlement of Guarda was on a small platform that was marked by an almost circular enclosure at the end of the Middle Ages. The streets

ITINERARY VIII Frontier Churches and Castles
Guarda

were not organised rationally, but took into account the nature of the terrain and the gates, of which there were probably five, that communicated with the outside, in the Mediaeval period. The streets are narrow and winding with some Manueline and some even earlier houses, such as those in Rua Direita and Rua dos Clérigos.

The Castle was situated on a dominating point inside the *enceinte*, but the clearest line of circulation was Rua Direita, which joined the Porta da Covilhã and the Porta dos Curros, the most distant gateways.

The Cathedral, also serving as the Parish Church, was another important focal point, being situated in the same square as the *Câmara* (Town Hall), a Manueline edifice. Two more parochial churches were linked to this parish and were a natural pole of attraction for the community. There was also an important Jewish community that lived here until the Manueline period. As decreed by D. Pedro I, the Jewish residential quarter had gates, which remained in place even after their official conversion in 1498.

Outside the gates, houses stretched beyond the walls and the most highly developed district in the Manueline era was the suburb around the Porta dos Ferreiros, in the Parishes of São Pedro and São Nicolau and close to the Franciscan Monastery.

It was here, too, that the annual fair was held. Lasting for two weeks, this extremely important event had been created by royal dispensation in 1255.

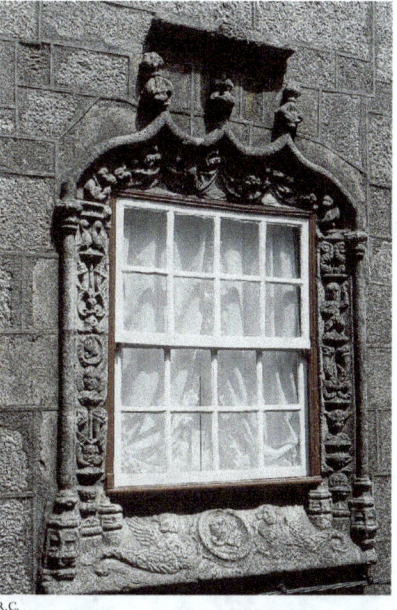

Guarda historic centre, Manueline window

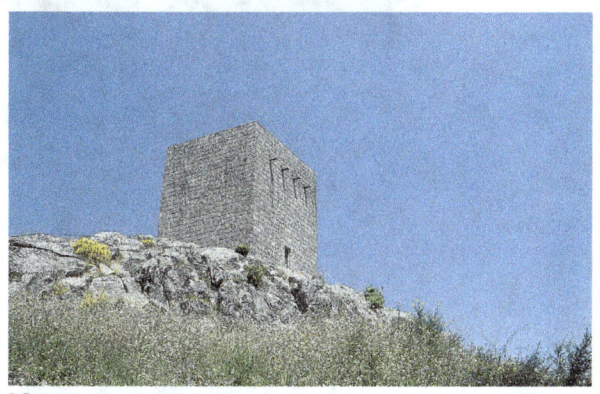

VIII.6.b Castle

Designated a National Monument. Information: Câmara Municipal (Town Hall Tel: 271 220220) or from the Tourist Office (Tel: 271 205530).

Guarda Castle Keep.

ITINERARY VIII   *Frontier Churches and Castles*
Guarda

Guarda Cathedral, general view.

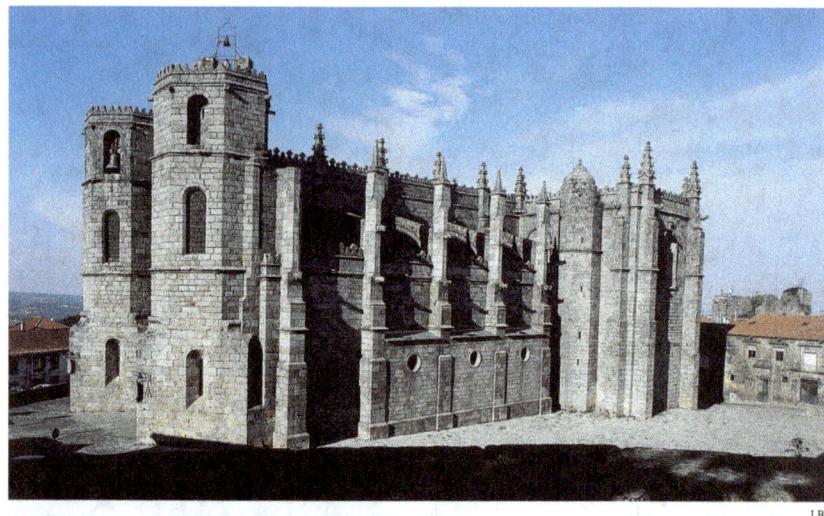

Guarda Cathedral, portal.

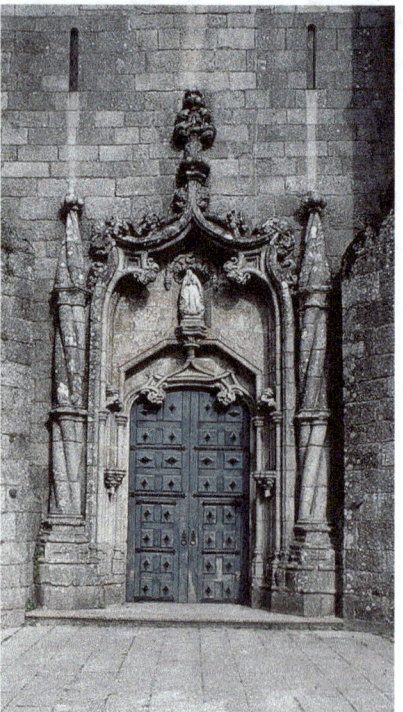

The Mediaeval Castle of Guarda, just as it was during the reign of D. Manuel I, still conserves the towers of the *enceinte*, the keep, gates and small stretches of wall. Begun by D. Sancho I, in the final years of the 12th century, it probably had at that time only the uppermost part of the castle built within the walls, where the main tower is today, and the keep. Work was carried out to enlarge the Castle in the time of D. Dinis and again in the time of D. Fernando. In the fighting between 1383 and 1385, the walls were badly damaged, so the last great Mediaeval restoration probably took place during the reign of D. João I.

Still to be seen are the towers, the Torre dos Ferreiros and the Torre Velha, as well as the gateways of Porta da Erva, Porta D'el-Rei and Porta dos Ferreiros, next to the fort of the same name, which is clearly Manueline in style.

VIII.6.c Cathedral

Praça Luís de Camões, also known as Praça Velha. (Tel: 271 211231). Designated a National Monument.
Opening hours: 09.00-12.30 and 14.00-17.00. Mass is held daily, 09.00-10.00. Closed on Mondays and the last weekend in each month, as well as January 1st, Easter Sunday, May 1st and December 25th.

Building began towards the end of the 14th century between 1392 and 1397, but the work in the traditional Gothic style is confined to the chancel and the transept. Work was begun again in 1504 and, from then until 1517, the brothers Pêro and Filipe Henriques, sons of the Master of Royal Works at Batalha, Mateus Fernandes, completed what was necessary on the lateral walls, building the front and pillars and covering the vessel of the church with very heavy vaulting. The Bishop, D. Pedro Gavião, whose coat of arms is emblazoned on the front and other parts of the edifice, sponsored the work.
The church, with its *flying buttresses* supporting the vaults, gives an impression of sturdy strength. It has two octagonal towers flanking the narrow front, which has a Manueline portal with naturalist elements. The interior has a nave and two aisles of unequal height separated by arches built in the 14th-century style and set on cruciform pillars. The transept terminates the main vessel with five bays with *cross-ribbed vaulting* with thick, rounded

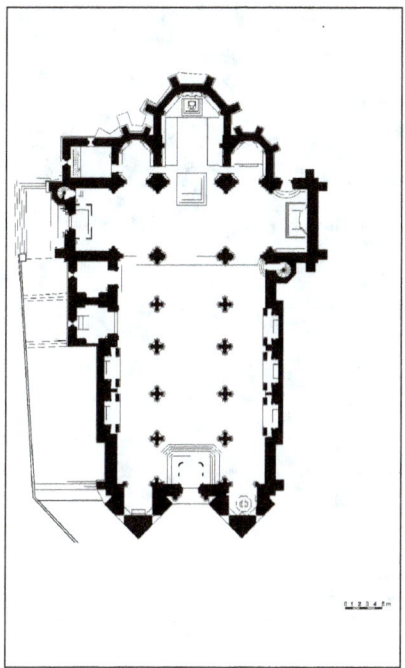

Guarda Cathedral, plan, Boletim da Direcção-Geral dos Edifícios e Monumentos Nacionais, No. 88.

ribs. There is a triple apse, with the chancel surpassing the side chapels.
The funerary chapel of D. João de Pina, the Protonotary, Apostolical and Royal Chaplain, as well as the keeper of the cathedral's treasure, opens on the left side, next to the transept. It has a Renaissance portal, even though this is actually a Late Gothic structure in the Manueline style. The tomb is housed in a niche in the same style which is from the same era as the recumbent statue of De Pina.

On leaving Guarda, follow the EN221. After the junction with the EN226, about 3 km. further on, there is a turning to Pinhel.

ITINERARY VIII *Frontier Churches and Castles*
Pinhel

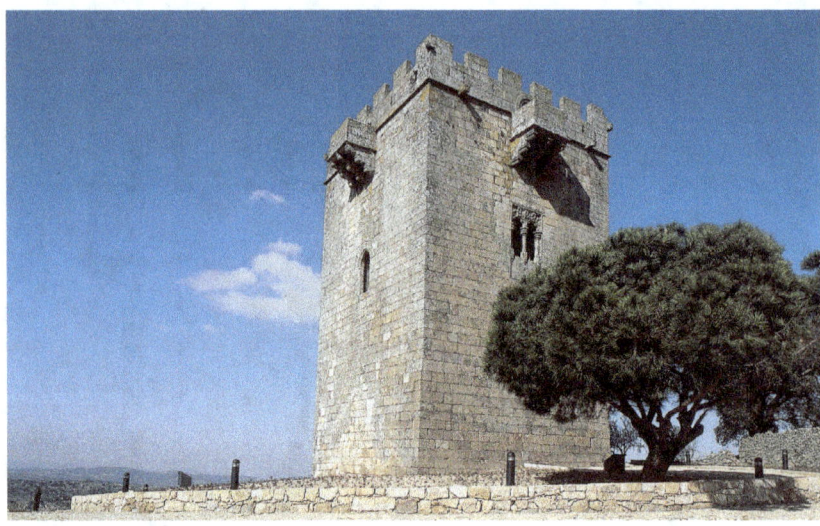

Pinhel Castle Keep.

VIII.7 **PINHEL**

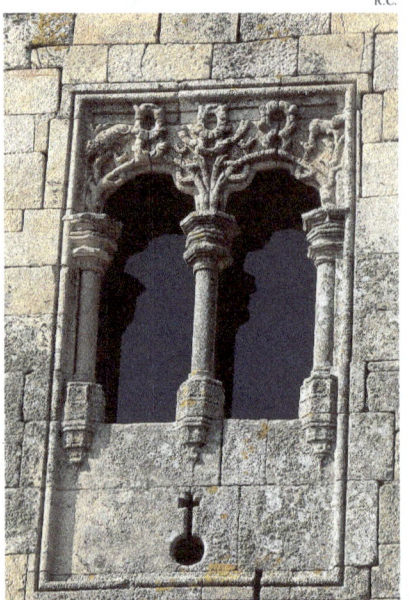

The city of Pinhel also owes its origins to the late 12th-century policy of D. Sancho I to establish and strengthen the frontier with León and Castile. The first charter dates from 1209, indicating that it was of sufficient size to deserve this distinction and the basic legislation for its future development.

Fundamental to this process of development was the introduction of the *Lei das Sesmarias* (a law designed to make ownership of the land conditional on tillage), decreed by D. Fernando, who also created an annual fair to attract traders from all over the region.

In 1510, Manuel I granted Pinhel a new charter.

Pinhel Castle, Manueline window.

VIII.7.a Castle

The Castle is reached via Rua de Santa Maria. Designated a National Monument. Information: Câmara Municipal (Town Hall Tel: 271 410000).

The Castle, like the town, was founded at the beginning of the 12th century, but all that remains today dates from Manueline improvements and consolidation built on structures of the 14th and 15th centuries.

The solid, square keep has a high entrance door on the first floor, which was reached by a set of retractable steps, and one of the finest Manueline windows in the Beira region, with a balcony and a double span with 15th-century columns in foliate *archivolts*. There is a cross-shaped embrasure, more ornamental than functional. The uppermost part of the castle, of which only traces are now visible, had other towers besides the two that remain, and communicated with the *enceinte* below.

VIII.7.b Church of Misericórdia and Pillory

Praça Sacadura Cabral. The Church is classified as a Building of Public Interest and the Pillory is designated a National Monument.

The Misericórdia Church was founded in the Manueline period and had a private chapel, though only the simple façade and the structure of the main vessel remain

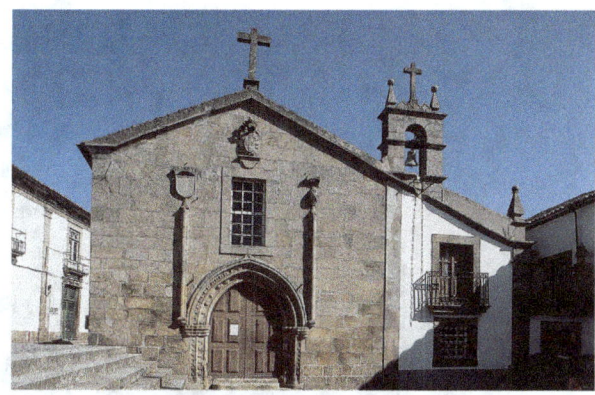

Church of Misericórdia, Pinhel.

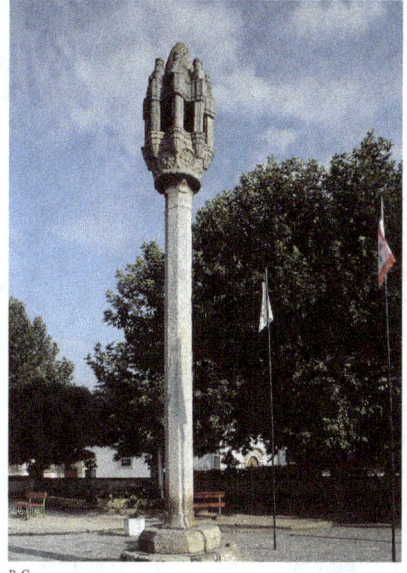

Pinhel Pillory.

from this period. The Gothic portal has inter-columnations decorated with foliate elements.

On leaving the church, in the same square, there is a Manueline pillory. It is quite simple with a two-step base and an octagonal pillar holding the lantern tur-

ITINERARY VIII Frontier Churches and Castles
Castelo Rodrigo

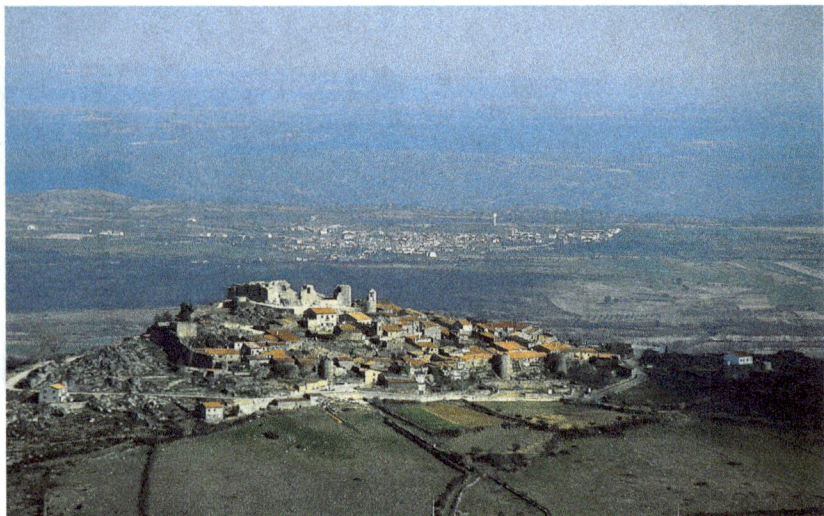

Castelo Rodrigo Castle and village.

ret, with decorative rosettes on the base, and a grooved top.

Retake the EN221 in the direction of Figueira de Castelo Rodrigo. After the junction with the EN332, the exit to Castelo Rodrigo is on the right.

VIII.8 CASTELO RODRIGO

A typical border settlement, built on a hill that dominates the surrounding region, Castelo Rodrigo was fortified from at least the 12th century onwards. It was brought under the Portuguese Crown in the time of D. Dinis, and gradually grew in importance until the first great Manueline reform, that gave the town's historic area the appearance that it still retains today. The town was granted a charter by D. Manuel I in 1508.

VIII.8.a Castle

1 km. out of town. Designated a National Monument. Information: Câmara Municipal (Town Hall Tel: 271 319000).
The Castle may be visited at any time.

D. Dinis had the first Portuguese Castle built here during the transition period of the 13th to the 14th centuries, though, at that time, it cannot have been much more than a small castle on the line of the hill. In the *Livro das Fortalezas*, the book in which Duarte D'Armas draws this castle and many others, the original construction is clearly visible and is distinguished by the lower than usual *enceinte* that surrounded the town. The drawings also indicate that the *curtain walls* were in a poor state of repair, mainly to the south, and were later restored. There was also a low *barbican* with embrasures on the northern side.

ITINERARY VIII   *Frontier Churches and Castles*
Castelo Rodrigo

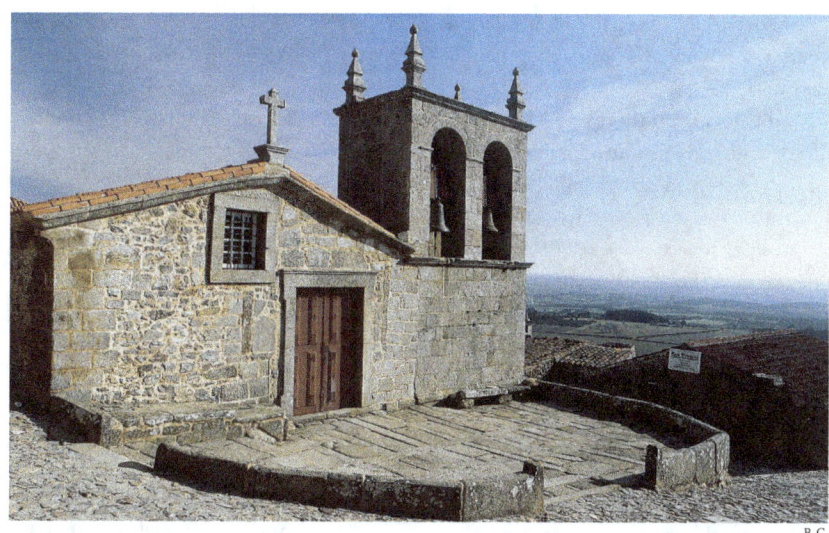

Nossa Senhora do Reclamador, Castelo Rodrigo Parish Church.

Despite the damage to which it was subjected at the beginning of the 19th century, the Castle still retains a large part of its Manueline walls with round towers.

VIII.8.b Nossa Senhora do Reclamador (Castelo Rodrigo Parish Church) and Pillory

Largo da Igreja. The church is classified as a Building of Public Interest, and the pillory is designated a National Monument. To arrange a visit to the interior, contact the President of the Junta de Freguesia (Parish Council Tel: 271 312642).

The Parish Church was profoundly remodelled in the 17th and 18th centuries, but its structure is still Manueline in style. Long and low, with six bays, it has the traditional rib arches that characterise this regional group.

Some of the Flemish sculptures, dating from the early 16th century, are of interest:

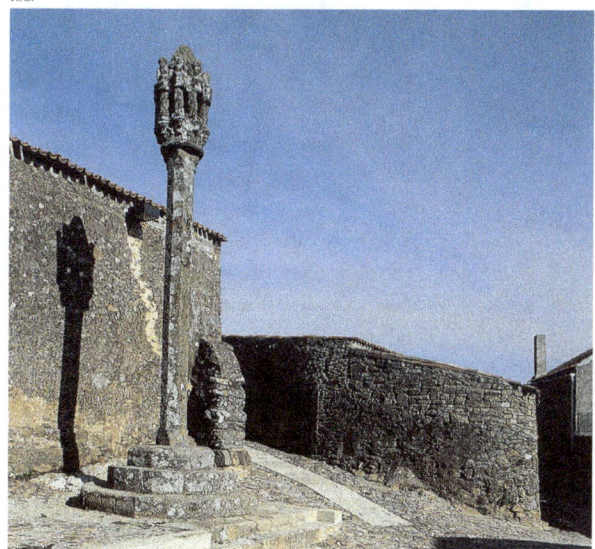

Castelo Rodrigo Pillory.

211

a *Calvary* and an exceptional *St John the Baptist* are possibly the work of Arnau de Carvalho.

Behind the church there is a Manueline pillory, with a lantern turret and two small columns set on an octagonal pillar, which in turn stands on a base of five steps.

To visit Vilar Torpim, retake the EN221 in the direction of Pinhel / Guarda. About 600 m. further on, there is a turning on the left leading to the EN332. Follow this road for about 6 km.

VIII.9 **VILAR TORPIM** (option)

VIII.9.a Nossa Senhora dos Prazeres (Vilar Torpim Parish Church)

Rua Padre João Mendes Garcia. The Church opens for Mass from Monday to Friday at 20.00, and on Sundays at 12.30. To visit the church at any other time, contact Sra. Laurinda (Tel: 271 377367), or call at her home in Rua do Meio, or alternatively, visit Sra. Maria Adelaide, in Rua da Igreja.

The structure of the Church is similar to those built at the beginning of the 16th century: wide with a single nave and ribbed arches. On the left-hand side is the Late Manueline vaulted funerary chapel of D. António de Aguilar with the recumbent statue of the knight who was a commendator of the Order of Christ.

The date on the inscribed stone on the floor is 1546. An early Renaissance painting of *Nossa Senhora da Piedade,* belonging to the chapel, has been placed in the chancel.

Retake the EN332 in the direction of Almeida for about 20 km. to the end of the road and then take the IP5 to Vilar Formoso.

VIII.10 **VILAR FORMOSO** (option)

VIII.10.a São João Baptista (Vilar Formoso Parish Church)

Largo da Igreja.
Opening hours: the Church opens for Mass from Monday to Friday at 18.30 in winter and at 19.30 in summer, on Saturdays at 19.00 in winter and 20.00 in summer, and on Sundays at 11.30. Outside these times, please contact the Centro de Acolhimento (Reception Centre Tel: 271 512554).

Like the Parish Church at Vilar Torpim, the Parish Church of Vilar Formoso is yet another typical example of this group of frontier churches built or re-built at the beginning of the 16th century. It has a single nave divided by long, low ribbed arches. The chancel has a polychrome *Mudejar* ceiling, as did the main vessel of the church before rebuilding was carried out.

MUDEJAR CEILINGS

Pedro Dias

Mudejar art is characterised by the influence of the Muslim aesthetic and technique in Christian territory. It blossomed in Reconquest Spain, but spread to other territories and was adopted for its brilliance, detail, intense colour and luxury. It is not surprising, therefore, to find *Mudejar* elements, mostly in the form of carpentry, in the upland areas of Aragón or Trás-os-Montes. But it nonetheless causes some perplexity to see the immense roofing of *par y nudillo* and *carpintería de lo blanco*, in Bolivia, Colombia and Mexico.

In Portugal there are a number of important works that are clearly influenced by Castile in the frontier Beira region. They are relatively modest ceilings, or the remains of roofing, mostly dating from the end of the 16th century, and that indicate the very extensive exchange between the two sides of the frontier, during the reign of D. Manuel I. This type of work can be seen in the churches of Escarigo, Leomil, Castelo Bom, Vilar Formoso, Castelo Mendo, Marmeleiro, Vila do Touro and Sortelha.

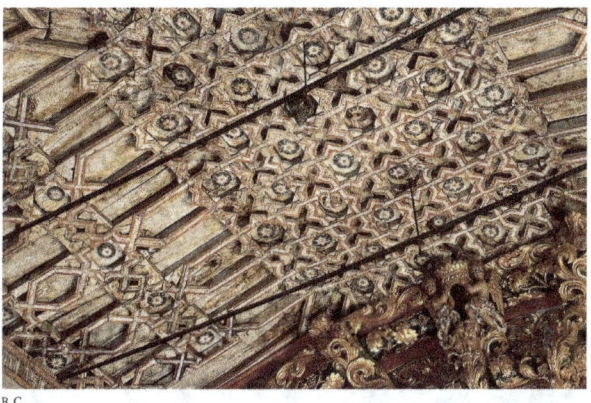

R.C.

Church of Escarigo, detail of the ceiling.

19th-Century Guarda Territory

"*Its territory is fertile in maize, rye, vegetables, greens, fruit and some wine; however, its vast pasturelands, which are magnificent, and where a great quantity of excellent livestock of different species are bred, constitute the main branch of agricultural industry; the most important being the export of cattle, wool, cheese and butter.*

Also the planting of mulberry bushes, which have developed very well here, making the breeding of silk worms prosper, and the spinning of silk, at which the women employ themselves almost exclusively; already with pleasing results, which, with time and improvement, will become a source of prosperity.

The Serra da Estrella, with its famed lakes, splendid waterfalls, singular grottoes and imposing rocks, makes the surroundings of Guarda very curious and picturesque.

There is also a great variety of both large and small game in the hills.

The Mondego is also abundant in fish."

Pinho Leal, *Portugal Antigo e Moderno,* Vol. III, Lisboa, 1871.

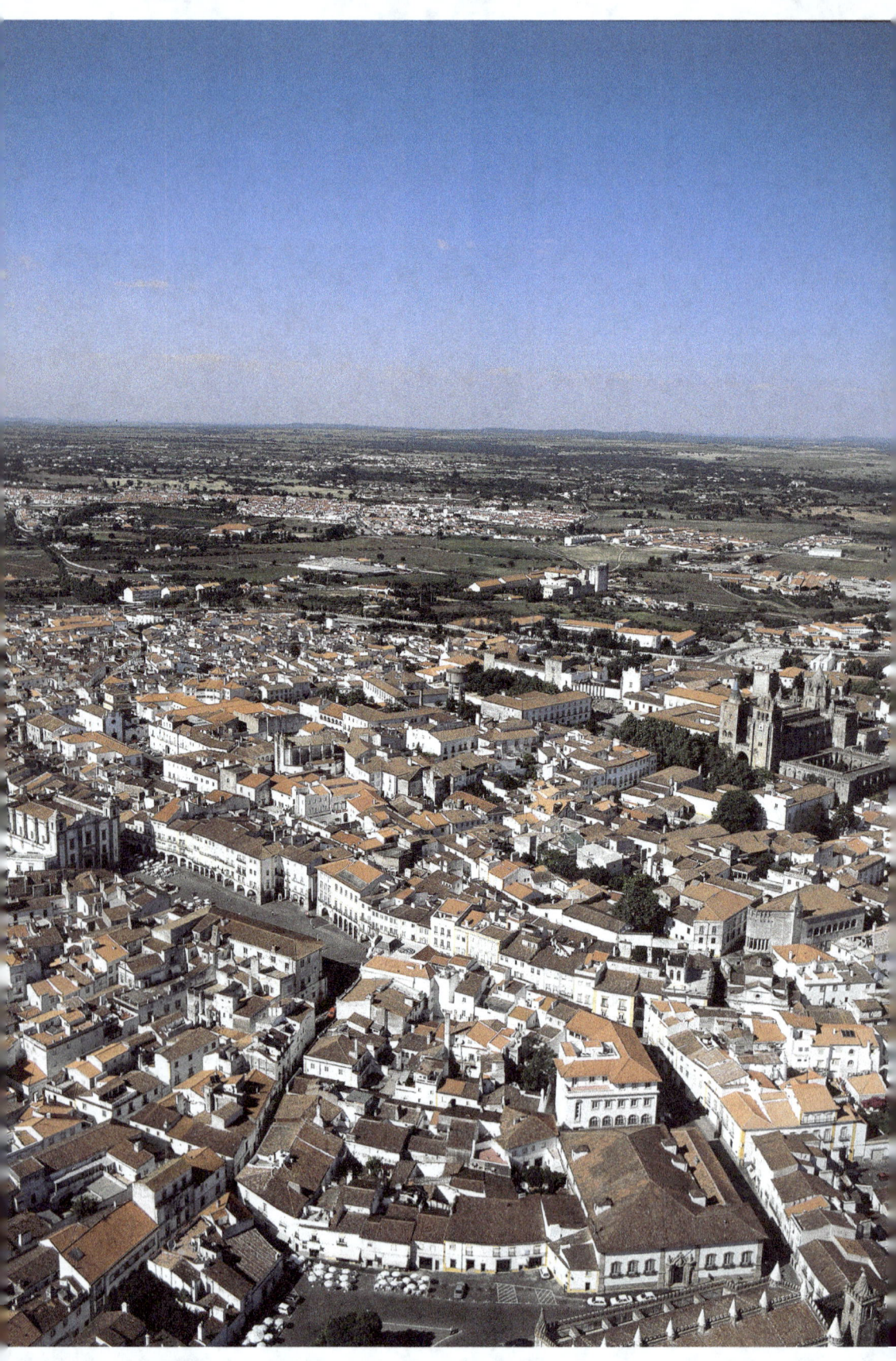

ITINERARY IX

Évora: City of the Court

Pedro Dias, Dalila Rodrigues,
Nuno Vassallo e Silva, Fernando Grilo

First day

IX.I ÉVORA

    IX.1.a City Walls
    IX.1.b Galeria das Damas, Paço Real (Royal Palace)
    IX.1.c Ruins of the Vimioso Palace
    IX.1.d Church of the Convent of São Francisco
    IX.1.e Cathedral Museum of Sacred Art
    IX.1.f Évora Museum
    IX.1.g Convent of the Lóios, or Convent of São João Evangelista
    IX.1.h Convent of São Bento de Cástris (option)
    IX.1.i Convent of Nossa Senhora do Espinheiro (option)

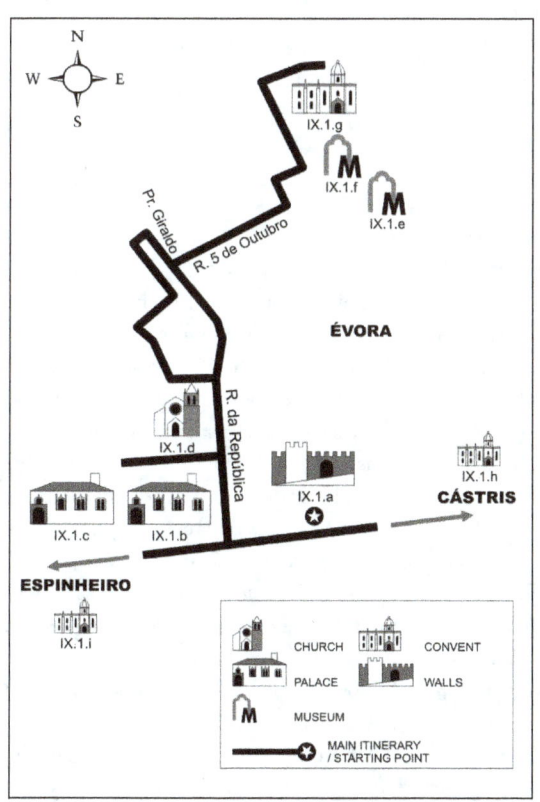

Aerial view of Évora.

ITINERARY IX   *Évora: City of the Court*

Évora

Towards the end of the Middle Ages and the beginning of the Modern Era, which coincided with the Golden Age of the Discoveries and the maritime expansion of the Portuguese, the city of Évora, in its cultural and artistic splendour, was unequalled on the Portuguese scene and became one of Europe's main centres of Renaissance culture.

The Portuguese monarchs of the Avis dynasty, attracted by the mild climate, fertile land and excellent hunting, spent much of their time in the area, and it was here that D. João II celebrated the marriage of the heir to the throne with the daughter of Ferdinand and Isabella of Spain. This solemn act presaged the possibility of Iberian unity and turned into one of the greatest celebrations ever witnessed in Europe in the late Middle Ages.

Towns in the province of the Alentejo, particularly those around Évora, grew and developed, as leading figures in the country became the Counts of Arraiolos, Vidigueira and Olivença. As populations settled, land was cultivated and religious institutions were built, as well as churches and manor houses. Courtiers played their part by constructing roads and adding to the defensive system.

The Court nobility settled in Évora and the surrounding district, following D. João II, D. Manuel I and D. João III, in particular, that lived in the city for many years. They wished to be near the king, to serve him and also to benefit from his consideration or friendship. They also commissioned works of art from the many artists who travelled there from all parts of Europe, as well as importing works from Flanders, Italy, Spain or the Far East. The result was the embellishment of the town with noble mansions belonging to the Counts of Sortelha, the Counts of Basto, the Counts of Vimioso, and with the beautiful houses of Vasco da Gama and Manuel de Sousa Sepúlveda. Artists, such as Nicolas Chanterène, Francisco Henriques, Olivier of Ghent, Frei Carlos, António and Francisco de Holanda, Francisco and Miguel de Arruda and Gil Vicente, had homes there too.

In the surrounding area, the nearby towns of Montemor-o-Novo and Arraiolos also thrived during this period.

X.1 ÉVORA

The history of Évora dates back to Roman times, as can be seen by the Temple of Diana, and it was also important in the Middle Ages when the city was shared with the Arabs, Hispano-Romans, Visigoths and Jews.

The old settlement was conquered from the Lusitanians by Decimus Junius Brutus, and, at the time of Julius Caesar, received the title *Liberalitas*. It was dependent on Mérida and was an important crossroads on the Roman road, with imposing monuments on the *Acropolis* and in the *Forum*.

At the end of the Roman Empire, the city was occupied first by the Visigoths

ITINERARY IX   *Évora: City of the Court*
Évora

and then by the Muslims, who formed an Arab elite, between 713 and 1165, the time of the Christian Reconquest. As Évora was the largest city between Lisbon and the Algarve, a number of Kings such as D. Afonso III, D. Dinis and D. Afonso IV chose to spend time there. Towards the end of the 14th century, the Lord High Constable D. Nuno Álvares Pereira maintained his main residence in Évora for 26 years. D. João II also showed a particular fondness for the city, living in Évora through some of the most dramatic moments of his reign.

A formidable wall that was dotted with towers encircled the town and defended the different quarters where Muslim, Jewish and Christian inhabitants peacefully co-existed. This wall had to be increased in size, so that it could encompass the new residential areas and religious institutions. In Manueline times, the city was remarkable for the beauty of its buildings and the wealth of its inhabitants, both lay and ecclesiastical.

Great churches such as the Cathedral, the largest of Portuguese Mediaeval sees, the huge Monastery of São Francisco or the modest Chapel of São Brás, were all girdled by the walls and have provided the city with a heritage of exceptional interest, along with the Muslim and Jewish Quarters and the Praça do Giraldo.

The remains of these glory days, and other more recent ones, are so remark-

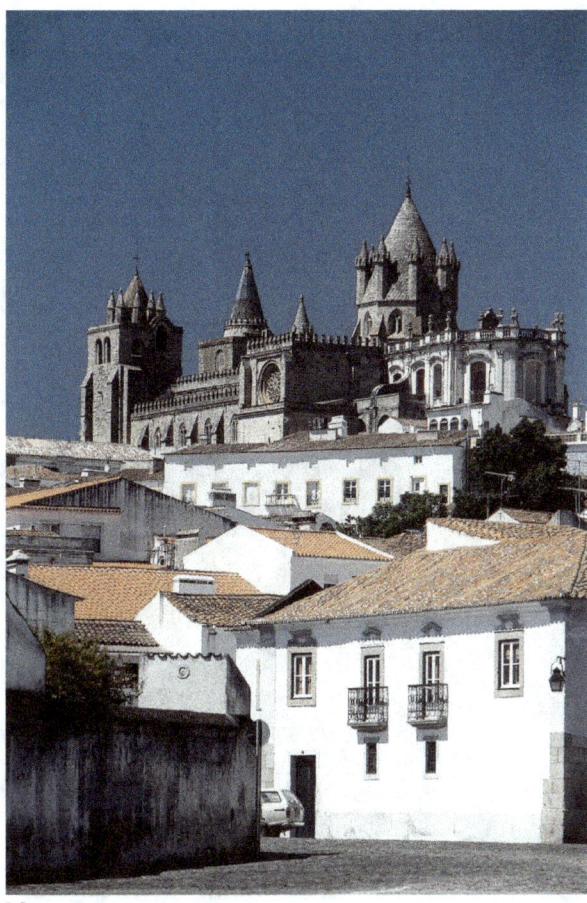
R.C.

able that UNESCO has placed the city on its World Heritage list.

It is possible to walk round the city and this is strongly recommended, as some of the places of interest are difficult to get to by car. There are a number of convenient car parks near the gates leading to the historic centre. There are two free car parks next to Rossio de São Brás.

Évora historic centre, with the cathedral in the background.

217

ITINERARY IX   *Évora: City of the Court*

Évora

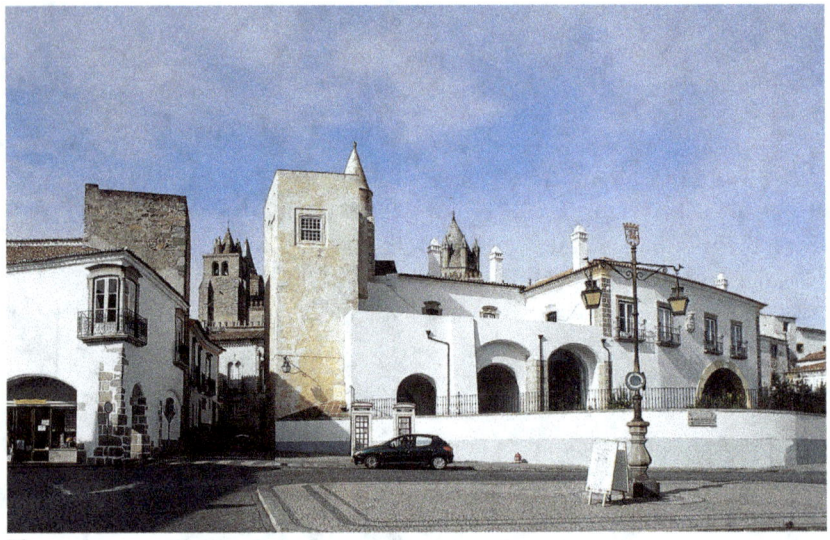

Évora City Walls.

IX.1.a City Walls

The original walls of the city stretched some 1,200 m. to form a circle with the Cathedral at the centre, though not much of these walls is still visible today. The new wall surrounds the whole of the historic centre of Évora, and is visible from all entrances to the city. Designated a National Monument. Information: Tourist Office (Tel: 266 702671).

The original walls of the city date back to Roman times, though they were restored during the Arab Occupation. At the time of the Reconquest by Geraldo Sem-Pavor, they were the strongest fortifications in the south of Portuguese territory.

In the mid-14th century, the *enceinte* was enlarged to take in the growing town, and also because many of the towers and *curtain walls* were old and fragile. Work went on for almost a century and what is to be seen today, in the Gothic style, dates from these restorations.

The oldest gateway is the Porta de D. Isabel, said to be Roman. The Porta do Moinho de Vento, in the new wall, was remodelled in 1517; both the Porta de Alconchel, built at the beginning of the 15th century, and the Porta da Lagoa, built at the end of the 15th century, have defensive towers. Powerful families used the battlements at various points to construct their town houses, such as the Paço de São Miguel de Freiria, the Paço dos Duques de Cadaval and the Paço dos Condes de Basto, all which still retain important details from Manueline times.

IX.1.b Galeria das Damas, Paço Real (Royal Palace)

The Royal Palace, also known as the Palácio de D. Manuel, is in the public garden. Designated a National Monument. It is currently used for exhibition purposes, its timetable varies according to the times of these exhibitions. Information Tel: 266 704101.

All that remains of the palatine complex of São Francisco de Évora is the so-called Galeria das Damas (Queen's Gallery), which underwent considerable restoration at the end of the 19th century.
D. Manuel I had a palace built in the Spanish *Mudejar* style on the lines of that of Ferdinand and Isabella of Spain, which he had seen on his visits to the neighbouring kingdom. The architects were Afonso de Pallos, Duarte de Medina and Pero de Trillo.
The building consists of two storeys: the ground floor, where only half the area is covered, whilst another part has medium-sized rooms; and the main floor, with a balcony on the top, has large windows and a turret with a pyramid-shaped *pinnacle*. Note the horseshoe arches and the *ajimeces* (paired arches) of the doors and windows, as well as the double arcade that divides the first floor into three, very typical of the early 16th-century Luso-Moorish style.

IX.1.c Ruins of the Vimioso Palace

In the public garden next to the Paço Real.

The fake ruins, started in 1866, and built on part of the new wall by the Italian scenographer, Cinatti, stand in the garden dominated by the Galeria das Damas. Built in the Romantic style of the period, the *Mudejar* windows and balconies are from the Palace of D. Afonso of Portugal, Bishop of Évora and Count of Vimioso, and the windows and balconies were from the original building that used to be in front of the cathedral.

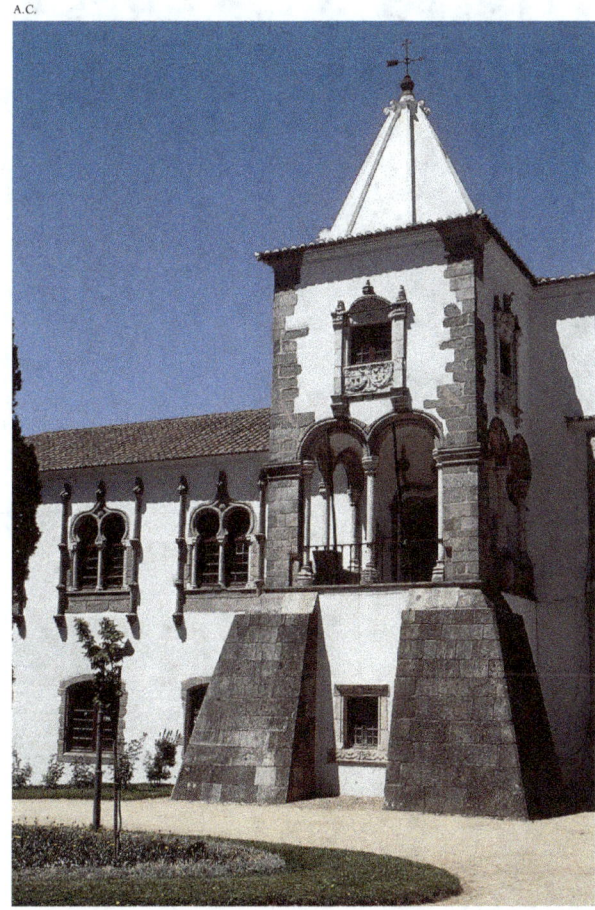

Paço Real, Galeria das Damas, Évora.

A.C.

Ruins of the Vimioso Palace, Évora.

Church of the Convent of São Francisco, Évora.

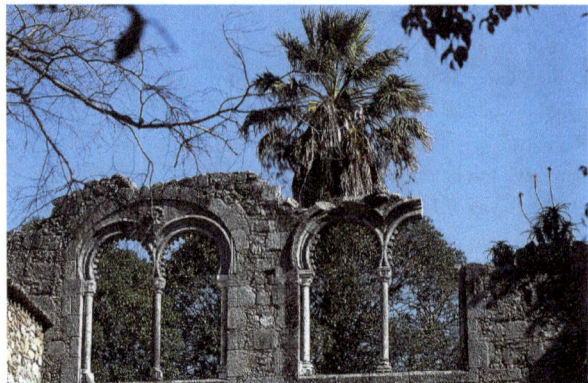

IX.1.d Church of the Convent of São Francisco

Praça 1º de Maio. (Tel: 266 704521). Designated a National Monument.
Opening hours: daily 08.00-18.00 in summer, and 09.00-13.00 and 14.30-17.30 in winter.

This mid-13th century Franciscan Monastery was always under the protection of the monarchy, the Royal Palace being built on adjoining land.
The building was restored in 1508 by the Master Builder, Estêvão Lourenço and is one of the most extravagant of the Manueline period. It stretches from a strong stonework porch with an elegant inner portal in marble, surmounted by the devices of D. Manuel I, who sponsored the work.
Crowned by decorative battlements, the traditional *pinnacles* were substituted by conical towers, which are very typical features of Alentejo brick architecture.
The large single nave has depressed ribbed vaulting, with only three bosses in each bay; the traditional ribbed arches are free standing, only meeting the intermediate ribs at the corbels. These ribs take the thrust of the vaulting onto the not very deep side chapels, which are also vaulted, but perpendicular to the nave, and act as buttresses. The chancel vault is much richer, with two stellar bays with elegantly decorated bosses. Early Renaissance paintings by Lisbon artists, disciples of Jorge Afonso, were included in the Baroque altars of the transept.

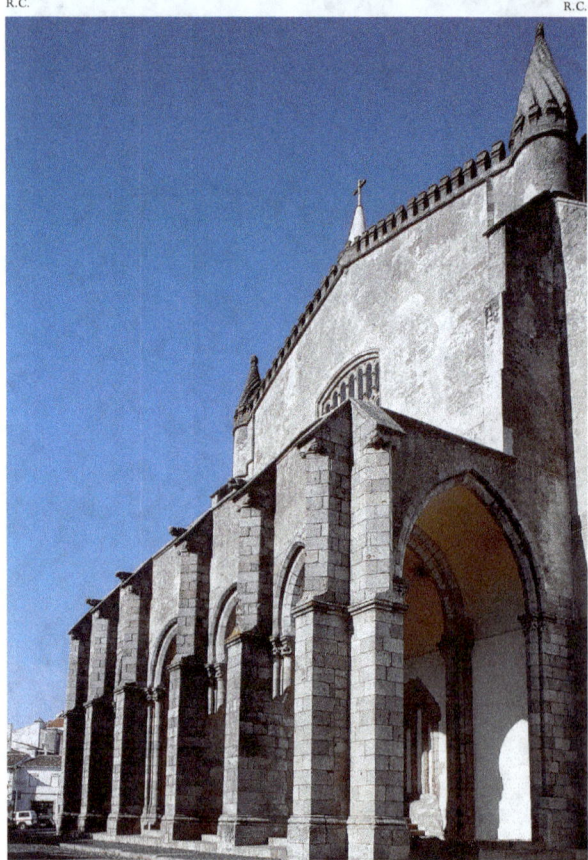

The Chapter House, with depressed ribbed vaulting on hexagonal pillars with ring capitals, also dates from the Manueline period.

The large church was erected during the reign of D. Manuel I, but the cloister by João of Alcobaça, who probably worked on the great Cistercian Abbey there, is earlier. It was in 1376 that João de Alcobaça was contracted to do this work in Évora by D. Fernando Afonso de Morais, the Commendator of the Order of Santiago. It is also known that in 1143, the Castilian Master Stonemason, Mestre Pero, was working on this building.

IX.1.e Cathedral Museum of Sacred Art

Largo do Marquês de Marialva, also known as Largo da Sé. (Tel: 266 759330).
Admission charge. Opening hours: 09.00-12.00 and 14.00-16.30, except on Mondays and December 25th.

A smaller, earlier cathedral in the Romanesque style was begun probably in 1186, and consecrated in 1204, when D. Paio was Bishop of the Diocese. The present building, begun between 1267 and 1283, has enormous cloisters: only one vaulted floor, in an evolved Gothic style, one of the best of 15th-century Portugal. The Capela do Esporão with Late Gothic ribbed vaulting and a Manueline/Renaissance transitional entrance arch, is on the left-hand side of the transept. The Baptismal Chapel is also Manueline and is closed by a grille dating from the same period, one of the few examples of its kind in Portugal.

The tower over the transept crossing, with its Manueline termination, is identical to those found in some older buildings, such as the Cathedrals of Salamanca and Zamora.

The collection in the Sacred Art Museum consists of sculpture, painting, vestments and, above all, ecclesiastical plate, beginning at the north tower and extending to the room above the sacristy, and running chronologically from the 15th to the 19th centuries.

The first room is dominated by the magnificent figure of the *Virgin of Paradise*, a French sculpture in ivory, donated to the Convento do Paraíso, in 1475. The Museum is particularly rich in silver and silver-

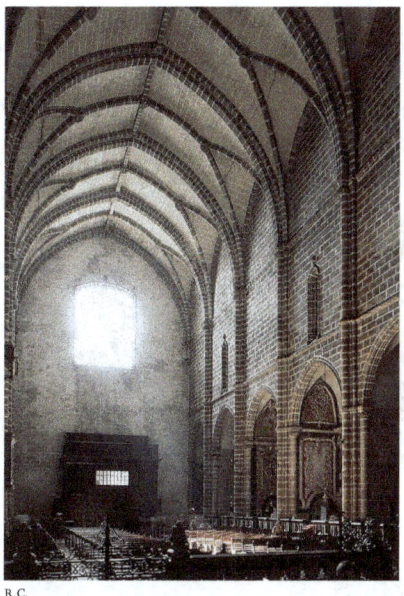

Church of the Convent of São Francisco, interior, Évora.

R.C.

ITINERARY IX   *Évora: City of the Court*
Évora

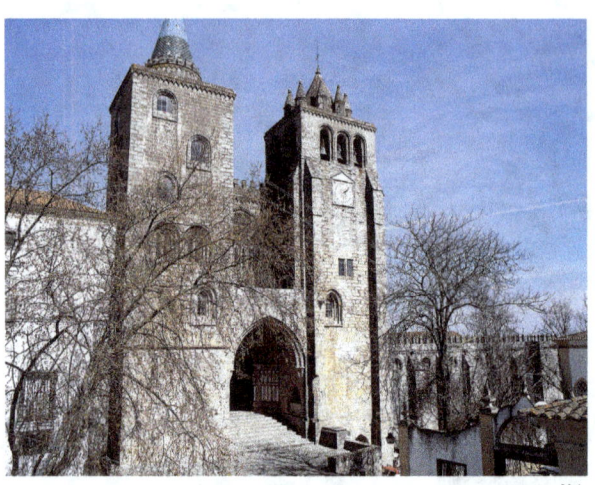

Évora Cathedral.

gilt, one item being a large silver-gilt monstrance with a very fine architectural upper part. It was made at the time when D. Afonso, the son of D. Manuel I,

IPM/J.R

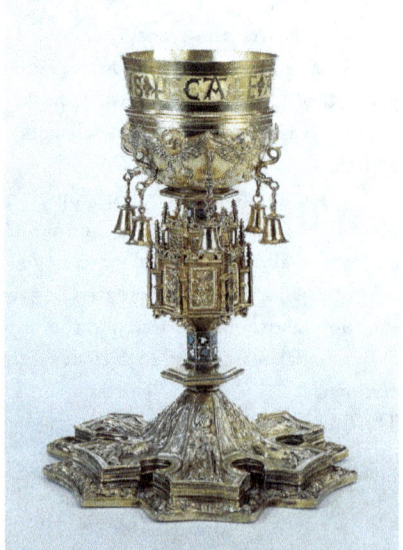

Silver-gilt chalice, Portuguese work, c.1530, Évora Museum.

was Bishop of Évora, between 1522 and 1540.

The most important item is the silver-gilt reliquary cross, ornamented with precious stones and the only one known from the time, but very like those represented in Manueline paintings. It has an imposing knot on the architectural part, which protects the figures of the New and Old Testament. The volute of the cross bears an elegant full-length figure of the Virgin. It probably belonged to Prince Henry the Navigator, also the son of D. Manuel I, and archbishop of Évora, from 1540 onwards.

IX.1.f **Évora Museum**

Largo do Conde de Vila Flor. (Tel: 266 702604).
Opening hours: Tuesday 14.00-17.30, Wednesday-Sunday, 09.30-12.30 and 14.00-17.30. Closed on Mondays and on January 1st, Easter Sunday, May 1st and December 25th.

The collection in the Museum contains some works of art from the Manueline period, and includes a very fine panel representing the *Annunciation* from Seville that is attributed to the workshop of Francisco Niculoso, who introduced majolica painting into Andalucia. This valuable painting has finely represented Gothic-style furniture and Renaissance ornamental elements in the framework of the scene, representing a chapel flanked by two columns ornamented with *grotesques*.

ITINERARY IX   *Évora: City of the Court*
Évora

The silver-gilt chalice, *c.*1515-1525, from the Ermida de São Bras is worthy of note because it has an architectural knot at the top of the stem that is very characteristic of the ornamental art of the period, where some Classical elements were already appearing. The stem is ornamented in black, white and turquoise *cloisonné*, and small fish support bells on the top. Saints are represented on the base.

Very little is conserved in the Museum, or indeed in the city, of the numerous paintings made for the retables of the monastery churches in Évora during the Manueline period. The retable in the Cathedral chancel, commissioned some time between 1485 and 1522 when D. Afonso de Portugal was bishop, is an exception with its 13 panels. *The Virgin of the Angels* or *Nossa Senhora da Glória* occupied the central space of the original retable, along with a sculpture that has since disappeared. The remaining 12 panels were organised in three overlapping, horizontal rows, in a symmetrical structure with three iconographic cycles. These were related to the birth and childhood of the Virgin: *Meeting of St Ana and St Joaquim at the Golden Gate, Birth of the Virgin, Presentation of the Virgin in the Temple* and *Marriage of the Virgin* were placed on the upper row of the retable. The series known as the *Nativity of Christ*, with the *Annunciation, Nativity, Circumcision* and *Adoration of the Magi* was in the middle, and on the lower part were the themes relating to Christ's childhood and times that were particularly painful for the Virgin Mary: *Presentation of Christ in the Temple,*

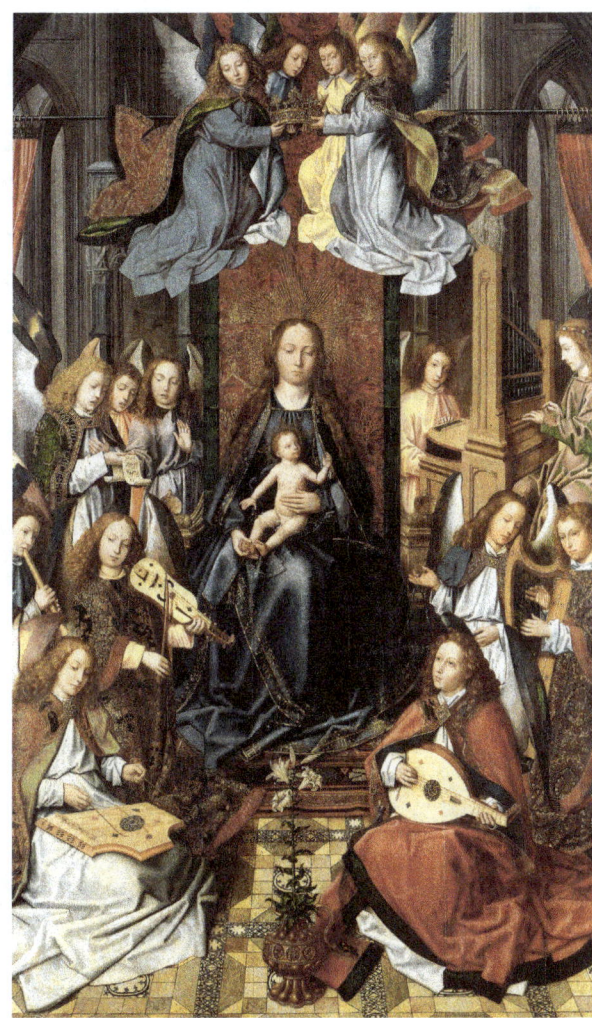

IPM/J.P

Flight into Egypt and *Jesus among the Doctors.* The series ended with the *Death of the Virgin.*

The retable was originally some 7-m.-high and 6-m.-wide, and consequently the upper rows of panels were positioned at a great height. The intention

Workshop of Gérard David, "Nossa Senhora da Glória", from the polyptych of Évora Cathedral, oil on oak, 1490-1500, Évora Museum.

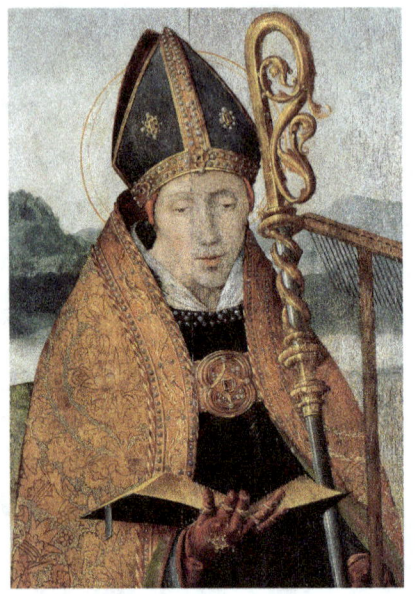

Frei Carlos, "São Brás", oil on wood, c.1530, Évora Museum.

to adapt the retable to the spectator's angle of vision is clearly visible in the spatial organisation of the compositions, particularly in the scaling of the successive planes and the emphasis on the figures in the foreground, which acquire a colossal scale. It is thought that painters from the Low Countries were specially contracted to do this work in Évora, and the retable does have a number of similarities with the work of the painter Gerard David, who headed one of the most prosperous workshops in Bruges.

The museum also contains another series of Flemish panels on the theme of the *Passion of Christ*, by two painters who became famous in Portugal, Francisco Henriques and Frei Carlos, both of whom worked in Évora.

Francisco Henriques, who died in Lisbon in 1518, was responsible for the retable paintings in the chancel and the side chapels of the Monastery Church of São Francisco, the majority of which are now housed in the Museu Nacional de Arte Antiga, in Lisbon. The collection in Évora contains a panel of the *Prophet Daniel judging Susana* from one of the side chapels. Frei Carlos was responsible for the retables in the Monastery Church of Espinheiro, where he took his vows in 1517, and from which a damaged panel of the *Adoration of the Shepherds* still survives.

Also of interest is a panel, clearly from Coimbra, representing *Two Holy Bishops* and bearing the coat of arms of Queen D. Leonor, the widow of D. João II.

IX.1.g **Convent of the Lóios, or Convent of São João Evangelista**

Largo do Conde de Vila Flor. (Tel: 266 704714 and ask for Sr. Jacinto Evaristo Carrageta). Designated a National Monument. The Monastery has been turned into a pousada, *so only part of the building may be visited. (Tel: 266 704051).*

Opening hours: winter 10.00-12.30 and 14.00-17-00, summer 10.00-12.30 and 14.00-18.00. Closed on Mondays and public holidays.

D. Rodrigo de Melo, the first Governor of Tangiers and Count of Olivença, began building work in 1485. At the end of 1491, he took Holy Orders, although the building work continued and was essentially completed in the first phase, when its patronage was taken over by the first Count of Tentúgal.

The history of the Monastery and the deeds of its founder are inscribed on a stone in the form of an elegant tent-shaped canopy held open by two angels to display the armorial bearings of the family and the inscription, which is to be seen on the left of the axial door, under the open portico.

Both the main door and the atrium are Late Gothic, superbly executed and clearly inspired by Batalha. The Church, with depressed Gothic vaulting and bosses, has one single nave and five bays, the first of which coincides with the upper choir, where there is an exhibition of works of art belonging to the Cadaval family, which owns the church and town house next to it. In the apse chapel, the ribbed vaulting is denser for aesthetic reasons.

As well as various Renaissance tombs, the church also contains a unique series of bronze memorials, specially commissioned for family graves, while others are in stone or in both stone and bronze. Those of D. Rodrigo de Melo and D. Isabel de Meneses are the oldest, both of them being depicted with great realism.

The Capela de Nossa Senhora do Rosário contains the memorials of D. Branca de Vilhena and Rui de Sousa, the former with an architectural framework imitating a Late Gothic niche, and the latter with foliage around the inscription. The most beautiful memorial, depicting Rui Pais and his wife praying, was undoubtedly made in Hainaut and is currently to be found in the upper choir.

The Monastery is built round a two-storey, vaulted cloister and was constructed in the first two decades of the 16th century; it is now largely occupied by a *pousada*. The emblematic, Alentejo *Mudejar* doorway to the Chapter House with its double tracery horseshoe arches is on the ground floor. It is surmounted by a representation of a stockade set in a medallion, the device of D. Rodrigo de Melo, which refers to his successful military campaigns in North Africa.

Other Luso-Moorish elements are also to be seen in other parts of the building, such as the *lavabo* (wash room) and refectory.

R.C.

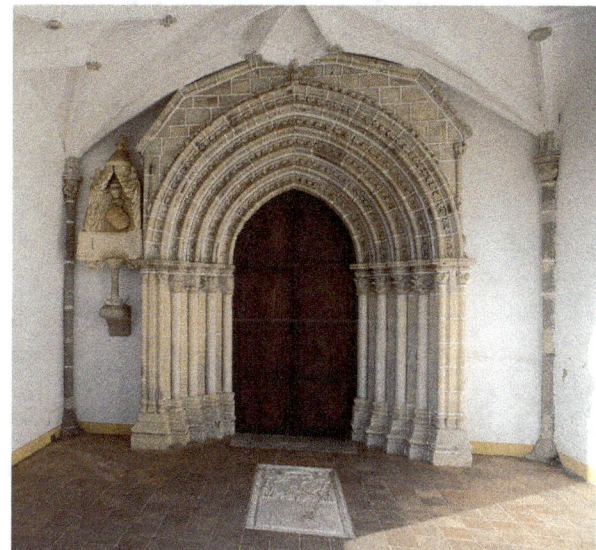

Church of the Convent of the Lóios, portal, Évora.

ITINERARY IX   *Évora: City of the Court*

Évora

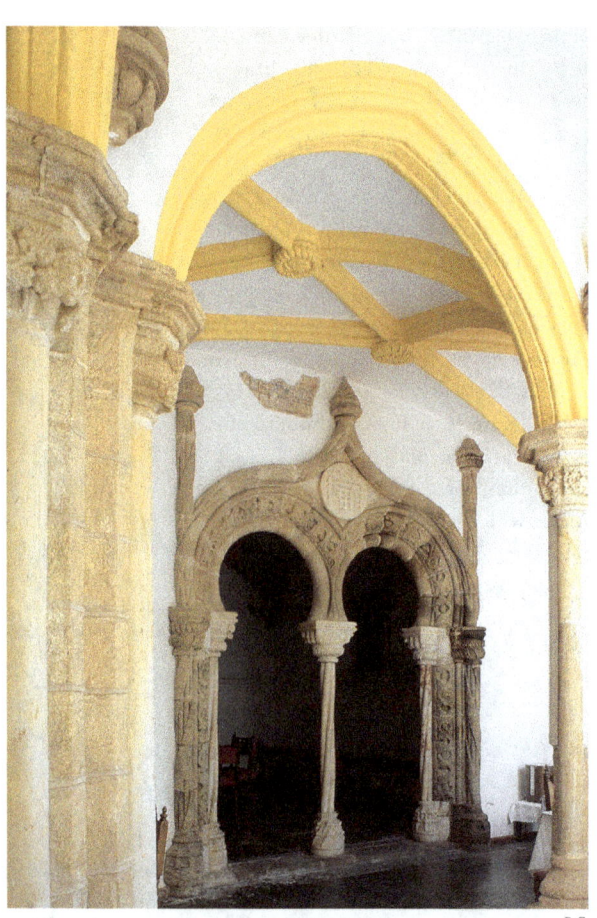

Convent of the Lóios, portal of the Chapter House, Évora.

IX.1.h **Convent of São Bento de Cástris** (option)

Situated about 2km. from Évora on the road to Arraiolos. The Monastery is signposted. Designated a National Monument. The church, cloisters and old refectory may be visited also. Information: Sra. Amélia Cambeta at Casa Pia (Tel: 266 760030).
Opening hours: Monday-Friday 09.00-12.00 and 14.00-17.00.

Situated on the outskirts of Évora, the Convent of São Bento de Cástris is one of the oldest in the Alentejo. The first church and complex was completed at the beginning of the 14th century, but, except for the entrance to the Chapter House, the rest was built later, dating from reforms undertaken in the Manueline era. The cloister was the work of the Master Builder, Estêvão Lourenço, which dates it to about 1520.

The atrium before the church has an arch with a partially twisted double *colonnette* and *archivolt*, followed by vaulting, though the portal is not original. The wide nave is covered with ribbed vaulting, with centred bays uniting four-part escutcheons and intermediate ribs with naturalist bosses, those in the centre bearing heraldic elements.

The two-storey cloister has double lowered arches, a peculiar structure somewhat similar to that of the Convento dos Lóios, so that they must have been the work of the same master builder. Though large in size, the materials are poor in quality, consisting of whitewashed and plastered brick, rather typical of the Alentejo Manueline architectural style.

IX.1.i **Convent of Nossa Senhora do Espinheiro** (option)

About 2km. north of Évora on the road to Estremoz. Take the road to Espinheiro cemetery. The Convent is private property and may only be visited with the permission of the owners. The funerary chapel of Garcia de Resende is contained within the monastery walls. The chapel and church are designated National Monuments.

This Monastery, probably founded by Bishop D. Vasco Perdigão in 1458, was an important religious centre in the second half of the 15th century, and throughout the 16th century.
Work was undertaken on the building in Manueline times and the living area, organised around a vaulted cloister, is of particular interest with its marked regional characteristics, similar to those of the *Convento de São Bento de Cástris* and the *Convento dos Lóios*. The building is smaller, but contains some interesting decorative elements, most notably the bosses on the vaulting ribs.
The utilitarian parts of the building are also vaulted, with brick and *arris vaulting*, a characteristic feature of the Alentejo. This is the case with the large *adega*, or wine cellar, c.1525. The cistern was built a little later, with more traditional roofing on strong pillars supporting simple ribs.
Set apart from the Monastery buildings is the Funerary Chapel of Garcia de Resende, one of the leading figures in Portuguese Humanism, who lived and died here. The contract to build the funerary chapel was signed in 1521, so that work on the small church with an open atrium, single vaulted nave and vernacular portal, must have been carried out immediately afterwards.
The floor is covered with *cuerda seca Mudejar* tiles made in Seville and also a 16th-century Renaissance memorial stone that was certainly sculpted by Nicolas Chanterène.

For Arraiolos, take the EN114-4 to the crossroads with the EN370, at Valeira, where you turn right in the direction of Arraiolos (27 km.).

ITINERARY IX

Évora: City of the Court

Pedro Dias, Dalila Rodrigues,
Nuno Vassallo e Silva, Fernando Grilo

Second day

IX.2 ARRAIOLOS
  IX.2.a Historic Centre
  IX.2.b Castle
  IX.2.c Church of Salvador
  IX.2.d Convent of the Lóios

IX.3 MONTEMOR-O-NOVO
  IX.3.a Castle
  IX.3.b Church of São Tiago
  IX.3.c Chapel of Nossa Senhora da Visitação

Painted Houses: Mural Painting in the House of Vasco da Gama

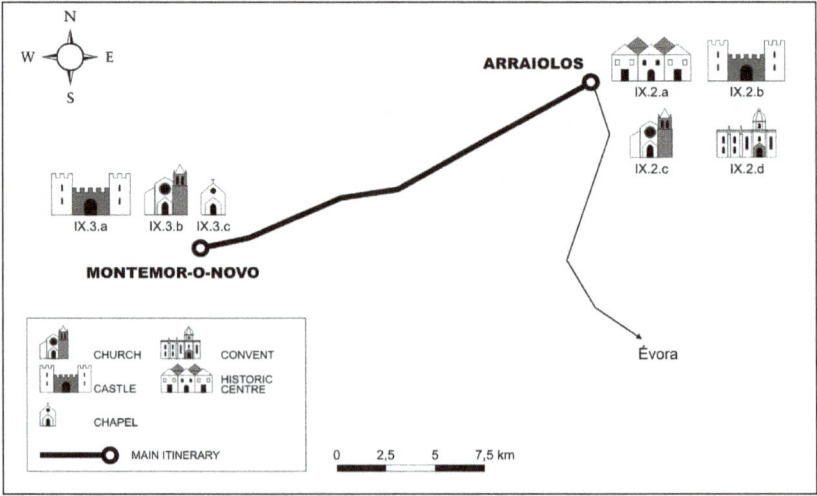

ITINERARY IX   *Évora: City of the Court*
Arraiolos

IX.2 ARRAIOLOS

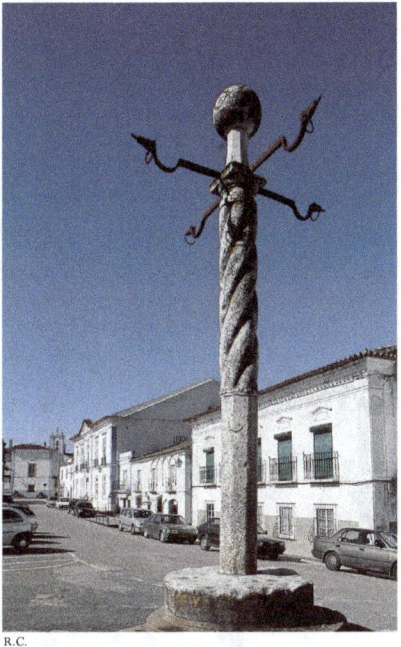

Arraiolos historic centre and Pillory.

Arraiolos was an important town throughout the Middle Ages, because it was Royal land. It was then granted to D. Nuno Álvares Pereira, who gave it to his grandson, the future Duke of Bragança, in 1422. The town was granted a charter by D. Manuel I, in 1514.

It was an important administrative and economic centre for this part of the Alentejo, and within its walls a cottage industry developed, from the beginning of the 17th century onwards, when handmade carpets made there began to incorporate Oriental designs, inspired by Turkish, Persian and Indian carpets.

IX.2.a Historic Centre

In the Old Quarter right in the centre of town, there are two Manueline features of particular interest. The first is the portal of the Espírito Santo Hospital, founded in 1409. The completed work was financed by the Duke of Bragança, D. Jaime and was finished by João Marques in 1525.

The second feature of interest is the pillory, erected in 1535, set on a four-step base, with a partially spiral shaft ending in a ball, the result of restorations carried out in the time of D. José I (1750-77), with the shackles in the shape of a horizontal cross.

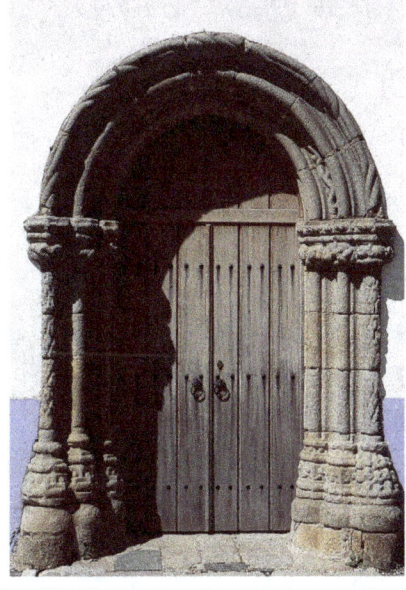

Hospital do Espírito Santo, portal, Arraiolos.

Arraiolos

Castle and the Church of Salvador, Arraiolos.

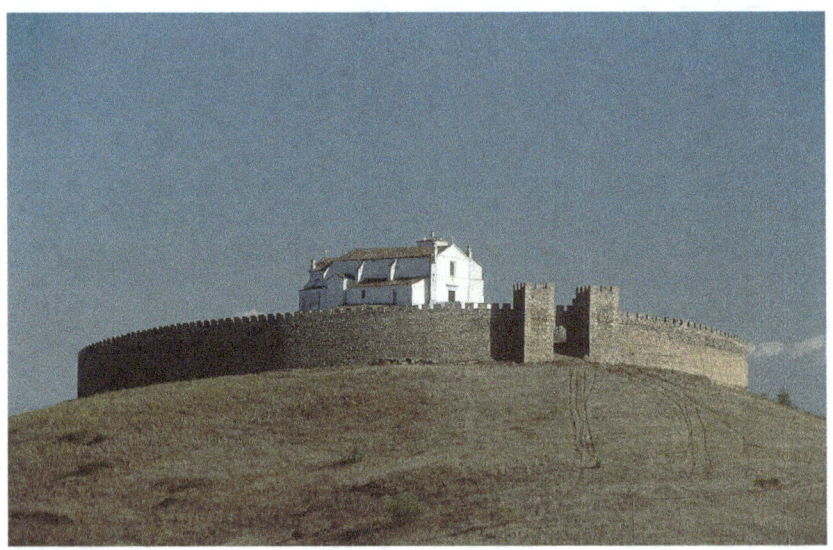

IX.2.b Castle

Designated a National Monument. Information: Tourist Office (Tel: 266 490240). The Castle may be visited at any time.

The Castle was built in the reign of D. Dinis in 1304; and the extremely well documented construction was the work of João Simão.
Besides the *enceinte* that sheltered the early settlement, it also had a house for the *alcaide*, or governor, during the Manueline era when it was regularly used, and it has remained largely the same up to the present time. The keep was remodelled after 1485, when work was also carried out to adapt the *curtain walls* next to the gateways, most notably the one around the parade ground, which was given wide crenellations.

IX.2.c Church of Salvador

The Church, which is contained inside the Castle, may be visited by contacting Sr. Teodorico Valente, at the Câmara Municipal (Town Hall Tel: 266 490240), or the Tourist Office (Tel: 266 490240).

Church of Salvador, Arraiolos.

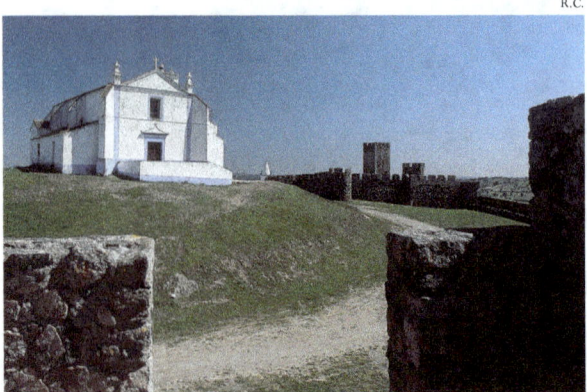

ITINERARY IX   *Évora: City of the Court*
Montemor-o-Novo

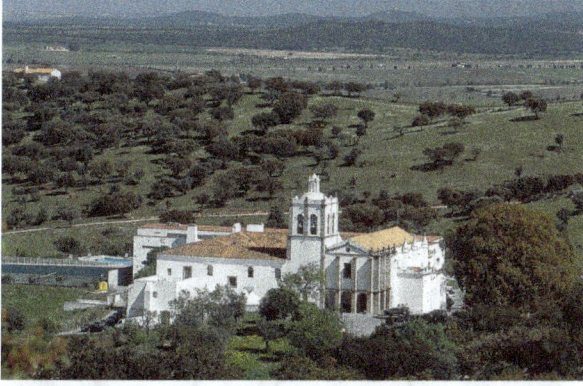

Convent of the Lóios, Arraiolos.

Opening hours: Fridays at 09.30-10.30 for the celebration of mass.

This Church existed before 1271, but the present-day structure dates from the beginning of the 16th century, when the Bishop of Évora, D. Afonso de Portugal, was its patron. Note the crossed Gothic vaulting with five bosses, and ribbed bays resting on addorsed *colonnettes*, which makes it appear that the old walls were used for the Manueline remodelling. The sacristy retains part of its original Late Gothic structure.

IX.2.d Convent of the Lóios

Herdade de Vale de Flores, about 1 km. from the centre of Arraiolos. Classified as a Building of Public Interest. The Convent currently houses the Pousada *de Nossa Senhora da Assunção. (Tel: 266 419340).*

Building started on the Convent in 1527, as a result of the donation of the site by João Garcês and Leonor de Abreu. All the royal family made notable contributions, even the king himself at that time, D. João III. D. Jaime, Duke of Bragança, paid entirely for the cloister.
The oldest part of the Convent is the church, which is reached through an open atrium with a typically Manueline naturalist doorway comprising a rounded arch and ball-flowered *archivolts* in the intercolumnations, foliate and rope-like capitals, with knots edging the extrados.
The heavy vaulting in the nave with five bosses, pulls together the depressed ribs from the

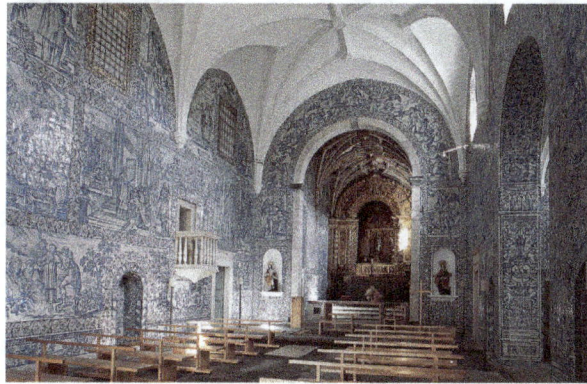

high, naturalistic corbels. The chancel is more richly vaulted and evolved, with well designed quatrefoils that meet in superbly decorated foliate bosses, to form two bays.

Church of the Convent of the Lóios, interior, Arraiolos.

Take the EN4 to Montemor-o-Novo (22 km.)

IX.3 MONTEMOR-O-NOVO

Like many towns and cities in the Alentejo province, Montemor-o-Novo originat-

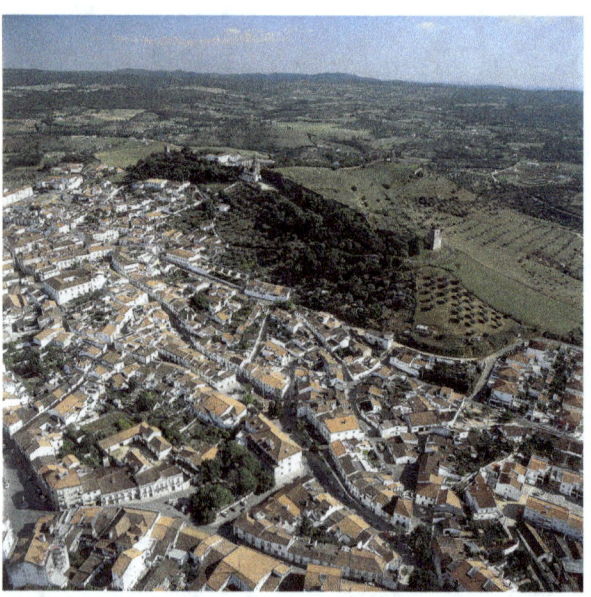

R.C.
Aerial view of Montemor-o-Novo.

ed from a Roman settlement, occupied and enlarged by the Goths and the Moors. D. Afonso Henriques conquered it in 1160, or thereabouts, and it remained part of the new kingdom for some time, before being granted a charter by D. Sancho I, in 1203. The town developed during the Middle Ages, various kings staying in the area and the Cortes Gerais, the General Assembly of the Kingdom, being held there in 1477 and 1481.

In January 1497, in the castle, D. Manuel I gave Vasco da Gama command of the first fleet of ships that left for India. The King definitively united Montemor-o-Novo to the Crown in 1498, and granted the town a new charter in 1503. It still preserves an important group of Mediaeval constructions and others dating from the 16th century. Where Late Gothic structures exist, they probably date from the time of D. João III, such as the Convento de Santo António, the Convento de Nossa Senhora da Saudação, the Hospital do Espírito Santo and even the Igreja da Misericórdia.

IX.3.a **Castle**

Designated a National Monument. Inside the Castle enclosure, in the Convento da Saudação, there is an Information Office, open from Wednesday to Sunday 10.00-13.00 and 14.00-17.00. Information: Câmara Municipal (Town Hall Tel: 266 898100, Ext. 397). The Castle is always open.

Montemor-o-Novo Castle was built during the Moorish period, but was considerably altered during the reign of D. Dinis. The circuit of the walls was practically defined with a perimeter that extended over 1.5 km., but the conservation work and strengthening lasted until the reign of D. Manuel I. The *alcácer* (alcazar) was in the most protected part and was known at the end of the Middle Ages as the Royal Palace. Considerable work was carried out here at the beginning of the 16th century and the famous cistern dates from this period. It has excellent fan-shaped ribbed vaulting set on pillars. The coat of arms of D. Manuel I is visible on the entrance to the guardhouse at the Porta de Vila.

The 20-m.-high Clock Tower is of particular interest, for its pyramid-shaped top

ITINERARY IX   *Évora: City of the Court*
Montemor-o-Novo

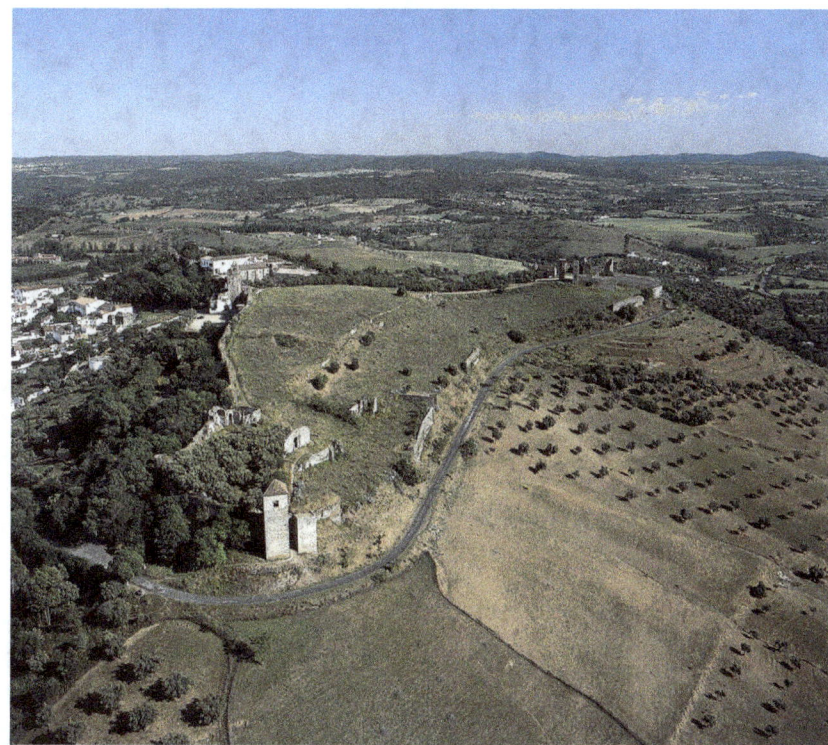

Aerial view of Montemor-o-Novo Castle.

Church of São Tiago.

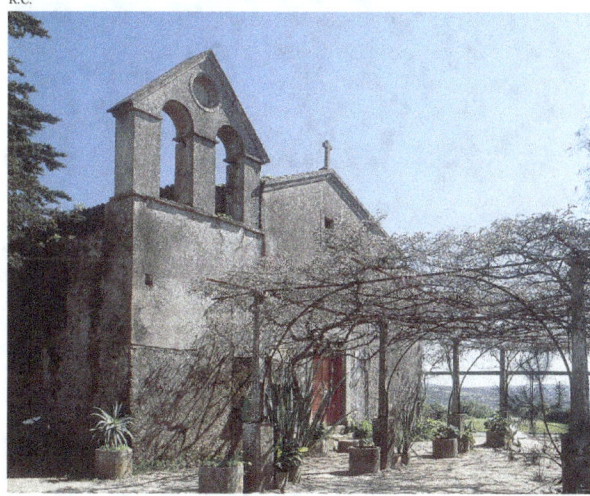

is very typical of the Manueline style used in the Alentejo.

IX.3.b Church of São Tiago

The Church is inside the Castle. Designated a National Monument.

The Church of São Tiago is in the enclosed part of the Old Town. Gothic in style, it was further added to in the reign of D. Manuel I. A former commandery of the Order of Santiago, it is of considerable interest as a construction, primarily the vaulting of the

Chapel of Nossa Senhora da Visitação.

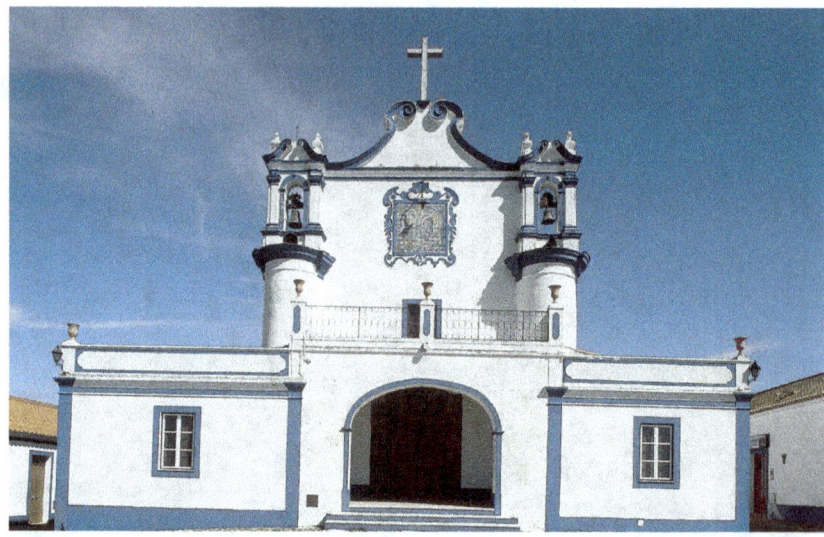

nave with its brick ribs. In fact, brick is used for most of the building, in an art that almost only appears in the southern third of the country. A memorial stone, dated 1511, and decorated with the National coat of arms, is dedicated to Francisco Frazão, magistrate, almost certainly indicating when the church was restored.

IX.3.c **Chapel of Nossa Senhora da Visitação**

1 km. from the centre of the city to the north east. Information: Parish House of Nossa Senhora da Vila (Tel: 266 892127).

Opening hours: daily 09.00-18.00.

The centre of a regional pilgrimage, the chapel was initially situated on the outskirts of the town, but nowadays it is completely integrated into the urban grid. There is nothing of the Late Gothic visible in the exterior, other than a fine and distinctly Baroque portal, dating from about 1515. The structure inside has magnificent vaulting mainly in the chancel, in a very advanced style with curved ribs, typical of those that were used from about the third decade of the 16th century onwards.

PAINTED HOUSES: MURAL PAINTING IN THE HOUSE OF VASCO DA GAMA

Pedro Dias

One of the most interesting reminders of Portuguese mural painting dating from the Manueline period is to be found in a 16th-century house in Évora that is traditionally associated with Vasco da Gama. The possibility of this house belonging to the famous navigator, although intriguing, comes from relatively late information, namely from the account given by Padre Francisco da Fonseca in his book *Évora Gloriosa*, and from *Livro das Visitações da Cidade d'Évora em 1591*.

The mural paintings, which were done at different times, are on a covered balcony with ribbed vaulting, and have been extended into a small oratory. The oldest painting, a formal concept marked by a certain ingenuity, is an extraordinary record of animal themes. There are no distinctions between the domestic and the wild, the real or the fantastic, and therefore, through a subversive disorderly discourse, the figures of affronted cocks, rabbits, deer, a leopard, and birds of various species, are brought together in a neutral and also ambiguous space, combined together more or less pacifically with fabulous, fantastic beings, such as mermaids with birds' or fishes' tails, dragons, or a mythical hydra with seven heads.

Related to the problematic imagery of the Discoveries — the decoration of the roof covering has a recurring theme of knotted ropes — this iconographic programme takes on special value by what it reveals of the profane art of this period. In an obviously Classical and erudite style, the lower frieze that forms a skirting board corresponds to a later period, but it again uses fantastic elements, following the repetitive schemes and stylised characteristics of the *grotesque*, in a frankly ornamental style.

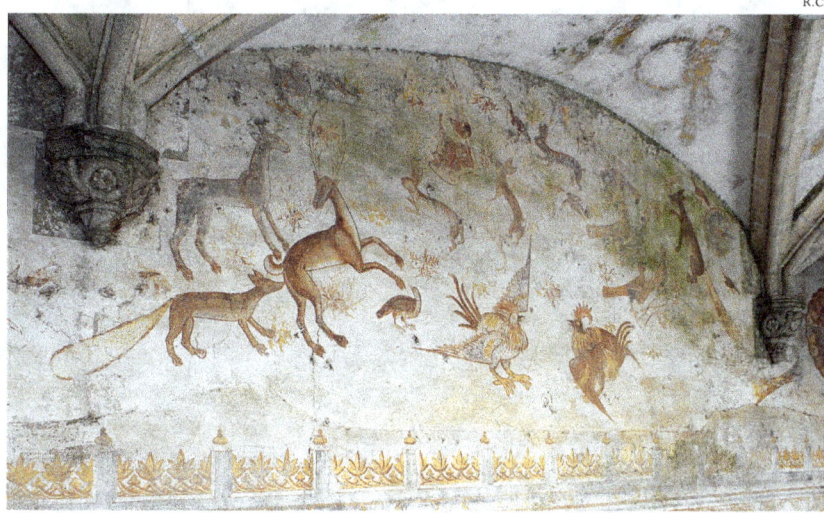

Mural paintings in Vasco da Gama's house, detail, Évora.

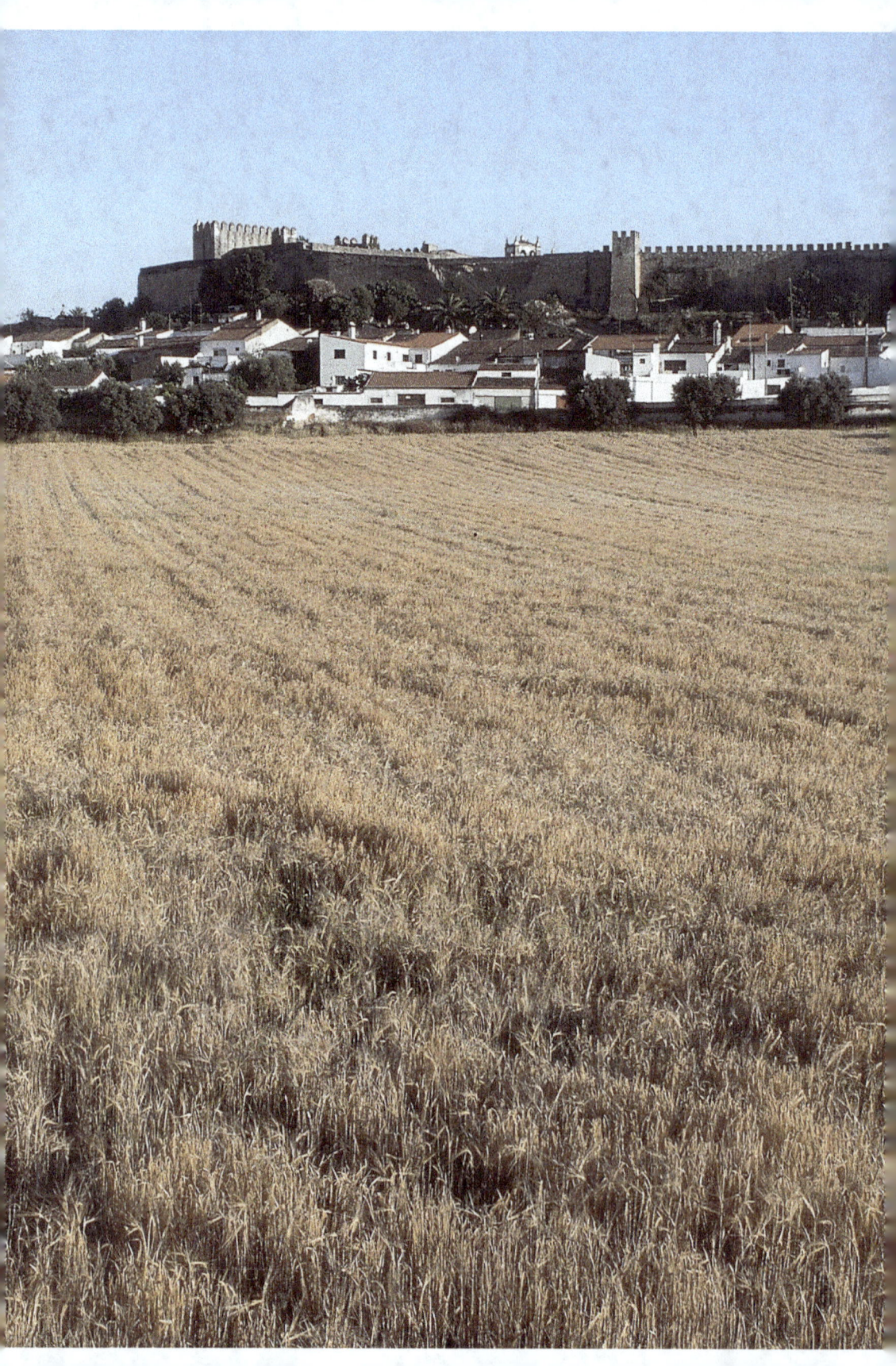

ITINERARY X

White Towns

Pedro Dias, Dalila Rodrigues,
Nuno Vassallo e Silva, Fernando Grilo

First day

X.1 VIANA DO ALENTEJO
    X.1.a Castle
    X.1.b Antiga Casa da Câmara
        (Former Town Hall)
    X.1.c Nossa Senhora da Anunciação
        (Viana do Alentejo Parish Church)
    X.1.d Church of Misericórdia

X.2 ALVITO
    X.2.a Historic Centre
    X.2.b Nossa Senhora da Assunção
        (Alvito Parish Church)
    X.2.c Casa da Câmara (Town Hall)
    X.2.d Castle
    X.2.e Chapel of São Sebastião

X.3 VIDIGUEIRA
    X.3.a Castle
    X.3.b Torre do Relógio
        (Clock Tower)
    X.3.c Ermida de Santa Clara
        (Chapel of St Clara)

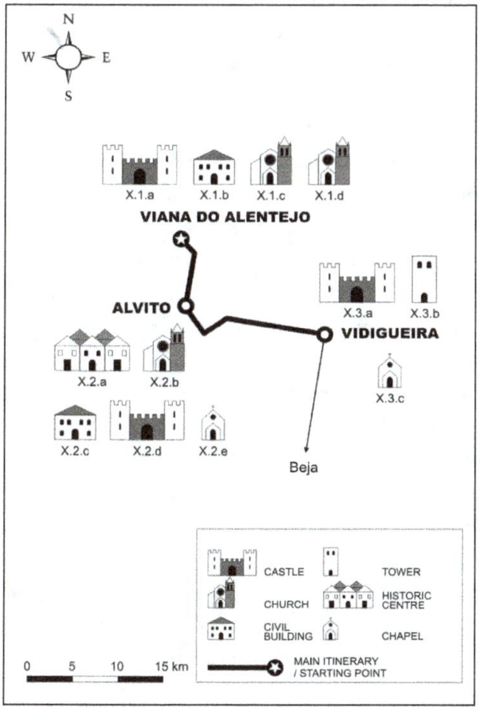

Serpa.

ITINERARY X   *White Towns*
Viana do Alentejo

The plains of the Alentejo, stretching as far as the eye can see, are green at the end of winter, and in spring, and golden in the hot summer and at the beginning of autumn. The colours are broken here and there by the blinding white smudges of towns with their immaculate whitewashed houses. These towns, often dating back to Roman times, when they grew up around extensive farms, were later to become Islamic and, even when conquered by the troops of D. Sancho I, still retained their southern character formed by the land and climate.

Today the townspeople still live from the sales of agricultural produce or the cattle they raise, though some have developed important cottage industries, such as woollen goods, and in particular the handmade carpets, first made in Arraiolos.

The people of the Alentejo did not prosper as in other parts of the country, but by the end of the 15th century, with many towns coming under the control of the monarchy, the Dukes of Bragança and other members of the Court nobility, things began to improve. Beja was made a city even before it became the see of the Diocese, but it was, most importantly, the residence of the Dukes of Bragança, D. Fernando and D. Beatriz, the parents of D. Manuel I, whilst, as is known, D. Fernando was also the brother of D. Afonso V.

These peaceful, white towns and their inhabitants have a relative view of time,

far from the hustle and bustle of modern-day life. Many doorways and window surrounds are still bordered in bright blue or ochre, as they were long ago, for this is seen as a way of warding off evil spirits. This is a journey with a warm welcome, excellent food and a fascinating heritage that includes reminders of Islamic times in the Iberian Peninsula, with Moorish or *Mudejar* architecture.

X.1 VIANA DO ALENTEJO

Viana do Alentejo was an important 15th-century town that belonged to the second Count of Barcelos, and then to D. Afonso V and his wife, before being absorbed into the domain of the Counts of Viana, namely D. Pedro de Meneses, Governor of Ceuta. Various Portuguese kings spent periods of time here, particularly D. Fernando I and D. João II.

An administrative centre, Viana developed with agricultural trade, benefiting from its strategic position on the Alentejo road network.

The town was granted a new charter by D. Manuel I, in 1517.

X.1.a **Castle**

The Castle can be reached through Largo de São Luís, or, if approaching from Praça da República, by Rua Cândido dos Reis. Designated a National Monument. To visit the Cas-

Viana do Alentejo

tle interior, contact Sr. Padre Manuel (Tel: 266 953133).

The pentagonal Castle of Viana do Alentejo, with cylindrical towers at the corners, originally dates back to the time of D. Dinis, who had an *enceinte* constructed with a perimeter of 400 "arms", approximately 880 m. What remains today, apart from the foundations, dates back to Manueline restorations, possibly by one or other of the Master Builders, perhaps either Martim Lourenço or the Arruda brothers, who lived in the Alentejo.
The fort had two gateways, and the highest and widest tower served as the keep. All the towers had conical roofs and a plastered, brick *pinnacle*, typical of the Alentejo. It is a fortress on the plains, with angled walls crowned by wide battlements with parapets, openings and slits ready to fire crossbows, which would date the building to about 1410. Outposts were set up in the lower part to prevent surprise attacks.
It is thought that the castle had a moat and that the gates had drawbridges, but all this has since disappeared.

X.1.b Antiga Casa da Câmara (Former Town Hall)

Praça da República (independent access from the castle). (Tel: 266 953106). The building is currently used as a library.

A.C.

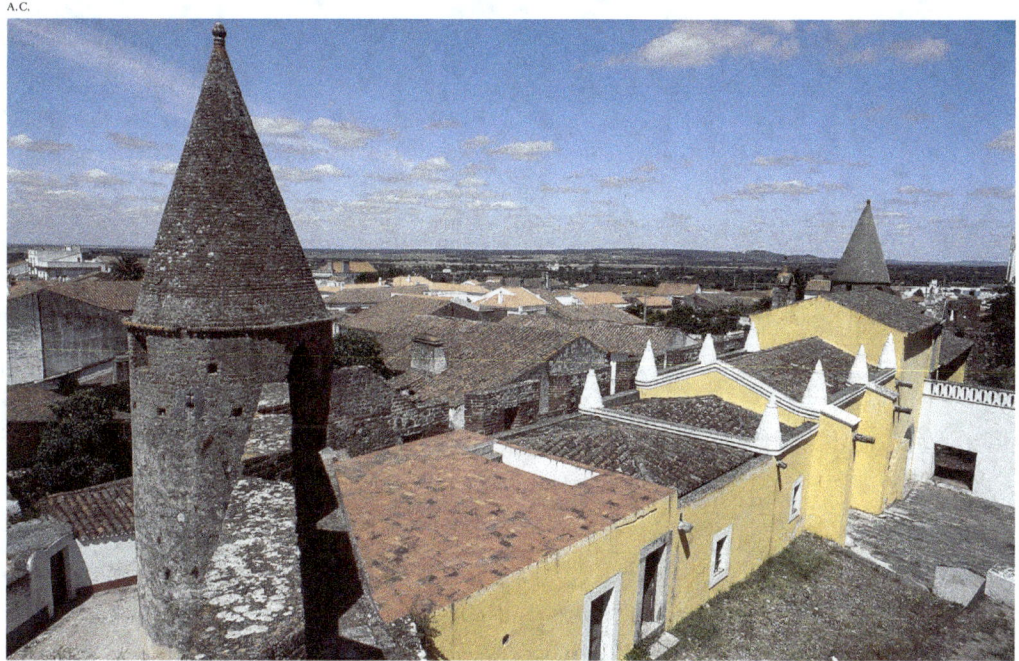

Viana do Alentejo.

ITINERARY X White Towns
Viana do Alentejo

Viana do Alentejo Castle.

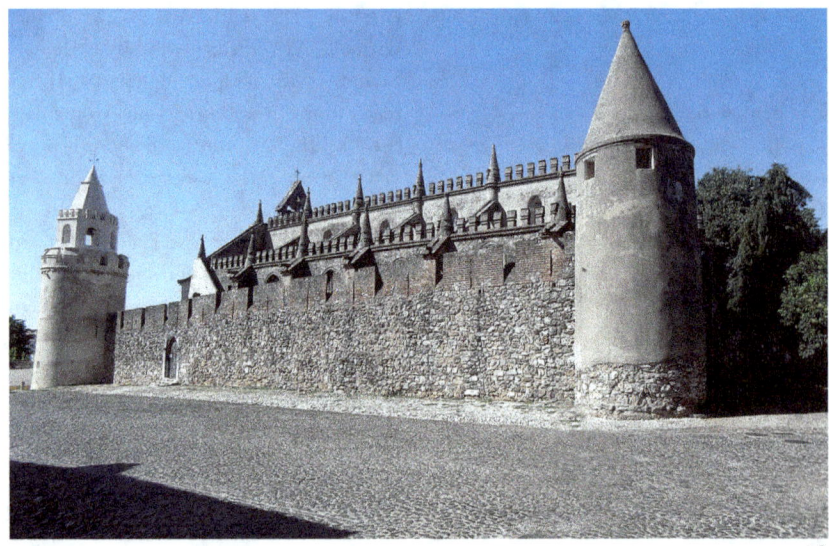

Opening hours: Monday-Friday 09.30-13.00 and 14.30-18.00.

The former Town Hall, dating from the 14th century, is inside the castle next to the wall and one of the gateways. In the 17th century, the building was transformed into the Church of Nossa Senhora da Assunção, though it is still possible to see some isolated Manueline features, which were reintegrated into the building some decades ago.

X.1.c **Nossa Senhora da Anunciação (Viana do Alentejo Parish Church)**

The Church stands inside the castle enclosure, in Largo de São Luís. Designated a National Monument. Information: Sr. Padre Manuel (Tel: 266 953133).

The Church may be visited and opens for mass: Monday-Friday at 8.00, Saturday at 9.00 and Sunday at 11.00 and 13.00.

One of the most remarkable Manueline buildings south of the River Tagus, the Parish Church dates back to the 13th century, although what can be seen today dates from the second and third decades of the 16th century.

The Portuguese Crown sponsored the work and it is quite possible that the Royal Master Builders from the Alentejo: Diogo and Francisco Arruda, or even Martim Lourenço, were involved in its construction. This is, however, only put forward as a hypothesis and lacks actual confirmation.

The church is complex in structure, with three aisles and five bays, a triple apse, with a chancel and two shallow side

White Towns
Viana do Alentejo

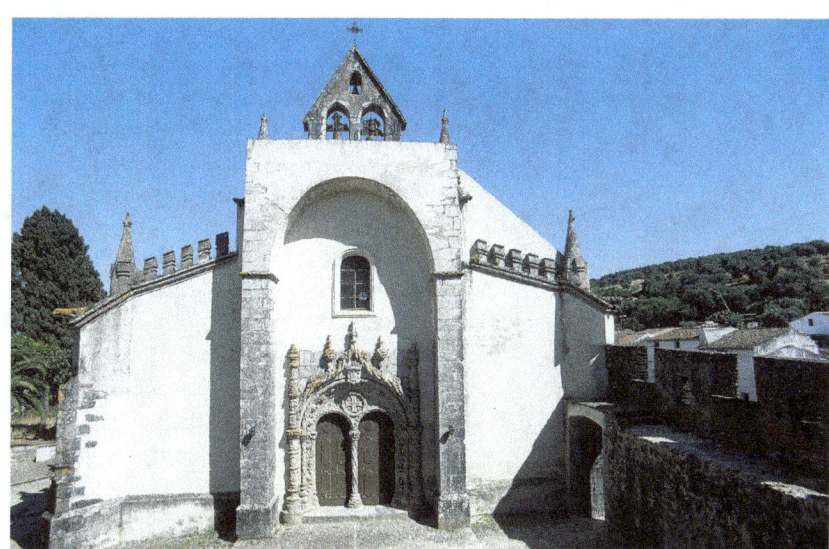

Nossa Senhora da Anunciação, Viana do Alentejo Parish Church.

chapels. The entire church is covered with angled ribbed vaulting on highly decorated octagonal piers, with foliate rings substituting capitals. Only the apse vaulting has a richer and more decorative network of ribs. The upper choir is set on lowered arches.

Outside, the buttresses support the thrust of the nave vaulting and provide reinforcement of the side aisles. The cresting is made up of decorative battlements and small conical *pinnacles*. The portal is a Manueline masterpiece where, on the concentric arches, architectural components have been completely replaced by foliate elements. A twisted pillar supports the twin arches and the *tympanum* with the Cross of Christ, which is surmounted by the royal coat of arms on the keystone of the *archivolts*, flanked by carved *pinnacles* at the sides, with those on the cresting holding armillary spheres.

The Romanesque interior remodelled in the Manueline style has some Late Gothic

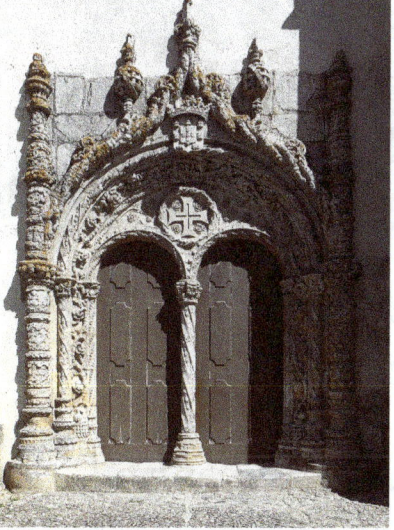

Nossa Senhora da Anunciação, Viana do Alentejo Parish Church, main portal.

ITINERARY X White Towns
Alvito

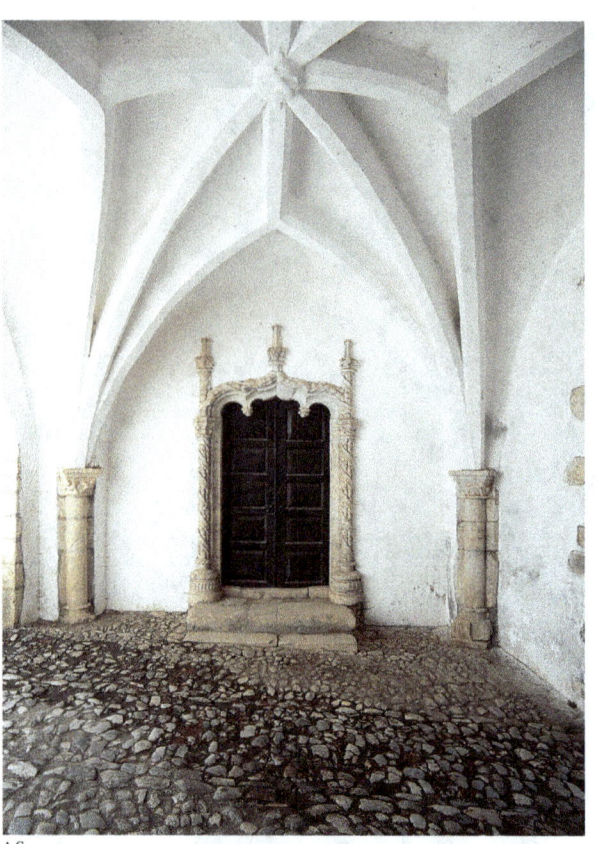

Church of Misericórdia, portal, Viana do Alentejo.
A.C.

inscribed stones and an altar frontal of *Mudejar* tiles produced in Seville.

X.1.d Church of Misericórdia

This Church is also situated inside the castle, next to one of the gates. To visit the interior, contact Sr. Padre Manuel (Tel: 266 953133).

The Santa Casa da Misericórdia, part of a national charitable institution, was founded in Viana do Alentejo, in 1516, and building work must have started immediately afterwards, as would seem to be suggested by the clearly Manueline structure.

The Church, situated against the wall next to one of the gates of the castle, but below the line of the battlements, is entered by an atrium covered by a Gothic rib vault, the same as that found in the former Town Hall. The magnificent polylobed naturalist portal appears to have been influenced by the doorway of the parish church, or possibly made by the same hands.

The interior of the Private Chapel of the Misericórdia is very simple, with the main vessel of the single nave ending in a chapel, preceded by a semi-circular *crossing arch*, with the bases of the columns and the capitals in fine foliate carving. The vaulting is simple and utilitarian.

Follow the EN257 to Alvito.

X.2 ALVITO

Alvito gained importance in the mid-12th century, when it came into the possession of the son-in-law and chancellor of D. Afonso III, D. Estêvão Anes. In 1279, it was transferred to the Order of the Most Holy Trinity (*Santíssima Trindade*), which did much to develop the region. By the end of the 14th century, it was already an important town, thanks to the contributions of various donors, and particularly

ITINERARY X   *White Towns*
Alvito

so in the 15th century when the second Baron of Alvito, D. Diogo Lobo da Silveira, built his palace there.
The town was granted a charter by D. Manuel I, in 1516.

X.2.a Historic Centre

Information: Tourist Office (Tel: 284 485440).

The Old Centre of Alvito shows how much it developed in the 16th century, as many traces of its Manueline past are still visible in the streets by the old castle, not only religious buildings but also doors and windows of secular buildings with carved or chamfered marble surrounds. Note the polylobed doors in Rossio de São Sebastião, or in Rua de Beja or the attractive Rua Nova.
The parish church and civil buildings, such as the Town Hall and the castle, mark the main areas, but the distribution and regularity of old Manueline houses is unusual for the time and indicates a higher standard of living for a significant proportion of the population.

X.2.b Nossa Senhora da Assunção (Alvito Parish Church)

Largo da Trindade. Designated a National Monument. To visit the interior, an appointment must be made through the Tourist Office (Tel: 284 485440).

This Church dates back to the 12th century, although, today, what remains is largely from the Manueline era or the beginning of the reign of D. João III. Considerable restoration and rebuilding of the present church took place when the first or second Baron of Alvito obtained permission to use it as his family pantheon. Later additions took place during the Renaissance, Mannerist and Baroque periods, but it is known that the essentials were completed by 1631, when an inspection was carried out.
The three-aisled, buttressed Church has a vaulted central nave with five bosses,

Manueline door, detail, Alvito historic centre.

A.C.

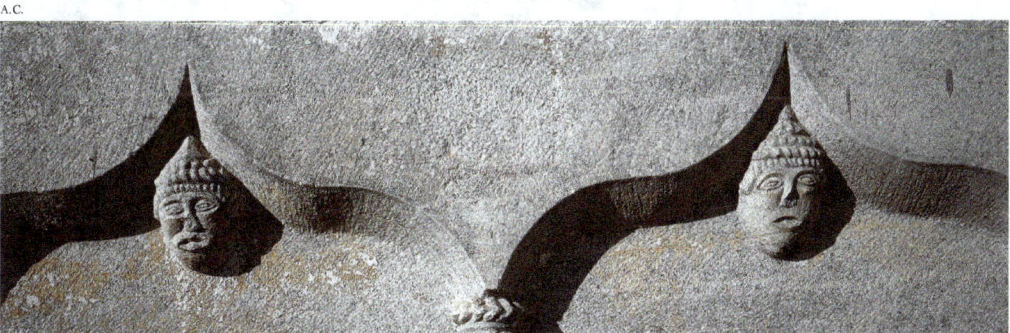

ITINERARY X *White Towns*
Alvito

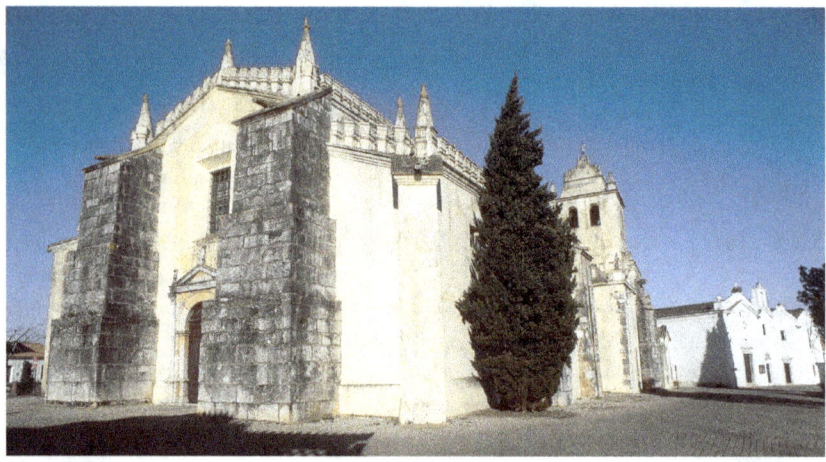

Nossa Senhora da Assunção, Alvito Parish Church.

while the octagonal arches dividing the aisles have naturalist rings in place of capitals. The older-style entrance arches of the transept are highly decorated and probably correspond to the first phase of the church's construction, since they were designed to house the tombs of the founding family, *Lobo da Silveira*, (Barons of Alvito).

The exterior of the Church is typical of the Alentejo Manueline period with decorative crenellations and traditional cone-shaped *pinnacles*. The tower dates from the early 16th century.

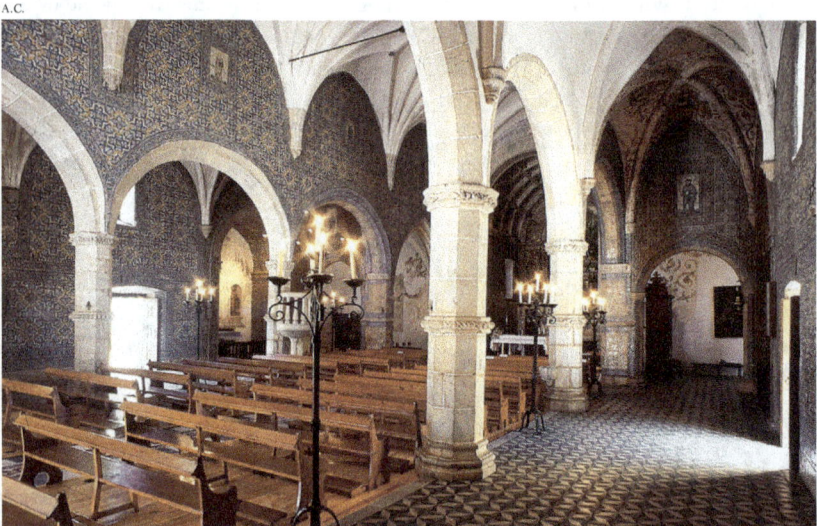

Nossa Senhora da Assunção, Alvito Parish Church, interior.

X.2.c Casa da Câmara (Town Hall)

Rua 25 de Abril, 64. (Tel: 284. 475266). The building still houses municipal services.
Opening hours: Monday-Friday 09.00-12.30 and 14.00-17.30.

Very little is left of the Manueline building, other than the clock tower, ending in a pyramidal *pinnacle* with a turret in each of the four corners, linked together by decorative battlements, typical of early 16th-century, Alentejo vernacular architecture. The main hall and meeting rooms are on the upper floor, which is reached by a side staircase from the street. The ground floor was used for other purposes.

X.2.d Castle

Now a pousada, *the Castle can be reached from Largo do Castelo. Designated a National Monument. Pousada do Castelo de Alvito Tel: 284 485343.*

Though the essential Manueline characteristics are still visible, the transformation of the castle into a *pousada* has mutilated this very fine example of domestic architecture, which had remained intact for five centuries.
Based on a slightly elongated rectangular plan and built around a courtyard, three sides are occupied by living quarters and the other by a high wall facing the kitchen garden.

The Mediaeval keep, almost square at the base, is about 11 m. in length, rising to a height of 25 m. At one of the corners of the main façade is the fountain turret; the other three towers are cylindrical, and typical of late 15th-century military architecture.
As a manor house on the plains, it was designed for defensive purposes, with many openings, high windows, double

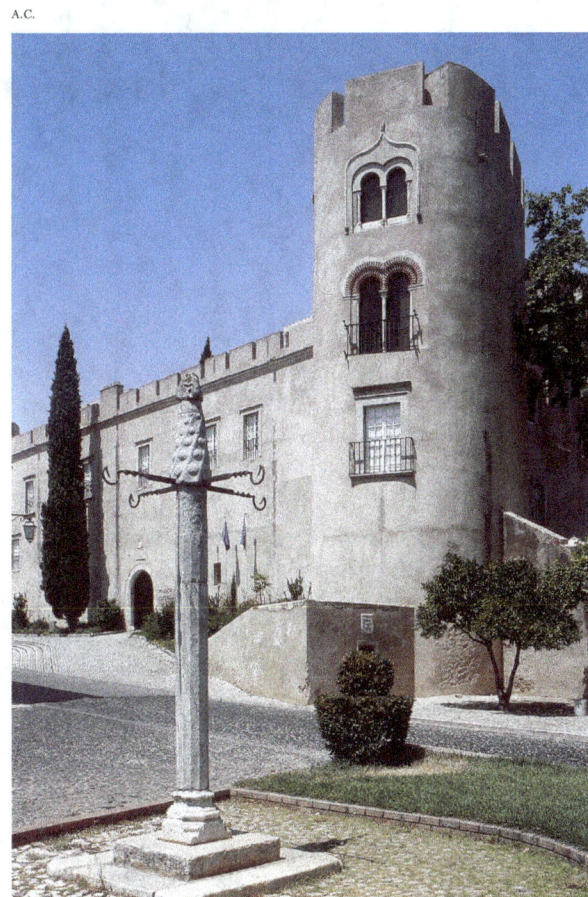

Alvito Castle.
A.C.

ITINERARY X   *White Towns*
Alvito

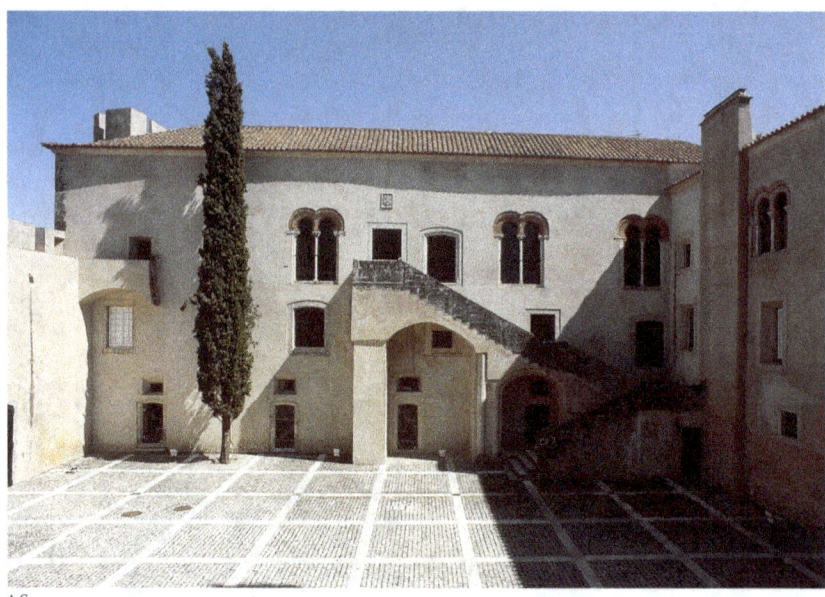

Alvito Castle, interior.

A.C.

balconies and horseshoe *Mudejar*-style arches. This characteristic is more marked in the interior of the courtyard, where the marble window frames of the central bay, and the double arches in brick, are reminiscent of the Galeria das Damas in the Royal Palace in Évora, for royal taste defined domestic architecture in the Manueline era.

According to the inscription over the door, the building was commissioned by D. Diogo Lobo da Silveira and was started in 1494, at the end of the reign of D. João II. It must have been completed by 1531, when D. João III stayed there with part of his Court. The Prince, D. Manuel, sworn in as heir to the throne, was also born here, although he was to die prematurely.

X.2.e **Chapel of São Sebastião**

Largo General Humberto Delgado, at the entrance to the town, in Rossio de S. Sebastião. Classified as a Building of Public Interest. The Chapel is usually open to visitors. If it is closed, ask at the local Tourist Office for permission to visit it. (Tel: 284 485440).

Decorative battlements surmount this small, rectangular Chapel, with cylindrical buttresses at the corners and on the side walls. The interior consists of one single nave with a rectangular vaulted chapel.

This building is similar in style to the Chapels of São Brás in Évora and Santo André in Beja.

For Vidigueira, follow the EN258 in the direction of Vila Ruiva / Vila Alva / Vila de Frades / Vidigueira.

X.3 VIDIGUEIRA

The town of Vidigueira developed at the end of the 14th century, with the successive transfer of patronage, placing it within the House of Bragança until 1519, when the navigator Vasco da Gama was made Count of Vidigueira, a title that was passed on to his descendants. It was around this time that various improvements were made to the town, to mark the importance that this family had in the region, as well as their influence on the policy towards the Far East. Among its members, for example, was D. Francisco da Gama, who, like his great grandfather, was Viceroy of India.

X.3.a Castle

The Castle can be reached via Rua da Cisterna, but only the exterior can be visited. Classified as a Building of Public Interest. Information: Tourist Office. (Tel: 284 436564).

Very little now remains of the Castle or fortified palace, other than some clearly Manueline walls and the keep. Although it already existed before this, when Vasco da Gama took possession of the town, he

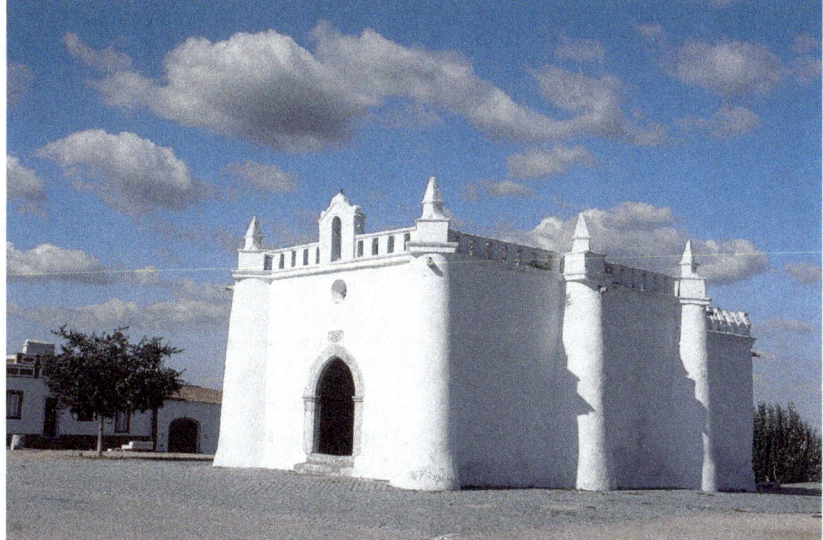

Chapel of São Sebastião, Alvito.

ITINERARY X   White Towns
Vidigueira

Vidigueira Castle.

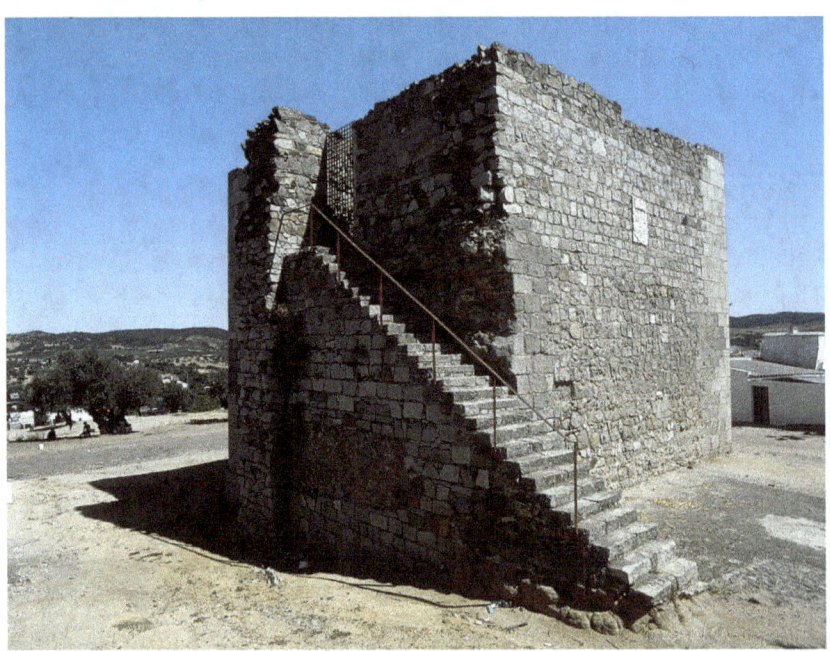

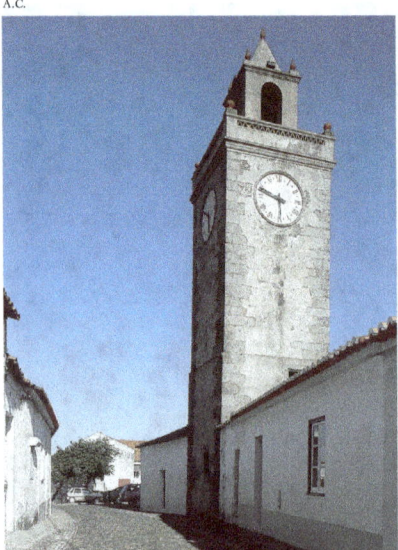

Clock Tower, Vidigueira.

had restoration work done on the castle, which included improvements to his main, or at least most emblematic residence, for he also had another important house in Évora.

X.3.b Torre do Relógio (Clock Tower)

Rua Miguel Bombarda.

Mediaeval in origin, the tower was restored and possibly added to at the beginning of the 16th century. One of the bells had an inscription stating that Vasco da Gama donated it in 1520.

ITINERARY X *White Towns*
Vidigueira

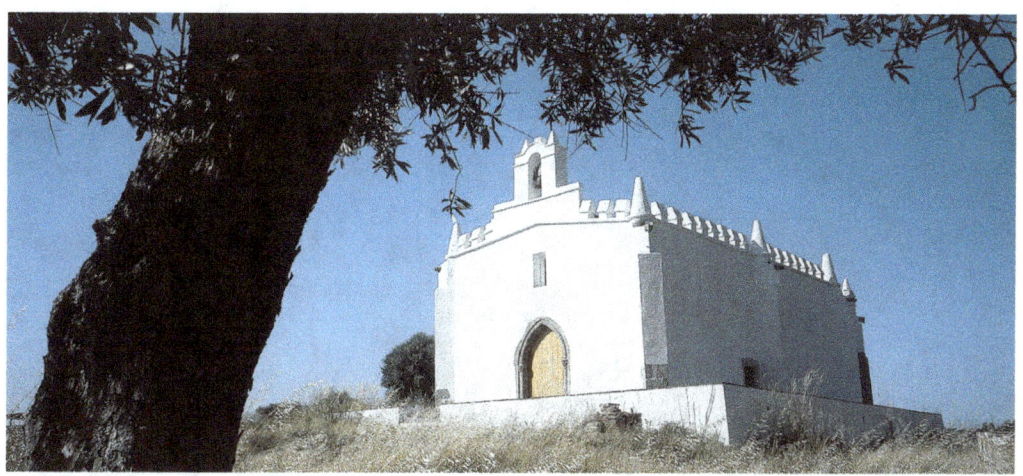

X.3.c **Ermida de Santa Clara (Chapel of St Clara)**

From either Évora / Portel or Beja / Cuba, take the main road to Rua de Santa Clara. Follow the dirt road to the Chapel. Classified as a Building of Public Interest. Information: Tourist Office (Tel: 284 434492).

This was a small Parish Church until, in 1540, it was rebuilt by Francisco da Gama, the son of the famous admiral. It has essentially retained its Manueline structure, probably dating from about 1520, but the main vessel of the church was altered later. The Manueline-style chancel is particularly fine, with a Late Gothic entrance arch with naturalist capitals, and ribbed vaulting with foliate decorative bosses.

The exterior is also Manueline, with buttresses, decorative battlements and conical *pinnacles*. The simple portal with a pointed arch is also Manueline.

Take the IP2 south for Beja.

Ermida de Santa Clara, Vidigueira.

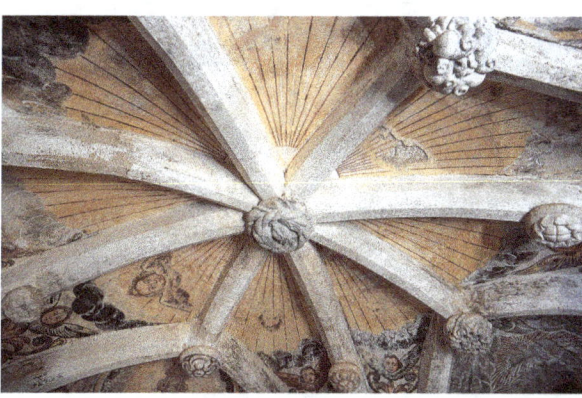

Ermida de Santa Clara, vaulted ceiling, Vidigueira.

249

ITINERARY X

White Towns

Pedro Dias, Dalila Rodrigues,
Nuno Vassallo e Silva, Fernando Grilo

Second day

X.4 BEJA
    X.4.a Chapel of Santo André
    X.4.b Historic Centre
    X.4.c Castle
    X.4.d Antigo Hospital de Nossa Senhora da Piedade
    X.4.e Convent of Nossa Senhora da Conceição and Museu Regional de Beja – Rainha D. Leonor
    X.4.f Convent of São Francisco

X.5 SERPA (option)
    X.5.a Castle

X.6 MOURA
    X.6.a Castle
    X.6.b São João Baptista (Moura Parish Church)

Queen D. Leonor

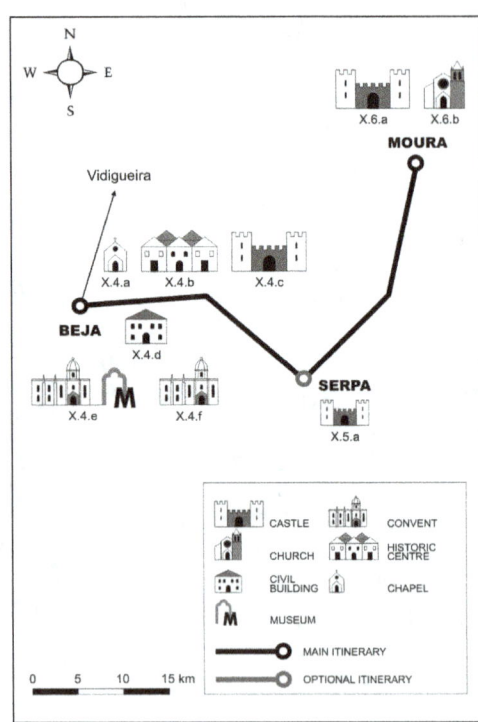

ITINERARY X *White Towns*
Beja

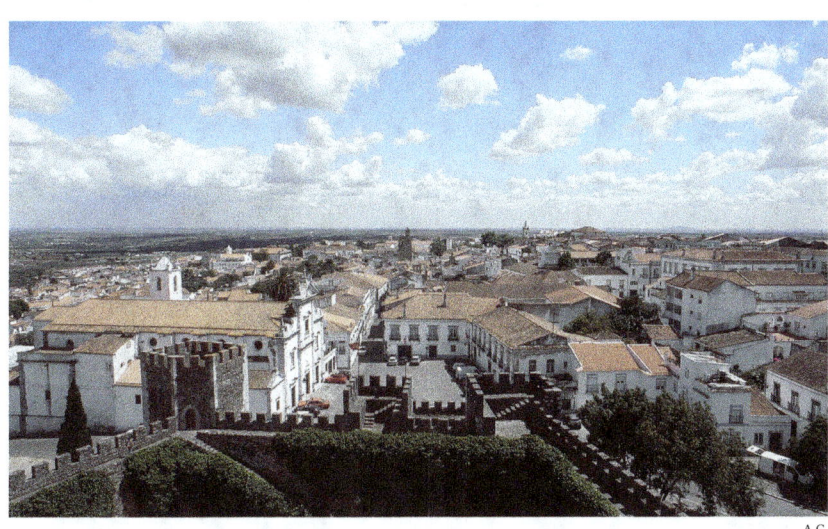

Beja historic centre.

X.4 BEJA

Beja was one of the most important Roman cities in the western peninsula, a position it maintained throughout the Islamic period, although successive, very destructive attempts were made to regain it by the Kings of Asturias and León. It was taken by D. Afonso Henriques, the first king, but was soon lost again and only came fully under the control of Portugal in 1232.

The town began to develop during the reign of D. Dinis, when the castle was rebuilt and various monasteries were founded. Considerable progress was made when the town was granted to Prince D. Fernando and his wife, D. Beatriz, with whom he founded one of the most powerful families in the country in direct competition with the House of Bragança. They were the parents of D. Leonor, and D. Manuel I.

These nobles endowed the town with important structures, building imposing residences and sponsoring religious orders, hospitals and the Misericórdia charitable organisation, amongst other works. During his reign, D. Manuel I elevated Beja to city status, making a number of improvements, many of which are still visible today.

X.4.a Chapel of Santo André

The Chapel is situated at the entrance to Beja on the EN121. Designated a National Monument. It can only be viewed from the outside.

ITINERARY X   White Towns
Beja

Chapel of Santo André, Beja.

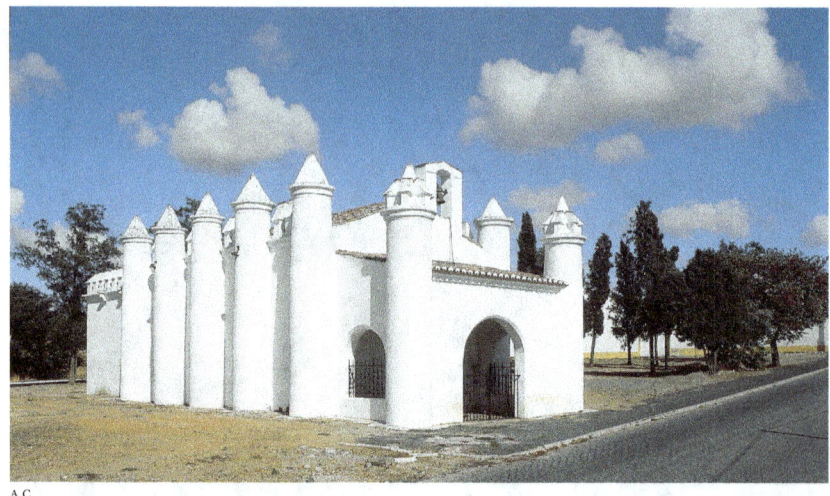

A.C.

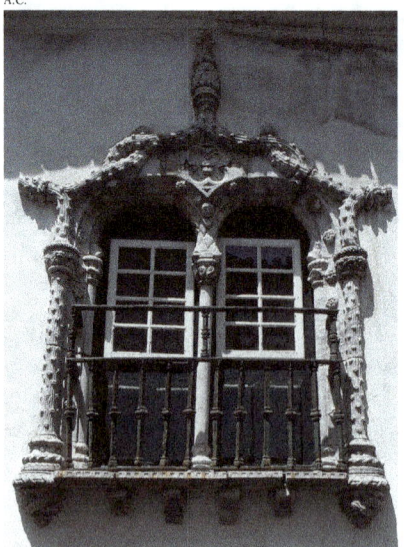

A.C.

Beja historic centre, Manueline window.

This Chapel or hermitage, is one of a series built in this region, all of them characterised by cylindrical buttresses at the corners and along the sides. This one also has a porch or covered atrium, and consists of one single nave and a square chapel, crowned by decorative battlements. The interior is very simple with ribbed vaulting in the apse.

After visiting the Chapel of Santo André, follow the signposts to the castle. There are two free car parks just before the entrance to the walled enclosure. From here, it is easier to see Beja on foot.

X.4.b Historic Centre

Information: Tourist Office (Tel: 284 311913).

Many vestiges of early 16th-century Manueline buildings are to be seen in the historic centre of Beja, which include parish and monastery churches, hospitals, the Town Hall, courts, the jail, etc., as well as numerous houses belonging to the wealthy middle class or members of the ducal household. The superb naturalist double-arched window in the Rua dos Mercadores, and the elegant rectangular doorway at No. 24, Rua do Esquivel, edged by a torus moulding and with rosettes on the intrados, are very finely detailed.

A stroll through the streets of Rua de São Gregório, Rua da Guia and Rua da Misericórdia brings many pieces of Manueline architecture to light. No. 43, Praça da República, boasts different doorways, two with simple low pediments; another with a double opening, surrounded by a rope and with large, prismatic capitals.

The pillory, with its naturalist decoration and twisted shaft erected in 1521, but largely reconstructed, is in the same square.

X.4.c Castle

Largo do Lidador, Rua D. Dinis and Rua Antero de Quental. Designated a National Monument.
There is an admission charge to visit the keep. Opening hours: 09.00-12.00 and 13.00-16.00 in winter, and 10.00-13.00 and 14.00-18.00 in summer. Closed on Mondays and public holidays.

The walls of Beja are the longest in the Baixo Alentejo and have largely retained the structure that they had in the reign

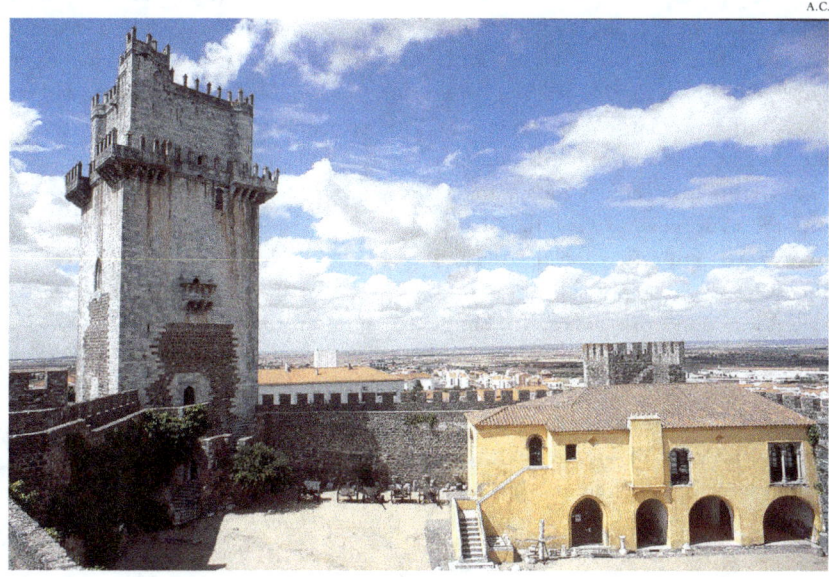

Beja Castle Keep.

ITINERARY X *White Towns*
Beja

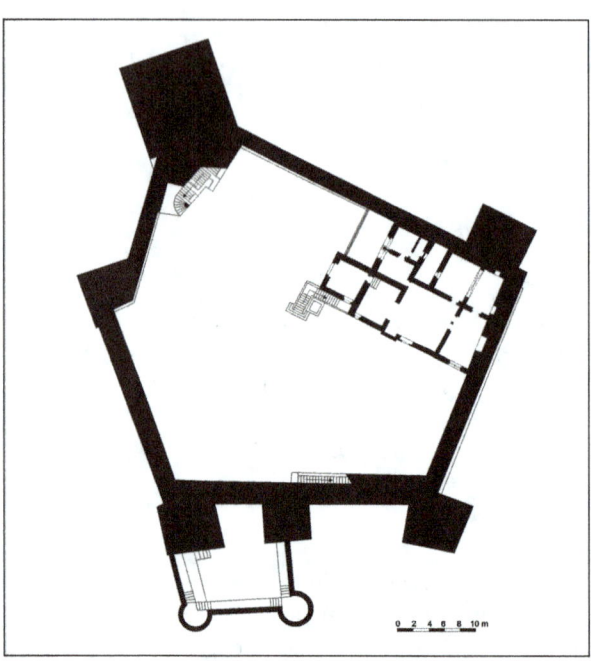

Beja Castle, plan, Boletim da Direcção-Geral dos Edifícios e Monumentos Nacionais, No. 77.

of D. Manuel I. They began with a Roman camp and were significantly enlarged during the Moorish occupation, but were largely destroyed by attacks by Christian troops. Restoration began in the 14th century and continued into the 15th century, when the Islamic fortress was entirely reconstructed and the 40-m.-high keep was built. Extensive restoration work was carried out in 1939.

The fortress and walls are easily distinguished, the latter enclosing the old Manueline part of the city with the main churches, such as the Igreja de Santa Maria, Igreja de Santiago and the Convento de Nossa Senhora da Conceição. Oval in shape, the walls had almost 40 towers, as well as dry moats and various gateways: Porta de Moura, Porta de Beja, Porta de Avis, Porta de Aljustrel and others, as well as wicket gates. The walls are high and strong with battlements and parapets all the way round.

The castle is pentagonal in shape and the parade ground contains the commander's residence, heavily restored and containing Manueline architectural features originating from demolition work carried out in other parts of the city, though it is clear from old photographs that the windows and arches on the façade are original.

The 15th-century keep, with three floors and vaulted ceilings, stands at one of the corners. The middle floor with its stellar vaulting, one of the finest and most complex of the Portuguese Gothic, is of particular interest. The upper part of the tower with its surrounding terrace and ample *machicolations* is also noteworthy.

X.4.d Antigo Hospital de Nossa Senhora da Piedade

Rua D. Manuel I. The former hospital is now used as a University and the Social Services Institute. Information (Tel: 284 327550).
Opening hours: weekdays only 09.00-12.30 and 14.00-17.30.

X.4.e Convent of Nossa Senhora da Conceição and Museu Regional de Beja – Rainha D. Leonor

Largo da Conceição. (Tel: 284 3232251). Designated a National Monument.
Admission charge. Opening hours: Tuesday-Sunday 09.30-12.30 and 14.00-17.15. Closed on public holidays.

D. Beatriz, the mother of D. Manuel I, founded the Royal Convent of Nossa Senhora da Conceição in Beja. The building dates back to at least 1469, but the final work was carried out in the 16th century during D. Manuel's reign, and, under his patronage, this became one of the richest religious institutions in the Alentejo.

Also known as the Misericórdia Hospital as it belonged to that charitable institution, the building was probably completed about 1511. The Manueline cloister has tall, narrow wings with elegant ribbed vaulting, prismatic corbels and decorative naturalist bosses.

The former Private Chapel, dedicated to St Mark, is an architectural jewel, with Gothic ribbed vaulting and a most elegant entrance arch with naturalist decorations.

The old hospital wards are very impressive, with their cruciform pillars supporting strong vaulting and pointed arches, although there is a total lack of decorative detailing as befits a building of this type. The bosses on the vaulting bear the royal arms of D. Manuel I, who was the patron of the institution.

A.C.

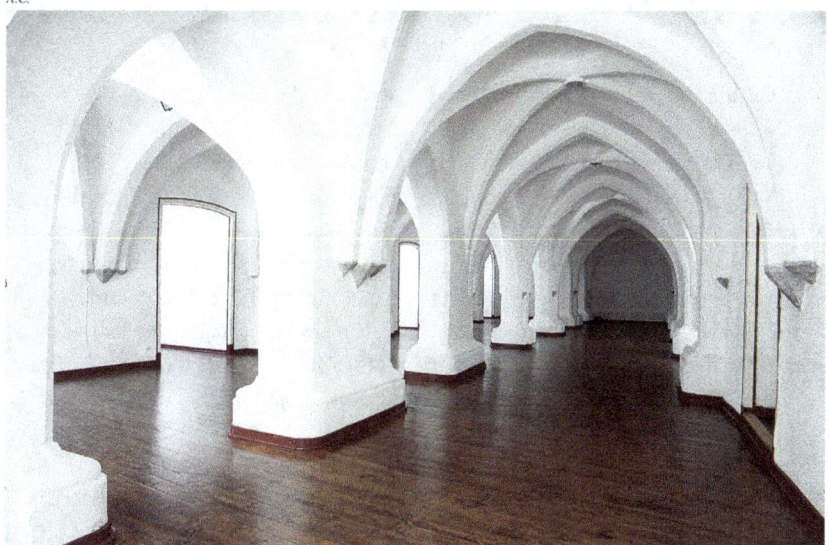

Former Hospital de Nossa Senhora da Piedade, ward, Beja.

Beja

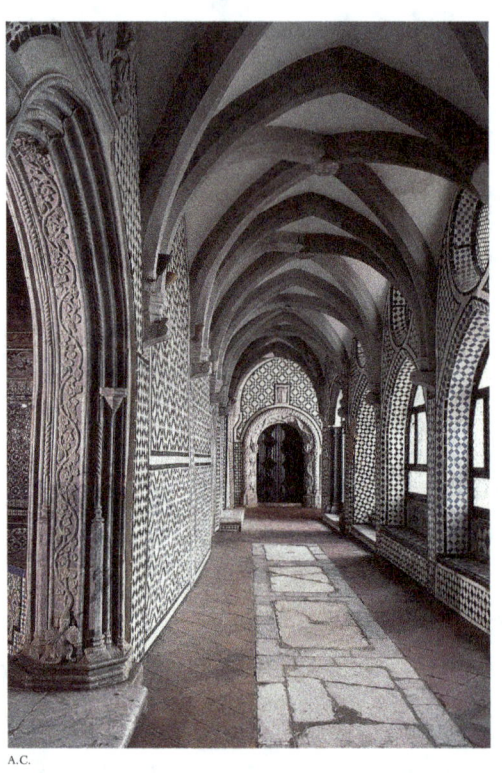
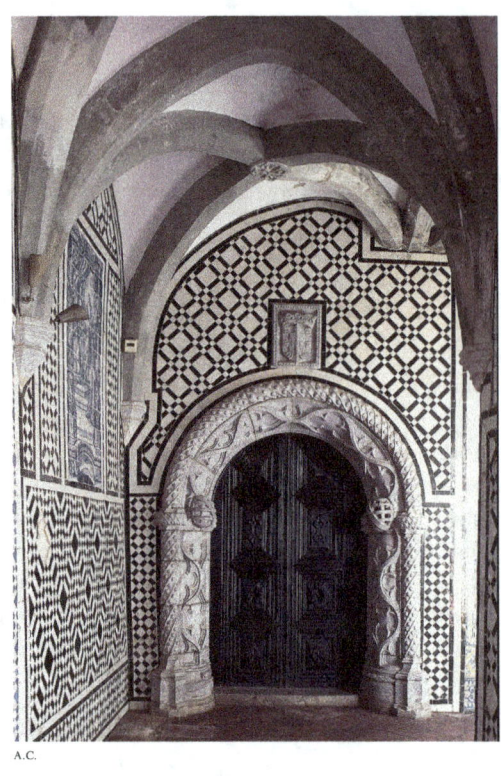

Convent of Nossa Senhora da Conceição, cloister, Beja.

Convent of Nossa Senhora da Conceição, door of the former refectory, Beja.

Neo-Gothic features have greatly altered the exterior, but the main door still remains in all the glory of the Flamboyant Gothic of Batalha. There is a double-arched Manueline window in the *Mudejar* style on the small upper balcony.

The cloister is of particular interest with four vaulted sides, each different and solid with little decoration. Note the former refectory door, exuberantly naturalist in style, with two armillary spheres on the doorposts.

The richly decorated Chapter House, with polychrome panels of Hispano-Moorish tiles from Seville and *Mudejar* in style, is also Manueline, though the entrance door is a little earlier.

The Beja Museum is installed in the convent and contains some interesting paintings, namely the *Nursing Virgin*, an example of minutely detailed Flemish realism and an *Ecce Homo* image, similar to a panel in the Museu Nacional de Arte Antiga in Lisbon. Both are highly enigmatic as regards author and materials used, but there seems to have existed a common prototype, associated with a very special religious phenomenon that existed between the 15th and 17th centuries. This prototype is the origin of a number of replicas, specifically the examples in Setúbal and Santa Clara in Funchal.

In the same collection, a panel with the figure of St Vincent is worthy of special attention, since it is an emblematic painting from a 16th-century workshop, probably situated in Coimbra. Unlike the case of the *Ecce Homo,* the author of this panel – perhaps Vicente Gil whose activity in Coimbra between 1498 and 1521 is documented – turns what is an accessory into an essential feature, with a special taste for dense material details. The coat of arms of Queen D. Leonor, who commissioned the painting, appears on the saint's alb.

In the field of decorative arts, it is necessary to mention the tapestry-shape panels of Hispano-Arabic polychromatic *azulejos* of the convent Chapter House, of the Manueline period too.

In the Museum we can also admire different groups of patterns of 16th century Sevillian *azulejos* made in the *cuerda seca* technique.

The most interesting piece, however, comes from China. It is the Pêro de Faria's blue-and-white porcelain porringer, dated 1541. This is one of the first Chinese works commissioned expressly by the Portuguese, and the association of this Governor of Malacca, a companion of Afonso de Albuquerque, a Viceroy of India, is noted in an inscription on the inside.

This rich collection includes a Late Gothic silver chalice and a small silver writing desk, which, it is said D. Manuel I donat-

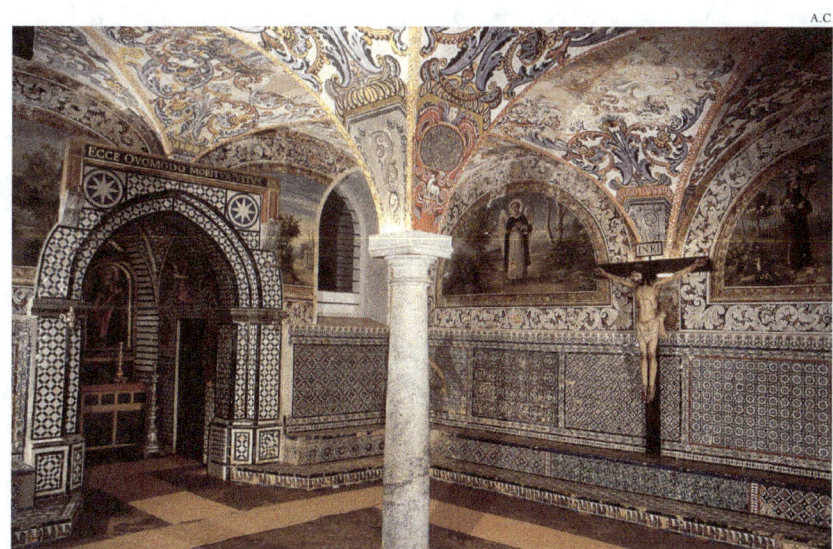

Convent of Nossa Senhora da Conceição, Chapter House, Beja.

ITINERARY X   White Towns
Beja

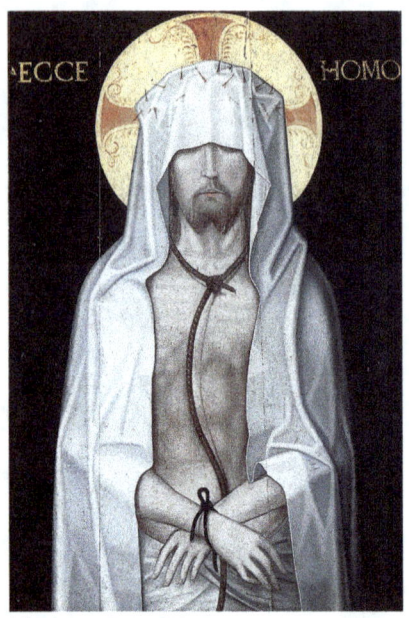

Unknow artist, "Ecce Homo", c. 1500, Beja Museum.

A.C.

ed to the city of Beja, though it is of a later date and may have been made to replace the original Manueline piece.
The Museum, named after Queen D. Leonor, also contains two remarkable 16th-century sculptures representing *St Sebastian*, though they are quite different in style. One is made of polychrome wood and was possibly the work of a Portuguese sculptor influenced by Flemish art, as can be seen by the posture, the treatment of volume and even the use of polychrome. The other one, made of stone, is also polychrome, but highly representative of Manueline workshops.

X.4.f **Convent of São Francisco**

Largo D. Nuno Álvares Pereira. Classified as a Building of Public Interest. The convent building has been adapted for use as a pou-sada (Pousada de São Francisco Tel: 284 328441).
Opening hours: visits should preferably take place after 14.00.

Founded in 1268, in the reign of D. Afonso III, the building underwent various alterations up to the Manueline era, when it reached its period of greatest splendour, although further work in the 18th century obliterated its lines, which have been partially recuperated by its restoration as a *pousada*.
The Gothic cloister, refectory and cistern date from the time of D. Manuel I, as does the 15th-century Gothic pantheon of the Andrade Friars, erected by builders trained at Batalha. The high, elegant cloister has ribbed vaulting set on corbels, and one of the sides opens onto the 15th-century Chapter House.
While the ribbed vaulting with five bosses in the refectory is more evolved, the ribbed vaulting set on mono-cylindrical pillars in the cistern, although utilitarian is, nevertheless, fascinating.

For Serpa, take the EN260 for about 30 km. To get to Moura, pass Serpa and turn left onto the EN255, a journey of about 28 km.

X.5 SERPA (option)

Castile and Portugal both fortified this important frontier town, until it passed definitively into the hands of the latter country, in the 13th century. It was occupied by the Moors and only began to develop in the 15th century, particularly during the Manueline period, with the restoration of the castle and the construction of many new houses and various religious and welfare institutions.

X.5.a Castle

The Castle can be reached through the old area next to Praça da República. Information: Tourist Office (Tel: 284 544727).
Opening hours: 09.00-12.30 and 14.00-17.30 in winter and 09.00-12.30 and 16.00-19.30 in summer. Closed on Mondays and public holidays.

The initial work from the Portuguese period must date from the reign of D. Dinis, at the end of the 13th century, but like all frontier towns, the castle and its walls were improved at the beginning of the 16th century. The walls and towers were reinforced and enlarged, and almost certainly the enclosure and new gates were built, two of which still remain, the Porta de Beja and the Porta de Moura.

The *curtain walls* of the *enceinte* and the towers were very well built, possibly by one of the Arruda brothers, and, from their design, they would appear to date to between 1510 and 1520.

X.6 MOURA

Moura probably existed before the Moorish invasion of 711, but only developed later. Conquered by D. Sancho II, in 1232, the town came under the Por-

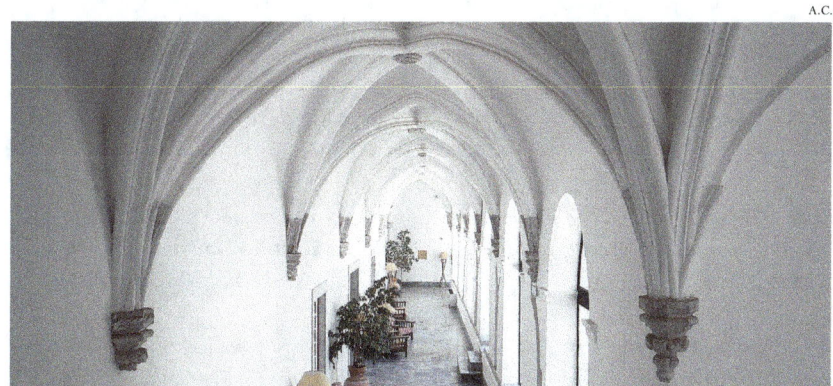

A.C.

Convent of São Francisco, cloister, Beja.

ITINERARY X   *White Towns*
Moura

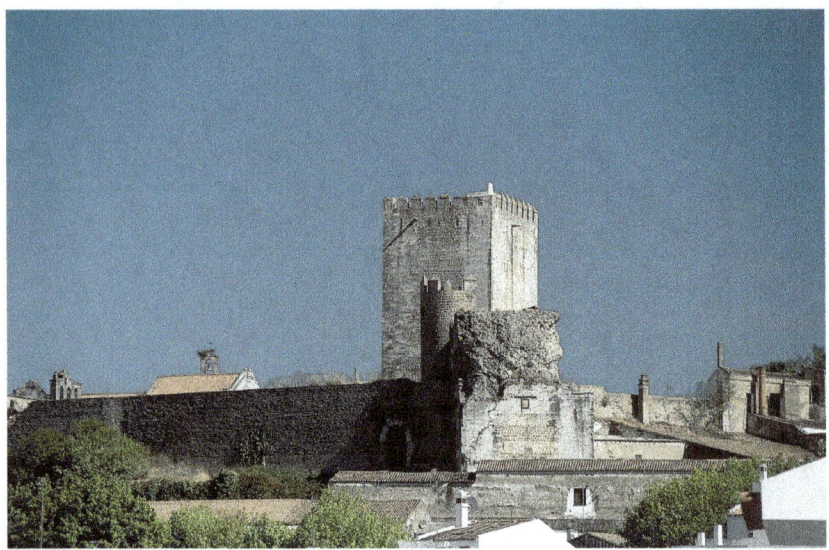

Moura Castle.

R.C.

tuguese crown later, being granted its first charter by D. Dinis, in 1292. Its position close to the frontier meant it was both an important stronghold and, at the same time, a suitable place for trade. D. Manuel I donated a new parish church and fortress, and sponsored other institutions such as the Convento do Carmo.

X.6.a Castle

The Castle is reached via Praça Sacadura Cabral. Classified as a Building of Public Interest. Information: Tourist Office (Tel: 285 251345).

The Castle dates back to the Islamic period, but it is most likely to have been significantly improved in the 12th century. Some of the castle's *lath-and-plaster* wall, with cylindrical or cubic towers, has been conserved from this time. In the late 13th century, in the reign of D. Dinis, major new work was carried out; the foundations of the old keep remaining from then. D. Manuel I had the castle rebuilt by the Master of Royal Works, Francisco de Arruda. This latter work may well date from between 1510 and 1520.

X.6.b São João Baptista (Moura Parish Church)

Praça Sacadura Cabral. Designated a National Monument.

White Towns
Moura

Opening hours: daily 09.00-18.00.

The original Church, dedicated to St John the Baptist, dates from the 15th century and amounted to little more than a small chapel, for at that time the Parish Church remained inside the castle walls. D. Manuel I, however, ordered a new church to be built from the foundations up, so that nothing now remains of the original building. This was one of the most important churches in the eastern part of the Alentejo and is similar in structure, at least in part, to the Parish Church of Golegã, another work that enjoyed Royal patronage. The relatively simple exterior has a sturdy side tower and a portal similar to that of Viana do Alentejo, but the interior is very fine. Elegant pillared arcades divide the three aisles; each with five bays, and there is no salient transept, whilst the triple apse has ribbed vaulting in the chancel with two bays and profusely decorated foliate bosses. The upper choir, pulpit and side door with naturalist decoration also date from the Manueline period.

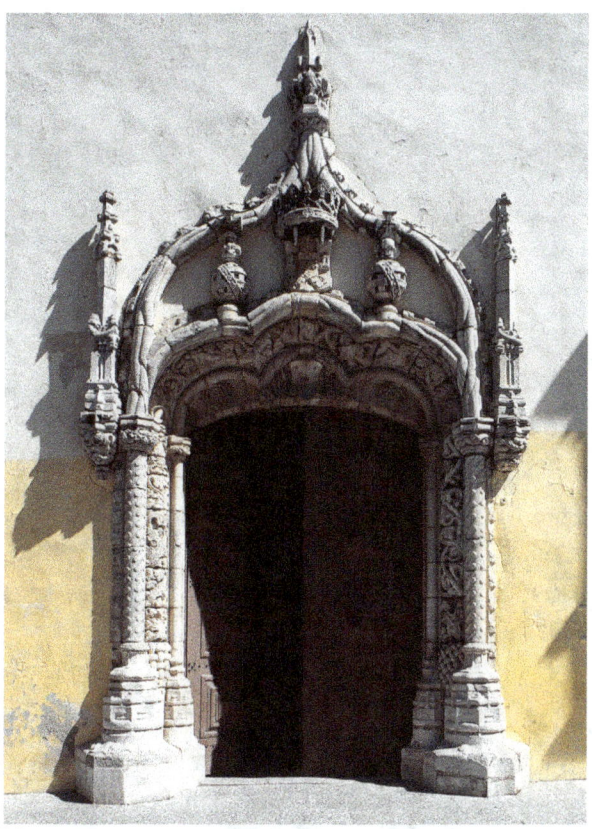

São João Baptista, Moura Parish Church, portal.

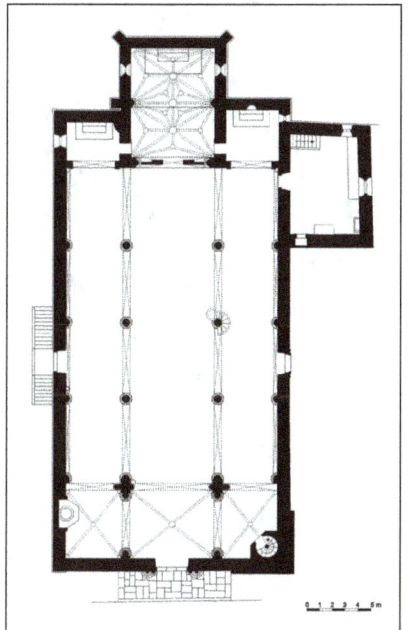

São João Baptista, Moura Parish Church, plan, Boletim da Direcção-Geral dos Edifícios e Monumentos Nacionais, No. 45.

ITINERARY X   *White Towns*
Moura

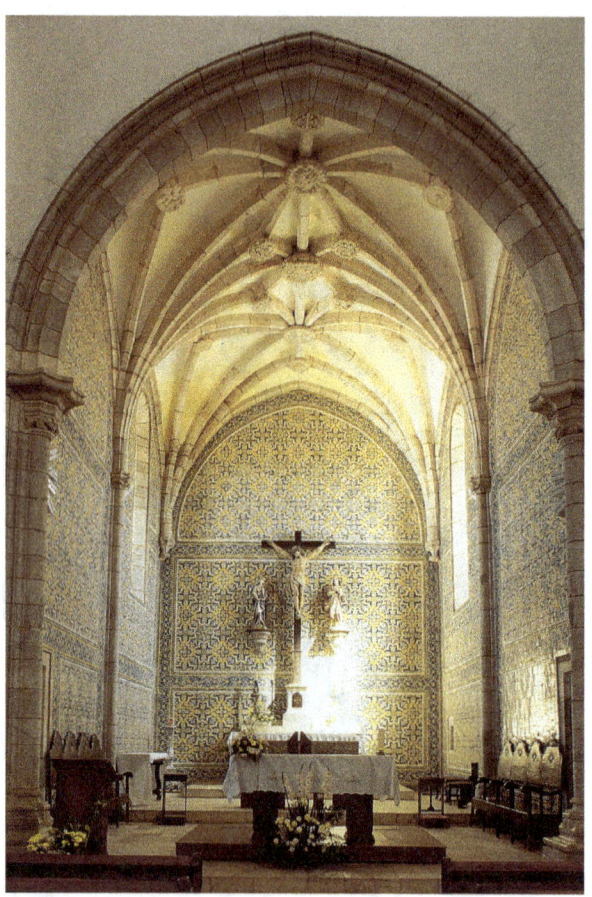

A.C.
*São João Baptista,
Moura Parish Church,
chancel.*

O Pulo do Lobo
Between the towns of Serpa and Mértola, the river creates a fearsome waterfall that makes a dreadful noise, frightening all who go near.
Duarte Nunes de Leão in his Descripção do Reino de Portugal, *referring to the waterfall wrote in 1599: "Here where the Guadiana falls is called Assonjo (waterfall, cascade, cataract, leap, etc.) because of the great noise, and thunder, that the water makes; falling from a high and narrow place that measures sixteen arms."*
The river drops into a chasm that is 100 metres wide and 80 arms (173 metres) high, flowing shortly before into two channels, so narrow that each one is not more than a metre wide; coming together again, they pass under a naturally formed stone bridge that leads from one side to the other of the river.
This waterfall is known by the name of Wolf's Leap.

Pinho Leal, Portugal Antigo e Moderno,
Vol. IX, Lisbon, 1871.

QUEEN D. LEONOR

Pedro Dias

Queen D. Leonor was one of the key figures in the history of Portugal in the second half of the 15th century, and the first quarter of the 16th century. Born in 1458, the daughter of the Duke and Duchess of Beja, D. Fernando and D. Beatriz, she was descended from the Kings of Portugal on both sides of her family. She married D. João II, whilst he was still a prince, in 1473, and ascended the throne on the death of her father-in-law, D. Afonso V, in 1482.

Her husband's reign was not without incident, due primarily to the plot hatched by the Dukes of Bragança and Viseu that lead to their deaths. However, with the help of her mother, the queen managed to protect her brother, D. Manuel, making it possible for him to ascend the throne in 1495. D. Leonor had only one son by her marriage to D. João II, Prince D. Afonso, who died in an accident at Santarém. Afraid that her husband's illegitimate son, Jorge de Lencastre, would become heir, she did everything possible to have D. Manuel named as successor, which did in fact happen.

The owner of considerable assets and estates, and acting as Regent in the absence of her brother in Castile, Queen D. Leonor dedicated much of her time to good works and founded the first Misericórdia charity organisation. She was also a great lover of the arts and amassed a very fine collection of works of art by leading European artists, housed in the Convento da Madre de Deus in Xabregas,

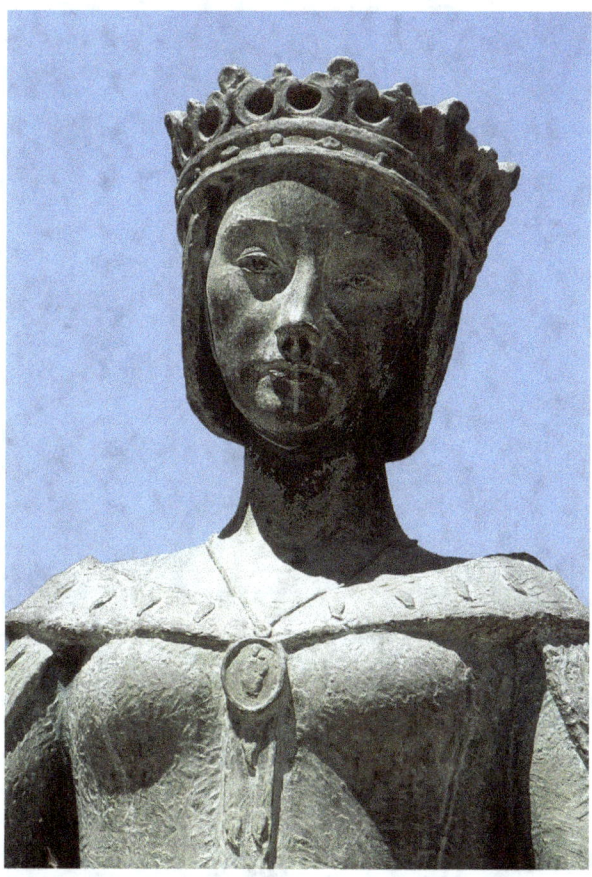

Statue of Queen Leonor, Beja.

Lisbon. The pieces included glazed terracotta from the workshops of the Della Robbias in Florence, and one of the finest works by the Flemish painter Quentin Metsys, as well as jewellery and other valuables from the Far East.

Queen D. Leonor died in 1525, during the reign of D. João III.

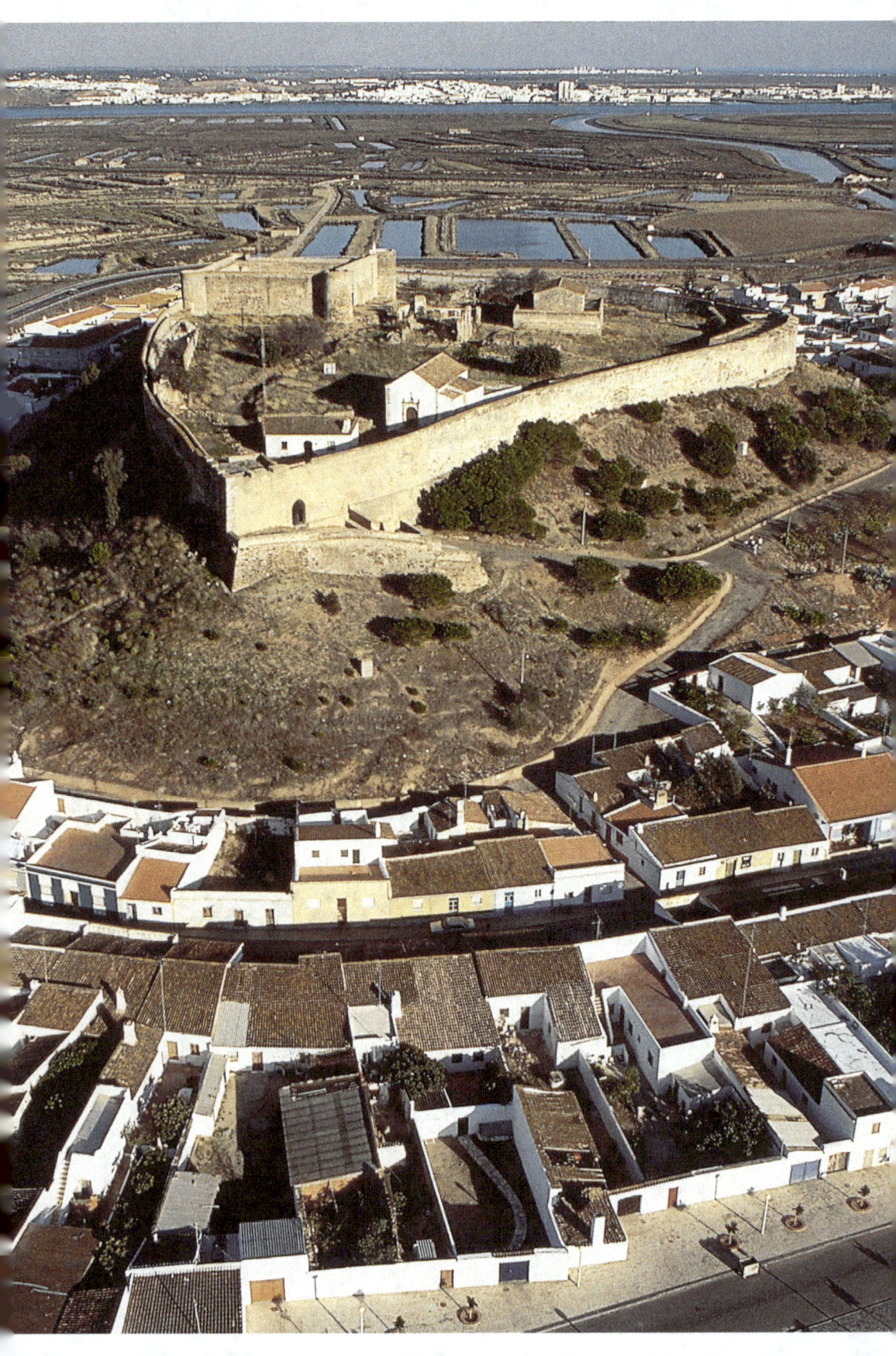

ITINERARY XI

Algarve

Pedro Dias, Dalila Rodrigues,
Nuno Vassallo e Silva, Fernando Grilo

First day

XI.1 CASTRO MARIM
    XI.1.a Castle

XI.2 TAVIRA
    XI.2.a Parochial Church of Santa Maria do Castelo
    XI.2.b Church of São José

XI.3 FARO
    XI.3.a City Walls
    XI.3.b Cathedral

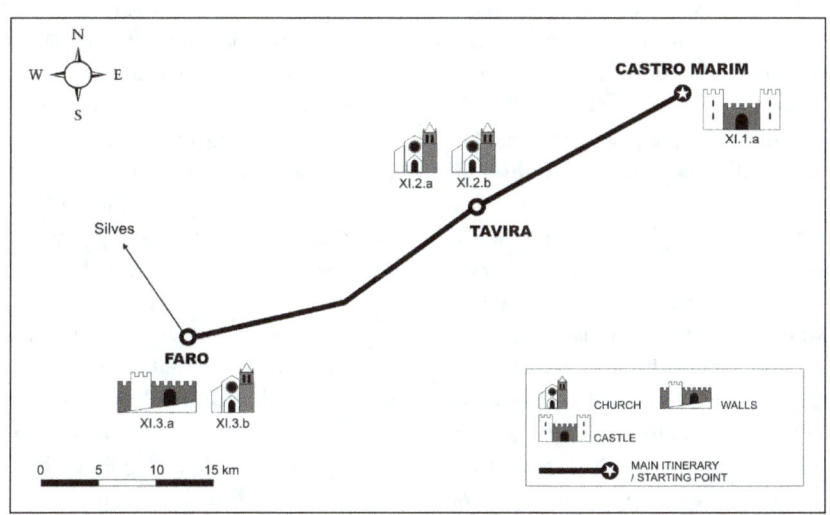

Aerial view of Castro Marim.

ITINERARY XI   *Algarve*

Castro Marim.

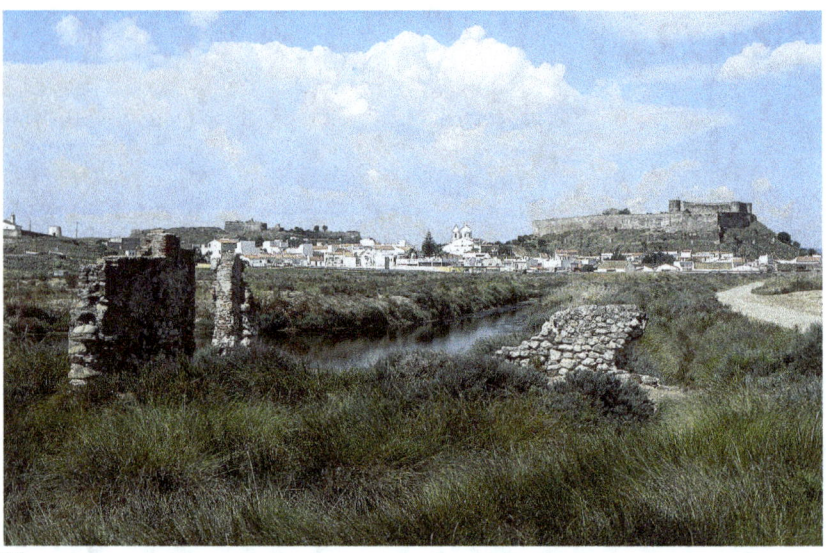

The history of the Algarve (Arabic, *Al-Gharb* "Sunset") is strongly linked to the maritime Discoveries. The fact that it is in the south of the country and of Europe, and on the route between the North Atlantic and Mediterranean, has made this region, for some 3,000 years, a rotating platform for people and cultures. Phoenicians, Carthaginians, Greeks, Romans, Goths, the people of Maghreb and Mauritania all passed this way, until, in the 13th century, the territory of the Islamic Gharb was brought under the control of the Portuguese Crown. The Algarve to this day retains its own characteristics, which, highlighted by its geography, make it a region quite distinct from others.

Prince Henry the Navigator, the initiator of the overseas adventure, settled close to Sagres where new methods of navigation and nautical instruments were tried out.

The long fishing and trading tradition of the Algarve naturally increased its participation in the Discoveries, and there were few families in the region whose sons did not go to sea.

The Algarve provided essential maintenance to the Portuguese fortresses in Morocco and the Atlantic islands of Madeira and the Azores, by supplying provisions, trading products, building materials and, above all, troops.

Tavira and Lagos in the main, but also Silves, Loulé, Faro and Cacela, grew and became wealthy towns, enriched by buildings that rivalled the beauty and technique of those of Islamic times. Today it is possible to visit legendary spots, such as the Ponta de Sagres, which now has a museum, or others that are perhaps more prosaic, such as Lagos, with its Manueline walls and slave market, or

ITINERARY XI *Algarve*
Castro Marim/Tavira

Tavira with its canals and port, the first refuge of the unfortunate people coming from Morocco.

D. Manuel I had a special affection for the Algarve because of the part its people played in Portuguese expansion, favouring its towns by promoting public, charitable and religious works. Unfortunately, many of these buildings were destroyed later in earthquakes, but Manueline memories have not been totally destroyed.

XI.1 CASTRO MARIM

This settlement came into the Portuguese orbit in 1242, during the reign of D. Afonso III, who granted it a charter, later confirmed by D. Dinis, in 1282 and by D. Manuel I, in 1504.

In 1313, D. Dinis made this the headquarters of the Order of Christ, when it took over the land and powers of the extinct Order of the Knights Templars in Portugal, and the Order remained here until 1334. In the Manueline era, it was the main centre for the defence of the River Guadiana and of considerable importance in supplying the Portuguese strongholds in North Africa.

XI.1.a **Castle**

The Castle is situated on the hill overlooking Castro Marim. Designated a National Monument. Information: Tourist Office (Tel: 281 531232).

Opening hours: 09.00-17.00, in winter, and 09.00-19.00 April-October.

Traces dating from the Iron Age have been found on the site where the Castle is built. The original fortifications were substituted throughout the Middle Ages, and its defences in the Manueline era are known through two drawings made by Duarte D'Armas for his book, *Livro das Fortalezas*. At that time, besides the quadrangular castle with round towers at the corners, which still exists today, there was a high keep and defensive *barbicans* at the gates as well as a surrounding wall that was lower and more irregular.

Follow the Via Infante (IP1) for Tavira. The exit is signposted, as well as access to Tavira by the EN397.

XI.2 **TAVIRA**

Tavira was re-conquered in 1242, by Paio Correia, and was granted to the Order of
A.C.

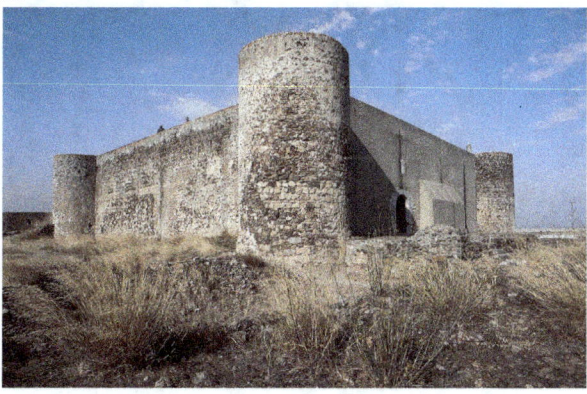

Castro Marim Castle.

ITINERARY XI *Algarve*
Tavira

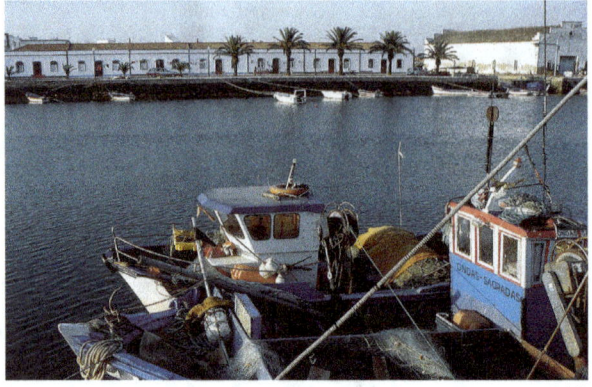

River Gilão, Tavira.

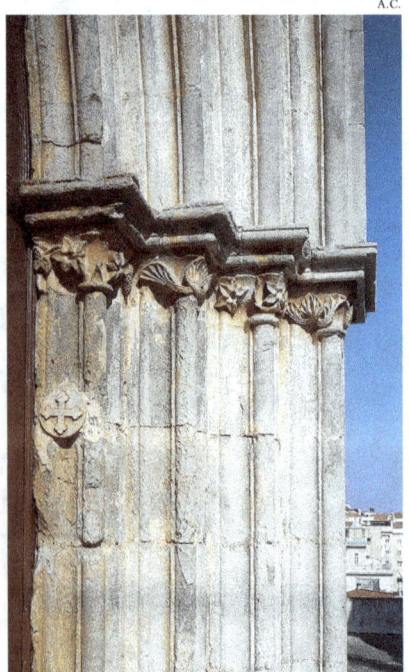

Church of Santa Maria do Castelo, detail of the portal, Tavira.

Santiago two years later. The military operations destroyed not only the greater part of the fortifications but also the houses.

The first re-construction of the castle was carried out during the reign of D. Afonso III, c.1266, and it was the first town in the Algarve to be granted a charter. The port flourished with the constant coming and going of vessels carrying various cargoes: men, ammunition and building materials to the Maghreb, and it was soon the most important town in the Algarve, being raised to city status by D. Manuel I, in 1520.

Manueline constructions and those from earlier periods have almost all disappeared, victims of a number of powerful earthquakes, but also due to the progress of the city in modern times, which led to the alteration and increase in administrative, industrial and religious buildings. The local people, enriched by the fishing industry and trade, improved their houses, though there are still traces of the Gothic period in churches such as the Igreja de Santa Maria do Castelo and the Manueline in the Igreja de São José, as well as in some of the houses situated along the bank of the River Gilão, with their chamfered lintels.

XI.2.a Parochial Church of Santa Maria do Castelo

Alto de Santa Maria, Largo Dr. Jorge Correia. (Tel: 281 325707). Designated a National Monument.
Opening hours: daily 10.00-17.30 in winter, and 10.00-19.00 in summer.

This 13th-century Parish Church is the oldest religious building in the city. It has retained traditional Gothic features, namely the lateral vaulting. The Manueline Chapel of Senhor dos Passos, has complex ribbed vaulting with the coats of arms of its donors and that of the Order of Christ on the bosses.

XI.2.b Church of São José

Praça Zacarias Guerreiro. For permission to visit the church, please contact the Misericórdia de Tavira (Tel: 281 322268).

The remains of the old Manueline Chapel of São Brás, the first headquarters of the Misericórdia charity organisation, have been integrated into the church. These are separate items, today serving as outbuildings of the 18th-century Church, but the vaulting of two chapels, one bearing the coats of arms of members of the local nobility, is of interest.

Take the EN125 in the direction of Olhão / Faro.

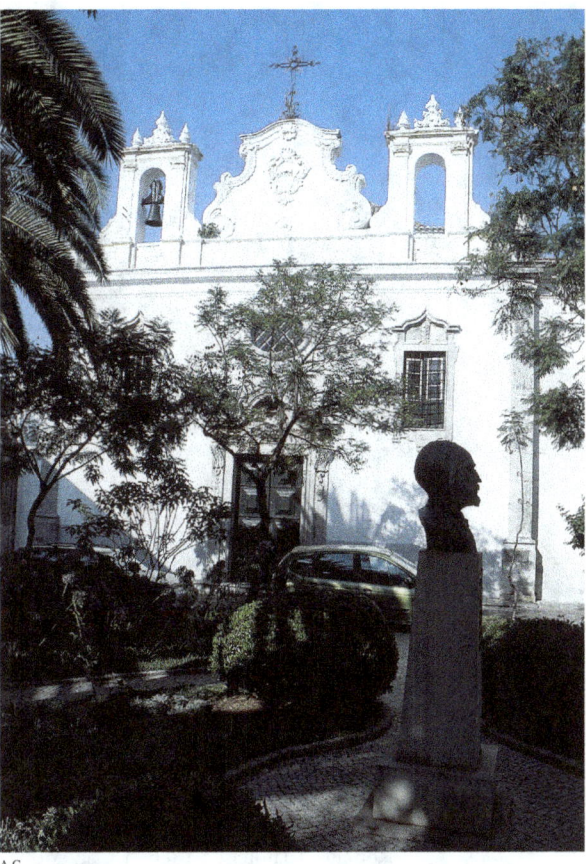

A.C.

Church of São José, Tavira.

> **Ria Formosa Natural Park**
> *Stretching some 60 km. along the Algarve coast, the park occupies an area of about 18 hectares, whilst a string of sandy islands and peninsulas protects a lagoon comprising a labyrinth of marshes, canals and islets. Thousands of birds nest and feed in the dunes, and the large number of botanical species makes this an area of special interest.*
>
> *The park may be visited via guided pathways from the Castro Marim Environmental Centre, or by taking a boat trip on the lagoon of Ria Formosa.*
>
> *For more information contact: Centro de Educação Ambiental de Castro Marim, 8700 Olhão (Tel: 289 704134/5).*

ITINERARY XI *Algarve*

Faro

Faro City Walls.

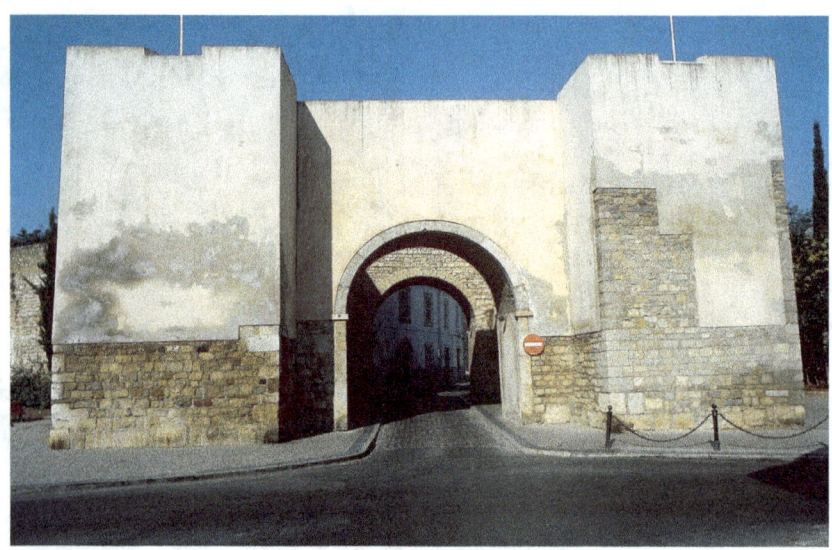

XI.3 **FARO**

In the 12th century, the City of Faro, a trading post between the Mediterranean and Atlantic, was one of the most important in the Muslim Gharb. Planned by the Romans, Islamicised after 713, and definitively conquered by D. Afonso III in 1249, it received its first charter in 1266. As Tavira and Silves gradually became more important, the structure of the town remained almost unaltered until the reign of D. Manuel I. In the 15th century, it had an important Jewish community, which established the printing press that produced the oldest Portuguese *incunabulum* in 1487. The town was granted a new charter by D. Manuel I, in 1504.

Leave your car in the free car park in Largo de São Francisco and walk around the walls and the enclosure where the cathedral is situated.

XI.3.a **City Walls**

A visit to the City Walls is best started in Largo de São Francisco. Classified as a Building of Public Interest. Information: Tourist Office (Tel: 289 800400).

The existing walls were restored in the time of D. Manuel I, although they were originally built much earlier. The general structure dates from the time of the Muslim emirs, as can be seen by the bases of some of the remaining towers and the surmounted arch of the town gate (Porta da Vila). The two *barbican* towers next to

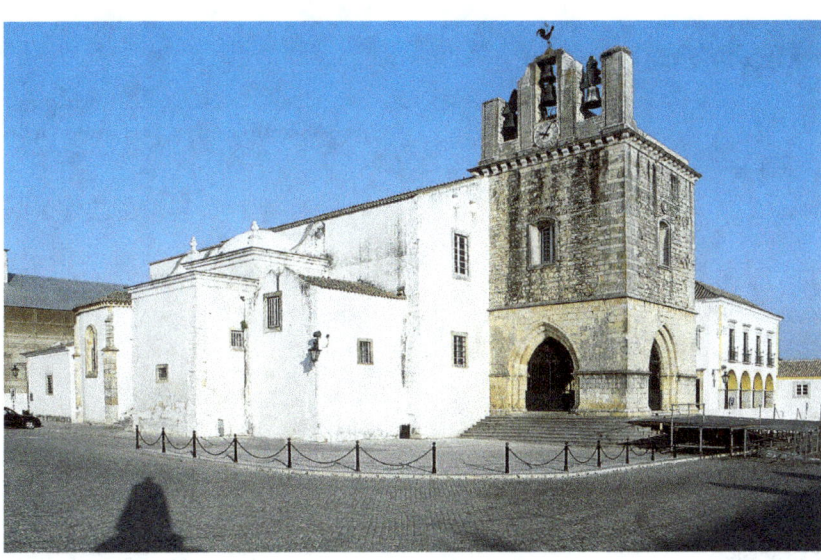

Faro Cathedral.

the Arco do Repouso must also date from the Almohad era.

XI.3.b Cathedral

Largo da Sé. Classified as a Building of Public Interest. Information (Tel: 289 806632).

In Manueline times, this was simply the Parish Church, Silves Cathedral being the only one in the Algarve. Begun in the 13th century, what can be seen today dates from the 15th century, and the beginning of the 16th century, such as the tower on the façade and the two transept chapels. The remainder was destroyed by earth tremors, and rebuilt in other styles. The three-aisled vessel of the church that existed at the time of D. Manuel I was also destroyed and was then modernised.

Take the EN125 to Lagoa; continue on the EN124-1 to Silves.

ITINERARY XI

Algarve

**Pedro Dias, Dalila Rodrigues,
Nuno Vassallo e Silva, Fernando Grilo**

Second day

XI.4 SILVES
        XI.4.a Cruz de Portugal (The Portuguese Cross)
        XI.4.b Cathedral

XI.5 ALVOR (option)
        XI.5.a Divino Salvador (Alvor Parish Church)

XI.6 LAGOS
        XI.6.a Historic Centre
        XI.6.b City Walls

XI.7 RAPOSEIRA
        XI.7.a Church of Nossa Senhora de Guadalupe

XI.8 SAGRES
        XI.8.a Fortress and Promontory

Prince Henry the Navigator

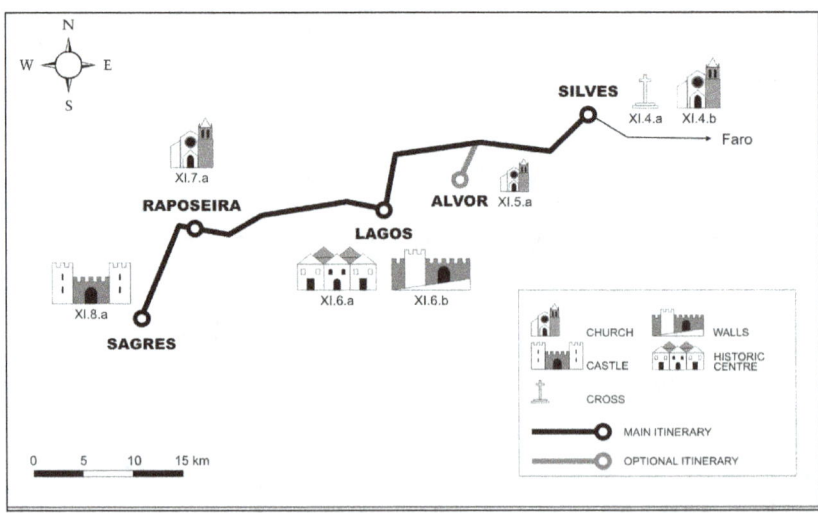

ITINERARY XI *Algarve*
Silves

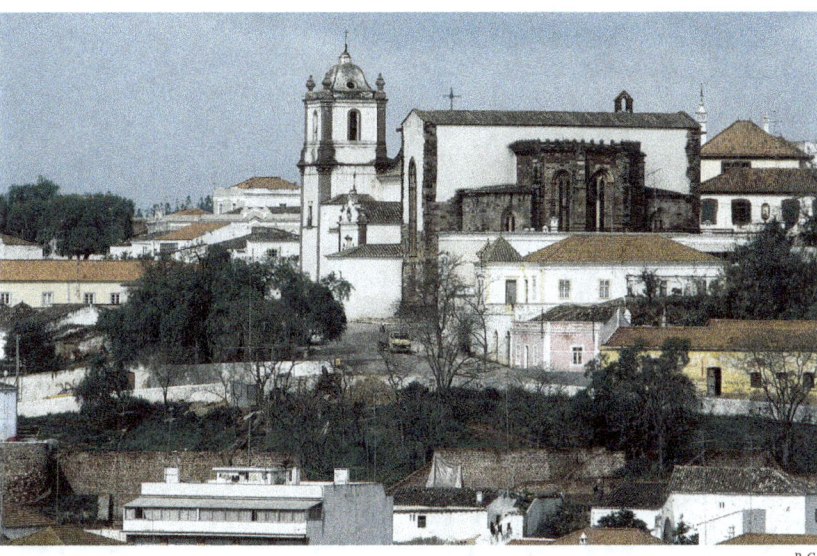

Silves historic centre.

XI.4 **SILVES**

*Information: Tourist Office
(Tel: 282 442255).*

This was the most important Muslim city in the south of present-day Portuguese territory. It was first settled in the Bronze Age and won from the Moors by D. Sancho I in 1189, though it was lost again shortly afterwards, and only became part of the Christian kingdom at the time of D. Afonso III, in 1240. Although other riverside towns became more important, Silves had been the see of the Algarve Diocese and had a castle, D. Manuel I, therefore, ordered the large cathedral to be built and the castle to be restored.

XI.4.a **Cruz de Portugal (The Portuguese Cross)**

In the lower part of Silves, next to the EN124. Designated a National Monument.

The *Cruz de Portugal* (the Portuguese Cross) is one of the loveliest Manueline crosses to have been conserved. According to documentation, it was customary for the local people to have crosses made to mark holy ground. The arms of the Gothic cross in honey-toned limestone are carved with foliate rosettes, and set in a niche supported by a profusely decorated column. The *Crucifixion* is represented on one side and on the other side is a *Pietà* with the Virgin holding the body of her dead Son.

ITINERARY XI   *Algarve*
Silves

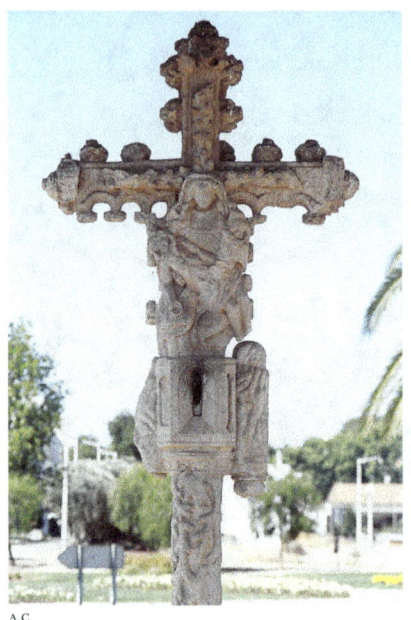

The Portuguese Cross, Silves.

A.C.

XI.4.b **Cathedral**

Rua da Sé. Designated a National Monument. Information: Casa Paroquial (Tel: 282 442472).
Opening hours: daily 08.30-18.30.

Building work began on the Cathedral during the reign of D. Afonso V, on the site of a previous 12th-century church. As it was still incomplete when D. Manuel I visited Silves in 1499, he ordered it to be rebuilt on a larger scale, as he considered the one being built to be far too small. The dividing arches of the aisles were erected at that time, as well as the side walls of the main vessel, the façade, and the wooden roof before the transept. The architecture, although sober and simple in line, is well designed, quite different from the more pop-

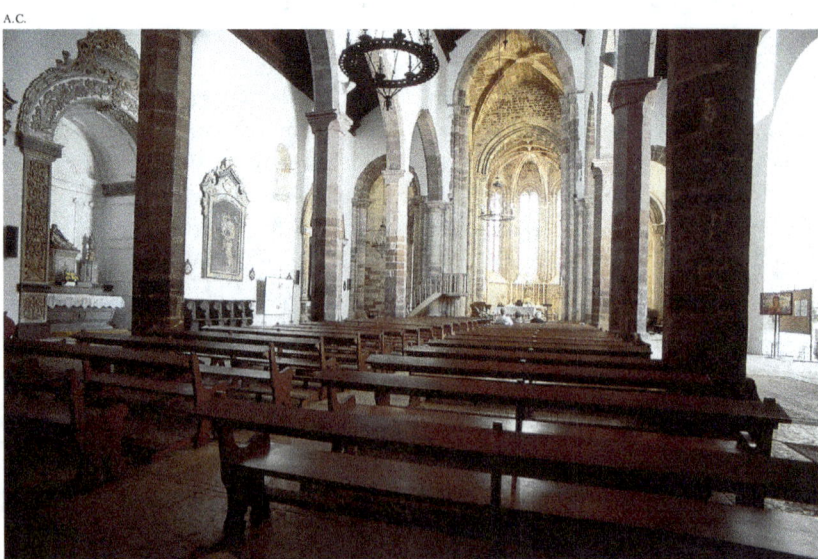

A.C.

Silves Cathedral, interior.

ular, exuberant decorative styles of the parish churches in the region. It has three aisles, divided by pillars supporting the wooden roof, and linking the main vessel of the church by a large transept to the triple apse in a traditional 15th-century Gothic style, on the lines of Batalha.

Retake the EN124-1 to Lagoa, then take the EN125 to Portimão. Follow the signs to Alvor.

XI.5 **ALVOR** (option)

XI.5.a **Divino Salvador** (Alvor Parish Church)

Largo da Igreja. (Tel: 282 459151). The portals are classified as a Building of Public Interest.
Opening hours: 09.00-21.00. Mass is celebrated in English on Saturday at 18.00.

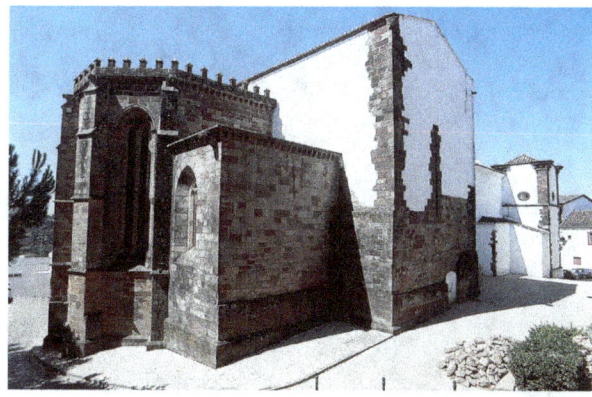

Silves Cathedral.

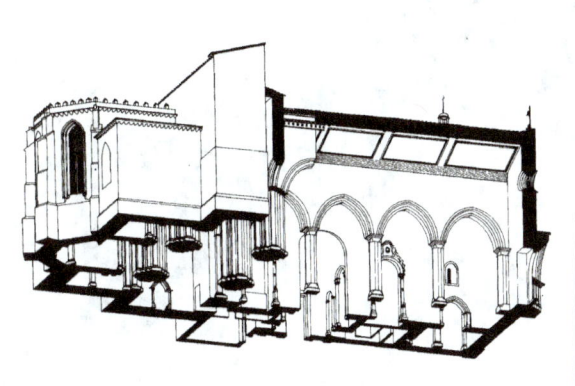

This is one of the few Manueline buildings in the Algarve to remain almost intact. The main portal is the loveliest and most complex in the region. A pruned tree trunk forms the external *colonnettes* and the main *archivolt* surrounds the frame made up of another *colonnette* and plain *archivolt,* that separate a simple inter-columnation with scenes sculpted in six registers superimposed on either side. The interior has three aisles, with four bays, separated by semicircular arches set on cylindrical columns, with large bases and crowned capitals, decorated with foliage, each one different from the others. All that remains of the Manueline apse is the *triumphal arch* of the chancel.

Silves Cathedral, axionometric drawing, Catalogue of the 18th Exhibition of Art, Science and Culture "The Portuguese Discoveries and Renaissance Europe", Lisbon, 1983.

Retake the EN125 to Lagos.

ITINERARY XI   *Algarve*
Lagos

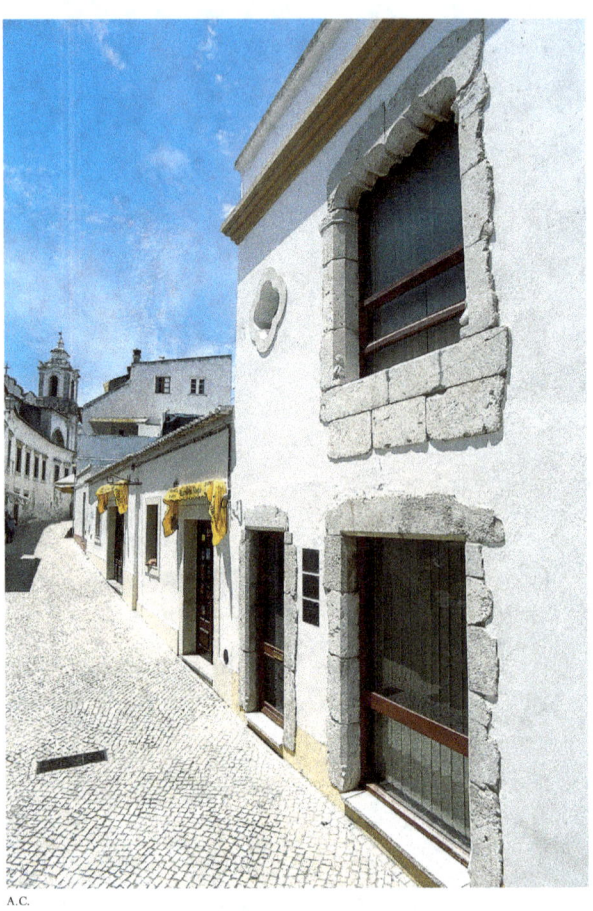
A.C.

Lagos historic centre.

XI.6 LAGOS

Dating back to the Roman era, at least, Lagos was an important centre during the Islamic period, but attained its peak during the period of the Discoveries. Prince Henry the Navigator was a frequent visitor, and D. Sebastião also sailed from the port on his ill-fated voyage to Alcácer-Quibir, from where he never returned.

In the 15th century, Lagos was a Portuguese naval research centre, and an obligatory departure and arrival point for Atlantic shipping. The fleet sailed from the port to conquer Ceuta, and Gil Eanes embarked here on the voyage during which he rounded Cape Bojador for the first time. On the death of Prince Henry the Navigator, in 1460, Lisbon took the lead in maritime navigation and trade, and within three years, the post for trading with Arguim was established in the capital.

Lagos continued, however, to supply fortresses in North Africa, leading D. Manuel I to order the reconstruction of its defensive walls.

XI.6.a Historic Centre

Guided visits may be booked at the Câmara Municipal (Town Hall Tel: 282 762055). Information: Tourist Office (Tel: 282 763031). The house with a Manueline window is situated at No. 2, Rua H. Correia da Silva.

The road layout of the old part of the city has remained largely as it was in the 16th century. The Manueline fortifications, with gateways leading to the beach and countryside, governed the basic outline, though these in turn were affected by the Muslim plan. Houses, warehouses and small businesses gradually occupied the ineffective Manueline defences, hiding the walls and taking over the towers and passages. Despite a series of earthquakes, there were very few alterations to the network of streets inside the city walls, other than the regularising of churchyards and the courtyards of religious buildings.

Some of the houses date from the 16th century and there is also a Manueline window, from which D. Sebastião is said to have addressed his troops before embarking for Morocco, in 1578.

XI.6.b City Walls

Jardins da Constituição. Designated a National Monument. A guided tour may be booked through the Câmara Municipal (Town Hall Tel: 282 762055).

The first walls built after the Reconquest appear to date from the time of D. Afonso IV, and therefore from the first half of the 14th century, although what is visible today was clearly begun by D. Manuel I, whose architects designed a traditional system of high, thick *curtain walls* with wide battlements, divided by square towers that were reinforced at the corners and gateways. On the Ribeira side, the long front has two towers to defend the main gate of the Porta de São Gonçalo, and a *barbican* was built later on high ground at the far end. The wall facing south is quite impressive with its more modern bastions, undoubtedly built at a later phase.

M.A.

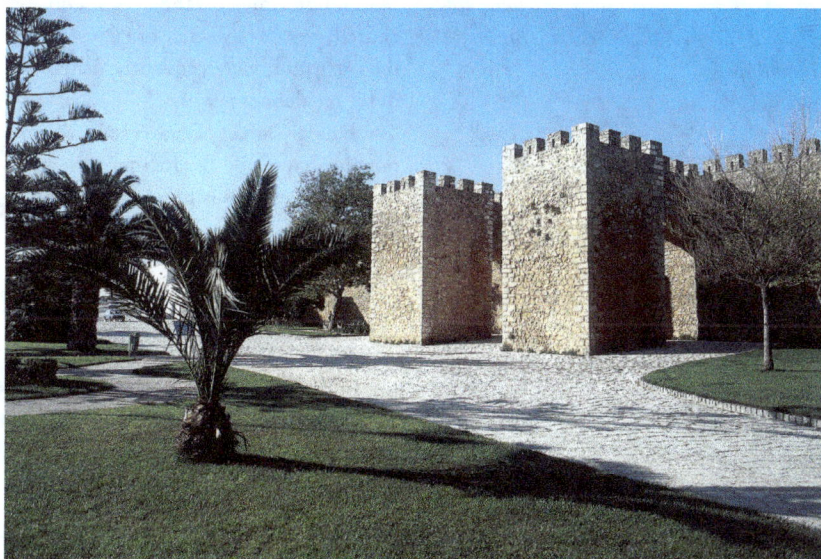

Lagos City Walls.

ITINERARY XI *Algarve*

Raposeira

Church of Nossa Senhora de Guadalupe, Raposeira.

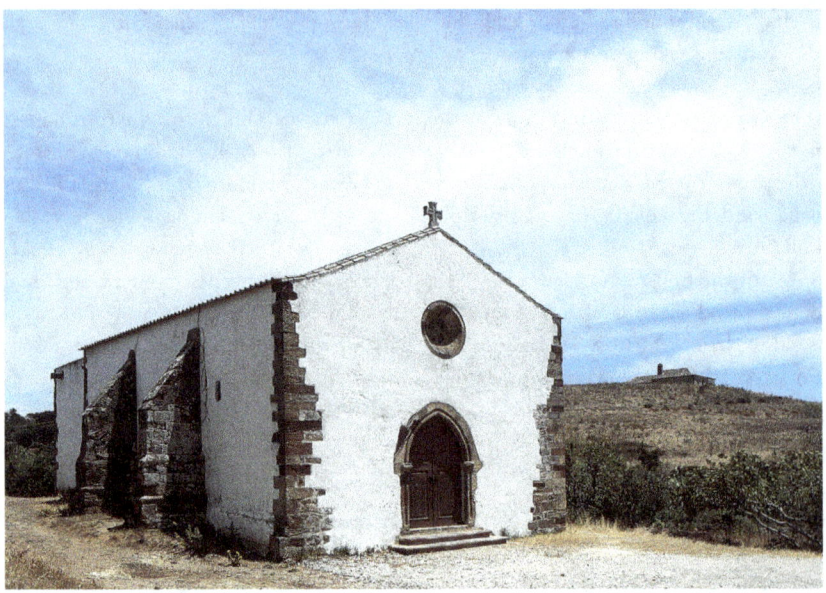

Take the EN125 in the direction of Vila do Bispo. After leaving Figueira, and before reaching Raposeira, on the right-hand side, is the Igreja de Nossa Senhora da Guadalupe.

XI.7 **RAPOSEIRA**

XI.7.a Church of Nossa Senhora de Guadalupe

*Quinta de Guadalupe, next to the EN125. Designated a National Monument.
Opening hours: 09.30-12.30 and 14.00-17.00, except on Mondays.*

This Church appears to date from before the 16th century, though it was built in Manueline times on the site of another church, possibly by order of Prince Henry the Navigator, who frequently visited one of his residences nearby.
The builder, a man of few resources, may possibly have used the former structure, and the decoration by local craftsmen gives the erudite motifs a somewhat rustic character.
The exterior is very simple: the portal has a pointed arch with a bull's-eye window above, and there are buttresses at the sides. In the interior, only the chancel is vaulted.

Retake the EN125 to Vila do Bispo. Follow the EN268 to Sagres.

XI.8 SAGRES

Information: Tourist Office (Tel: 282 624873).

XI.8.a Fortress and Promontory

Opening hours: 10.00-18.00 in winter, and 10.00-20.30 in summer (May-September). The modern building is used for temporary exhibitions, which also provides educational information about the site and may also be visited.

The promontory, the fortress and, most of all, legend marks Sagres. It was thought to have been here that Prince Henry the Navigator founded his famous "Sagres School", where the art of navigation was studied and mariners trained. Although this tradition has been destroyed by solid arguments, the place still lives upon the myth. It is true that Prince Henry did have one of his residences nearby, in Raposeira, where he had a *quinta*, and it also seems to be true that techniques, ships and instruments were tested in the bay at Sagres and São Vicente.

In the Manueline era, there was a sufficiently large population for the area to be designated a parish. There was also a fortress on the promontory that developed naturally, making a wall that isolated the area. The wall enclosed the Chapel of Nossa Senhora da Graça, houses, barracks and other constructions. The present fortifications were completed in 1793.

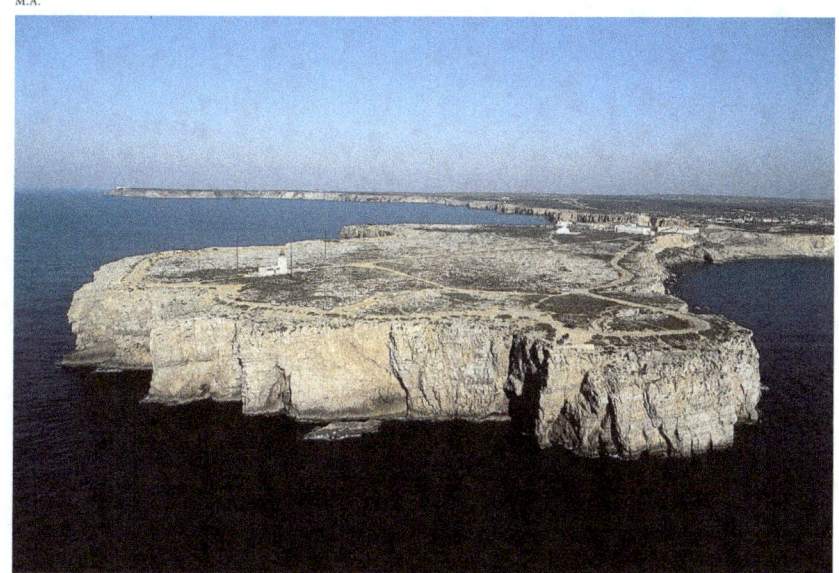

Sagres Fortress and Promontory.

ITINERARY XI *Algarve*

Sagres

The Sacred Promontory
"On this far tip of the continent of Europe where the coast curves towards the North, on this arid, deserted land, facing a foaming, harsh sea, men's memories have accumulated since distant times. Few places on the globe so isolated from the world can be found linked to so many grandiose recollections of Myth and History. The cultured traveller is seized by an almost religious awe and by a holy disturbance — so many are the ancient fears, the wonderful legends and adventures that this place evokes. To the Greeks and Romans, this was the **Promontorium sacrum**, where they could see the sun, as it sank, one hundred times larger than in other parts of the world and hear the amazing sound of the star as it drowned in the waves. It was here, according to Artemidon, that the gods 'came to rest at night from their works and journeys across the world.' The Christians in their turn created a new myth that the body of St Vincent came to rest here after his martyrdom, as his relics were taken from here later (in 1173) to be sheltered in the cathedral in Lisbon.

Long before Portugal was an independent kingdom, the Christians erected the Temple of the Raven there, to which al-Idrisi referred, and where the faithful made pilgrimages and offerings. 'On the top of the edifice,' says the Arab geographer, 'are ten ravens that never leave that spot, the priests from the church tell amazing things about them... It is impossible to go there without taking part in the sumptuous banquet the people from the church offer the visitor — an old custom that they never fail to observe.'"

Sant'Ana Dionísio, **Guia de Portugal**, *Vol. II, Lisbon, 1927.*

PRINCE HENRY THE NAVIGATOR

Pedro Dias

Prince Henry was the fifth son of D. João I and Philippa of Lancaster. He was born in the city of Oporto on March 4th, 1394 and died in Sagres, on November 13th, 1460.

Educated in the atmosphere of the Portuguese Court, where his mother lay down the law, he soon displayed an interest in the Arts and attained a high degree of culture and knowledge, while maintaining an interest in Chivalry, which was fashionable among the princes of his time. When he was 21 years old, he took part in the first act of Portuguese expansion, the Reconquest of the Christian city of Ceuta in North Africa, in 1415. He was given the task of governing the city and, from then on, he was the prime enthusiast for maintaining the Portuguese presence in Morocco and carrying out Atlantic exploration.

He was made a duke within his own household, whilst his squires and servants set out to sail the seas and, within a few decades, with unprecedented vigour they brought back knowledge of unknown African lands and many of the North Atlantic islands. Henry brought together experts of various nationalities and creeds, absorbing classical culture mingled with new experiences to open a new era in the life of Humanity.

A pious man, but also very pragmatic, he crossed the sea to fight in Morocco, travelled constantly between the Court and the Algarve and administered the Order of Christ, which he placed at the service of the overseas expansion.

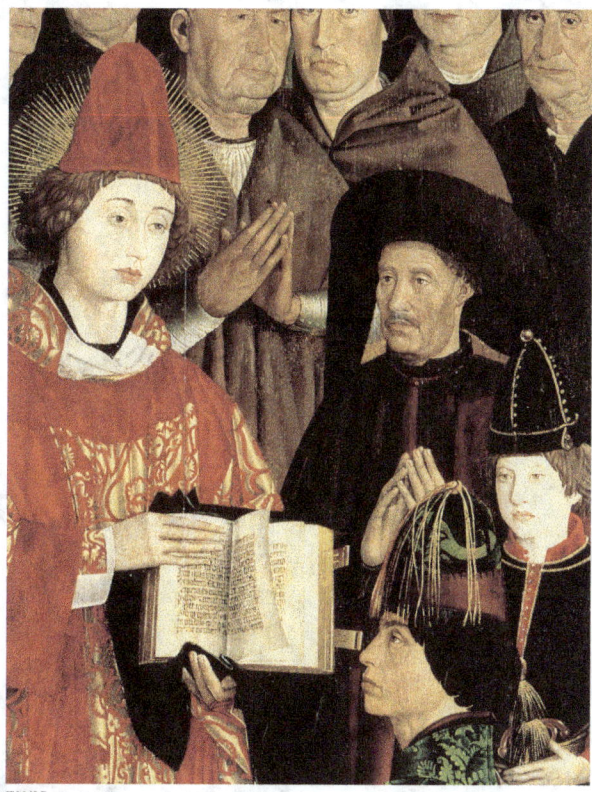

He brought immigrants from the Northern of Europe to settle the islands of the Azores and Madeira, gave privileges to Italians and Catalans, for helping in this great adventure, and, when he died, his men had already reached Sierra Leone and the Cape Verde archipelago. He dreamed of reaching the lands of Prester John and even India; he may not have succeeded, but he enabled the princes who succeeded him to do so.

Polyptych of St Vincent (Prince's Panel), detail, Museu Nacional de Arte Antiga, Lisbon.

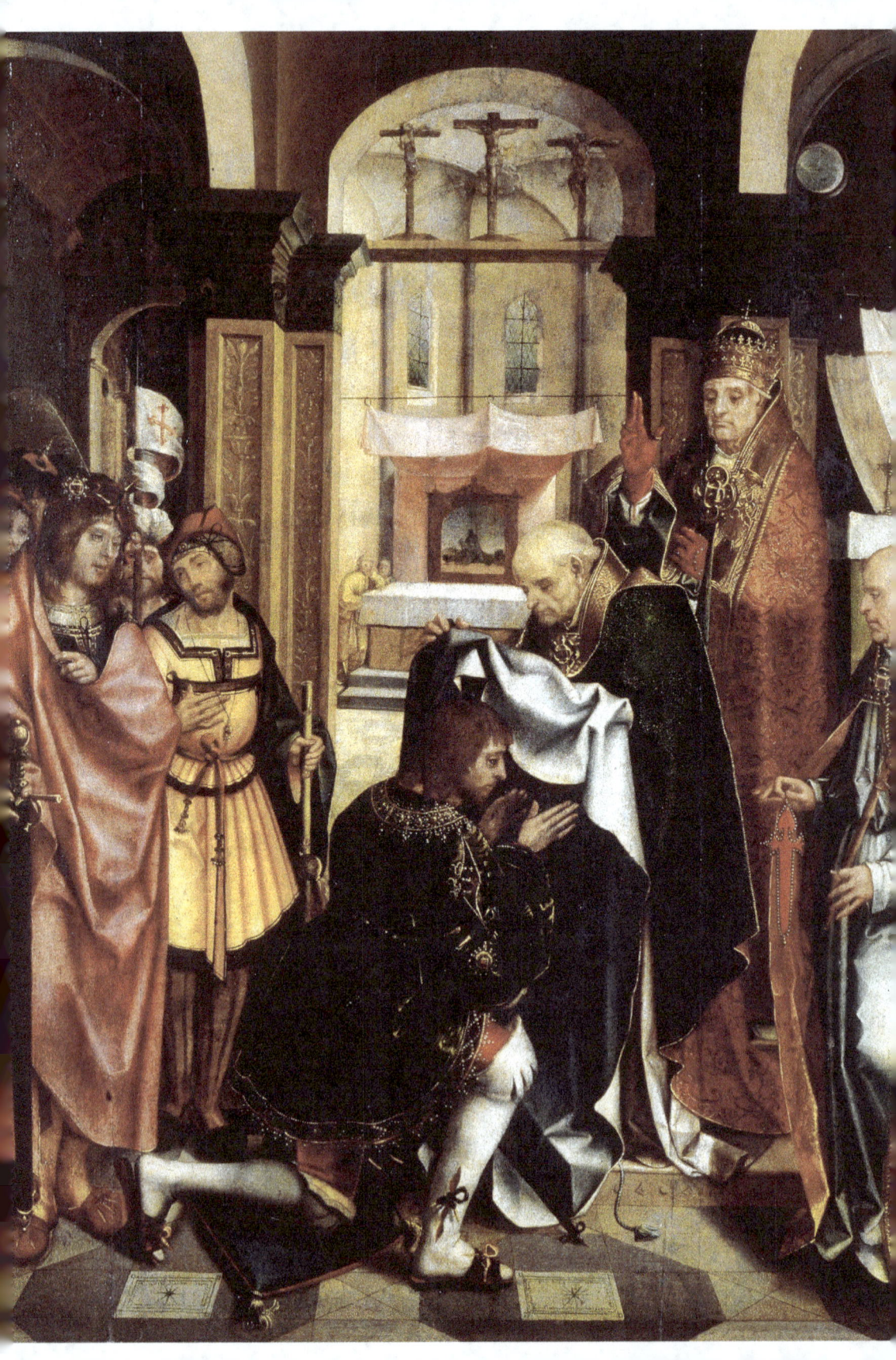

ITINERARY XII

The Military Order of Santiago

Pedro Dias, Dalila Rodrigues,
Nuno Vassallo e Silva, Fernando Grilo

XII.1 SINES
    XII.1.a Castle
    XII.1.b Chapel of Nossa Senhora das Salas

XII.2 SANTIAGO DO CACÉM
    XII.2.a Castle
    XII.2.b Santiago (Santiago do Cacém Parish Church)

XII.3 ALCÁCER DO SAL
    XII.3.a Castle

XII.4 SETÚBAL
    XII.4.a Historic Centre
    XII.4.b Convent of Jesus
    XII.4.c Setúbal Municipal Museum
    XII.4.d São Julião (Setúbal Parish Church)

XII.5 PALMELA
    XII.5.a Castle
    XII.5.b Church of Santiago

XII.6 ALCOCHETE
    XII.6.a São João Baptista (Alcochete Parish Church)

Vasco da Gama

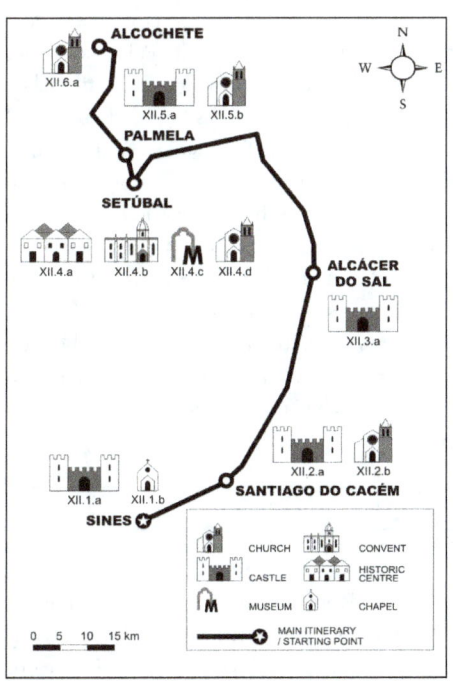

Master of Lourinhã, "Investiture of a Master of the Order of Santiago", oil on wood, c.1520-25, Museu Nacional de Arte Antiga, Lisbon.

283

ITINERARY XII   *The Military Order of Santiago*

Sines

The Military Order of Santiago, one of the most important in the Reconquest of peninsular territory from the Moors, traditionally dates back to the time of Ramiro I of León (842-850). However, its formal structure was only acquired much later, in *c.*1160, coinciding with the increase in the worship of St James (São Tiago), whose body was said to have been found in Compostela, with the military advances to the south. Fernando II of León officially established the Order in 1170, with its headquarters at Cáceres in present-day Spanish Extremadura.

Arruda dos Vinhos was probably the first town in Portugal to host the headquarters of the Order in the time of D. Afonso Henriques, the first king, who later increased the Order's territory to include Alcácer do Sal, Almada and Palmela, a donation confirmed by his son, D. Sancho I.

The Order of Santiago, also known as the Order of the Gladiators, was to split into two, with the Portuguese branch having its headquarters in Palmela. This became the central power controlling a vast region along the banks of the River Sado, reaching both into the Alentejo, and as far as the estuary of the River Tagus.

At the beginning of the 15th century, other military orders became more important, particularly that of the Order of Christ, although in 1491, D. Jorge, the natural son and heir presumptive of D. João II, was made Master of the Order of Santiago, after the tragic death of Prince D. Afonso. This attracted important families, who were granted commanderies, and from which many of the leading figures of the Discoveries originated, among them Vasco da Gama and many members of his family.

The region became more or less the fiefdom of the prince D. Jorge, who retained his importance on the national political scene even when his cousin, D. Manuel, Duke of Beja, ascended the throne in 1495. Careful administration made these towns some of the most prosperous in the kingdom and led to a spate of building that included everything from houses to Town Halls, churches, monasteries, convents, prisons, warehouses and, of course, castles. The hand of D. Jorge was visible everywhere, starting with the Palmela Castle, overlooking from on high the fertile valley of the River Sado. His tomb is to be found in the Igreja de Santiago inside the castle.

There are still other reminders of the early days of the Order, such as churches in Alcácer do Sal, and traces of Islamic occupation, such as the walls of the castle in this same town. Two of the leading figures in Portuguese history were born in this area, D. Manuel I, in Alcochete and Vasco da Gama in Sines.

XII.I **SINES**

The Roman occupation of Sines is documented, but it only became important as a fishing port during the Islamic period.

ITINERARY XII   *The Military Order of Santiago*
Sines

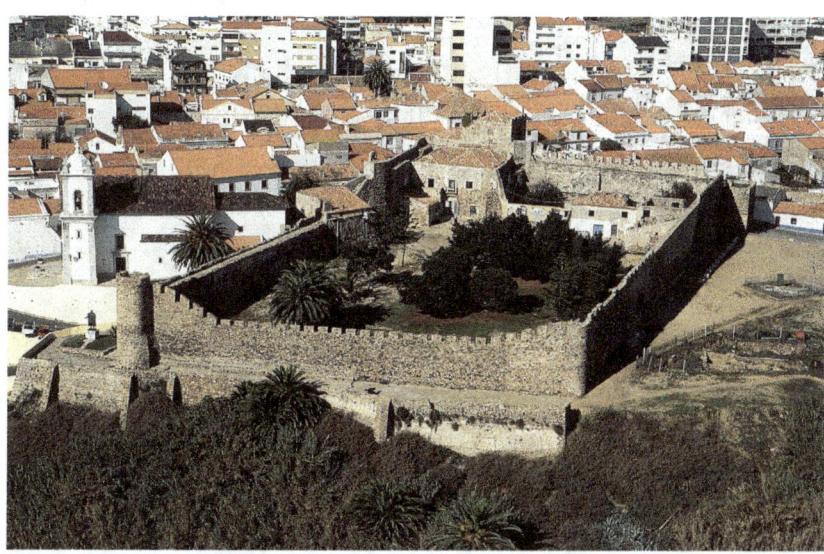

Aerial view of Sines Castle.

The Knights Templar recaptured the town, which came definitively under the Portuguese Crown in 1217, in the time of D. Sancho II. During the Middle Ages, it lived in the shadow of the Order of Santiago and was the residence of the Da Gama family, which produced Vasco da Gama, the commander of the first fleet to find the sea route between Portugal and India. D. Manuel I granted the town a new charter in 1512.

XII.1.a Castle

The Castle is reached via Largo João de Deus. Classified as a Building of Public Interest. The Tourist Office is inside the castle (Tel: 269 634472).
Opening hours: daily 10.00-12.00 and 14.30-18.30 October-April, and 09.00-12.00 and 14.00-18.30 May-September. Closed on December 25th and May 1st.

The original castle probably dates back to Muslim times, though it underwent extensive alterations again in the 14th century, and during the reign of D. Manuel I, the central part still conserving the same outline. Four *curtain walls* from this period form a small rectangle, reinforced at the corners. The governor's residence with paired windows, where Vasco da Gama was probably born, is on one of the corners, next to the considerably altered keep.
A partially artificial platform was created for the construction and used for the building of a low *barbican*. A continuous parapet and battlements run round the walls, many of them rebuilt some decades ago.

ITINERARY XII   *The Military Order of Santiago*
Santiago do Cacém

Chapel of Nossa Senhora das Salas, Sines.

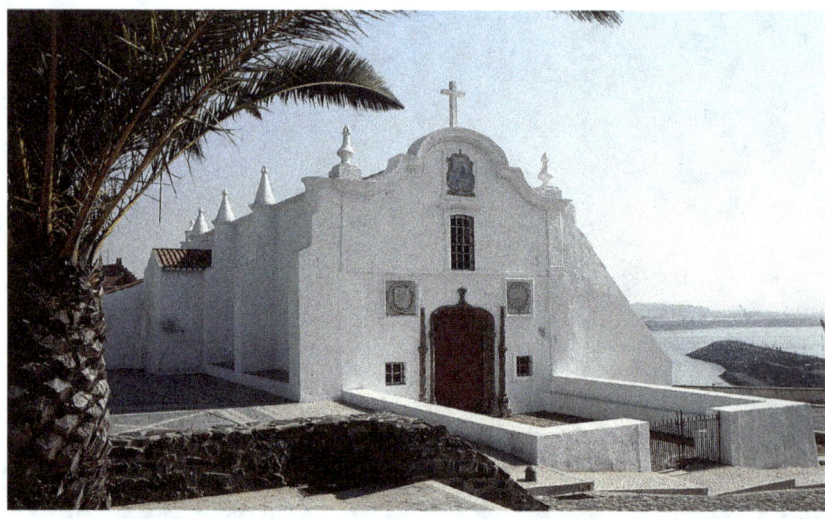

XII.1.b Chapel of Nossa Senhora das Salas

Rua de Nossa Senhora das Salas. Designated a National Monument.
Opening hours: Friday at 19.00 for mass, and at weekends in the summer 12.00-19.30.

Chapel of Nossa Senhora das Salas, interior, Sines.

This 14th-century Chapel was completely reconstructed during the Manueline period on the initiative of Vasco da Gama, his successors carrying on the work until at least 1529. A small, simple structure consisting of one single nave, it has only one chapel in the apse, although this is completely vaulted which is unusual in buildings of this size. The portal is Late Gothic, naturalist in style, with a keel arch surmounted by the royal coat of arms.

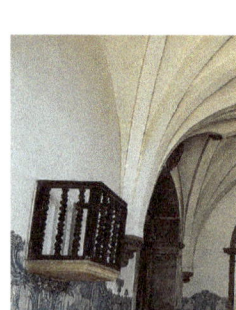

Take the IP8. Where the road forks with the IC8 and EN120, take the latter to Santiago do Cacém.

XII.2 SANTIAGO DO CACÉM

The origin of the town is linked to the development of the nearby Roman city of Miróbriga, the ruins of which bear witness to this once highly important regional cen-

ITINERARY XII   *The Military Order of Santiago*
Santiago do Cacém

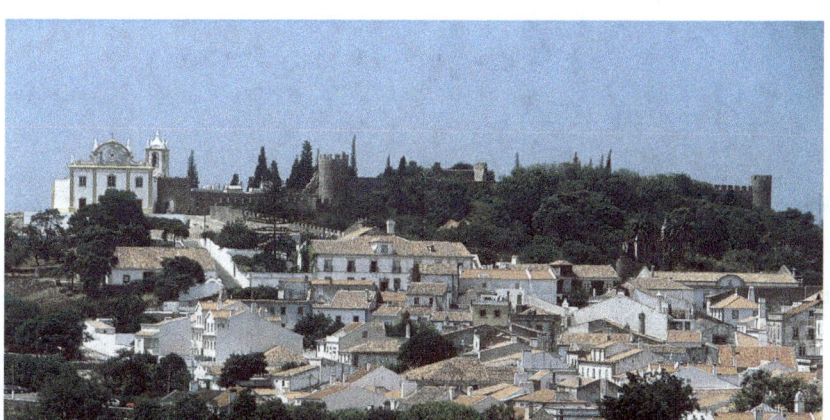

General view of Santiago do Cacém.

R.C.

tre. The historic centre of the town became important during the Islamic period when an imposing castle was built. The first Reconquest took place in 1157 at the time of D. Afonso Henriques, but the town only became a definitive possession of the Portuguese Crown in 1217.
Like all the towns in the region, its development was due to the Order of Santiago. It was one of the principal commanderies and was granted a new charter by D. Manuel I in 1512.

XII.2.a Castle

Designated a National Monument. Viewing of the Castle is from the outside only. Information: Tourist Office (Tel: 269 826696).

Nothing can be seen today of the original Islamic construction, and the present shape of the building, an irregular rectangle about 200 m. in length and a little more than 30 m. wide, is the result of changes made after the Christian Reconquest in the 13th century. Improvements were also carried out at the end of the 14th century, and in the 15th century, and from this period there are still remains of not only some sections of the walls, but also many towers. During the Manueline period, the castle was again

R.C.

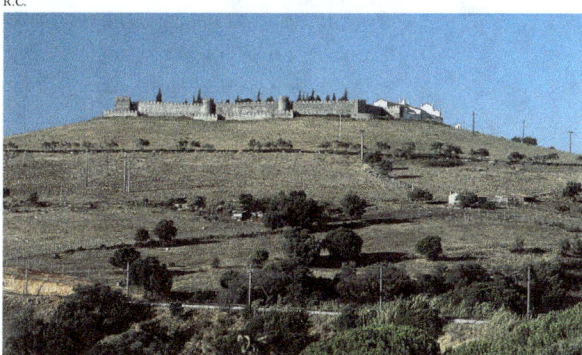

Santiago do Cacém Castle.

ITINERARY XII *The Military Order of Santiago*
Alcácer do Sal

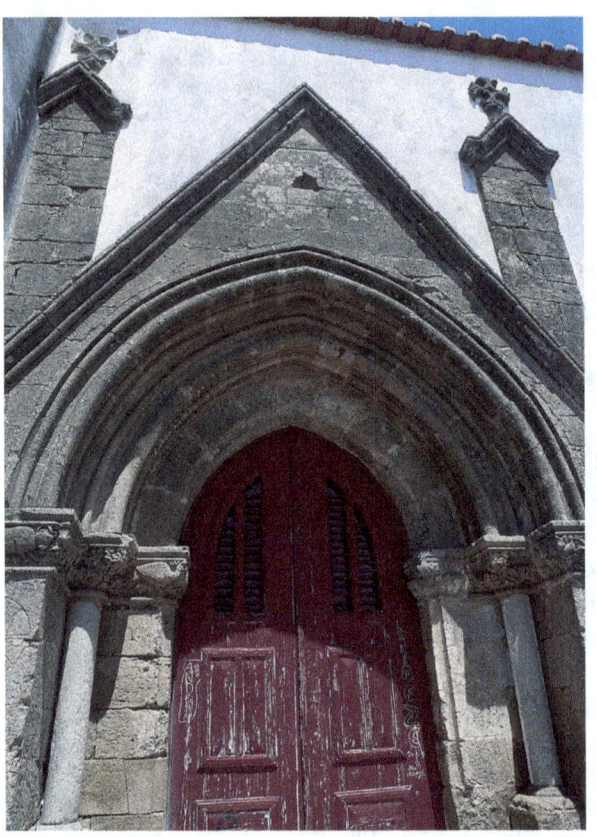

Santiago do Cacém Parish Church, side portal.

R.C.

repaired. Although this was to be the final reconstruction, time has taken its toll on the enclosure, gateways and the *curtain walls*, which nonetheless still give an impression of what it looked like during the reign of D. Manuel I.

XII.2.b **Santiago (Santiago do Cacém Parish Church)**

Situated next to the castle. Designated a National Monument.

Opening hours: Tuesday-Friday 10.00-12.00 and 14.00-17.00, Saturday and Sunday 14.00-17.00. Closed on Monday and Public Holidays.

The Church is essentially 14th-century, although it underwent changes afterwards, mainly in the early 16th century. Its Perpendicular Gothic portal is in the style of that in Batalha. The interior has three aisles supported by Gothic arcades and pillars.

Take the EN261 to the IP8 and then head northwards along the A2, taking the exit to Alcácer do Sal.

XII.3 ALCÁCER DO SAL

Alcácer do Sal was the old Roman settlement of *Salácia*, a name derived from the production of salt, which was its principal source of income, and also important in a regional context. Taken from the Moors in 1158, who retook the town shortly afterwards, only in 1271 did it become part of the land of the Portuguese Crown and was then granted to the Order of Santiago. With the advent of the great voyages of the Portuguese Discoveries, the economy thrived and an important middle class was formed, as salt became even more important for the conservation of provisions. D. Manuel I, who granted Alcácer do Sal a new charter in 1516, married Maria of Castile, the daughter of Ferdinand and Isabella of Spain, in the Igreja do Espirito Santo in the town, in 1501.

ITINERARY XII   *The Military Order of Santiago*
Setúbal

XII.3.a Castle

Designated a National Monument. Some rooms of the Castle has been converted into the Pousada D. Afonso II. Tel: 265 613072.

The Castle at Alcácer do Sal has essentially retained its late 11th and 12th-century, Islamic lines, and part of the existing *lath-and-plaster* walls and towers, mainly turrets on the south and north sides, date from this period.
From the 14th century onwards, the Order of Santiago carried out extensive work on the Castle, mainly consolidating the *curtain walls* and towers; the last reforms took place during the Manueline period, when the fortress was improved and made larger.
Within the Castle enclosure there are two 14th-century Gothic churches, the Igreja de Santa Maria and the Igreja do Senhor dos Mártires.
A.C.

Take the A2. At the junction with the A12, take this latter motorway to Setúbal.

XII.4 SETÚBAL

Set on the estuary of the River Sado, the Port of Setúbal was, besides the sea traffic, an important region for both fishing and salting in Roman times. Following the Christian Reconquest, the town received a further boost after a period of stagnation. It was linked to the Order of Santiago da Espada, and was granted a charter in 1249.
There are still some traces of the town walls, built in 1343, during the reign of D. Afonso IV.
By the end of the 15th century, due to the revenue from the salt trade and other products, Setúbal was making considerable tax contributions to Crown coffers. D. João II, who married his cousin Leonor

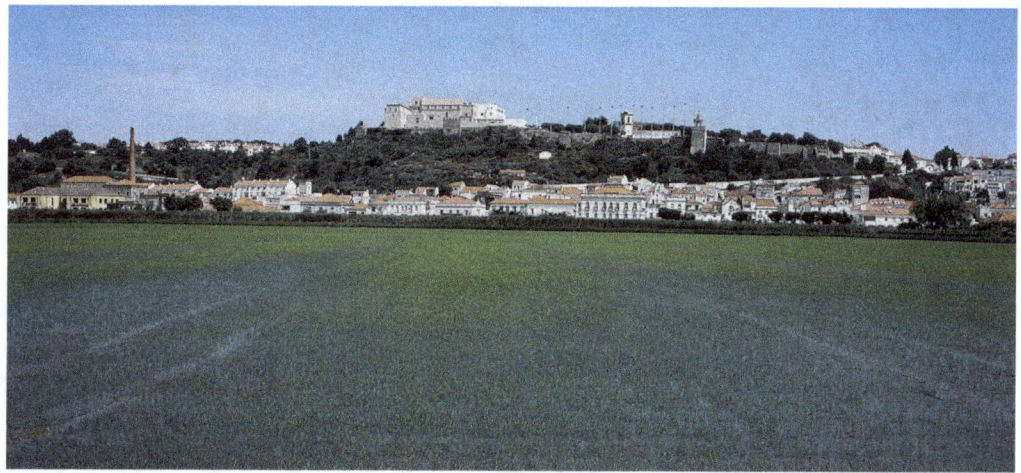

General view of Alcácer do Sal Castle and town.

ITINERARY XII The Military Order of Santiago
Setúbal

in the town in 1471, made a number of improvements, building an aqueduct and regulating the urban area that had spread beyond the 14th-century walls.

D. Manuel I took great interest in the town, ordering two parish churches to be built as well as the Town Hall, the prison, slaughterhouses, a leper hospital and corn market. The Master of the Order of Santiago, D. Jorge de Lencastre, the natural son of D. João II, had a residence in the town and was also a patron of local institutions.

XII.4.a Historic Centre

The Casa das Quatro Cabeças at No. 44, Rua Fran Pacheco (formerly Rua Direita de Troino), the portal of the Leper Hospital at No. 17, Avenida Manuel Maria Portela, the Convento of São João in Rua Almeida Garrett and the Igreja de Santa Maria in Largo de Santa Maria. Information: Tourist Office (Tel: 265 539120).

In Setúbal, Manueline architectural remains are found mostly on the slope where the Church of Santa Maria stands. The imperfect rectangular outline of the old Mediaeval walls is still visible today and the Porta do Sol gateway has survived. Besides the arches of Santa Maria, the doorway of the Convento de São João, the portal of the Leper Hospital and the Casa das Quatro Cabeças (the House of Four Heads), Setúbal still retains a number of Manueline doorways and windows in houses that are a reminder of a time when the port was one of the main supply bases for navigation and sea trade and the streets were named after merchants (Rua dos Mercadores), basket makers (Rua das Canastras), coppersmiths (Rua da Caldeiros) and so on. There is a simple but elegant polylobed lintel at No. 3, Travessa de São José, and a more highly decorated one at No. 45, Rua de António Granja. Most houses, however, have grooved doorposts with a lower three-lobed arch, included in the plain exterior lintels.

XII.4.b Convent of Jesus

Praça Miguel Bombarda (formerly Largo de Jesus). The Church, Cloister and Chapter House are classified as a National Monument.
Opening hours: Tuesday-Saturday 9.00-12.30 and 14.00-17.30. Closed on Sunday, Monday and public holidays.

The Convento de Jesus was founded in 1489 by D. Justa Rodrigues, wet nurse to D. Manuel I, when the latter was still only

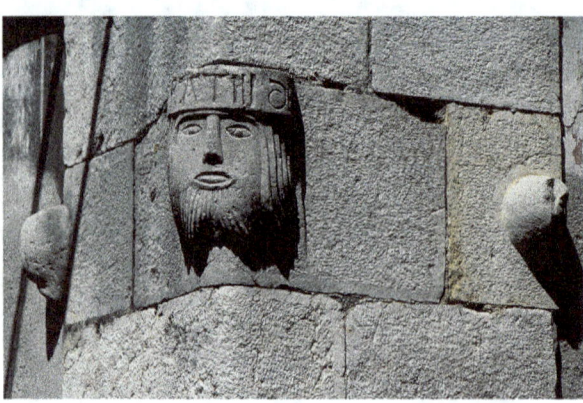

The House of the Four Heads, detail, Setúbal historic centre.

ITINERARY XII   *The Military Order of Santiago*
Setúbal

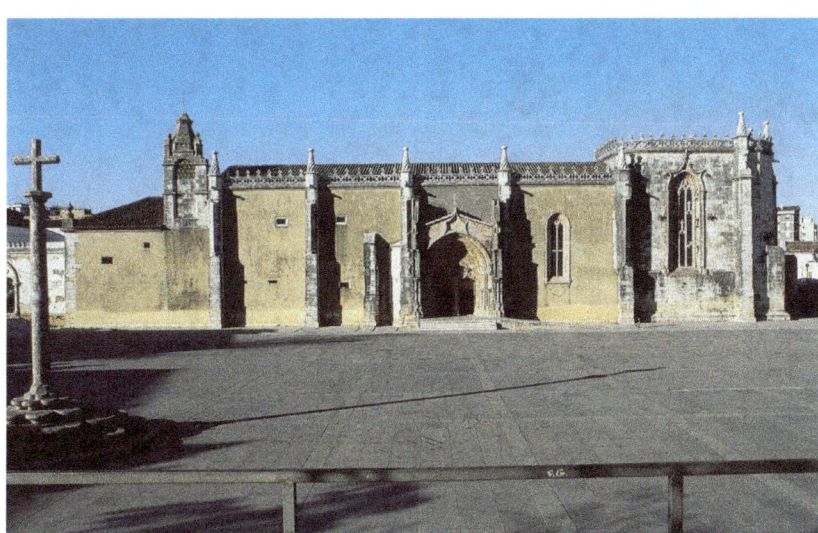

Convent of Jesus, Setúbal.

the Duke of Beja, and Administrator of the Order of Christ. The first stone was laid on August 17th 1490, and two years later, during a visit by D. João II, the ceremony was symbolically repeated. It is known that the Master of Works, Boytac, worked there before 1490 and the initial project was certainly his, although only a small part of what remains today is his work.

When D. Manuel I ascended the throne, the original plan was altered to make a larger church and more ample residential quarters. The walls of the church, the crypt below the chancel, and the upper and lower choirs, date from the early times of the construction, and possibly the plan for the cloister, completed in 1520, also dates from the 15th century. The church has three aisles rising to the same height, separated by twisted columns in polished stone from the Serra da Arrábida. The chancel, higher and better built, was begun in 1520 by master masons who had worked on the Mosteiro dos Jerónimos in Lisbon. It has rich, complex vaulting with curved ribs forming a quatrefoil. The stained

Church of the Convent of Jesus, axionometric drawing, Catalogue of the 18th Exhibition of Art, Science and Culture "Os Decobrimentos Postugueses e a Europa do Renascimento", Lisbon, 1983.

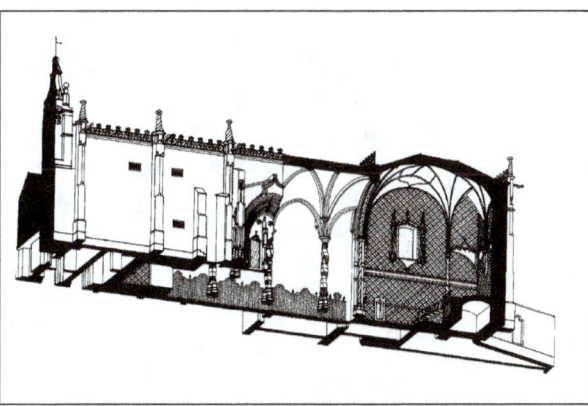

291

ITINERARY XII   The Military Order of Santiago
Setúbal

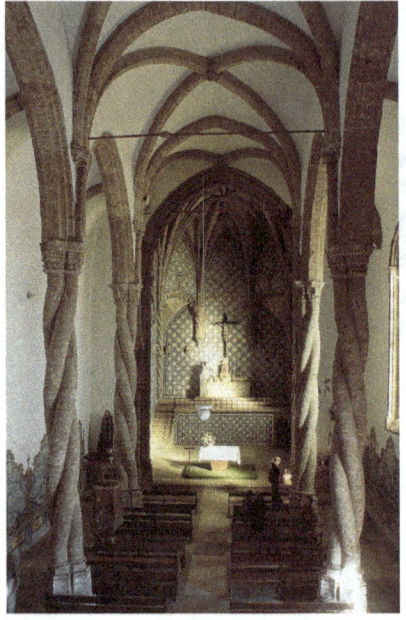

Church of the Convent of Jesus, interior, Setúbal.

Reliquary of Nossa Senhora da Anunciada, 1520, Setúbal Municipal Museum

chancel, the niche in the sanctuary, the altar-niche in the sacristy, and the blind window on the left-hand side of the apse.

The large cloister has two storeys and arcades with pointed arches, only broken by openings to the garth. The covered *lavabo* (wash room), an addition to the quadrangular plan, is at the opposite end of the church and has beautifully designed corbels with heads in high relief.

XII.4.c Setúbal Municipal Museum

The Museum is housed in the Convento de Jesus; the entrance is in Rua do Balneário Dr. Paula Borba. (Tel: 265 537890).

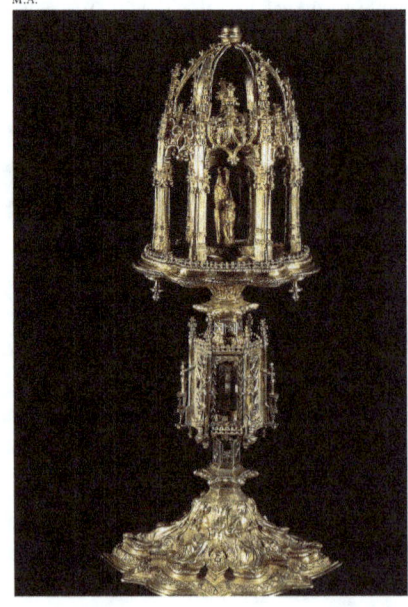

glass windows were only completed in 1539.

The main vessel of the church was not the work of the same designer and must have been the result of a decision by D. João III to complete the building as quickly and as cheaply as possible. It is lower than the apse and retains the buttresses of the initial work on the exterior, while the doorway is Late Gothic in design.

There is an interesting series of *Mudejar* tiles from Seville with inscriptions evoking death in the funerary crypt. The entire church has highly complex decorative elements in the Late Gothic style that are excessively naturalist in taste, as is the case with the triangular shaped part of the vault in the

ITINERARY XII *The Military Order of Santiago*
Setúbal

Opening hours: 9.00-12.00 and 13.30-17.30, Tuesday-Saturday. Closed on Sunday, Monday and public holidays.

The Museum is housed in buildings that formerly belonged to the Convent of Jesus and which contains a number of masterpieces from the Manueline era. Firstly, there is an extraordinary series of 14 panels that include the retable from the Monastery chancel that was almost certainly directed by the Court Painter to D. Manuel I, Jorge Afonso, and can be dated to between 1520 and 1530.

This large retable followed an iconographic plan in three levels corresponding to three cycles: the *Passion of Christ*, the *Childhood of Jesus* and the *Franciscan Saints*. The *Assumption of the Virgin* was probably also depicted, as usual in the centre, and there would have been a magnificent *Calvary* at the top. The use of various inspirational sources can be seen in another panel, the *Apparition of the Angel to St Clare, St Agnes and St Colette*, which reproduces the same theme as the painting by Quentin Metsys, also in this Museum, where the master has altered the architectural background to a Manueline building, which bears the coat of arms of Queen D. Leonor on the portal. Among the ambiguities that tend to characterise painted architecture during this period are other panels with Renaissance elements, such as the *Annunciation*, with its classical portal surmounted by a shell.

The collection of silver and silver-gilt items contains some fine Manueline pieces donated by D. Manuel I and even by Ferdinand and Isabella of Spain, though the most important ensemble is from the Brotherhood of Nossa Senhora da Anunciada, which was integrated into the Misericórdia charity organisation in Setúbal in the 19th century. Dating from the end

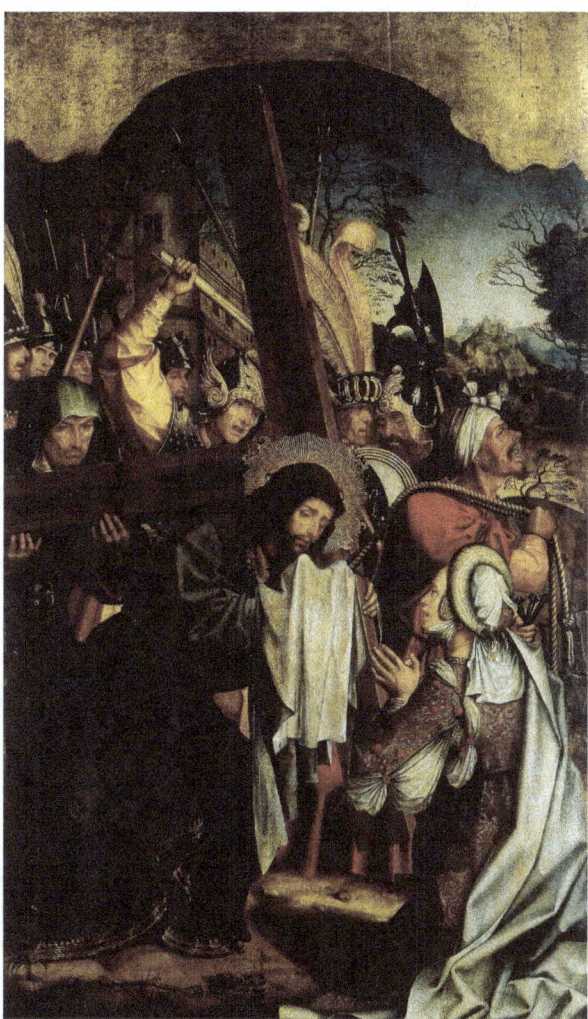

IPM/J.P.
Jorge Afonso, "Christ and St Veronica", from the retable of the Convent of Jesus, 16th century, Setúbal Municipal Museum.

ITINERARY XII   *The Military Order of Santiago*
Setúbal

of the reign of D. João II, it includes an elegant cross in rock crystal, mounted in silver-gilt, the gift of the king's chancellor, Nuno Gonçalves. An elegant silver-gilt chalice dating from the same period is decorated with foliate motifs, with an architectural-style knot and representations of the Virgin Mary, St Peter and St James on the base.

The remarkable reliquary of *Nossa Senhora da Anunciada* from a Lisbon workshop is, like many works of the period, an architectural fantasy structure, protecting an ivory image of the Virgin in a silver and glass case under a *baldachin*. In the knot on the stem is a relic of Christ's Crown of Thorns, set between pieces of glass.

Surprising in its rarity is a small silver bottle of holy oil that dates back to the first half of the 16th century and recalls some items of Chinese porcelain that were then being imported from the Far East.

XII.4.d São Julião (Setúbal Parish Church)

Praça do Bocage. Designated a National Monument.
Opening hours: daily 08.30-12.00 and 15.00-18.00, and on Sundays 08.30-12.00 and 17.30-18.30. (Tel: 265 523723).

The Church was altered and enlarged in 1515 by order of D. Manuel I, when there was a considerable increase in population and the monarch was keen to enhance the town with suitably majestic buildings. João Favacho, who almost certainly worked on the Mosteiro dos Jerónimos, carried out the work between 1516 and 1519.

Various earthquakes affected the city, mainly that of 1755, which destroyed almost all the Manueline work, leaving only two portals and the bell tower. The North Door is extraordinarily exuberant, combining naturalist elements with others based on silver and fabric designs. The axial door is simpler but also heavily naturalist, with twisted arches ending in canopies.

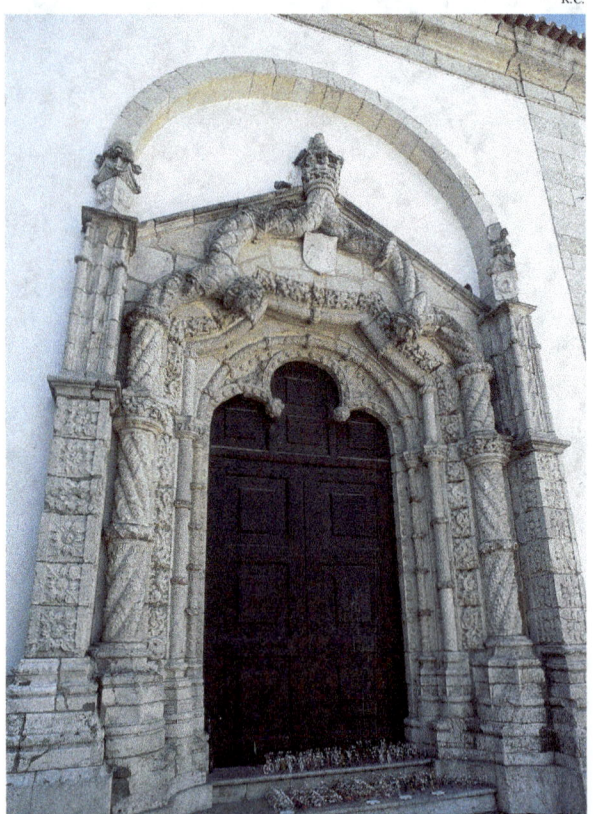

Setúbal Parish Church, portal.

R.C.

294

ITINERARY XII *The Military Order of Santiago*
Palmela

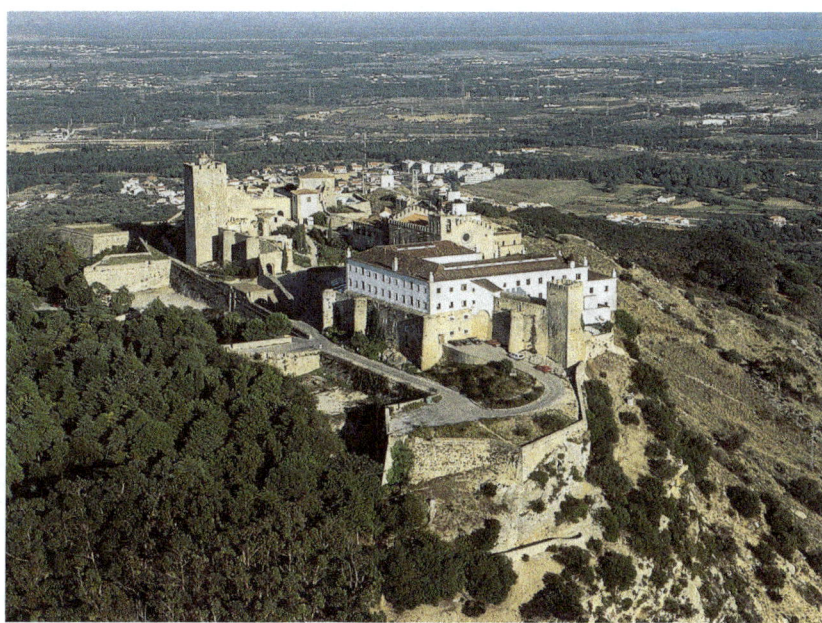

Aerial view of Palmela Castle.

Reserva Natural do Sado
The Sado Nature Reserve, to the south-west of Setúbal, covers some 23 hectares of what is, for the most part, canals, creeks and marshes. Among the many species to be seen here are otters and badgers and birds such as the white stork, the marsh harrier or migratory birds like the wood pigeon. Among the reserve's many attractions are its flora, lagoons, the river estuary and a large area of pine forest.

For further information, contact: Reserva Natural do Estuário do Sado, Praça da República, 2900 Setúbal. (Tel: 265 524032).

Take the A2 in the direction of Lisbon and exit at Palmela.

XII.5 **PALMELA**

The town and castle of Palmela were won back from the Moors by the troops of D. Afonso Henriques in 1148, although it was briefly re-occupied shortly afterwards. The first King of Portugal then granted it to the Order of Santiago da Espada, and it was granted a charter in 1185. It was the main castle in the region and, in the second half of the 15th century and the first half of the 16th century, it benefited from the patronage of the Master of Santiago, D. Jorge, the natural son of D. João II. He was responsible for many improvements, including the maintenance and enlargement of the castle and the completion of the Igreja de Santiago.

ITINERARY XII   *The Military Order of Santiago*
Palmela

Palmela Castle.

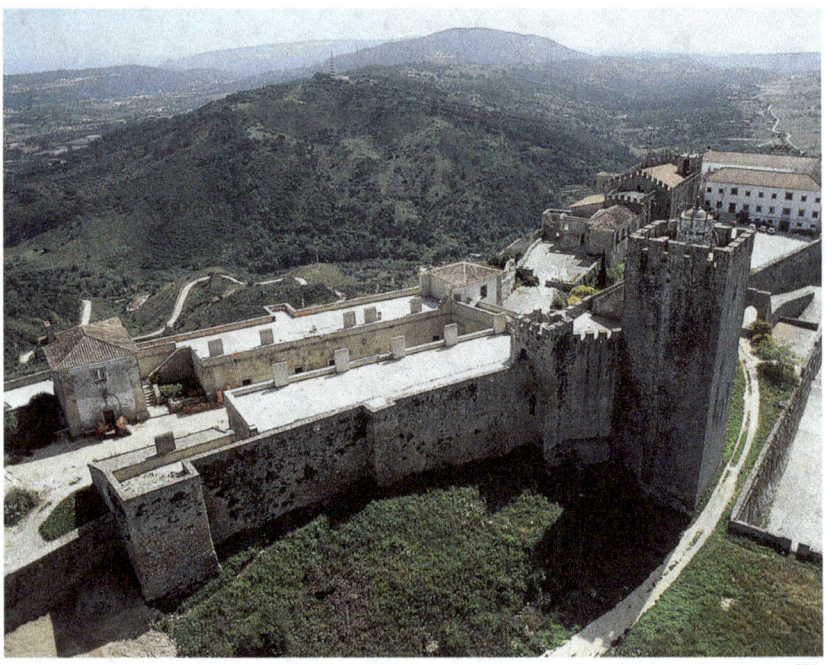

XII.5.a Castle

The route to the castle is signposted. Designated a National Monument. Try to make time to visit the Museu Municipal de Palmela in the former parade ground, which has five rooms containing archaeological finds from excavations carried out in the fortress. Information Tel: 21 2331580 / 21 2331669.

The Castle, adapted to the irregular topography and with high, strong walls reinforced by towers in the corners and at the weaker parts of the curtain walls, is typical of the architecture of the Middle Ages. The residences and monk's chapel are inside the upper part of the Castle. The 15th-century or early 16th-century adaptations can be seen in the keep with its long embrasures and wide battlements.

XII.5.b Church of Santiago

The Church is situated inside the castle enclosure. (Tel: 21 2331669 / 21 2331580). Designated a National Monument.
Opening hours: daily 10.00-12.30 and 14.00-18.00 (20.00 in summer), except on Mondays.

The Church and the Monastery, built on the initiative of the prince D. João, the son of D. João I, were started about 1443.

ITINERARY XII   *The Military Order of Santiago*
Alcochete

Work continued for some time and produced a plain Gothic building, very similar to that of the Mosteiro da Batalha. D. Jorge de Lencastre, Master of the Order of Santiago, who was buried in a Manueline-style wall niche built shortly before his death in 1551, ordered the last alterations that were carried out in 1508.

Take the A2 towards Setúbal and, at the crossroads with the A12, take this latter road in the direction of Lisbon to Alcochete.

XII.6 ALCOCHETE

From very early times, the position of the town on the Tagus estuary made it ideal for fishing and trade between the two banks. In the Moorish period, the lime-kilns there were already of some importance and the name of the town came from the Arab *al-Kuxat*. The area supplied Lisbon with lime and firewood for several centuries.

D. Manuel I was born in Alcochete, on May 31st 1469, at the Palácio de D. Beatriz, named after his mother, which was almost totally destroyed in the earthquake of 1755. Prince D. Fernando and his private court also lived here for quite some time.

XII.6.a **São João Baptista**
         (Alcochete Parish Church)

Situated in Largo de S. João. (Tel: 21 2340166). Designated a National Monument.

M.A.

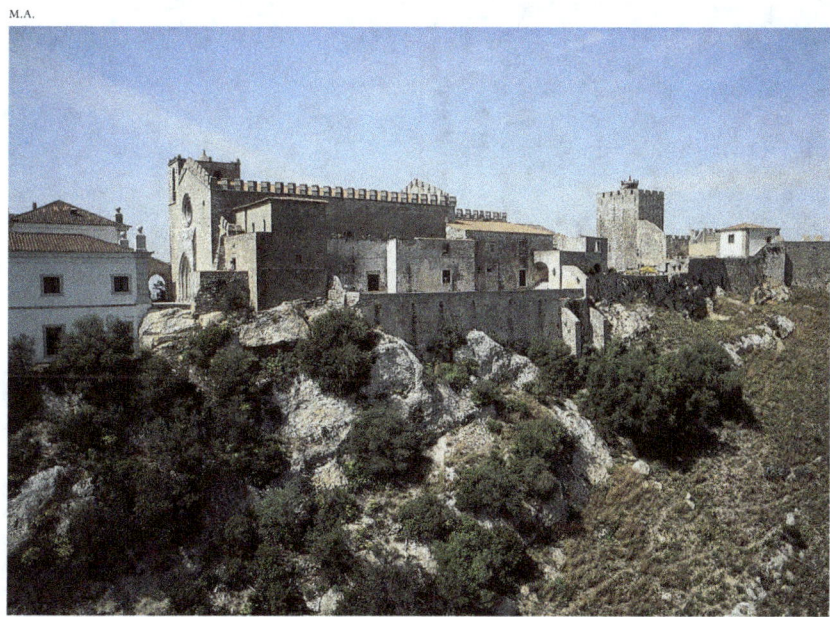

Church of Santiago, Palmela.

297

ITINERARY XII   The Military Order of Santiago
Alcochete

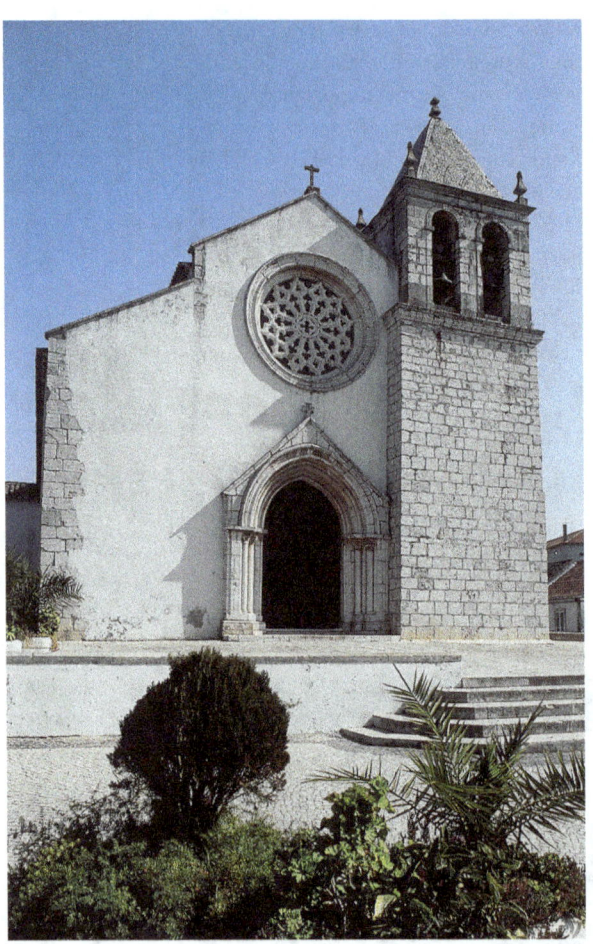

Church of São João Baptista, Alcochete Parish Church, main façade.

Opening hours: 08.00-12.30 and 15.00-20.00. Closed on Monday, Thursday and Sunday afternoons. Open on Saturdays: 08.00-12.30 and 17.00-20.00.

The Parish Church underwent considerable changes during the Manueline era, although it still retains some 15th-century features, such as the axial and lateral portals. The main vessel of the Church is composed of three aisles with four bays, with mono-cylindrical pillars supporting pointed arcades with octahedral capitals. There is only one modern chapel in the apse, but on the left-hand side there is another low chapel with Late Manueline ribbed vaulting.

VASCO DA GAMA

Pedro Dias

Vasco da Gama was born in Sines in *c.*1468. His father was Estêvão da Gama and he and most of his family were linked to Atlantic navigation. It is very likely that he sailed to North Africa or nearby islands while still quite young.

His prestige was such that at only 30 years of age he was given command of the fleet that was to make the first voyage between Europe and India. He left Lisbon on July 8th 1497, taking his brother Paulo, who was to die on the return journey and was buried at Terceira in the Azores, and Nicolau Coelho, certainly the best seaman of the time, as pilot.

On his arrival in India the following year, Vasco da Gama tried to make an alliance with the *Samorim* or King of Calicute, but the various intrigues of Muslim merchants who had huge interests at stake made this impossible. He stopped at the island of Angediva, a few dozen kilometres to the south of Goa, and began his return journey on October 5th 1498, disembarking in Lisbon in August 1499.

The voyage started regular contacts between the East and West, with the Portuguese discovering the sea-route to Japan in 1543.

Vasco da Gama was made Count of Vidigueira and, in 1504, he returned to India. He died as Viceroy in Cochin in 1524, and his descendants continued to be leading figures in the Far East for many generations.

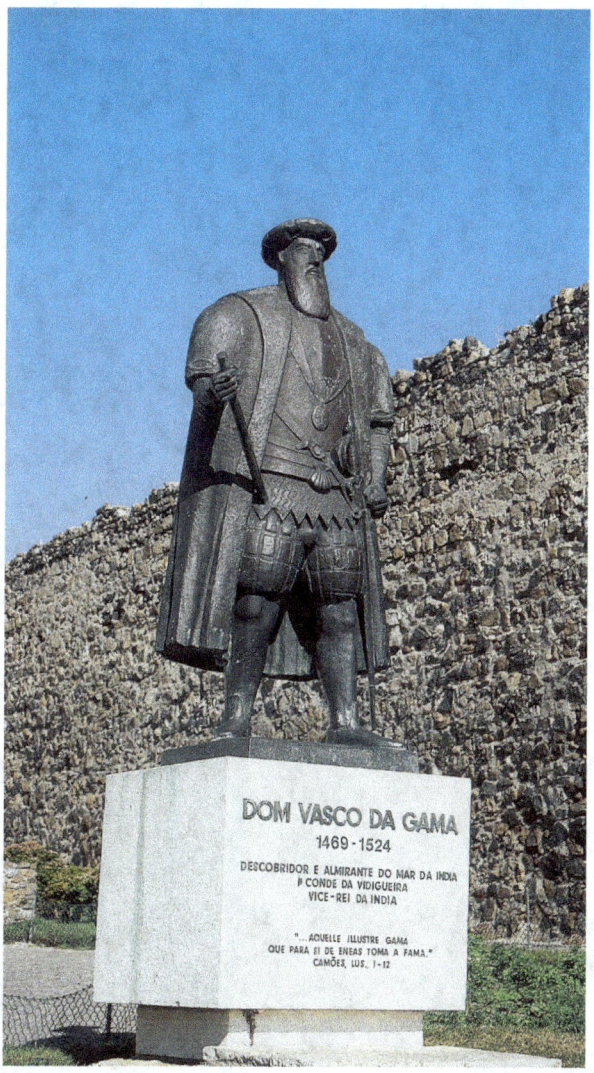

Statue of Vasco da Gama, next to Sines Castle.

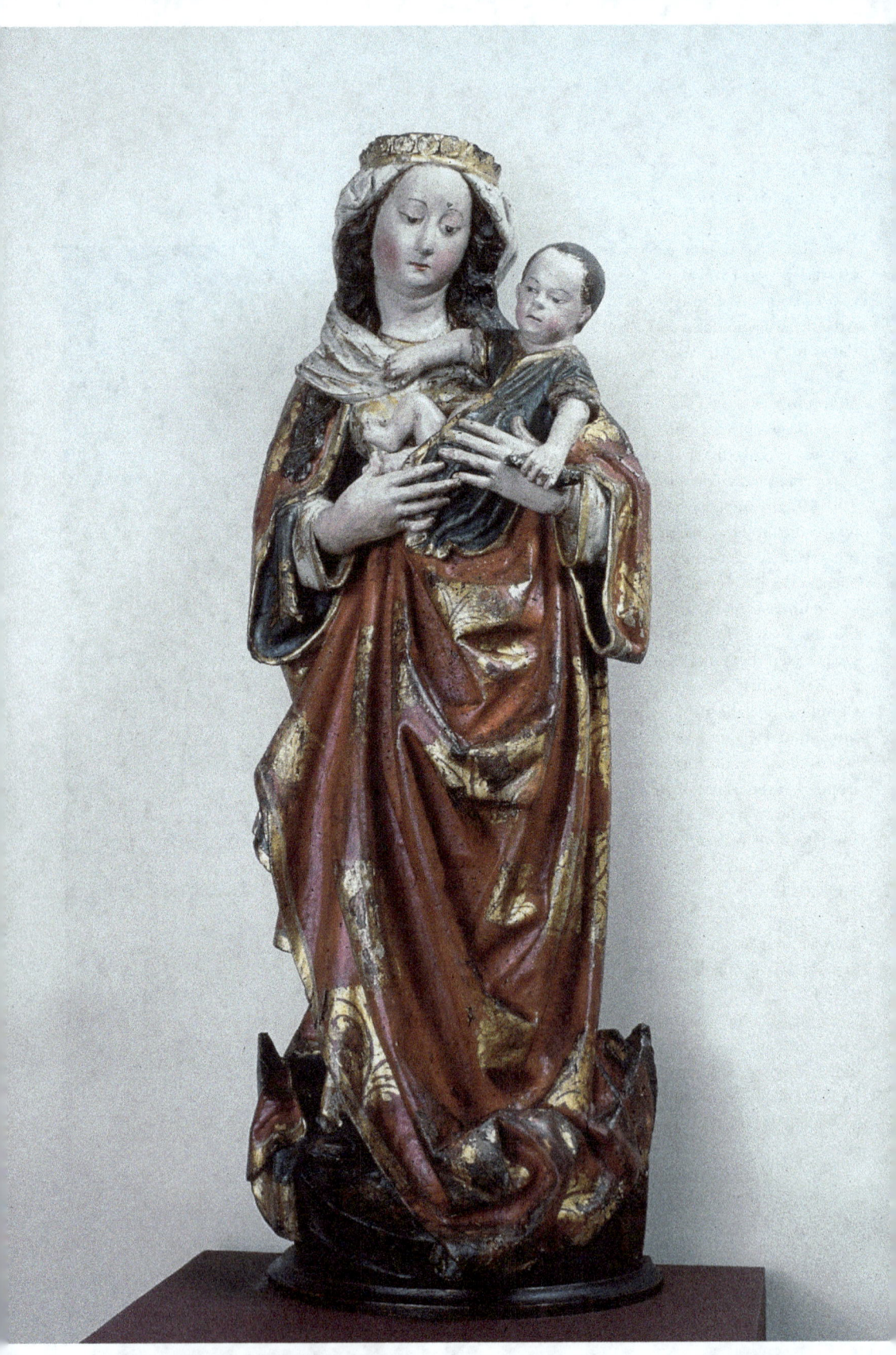

ITINERARY XIII

The Island of Madeira:
Between Portugal and Flanders

Pedro Dias, Dalila Rodrigues,
Nuno Vassallo e Silva, Fernando Grilo

First day

XIII.1 FUNCHAL
    XIII.1.a Historic centre
    XIII.1.b Cathedral
    XIII.1.c Alfândega Velha (Old Customs House)
    XIII.1.d Chapel of Corpo Santo
    XIII.1.e Museum of Sacred Art
    XIII.1.f Convent and Church of Santa Clara

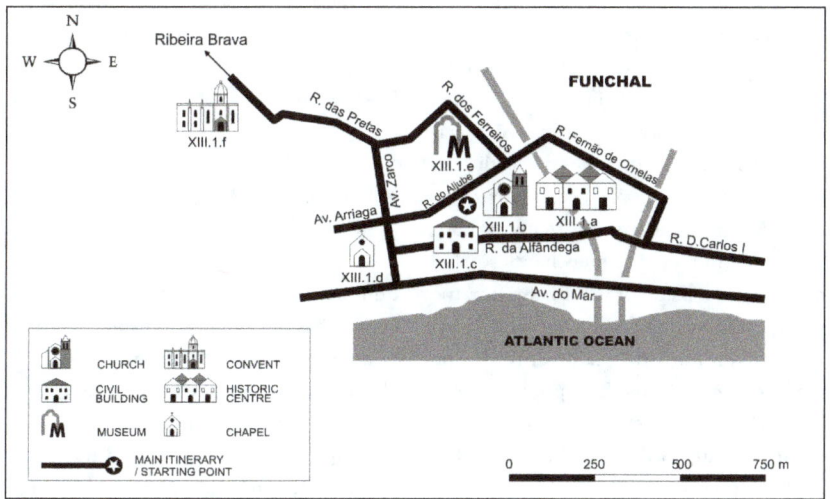

"The Virgin and Child", Flemish sculpture that once belonged to Machico Parish Church, c.1510, Museu de Arte Sacra do Funchal.

ITINERARY XIII   The Island of Madeira: Between Portugal and Flanders

Funchal

The Island of Madeira, covering an area of 741 sq. km., is the most important in the archipelago, a mere 1,000 km. from Lisbon and a little over 500 km. from Cape Djouchi on the African coast.

Porto Santo, 41 sq. km in size and 50 km. from Madeira, along with the Selvagens and Desertas and a handful of dispersed rocks, completes the archipelago. João Gonçalves Zarco officially discovered these uninhabited islands in 1419. Their relative proximity to Portugal encouraged settlers and they soon became natural extensions of the kingdom and a regular stopover point for vessels sailing south, as well as providing support for the Portuguese fortresses in Morocco.

The first inhabitants included members of the lower nobility and squires of Prince Henry the Navigator's Household, ennobled for their deeds in the Maghreb. The ordinary people came from various parts of the kingdom, and very many soon rose to a privileged status.

The introduction of sugar cane created an agriculture based on a single crop, broken only by the planting of wheat, which was in short supply at the end of the 15th century. The European preference for sugar from Madeira meant that many Italian, Flemish and German merchants settled on the island, some of whom also became producers, putting down roots and creating new families that later entered the ranks of the nobility. The population of European origin grew very quickly, numbering about 18,000 by the end of the 16th century.

Another important factor in the development of the archipelago was the creation of the Diocese of Funchal, by Pope Leo X, in 1514, at the insistence of D. Manuel I. All the Portuguese overseas territories depended on the new Episcopal see, both those already discovered and those that would later be so. It became an Archdiocese in 1533.

The Manueline epoch was heavily marked by Flemish influences, as many works of art placed on altars in churches, chapels and oratorios were imported from Flanders and surrounding regions. These consisted largely of painting and sculpture, much of which is still to be seen today in museums and churches on the Islands.

Besides excellent Manueline architecture, with its *Mudejar* ceilings of Hispano-Moorish tradition, paintings and sculptures were imported from Flanders or made by Flemish masters living in Madeira, proof of the close relationship between Portugal and the northern Europe at the time of the Discoveries.

XIII.1 FUNCHAL

Funchal, the Capital, and largest urban centre, has been important since the time of the early settlers. Its privileged setting, allowing for an easy approach by sea, together with its sheltered bay and protecting hills, meant that its future development was ensured. The first buildings

ITINERARY XIII   The Island of Madeira: Between Portugal and Flanders
Funchal

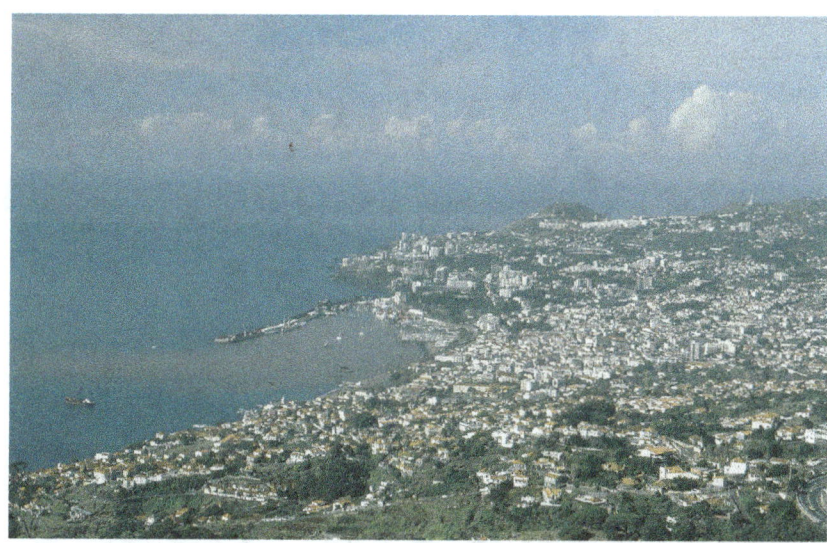

Panoramic view of Funchal.

erected here, undoubtedly not very far from the shore, consisted of simple huts, built to house the early settlers and extremely poor hut-like churches. After the churches had been built, the first house to be constructed in stone was that of Constança Rodrigues, the granddaughter of the discoverer of Madeira, João Gonçalves Zarco. A certain João Manuel followed this with a house built in white cedar that caused something of a stir as it was higher than the others and so was regarded as an affront not only to the neighbourhood but also to the Crown.
The oldest surviving edifice is the Torre do Capitão (the Captain's Tower, now in the Parish of Santo António, in Funchal), situated on the Alto de Santo Amaro, a modest square building with two embrasures and a doorway with a pointed arch.

The area that is to be visited in this itinerary covers the neighbourhoods around the cathedral and Santa Maria. It is divided by two streams crossed by a series of bridges, completely covered in some places by luxuriant bougainvillaea.

XIII.1.a Historic centre

It is recommended that you begin your visit at the Cathedral, continue to Alfândega Velha and then to the Capela do Corpo Santo, returning by Largo do Pelourinho and Rua Direita, all of which streets cover the centre that existed in Manueline times.
Information: Tourist Office (Tel: 291 211900).

The General Administrators of the Order of Christ, D. Fernando, D. Diogo and the

ITINERARY XIII   The Island of Madeira: Between Portugal and Flanders
Funchal

Fortaleza de São Lourenço, c.1535, Funchal historic centre.

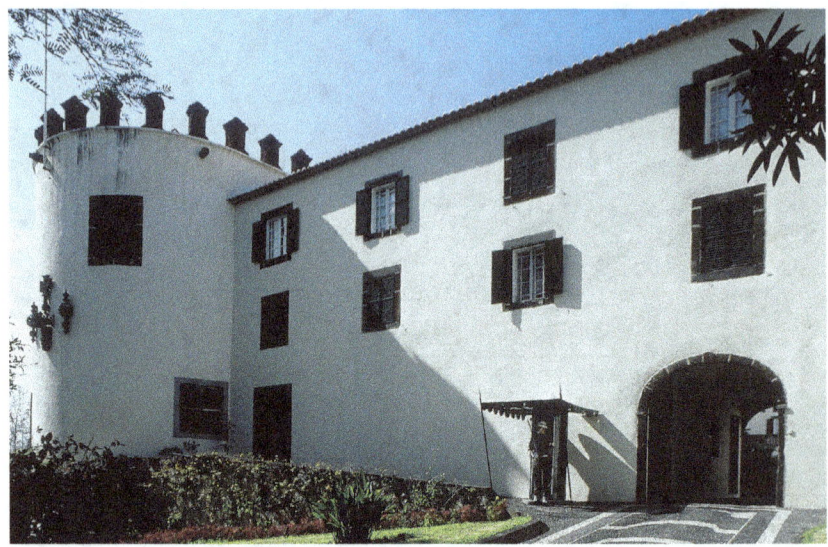

Duchess D. Beatriz, when D. Manuel was still a minor, and naturally D. Manuel himself, were responsible for the first public buildings. In June 1489, the Municipal Council also promoted some of the work, such as the Ribeira das Casas (a wooden bridge, since replaced), built in the same style as the bridge next to the jail and linking Rua Direita and Rua dos Ferreiros. In 1495, further suggestions for building roads and stone bridges were put forward by D. Manuel's governing magistrate, but the people of Funchal reacted adversely on hearing how much it would cost them in municipal taxes and quashed the plan.

People had settled according to the natural lie of the land, particularly along streams, but, at the time of D. Manuel I, an interest was taken in the layout of Funchal and the necessary fortifications. The first attempt at fortification took place in 1476, when the Princess D. Beatriz, D. Manuel's mother governed, and the second Donatory-Captain asked her for a construction to defend the port, but she too pleaded lack of funds.

As to the centre of the town, D. Manuel's idea was that all the important buildings should be constructed around a square, Campo do Duque. These included the Town Hall, Notary Offices, Audience Chamber, the Misericórdia charity organisation, and the Cathedral, although only the last named has survived to the present day. The main network of roads spread out from this square, much of which remains unchanged today. Another important space was represented by the Largo do Pelourinho, where the pillory stood.

The main streets continue to be Rua Direita and Rua dos Mercadores (now called Rua da Alfândega), the latter linking the fortress to Santa Maria do Calhau and being the street where all the most important merchants lived and worked with other traders from England and Flanders.

XIII.1.b **Cathedral**

Largo da Sé. (Tel: 291 228155). Designated a National Monument.
Opening hours: Monday-Saturday 09.00-11.00 and 16.00-17.30.

The Cathedral, begun about 1493 and still fortunately surviving almost intact, was the most important building erected during the Manueline era. D. Manuel I proposed it himself, and appointed João Gomes to oversee the work. However, due to constant misunderstandings and unforeseeable delays, work only began definitively in 1502, largely as a result of the king's personal commitment. The Cathedral was completed in 1517 under the Master Mason, Pêro Anes, assisted by Gil Eanes. The role of the latter artist has been the subject of much discussion, so that he has to be understood as acting as the Master of Works, in other words: number two in the hierarchy on the building site.

The fact that the Cathedral's construction took many years is verified by the king's financial contributions, as noted in documents from 1517 and 1521. Although a project that was developed much later, the wide church was simi-

R.C.

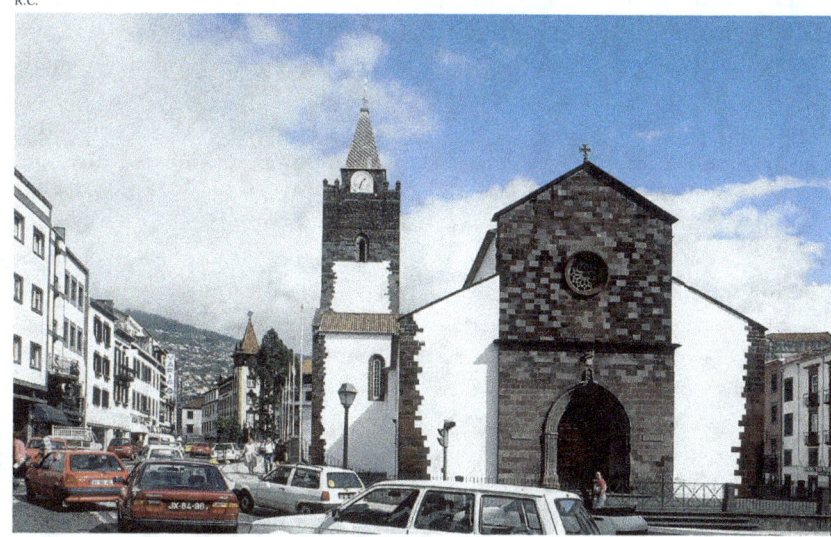

Funchal Cathedral.

ITINERARY XIII   *The Island of Madeira: Between Portugal and Flanders*

Funchal

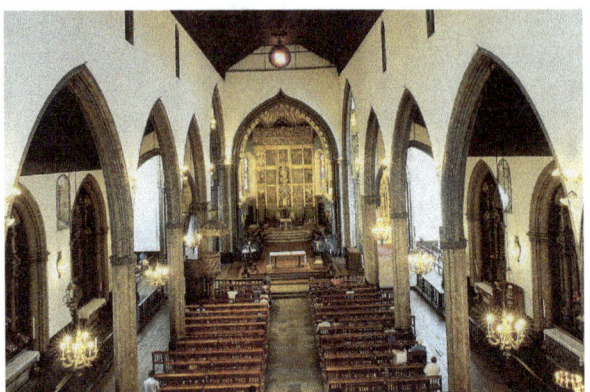

R.C.

Funchal Cathedral, general view of the interior.

lar to the model that had been used for the most important churches in mainland Portugal since the 13th century. It has three aisles with five bays, a projecting transept and apse, with three parallel rib-vaulted chapels. The carved bosses of the chancel vaulting, bear the royal coat of arms, an armillary sphere and the Cross of Christ. The *Mudejar* ceiling with its stylistic geometric designs, and roses in inlaid cedar wood, is particularly fine, although the pictorial decoration is in the Central European Renaissance style.

The volumetric interior structure is reflected in the exterior scheme: the central part of the façade is higher than the sides. At the east end there is an elegant tower with a *spire* that was used as a belltower and probably as a watchtower too. A flamboyant garland completes the roof, covering of the apse chapels. The main portal is in the typical Late Gothic style: a pointed arch set on seven parallel *colonnettes* that extend to the capitals of the same number of *archi-*

volts. Only the penultimate one is decorated.

The Manueline retable with its three tiers of panels, joined by delicate wood carving and some important figures, is the only one of its kind to have remained intact in its place of origin amongst the many that were made at that time in Portugal. Although various alterations were introduced over the years, including a Baroque statue in the central niche, it is only the poor state of conservation of the retable that impedes a full appreciation of its original sumptuousness. Little is known of the painter, the "Master of Lourinhã", who is said to have been from the Low Countries, but he and his team certainly demonstrate the stylistic processes of painters from this part of Europe. Be that as it might, Portuguese painters who were famous at that time, and particularly those working within the Court, were greatly influenced by imported Flemish painting, appreciating the mimetic expression of reality. The work can therefore be dated to around 1515, painted by an unknown artist, but directly linked to painters from the Lisbon circle.

The magnificent choir stalls in the chancel probably date from between 1508 and 1512, and are still located in their original position in a remarkably good state of conservation. Similarly the choir stalls must be considered the work of an unknown Flemish master, consisting of two rows of seats, the higher one having canopies and backs, whilst the second

ITINERARY XIII   The Island of Madeira: Between Portugal and Flanders
Funchal

row has just a carved frieze, already displaying Renaissance taste.

The retable here also displays remarkable woodwork, revealing the influence of Olivier of Ghent, although a Flemish master working in Madeira probably produced them.

The relief sculptures are of the highest quality, as can be seen in the beautifully carved figures of the apostles, in the niches that separate these figures, and in the decorative friezes. According to tradition, the quality of the carving was such that they were not originally gilded so as to highlight the sculpted lines. The gilding was added in 1755.

XIII.1.c Alfândega Velha (Old Customs House)

The present-day building, flanked by Rua da Alfândega, Largo Dr. António José de Almeida and Avenida do Mar, is the result of both Manueline and Pombaline influences and comparatively recently it has been adapted to house the Regional Legislative Assembly. (Tel: 291 223133). Designated a National Monument. Opening hours: Monday-Friday 09.00-12.30 and 14.00-17.30.

D. Manuel I ordered the construction of the Customs House, and Pêro Anes, who also worked on the cathedral, was responsible for erecting it in 1508. In this enterprise, he had the help of a certain Bartolomeu.

A 17th-century drawing shows the two-storey Manueline structure made up of two parallel wings, as can be seen by the line of the roof. The doors and windows were surrounded by stonework and the main floor had a panel that divided the window openings. The northern doorway had a lowered arch and foliate capitals. The Casa do Despacho (Dispatch Office), on the ground floor, is divided by parallel arcades of three depressed arches on cylindrical pillars with naturalist

R.C.

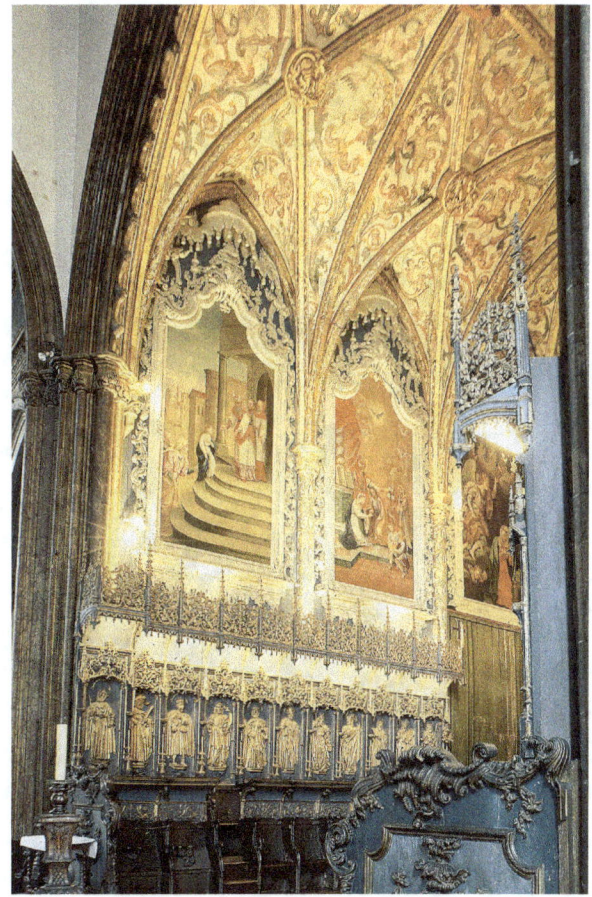

Funchal Cathedral, chancel.

307

ITINERARY XIII   The Island of Madeira: Between Portugal and Flanders
Funchal

capitals, with the same design as that of the corbels. The chamfered pillars and arches are solid and imposing, as is the *Mudejar* ceiling of the Casa dos Contos (Counting Office), in the style of those of the cathedral aisles and transept with tracery, roses and geometric designs. The main door and windows opened onto a terrace overlooking the sea. On the eastern side, the building was more compartmentalised, and there are still two small Manueline doors; on the upper floor the smaller rooms also has *Mudejar* ceilings.

XIII.1.d Chapel of Corpo Santo

Largo do Corpo Santo. Classified as a Building of Public Interest. For guided visits, contact DRAC (Tel: 291 211830).
Opening hours: Monday-Friday 10.00-12.30 and 14.00-17.30, except for public holidays.

The Chapel, founded by sailors and fishermen, stands at the end of the former settlement at Cape Calhau and dates back to the mid-15th century. Probably initially made of wood and thatch, the stone building was erected at the end of the 15th century, and it conserves from that time the essential parts, mainly the pointed arch of the portal without capitals.
An inscription on one of the stones shows that considerable alterations were carried out in 1594, whilst over the years the interior of the chapel has been successively decoratively enriched.

XIII.1.e Museum of Sacred Art

In the former Episcopal Palace, the Museum entrance is at No. 21 Rua do Bispo. (Tel: 291 228900). Designated a National Monument.
Admission charge. Opening hours: 10.00-12.30 and 14.30-18.00 Tuesday-Saturday,

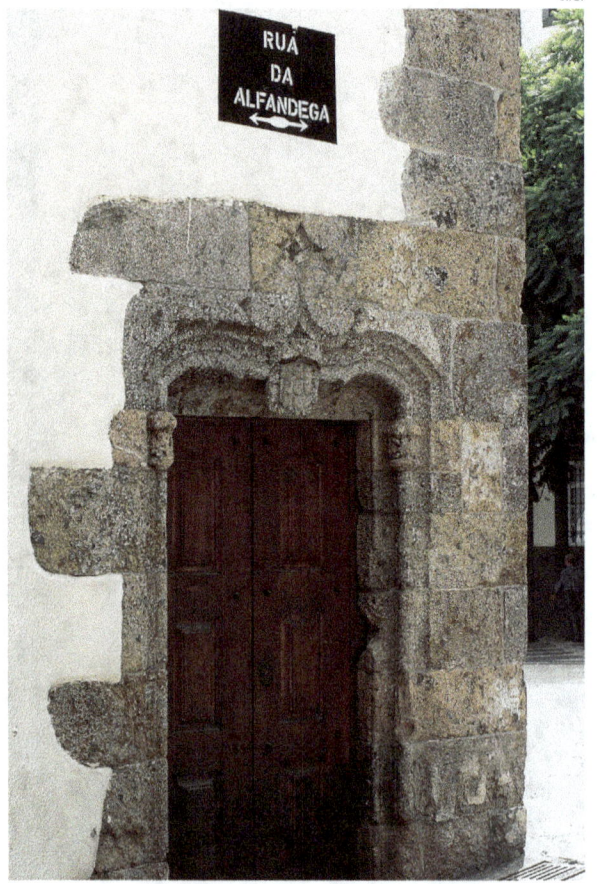

The Customs House, portal, Funchal.

ITINERARY XIII   The Island of Madeira: Between Portugal and Flanders
Funchal

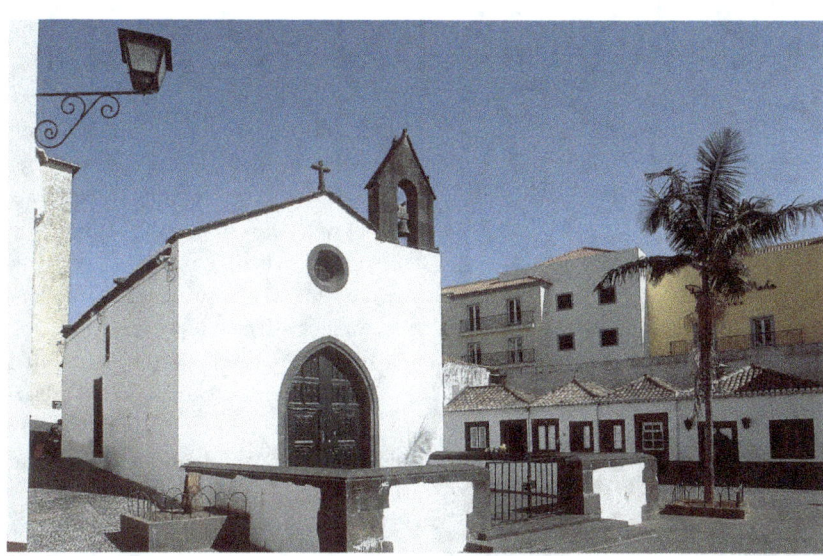

Chapel of Corpo Santo, Funchal.

R.C.

and 10.00-13.00 on Sunday. Closed on Monday and public holidays.

The Museum of Sacred Art contains some highly important pieces of Manueline gold- and silverwork, almost all from a posthumous donation made by D. Manuel I to Funchal Cathedral of 21 religious objects in silver. The donation was made in 1528, seven years after the death of D. Manuel I.
The collection includes a huge processional cross, the largest of its kind in Portugal and belonging to yet another donation from the king.
As is the case with the famous Monstrance of Belém, now housed in the National Museum of Ancient Art in Lisbon, the king's device, or the armillary sphere, is very clearly highlighted, so that the donor's memory is not forgotten.

Another of the king's offerings is a small but lovely *porta-pax*, undeniably one of the most remarkable pieces of its kind amongst the whole of Portuguese gold- and silverware. The *porta-pax* reproduces a Renaissance portico supported by Corinthian columns, with the arms of Portugal flanked by two winged figures under the entablature. The freestanding, albeit very badly damaged figure of the Eternal Father crowns the composition, finished on both sides by fantastic creatures. In the centre is a chased relief of the *Adoration of the Magi*, and five precious stones (hyacinths) complete the decoration.
Another unique although small Manueline image is that of Our Lady, originating from the Fraternity of Our Lady of the Rosary from Funchal Cathedral and executed by a workshop in Lisbon. It

ITINERARY XIII   The Island of Madeira: Between Portugal and Flanders
Funchal

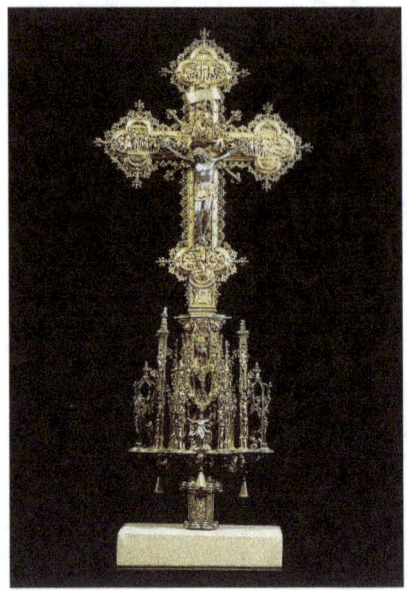

Processional Cross, c.1520, Museum of Sacred Art of Funchal.

IPM/J.P

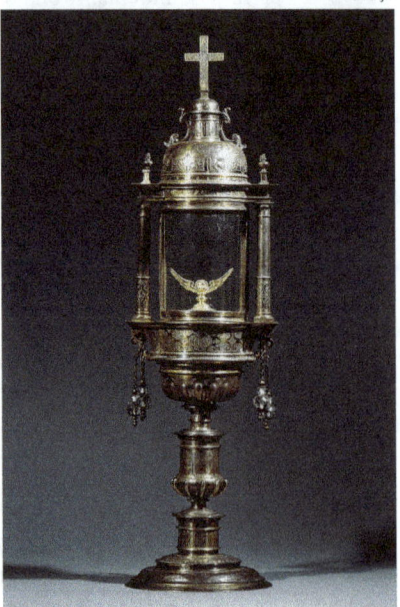

Chalice-Monstrance, c.1600, Museum of Sacred Art of Funchal.

IPM/J.P

represents a freestanding figure of the Virgin, her hands in an attitude of prayer and her face raised to Heaven. Both the face and hands have been painted. The modelling of her costume, the almost musical rhythm of the pleats in her mantle, resting on the base of the image shaped like a rose, all help to make this a unique piece amongst Manueline silver sculptures.

No less remarkable is the Manueline chalice also from Funchal Cathedral, which still retains its original highly decorative enamel on the stem and knot.

The collection of paintings, which come from various religious institutions on the Island, again underlines the importance of Flemish painting in Manueline times. With few exceptions, the collection is made up of large panels indicating that they were mostly specific commissions and not bought on the open market. In fact, the importation of painting was largely due to royal donations and private commissions by the local nobility; not forgetting that ample funds were available from sugar production and the flourishing trade with Flanders. Whilst the existing documentation provides some information about the private commissioning of works by the powerful land-owning nobility, namely through clauses contained in wills, the paintings themselves also testify to the direct involvement of this social sector.

The magnificent triptych of the *Descent from the Cross*, attributed to the Flemish

ITINERARY XIII   The Island of Madeira: Between Portugal and Flanders
Funchal

painter Gérard David and his collaborators, is an example of this patronage. The triptych depicts Portraits of the donors accompanied by St James the Greater, on the left-hand side, and St Bernardino on the right. In another triptych of St James the Less and St Philip, attributed to Pieter Coeck van Aeist, the third and fourth patrons of Funchal, Simão Gonçalves da Câmara and his son João, are depicted on the outer panels with their wives and families.

The importance of each picture in this fascinating museum means that it is not possible to pinpoint any single piece from it for particular observation, but the triptych of *St Peter, St Paul and St Andrew*, attributed to the painter Joos van Cleve, enables the visitor to see the expressive strategies and resources used by the so-called Flemish "primitives". In the foreground, the apostles in opulently coloured, flowing robes are outlined against an extraordinary landscape, with the pleats and folds effectively suggesting anatomical volume. The landscape is treated with impressive tactile realism, gradually changing colour from browns to blues, as the figurative elements lose definition and scale. With a remarkable ability to handle perspective, the painter suggests enormous spatial depth, which he uses in the central panel to represent St Peter on the Sea of Galilee.

The landscapes and the objects depicted in these paintings, used as scenarios or accessories to religious themes, later acquired an autonomous value in new types of paintings, specifically still-life and landscape painting. These apparently profane secondary objects and figures of mere decorative value had a symbolic significance that needs to be decoded. On the reverse of the side panels, and only visible when the triptych is closed are paintings of *The Virgin* and the *Angel of the Annunciation*.

The importance of Madeira during the Manueline period is also reflected in sculptures that ranges from miniature

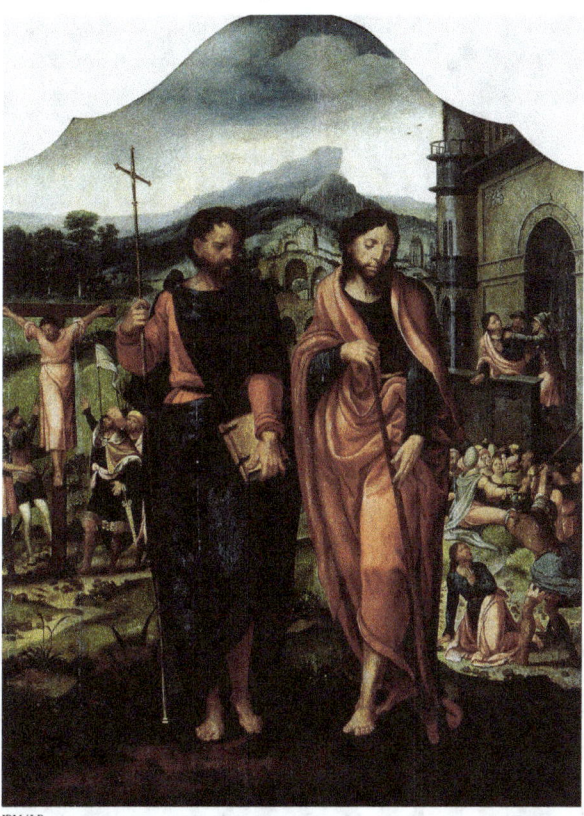

IPM/J.P

Attributed to Pieter Coeck van Aeist, "St James, St Philip and Patrons", central panel from the triptych of St James the Less and St. Philip, from the Church of Socorro, oil on oak c.1527-1531, Museum of Sacred Art, Funchal.

311

pieces made in specialised workshops in Malines, to commissions from workshops in the Antwerp area, and which include complete retables, such as the *Reis Magos* (Three Kings) from a chapel of the Estreito da Calheta. The Museum has a number of high quality paintings most notably those that represent the *Virgin and Child* from places such as the Parish Churches of Ponta do Sol, Machico or Ribeira Brava. There are also some exemplary expressive examples of *The Deposition of Christ* in the Museum. Isolated images, such as that of *St Sebastian*, also arrived on the island. Although this latter figure is now housed in the Museum, it belonged to the chapel of the same name. There is also another *Virgin and Child*, originating from the Capela of Nossa Senhora da Ajuda.

XIII.1.f Convent and Church of Santa Clara

The entrance to the Convent is at No. 15 Calçada de Santa Clara. The Convent buildings also face onto Calçada do Pico and Rua das Cruzes. (Tel: 291 742602). Designated a National Monument.
Opening hours: daily 10.00-12.00 and 15.00-17.00.

Construction of the 15th-century Convent of Santa Clara in Funchal, founded by João Gonçalves da Câmara, was started in 1492, and it was only five years later that the first nuns arrived from Setúbal to take up residence. The complex was built round an earlier, smaller chapel, with a Gothic portal that is still used as an entrance today.
The exceptional but simple Gothic cloister, with pointed arches remains and, inside, the significantly modified church contains the Flamboyant Gothic tomb of Martim Mendes de Vasconcelos, the son-in-law of João Goncalves Zarco.
A series of *azulejos* almost completely covers the floors of the upper and lower choirs, a total of almost 4,000 *cuenca* tiles covering some 90 sq. m., with eight different geometrical patterns and two with phytomorphic elements. The body of the tiles is covered with lead glaze to produce different shades of green. A panel

Attributed to Joos van Cleve, "The Annunciation", panel from the triptych of Bom Jesus, from the Church of Recolhimento do Bom Jesus da Ribeira, oil on oak, c.1520, Museum of Sacred Art, Funchal.

IPM/J.P

like a square carpet, or medallion made up of 100 tiles in the same colours, was placed in the centre of the upper choir. *Mudejar* taste was also a feature of the tracery decoration of the ceiling, which is clearly suggested by some of the oldest vestiges.

The lower choir was considerably remodelled in later periods, mainly in the mid-18th century, but the *Mudejar* flooring was maintained and has recently been uncovered and restored. This unique ensemble is an expression of refined taste, economic capacity and knowledge of how to adapt the best materials to everyday use.

Leave Funchal in the direction of Ribeira Brava, following the R101 towards Câmara de Lobos / Estreito de Câmara de Lobos / Campanário to Ribeira Brava (21.3 km.)

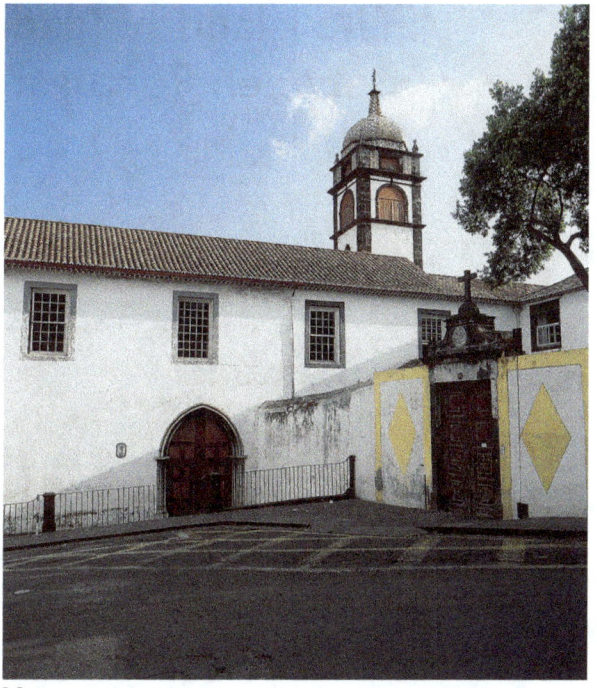

Convent of Santa Clara, Funchal.

ITINERARY XIII

The Island of Madeira: Between Portugal and Flanders

Pedro Dias, Dalila Rodrigues,
Nuno Vassallo e Silva, Fernando Grilo

Second day

XIII.2 RIBEIRA BRAVA
    XIII.2.a São Bento
        (Ribeira Brava Parish Church)

XIII.3 PONTA DO SOL
    XIII.3.a Nossa Senhora da Luz
        (Ponta do Sol Parish Church)

XIII.4 CALHETA
    XIII.4.a Espírito Santo
        (Calheta Parish Church)

XIII.5 SANTA CRUZ
    XIII.5.a São Salvador
        (Santa Cruz Parish Church)

XIII.6 MACHICO
    XIII.6.a Nossa Senhora da Conceição
        (Machico Parish Church)

Porto Santo

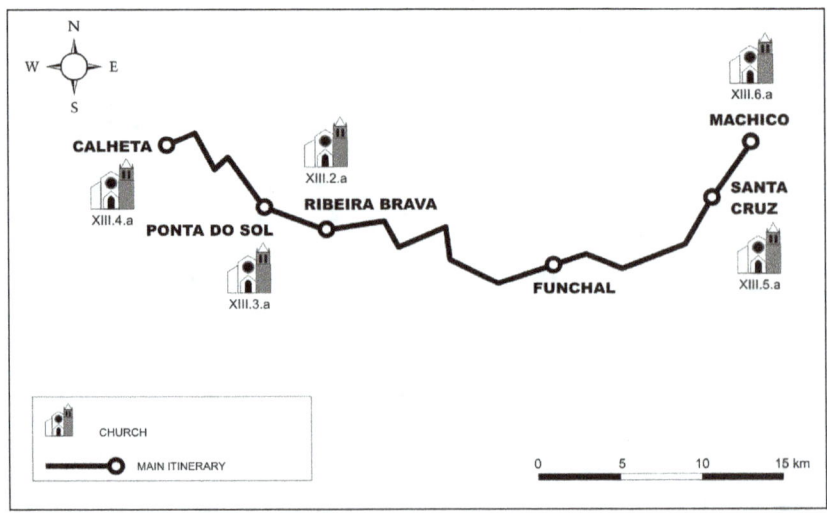

The South Coast of Madeira

The development of the Island of Madeira, from the arrival of the first settlers, took place largely in the south of the island, where the coast facilitated disembarkation and communication, due to bays, cliffs, winds and tides. More gentle valleys encouraged planting of different species for the inhabitants' use, and sugar cane was also planted on these slopes and sugar mills were built on the respective terraced *levadas* (irrigation channels).

It is hardly surprising that these areas produced some of the most important pieces of art and architecture of the Manueline era, and from Caniçal to the Estreito da Calheta there are many villages that deserve a visit. We have chosen only those that seemed most significant for this particular guide, which does not imply any disinterest in the beautiful surrounding landscape or other urban settings, with their memories of different times and other economic cycles.

XIII.2 RIBEIRA BRAVA

XIII.2.a São Bento (Ribeira Brava Parish Church)

The Church is situated in the centre of the town with entrances in Largo da Matriz and Rua do Visconde da Ribeira Brava. (Tel: 291

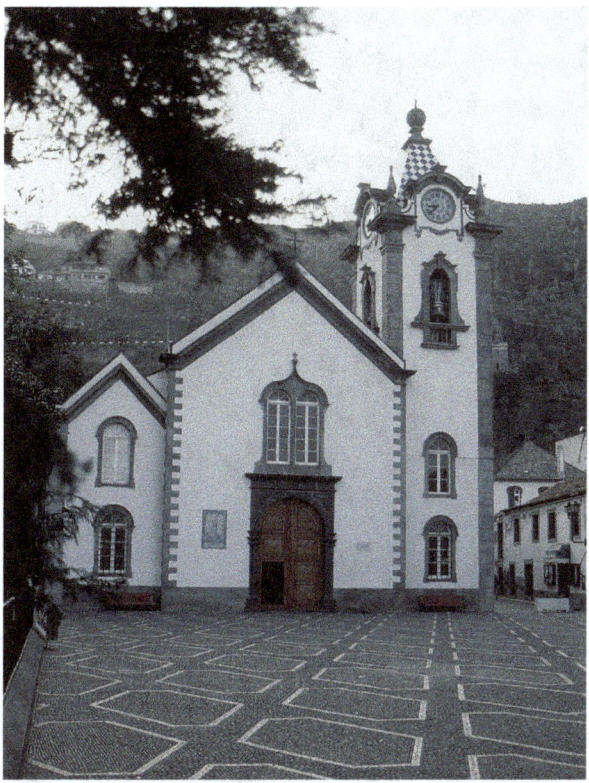

Ribeira Brava Parish Church.

952172). Classified as a Building of Public Interest.
Opening hours: 07.00-12.00 and 15.00-18.00 Monday-Saturday.

The Parish Church of Ribeira Brava was, originally, a small chapel dedicated to São Bento. It was founded at the time of the Duke of Beja, D. Fernando's government, the brother of D. Afonso V, and the father of D. Manuel I, although the oldest parts date back to the Manueline era when the church was completely modified. Flood-

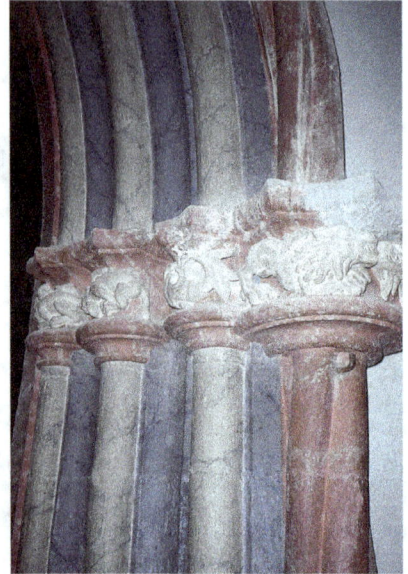

Ribeira Brava Parish Church, detail of interior.

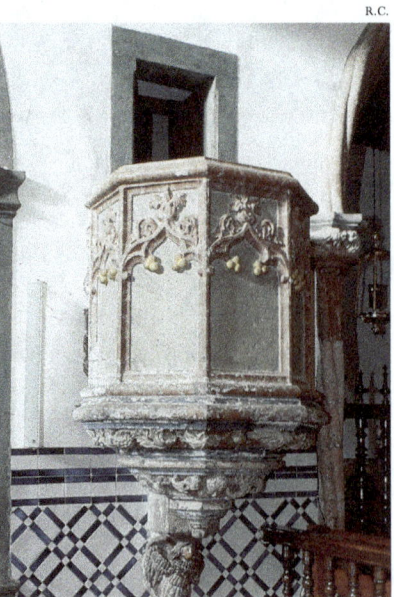

Ribeira Brava Parish Church, pulpit.

ing, that destroyed part of the church precipitated new work resulting in a Neo-Gothic nave and aisles and a more recent façade.

The entrance arch to the Chapel of the Holy Sacrament dates from the Manueline period and the naturalist elements on the capitals of the *archivolts* were rare in the early years of the 16th century. The structure is Flamboyant Gothic on the lines of Batalha Monastery, emphasising the newly acquired enthusiasm for the exotic that marked Madeiran architecture at the beginning of the 16th century.

The pulpit, with an exceptional corbel of an angel with a *phylactery,* and the baptismal font, were the work of the same master mason; an able builder with a talent for decorative sculpture.

On leaving Ribeira Brava retake the R101 to Ponta do Sol (3.3 km.).

XIII.3 PONTA DO SOL

XIII.3.a Nossa Senhora da Luz (Ponta do Sol Parish Church)

The Church is situated in the centre of the town, separated from the surrounding houses. Classified as a Building of Public Interest.

The Parish Church in Ponta do Sol has been documented since 1486, when Rodrigo Anes had the church built. It

ITINERARY XIII The Island of Madeira: Between Portugal and Flanders
Calheta

was dedicated to St Mary and had a tomb in the chancel where he wished to be buried, although since then a lot of work has been carried out on the building, beginning in the early 16th century.

Built on a simple plan with only one rectangular nave and apse, there are two Late Gothic side chapels by the crossing, acting as a false transept. The one on the left has ribbed vaulting, but the chapel on the right has only an entrance arch. The same taste and style are obvious in the delicate lines of the arch of the present Chapel of the Holy Sacrament, with delicate wood carving and a fine representation of phytomorphic elements. The late 16th-century *Mudejar*-tracery ceiling of the chancel is of particular interest.

Take the R101 for Calheta, in the direction of Madalena do Mar to Calheta (7 km.).

XIII.4 CALHETA

XIII.4.a Espírito Santo (Calheta Parish Church)

The Church is situated on the Estrada da Calheta. The courtyard is walled; enter by the wrought-iron gates. Classified as a Building of Public Interest.

The Parish Church has retained its Manueline structure, although it was heavily restored in 1604 and 1609, which raises problems as to the dating of the ceilings. It seems that the Royal Master of Works, Jerónimo Jorge, took down and adapted the *Mudejar* ceiling and eventually replaced missing elements, or completed new areas.

The structure of the ceiling is complete, with the central octagonal panel lengthened by a golden central *almocarabez*

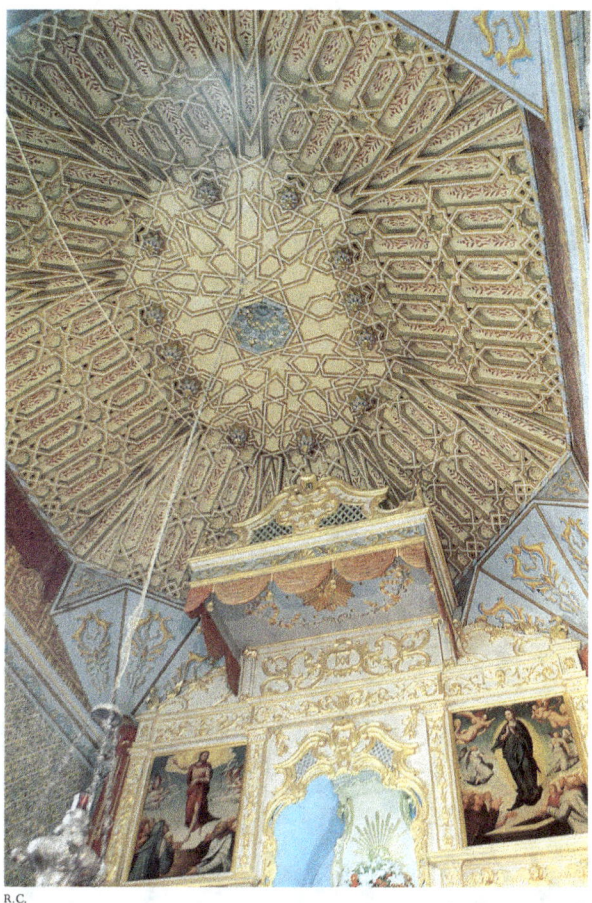

R.C.

Ponta do Sol Parish Church, Mudejar ceiling.

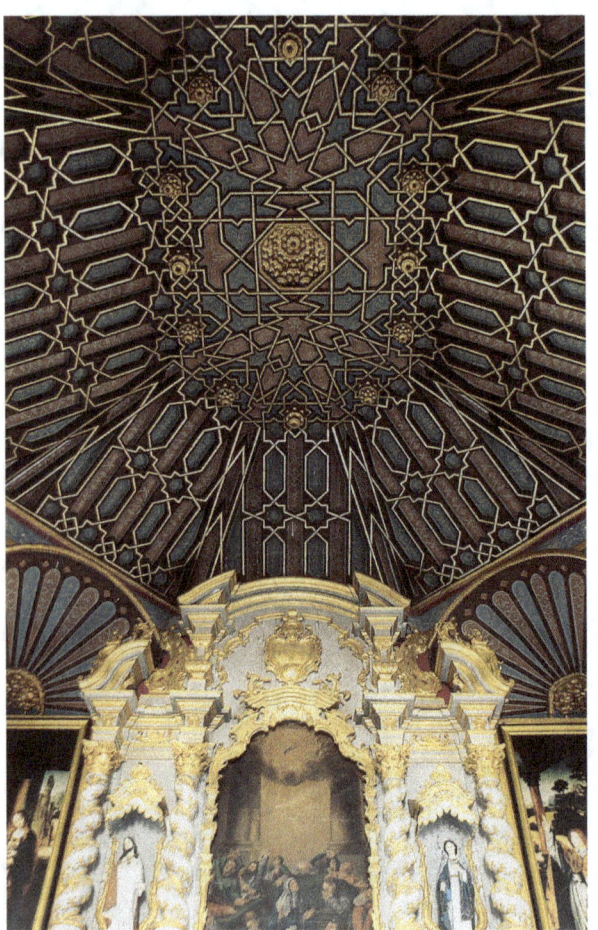

Calheta Parish Church, Mudejar ceiling.

For Santa Cruz, follow the R204 to São Gonçalo / Caniço / Santa Cruz.

XIII.5 SANTA CRUZ

XIII.5.a São Salvador (Santa Cruz Parish Church)

The Church is situated in the centre of town, flanked by a garden with trees. Classified as a Building of Public Interest.
Opening hours: daily 08.00-19.00.

Documents relating to the Parish Church of Santa Cruz indicate that it dates back to 1479, when Gil Eanes built the Chapel of Jesus in the early building that was to be substituted by the "New Church", so-called in contrast to the previous "Old Church". However, there is also a lot of information about the resultant building that has survived to the present day and was dedicated to São Salvador.

On January 25th 1502, D. Manuel I ordered the local inhabitants to complete the main vessel of the church and told the *almoxarife*, or administrator, to begin work on the chancel, for which the King was responsible as patron, although it was then donated to João de Freitas for his tomb. In 1508, the building work was being directed by the Master Builder, Fernão Mouseiro, whose first assistant was a certain Diogo. Work

(bow-shaped) and eight oblique trapeziums that support the sides and the inevitable vaulting in the corners, here in the shape of inverted shells. The design, based on interlinked eight-pointed stars and lozenges, is good both in the centre and round the edge. The small reticulated *corbelling* and *architraves* in the nave are also in the *Mudejar* style.

ITINERARY XIII   The Island of Madeira: Between Portugal and Flanders
Santa Cruz

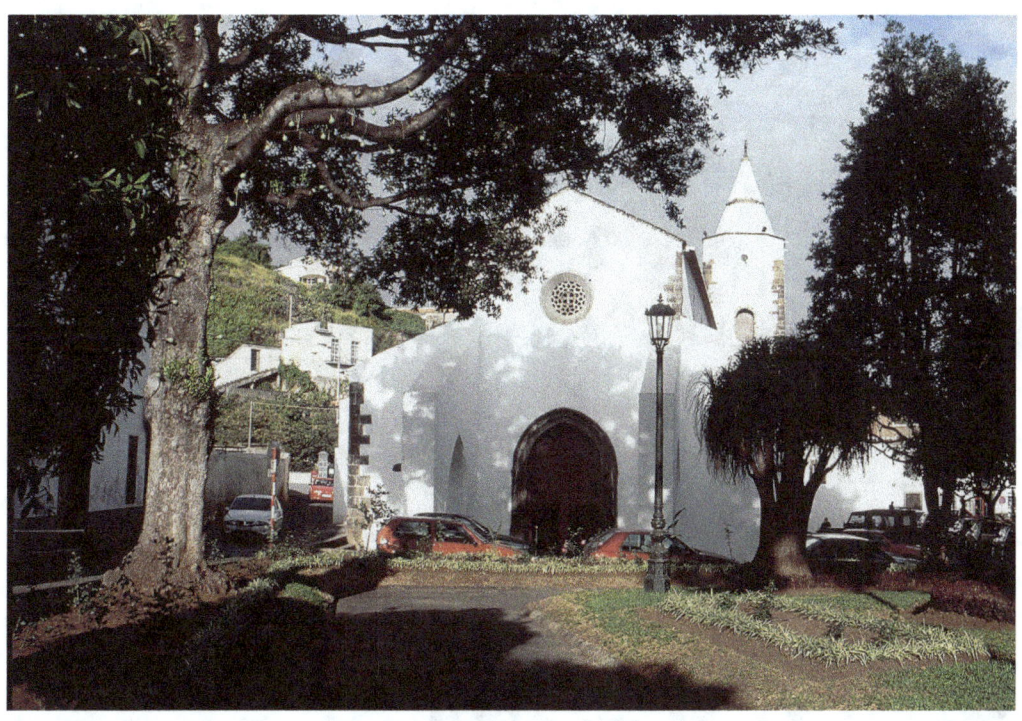

lasted for several years, at least until 1511.

The façade, showing the different heights of the nave, has two large buttresses built after the Manueline period, and a Gothic portal with columns of various diameters alternating with foliate capitals surmounted by a bull's-eye window. The Manueline bell- and watchtower with its belfries and pyramidal *spire* rises at the apse end; a good example of the typical Manueline towers that have since disappeared from other parish churches on the island.

The main vessel is divided into three separate aisles by simple, unornamented arcades. The apse is covered by ribbed vaulting, that forms an octagonal shape in the centre with decorated bosses displaying the Royal arms, the shield of Portugal, and the Cross of Christ. The double door of the sacristy, divided into two by a central pillar, is of an unusual design and ornamental richness, with elegant, lowered polylobed arches and half spheres decorating the *archivolt* and walls. The Late Gothic side chapel of São Tiago (St James), built by João de Morais before 1522 is also of interest, with armorial bearings on the keystone of

Church of São Salvador, Santa Cruz Parish Church.

ITINERARY XIII   The Island of Madeira: Between Portugal and Flanders
Machico

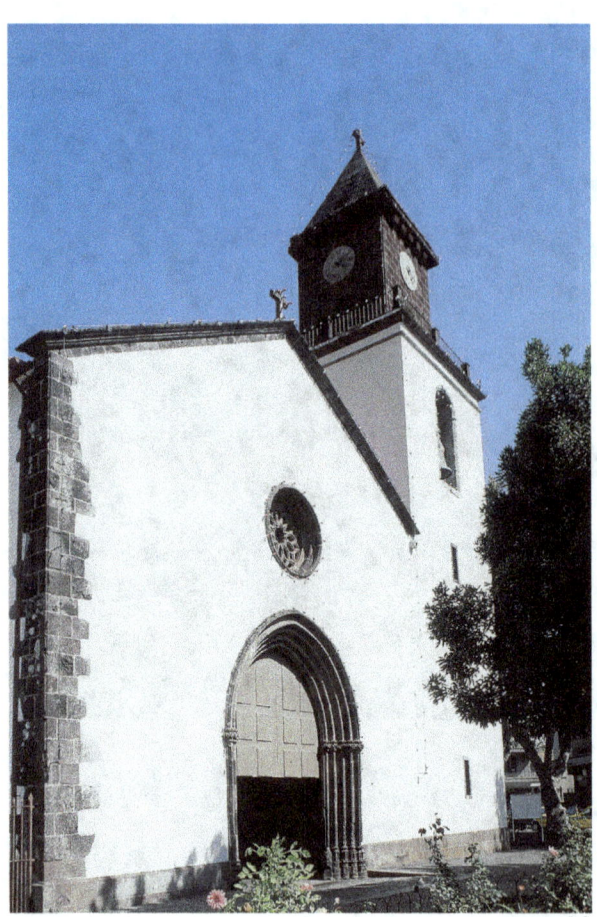

Machico Parish Church.

If heading for Machico, you should return to the R101 and head in the direction of Santa Cruz / Água de Pena / Machico.

XIII.6 MACHICO

XIII.6.a Nossa Senhora da Conceição (Machico Parish Church)

The Church is set among trees in the centre of the town. (Tel: 291 965139). Classified as a Building of Public Interest.
Opening hours: daily 09.00-18.00.

The Parish Church has retained its Manueline structure, despite a great deal of restoration. The first Master of Works was Pedro Álvares, to whom various payments were made in 1511. Documents also exist asking for estimates for work to be done on the chancel in 1521.
Much of the building material, mainly cedar, was ordered from Flanders in the middle of 1526, and the work was completed in 1529. The work in the chancel was ongoing, for in 1535 it was open to the sky and had to be demolished and started again. The work was finally declared finished by Grão Vasco on April 28th 1537, although the exterior ornamentation and the roof crenellations still remained to be done, completed two years later.

the semicircular entrance arch and naturalist capitals.
The funerary niche belonging to Micer Batista, a knight and merchant from Genoa who lived in the town, is in the same style and is dated 1516. Also note the open niche next to the baptismal font, designed to serve as a cupboard, which is a good example of the Manueline style.

The structure of the Church is essentially Manueline. The portal on the frontage has a Gothic arch and five elegant Doric columns with finely decorated naturalist capitals made in stone indigenous to the island. Above is a small bull's-eye window dating from the same period. Another portal with imported white marble columns faces the square.

The interior is essentially Manueline, although various additions have been made over the years. The chancel arch is Late Gothic, as are the three side chapels; two forming a false transept and the other standing against the left wall. The first two contain ribbed vaulting with five bosses, typical of the style used in Batalha, while the third is plainer with simple crossed ribs.

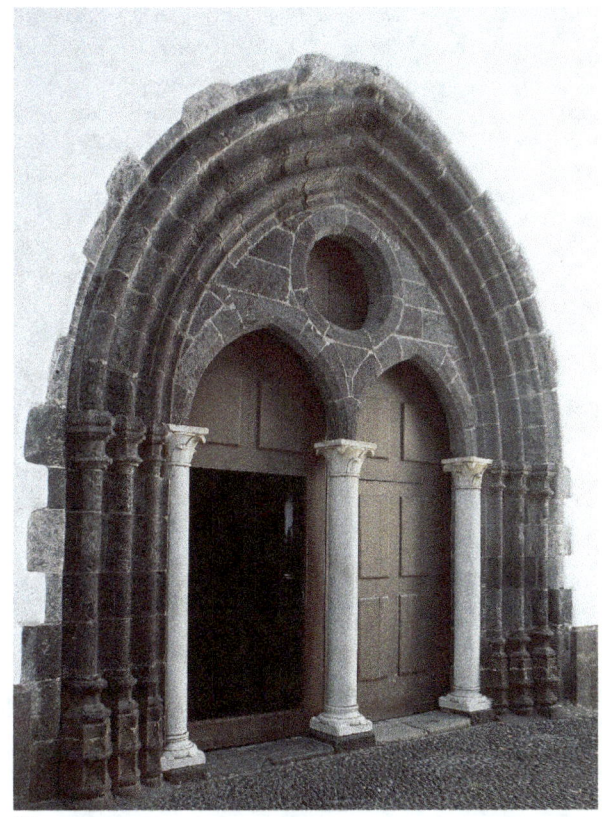

Machico Parish Church, side portal.

PORTO SANTO

"The island of Porto Santo is small, but cool, with good air and healthy, although it does not have good water, for it is dry and has few trees or bushes, the main ones (not counting dragon trees) being junipers and heather. It is on the route, when going from Lisbon to Madeira, from which it is twenty leagues from port to port, that is from the port of the Town to the port of Funchal, and from land to land it is twelve leagues. The part to the north is thirty-three degrees high. It is small and almost round, three leagues long and one and a half wide, or a little more.

In the port of Cagarras, so called because there are many grebes on the rock, which is on the eastern side, on the Northeast of the island, a long salt stream flows to the sea.

From the port of Frades, a little more than half a league away, going west by the same part of the South, is a small round island, half a league from the shore, both to the North and South of it. With high rocks all round, it has a large field on top, measuring about 150 hectares of land, where there are many dragon trees, and that is why it is called Dragoeiros island; it also has wild olive trees, and there are many goats, grebes and rabbits of many colours.

Half a league to the west of Dragoeiros island, on the same southern side, there is a large round rock like a small island, which (seems) from here to be someone lying down asleep, and which used to be called the Penedo do Sono, Rock of Sleep.

From the Rock of Sleep to the island of Boqueirão, it is a little more than a league and a half, which is at the last western point of the island, all the sand is white without a single stone and the bay is not very curved, nor does it have large headlands to the sea, so boats can sail out to sea in any weather from the port that is in the middle of the bay and beach, and that is why the port is called Vila de Porto Santo.

Finally, the island of Porto Santo is very healthy, with good fresh air, although it is small, three and a half leagues in length and more or less one and a half wide (as I have said); and it has little water, as it is dry and has few trees, and the main tree is the juniper tree (except for the dragon trees) and heather. And in many parts of the island, Nature has produced many dragon trees, the trunk of which makes wood, and many are so thick that only one trunk will make a boat, such as there are today, that are big enough for six or seven men to go fishing in them, and troughs that hold five quarters of corn. Much use is made of the wood, for which a tenth is paid to the king, and they make use of dragon's blood, highly prized in pharmacy; these dragon trees have a round fruit, that when it is ripe, is very yellow, and very sweet, and when there were many dragon trees they fattened the pigs with this fruit (which are like hazelnuts, and are thus called little apples), there are already few and they will be missed, for use in the pigs' troughs, for they are very light, as they are dry, and also in slices."

"A description of the island of Porto Santo and its abundance and inhabitants", in Gaspar Frutuoso, *Saudades da Terra*, 1560.

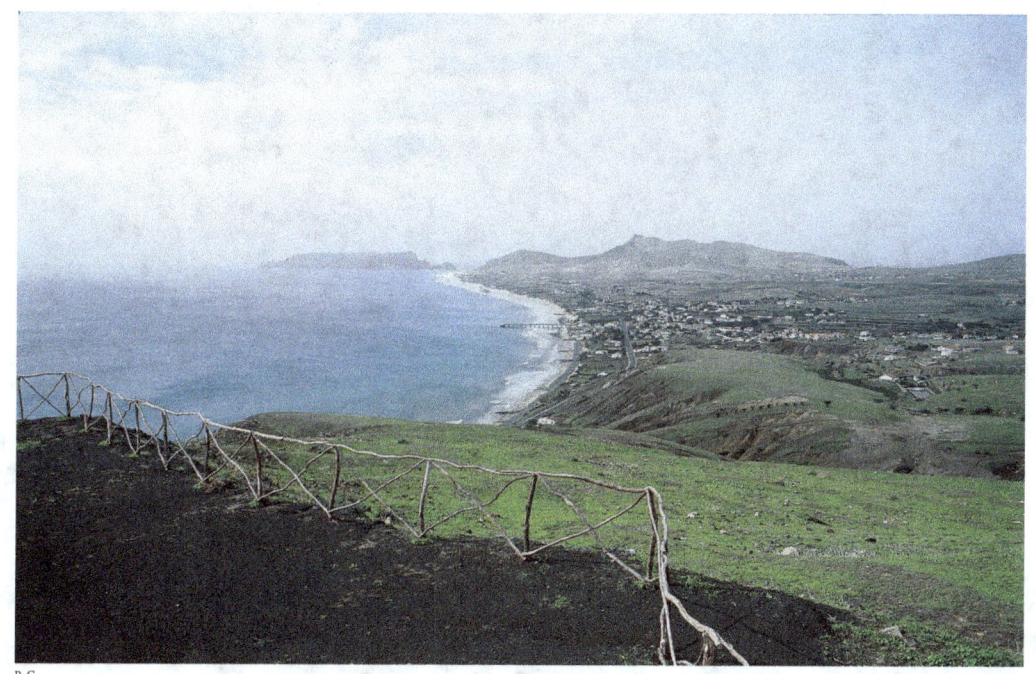

General view of Porto Santo.

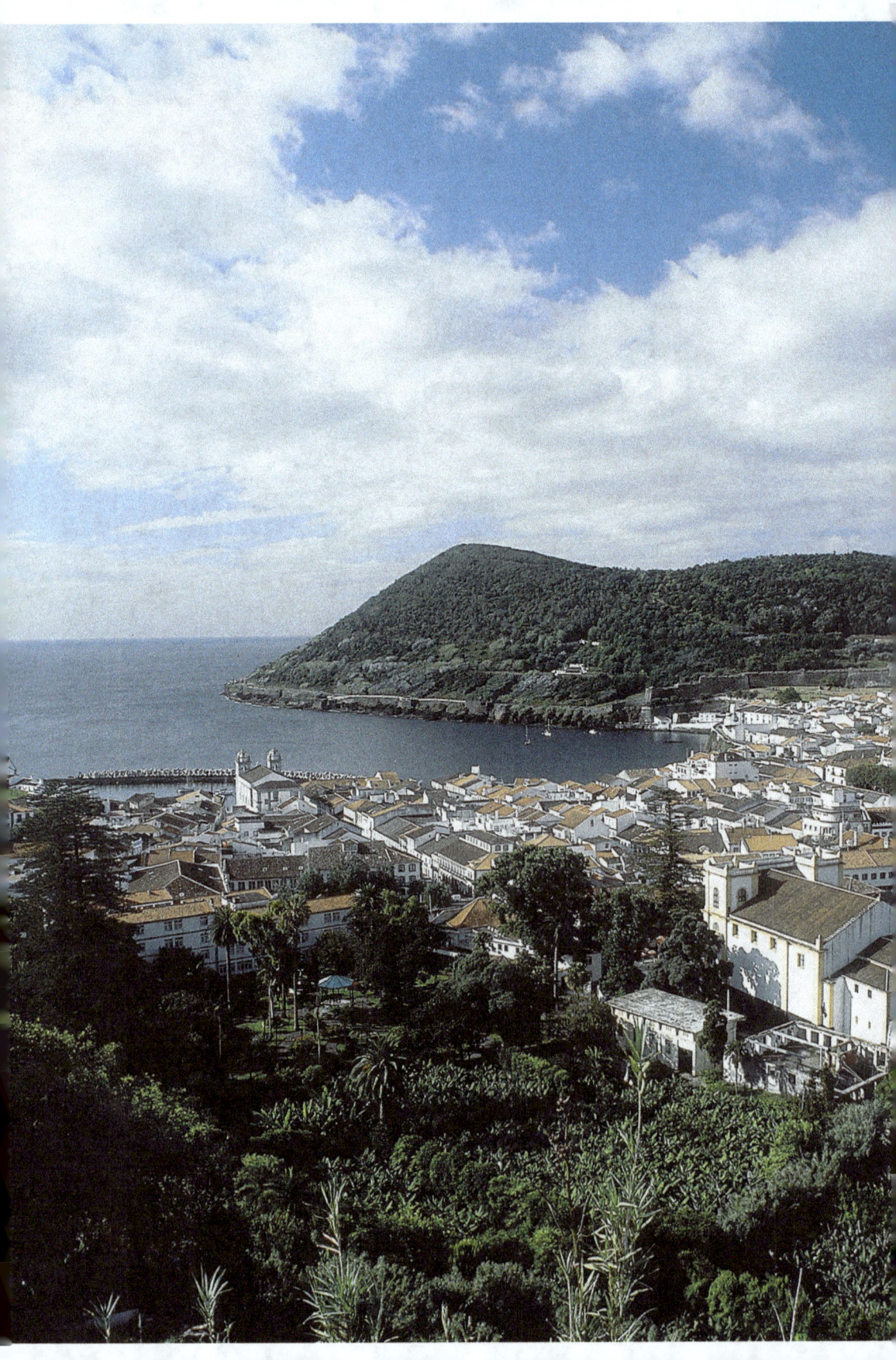

ITINERARY XIV

The Azores on the Routes West and East

Pedro Dias, Dalila Rodrigues,
Nuno Vassallo e Silva, Fernando Grilo

First Day

XIV.1 **PONTA DELGADA**
      XIV.1.a São Sebastião (Ponta Delgada Parish Church)
      XIV.1.b Carlos Machado Museum

XIV.2 **VILA FRANCA DO CAMPO**
      XIV.2.a São Miguel Arcanjo (Vila Franca do Campo Parish Church)

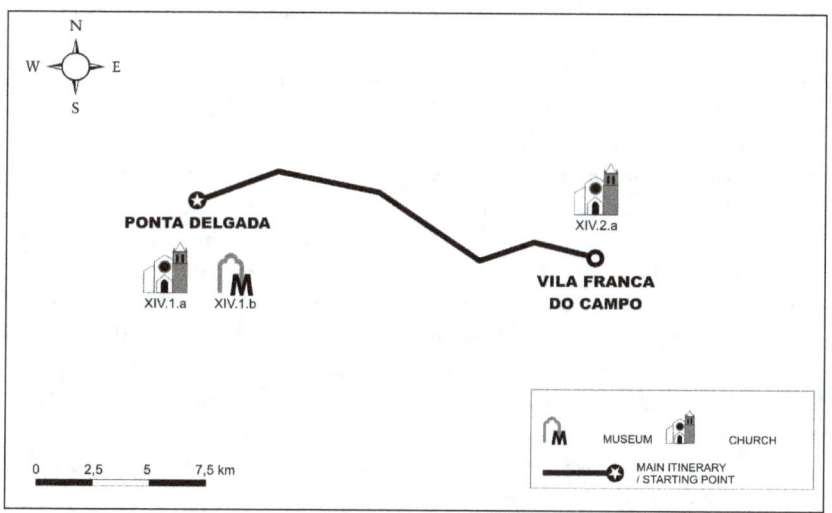

Bay of Angra do Heroísmo.

ITINERARY XIV   The Azores on the Routes West and East

Situated in the Atlantic Ocean, half way between Europe and America, the nine islands in the Azores archipelago seem to have been drawn with reasonable precision on Catalan and Italian charts, before the official date of their discovery. This would mean that the islands were discovered before Gonçalo Velho Cabral arrived at the Island of Santa Maria, c.1431, spending the following years at São Miguel, Terceira, Faial and Pico. The first specific reference to this fact is a letter from Prince Henry the Navigator, dated July 2nd 1439, in which he informed his brother the Prince Regent, D. Pedro, Duke of Coimbra, that he had turned sheep loose on the islands and asked whether he agreed that the islands should be colonised. There were still two more islands to be discovered or rediscovered, Flores and Corvo, which were reached by Diogo de Teive, in 1452.

D. Pedro de Coimbra took a constant interest in the Azores, obtaining various benefices from his nephew, D. Afonso V, for the inhabitants and territory of São Miguel. Prince Henry the Navigator had already decided on the settling of the Island of Santa Maria, and substituted D. Pedro in this enterprise with the explicit support of his sister D. Isabel, Duchess of Burgundy, as Portugal lacked the human resources for such a venture. This accounts for the large number of Flemish settlers in the Azores, particularly on the Island of Faial, which was to have such a notable influence on artistic production and taste. Names appeared such as Van Aard, Govaert, Groot, der Haghe: some were of distinguished families; others were simple artisans, and yet others had been sent into exile. Jacomo de Bruges had been living in Oporto, but left to settle in Terceira with a number of compatriots, as well as people from the north.

The first captaincy was made up of the Islands of Santa Maria and São Miguel, which was divided into two in 1474. Twenty years earlier, Prince Henry the Navigator had set up a commandery under Gonçalo Velho, granting him powers under the Order of Christ. This Order was to provide religious support for the settlers, but almost immediately Franciscan monks and other religious Orders joined them. The first monastery in the Azores at Vila Franca do Campo, on the Island of St Miguel, was destroyed by an earthquake in 1522 and replaced by another, dedicated to Nossa Senhora do Rosário. Other religious institutions that contributed to the development of the islands were the Convento de Nossa Senhora da Guia (generally considered to have been the first of them all), situated at Angra and dating back to 1452, and six nunneries in Vila da Praia, Vila Franca do Campo, Horta, Ponta Delgada, Ribeira Grande and Angra, although these were not built until the 16th century.

Agricultural produce was of primary importance, particularly wheat, as Portugal was chronically short of this staple crop and, additionally, the needs of the forts in Morocco were also great. Cattle was bred and there was a flourishing export trade in wood, of great value to the textile trade in Northern Europe.

ITINERARY XIV   *The Azores on the Routes West and East*
Ponta Delgada

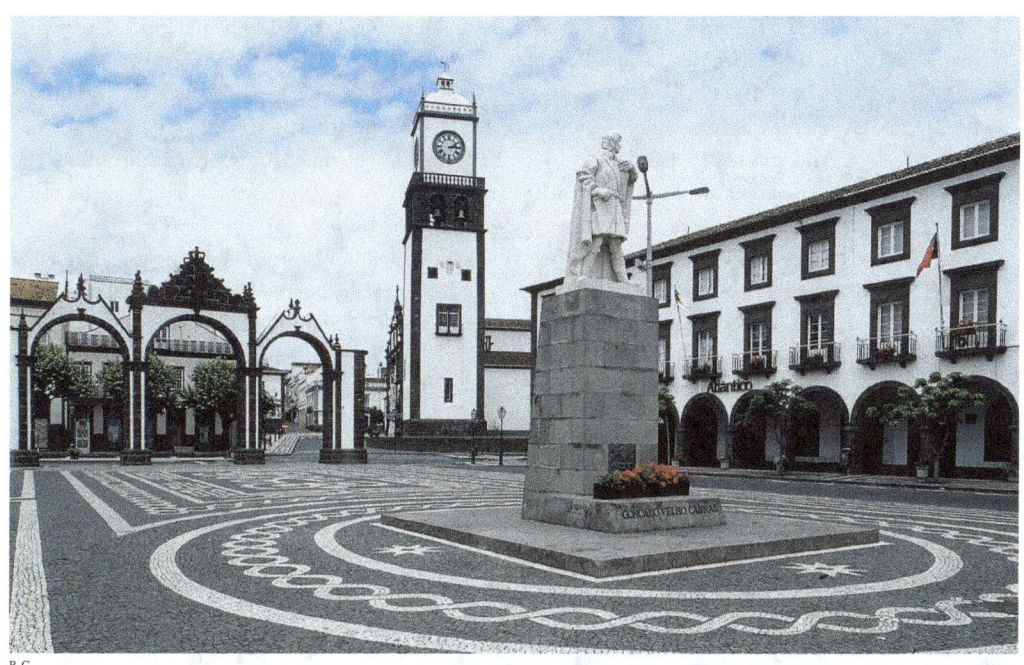

Ponta Delgada historic centre.

XIV.I PONTA DELGADA

At the end of the 15th century, with the opening of the sea route to the Americas and India, the islands became increasingly important, particularly Angra, the capital of the Island of Terceira, which was soon elevated to city status and the see of a new Diocese, in 1534.

From 1518 onwards, the number of vessels stopping over en route to India increased rapidly and, between then and 1598, the fleet sailing to the Americas stopped there 42 times to store chests filled with gold and silver from the New World. The constant turnaround of Atlantic maritime traffic provided the islands and their populations with essential employment in the service industries.

The Island of São Miguel, or the "Green Island" as it is known, is the largest in the archipelago, with an area of almost 760 sq. km., oblong in shape and measuring 65 km. in length and 12 km in width. The scenery is particularly breathtaking with high peaks and lakes in the craters of extinct volcanoes, as well as a diverse array of flora.

The island was discovered between 1426 and 1439, the year when colonisation began. The main town is Ponta Delgada, although there are other cities and towns remarkable for their artistic

327

Ponta Delgada

heritage, such as Ribeira Grande and Vila Franca de Campo, in relation to, primarily, the Baroque period. Earthquakes, however, such as that in 1522, and the comparative fragility of early constructions, have meant that little has survived from these early times other than two churches and a few items in various museums.

The oldest references to Masters of Works date back to 1507, when the *fidalgos*, the gentry, in Ribeira Grande signed a contract with a Biscayan Master, João de la Pena to build a local church, which unfortunately did not last very long, and had to be rebuilt. Fernão Álvares, a Portuguese, who lived in São Miguel from 1514 and spent almost all his life in the Azores, built a stone bridge in the town in 1520.

Building flourished during the Manueline period due to the rapid economic and social development. There did not seem to be any one architectural language, but rather a diversity corresponding to the different origins of these master craftsmen and, obviously, the extremely long time that the Late Gothic period lasted. The strongly structured vaulting has a complexity of ribs that is not to be found elsewhere, and can only be put down to the constant earth tremors. Whatever the reason, this was one of the high points in the history of architecture in the Azores and one of the peaks of both the Portuguese and European Late Gothic style.

XIV.1.a São Sebastião (Ponta Delgada Parish Church)

Largo da Matriz (entrance by the side door). (Tel: 295 904554). Classified as a Building of Public Interest.

Opening hours: daily 09.00-12.00 and 13.00-18.00 in winter, and 08.30-20.00 in summer, Saturday 09.00-12.30 and 17.00-18.30.

There is also a small Museum of Sacred Art in the Church, open on weekdays and outside the hours of worship.

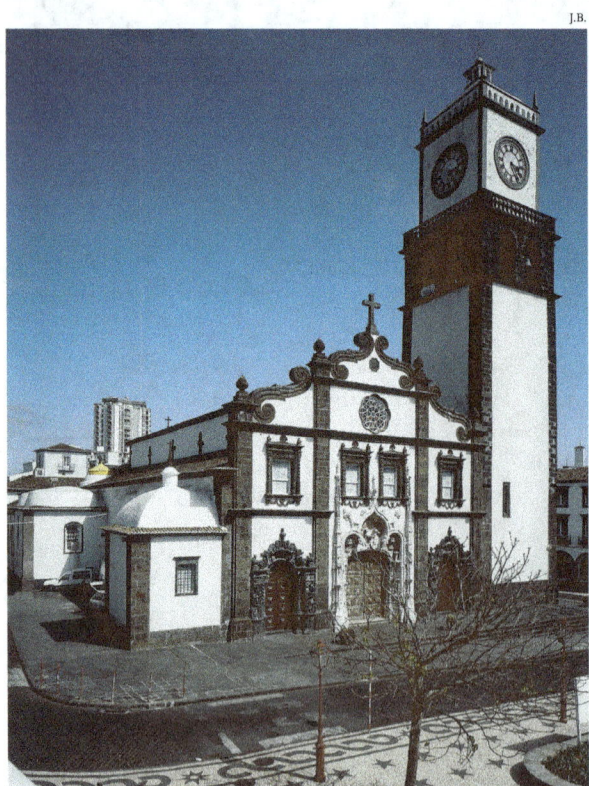

Church of São Sebastião, Ponta Delgada Parish Church.

J.B.

ITINERARY XIV *The Azores on the Routes West and East*
Ponta Delgada

This well-documented Parish Church, dedicated to St Sebastian, has three outside portals with vaulting similar to that of chapels in the Late Gothic style, although various Renaissance features are already evident. There was an earlier building on the site built before 1514, but the work on this Church took place between 1533 and 1545. The Master of Works was a certain Lúpedo, who contracted the work for 1,350,000 *reais*, an enormous sum at the time. He was, however, replaced by Afonso Fernandes who was expressly chosen by the Court. The stone for the portals, carved by Nicolau Fernandes and André Fernandes, was sent to Ponta Delgada from Portugal. The masonry was by the brothers, Estêvão da Ponte and Brás da Ponte, whilst the carpentry was by Diogo Dias, Pêro Fernandes and Diogo Alves.

There are Italianate early Renaissance *grotesques* on the portals and capitals with fantastic images. The structure is extremely complex and was clearly designed to emphasise the power and economic wealth of those who commissioned it.

The unusual ribbed vaulting in two of the chapels is of interest: one is traditional with five bosses, whilst the other has the essential elements to form a circumference by joining the secondary bosses. The vaulting in the chancel is even more complex and is divided into two areas over the choir and the apse. The *crossing arches* are well marked and the master created a dense grid of decorated rib segments that guaranteed greater security, particularly in a Church that had previously been damaged by several earthquakes.

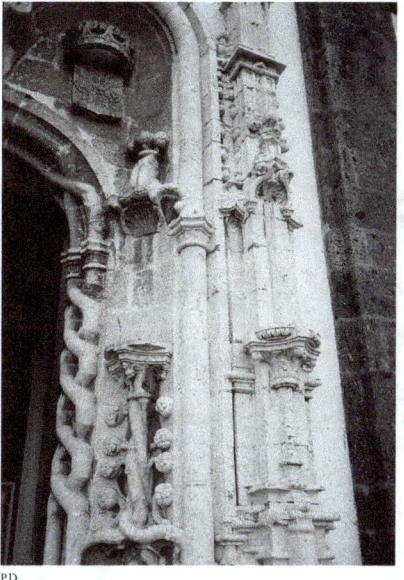

Ponta Delgada Parish Church, detail of the portal.

XIV.1.b Carlos Machado Museum

The Museum is housed in the former Convento de Santo André in Rua João Moreira. (Tel: 296 283814). Classified as a Building of Public Interest.

Opening hours: winter 10.00-12.00 and 14.00-17.00 Tuesday-Friday, and 14.00-17.30 at weekends; in summer 09.30-12.30 and 14.00-17.30 Tuesday-Friday, and 14.00-17.30 at weekends. Closed on Mondays.

The Museum is installed in the Baroque Monastery of Santo André, dating back to

ITINERARY XIV   The Azores on the Routes West and East
Ponta Delgada

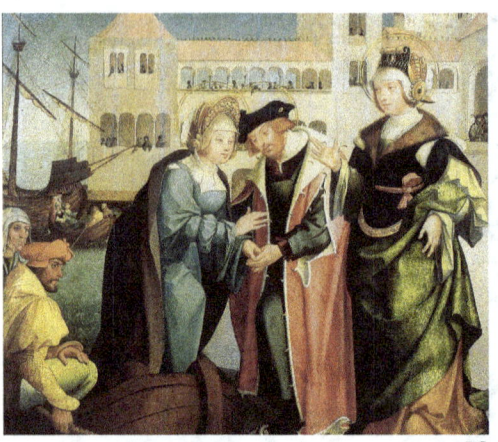

Portuguese school, "Martyrdom of St Veríssimo, St Máxima and St Júlia – Disembarkation in Lisbon", oil on wood, 16th century, Museu Carlos Machado, Ponta Delgada.

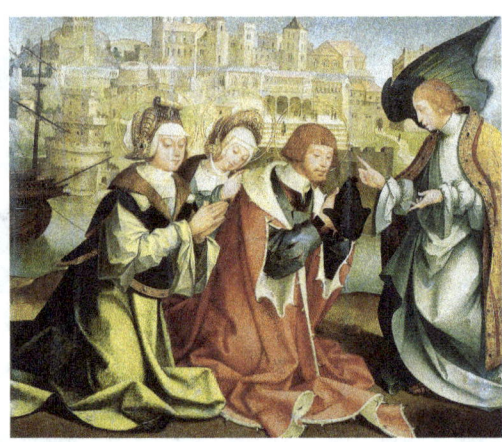

Portuguese school, "Martyrdom of St Veríssimo, St Máxima and St Júlia – Annunciation of the Martyrdom", oil on wood, 16th century, Museu Carlos Machado, Ponta Delgada.

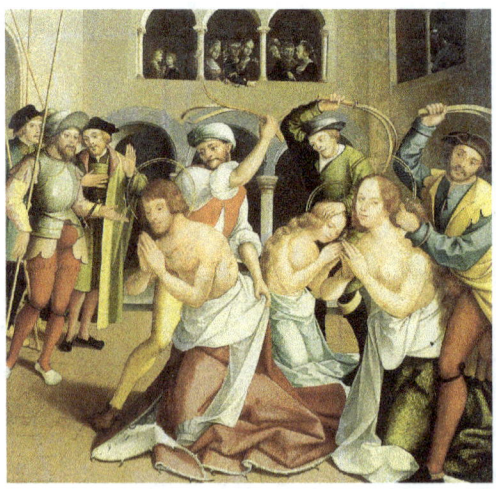

Portuguese school, "Martyrdom of St Veríssimo, St Máxima and St Júlia – Flagellation", oil on wood, 16th century, Museu Carlos Machado, Ponta Delgada.

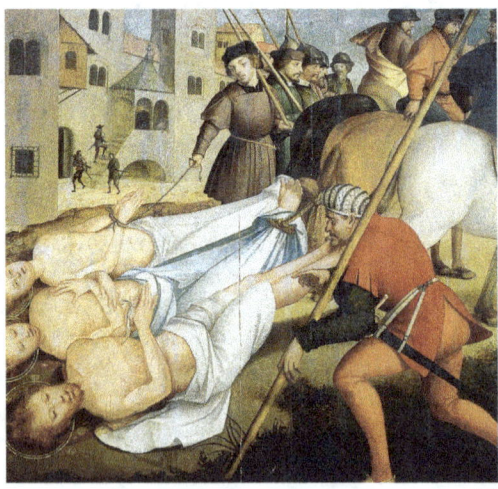

Portuguese school, "Martyrdom of St Veríssimo, St Máxima and St Júlia – Death by Dragging", oil on wood, 16th century, Museu Carlos Machado, Ponta Delgada.

the 17th and 18th centuries. The collection contains a number of old paintings from various workshops in Portugal.
Two panels, which must have belonged to the *predella* of a Manueline altarpiece represent *St Catherine*, *St Barbara*, *St Margaret* and *St Apollonia* and bear the unmistakable stamp of the "Masters of Coimbra". They were donated to the Museum by the heirs of Vasco de Bensaúde. There is an accentuated schematism in the drawing of the figures and a total absence of characterisation in the faces, in an almost disconcerting process of simplification. On the other hand, the work is excellent as regards the garments and adornments, which display extraordinarily patient craftsmanship.
Another important series is made up of four panels, measuring 73cm. x 83cm., evoking the *Martyrdom of St Veríssimo, St Máxima and St Júlia*. Also donated by the Bensaúde family, it can certainly be attributed to one of the best workshops in Lisbon, at the end of the reign of D. Manuel I. Particularly relevant is the *Disembarkation*, as it represents the Paço da Ribeira in Lisbon, where a caravel is tied up at the quayside. Other references to the Manueline palace in the capital also appear in the paintings of the *Flagellation* and *Death by Dragging*. These saints were actually martyred in Lisbon in Roman times, so that the artist, undoubtedly someone who had learned and worked with Jorge Afonso, decided to paint a scenario that existed at that time, resulting in a clear identification of each site for each different martyrdom scene.

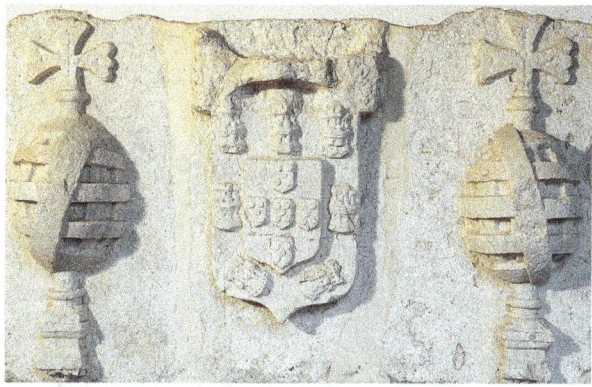

Emblazoned, limestone, 16th century, Museu Carlos Machado, Ponta Delgada.

There are a number of other examples of Manueline art in the Museum, including some that illustrate the meeting of Western and Eastern cultures as a result of the Portuguese Discoveries. There is the stone with the royal coat of arms, the armillary sphere, and the Cross of Christ, made in cretaceous limestone in Lisbon, which belonged to the Palace of the Counts of Ribeira Grande. There is also the lintel with a *canopied arch* from the Convento de Santo André in Ponta Delgada, along with various decorative features from other contemporary constructions in either trachyte or ignimbrite: an armillary sphere, a gargoyle, a font and a vaulting boss, among other pieces.
Of special note are the Luso-Oriental works, particularly a series of sculptures in ivory from Goa and Ceylon.

Leave Ponta Delgada in the direction of Vila Franca do Campo and follow the ER1-1 towards São Roque / Lagoa / Água de Pau /

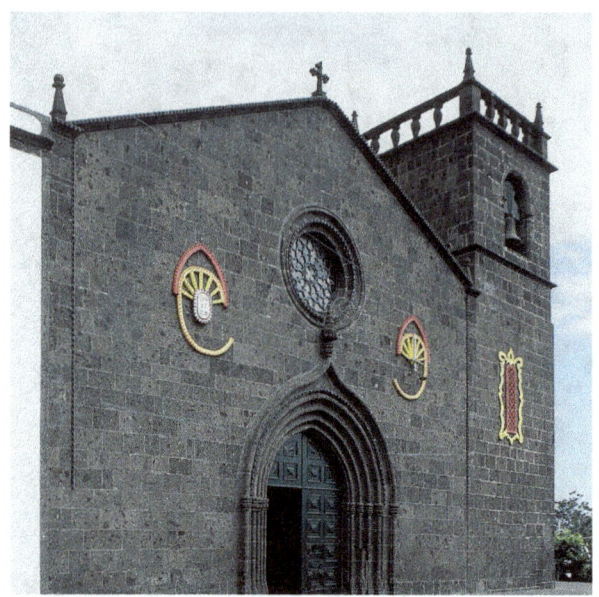

Church of São Miguel Arcanjo, Vila Franca do Campo Parish Church.

Ribeira Chã / Água do Alto and, finally, to Vila Franca do Campo (20 km.).

XIV.2 VILA FRANCA DO CAMPO

Vila Franca do Campo was the capital of the Island of São Miguel until 1522, when it was completely destroyed by an earthquake that killed most of its inhabitants. The houses were rebuilt in the same places, as were the churches and chapels. In the following centuries, the town developed and has fine examples of Mannerist and Baroque architecture. The Parish Church, dedicated to St Michael, is all that remains from the early years of the 16th century.

XIV.2.a São Miguel Arcanjo (Vila Franca do Campo Parish Church)

Rua Teófilo Braga. Information: Câmara Municipal (Town Hall Tel: 296 539100). Opening hours: daily 08.00-18.00, on Saturdays 08.00-12.00, and on Sundays 08.00-18.00.

The Parish Church dates back to the time of D. Manuel I, though it has the appearance of a traditional mid-15th-century Gothic building. The main portal is in the form of a *canopied arch* ending in a foliate rosette, and there are four small columns on either side that continue into the *archivolts*. The capitals form a foliate ring and have highly developed *abacuses*. The complex bases are in the Flamboyant Gothic style.

To reach Angra do Heroísmo, on the Island of Terceira, there are two choices: either by boat (see timetables for Angra do Heroísmo) from Ponta Delgada (170 km./5 hours), or by plane from the city airport.

ITINERARY XIV

The Azores on the Routes West and East

Pedro Dias, Dalila Rodrigues,
Nuno Vassallo e Silva, Fernando Grilo

Second Day

XIV.3 ANGRA DO HEROÍSMO
        XIV.3.a Fortifications
        XIV.3.b Museum of Angra do Heroísmo

XIV.4 SÃO SEBASTIÃO
        XIV.4.a São Sebastião (São Sebastião Parish Church)

XIV.5 PRAIA DA VITÓRIA
        XIV.5.a Santa Cruz (Praia da Vitória Parish Church)
        XIV.5.b Church of Senhor Santo Cristo das Misericórdias

The 16th-Century Furniture Factory on the Island of Terceira

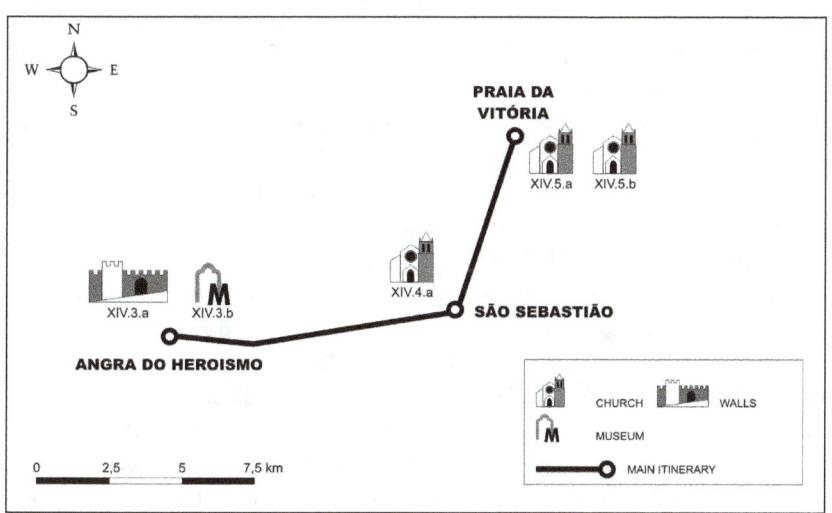

ITINERARY XIV   The Azores on the Routes West and East
Angra do Heroísmo

Angra do Heroísmo, Terceira Island.

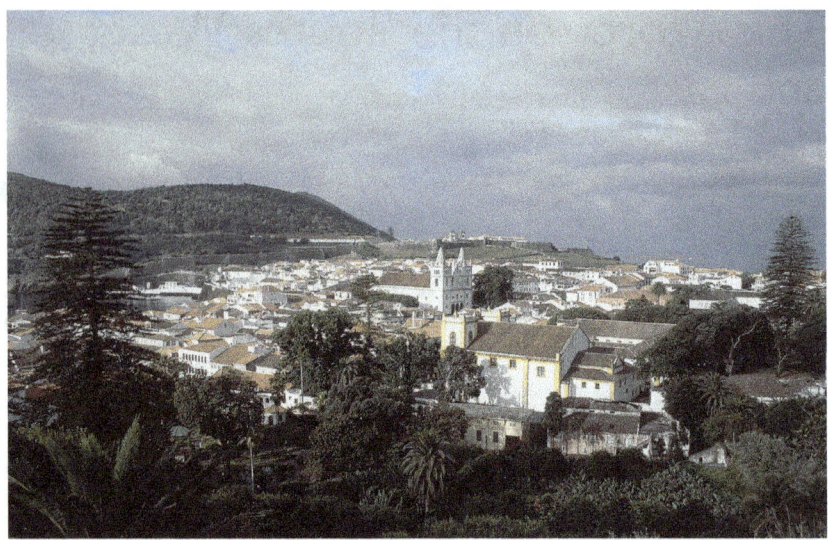

R.C.

This island, also oblong in shape, covers an area of approximately 382 sq. km., being 29 km. in length, and 17.5 km. in width, at its widest point. Initially called *Ilha de Nosso Senhor Jesus Cristo* or *Ilha do Bom Jesus*, the island was colonised in 1450, by Jacomo de Bruges, from Flanders.

This was a regular port of call for North Atlantic shipping and a meeting place for the fleets returning from the Far East. Vasco da Gama dropped anchor here on his inaugural voyage to India in 1497 and 1498, and his brother, Paulo da Gama, died here on their return and was buried in the Convento de São Francisco.

The considerable maritime traffic between both West and East gave the arts on the island their own unique stamp, mixing the aesthetics of Europe and Asia, particularly with regard to furniture and sculpture, at times made in materials brought from the Americas, such as precious metals, stone or wood.

XIV.3 ANGRA DO HEROÍSMO

Due to its extraordinary artistic wealth, the city of Angra was declared a World Heritage site by UNESCO in 1983.

Angra, situated by the sea on the South Coast, and made the see of a new Diocese in 1534, developed in the form of a rational, right-angled grid, in which the blocks of houses were built in a solid bourgeois style, with shops and workshops on the ground floor. An enormous defensive complex was naturally set up to protect the city, and other vulnerable parts of the island. At the same time, a number of religious Orders also built churches, monasteries and convents, and, in the 17th century, the Society of Jesus constructed one of its largest overseas colleges. As the historian Gaspar Frutuoso wrote at the end of the 16th century, *"Angra [was] the universal port of call to the west known throughout the world as the heart of all the islands"*. At that time, it had a population of between 5,000-6,000 inhabitants.

XIV.3.a Fortifications

The Forte de São João Baptista is situated on Monte Brasil, from where there is a good panoramic view of the fort. It can be visited during the daytime. Classified as a Building of Public Interest.
The Forte de São Sebastião, also known as the castelinho, *is at Porto das Pipas. Classified as a Building of Public Interest.*

From the Manueline period onwards, the importance of the Azores grew, due to a similar increase in the number of voyages to the Far East, Spain, America and Brazil. This led to the construction of fortifications: the Forte de São João on Monte Brasil, on one side, and the Forte de São Sebastião, at Porto das Pipas, on the other side, to protect the ports, population, and the fleets that guarded the seas. The vessels laden with merchandise were a tempting prize for pirates and privateers, who also sought logistical support and provisions in the Islands of the Azores before launching their attacks. In 1542, a plan was put forward to erect some settlements walls and bulwarks, but it was several years before these became effective, despite the warnings that Bartolomeu Ferraz made to D. João III in the following year, about the need to fortify the islands against French pirates.

Later the Purveyor to the fleets took on the task of preparing the most suitable terrain both in Angra and Ponta Delgada, and construction of the Fortress of São Brás was underway by 1551.

The engineer and architect, Isidoro de Almeida, designed the forts, assisted by Manuel Álvares. When French corsairs attacked Madeira, an expedition of highly qualified fortification experts was sent to the islands to provide advice. Pompeo Arditi and Tommazo Benedetto de Pesaro were in São Miguel in the spring of 1567 and then went on to the Islands of Terceira, São Jorge, Faial and Santa Maria.
A general plan for the defence of the islands was put forward by Pedro de Maeda

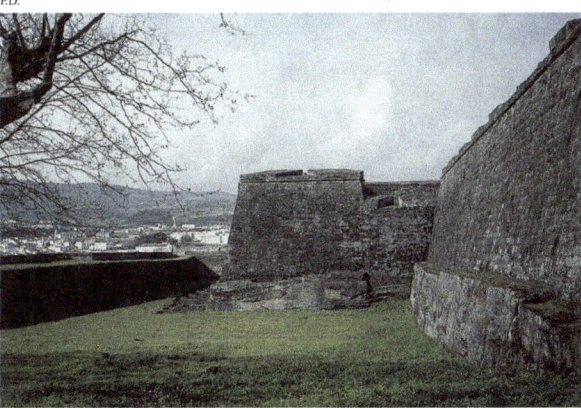

Fort of São João Baptista, Angra do Heroísmo.

ITINERARY XIV The Azores on the Routes West and East
Angra do Heroísmo

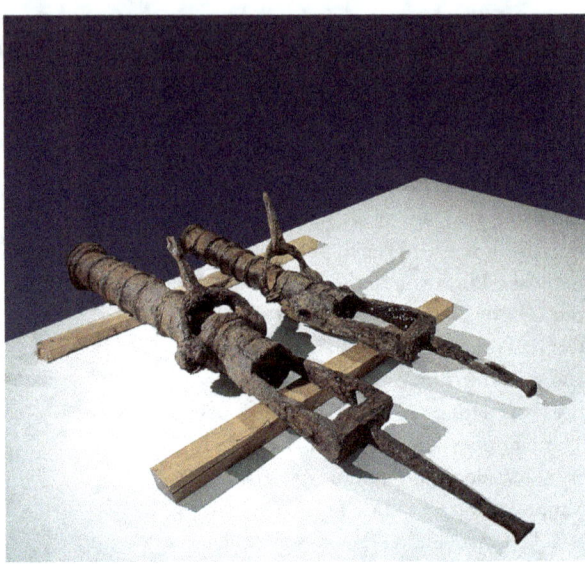

R.C.

"Veuglaire" launching cradle, mediaeval shipyard on the Portuguese coast, wrought iron bars and rings, 15th century, Angra do Heroísmo Museum.

XIV.3.b Museum of Angra do Heroísmo

The Museum entrance is in Ladeira de São Francisco. (Tel: 295 213147). The former Convento de São Francisco is classified as a Building of Public Interest.
Opening hours: winter 10.00-12.00 and 14.00-17.00 Tuesday-Friday, and 14.00-17.00 at weekends; summer 09.30-12.30 and 14.00-17.30 Tuesday-Friday, and 14.00-17.30 at weekends. Closed on Mondays.

The Museum is in the former Convento de São Francisco and was one of the first religious institutions to be founded overseas by the Portuguese. Vasco da Gama buried his brother, Paulo, here who died on the way back from the first voyage to India, in 1499. The collection contains a number of architectural features from Manueline buildings, including the actual Museum itself, as well as the Old Chapel of Nossa Senhora da Guia.
The theme of the permanent exhibition is *Land and Sea: a History of the Atlantic,* which illustrates life in the Azores in general, and in Terceira in particular, from its discovery and first settlement to the present day. It is organised as follows: Knowledge of the Islands of the Azores; Angra, the Azores and the World; From Captaincy-General to Liberalism and, finally, Formation of Contemporary Azores.
The Museum contains replicas of vessels and other nautical artefacts, some beautiful 19th-and 20th-century photographs, as well as many other works of art and original utensils, ranging from arms to

in 1577, and then another in 1592, by João de Vilhena. Although these constructions are outside the time frame fixed for this exhibition, it is nonetheless undeniable that they are the direct result of the navigations and maritime discoveries that are of particular interest to us here.
The Court never ceased dreaming up new and more powerful forts. By 1590, elaborate projects had been drawn up as part of an overall plan by D. António de la Puebla, which was then carried out by João de Vilhena. The Italian fortification expert, Tiburzio Spanochi, designed the Fortaleza de São Filipe on Morro Brasil, in Angra, which took decades to build, only being completed in 1643. As this was the Restoration period, and Philip of Spain no longer ruled the fort, it was, therefore, named São João (St John), after the new Portuguese king, D. João IV.

cartography, and from sculpture to painting, religious objects, Indo-Portuguese pieces and local furniture and sculpture.

For São Sebastião, take the ER1-1, passing through Ladeira Grande, Feteira and Porto Judeu de Cima. The journey affords splendid views for about 13 km.

XIV.4 SÃO SEBASTIÃO

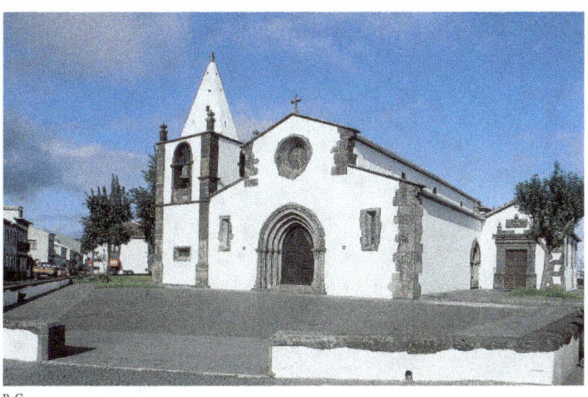

São Sebastião, one of the most important towns on the island of Terceira, was granted a charter in 1503, and was one of municipalities that developed most during the Manueline period due to its position between Angra and Praia, which justified the building of a large parish church.

São Sebastião Parish Church, Terceira Island.

XIV.4.a São Sebastião (São Sebastião Parish Church)

Largo de São Sebastião. Classified as a Building of Public Interest.

The Late Gothic Parish Church has remained almost intact. Over the years, it underwent considerable restoration work, during which almost all the later additions, some of great historic and aesthetic interest, such as carved gilded woodwork, were destroyed.
The interior has three aisles with six bays, the nave being higher than the side aisles. The transept is made up of two quadrangular chapels, perpendicular to the main vessel of the church, but out of line with the aisles. They are covered with well-designed stellar vaulting, with crosses, escutcheons and straight intermediate ribs, which are

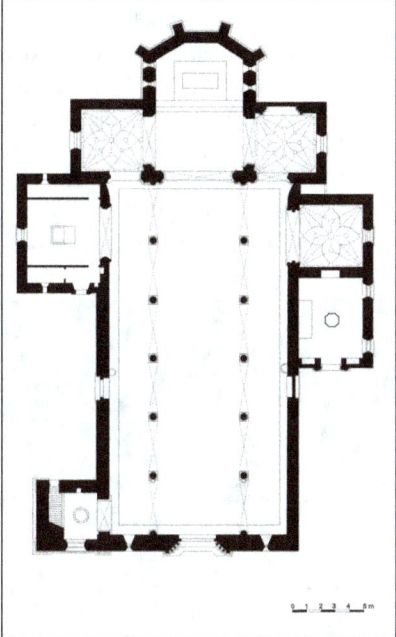

Church of São Sebastião, plan, Boletim da Direcção-Geral dos Edifícios e Monumentos Nacionais.

Praia da Vitória

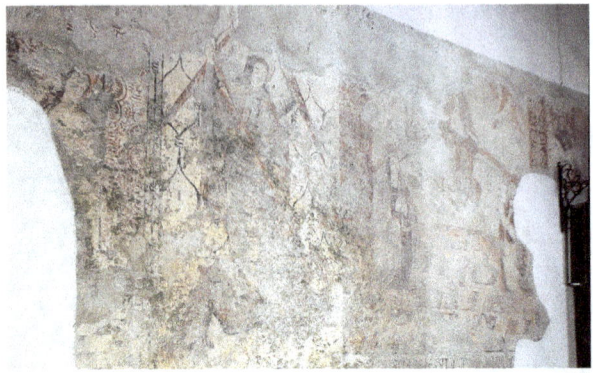

Frescoes in the Church of São Sebastião, São Sebastião Parish Church, Terceira Island.

then connected by curved sections. The chapel on the right-hand side has the same type of vaulting. The ribs, columns and archivolts, as well as the bosses, are all Late Gothic in style. The chancel has Renaissance vaulting, but the wall structure with buttresses is possibly earlier.

The important series of frescoes on the side walls have decorative Renaissance elements, although they reflect the taste of a master trained in the Late Gothic style.

Continue on the ER1 to Praia da Vitória (8 km.).

XIV.5 PRAIA DA VITÓRIA

Praia da Vitória was the headquarters of the first captaincy of the Island of Terceira, from 1456 to 1474, at the time of the first settlers. Despite being overtaken by Angra, the town developed extensively, and was granted a city charter in 1640. It retains an important architectural heritage from this period, which includes the Parish Church and the *Igreja do Senhor Santo Cristo das Misericórdias*. The famous Battle of Salga took place here, in 1581. The following year, D.

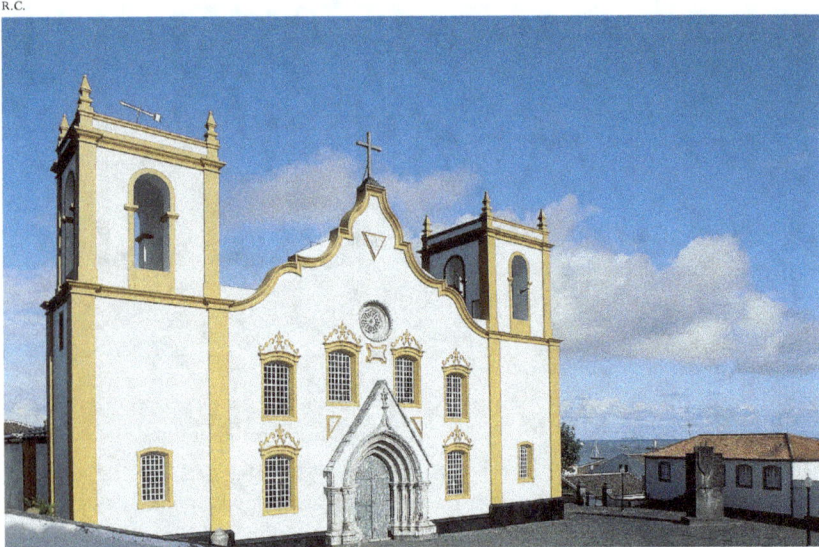

Santa Cruz, Praia da Vitória Parish Church.

António, the Prior of Crato at war with his cousin Philip II of Spain, was acclaimed king here, though it was Philip who ended up consolidating his position on the throne of Portugal.

XIV.5.a Santa Cruz (Praia da Vitória Parish Church)

In Ladeira de São Francisco. (Tel: 295 542100). Classified as a Building of Public Interest.
Opening hours: Monday-Friday 14.00-19.00, and on Saturdays and Sundays 09.00-12.00.

The Parish Church has retained a number of Manueline characteristics, though most of the building dates from the 18th century. It has interesting naturalistic decorative elements and anthropomorphic figures. Inside, the side chapels of São Francisco and Senhor dos Aflitos have entrance arches bordered with a carved-rope design, and depressed rib vaults, with crosses, escutcheons and intermediate ribs forming quatrefoils, together with curved segments. The main portal, built in 1517 according to the date on the front of the church, has naturalistic elements and also a conical canopy, in the mid-15th-century Batalha style.

XIV.5.b Church of Senhor Santo Cristo das Misericórdias

Churchyard of the Igreja de Santo Cristo. Opening hours: 09.00-17.00 Monday-Friday and in the afternoon at the weekends.

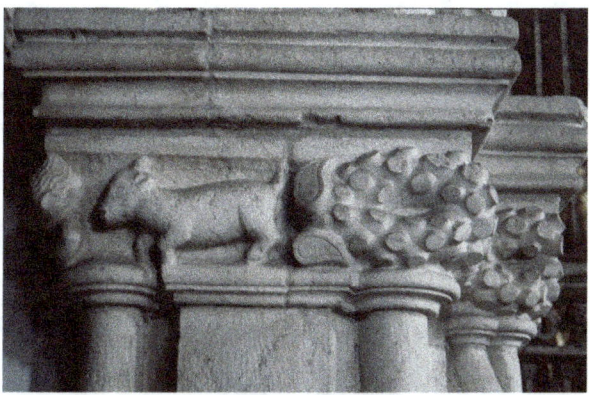

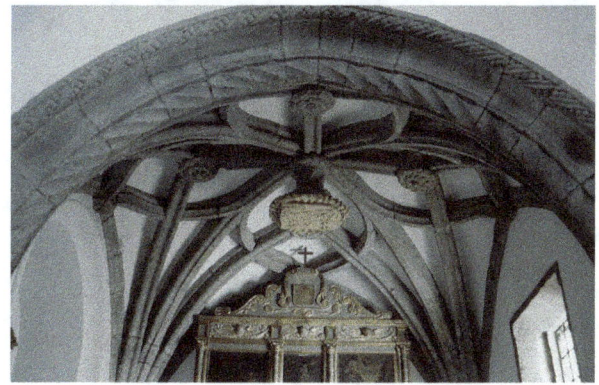

The Misericórdia Church was completely re-modelled in the 18th century, but has many Late Gothic works of art dating from the Manueline period and the beginning of the reign of D. João III. The panels, oil and tempera painted on cedar wood show a strong Flemish influence, though they are repainted here and there, which makes analysis difficult.
The damaged central, almost quadrangular, panel represents the *Descent of the Holy Ghost upon the Virgin and the Apostles*. The furniture, architecture and atmosphere

Praia da Vitória Parish Church, capitals.

Praia da Vitória Parish Church, interior.

Praia da Vitória

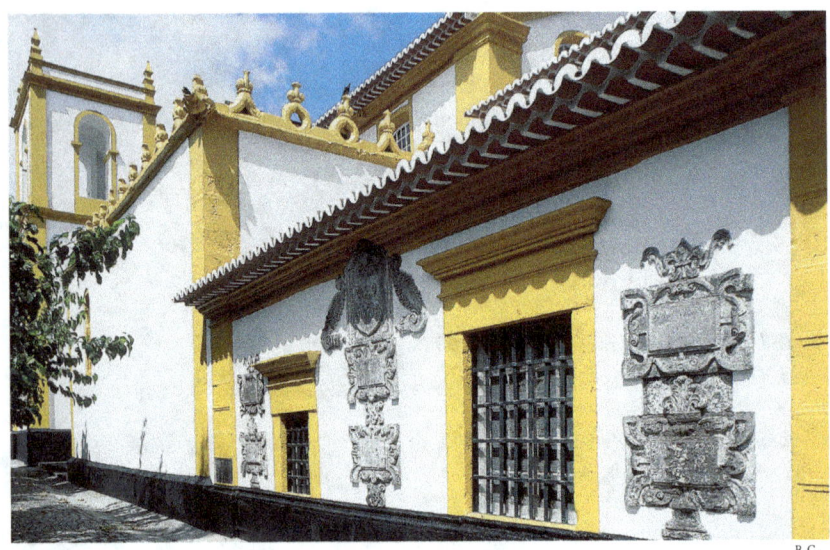

Praia da Vitória Parish Church, side façade.

are Gothic; the human figures are based on 16th-century models from workshops in both Ghent and Bruges.

There is some attempt here at perspective, but the human body is not handled very effectively. It is clear that the painter had studied the masters, and had even perhaps been an assistant in a Flemish workshop before finding his way to the Azores. Everything about the work is pure conjecture, as there is no other identical or slightly similar.

The panels of the *Apparition of Christ to the Virgin* and *Christ ascending into Heaven*, c.1530, are stereotypes, but display better craftsmanship, avoiding the errors of the central panel of this ensemble, that must originally have been a triptych.

THE 16TH CENTURY FURNITURE FACTORY ON THE ISLAND OF TERCEIRA

Pedro Dias

For many years, scholars in the field of the Decorative Arts wondered about the origin of a type of furniture with carved decoration that combined Eastern and Western models. Recent studies confirm that they were made on the Island of Terceira, from the 16th century onwards. The Dutchman Huyghen van Linschoten wrote in 1596:

"The island has a lot of excellent wood, namely cedar, which is so abundant that they make boats and carts and other bulky objects from it. Most of it is firewood, so it is considered to be of little value, because of its great abundance. There is another type of wood called dogwood; it is very pretty, with a reddish colour. There is also another type, which is called white wood, for it is as white as chalk. And there is yet another type, which is perfectly yellow in its natural state without being coloured. This is why many good craftsmen and carpenters who live in Terceira make many lovely things with great skill, such as desks, cupboards, boxes and a thousand and one other objects, which are taken to Portugal in quantity and are much esteemed, as much for the beauty of the wood as for the skill of the work, mainly by the people in the Spanish India fleet, who always go there to pick up fresh stores. Many of these pieces are sold, for they are amongst the best and most carefully made objects in Spain and Portugal, although they do not compare with the desks and artistic objects from Nuremberg and such regions. However, the quantity of timber on the island is greater than in all other places, for, besides the woods mentioned, the aforesaid Spanish fleets also bring a thousand other varieties of wood, a marvellous sight to behold, for they come in all colours that it is possible to imagine, so that it would be difficult to paint them more splendidly. On the island of Pico, 12 leagues from Terceira, there is a wood called yew. It is very beautiful and royal, so it is forbidden to cut it, unless it is for the king or for his official. It is a wood that is as hard as iron, which, when worked, has a red camlet colour inside, with the same lines, and the older and more used it is, the prettier is the colour, so it is worth taking care of it, in truth it is."

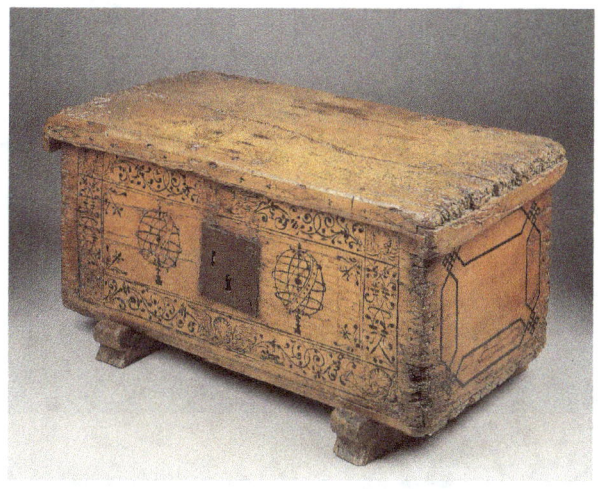

Azorean chest, manufactured in Angra, 16th century, private collection.

GLOSSARY

Abacus	Upper part of a capital, which supports the architrave or from which the arches spring.
Alcácer (alcazar)	Palace, in its Muslim sense; a castle or redoubt of the fortress or parade ground, where the *alcaide* or governor lived.
Alcáçova	Arabic *al-qasaba,* a castle or fortress.
Alcaide	Until the end of the middle Ages, custodian and defence of a castle or fortress under oath.
Ambulatory	Gallery used in large churches, representing the generally semi-circular continuation of the aisles. The circle surrounding the chancel.
Architrave	Lower part of the entablature, which makes immediate contact with the capital. Its dimensions and decoration vary according to the orders. By analogy, it also refers to a stone beam supported by columns or pillars.
Archivolt	Series of mouldings or arches following on from one another in a portal, door or window; moulding around the extrados of an arch.
Azulejo	(From Arabic *al-zellige.*) Smalted tile with designs used as decoration both in interior and exterior walls.
Arris vaulting	Vaulting resulting from the juxtaposition of two tunnel vaults, forming sharp edges.
Baldachin	Originally a canopy made of material, now an architectural finish that may have various forms, sometimes placed over altars in Baroque churches.
Barbican	Low walls that surrounded and defended the moat and reinforced the walls of the parade ground.
Canopied arch	Arch formed from two concave lines that meet at the top and then curve to form convex lines.
Carpintería de lo blanco	Art of assembling wood structures, for a framework or a bridge, etc.
Charola (Rotunda)	Same as an ambulatory.
Cloisonné	Decorated in enamel, in compartments formed by fillets of metal.
Colonnette	Elongated column with small diameter.
Conventus	Name given to the assembly convened by the governor of a Roman province for the administration of justice. Later, the name would be extended both to the city and the district where these activities took place.
Corbelling	Projections from a wall, at regular intervals, designed to support cornices and balconies.
Cornice	Top part of an entablature. A sequence of projecting mouldings used to crown pedestals, pediments, balustrades, etc. Used for draining water, they may also divide the wall into storeys; a decorative element that breaks the monotony of the building or accentuates certain lines.

Glossary

Crossed (cross-ribbed or quadripartite) vaulting	Vaulting composed of four equal sections, with projecting ribs. Each of the sections may be divided by secondary ribs, known as liernes and tiercerons, comprising two ribbed arches and two side arches supported on the piers.
Crossing arch	Arch that separates the main vessel of the church from the chancel; also known as the 'triumphal arch'.
Cryptoporticus	Portico or semi-subterranean gallery used in Roman architecture as an artificial foundation for Roman villas and gardens.
Cuenca tiles	Ceramic, with sunken-relief designs obtained by the pressure of a mould and then coloured completely with the enamels deposited in the hollows or *cuencas* delimited by a lip or *arista*.
Cuerda seca	Ceramic technique that consists of the separation of different coloured enamels by means of a line of oil-based paint.
Curtain wall	Section of the wall between two towers or bulwarks.
Enceinte	An enclosure, generally the whole area of a fortified place.
Flying buttress	Sloping arch springing from an outer buttress, supporting the thrust of the vertical and horizontal pressures from the vaults.
Galilee	Construction that preceded the façade of churches, juxtaposed with the portal, throughout its width, or else extending beyond it.
Grisaille	A method of painting in grey monochrome, giving the impression of low relief. Above all, it was used in decorative painting and also in European "primitive painting", on the back of the side panels of a triptych.
Grotesque	Form of wall decoration that mixes human figures, animals, fantastic and stylised figures, with medallions, effigies, etc.
Hall-church	Church in which the nave and aisles have approximately the same height, resulting in a completely unified space.
Hood mould	Gable originating in the triangular pediment that framed the upper part of the archivolts of church portals and other constructions.
Incense boat	Small vase, in the shape of a boat, in which incense is placed to be transported to the thurible, at religious ceremonies.
Incunabulum	Book printed before 1501.
Lath-and-plaster	Ancient building process, involving the use of plaster, with sand and cracked stones, bound together with clay; wall raised on a framework of laths covered with soft clay.
Machicolation	Military balcony appearing on keeps, secondary towers and entrance gateways, in the corners of battlements and in the middle of walls.

	It is supported by projecting corbels, with large openings (machicolations) in the floor, and consists of a small parapet with battlements.
Merlons	Square projecting part of the parapet of a fortress, placed between two embrasures at regular intervals.
Mozarab	A member of the Christian minorities, tolerated by Islamic right as tributaries and who lived in al-Andalus holding on to their religion and ecclesiastic and judicial organisation.
Mudejar	A Muslim allowed to remain among Christian conquerors, without converting, in exchange for a tribute. The adjective also refers to the arts representing handicraft traditions started under Islamic rule and continued for their Christian «customers» following their conquest of a region.
Namban	Japanese art of Western inspiration; refers to the 16th and 17th centuries; Japanese objects conceived with European forms and functions.
Oppidum	Fortified Roman town.
Par y nudillo	*Parhilera* timberwork, in which a horizontal beam known as a *nudillo* is placed between the uprights, in order to obtain greater support and to prevent them from warping.
Phylactery	Band of fabric, as represented in painting or sculpture and used to display a motto or a set of ritual terms.
Pilaster	Four-sided pillar, embedded in the wall, with proportions and decorations that are identical to those found in the Classical Orders.
Pinnacle	Small terminal pyramid of a buttress, flying buttress, dome or spire.
Platband	Fascia (wall, rail, balustrade, etc.) around a terrace or roof.
Polyptych	Retable with more than three fixed or movable panels. A retable with three panels is known as a triptych.
Porta-pax	Plate of metal, wood, ivory, etc., holding an image or signs in relief that was kissed in the solemn masses during the "peace ceremony".
Predella	Upper step of an altar; panels that form a frieze in the lower part of a retable, either included in the composition or remaining separate from this.
Pyx	Vase, generally cylindrical in shape, in which the Holy Sacrament is kept.
Scriptorium	(Pl. scriptoria) A room in a monastery where manuscripts were copied and illuminated.
Spire	Cone or pyramid-shaped pinnacle at the top of towers or belfries.
Thurible	Metallic vase, generally a valuable one, closed by an *opercle* (lid) and held by chains, used at religious ceremonies for burning incense.

Tondo	(Italian, pl. *tondi*) Circular painting or carving in relief.
Triumphal arch	See *crossing arch*.
Tympanum	Triangular space from Classical architecture, bounded by the cornices of the pediment and normally decorated; semicircular space between the lintel and archivolts of the portal.
Voussoir	Six-sided wedge-shaped stone, forming an integral part of an arch or vault.

KINGS AND QUEENS OF PORTUGAL

1st DYNASTY (1139–1383)

D. Afonso Henriques (b. 1094 – R. 1139 – d. 1185)
D. Sancho I (b. 1154 – R. 1185 – d. 1211)
D. Afonso II (b. 1185 – R. 1211 – d. 1223)
D. Sancho II (b. 1207 – R. 1223 – d. 1248)
D. Afonso III (b. 1210 – R. 1248 – d. 1279)
D. Dinis (b. 1261 – R. 1279 – d. 1325)
D. Afonso IV (b. 1291 – R. 1325 – d. 1357)
D. Pedro I (b. 1320 – R. 1357 – d. 1367)
D. Fernando (b. 1345 – R. 1367 – d. 1383)

2nd DYNASTY (1385–1580)

D. João I (b. 1357 – R. 1385 – d. 1433)
D. Duarte (b. 1391 – R. 1433 – d. 1438)
D. Afonso V (b. 1432 – R. 1438 – d. 1481)
D. João II (b. 1455 – R. 1481 – d. 1495)
D. Manuel I (b. 1469 – R. 1495 – d. 1521)
D. João III (b. 1502 – R. 1521 – d. 1557)
D. Sebastião (b. 1554 – R. 1557 – d. 1578)
D. Henrique (b. 1521 – R. 1578 – d. 1580)

3rd DYNASTY (1580–1640)

D. Filipe I (b. 1527 – R. 1580 – d. 1598, Felipe II of Spain)
D. Filipe II (b. 1578 – R. 1598 – d. 1621, Felipe III of Spain)
D. Filipe III (b. 1605 – R. 1621–1640 – d. 1665, Felipe IV of Spain)

4th DYNASTY (1640–1910)

D. João IV (b. 1604 – R. 1640 – d. 1656)
D. Afonso VI (b. 1643 – R. 1656 – d. 1683)
D. Pedro II (b. 1648 – R. 1667 – d. 1706)
D. João V (b. 1689 – R. 1706 – d. 1750)
D. José (b. 1714 – R. 1750 – d. 1777)
D. Maria I (b. 1734 – R. 1777 – d. 1816)
D. João VI (b. 1767 – R. 1816 – d. 1826)
D. Pedro IV (b. 1798 – R. 1826 – d. 1834)
D. Miguel (b. 1802 – R. 1828 – d. 1866)
D. Maria II (b. 1819 – R. 1826 – d. 1853)
D. Pedro V (b. 1837 – R. 1853 – d. 1861)
D. Luís (b. 1838 – R. 1851 – d. 1889)
D. Carlos (b. 1863 – R. 1889 – d. 1908)
D. Manuel II (b. 1889 – R. 1908-1910 – d. 1932)

CHRONOLOGY

1415	Ceuta is reconquered from the Moors.	1495	D. João II dies and D. Manuel I is acclaimed king.
1426	Work is carried out on the apse of Guarda Cathedral.	1496	Expulsion of the Jews. D. Manuel I orders the reconstruction of Alvor Castle.
1428	The painter Van Eyck travels to Portugal.	1498	The Misericórdia charitable organisations are founded.
1433	D. João I dies and D. Duarte ascends the throne.		Boytac is awarded an annual pension of 8,000 *reais* for his work on the Igreja de Jesus in Setúbal.
1438	D. Duarte dies and D. Pedro begins his period of regency on behalf of D. Afonso V.	1499	D. Manuel I orders the re-building of Silves Cathedral. Extensive building work is carried out on the Convento de Cristo in Tomar.
1449	Battle of Alfarrobeira and death of D. Pedro.		
1450	Nuno Gonçalves is made the official painter of D. Afonso V.		
1460	Prince Henry the Navigator dies.	1500	Brazil is discovered by Pedro Álvares Cabral. Extensive work begins on the Paço da Ribeira, in Lisbon. Sancho Garcia is placed in charge of the work at Vila do Conde Parish Church.
1471	Asilah is taken. Nuno Gonçalves is made painter of the works in Lisbon.		
1481	D. Afonso V dies and D. João II ascends the throne.		
1485	Work begins on the building of the Convento dos Lóios, in Évora.	1501	Work begins on the building of the Mosteiro dos Jerónimos.
1490	Duke of Beja, D. Manuel, builds the Igreja de São Tiago, in Soure.	1502	The Convento de Santo António is built at Serpa. Work begins on Funchal church (later cathedral), directed by Pêro Anes. Work is carried out on the Convento de São Domingos, in Lisbon. Performance of Gil Vicente's first morality play (*Auto da Visitação* or *Monólogo do Vaqueiro*). The play is written in Spanish to celebrate the Queen D. Maria (the mother of D. João III), giving birth. Damião de Góis is born. First reference to the painter Vasco Fernandes.
1491	Work begins on the Igreja dos Lóios, in Évora.		
1492	The Hospital Real de Todos-os-Santos (Royal Hospital) is founded in Lisbon. The Jews are expelled from Spain. Colombus undertakes his first voyage.		
1493	Construction work begins on Funchal Cathedral.		
1494	The Treaty of Tordesilhas is signed between Portugal and Spain. The first printing press is founded in Portugal. João Rianho is appointed Master of Works at Vila do Conde Parish Church.	1503	An agreement is signed with the Welsers for the sale of goods from India. Nuno Vaz is appointed Master of Carpentry for the city of Lisbon.

	Work is carried out on the Igreja de S. Julião, in Lisbon. Work is completed on the Igreja da Misericórdia in Asilah, in Morocco. First trading post is built in Cochim.		is made the inspector and supervisor of all painting works in the kingdom of Portugal. Francisco Danzilho works on the walls of Almeida, Castelo Rodrigo and Castelo Bom.
1504	Pêro and Filipe Henriques put finishing touches to Guarda Cathedral. The chancel of the Collegiate Church in Barcelos is completed.		Work finishes on the Igreja do Pópulo, in Caldas da Rainha. Diogo de Arruda works on the bulwarks at Paço da Ribeira, in Lisbon.
1505	Reconstruction of Viseu Cathedral begins.		Work is carried out on the Convento da Conceição, in Beja.
1506	The Belém Monstrance, commissioned from the workshop of Mestre Gil Vicente, is completed. Pedro Afonso works in La Laguna, in the Canary Islands. Fernão Gomes is appointed Master of Works at the fortress in Kilwa (Quiloa). Tomás Fernandes is appointed Master of Works for the fortifications in the Indian Ocean. João Vaz directs works on the Fortress at Sofala, in Mozambique. The castle is built on the Island of Socotra (in present-day Yemen).	1509	Pêro Anes builds the Customs House in Funchal. Fernão Mouseiro directs work on the Igreja de Santa Cruz, on the Island of Madeira. Pêro de Carnide is placed in charge of the work to enlarge the Palácio da Vila in Sintra. Mateus Fernandes completes the arch of the Capelas Imperfeitas (Unfinished Chapels) in Batalha. João de Castilho completes work on the chancel of Braga Cathedral. Boytac works on the Mosteiro da Batalha.
1507	Tomás Fernandes begins building the Fortress at Ormuz, in the Persian Gulf. Boytac begins the reconstruction of the Igreja de Santa Cruz, in Coimbra. Boytac directs work at the Convento da Pena, in Sintra. Martim Lourenço is appointed Master of Works at the Convento de São Francisco, in Évora. João de la Penha begins building Ribeira Brava Parish Church. Work begins on building the Fortress at Safi, in Morocco.	1510	Lopes Fernandes collaborates in building the Hospital de La Laguna, in the Canary Islands. Work begins on the Church at Cochim, on the Malabar Coast in India. Work is completed on the Igreja de São João Baptista in Tomar. Boytac inspects the building work at Asilah in Morocco. Diogo de Arruda begins work on the Convento de Cristo in Tomar. Francisco de Arruda rebuilds the walls of Moura, Mourão and Portel.
1508	Jorge Afonso is appointed the Royal painter of D. Manuel I, and		Pêro Gallego builds the Convento de Santa Ana in Viana do Castelo.

Chronology

| | The walls of Lisbon and Évora are repaired.
The Manueline body of the Ducal Palace in Vila Viçosa is constructed.
Work begins on the walls of Goa.
The chronicler Fernão Mendes Pinto is born. |
| 1511 | João de Castilho finishes the work on Vila do Conde Parish Church.
Francisco Danzilho is Master of Works at Alcácer Ceguer, in Morocco.
Tomás Fernandes builds the Castle and Fortress of Malacca. |
| 1512 | Francisco Henriques travels to Flanders, as head of a trade mission related to the selling of spices. |
| 1513 | Boytac is contracted to complete the Igreja de Santa Cruz, in Coimbra.
João de Cáceres is appointed Master of Royal Works, on the Island of Madeira.
The knotted vaulting is completed in Viseu Cathedral.
Diogo Pires, the Elder, builds the Capela dos Almeida in Vouzela Church.
Fernão Pires works on Mértola Castle. |
| 1514 | Work begins on Batalha Parish Church.
Boytac works at the Mosteiro da Batalha.
Francisco and Diogo de Arruda are in Africa, working at Ceuta, Safi and Azamor in Morocco.
Afonso Gonçalves works on the stores and warehouses at Lisbon docks.
Fernão Álvares works in Ponta Delgada, in the Azores. |

| | Rodrigo Afonso begins building the Capela de São Jerónimo, in Belém (Lisbon).
Work begins on the Fortress of Mazagan (Mazagão, present-day El-Jadida), in Morocco.
Martim Lourenço is appointed Master of Works at Alcácer Ceguer, in Morocco. |
| 1515 | João de Castilho completes the Chapter House of the *Convento de Cristo*, in Tomar.
Mateus Fernandes dies, and his son, also called Mateus Fernandes, takes over his work.
Boytac is placed in charge of work at the Mosteiro dos Jerónimos in Lisbon.
Francisco Arruda begins the construction of the Torre de Belém, in Lisbon. |
| 1516 | João de Castilho replaces Boytac as the Master of Works at the Mosteiro dos Jerónimos.
Pêro and Francisco Henriques complete work on Guarda Cathedral.
André Pires is appointed Surveyor of Works to the city of Lisbon.
Brás Martins and Francisco Esteves work on the Paço dos Estaus of Lisbon.
João Favacho builds the Igreja de São Julião, in Setúbal.
Pêro Gomes builds the Customs House at Safi, in Morocco.
Francisco del Barco is Master of Works at the fortifications in Asilah.
The Convento de São Francisco is built at Asilah.
Gonçalo de Évora is appointed Master of Works at the Fortress of Ormuz, in the Persian Gulf. |

Chronology

	Tomás Fernandes is awarded an annual pension for services in the Far East.	1519
1517	Nicolas Chanterène works on the main portal of the Mosteiro dos Jerónimos.	

1517
Tomás Fernandes is awarded an annual pension for services in the Far East.
Nicolas Chanterène works on the main portal of the Mosteiro dos Jerónimos.
Marcos Pires takes charge of the work on the Mosteiro de Santa Cruz, and the Paço Real in Coimbra.
Work re-commences on Azurara Parish Church.
Brás Rodrigues, Bastião Afonso, João Pires and Luís Gomes work on the Paço da Ribeira, in Lisbon.
Work commences on the Convento de São João, in Setúbal.
Work begins on the Igreja de Nossa Senhora da Assunção in Elvas.
Praia da Vitória Parish Church in the Azores is completed.
Work is carried out on the Convento de São Francisco, at Safi in Morocco.
Leonardo Vaz begins work on the refectory of the Mosteiro dos Jerónimos, in Lisbon.

1518
João de Castilho takes charge of the building work at the Mosteiro de Alcobaça and builds the side portal and cloister at the Mosteiro dos Jerónimos.
Diogo de Castilho begins to work in Coimbra.
Diogo de Arruda begins work on the Castelo Novo, in Évora,
Work begins on the Convento de São Bernardo, in Portalegre.
The Parish Church is built at Mazagan, in Morocco.
Cristóvão Fernandes, Álvaro Anes and João Rodrigues build the Convento de Santa Clara, in Estremoz.

1519
Boytac works on the Mosteiro da Batalha.
The Cathedral is built at Safi, in Morocco.
Cristóvão Martins is declared Master of Royal Works at Asilah.
Pedro Nunes is appointed Master of Works at the Paço Real in Almeirim.
The Torre de Belém is completed.
Fernão de Magalhães (Magellan) sets off on his first voyage to circumnavigate the world.

1520
Brás Rodrigues works on the Armoury, in Lisbon.
Afonso Pires, Luís Gomes and Gil Fernandes work on the Mosteiro de São Francisco, in Lisbon.
Work begins on the cloister of the Convento de São Bernardo, in Portalegre.
Estêvão Lourenço builds the cloister of the Convento de São Bento de Cástris, in Évora.
Fernão Álvares is contracted to build the bridge at Ribeira Brava.
Mestre Álvaro takes over from Antão Pires as Master of Works at Azamor.
Gonçalo Mateus is appointed Master of Royal Works at Alcácer Ceguer.

1521
The architect Marcos Pires dies.
The Cloister of Silence is completed at the Mosteiro de Santa Cruz, in Coimbra.
Work is carried out on the chancel of Machico Parish Church, in Madeira.
The Convento de São Francisco is built in Goa.
D. Manuel I dies and D. João III ascends the throne.

351

1522	João de Castilho begins the vaulting of the Igreja dos Jerónimos, in Lisbon. Diogo de Castilho builds the chancel of the Church at the Mosteiro de São Marcos. João Álvaro and Álvaro Anes complete the cloister of the Convento de Espinheiro, in Évora.		The Chapel of Nossa Senhora da Conceição is built in the Convento de Santa Clara, in Vila do Conde.
		1527	Diogo de Castilho recommences work on enlarging the Mosteiro de Santa Cruz, in Coimbra.
		1528	Diogo de Castilho completes the chancel of Atalaia Church, in the Ribatejo.
1523	Work is carried out on churches in Évora, Alcobaça, Cela, Alvorninha and Aljubarrota.	1529	Diogo de Castilho builds the chancel of the Church in Góis, and the Palace of D. Luís Silveira. João Português builds the Church of the Convento de Celas, in Coimbra.
1524	Diogo de Castilho is appointed Master of Royal Works in Coimbra. Duarte Coelho builds the cloister of Lamego Cathedral. Work is completed on the Mosteiro de São Domingos, in Lisbon. Pero de Trillo works on the Convento de São Francisco, in Lisbon. Diogo Fernandes and Pedro Pexão are in charge of the work on the Palácio da Vila, in Sintra.		
		1530	Work is completed on the Igreja de São Quintino, in Sobral de Monte Agraço. The Church of the Convento de São Bernardo is completed in Portalegre. Diogo Dias from Lisbon builds the Paço da Audiência, in Lima, Peru.
1525	Diogo de Arruda is appointed Master of Works of the Royal Residences in Évora. Work begins on the Capela dos Coimbras, in Braga. João Marques builds the portal of the Hospital do Espírito Santo, in Arraiolos. The Castelo de D. Teodósio is begun in Vila Viçosa. Basic work is completed on the Castle at Calicut, in India. Bernardo Anes is Master of Works at the Mosteiro de Almoster.	1531	Diogo de Arruda dies and his brother, Francisco, continues his work. Work is carried out on the Castle at Évora Monte.
		1532	Batalha Parish Church is completed.
		1533	Pêro Garcia works on the Convento de Santo António, in Ferreirim. Work begins on Ponta Delgada Parish Church, in the Azores.
		1534	Diogo de Castilho builds the chancel of Trofa do Vouga Church.
		1535	The Chapel of D. Fradique is built in the Igreja de São Francisco, in Estremoz.
1526	Fernando Gil carries out work on the Casa da Câmara (Town Hall), slaughterhouses and other buildings in Setúbal.	1536	The Torre dos Azevedos is built near Barcelos.

HISTORICAL PERSONALITIES

Afonso Domingues (d. 1402)
Master architect, who worked on the Real Mosteiro de Santa Maria da Vitória, (Monastery of Batalha) from 1387–88 to 1402 and is believed to have drawn up the first plan of the building.

Aires Gomes da Silva
Nobleman at the Court of D. Manuel I and protector of the Hieronymite monks in Coimbra, where he is buried in the Mosteiro de São Marcos. He commissioned a monumental retable by Nicolas Chanterène for the Monastery Chancel.

António Carneiro (1460-1545)
In 1482, he held the post of Official Scribe to D. João II, and later to D. Manuel I. In 1500, he was granted the captaincy of the Island of Príncipe. Appointed Secretary of State in 1509, he conducted important negotiations, keeping chancery records and dealing with diplomatic correspondence.

Arnau de Carvalho
Master woodcarver and sculptor from Northern Europe, mainly working in Northern Portugal and Galicia. His work in Portugal shows the Flemish influences at the Court of D. Manuel I. He collaborated as a woodcarver, with the painter Vasco Fernandes (Grão Vasco).

Boytac (d. 1525)
Famous architect that lived and worked in Portugal in the late 15th and early 16th centuries. As from 1504, he received a series of Royal commissions. One of the greatest of Manueline architects, his work includes the Church of the Mosteiro de Santa Maria de Belém (Lisbon). He died in 1525 and was buried in the Mosteiro de Santa Maria da Vitória (Batalha), where he had worked for the last years of his life.

Brás de Albuquerque (or Afonso de Albuquerque) (1501-1581)
Son of the Governor of India, Afonso de Albuquerque. He was baptised Brás at the suggestion of D. Manuel I, but used the name Afonso in memory of his father. Was Comptroller of the Treasury and presided over the Lisbon Senate during the reign of D. João III. He spent some time in Italy and was profoundly influenced by its culture, building in the Italian style, the Quinta da Bacalhôa, Azeitão, incorporating a belvedere and a lakeside pavilion.

Cristóvão de Figueiredo
16th-century painter, who was known to be active from 1515 to 1543 during the reigns of D. Manuel I and D. João III. Apprenticed to Jorge Afonso, whose niece he married. From 1513, he was painter to the Cardinal-Prince D. Afonso, and worked in partnership with Gregório Lopes and Garcia Fernandes.

Della Robbia
Family of Italian sculptors, active in the 15th and 16th centuries, who became famous for their works in *majolica*, a process of painting and glazing the terracotta. There are a number of items from this workshop in the Museu de Arte Antiga, Lisbon, including *tondi*, altar frontals and sculptures.

Diogo Ortiz de Vilhegas, Dom (Diego Ortiz de Villegas)
Born in Calzadilla, León, he came to Portugal in 1476 as Chaplain to Queen Joana. In 1491, D. João II appointed him Bishop of Tangiers, and three years later he became his principal chaplain. In 1482, he presided over the *Junta dos Matemáticos* (Council of Mathematicians). He became Bishop of Ceuta in 1500 and, four years later, Bishop of Viseu, where he sponsored the construction of the Manueline vaulting in the cathedral. D. Manuel I made him Tutor to the Royal princes and also, in 1517, named him executor of his will. Wrote the treatise entitled *Catecismo Pequeno*.

Diogo de Azambuja (1432-1518)
Began by serving the son of Prince D. Pedro, Duke of Coimbra, whom he had followed into exile. In 1458, he fought the Castilians at Alcácer Ceguer, on the side of D. Afonso V. In 1487, appointed Quartermaster General of military warehouses by D. João II. Continued to serve the crown during the reign of D. Manuel I, especially in North Africa, where he had a number of fortresses built.

Diogo de Castilho (Diego del Castillo) (c.1493-1574)
Born in Santander, came to Portugal, as did his brother João de Castilho, to follow an artistic career. Worked on important buildings such as Santa Maria de Belém. He went to live in Coimbra, having been appointed Master of Royal Residences. Castilho was one of the most important architects of the period, on a par with Jean de Rouen, with whom he collaborated for many years. He was made a Citizen of Oporto in 1527 and, 20 years later, was made a Knight of the Royal Household.

Diogo de Arruda (d. c.1531)
Engineer and architect, who was active from 1508 to 1531. He and his brother, Francisco de Arruda, were two of the most outstanding creators of Manueline art. He worked at the Royal Palaces at Santarém, as well as many others. He distinguished himself as a military architect, mainly constructing fortifications in Africa.

Diogo Pires-o-Moço (Diogo Pires the Younger)
Sculptor, who was active in Portugal from 1491 to 1530 and was probably the son of Diogo Pires designated "the Elder". One of his most important works is the tomb of Diogo da Azambuja, in the Igreja dos Anjos, Montemor-o-Velho. His other work includes the altar frontal in the Sé Velha in Coimbra (1491); the tumulary stone of Bishop D. Álvaro; and the *Guardian Angel of the Kingdom*, all in the Museu Nacional Machado de Castro, in Coimbra. He, and the artist Diogo Mendes, probably worked together on the three tombs in the chancel of the Igreja de São Marcos.

Diogo Pires-o-Velho (Diogo Pires the Elder)
Sculptor, who worked in Coimbra in the last quarter of the 15th century. His work includes various representations of Our Lady, one of which, dating from 1481, is in the Parish Church of Leça da Palmeira.

Diogo de Sousa, Dom (1461-1532)
Attended the Universities of Salamanca and Paris and was a leading figure in the introduction of Humanism into Portugal. In 1493, D. João II sent him to Rome to render obedience on his behalf to Pope Alexander VI, and in 1505 D. Manuel I sent him for the same purpose to Julius II. He was named Archbishop of Braga in the same year. On his death, he was buried in the tomb he had commissioned, in the Chapel of Jesus in Braga Cathedral.

Diogo de Torralva
Son-in-law of Francisco de Arruda. He worked as an architect from 1520 to 1554. Two of his most important works are the Igreja da Graça in Évora, and the D. João III cloister in the Convento de Cristo, Tomar.

Egas Moniz (d. 1146)
Became famous for the legend that gave him the role of hostage when D. Afonso Henriques reneged on his pledge to Alfonso VII of León, during the siege of Guimarães. He was the most important person at the Court of D. Afonso Henriques, having been nominated High Steward. He was buried in the Mosteiro de Paço de Sousa, which he had endowed and enriched.

Fernão Muñoz (Fernán Muñoz)
Stonemason and sculptor from Biscay, who worked with João de Castilho on Caminha Parish Church. He was possibly the same master who was later responsible for the sculptural monuments of the prophets, left unfinished by Oliver of Ghent in the Rotunda of the Convento de Cristo in Tomar.

Francesco da Cremona
Italian architect commissioned by D. Miguel da Silva, Bishop of Viseu, to build the cloister of Viseu Cathedral and other important works at the mouth of the River Douro.

Francisco Arruda (d. 1547)
Royal architect, he is known to have been working with his brother on the Convento de Cristo (Tomar) in 1512. Two years later, he was listed as one of the Masters of Works at the Mosteiro de Santa Maria de Belém, Lisbon. He built the Torre de Belém, by the river in Lisbon between 1515 and 1519. Among his well-known works are the Church of Conceição in Elvas, and the aqueduct of Água de Prata, Évora.

Historical Personalities

Francisco Henriques (d. 1518)
A painter of Flemish origin, who settled in Portugal in about 1500. He married the daughter of Jorge Afonso, another important painter. At the time of D. Manuel I, he was regarded as the best painter in the land. His work is to be seen at the Igreja de São Francisco in Évora, and in various other museums and churches.

Frei Carlos
A painter of Flemish origin, who worked in the first half of the 16th century. He died before 1553 at the Convento do Espinheiro, on the outskirts of Évora, where he took his vows as a monk.

Gaspar Vaz (1490-1569)
His work is documented from 1514 to 1568. He initially worked in Lisbon in the workshop of Jorge Afonso, along with painters such as Vasco Fernandes, Garcia Fernandes, and Gregório Lopes. He is known to have collaborated on various works, although no signatures or dates are known.

Garcia Fernandes
Painter, who was active from 1514 to 1565. He was apprenticed to Jorge Afonso, along with Gregório Lopes and Cristóvão de Figueiredo, with whom he painted the retable at Ferreirim, which led to them later being described as the "Masters of Ferreirim". His work is found in various parts of the country.

Gil Eanes
Initiated European navigation to the south of Cape Bojador, having finally rounded the Cape in 1434, after 12 years of consecutive attempts. He managed to sail 50 leagues along the West Coast of Africa. Prince Henry the Navigator made him a Squire in his Household.

Gil Vicente (c.1465-c.1536)
A 16th-century goldsmith and poet. His most important work is the famous gold monstrance, the Custódia de Belém, a superb example of Portuguese religious craftsmanship. He worked in the service of Queen Leonor, and also as Master of the Scales, at the Mint in Lisbon.

Gregório Lopes (d. 1550)
Well-known painter from the first half of the 16th century, whose work is documented in Lisbon between 1513 and 1550. He was Court painter to D. Manuel I and D. João III, as well as a Knight of the Order of Santiago. He produced works for the Mosteiro de São Francisco, in Lisbon, the Mosteiro de Ferreirim and the Convento de Cristo, among others.

Gualdim Pais (1118-1195)
Member of the nobility, distinguished by his feats during the Reconquest. He was the Master, the first in Portugal, of the Military Order of the Knights Templar from 1157 to 1195, a post

he occupied until his death. After the Reconquest, he was placed in charge of the defences along the River Tagus and was granted extensive lands, upon which the Templars began to build the Castle of Tomar in 1160.

Houdart (Odart)
French sculptor who arrived in Portugal, from Toledo, in the first half of the 16th century; a number of his works remain in Toledo. A highly skilled artist in working with clay, he produced several remarkable pieces, most notably a *Last Supper*, which he made for the Mosteiro de Santa Cruz in Coimbra and which is now to be found in the Museu Nacional Machado de Castro, also in Coimbra.

João de Castilho (Juan del Castillo) (1490-1551)
A Biscayan architect, born in Santander. He studied art, and civil and military architecture, in Naples. He is known to have been working in Portugal, as early as 1517, on the Mosteiro de Santa Maria de Belém, where he was Master of Works from 1522 onwards. He also worked on the Convento de Cristo (Tomar), the Mosteiro de Alcobaça, and the Mosteiro de Santa Maria da Vitória (Batalha). He was responsible for the building of an important bastion in Mazagan (Mazagão).

João de Ruão (Jean of Rouen) (d. 1580)
French sculptor, who arrived in Portugal in *c.*1517 and remained in the country until his death. Much of his work was done in the centre and north of the country, where he produced numerous retables and figures. He played a key role in introducing Renaissance elements into Portuguese sculpture.

Jorge Afonso (*c.*1475-1540)
He was appointed Court painter in 1508, and was Inspector and Master of the King's paintings during the reigns of D. Manuel I, and D. João III. Two of his many outstanding works are the paintings in the Rotunda, the original 16-sided church of the Templars, in the Convento de Cristo in Tomar, and scenes depicting the Childhood of Christ, part of a series, in the Igreja de Jesus in Setúbal. He was an excellent painter, remarkable for his drawing, use of colour and the balance of his compositions. He influenced an entire generation of Renaissance painters, maintaining an active school in Lisbon.

Jorge de Almeida, Dom (1458-1543)
He was the brother of the first Viceroy of India, D. Francisco de Almeida. At the age of only 25, only just a member of the clergy, he was elected Bishop. He was admitted to the priesthood in March 1485, and was consecrated Bishop in 1488. He was bishop for more than 60 years, during which time he commissioned building work, and made alterations and additions primarily to the Sé Velha in Coimbra. He contracted Oliver of Ghent to execute the monumental retable in the chancel, as well as other architectural and decorative works. He wrote *Constituições do Bispado,* in 1521, a work that remains as a valuable document for the study of this period.

Luís de Camões (c.1524-c.1580)
One of the most important figures in 16th-century literature. He was the author of *Os Lusíadas* (The Lusiads), first published in 1572, which is generally considered to be a masterpiece of Renaissance literature and in which he describes the epic feats of those taking part in the Portuguese Discoveries. He is known to have led a passionate and ill-fated life. Twice sent into exile, he travelled along the African coast and to the Far East, where he fought in several battles.

Machim
Flemish sculptor, active in Portugal in the first half of the 16th century, who designed the beautifully executed altar frontal of Guarda Cathedral.

Manuel Vicente
Son of the painter Vicente Gil, he followed his father's profession and worked in Coimbra from 1521 to 1530.

Marcos Pires (d. 1521)
Architect responsible for the work on the Mosteiro de Santa Cruz in Coimbra, where he designed the Cloister of Silence.

Mateus Fernandes (d. 1515)
Worked in Santarém, as well as on the fortifications in Madeira, and the Mosteiro de Alcobaça. From 1490, he was one of the most important Masters of Royal Works at the Mosteiro de Santa Maria da Vitória (Batalha). He is thought to have been responsible for the portal, dated 1509, leading into the Unfinished Chapels, the pantheon of D. Duarte, which is remarkable for its superb aesthetic quality.

Mestre da Lourinhã
Anonymous painter, who was active during the first half of the 14th century. A number of his works have been identified by comparing his painting entitled *John the Baptist,* in the Misericórdia Church at Lourinhã, with other works to be found in the Museu de Arte Antiga in Lisbon, and at other places. This has not been straight forward due to similarities with the work of Frei Carlos.

Miguel da Silva, Dom (1480-1556)
Son of the first Count of Portalegre, he studied at the universities of Lisbon, Paris and Sienna. In 1514, D. Manuel I appointed him Ambassador to the Papal Court. He lived in Rome, and was a friend of the Popes Leo X and Clement VII, and also of the painter Raphael. On his return to Lisbon, in 1525, D. João III made him Bishop of Viseu, and his confidential scribe. In 1541, he was appointed Cardinal, against the wishes of the king, which led him to flee to Rome, where he then settled. He was responsible for sending the architect, Francesco da Cremona, to Portugal, who carried out a number of works, including that in the cloister of Viseu cathedral.

Nicolas Chanterène

French sculptor, who was active in Portugal from 1517 to 1551. A remarkable artist, he was a friend of the Humanists and a pioneer in introducing the Renaissance style into Portugal. He sculpted works in Lisbon, namely the axial portal of Santa Maria de Belém, the retable of the Palácio da Pena in Sintra, and work in Coimbra and Évora, all of which reveal his artistic and intellectual stature.

Nuno Gonçalves

Painter, who was active between 1450 and 1492. He was appointed Court Painter to D. Afonso V on 20th July 1450, and was responsible for a number of important 15th-century paintings. In 1470, he was made a Knight of the Royal Household and, a year later, became the official painter for the City of Lisbon.

Oliver of Ghent (Olivier de Gand)

Highly skilled Flemish sculptor and woodcarver, and the author of the monumental retable of the Sé Velha in Coimbra, one of the most superb pieces in the panorama of Flemish sculpture in Portugal. Commissioned by D. Manuel I, he made an extraordinary series of larger-than-life-size sculptures in wood, for the Rotunda of the Convento de Cristo in Tomar.

Pedro Álvares Cabral (1460/70-1520)

Born in Belmonte, the son of the Governor General of Belmonte, he soon entered Court circles, marrying one of the daughters of Afonso de Albuquerque, and being granted an annuity by D. João II, although the services that he actually performed are not known. He was in command of the fleet that first sighted Brazil on 22nd April 1500, where he anchored two days later, in a spot he called Porto Seguro.

Pedro de Meneses, Dom (d. 1437)

Son of the first Count of Viana do Alentejo who, in 1383, on the succession of D. Fernando, left with his family for Castile. He took part in the Conquest of Ceuta, where he was made a knight. He became Governor of the City and defended it against Moorish attacks for 22 years. He was made Count of Vila Real, by D. João I and also became the second Count of Vila Real in 1424.

Pêro de Alcáçova Carneiro (1515-1593)

Born in Lisbon, he was the son of the Secretary of State, António Carneiro. From 1545, he was Privy Councillor to D. João III, but was dismissed by D. Sebastião. He was later reinstalled and accompanied D. Sebastião to the meeting with Philip II of Spain, at Guadalupe. Later, the Cardinal-King D. Henrique exiled him to Torres Vedras, blaming him for the unfortunate expedition to Africa that resulted in D. Sebastião's death. He favoured a pro-Spanish policy and was made Count of Idanha-a-Nova, in 1582.

Pêro Henriques
Son of the Master of Works at the Mosteiro de Santa Maria da Vitória (Batalha), Mateus Fernandes, and the brother of Filipe Henriques. Both brothers were Masters of Works at Braga cathedral between 1504 and 1516.

Quentín Metsys (c.1465-1530)
Painter of Flemish origin, that had a considerable following in Portugal. Some of his paintings are to be seen in Coimbra, particularly in the Mosteiro de Santa Cruz, and in the Museu Nacional Machado de Castro.

Rodrigo de Pontecilla
Spanish sculptor, who worked at Santa Maria de Belém, directing and executing work on the Chapter House portal.

Sesnando, Dom
Governor of Coimbra and the son of a Mozarab family that owned considerable estates in the Tentúgal region near Coimbra. He was taken to Seville as a prisoner of the Muslims in 1026. He occupied important positions in the Arab Court as a minister and a member of the Supreme Council. He took refuge with Fernando the Great, King of León and Castile, counselling him to take Coimbra. On 9th July 1064, after a six-month siege, the city fell and he was appointed Governor, and granted the title of Count. He took part and played an important role in other Conquests.

Tomé Velho
Mannerist sculptor, who was a student of Jean de Rouen. He produced important work, primarily in the city of Coimbra.

Vasco da Gama (c.1468-1524)
Navigator and Captain-General of the fleet which completed the discovery of the sea route to India. He set sail on the Great Voyage from Lisbon in 1497, destined for Calicut, and taking with him 3 carracks and a supply ship. On returning to the capital, D. Manuel I appointed him Admiral-in-Chief of the Indian Sea. Vasco da Gama made further voyages to India in 1502 and 1524, the latter journey being undertaken when he was already Viceroy.

Vicente Gil
Painter to D. João II, who is known to have been active in Coimbra from 1498 to 1525. The father of Manuel Vicente.

BIBLIOGRAPHY

ALMEIDA, Carlos Alberto F. de, *Alto Minho*, Lisbon, 1987.

ALPUIM, Maria Augusta de, and VASCONCELOS, Maria Emília, *Casas de Viana Antiga*, Viana do Castelo, 1983.

ALPUIM, Maria Augusta de, *A Sé Catedral de Viana do Castelo*, Viana do Castelo, 1984.

ÁLVAREZ VILLAR, Julián, "Ecos hispánicos del manuelino", in *As Relações Artísticas entre Portugal e Espanha na Época dos Descobrimentos*, Coimbra, 1987.

ALVES, Alexandre, "Artistas espanhóis na cidade de Viseu nos séculos XVI e XVII", in *As Relações Artísticas entre Portugal e Espanha na Época dos Descobrimentos*, Coimbra, 1987.

ALVES, Ana Maria, *Iconografia do Poder Real no Período Manuelino*, Lisbon, 1985.

ALVES, Lourenço, "Do gótico ao manuelino no Alto Minho, Monumentos religiosos", in *Caminiana*, Caminha, 1984.

ALVES, Lourenço, "Do gótico ao manuelino no Alto Minho, Monumentos religiosos" in *Caminiana*, Caminha, 1986.

ARAGÃO, António, *Para a História do Funchal*, Funchal, 1979.

ATHAÍDE, Luís Bernardo Leite d', "Património de arte em S. Miguel", in *Insulana*, Ponta Delgada, 1953.

ATHAÍDE, Luís Bernardo Leite d', "*Etnografia, Arte e Vida Antiga nos Açores*", Coimbra, 1974.

AVERINI, Ricardo, "Storia dell'arte portoghese", in *Estudos Italianos em Portugal*, Lisbon, 1970.

AZEVEDO, Carlos de, *Solares Portugueses*, Lisbon, 1969.

BARREIROS, Manuel de Aguiar, *A Egreja de Villar de Frades no Concelho de Barcelos*, Porto, 1919.

BARREIROS, Manuel de Aguiar, *A Capella dos Coimbras*, Porto, 1922.

BARREIROS, Manuel de Aguiar, *A Capella de Nossa Senhora da Conceição (Braga)*, Porto, 1923.

BATALHA, Matriz da, *Boletim da Direcção-Geral dos Edifícios e Monumentos Nacionais* No. 13, Lisbon, 1938.

BORGES, Nelson Correia, "Artistas e artífices espanhóis em Portugal durante o barroco e o rococó", in *Relaciones Artísticas entre Portugal y España*, Salamanca, 1986.

CARITA, Helder, and Amaro, Clementina, "A Casa dos Bicos", in *Catálogo da XVII Exposição Europeia de Arte, Ciência e Cultura*, Lisbon, 1983.

CASTILHO, Júlio de, *Lisboa Antiga*, Lisbon, 1935–1966.

CASTILHO, Júlio de, *A Ribeira de Lisboa*, Lisbon, 1941.

CORREIA, José Eduardo Horta, *A Arquitectura Religiosa do Algarve de 1520 a 1600*, Lisbon, 1987.

CORREIA, Vergílio, *As Obras de Santa Maria de Belém*, Lisbon, 1922.

CORREIA, Vergílio, *Mosteiro da Batalha*, Porto, 1928.

CORREIA, Vergílio, "*A Arte no Séc. XVI*", in *História de Portugal*, Vol. V, Barcelos, 1933.

CORTEZ, Fernando Russel, "Artistas portugueses que trabalharam na Galiza nos séculos XVI e XVII", in *As Relações Artísticas entre Portugal e Espanha na Época dos Descobrimentos*, Coimbra, 1987.

DIAS, Pedro, *A arquitectura de Coimbra na Transição do Gótico para a Renascença, 1490-1540,* Coimbra, 1982.

DIAS, PEDRO, "O MANUELINO", in *História da Arte em Portugal,* Vol. V, Lisbon, 1986.

ESPANCA, Túlio, *Inventário Artístico de Portugal – Concelho de Évora,* Lisbon, 1966.

ESPANCA, Túlio, *Inventário Artístico de Portugal – Distrito de Évora,* Lisbon, 1966–1978.

ESPANCA, Túlio, *Inventário Artístico de Portugal – Distrito de Évora, Concelho de Arraiolos, Estremoz, Montemor-o-Novo, Moura e Vendas Novas,* Lisbon, 1975.

FERREIRA, Manuel Juvenal Pita, *A Sé do Funchal,* Funchal, 1963.

FREITAS, Eugénio de Andrea da Cunha e, "Os mestres biscainhos na Matriz de Vila do Conde, João Rianho, Sancho Garcia, Rui Garcia, e João de Castilho", in *Anais da Academia Portuguesa da História,* Lisbon, 1951.

FREITAS, Eugénio de Andrea da Cunha e, "*Igreja de Nossa Senhora da Oliveira. Notícia histórica*", in *Boletim da Direcção-Geral dos Edifícios e Monumentos Nacionais,* No. 128, Lisbon, 1981.

GONÇALVES, António Augusto, *Estatuária Lapidar no Museu Machado de Castro,* Coimbra, 1923.

GONÇALVES, António Nogueira, *Inventário Artístico de Portugal – A cidade de Coimbra,* Lisbon, 1947.

GONÇALVES, António Nogueira, *Inventário Artístico de Portugal – Distrito de Aveiro, Zona Sul,* Lisbon, 1959.

GONÇALVES, António Nogueira, *Estudos de História da Arte da Renascença,* Coimbra, 1979.

GONÇALVES, António Nogueira, "Lamego. Sé Catedral", in *Guia de Portugal,* Vol. V, tomo II, Lisbon, undated.

GOULÃO, Maria José, "Alguns problemas ligados ao emprego de azulejos mudéjares em Portugal nos séculos XV e XVI", in *As Relações Artísticas entre Portugal e Espanha na Época dos Descobrimentos,* Coimbra, 1987.

GUERRA, Luís Figueiredo da, *Viana e Caminha,* Porto, 1929.

HAUPT, Albrecht, *A Arquitectura da Renascença em Portugal,* Lisbon, 1924.

HOOYKAAS, R., *Os Descobrimentos e o Humanismo,* Lisbon, 1983.

IRIA, Alberto, *O Algarve e os Descobrimentos,* Lisbon, 1956.

JÚDICE, Pedro Mascarenhas, *A Sée o Castelo de Silves,* Gaia, 1934.

KARLINGER, Hans, *Arte gótica,* Madrid, 1932.

KEIL, Luís, *Inventário Artístico de Portugal – Distrito de Portalegre,* Lisbon, 1943.

LIMA, Batista de, "A Igreja de S. Sebastião da Terceira", in *XVI Congrès International d'Histoire de L'Art,* Lisbon, 1949.

MANIQUE, Luís de Pina, *A Arquitectura Manuelina de Alvito,* Lisbon, 1949.

MOREIRA, Rafael, "Arquitectura militar do Renascimento em Portugal", in *A Introdução da Arte da Renascença na Península Ibérica,* Coimbra, 1980.

MOREIRA, Rafael, "Arquitectura", in *Catálogo da XVII Exposição de Arte, Ciência e Cultura do Conselho da Europa, Museu de Arte Antiga I,* Lisbon, 1983.

MOREIRA, Rafael, *Jerónimos,* Lisbon, 1987.

PEREIRA, Gabriel, *Estudos Eborenses. O Mosteiro de Nossa Senhora do Espinheiro*, 2a edition, Vol. I, Évora, 1947.

RIBEIRO, Bartolomeu, *Convento de Santo António do Varatojo*, Braga, 1956.

SANTOS, Reinaldo dos, *A Torre de Belém, Estudo Histórico e Arqueológico*, Lisbon, 1922.

SANTOS, Reinaldo dos, *A Torre de Belém*, Coimbra, 1922.

SANTOS, Reinaldo dos, "Madre de Deus", in *Guia de Portugal*, Vol. I, Lisbon, 1924.

SANTOS, Reinaldo dos, *O Estilo Manuelino*, Lisbon, 1952.

SANTOS, Reinaldo dos, "O Portal da Igreja Matriz de Vila do Conde", in *Vila do Conde*, nº 3, Vila do Conde, 1961.

SANTOS, Reinaldo dos, *Oito Séculos de Arte Portuguesa*, Lisbon, n.d.

SEGURADO, Jorge, *A Igreja de S. João de Moura*, Lisbon, 1929.

SEGURADO, Jorge, "Da génese da Igreja de S. João de Moura", in *Belas Artes*, Lisbon, 1975.

SEQUEIRA, Gustavo de Matos, *Inventário Artístico de Portugal – Distrito de Leiria*, Lisbon, 1955.

SOARES, Joaquim, and Silva, Carlos Tavares da, *Património Construído de Setúbal, Época dos Descobrimentos*, Setúbal, 1983.

SOUSA, A. D. de Castro e, *Memória Histórica sobre a Origem da Fundação do Real Mosteiro de N. S. da Pena, situado na Serra de Sintra*, Lisbon, 1945.

SOUSA, J. de, *A Torre de Belém, Castelo de Sam Vicente a par de Belém*, Lisbon, 1959.

SOUSA, Nestor de, *A Arquitectura Religiosa de Ponta Delgada nos Séculos XVI a XVIII*, Ponta Delgada, 1986.

TAROUCA, Carlos da Silva and CHICÓ, Mário Tavares, "Igreja do Lóios de Évora", in *A Cidade de Évora*, Évora, 1945.

TEIXEIRA, Garcez, "A casa do capítulo incompleta do Convento de Cristo", in *Lusitânia*, Vol. III, Lisbon, 1925.

VALADARES, Álvaro de, "História das igrejas do Algarve", in *O Algarve*, Faro, 1958.

VALADARES, Álvaro de, "A Arte no Algarve", in *O Algarve*, Faro, 1958-1959.

VASCONCELOS, Joaquim de, *Da Arquitectura Manuelina*, Coimbra, 1885.

AUTHORS

Pedro Dias

Born in Coimbra in 1950, he is Professor of History of Art at Coimbra University.
He has undertaken research work in Spain, Italy, Holland, Germany, France, Brazil and India, both with scholarships from the National Institute of Scientific Research and the Fundação Calouste Gulbenkian, sponsored by UNESCO and the European Union.
He has held the following posts: Director of the Art History Institute at Coimbra University, Director of the Museu Nacional Machado de Castro, Delegate of the Office of the Secretary of State for Culture for the Central Region of Portugal, Member of the Editorial Board of Imprensa Nacional-Casa da Moeda, Member of the Consultative Board of the Portuguese Institute of Architectural and Archaeological Heritage, and Member of the Scientific Committee of the National Commission for the Commemoration of the Portuguese Discoveries.
He is a member of the National Academy of Fine Arts, the Real Academia de Bellas Artes de San Fernando in Madrid, the Real Academia de Bellas Artes de la Puríssima Concepción in Valladolid, and the International Committee for the History of Art, as well as president of the Portuguese Section of this same committee.
Three of his books have been awarded the José de Figueiredo Prize by the National Academy of Fine Arts: *A Arquitectura de Coimbra na Transição do Gótico para a Renascença*, in 1982; *Nicolau Chanterene escultor da Renascença*, in 1987; and *A Arquitectura Gótica Portuguesa*, in 1994. He was also one of the authors of the book *Flandre et Portugal*, which was awarded the Belgian Duc d'Arenberg Prize in 1991. In 1983, he was awarded the Medal of Merit in Fine Arts – Gold Class.
Amongst his latest publications are: *Os Portais Manuelinos do Mosteiro dos Jerónimos*, Coimbra, 1993; *A Viagem das Formas*, Lisbon, 1995; *A Escultura Maneirista Portuguesa*; *Subsídios para uma Síntese*, Coimbra, 1995; *O Fydias Peregrino*; *Nicolau Chanterene e a Escultura Europeia do Renascimento*, Coimbra, 1996; *História de Arte Portuguesa no Mundo (1415–1822). O Espaço do Índico*, Lisbon, 1998; *História da Arte Portuguesa no Mundo (1415–1822). O Espaço Atlântico*, Lisbon, 1999; *Arquitectura dos Portugueses em Marrocos, 1415 a 1769*, Coimbra, 2000.
He has been involved in the organisation of several important exhibitions, having been the Scientific Curator of a number of them, such as *O Tempo das Feitorias*, in 1991, at Antwerp Royal Museum; *A Arte da Época dos Descobrimentos*, at Museu Nacional de Arte Antiga in Lisbon, in 1992; *Álvaro Pires de Évora, um pintor Português no Quattrocento Italiano*, in Lisbon, at the Torre do Tombo, in 1994; *O Rosto do Infante*, in Tomar and Viseu, also in 1994; *Reflexos: Símbolos e Imagens do Cristianismo na Porcelana Chinesa*, at the Museu de São Roque, in Lisbon, in 1997; and *O Brilho do Norte. Escultura e Escultores do Norte da Europa em Portugal. Época Manuelina*, at the Palácio da Ajuda in Lisbon, in 1997.

Dalila Rodrigues

Born at Granja de Penedono in 1960, she has a Ph.D. in the History of Art from Coimbra University. She is the Director of the Museu Grão Vasco and Lecturer at the Instituto Superior Politécnico de Viseu.
She is a specialist researcher in the History of Portuguese Painting and has participated in various research projects, collaborating with several national institutions, such as the Portuguese Institute of Museums, the Portuguese Institute of Architectural Heritage and the Library and Reading Support Department of the Fundação Calouste Gulbenkian. She has undertaken research projects in the USA, with the support of the Luso-American Development Foundation, and in India, with the support of the National Commission for the Commemoration of the Portuguese Discoveries.

She was curator of the *Grão Vasco e a Pintura Europeia do Renascimento* exhibition (CNCDP, Palácio Nacional da Ajuda 1992); and the *Mestres de Ferreirim* section of the 3ª Bienal de Arte exhibition (Fundação Cupertino de Miranda, Museu de Lamego, 2001).
She was awarded scholarships by both the Fine Arts Department of the Fundação Calouste Gulbenkian and PRODEP. She has participated in various conferences in Portugal and abroad and is the author of several publications, articles, essays and papers.

Fernando Jorge Artur Grilo

Born in Lisbon in 1962, he has a Ph.D. in the History of Art from Lisbon University. He lectures at the Faculdade de Letras da Universidade de Lisboa on the History of the Art of the Renaissance, Mannerism and the Baroque, having published several works in this field.
He has participated in various research projects, in particular with the Art History Institute of the Faculdade de Letras da Universidade de Lisboa, on the *Medusa* projects – *Quarries exploited for the Mosteiro da Batalha. History of quarrying in the construction and restoration of the monument*, and *The Art of the resettlement of Portuguese territory: Testimonies to Christian activity in the west of the Iberian Peninsula between the 9th and 11th centuries*.
A scholarship was awarded to him by the Fundação Calouste Gulbenkian; following his work on Spanish, French and Italian archives. He was Deputy Scientific Curator of the *O Brilho do Norte. Escultura e Escultores do Norte da Europa em Portugal. Época Manuelina*, held at the Palácio Nacional da Ajuda, in 1998. He has participated in various conferences and is the author of several books and articles, namely "O Gosto do Olhar. A colecção de pintura do Banco Mello", "Andrea Sansovino em Portugal no Tempo de D. Manuel" and "Nicolau Chanterene. Um escultor do Renascimento em Évora".

Nuno Vassallo e Silva

Born in Lisbon in 1961, he is a graduate in the History of Art, variant of the History degree at the Faculdade de Letras da Universidade de Lisboa.
He has been Assistant Director of the Museu Calouste Gulbenkian since 1999.
He is currently working on his Ph.D. thesis, entitled *Ourivesaria e Objectos Preciosos Indianos para Portugal*, for which he has won a scholarship from the Fundação Oriente.
His areas of specialisation are the History of Decorative Arts in Portugal (Jewellery and Gold- and Silverwork), the production of precious objects in Portuguese India and the history of art collecting.
He has worked with various cultural institutions such as the Museu Nacional de Arte Antiga, the Portuguese Institute of Architectural Heritage, the Galeria de Pintura do rei D. Luís and the Palácio Nacional da Ajuda. He was curator of the Museu de São Roque/Santa Casa da Misericórdia de Lisboa.
He has been the curator of several exhibitions, namely: *No caminho do Japão* (1993), *Tesouros Artísticos da Misericórdia do Porto* (1995), *O Púlpito e a Imagem* (1996), *A Herança de Rauluchantim* (1996), *Esplendor e Devoção: Relicários de São Roque* (1998), *Arte do Retrato: Quotidiano e Circunstância* (1999) and *Exotica: Portugals Entdeckungen im Spiegel fürstlicher Kunst – und Wunderkammern der Renaissance* (2000), in partnership with Helmut Trnek.
He has written a number of books, including *Joalharia Portuguesa/Portuguese Jewellery* (1996) and *Colecção de Ourivesaria do Museu Alberto Sampaio* (1998), as well as various articles, essays and papers that he has given at conferences in both Portugal and abroad.

www.ingramcontent.com/pod-product-compliance
Lightning Source LLC
Chambersburg PA
CBHW050047230526
45470CB00004B/1429